Science World 3

Peter Stannard
BSc, DipEd

Ken Williamson
BSc (Hons), DipEd

Consultants
David Greig   Brighton Secondary School
Donna Brookes   Buckley Park College
Susan Grant   Northland Secondary College
Kelly Camilleri   Werribee Secondary College
Kathryn Middleton   Fairhills High School
Peter Jeans   Colac High School

Technical art
Brent Hagen   Chris Dent

Cartoons
Chris Dent

Second Edition

MACMILLAN

First edition published 2001 (reprinted 5 times)
Second edition published 2007 by
MACMILLAN EDUCATION AUSTRALIA PTY LTD
627 Chapel Street, South Yarra 3141

Visit our website at www.macmillan.com.au

Associated companies and representatives
throughout the world.

National Library of Australia
cataloguing in publication data

Stannard, Peter.
    ScienceWorld. 3.

    2nd ed.
    Includes index.
    For year 10 students.
    ISBN 978 1 4202 1218 1.

    1. Science—Problems, exercises, etc.—Juvenile literature.
    2. Science—Study and teaching (Secondary).
    I. Williamson, Ken. II. Title.

500

Publisher: Ben Dawe
Project editor: Kirstie Innes-Will
Technical illustrators: Brent Hagen and Chris Dent
Cartoonist: Chris Dent
Cover and text designer: Dimitrios Frangoulis
Photo permissions: Debbie Gallagher
Typeset in Sabon, Univers and Helvetica Condensed by Dimitrios Frangoulis
Cover and title page images: cover image copyright © Oceanwide Images/
Mark Simmons; Photolibrary/Creatas for water image on front cover, spine, back
cover and title page

Printed in Malaysia

Acknowledgments
The authors would like to thank Chuck Forzatti of Siena College for
advice and suggestions, and those students from St John's College
who helped with photographs.

The authors and publisher are grateful to the following for
permission to reproduce copyright material:

Photographs

Photographs
AAP/Associated Press/NASA TV, p. 327 (centre); Aberdeen
Foundries, <www.aberdeenfoundries.co.uk>, p. 300; Satellite image
originally produced by the Australian Bureau of Meteorology from
the geostationary satellite MTSAT-1R operated by the Japan
Meteorological Agency, p. 318 (top); Anteater Publications, pp. 1, 3,
5, 6, 12, 18, 19 (top), 21, 25, 26, 33, 35, 37 (top and bottom right),
43, 46 (bottom), 47, 50, 51, 56, 60, 65, 66, 73, 80, 82, 89, 91, 93,
100, 101, 122, 147, 155 (bottom), 157, 164, 166 top, 168, 173, 184,
185 (left), 186, 198, 200, 208, 210, 211 (top), 213 (top and bottom
left), 222 (top left), 225, 228, 235, 247, 258, 259, 262, 268, 276,
283 (bottom), 287, 288, 293, 298, 303, 318 (bottom),
<www.biocrawler.com/encyclopedia/Nanotechnology>, p. 272;
Coo-ee Historical Picture Library, p. 273; Coo-ee Picture Library,
pp. 222 (bottom), 223; Corbis/© D. Robert & Lorri Franz, p. 189;
DigitalVision, p. 58; Robert Sparkes Photographer, dragster.com.au,
p. 104; ESA/CNES/ARIANESPACE, p. 308; IKONOS satellite image
courtesy of GeoEye/SIME. Copyright 2007. All rights reserved,
p. 317 (left); Getty Images, p. 230 (top and bottom), /AFP, p. 314,
/Cancan Chu, p. 159, /Lester Lefkowitz, p. 127, /Ken Lucas, p. 220,
/David McGlynn, p. 155 (top), /Kelvin Murray, p. 29, /Michael
Rosenfeld, p. 275, /Issouf Sanogo, p. 211 bottom, /Jeff Sherman,
p. 279, /Robin Smith, p. 142, /Ryan/Beyer, p. 46 (top), /Space
Frontiers, p. 136 (top); Goodyear Tyres (South Pacific Tyres Pty Ltd),
<www.goodyear.com.au>, p. 113; Great Southern Stock © Brian
Carr, p. 297; David Greig, p. 139; Healesville Sanctuary, Zoos
Victoria, p. 217 (top); India Tourism, Sydney, www.india.com.au,
p. 305; iStockphoto, pp. 161, 271, /Tamara Bauer, p. 212, /Flavia
Bottazzini, p. 166 bottom, /Alan Collins, p. 185 (centre and right),
/Darinburt, p. 248, /Daniel Gale, p. 32, /David Gilder, p. 199 left,
/Richard Gunion, p. 270 (bottom), /Carmen Martínez Banús, p. 199
(right), /Steve McWilliam, p. 217 (bottom), /David Philips, p. 283
(top), /Mike Salrin, p. 207 top, /Nico Smit, p. 213 (bottom right),
/Nicola Stratford, p. 301, /Moritz von Hacht, p. 68; Lochman
Transparancies/Jiri Lochman, p. 218; Lonely Planet Images/Jason
Edwards, p. 207 (bottom); <www.macgen.com.au>, p. 138; Mary
Evans Picture Library, p. 219; NASA, pp. 306 (top), 320, 325, 326,
327 (top); NHTSA, <www.nhtsa.gov>, p. 114; Photo copyright Palm
Press, Inc. from the Estate of Dr Harold Eugene Edgerton, p. 109;
Photodisc, p. 222 (top right); PhotoEssentials, p. 307; Photolibrary,
p. 226, /Garden Picture Library/Friedrich Strauss, p. 209, /Stefan
Mokrzecki, p. 270 (top); Photolibrary/Photo Researchers, Inc.,
p. 238, /Biophoto Associates, p. 179 (top), /Nancy Hamilton, p. 190;
Photolibrary/Science Photo Library, pp. 156, 315, /Samuel Ashfield,
p. 171, /Ian Boddy, p. 55, /Dr Jeremy Burgess, p. 19 (bottom),
/CC Studio, p. 37 (bottom left), /Deep Light Productions, p. 54,
/Michael Donne, p. 179 (bottom), /Eye of Science, p. 216, /NASA,
pp. iv, 303 (bottom), 322, 323, 328, /Philippe Plailly, p. 204, /Sinclair
Stammers, p. 193, /Volker Steger, p. 86, /David Vaughan, p. 317
(right); Plug&Power, <www.plugandpower.com.au>, p. 136
(bottom); © Rolex/Xavier Lecoultre, p. 151; Toyota Motor
Corporation Australia, p. 289.

Other material
Choice magazine test data, with permission of the Australian
Consumers' Association (ACA) <www.choice.com.au>, pp. 26–28;
Bar graph data 'Energy used per person per year in selected
countries', includes data from *BP Statistical Review of World Energy*,
June 2006, used with permission, p. 128; Table data 'Table of energy
reserves', includes data from *BP Statistical Review of World Energy*,
June 2006 & data from Australian Uranium Association, used
with permission, p. 129; Table data 'Table Australia's production
and consumption of oil', *BP Statistical Review of World Energy*,
June 2006, p. 129; Table outlining performance of Holden Astra
and Mazda RX-8 Turbo, by Peter Robinson and *Wheels* Magazine,
Wheels magazine, September 2005, used with permission, p. 104.

While every care has been taken to trace and acknowledge copyright,
the publishers tender their apologies for any accidental infringement
where copyright has proved untraceable. They would be pleased to
come to a suitable arrangement with the rightful owner in each case.

Contents

Transition science

Science World 3 is designed to help you make the transition from the junior school to the senior school. It will help you clarify the ideas you have about science subjects which you may study in Year 11. If you are not sure what senior biology, chemistry and physics are like, the chapters in this book will give you some idea. Work in small groups to discuss these questions.

1 To solve everyday problems you often need to **work scientifically.** What does this mean?

2 Which chapters in this book are mainly about working scientifically?

3 You use the skills of working scientifically in the four areas of science below. Check the contents list on the previous page. You will notice that the chapters are grouped. Browse through the Physics chapters to get an idea of what physics is like. Do the same for the Biology, Chemistry and Astronomy chapters.

4 Which of the four areas do you like best? Why?

5 Which of the four areas would you need to study environmental science? Explain.

6 Whether or not you do science next year, this book explores and encourages debate about the relationships between science, society and technology. It contains many ideas and issues that you will hear about in the news and discuss with others. For instance:
  - experiments using animals (pages 7–8)
  - use of nuclear power (Chapter 6)
  - lighting homes in remote villages around the world (page 151)
  - gene technology and cloning (Chapter 9).

Do you think that science can solve all our problems? Explain.

Physics is the study of how objects, from the very tiny to the very big, behave.

> Yeah, hi Dad. Er, I've got some good news. The crumple zones and air bags in your new car work really well.

Chemistry is the study of matter, of natural and processed materials. You study what substances are made of and how they react with each other.

> Erk! Some H_2O has permeated the NaCl

Biology is the study of life and living things.

> No way am I gonna grow up to be like my father

Astronomy is the scientific study of the universe and all it contains.

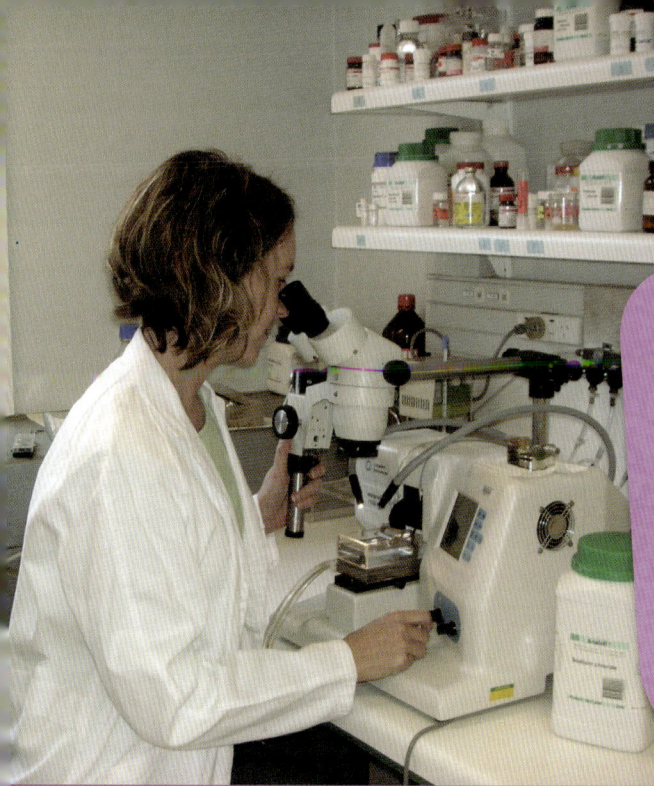

Science is investigating

Getting Started

Science skills can be used to solve everyday problems. For example, suppose Emily's bicycle has a flat tyre and she wants to know why. Emily and her friend Nick investigate this.

Emily: *Hey Nick, my front tyre is flat! There must be a leak somewhere. We'll have to find out where the air is getting out before we can fix it.*

Nick: *Perhaps there's a nail in it.*

Emily: *I can't see one.*

Nick: *There might be a cut in the tyre.*

Emily: *No, it seems OK.*

Nick: *What about the valve? Someone told me you can test it by putting some spit on it. If air is getting out a bubble will form in the spit.*

Emily: *I'll try that . . . Hey look, the bubble is slowly getting bigger.*

Nick: *Then the valve must be leaking.*

Emily: *Well, let's go and get a new valve.*

In their investigation Emily and Nick used several science skills. Try to identify the following in their conversation:

● observations
● inferences
● an experiment
● a prediction

1.1 Steps in investigating

Planning an experiment

There are four main steps in a scientific experiment, as shown.

> What I'm going to find out is ...

1 **Planning the experiment**

★ Identify the problem.
★ Identify the variables.
★ Write a research question or a hypothesis that can be tested.
★ Work out which variable you will change, which you will measure and which you will control.
★ Work out the method and select the equipment you will use.

2 **Conducting the experiment**

★ Carry out the experiment.
★ Observe, measure and record data.

> I could probably improve my experiment if ...

3 **Processing data**

★ Organise the data, draw graphs and do calculations.
★ Identify patterns in the data and relationships between the variables.
★ Use scientific knowledge to explain the patterns and relationships.

> An experiment is simply a fair test.

> Now—what does all this mean?

4 **Evaluating the experiment**

★ Evaluate the design of the experiment and the methods used.
★ Discuss the results. Are they reliable?
★ Evaluate the findings in relation to the original problem, question or hypothesis.
★ Write a conclusion. Make sure it is valid.

Activity

Planning an experiment

Imagine you work for a motoring organisation. You have read an overseas report that says that the brand of tyres used on a car makes little difference to its stopping distance when braking in an emergency. You decide to investigate this claim under Australian conditions, using the steps in investigating on the previous page.

1 In your own words, write down the problem to be investigated.

2 Rewrite the problem as a hypothesis—a generalisation that can be tested by an experiment.

3 What are the variables involved; that is, what factors could affect the results of the experiment?

4 What method will you use to test your hypothesis?

5 Which variable will you purposely change in your experiment? This is the independent variable.

6 Which variable will you measure? This is the dependent variable.

7 Which variables will you need to control?

8 What equipment will you need?

9 What data will you collect and how will you record it?

10 How will you know whether your hypothesis is correct or not?

Evaluating an experiment

When you have finished an experiment you should think carefully about how successful it was and whether you could improve it. This is called *evaluating an experiment*. For example, were you able to make accurate measurements? Did you repeat your measurements and calculate an average? The more measurements you make the more *reliable* the average will be, but three measurements are usually enough.

After evaluating the experiment, you may need to repeat it with some modifications. You also need to be able to evaluate other people's experiments. Scientists do this often, and they sometimes do the experiments themselves to see if they obtain the same results. They may be able to suggest ways to improve the experiment.

It is also important to check any conclusions or generalisations made from the data collected in an experiment to make sure they are logical or *valid*. Sometimes poor thinking or reasoning can lead to incorrect or invalid conclusions. Also, not everyone will reach the same conclusions after analysing the same data.

In the next activity you can practise evaluating an experiment and a conclusion.

Activity

Part A: Evaluating an experiment

The manufacturer of a brand of paintbrush has made the following claim:

Scientific tests show that Super Soaker has a greater paint pick-up than any other brand.

Five brands of paintbrush were tested as follows.

1   Paint was added to the tray until the reading on the electronic balance was 500 g exactly.

2   The first brush was attached to the lever. It was lowered into the paint, then lifted out.

3   The new mass of the tray plus paint was recorded, and the mass of paint picked up was calculated by subtraction.

4   The same procedure was followed for all five brushes.

5   The test was repeated 4 times for each brush and the masses were averaged. The results in the data table on the right show the average masses.

- What variables would need to be controlled in this experiment?
- Are the results reliable? Give a reason for your answer.
- Do you consider the manufacturer's claim to be correct? Explain.
- How could you improve the experiment?

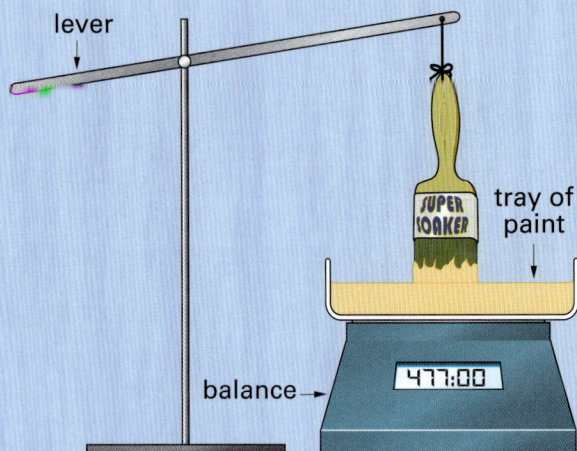

lever

tray of paint

balance

477:00

Brand of paintbrush	Final mass of tray plus paint (g)	Mass of paint picked up (g)
Bettabrush	478	22
Easy Paint	491	9
Slurp	485	15
Super Soaker	**477**	**23**
Thickbrush	483	17

Part B: Evaluating a conclusion

James and Tjanda wanted to know which was the best all-purpose pesticide. To do this they recorded the death rate for flies, mosquitoes and spiders using four different pesticides.

James concluded that Bingo was the best all-purpose spray, but Tjanda said that No More Flies was the best.

- Who do you agree with? Explain your choice clearly.

Pesticide	Percentage death rate		
	Flies	Mosquitoes	Spiders
Bingo	80	60	60
Bugaway	30	20	90
No More Flies	95	100	15
Zap	40	40	40

Investigating Velcro

In the experiment on the next page you will investigate the strength of a Velcro strip. Before you do this, however, you need to know something about Velcro.

Activity

Your teacher will give you a small piece of Velcro (both hook and loop strips). Examine both strips using a hand lens or stereomicroscope.

- Sketch the appearance of the surface of both strips.
- Explain how the two strips link together.
- Can you make a join with two pieces of tape of the same type? Explain.

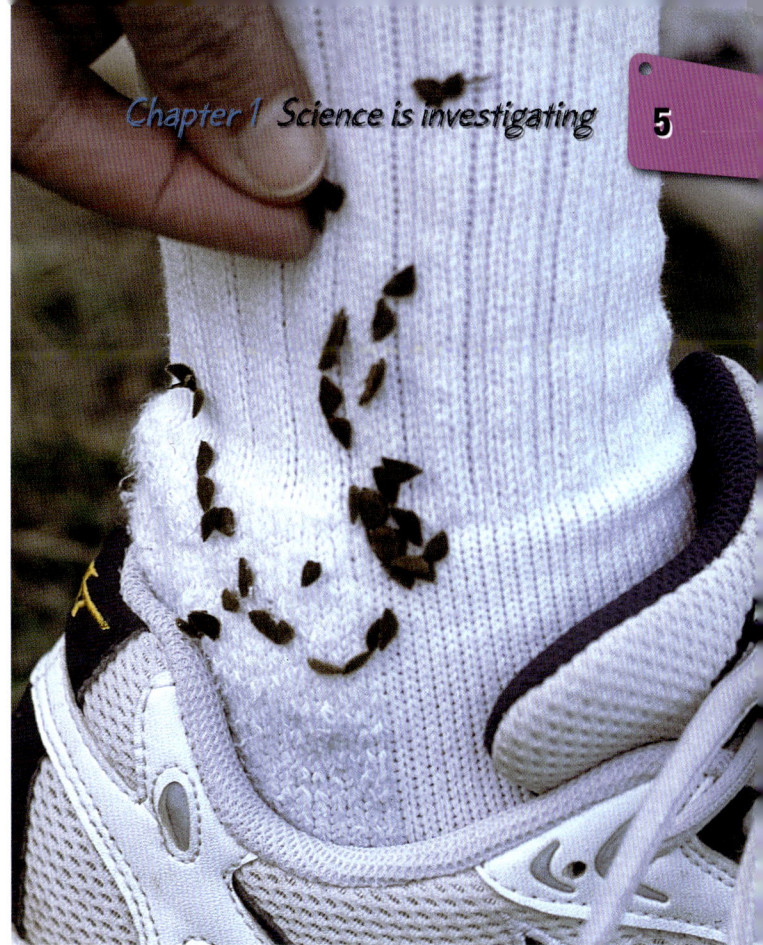

Fig 5 Velcro weed sticking to socks

Velcro

Velcro is a trademark name from the French words *velours* (velvet) and *crochet* (hook). A Swiss engineer Georges de Mestral had the idea for Velcro after getting burrs caught in his clothing and in his dog's fur while walking in the forest. When he examined the burrs under a microscope he found tiny hooks that could attach themselves to anything with loops in it, like hair or cloth. Velcro (or nylon press tape) is made in two parts, one with hooks and one with loops. It is now a universal fastener, for everything from disposable nappies to sandals.

A 5 mm square piece of Velcro may contain 3000 hooks and loops, although they will not all be hooked together. Two 5 cm squares pressed together can support the weight of a person weighing 80 kg! You may have seen Velcro jumping, where a person leaps off a trampoline and sticks to a Velcro wall.

As the diagram shows, less force is required to detach Velcro when it is pulled off at an

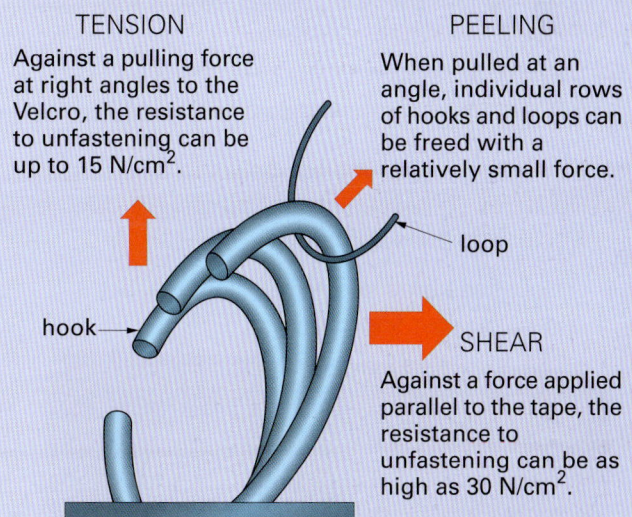

TENSION
Against a pulling force at right angles to the Velcro, the resistance to unfastening can be up to 15 N/cm^2.

PEELING
When pulled at an angle, individual rows of hooks and loops can be freed with a relatively small force.

loop

hook

SHEAR
Against a force applied parallel to the tape, the resistance to unfastening can be as high as 30 N/cm^2.

angle than when it is pulled at right angles or parallel to the Velcro. This is because you are pulling a single row rather than all the hooks and loops together. This smaller force is sufficient to disconnect one row after another, producing the familiar ripping sound.

Experiment
TESTING VELCRO

Research questions

Rachel is thinking of buying a new pair of training shoes which use a Velcro strap instead of laces. She likes the idea because it is so easy to change into and out of her shoes.

Rachel is fascinated with the Velcro idea and wants to check whether the information on Velcro on the previous page is correct.

These are some of the questions she would like answered.

1 What peeling force is needed to unfasten the Velcro strip?

2 What shear force will be necessary to undo the strap off her shoe?

3 Will the strap keep its strength if it is unfastened and fastened many times?

4 Will the strength of the strap be affected by grit and material fluff that gets caught in the Velcro?

Designing your experiment

1 Work in a small group and discuss which test or tests you would like to do.

2 Write a hypothesis for your experiment.

3 Make a list of the equipment you will need.

4 Write a draft of your plan, including the variables you will be controlling and the data you are going to record.

5 Discuss the draft design with your teacher, then write your final design.

Hints and tips

1 You can buy hook and loop strips in cheap variety stores or in fabric stores.

2 You should record the results of the tests as the force used (in newtons) per area of Velcro (for example, per cm²).

3 You will have to design a clever way to attach the force measurer (usually a spring balance) to the Velcro. Stitching, using a small clamp or gluing are three possible methods.

Planning and Safety Check

- Do a risk assessment to identify any safety hazards and decide on necessary precautions.
- Prepare a data table for your results. Remember, your results will be more reliable if you take at least three measurements and find the average.

Writing your report

Write a report of your experiment using the six headings Title, Aim, Materials, Method, Results, Discussion and Conclusion.

Your description of what you did needs to be good enough so that if someone else follows your method they will get very similar results. A diagram will help.

In the discussion, say how well your method worked and suggest how you might be able to get more reliable results.

In your conclusion you need to answer the research questions you investigated.

Science in action

Experiments using animals

No new drug can be put on the market until extensive information has been obtained on the effects it is likely to have on humans. One tragic example where this was not done properly was with the drug thalidomide. It was used in the 1950s to stop morning sickness and as a sleeping pill by pregnant women, but was later identified as a cause of deformities in newborn babies.

New drugs are usually tested first on laboratory animals, mainly rats and mice. Sometimes animals are also used to test the safety of food additives and household cleaning products. However, many people feel that this testing is unethical, and for this reason very few cosmetics are now tested this way.

Experiments involving living things require special methods. This is because no two individuals are the same. Also, it is not possible to control the behaviour of live subjects, or to control attitudes if people are used. However, scientists take care to control as many variables as possible. For example, if they were using mice they would control the following variables:

- genetic differences—all mice would be descended from the same stock
- age—all mice would be the same age
- environment—all mice would be kept in similar cages and be given the same food and water
- no diseases—the mice would be kept in the best of health.

When conducting such experiments scientists normally use a test group and a control group. The test group is given the drug and the control group is not. Any differences in response can then be said to be caused by the drug.

Experimenting on people

When experimenting with people, it is important that the subjects do not know whether they are in the test group or the control group. Suppose a drug company wants to test a new drug which they claim can help smokers give up smoking. A test group and a control group are given tablets—real ones for the test group and fake ones for the control group. However, the volunteers do not know which tablets they have been given. The fake tablets are called **placebos (pla-SEE-bows)** and appear to be exactly the same as the real tablets. After several months, the smoking behaviour of the volunteers is checked, and conclusions can then be drawn. This procedure is called a **blind experiment** because the subjects are unaware of (or blind to) whether they are in the test group or the control group.

A blind experimental design helps to overcome differences in the attitudes of the people involved in the trial. Some people may want to give up smoking more than others, and some may think that no treatment will work for them. Despite this special experimental design, however, the results may still be inconclusive. For example, suppose 20% of the test group give up smoking and 10% of the control group give up smoking. Before you can draw a conclusion from this, you need to analyse the data to decide whether the differences could have arisen by chance alone or whether there are real differences.

In some experiments the scientists are 'blind' as well as the subjects. This design is called a **double-blind experiment**. Suppose a scientist wanted to test a new ingredient X which is supposed to reduce acne (pimples). She could arrange for a large number of bottles of lotion to be made, half with X in them and half without. The bottles could then be numbered and given to volunteers to use. With this design, however, neither the volunteers nor the scientist would know which volunteers were using ingredient X and which were not. The scientist could then judge the effect on the pimples of each volunteer without prejudice. Only after the experiment would the scientist find out who had been given ingredient X.

The Venetian Bros Laboratory specialises in double blind experiments.

Ethical or unethical experiments?

Some people say it is unethical for researchers to give sick people placebos, or no treatment, if effective treatments are already available.

A needle-exchange study with heroin addicts was conducted in 1997 in Anchorage, Alaska. Half of the addicts were given needles and the other half were not. The study was to see how many in each group got hepatitis B, even though there is an effective hepatitis B vaccine. The vaccine was offered to all participants after the study, but critics of the study claim it was designed to prove that needle-exchange programs work, rather than to help the addicts.

Questions

1 Explain the differences between a blind experimental design and a double-blind experimental design.

2 Suppose a drug company has developed a new drug called Nodec which they claim will reduce tooth decay. They arrange to test Nodec at your school using this method:

- Company representatives visit the school to explain the experiment and call for volunteers.
- They select 100 students and each student is examined to record the number of fillings.
- Each student is given a jar of tablets—either Nodec or a placebo. Students are to take one tablet each day. The drug company claims that their representatives do not know who is given Nodec and who is given the placebo.
- After 6 months the students are examined again

and the data recorded. When the trial is complete, the drug company sends the following summary to the school.

	Total number of fillings	
	Before	After
Placebo (50 students)	56	73
Nodec (50 students)	47	59

a Evaluate the design of the experiment and the results obtained.
b On the basis of this experiment, would you use Nodec? Explain.

3 In a group discuss whether animals should be used to test drugs, cosmetics and other products intended for use by humans. You could research this topic on the internet or have a class debate.

4 Consider the Anchorage needle-exchange program described above.
a Do you think this study was ethical? Explain.
b Two of the principles of the Declaration of Helsinki (October 2000) are:
- Medical progress is based on research which ultimately must rest in part on experimentation involving humans.
- In medical research on humans, considerations relating to the well-being of the human should take precedence over the interests of science and society.

Were these principles used in the Anchorage needle-exchange study? Explain.

Hmm, I don't think Nodec has had the desired effect on this particular subject.

Check!

1 Match these four words with the four statements below:

inference   observation

hypothesis   prediction

  a My pulse rate is 56 beats per minute.

  b My pulse rate will increase when I run.

  c The more active you are the higher your pulse rate.

  d I think my pulse rate is caused by my heart beating.

2 What is a variable? Why is it so important to control variables in an experiment?

3 Write down in the correct order the four steps in an investigation.

4 a A magnet moving in and out of a coil of wire generates an electric current. What variables could be changed to produce a larger electric current?

  b Milk left open out of a refrigerator turns sour much more quickly than unopened milk kept in a refrigerator. What variables can affect the rate at which milk turns sour?

  c When a hot concentrated solution of copper sulfate was poured into a watch glass, small crystals started to grow around the edge of the solution. What variables could influence the growth of these crystals?

5 Jessica set up 5 pots, each containing 10 small cabbage plants. Each plant was 4–5 cm tall, and each pot had the same amount of soil in it. On the day after the cabbages were planted Jessica added different amounts of liquid fertiliser to each pot. From then on she watered the plants the same amount each day. She observed the growth of the plants over 10 days, and her results are shown below.

Jessie seemed unaware of the plants' attempts at telepathic communication.

  a What problem was Jessica investigating?

  b What variables did she control in her test?

  c What conclusions can you draw from her results?

Pot	Amount of liquid fertiliser added (mL)	Observations after 10 days	
		Colour of leaves	Average height (cm)
1	none	pale green	8
2	5	green	8
3	10	green	15
4	15	green	16
5	20	yellow	8

6 Dominic is a keen tennis player and has played on several different surfaces. He wants to know which surface causes balls to bounce highest. Design an experiment to answer this question. Make sure you list all the variables Dominic will have to control.

7 Work in a group and discuss how you investigate these research questions.

  a Which coloured flowers do bees prefer?

  b Do the phases of the moon affect the weather?

8 Tom wanted to find out which type of nut contained the most stored energy. For each nut he followed the steps in the box below.
  a Do you think Tom's conclusions would be valid?
  b How could he improve his experiment?

1   Put some water in a test tube and clamp it in place as shown.

2   Measure the temperature of the water.

3   Pick up the nut using a metal skewer and light it in a burner.

4   Heat the water in the tube using the flame from the nut.

5   Note the increase in temperature of the water.

6   Repeat steps 1 to 5 for the other nuts.

 ## challenge

1 Suggest why Velcro loses strength when it collects thread or fluff (called lint) during washing.

2 a For each of the following hypotheses write down the independent variable and the dependent variable.

  A Punch brand batteries last longer than GoGo batteries.

  B Small marble chips dissolve more quickly in acid than large chips do.

  C Light-coloured clothing is cooler to wear than dark-coloured clothing.

  D Iron rusts faster in sea water than in fresh water.

  E The chirp rate of crickets increases in warmer weather.

  b Design an experiment to test one of the hypotheses in **a**.

3 Four pairs of students carry out an experiment into the effects of exercise on pulse rate. Their methods are as follows.

  A Kiri and Monique run on the spot for 2 minutes then take each other's pulse.

  B Drew runs on the spot for 2 minutes. Felicity then measures his pulse.

  C Samara takes Mimaki's pulse while Mimaki is seated. Mimaki then runs on the spot for 2 minutes and Samara takes her pulse again.

  D Adam runs on the spot for 2 minutes then takes his own pulse. Bradley sits and takes his pulse.

Evaluate the method used by each pair of students. Which students are most likely to be able to make a valid conclusion about the effect of exercise on pulse rate? How could their experiment be improved?

4 When planning an experiment it is a good idea to use your knowledge of science to change the question you are investigating into a hypothesis. For example:

Question: Which part of your skin is most sensitive to touch?

Hypothesis: Fingertips are the part of your skin most sensitive to touch.

Use your knowledge of science to change the following questions into testable hypotheses.

  a Which objects are attracted to a magnet?

  b Do plants grow better under green plastic or clear plastic?

  c What is steam?

  d What causes silver to tarnish?

1.2 Processing data

Once you have done an experiment and collected your data you need to organise and display it. This makes it easier to identify any patterns or trends in the data. It also makes it easier to discover any cause-and-effect relationships or links between the variables. That is, does increasing (or decreasing) one variable have any effect on another variable?

Over 300 years ago an English schoolteacher called Robert Hooke found a relationship between the amount a spring stretches and the force used to stretch the spring. You can repeat Hooke's experiment yourself on the next page.

Skillbuilder

Drawing lines of best fit

In the next investigation you are going to use your data to draw a graph to show the relationship between two variables.

You will find that the points you plot on the graph will lie close to, but not exactly on, a straight line. You need to draw a **line of best fit**, rather than joining all the points. A line of best fit averages out any errors you made in your measurements in the investigation.

If you need help in drawing lines of best fit, the animation will show you how it is done.

For help with drawing lines of best fit, open the **Drawing a line of best fit** animation on the CD.

Working with technology

Science in action

Writing a science magazine article

Robert Hooke 1635–1703

Robert Hooke has been described as the greatest experimental scientist of the 17th century. Yet he is not nearly as famous as his arch-rival, Isaac Newton.

Your task is to research information about Robert Hooke and write an interesting science magazine article (maximum 500 words) about him.

Structure of the science article

Here are some hints and tips on writing an article for a science magazine.

- Write more of a human interest story than a science story.
- The *introduction* is very important. You should entice your reader with emotion, drama, descriptions and quotations.
- The *body* of the article needs to expand the ideas from the introduction.
- The *conclusion* should be short and punchy and remind the reader of the key points of the story.
- Write in the active voice, eg 'Robert Hooke used his artistic talents to draw the organisms he saw with his newly invented microscope.'
- Avoid lengthy paragraphs. Two or three sentences will do for each paragraph.

Suggestions

- Use the websites below or search for *Robert Hooke* in your browser.
- Write your article on a word processor. You can download images from the websites.
- Make sure your article is scientifically and historically accurate. Don't make up information!

WEBwatch

Go to www.scienceworld.net.au and follow the links to the websites below.

Robert Hooke (1635–1703)

This site contains useful information and links to other sites.

Robert Hooke

This site is dedicated to Robert Hooke and has useful information and pictures which can be downloaded.

Robert Hooke—natural philosopher, inventor …

Interesting site with a large amount of information about his discoveries and achievements.

Investigate

1 HOOKE'S SPRING

Research question

What is the relationship between the force (load) on a spring and the extension of the spring?

Materials

- helical spring
- 50 g mass hanger and standard masses
- stand and clamp
- metre rule
- brick or other heavy mass
- graph paper

Planning and Safety Check

- Use the research question above to write a hypothesis linking the load and the extension of the spring.
- List the steps you will take in your experiment. Use the photo as a guide to setting up your apparatus.
- Draw up a suitable data table in which to record the load (mass added) and the extension (amount of stretch) of the spring.
- List any safety issues.

Planning hints

1 To find the load in newtons, divide the mass (in grams) by 100.

Working with technology You could enter your data into a computer spreadsheet such as *Excel*.

2 After adding the first mass, remove it and check that the spring returns to the zero mark. If it does not, you may not be able to form a valid conclusion from your results. Continue in this way by adding extra masses and recording the extensions. (If the spring does not return to the zero mark between measurements, it is best to stop the experiment and try another spring.)

Discussion

1 Look closely at your data. Do they support your hypothesis?

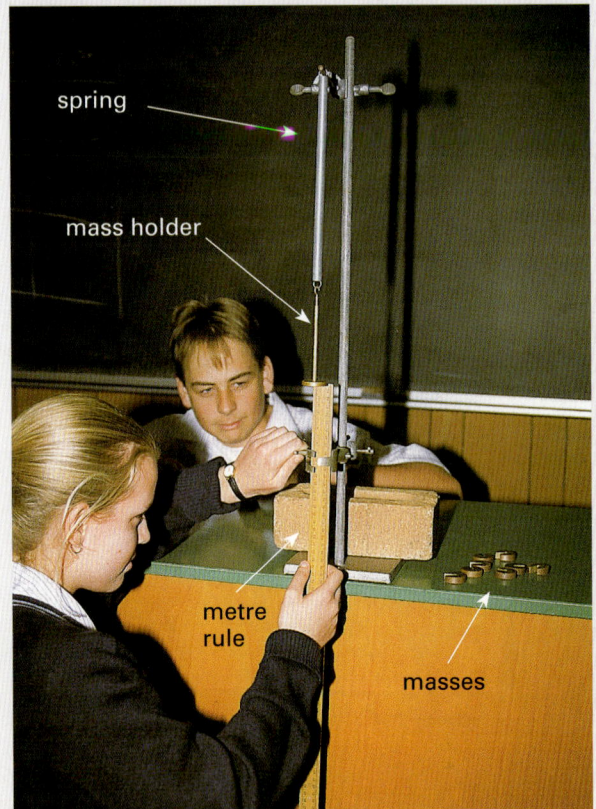

spring

mass holder

metre rule

masses

2 Which is the independent variable (the one you purposely changed in the experiment)?

3 Which is the dependent variable (the one you measured)?

4 Use graph paper to draw a line of best fit as shown below.

5 Compare your data with the data collected by other people. Explain any differences.

Spring extension vs load

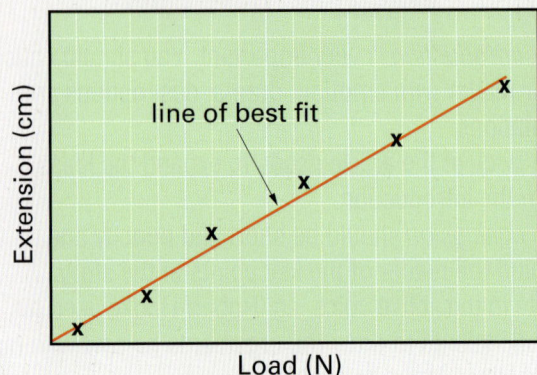

line of best fit

Extension (cm)

Load (N)

Interpreting graphs

Graphs are a very useful way of displaying patterns or trends in data. For example, the graph in the previous experiment shows that the extension of the spring and the load on the spring are directly related to each other. An increase in one variable causes an increase in the other. Similarly, a decrease in one causes a decrease in the other. The fact that the graph is a straight line means that the increases or decreases are proportionally equal. For example, if you double the load you double the extension, and if you triple the load you triple the extension.

Sometimes an increase in one variable causes a decrease in the other. For example, the number of hits on an archery target decreases as the distance from the target increases. In this case the variables are inversely related.

Note that a line of best fit does not go through all the points, but it does go close to them. It tends to 'average' the points and reduce any inaccuracies due to the experimental method used. It is also possible to draw a curve of best fit, as shown below.

Hits on archery target

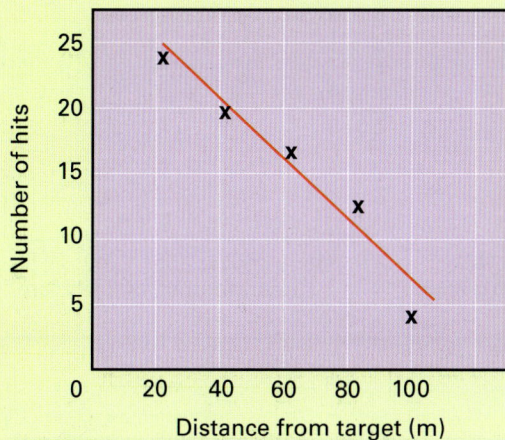

Growth of plant

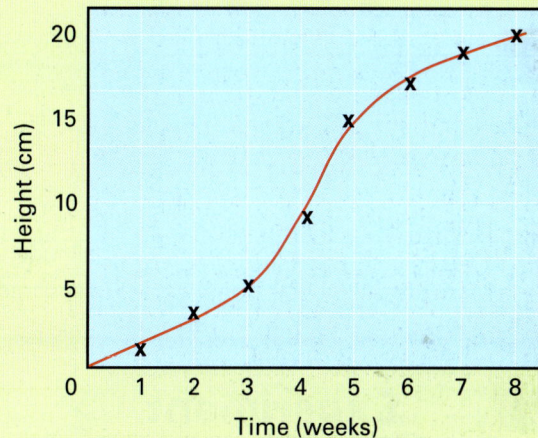

Predicting from graphs

Graphs not only show patterns but can also be used to make predictions. If the prediction is *between* two measurements the process is called **interpolating** (in-TERP-oh-late-ing). On the graph on the right, for a load of 3.5 N you can predict a spring extension of about 20 cm.

It is also possible to make predictions for values *beyond* the measured values. This process is called **extrapolating** (ex-STRAP-oh-late-ing). For example, for a load of 7 N you can extend the straight line and predict an extension of about 40 cm. However, the graph may not be a straight line at that point—for example it may curve upwards. (This is what happens if the spring does not return to its original length when the load is removed.) If this is the case your prediction of a 40 cm extension for a load of 7 N will be far too

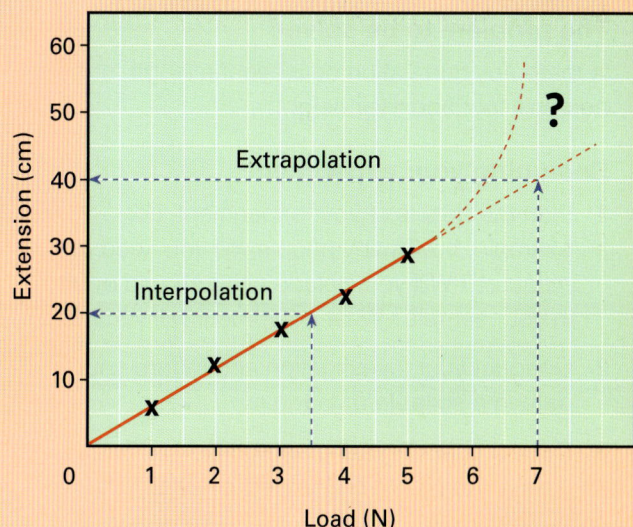

small. This is why you often see widely different predictions for such things as world population or global warming.

Scatter graphs

Suppose you want to see if there is a relationship between the mass and the height of students. You simply plot all the points and look for any *pattern* in the scatter of the points. This type of graph is called a **scatter graph**.

In Graph 1 there is an obvious trend. The taller the student, the heavier they are likely to be. There is a direct relationship between the two variables. We say there is a *high* **correlation** between them. In fact, you could draw a line of best fit through the points.

In Graph 2 there is no direct relationship, but there is *some correlation*. Most plants tend to grow in soils with water content between 10 and 25 g/100 g water.

In Graph 3 there is no relationship between the size of a person's head and their intelligence. There is *no correlation*.

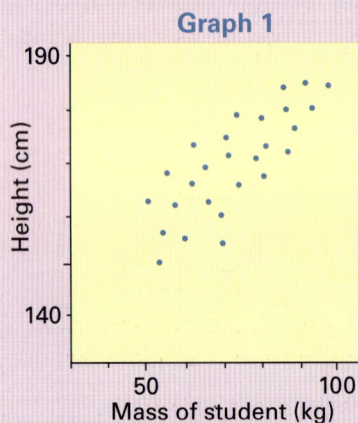

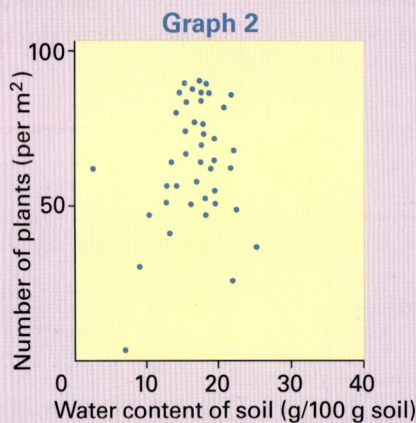

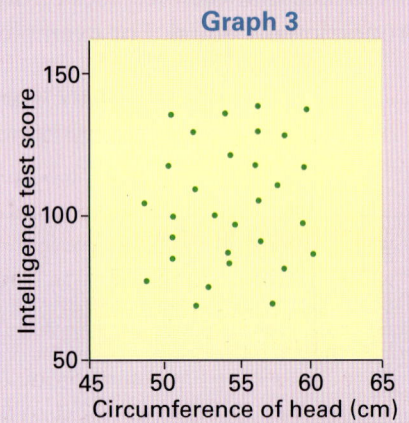

Graph 1

Height (cm) vs Mass of student (kg)

Graph 2

Number of plants (per m²) vs Water content of soil (g/100 g soil)

Graph 3

Intelligence test score vs Circumference of head (cm)

Experiment
MEASURING FEET

The problem to be solved

Is there any correlation between the length of a person's foot and their height?

Designing your experiment

1 Plan the details of your experiment. For example, how many people will you need to measure? Will you include children and adults in your sample? What equipment will you need?

2 Conduct your investigation and record your data in a suitable data table.

3 Draw a scatter graph of height versus foot length. Comment on the degree of correlation.

4 Write a report of your experiment, including the answer to the problem. Finally, evaluate the method you used. Are there things you could do to make your results more reliable?

Shouldn't we take our shoes off for this experiment?

If someone else did this experiment, do you think they would obtain the same results? Explain your answer.

Check!

1 Joshua investigated how far a wind-up toy frog moved with different numbers of turns of the winder.

Number of turns	Distance travelled (cm)
5	23
10	47
15	70
20	90
25	117

a Use his results to draw a graph of best fit. (Try to make the graph fill the whole sheet of graph paper.)
b Write a generalisation linking the number of turns and the distance travelled.
c Use your graph to predict how far the frog will go with 12 turns.
d How many turns are needed to make the frog go 1 metre?

2 Plot the following data on a graph.

Air temperature (°C)	Distance hiked in one hour (km)
9	8.6
15	6.4
22	4.3
25	3.2
30	2.1

a Draw a line of best fit.
b Write a statement describing the relationship between the two variables.
c Use the graph to predict how far you would expect to be able to hike at 20°C and at 35°C.
d Which of these two predictions do you think is more accurate? Why?

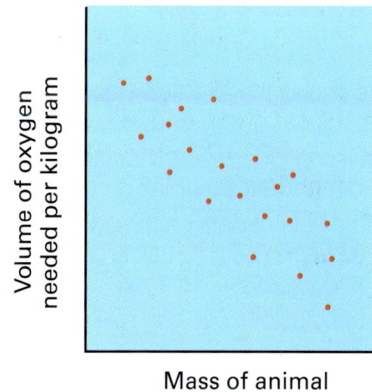

Mass of animal

3 The scatter graph above shows the results of an investigation.
a What was being investigated?
b Is there any correlation between the two variables? Explain your answer.
c Write a statement describing the relationship between the two variables
d Suggest a reason for the relationship.

4 Look at the four scatter graphs below. Which ones show:
• a high correlation between the variables
• a low correlation between the variables
• no correlation between the variables
Give a reason for each choice.

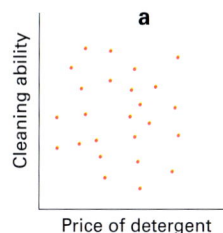

a
Price of detergent

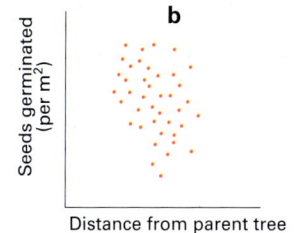

b
Distance from parent tree

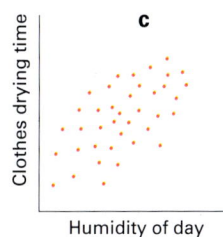

c
Humidity of day

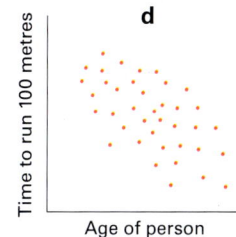

d
Age of person

challenge

1 The table shows the average stopping distance of a car on dry and wet roads.

  a Which is the independent variable and which is the dependent variable?

  b Plot both sets of data on the one graph and draw curves of best fit. Label one curve 'dry road' and the other 'wet road'.

  c What conclusions can you make from the graph?

  d What variables do you think would have been controlled in this investigation?

Speed (km/h)	Stopping distance (m)	
	Dry road	Wet road
0	0	0
20	8	8.5
40	20.5	22
60	38	43
80	60.5	71
100	87.5	106
120	119	149

2 Use the scatter graph below to answer the questions at top right.

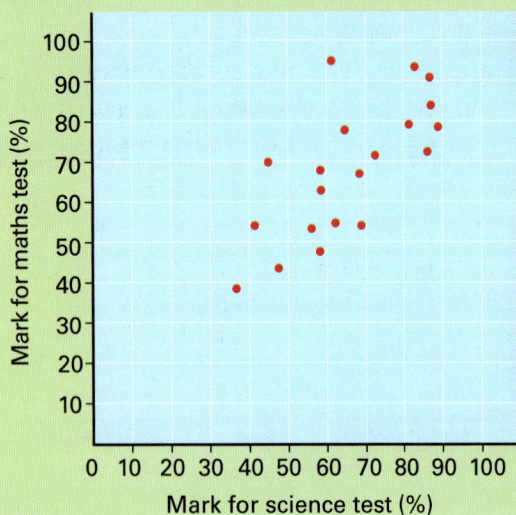

a Which two variables are plotted on the graph?

b What was the highest mark on the science test?

c What was the lowest mark on the maths test?

d What correlation is there between the two sets of marks?

e Draw a line of best fit through the points.

f If a student obtains a score of 70% on the science test, predict their score on the maths test.

g Compare your prediction with those made by others. Explain any differences.

3 Write a sentence to describe the relationship between the variables in each of the six graphs below.

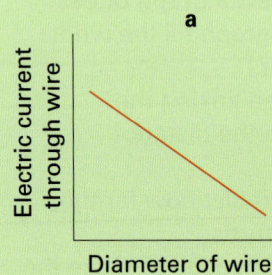

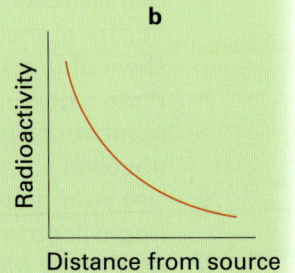

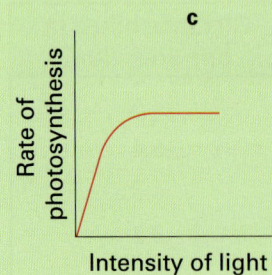

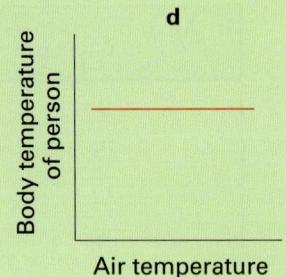

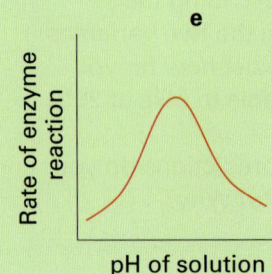

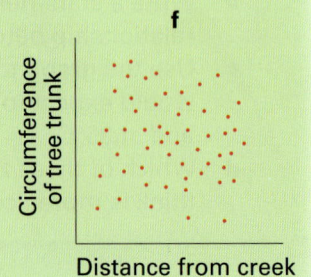

1.3 Collecting data

Some science investigations require you to collect data in the field. For example, you might be investigating the conditions of the water in a creek. You will have to take water samples and measure the pH, temperature and the amount of dissolved nutrients such as nitrates and phosphates, and test the clarity of the water. You might also want to find out the types and numbers of organisms that live in the creek.

Let's look at some techniques to collect data in the field.

Estimating numbers in a population

Some organisms, such as barnacles, are fixed in place in their habitat, while most other organisms are mobile and move from place to place. Different techniques are needed to study and count fixed and mobile organisms.

In field studies you can usually never count every organism in a population. You have to use methods to *sample* the population, and then *estimate* the total number.

The quadrat method

This method is used to study populations that are fixed in position. A **quadrat** is a square frame made of plastic, wire, wood or even string, which can be used to sample the organisms in a particular area.

Suppose you need to estimate the population of barnacles and molluscs in an area of a rocky shore. Quadrats vary in size but are usually 1 m × 1 m square; however, this is far too large to count small rocky shore organisms. A suitable quadrat might be 200 mm × 200 mm.

You can use the quadrat to count the various organisms in a number of different places chosen at random in the area. For a reliable estimate you should sample at least 10 places. The data can then be used to estimate the various populations in the selected habitat, or the population density per square metre.

Suppose you were studying a rocky shore and wanted to estimate the number of barnacles in a 10 m × 5 m area. You drop your 200 mm × 200 mm square quadrat at random over the selected area. You do this ten times and each time count the number of barnacles inside the quadrat.

Number of barnacles in each of the 10 quadrats:

5, 9, 5, 8, 11, 14, 7, 5, 10, 6 Total = 80 barnacles

$$\text{Area of 1 quadrat} = 200\,mm \times 200\,mm$$
$$= 0.2\,m \times 0.2\,m$$
$$= 0.04\,m^2$$
$$\text{Area of 10 quadrats} = 10 \times 0.04$$
$$= 0.4\,m^2$$

$$\text{Population size} = \frac{\text{no. of barnacles in 10 quadrats}}{\text{area of 10 quadrats}} \times \text{total area}$$

$$= \frac{80}{0.4} \times 50$$

$$= 10\,000 \text{ barnacles}$$

The capture–recapture method

This sampling method is used to estimate mobile populations of organisms. In this method a sample of the population is caught, counted and tagged. The organisms are then released back into the habitat. After some time when they have dispersed throughout the population, a second sample is taken. Some organisms will be tagged, others will be untagged. Both are counted and an estimate is calculated as shown below.

Suppose 200 fish were caught in a lake. They were tagged and released. One month later, 100 fish were caught. Among these were 25 tagged fish that had been caught previously.

The capture–recapture method works on the principle that the proportion of tagged fish in the second sample is the same as the proportion of tagged fish in the total population.

$$\text{Proportion of tagged fish in 2nd sample} = \frac{25}{100}$$

$$\text{Proportion of tagged fish in 1st sample} = \frac{200}{\text{total}}$$

$$\frac{25}{100} = \frac{200}{\text{total}}$$

$$\text{Therefore, total} = \frac{100}{25} \times 200$$

$$= 800 \text{ fish}$$

So you can estimate there are 800 fish in the lake.

Investigate

2 ESTIMATING POPULATIONS

Aim

To estimate the size of a population using the quadrat and capture–recapture methods.

Materials

- a large container of plastic-coated, coloured paperclips
- 1 m of heavy wire (fencing or coathanger wire)
- at least 5 m of string
- bar magnet (optional)

Planning and Safety Check

- It is best to work in groups of 3 or 4.
- Carefully read through the Method for Part A and B and decide which part you will do first.
- Prepare data tables for your results in both parts.

PART A
Quadrat method

Method

1 Bend the wire into a 200 mm x 200 mm square frame. This is your quadrat.

2 Count the paperclips. Then scatter them over an area of at least 2 m x 2 m in the room or outside.

Instead of dropping the quadrat at random, you will use a *transect*. This is a line across your area along which you place your quadrats. You take your 10 samples along this line.

3 Have two people hold the ends of the string and *without looking* lay it across the area containing the scattered paperclips.

4 Use the quadrat to take 10 samples along the transect.

   Count and record the number of paperclips.

Discussion

1 Find the total number of paperclips in the 10 quadrats.

2 The area of the 200 mm x 200 mm quadrat is 0.04 m^2. Find the total area of the 10 quadrats.

3 Use the equation below to estimate the population of paperclips.

$$\text{Population size} = \frac{\text{no. of paperclips in 10 quadrats}}{\text{area of 10 quadrats}} \times \text{total area}$$

4 How does the estimated paperclip population compare with the known count of paperclips?

5 Calculate the population density in numbers per square metre. (Use the estimated population.)

6 Suggest ways to improve this investigation so that you obtain more accurate results.

7 What is the advantage in taking samples along a transect? Can you think of another way to sample the population which will give you reliable results?

PART B
Capture–recapture method

Method

1 Empty the container of paperclips on the desk. Select a colour and count all the paperclips of this colour. These represent your *tagged* paperclips in the total population.

   ✎ Record this number.

2 Return the paperclips to the container and mix them up well.

3 Use a small container about the size of an eggcup or a kitchen measuring spoon to scoop out some paperclips. Alternatively you can dip a bar magnet into the paperclips.

4 Count the number of paperclips in the sample and also the number of the selected colour (tagged) paperclips.

   ✎ Record your results.

5 Return the sample to the container, mix well and repeat Steps 3 and 4 for a total of 10 samples.

Discussion

1 Use the ratio formula below to calculate the estimated population size for each of the 10 samples.

$$\frac{\text{total no. tagged}}{\text{population size}} = \frac{\text{no. tagged recaptured}}{\text{no. in sample}}$$

2 Find the average population size for the 10 samples. Compare this with the known size of the population of paperclips.

3 Comment on the reliability of your results. Could you improve your method?

4 This method assumes that the number of individuals in a population remains the same throughout the sampling. Would this be true of a population of fish in a lake? What factors might affect this assumption?

Sampling in the field

Collecting data on the types and numbers of organisms is one part of a field study; obtaining data on the physical factors in the environment is the other part.

   You know from previous studies in science that physical or abiotic factors such as temperature, availability of water, soil types and soil nutrients, and the pH of water and soil play a large part in determining the abundance and distribution of organisms in a particular habitat.

Fig 26 The rapid growth of blue-green algae is due to high water temperatures and large amounts of nutrients dissolved in the water.

Investigate

3 SAMPLING PHYSICAL FACTORS

Aim

To practise various techniques for sampling physical factors in the environment such as temperature, pH, dissolved salts and dissolved oxygen.

This investigation is best done in the field. If this is not possible you will be supplied with 4 buckets of creek or pond water. Assume that each bucketful of water has been collected from one of four sites in a creek as shown in the diagram.

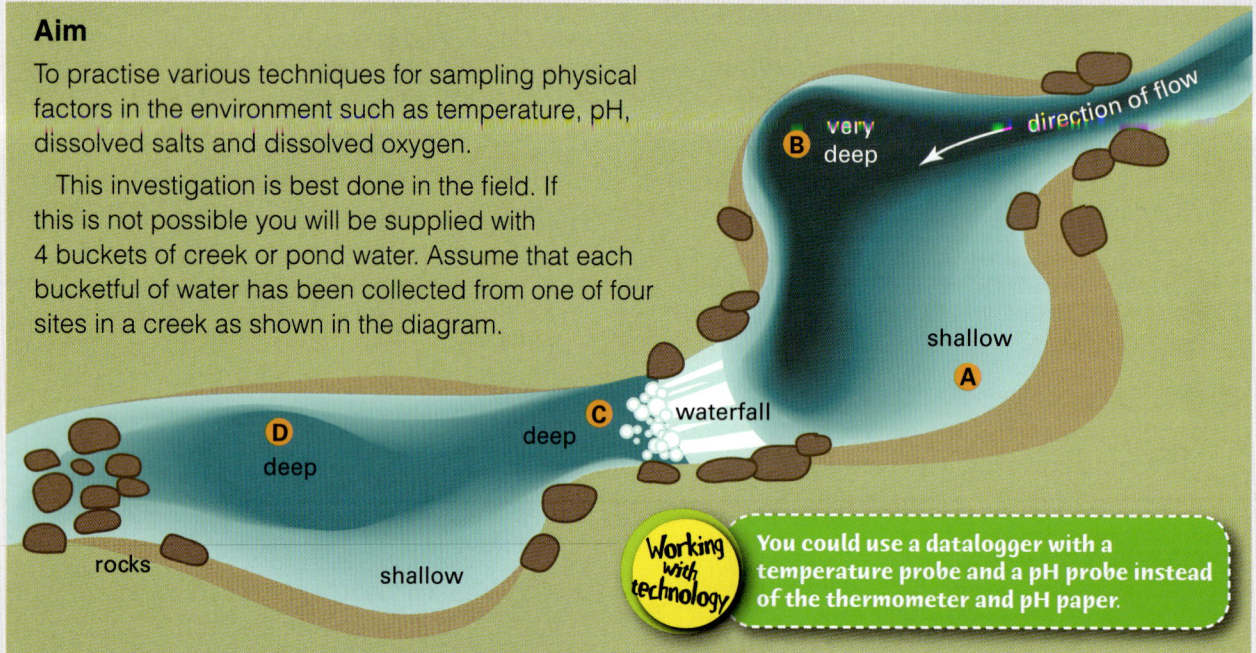

direction of flow

B very deep

shallow **A**

C deep   waterfall

D deep

rocks   shallow

Working with technology
You could use a datalogger with a temperature probe and a pH probe instead of the thermometer and pH paper.

Planning and Safety Check

- Work in groups of 3 or 4.
- Carefully read through each part. Make sure you know what to do. Decide which part your group will do first, then discuss this with your teacher.
- Prepare data tables for your results in each part.
- Make a list of the safety issues in each part. Your teacher will discuss these as a class before you start.

PART A
Temperature and pH

Materials

- 4 buckets of pond water or specially prepared water
- two 100 mL beakers or glass jars
- thermometer
- pH paper, universal indicator solution and colour card, or swimming pool pH kit
- distilled water

Method

1. Make sure your beakers are clean and rinsed in distilled water.

2. Number the buckets. Take about half a beakerful of water from the first bucket.

3. Use the equipment to find the temperature and pH of the water.
   Record the results in the data table.

4. Tip out the water and rinse the beaker in distilled water.

5. Repeat Steps 2 and 3 for the other 3 buckets of water and record your results.

Discussion

1. Why is it necessary to rinse the beakers in distilled water after each test?

2. Reliable results are obtained when you take a number of samples and average the results. Would you average the data from all four sites in the creek or just some of the sites, or use individual readings? Use the map of the creek to justify your answer.

PART B
Conductivity

Conductivity is a measure of the amount of dissolved salts (nutrients) in the water. Water from a salt water swimming pool is tested for conductivity to determine how much dissolved salt is in the water.

A conductivity probe contains two metal electrodes. When the battery is switched on and the electrodes are dipped into the water, the ions in the water carry the current between the electrodes. A meter reads how much current flows. This reading is proportional to the concentration of the dissolved salts.

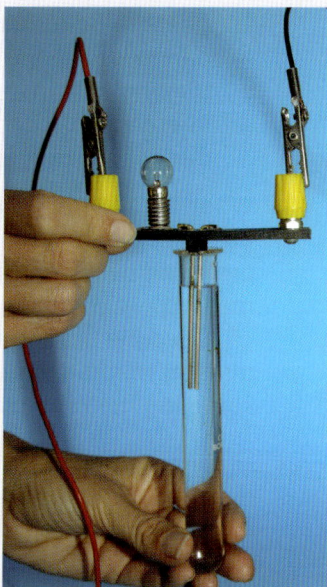

Materials
- 100 mL beaker or glass jar
- conductivity kit or datalogger with conductivity probe

Method
1 Clean the beaker and rinse it in distilled water.
2 Take a sample of about 50 mL from one of the buckets of water. Record the number of the bucket.
3 Use the equipment to find the conductivity of the water.
   Record your results in the data table.

Discussion
1 Calculate the average conductivity of all four samples.
2 What conditions would change the conductivity of the water in a creek?

PART C
Dissolved oxygen

Dissolved oxygen (DO) is a very important factor in determining the distribution and abundance of aquatic organisms. Some organisms can survive only in water with high levels of dissolved oxygen, while others can tolerate very low levels.

Materials
- 100 mL beaker and glass jar with screw lid
- oxygen meter with probe, or DO test kit

Note: Your teacher will show you how to use the oxygen meter and probe if your school has one. Alternatively you will be shown how to use the dissolved oxygen (DO) test kit.

Method
1 Clean the beaker and rinse it in distilled water.
2 Without disturbing the surface of the water too much, slowly dip the beaker into a bucket of water and collect about 70 mL of water.
3 Use the oxygen meter or the DO test kit to find the level of dissolved oxygen in the water.
   Record your results in the data table.
4 Repeat Steps 1 to 3 for the other buckets of water.
   Record your results.
5 Take another water sample from any bucket and pour it into the glass jar. Screw the lid on and shake vigorously. Then test for DO.
   Record your results.

Discussion
1 Compare the DO in the shaken jar with the water in each of the buckets. Account for the differences.
2 Why was it necessary to avoid disturbing the water when you took your samples from the buckets?
3 What biotic and abiotic factors might change the level of dissolved oxygen in a creek?

Check!

1 Match the words in the list below with their descriptions.

sample   quadrat   conductivity
transect   population   abiotic

a A measure of the concentration of ions in water

b A square frame used to count organisms in a particular area

c A line across a selected area which is used as a guide to sample organisms

d A number of organisms of the same kind in a particular area

e A small group of organisms selected from the total population

f The physical or non-living factors in the environment

2 The table (top right) shows the number of dandelion plants in a grassy area in 1 m x 1 m quadrats taken along a transect. The grassy area measured 10 m x 25 m.

Quadrat	1	2	3	4	5	6	7	8	9	10
Number of dandelion plants	4	4	9	9	11	6	8	9	7	4

a Find the total number of dandelions in the 10 quadrats.

b Use the equation on page 17 as a guide to find the total population of dandelions in the grassy area.

c Use the data in the table to make an inference about the distribution of dandelions in the grassy area.

3 When sampling populations of organisms in the field, the quadrat method is sometimes preferred over the capture–recapture method.

Describe the situations in which the quadrat method would be the better sampling method to use.

challenge

1 The grid below shows the number of feral horses in a particular area. The horses were photographed from an aircraft and the positions of the horses (●) were placed on the grid shown.

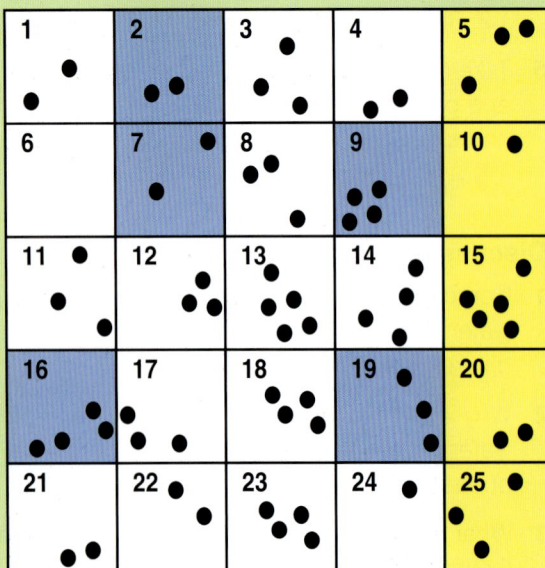

Biologists want to estimate the size of the horse population so they can study their habits and try to reduce the damage that they cause to native wildlife.

The biologists used the quadrat method to sample the horses. They selected 5 squares at random (shown in blue) and also 5 squares along a transect (shown in yellow).

a Use the random squares (blue) to estimate the size of the horse population.

b Now use the transect squares (yellow) to estimate the horse population.

c Do your answers for **a** and **b** indicate that one method gives a more accurate estimate of the total horse population than the other? Explain.

d Select another 5 squares to show that results can vary when using the quadrat method. How did you select the quadrats?

e Why was the quadrat method used by the biologists? Could the biologists have used the capture–recapture method instead? Give reasons for your answer.

MAIN IDEAS

Copy and complete these statements to make a summary of this chapter. The missing words are on the right.

1 The four main steps in a scientific investigation are _____, doing the experiment, processing the data and _____ the experiment.

2 To obtain _____ results in an experiment you usually need to take repeated measurements and calculate an _____.

3 To evaluate an investigation you think about how you could improve the experiment and whether your conclusions are _____.

4 Processing data involves looking for _____ or trends showing relationships between the _____ being investigated.

5 Graphs of best fit drawn from experimental data can be used to make _____.

6 _____ graphs can be used to check what correlation there is between two variables.

7 Both the _____ method and capture–recapture method can be used to _____ the size of a population.

average
estimate
evaluating
patterns
planning
predictions
quadrat
reliable
scatter
valid
variables

Try doing the Chapter 1 crossword on the CD.

Working with technology

REVIEW

1 In testing the effectiveness of a dishwashing detergent you would not need to consider:
A the amount of detergent used
B the time of day
C the temperature of the water
D how the dishes were washed

2 Glen did an experiment to find out if fertiliser affects the amount of oxygen a water plant makes. He used the apparatus shown below. A suitable control for this experiment would be to use the same apparatus but without the:
A water plant
B test tube
C fertiliser
D water

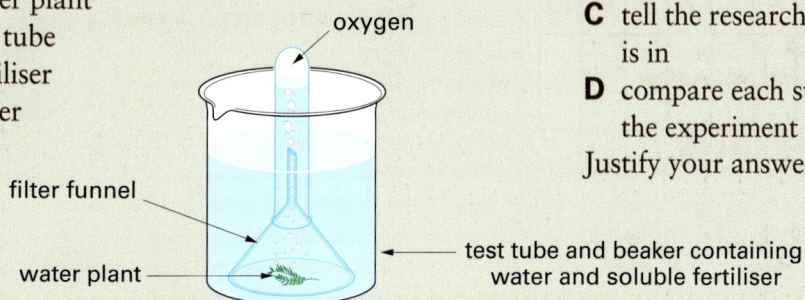

oxygen

filter funnel

water plant

test tube and beaker containing water and soluble fertiliser

3 From coral, a drug company has isolated a chemical (Z), which they claim reduces acne. They select 200 students with acne and photograph the areas of skin affected. Half of the students (the test group) are given a lotion containing Z. The other half (the control group) are given an identical lotion except that it contains no Z. To make this experiment a fair test of ingredient Z, the drug company should *not*:
A release any details of the trial to the public
B give identical-looking lotion to all students
C tell the researchers which group each student is in
D compare each student's acne before and after the experiment
Justify your answer.

4 A biologist found that if you eat a meal containing a lot of carbohydrates your blood sugar level rises rapidly then drops off almost as rapidly. If you eat a meal containing a lot of protein, your blood sugar level rises more slowly to a lower peak. It also drops more slowly, but it does not fall as far as with a high carbohydrate meal.

Which graph correctly shows these findings?

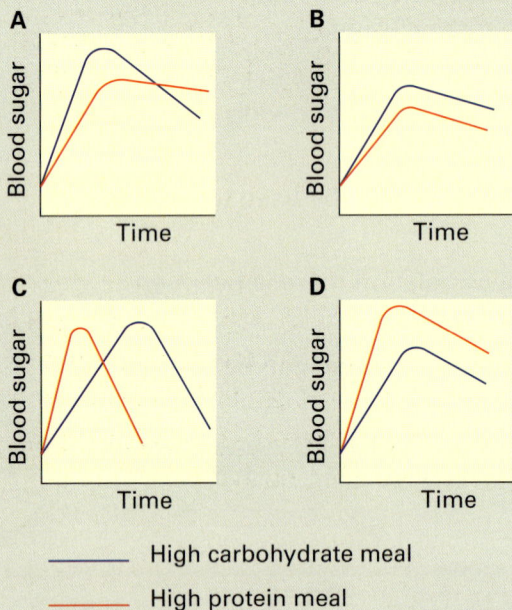

A B C D graphs with axes Blood sugar (vertical) and Time (horizontal)

——— High carbohydrate meal

——— High protein meal

5 Describe how you would use the capture–recapture method to estimate the population of mullet in a section of a river.

6 Two students used the quadrat method to estimate the population of periwinkles on a rocky platform close to the water's edge. The rocky platform measured 20 m × 5 m, and ten 1 m × 1 m quadrats were sampled along a transect.

Quadrat	1	2	3	4	5	6	7	8	9	10
Number of periwinkles	10	12	15	13	12	9	16	14	10	9

a Find the total number of periwinkles in the 10 quadrats.
b Estimate the periwinkle population on the rocky shore platform.

c Suggest why the quadrat method was used by the students instead of the capture–recapture method.

7 Nancy and Daniel were both given a new bicycle for Christmas. Nancy's was a mountain bike with 22 gears and Daniel's was a BMX with 10 gears. Nancy argued that her bike was safer because its larger wheels meant it would stop more quickly than Daniel's BMX with smaller wheels.

To settle the argument Nancy and Daniel rode their bikes down a hill and braked when they reached a particular spot on the road. Nancy stopped in 22 m and Daniel stopped in 14 m. Daniel claimed that Nancy was wrong— small wheels stop you more quickly than large wheels.

a What Nancy and Daniel did was not a fair test of wheel size and braking ability. List at least three uncontrolled variables that could have affected the results.
b Suggest ways in which Nancy and Daniel could improve their test.

8 Chung investigated the relationship between the diameter of ropes and their breaking strain.

Diameter of rope (cm)	Breaking strain (kg)
1	400
2	500
3	750
4	950
5	1100

a Use Chung's results to draw a graph of best fit.
b Write a statement of the relationship between the two variables.

Check your answers on page 331.

2 Consumer science

Getting Started

Ella is planning to buy a mobile phone. This will make a large hole in her savings, so she wants to make the correct choice. Her friends have plenty of suggestions, but how can she sort out this advice?

- Arrange the advice in the cartoon into a flow chart that shows the order of the steps Ella should take in deciding which phone to buy.
- Compare your flow chart with other people's. Discuss any differences.

LAURA: Where can you get information about the product?

KATE: Is it value for money?

MING SHANG: Describe the type of product you need.

CHELSEA: What effect will buying this have on the environment?

CLINTON: Check the reliability of all the information.

NIKKI: Test each of the alternatives.

LACHLAN: Find out what the alternatives are.

ZACK: How well does this choice match what you wanted in the first place?

SANAA: Reconsider your decision.

BEN: What are the advantages and disadvantages of each alternative?

MIKAELA: Decide what you mean by quality.

MAI: Make a decision.

2.1 Consumer testing

We are all consumers because we eat food and belong in a food web. However, the word 'consumer' is used with another meaning: it is used to describe someone who buys something. Every time you go to the shops and buy something, you are a *consumer*. It does not have to be food. It could be clothes, electrical goods, sporting equipment or even electricity.

Testing mobile phones

There are many articles published in newspapers and magazines to help consumers choose which products to buy. *Choice* magazine is one such publication, and their investigators recently tested mobile phones. The six steps used in their investigation are shown on the right and on page 28.

STEP 1: Decide which product you want to test

Mobile phones are very popular with all ages of people. They are packed with features and functions you may love—or never use. The *Choice* investigators tested 45 GSM models.

STEP 2: List the features you want to test

Choice decided to test the 10 features listed below.

STEP 3: Design a fair test for each feature

To check for durability the testers put the phones in an 80 cm barrel that was then turned, simulating falls from a table or out of a shirt pocket. After 5, 15 and 25 turns the phones were checked for damage.

STEP 4: Do the tests and record the results

See the table on the next page.

1 How good is the battery?

2 Sensitivity—how well does the phone deal with a weak signal?

3 How easy is it to use the basic functions?

4 How easy is the keypad to use (ergonomics)?

5 How good is it for SMSing?

6 What is the sound quality?

7 What is the quality of the digital camera pictures?

8 How many different features does it have (versatility)?

9 How big is it? How heavy is it (portability)?

10 How tough is it (durability)?

Brand/model (in rank order)	A	B	C	D	E	F	G	H
Overall score*	68	68	63	63	61	60	59	55
1 Battery score	63	62	78	49	55	76	49	39
2 Sensitivity	80	75	69	72	70	66	74	66
3 Everyday use	76	89	81	65	73	56	47	62
4 Ergonomics	63	59	54	69	46	45	51	63
5 SMS	74	70	61	76	68	63	58	67
6 Sound	62	67	51	61	53	54	47	52
7 Picture	50	54	47	51	52	43	60	37
8 Versatility	73	68	62	63	64	49	84	57
9 Portability	59	66	41	70	67	65	49	71
10 Durability	75	65	68#	61	59#	61	78#	53
Battery life (h)†	5.1	6.0	7.7	3.9	4.8	7.6	3.8	3.0
Charge time (min)	171	120	132	120	118	158	77	94
Voice dialling	✓		✓		✓		✓	
Voice recording	✓	✓	✓	✓	✓		✓	✓
Email	✓	✓		✓	✓	✓	✓	
Weight (g)	123	99	126	92	97	99	130	87
Dimensions (mm)	88x47x23	93x47x25	98x48x27	108x47x20	98x53x15	107x46x19	102x50x23	105x47x19
Price ($)	639	999	649	399	999	179	619	349

Reprinted from the June 2005 edition of *Choice* with the permission of the Australian Consumers' Association (ACA).

* Combined score for features 1–10
\# Defective after tumble test
$\dagger$ An average for different use patterns

STEP 5: Interpret the results and write a report

Most mobile phones can take digital photos and send them to someone else. However, the quality is poor compared with digital cameras. While phone A was rated the best overall, it may not be the best on a particular feature, eg weight. So if a particular feature is essential to you, a model further down the table, which doesn't have a major weakness, may be the one for you.

STEP 6: Decide on the best product

Value for money

When deciding which product to buy, you should consider *value for money*. With the mobile phones tested by *Choice,* A and B had the same overall score, but A was cheaper.

To find value for money for products in containers, you can divide the cost by the net mass, as shown below, to calculate the cost per gram or per millilitre. With solutions, you may need to consider the concentration of the solution as well as the volume. For example, 500 mL of a 10% bleach solution should last longer than 500 mL of a 5% solution, since you need to use only half the amount each time.

You also need to consider the lifetime of the product. For example, an alkaline battery that lasts twice as long but costs three times as much is not the best value for money.

Rating panels and surveys

It is easy to compare products when you have tested them by measuring something, for example the weight of a mobile phone, or by noting whether or not it has a particular feature. Such tests are said to be **objective tests**.

In other tests you cannot be as objective. For example, the performance of a mobile phone, eg ease of use, is based on opinion—what one particular person thinks. Such tests are said to be **subjective tests**. To make the results of such tests easier to compare you can ask people to give the product a *rating*. For example:

or

| borderline | OK | good | very good |

| 1 (very poor) | to | (excellent) 10 |

For this sort of test you need a number of people (a *panel*). If you want an overall rating you can then average the results.

Another method used to collect consumer information is a **survey**. For example, you might want to do a survey on the reliability of various makes of cars. When carrying out such a survey you obviously cannot ask *all* users of the make you choose (eg Holdens).

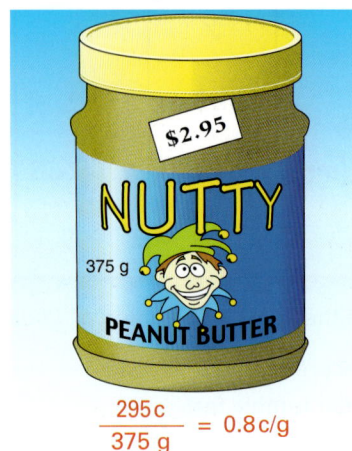

$$\frac{193c}{200\,g} = 1.0\,c/g$$

$$\frac{239c}{375\,g} = 0.6\,c/g$$

$$\frac{295c}{375\,g} = 0.8\,c/g$$

Fig 3 Which is the best value for money here?

Instead you use a **sample**—in this case, only selected car users. You need to choose this sample carefully so that it represents the whole group and not just a part of it. For example, you would need to sample car users of different ages from different areas of Australia. Making the sample size as large as possible improves the results, and helps to overcome prejudice or bias.

To conduct the survey you can either interview people or send them a printed list of questions called a *questionnaire*. These questions must be worded in a way that will make the results as objective as possible. For example, instead of asking *How reliable is your car?* it would be better to ask *How many times did your car break down in the last year?*

Fig 4 Taste is a subjective test. When comparing wines, judges rate the wines on criteria such as taste, colour and aroma.

Investigate
4 A TASTE TEST

Aim
To use a panel to assess the quality of a type of drink or food.

Method
1 Select about three different brands of a particular product, eg orange juice, lemonade, sandwich spread, yoghurt or hamburgers.

2 Decide on the criteria you will use to assess the product, eg flavour, colour, texture, sweetness, smell.

3 Design a data table to record your results.

4 Set up a tasting panel of at least four people. Blindfold them.

5 Have two samples of each product. This lets you compare people's ratings of the same product to see if they are 'reliable' tasters.

6 Give the samples to the tasters in a mixed order, and ask them to rate each on a scale of 1 to 10, using the criteria from Step 2.

7 Record the ratings in your data table and analyse them.

Discussion
1 Why were the testers blindfolded?

2 Which product did each person give the highest rating? Which did they give the lowest rating?

3 Did all tasters give their highest rating to the same product?

4 What is the average rating for each product?

5 Can you suggest any improvements to your test? Explain.

Conclusion
Write a brief conclusion for your test.

Experiment
CONSUMER TESTING

Imagine you work for a consumer magazine. Your boss has asked you to choose a consumer product and apply the six steps below to compare different brands. She wants you to write up your findings for the next issue of the magazine.

STEP 1: Decide which product you want to test

There are lots of products to choose from, and here are some suggested research questions.

- Which drink contains the most sugar or the most vitamin C?

- Which stain remover works best?

- Which chewing gum keeps its flavour the longest?

- Does a fine point biro last longer than a medium point one?

- Believe it or not, breakfast cereal contains tiny particles of iron, but which brand contains the most?

STEP 2: List the features you want to test

You can get further ideas from *Choice* magazine. You could also go to www.scienceworld.net.au and follow the links to the websites below:

Choice

Science Fair Project Ideas

STEP 3: Design a fair test for each feature

Remember to apply what you have learnt about working scientifically and doing projects.

- Write an aim that makes it clear what it is that you are investigating. This is usually in the form of a research question like the ones in Step 1.

- Write a plan that outlines what you intend doing and how you will make any tests fair. It is a good idea to test each product three times and average your results.

- List the equipment you will need.

- Before starting your experiment check with your teacher whether the equipment is available and whether what you are planning to do is safe.

STEP 4: Do the tests and record the results

Present your data in a way which helps show any patterns or trends in it.

STEP 5: Interpret the results and write a report

- What is the answer to your research question?

- Are your results what you expected? Did you control the variables properly? Could you improve your results by changing your method or repeating measurements?

STEP 6: Make a decision on the best product

Your findings should be *reliable*. For instance, you should be able to defend your tests if a manufacturer says your results are inaccurate. If someone else repeats your tests, would they obtain similar results?

Hey Chris, did you work out which cereal has the most iron in it?

Check!

1 Use the table on page 27 to answer these questions about the mobile phone investigation done by *Choice*.
   a Which is the heaviest of the phones tested by *Choice*?
   b Which do you think would be the best phone if you do a lot of SMSing?
   c Which phone would take the best photos?
   d Which phone would be the best where there is a poor signal?
   e Which phones failed the tumble test?
   f What similarities and differences are there between the Brand A and Brand B phones? Which would you buy? Why?
   g According to the *Choice* results, are the most expensive phones the best?
   h What is meant by the ergonomics of a phone?
   i On average, how long do mobile phone batteries last?
   j Which of the *Choice* tests do you think would be subjective? Explain your answer.
   k Which of the phones is the smallest? Explain your answer.

2 Margarita was worried that there was too much juice and not enough fruit in a certain brand of tinned fruit, so she did a test. Here are her results.

   mass of unopened can   = 550 g

   mass of opened can after   = 400 g
   juice has been drained off

   mass of empty can   = 50 g

   a What is the total mass of the contents of the can? (This is the *net* mass.)
   b What is the mass of juice in the can?
   c What is the mass of solid fruit in the can?
   d What percentage of the can's contents is solid fruit?

3 List four tests you could use to decide which brand of correction fluid to buy.

4 Look at the bar graph below showing the amount of protein in an average serving of two breakfast cereals.

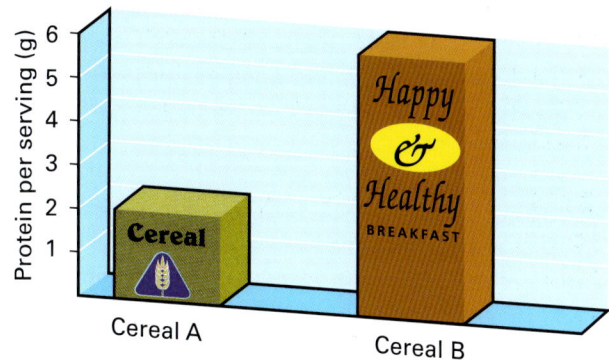

   a Based on this graph, which cereal do you think is better for your health? Explain.
   b The recommended daily amount of protein is 50–100 g. Does this change your answer to a? Explain.

5 Kyra asked three people to do some tests on hamburgers using this five-point scale:
   5 Yummy
   4 Not bad
   3 Nothing special
   2 Not very nice at all
   1 Yuk! I'd rather starve

   Each person tested each hamburger twice. The results are shown below.
   a Calculate the average rating for each of the hamburgers.
   b Rate the four hamburgers in order of popularity.
   c Who was the most reliable taster—that is, the person whose ratings for the same hamburger are the closest?

	Yasmin		Felicity		Kelly	
Fast food chain A	3	2	3	1	3	3
Fast food chain B	5	4	4	3	4	4
Homemade	3	4	3	5	4	3
Corner store	5	5	4	2	5	4

challenge

1 You want to test how effective various sunscreens are. What variables could affect the results of your test?

2 Blake is looking for a new boogie board.
   a What features do you think he should be looking for?
   b What tests could he do?

3 Choose a test report that interests you from *Choice* magazine and write a summary of it. In your summary, make sure you give the aim of the investigation, what tests were done, the results and the conclusions.

4 How would you test which of four different science textbooks was the best?

5 There are three options for providing nappies for a baby. List at least three advantages and three disadvantages of each option. Then, as a group, decide which you consider the best option and why.

Option 1: Use re-usable cloth nappies. Parents who use this method buy about 30 nappies (about $2.50 each) and wash them at home after use. Remember there are costs (about $6.50 per week) for washing powder, disinfectant, hot water and electricity to run the washing machine and perhaps the clothes dryer. Assume the cloth nappies last about a year.

Option 2: Use re-usable cloth nappies and pay a nappy service to collect the dirty nappies and replace them with clean ones. The nappy service washes the nappies for you. Nappy services charge about 44 cents per nappy, and about 60 nappies are required each week.

Option 3: Use disposable nappies. These cost about 31 cents each.

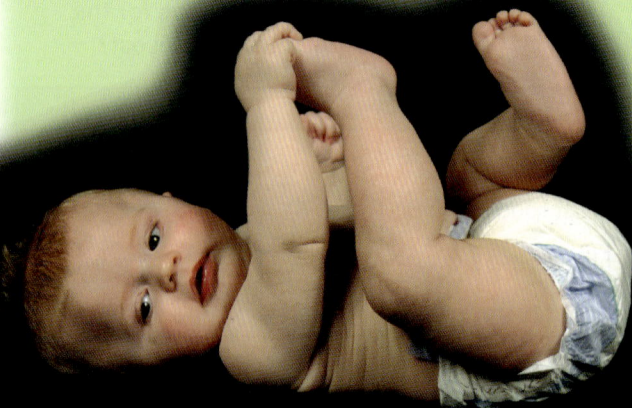

6 Examine the advertisement below and answer the following questions.
   a Why is the person in the advertisement a middle-aged male with a white coat and glasses? What is he meant to represent? Do consumers trust this sort of person more than others?
   b There are many products whose names suggest they are 'green', like *Eco-gentle*. What advantages do the manufacturers expect to gain from this?
   c Is it realistic to say the product has no effect on the environment?
   d Can experiments prove the safety and effectiveness of the product? Explain.
   e Is there anything special about tests carried out in universities? Why might advertisers include this type of statement?
   f What does the word 'hypo-allergenic' mean? Do you think many consumers would know? Why do you think this word was used in the advertisement?

For tough stains...

You know that you can trust Eco-Gentle stain remover.

...Eco-Gentle
- Eco-Gentle is a revolutionary approach to stain removal.
- It will remove stains from every type of fabric without damage.
- University experiments have proven the safety and effectiveness of this product.
- It has absolutely no impact on the environment, and is hypo-allergenic.

Eco-Gentle

2.2 Options

There are six options for you to choose from. Each one has something to do with making decisions about which product to buy or about safety aspects of a product. You can use these summaries to help you decide which options to do.

OPTION 1

VISCOSITY OF OILS   page 34

You find out about the viscosity of oils, and conduct an experiment to find out how the viscosity changes as the temperature changes.

OPTION 2

TESTING GLUES   page 36

You plan and conduct various consumer tests on different brands of glue, along the lines of the *Choice* mobile phone tests.

OPTION 3

FIRE DANGER   page 37

You investigate whether fabrics can be made less flammable by treating them with a fire retardant.

OPTION 4

FOOD ADDITIVES   page 39

You learn about food labels and the different types of food additives, then test for sulfur dioxide in foods.

OPTION 5

DISPOSABLE NAPPIES
page 42

You compare the effectiveness of different brands of disposable nappies.

OPTION 6

COSMETICS   page 43

First you find out what an emulsion is, then you make your own cleansing cream and compare it with commercial cleansing creams.

Experiment
VISCOSITY OF OILS

Research question

How does the viscosity (thickness) of oil change as the temperature is changed?

Designing your experiment

Read through the Planning hints, then work in a small group to design your experiment. Make a list of the materials you will need.

   Include in your design an assessment of the safety issues you will address when you do the experiment.

   Show your draft design, materials and risk assessment to your teacher for approval. Do not start your experiment without a signed approval from your teacher.

Planning hints

1   Write a testable hypothesis linking the viscosity of the oil to its temperature.

2   You can measure the viscosity of the oil by dropping a ball bearing through it. The longer it takes to fall, the more viscous the oil is.

3   You can use a magnet to retrieve the ball bearing from the bottom of the cylinder.

4   You don't want the fall time to be too short, so you need a tall measuring cylinder. You could experiment with a long tube, eg an old burette works well. You could also use a marble or something similar instead of a ball bearing.

5   Another method is to put the oil in a long tube, leaving an air bubble. When you tip the tube upside down you can measure how long the bubble takes to move *up* the tube.

6   You should do each measurement three times, then calculate an average fall time.

7   To cool the oil, put it in a refrigerator.

8   To warm the oil, heat it in a beaker on a hotplate, but **do not heat the oil above 50°C**.

9   Remember to control all variables except the temperature of the oil.

10 Graph your results and draw a line of best fit through the points. (It may be curved.)

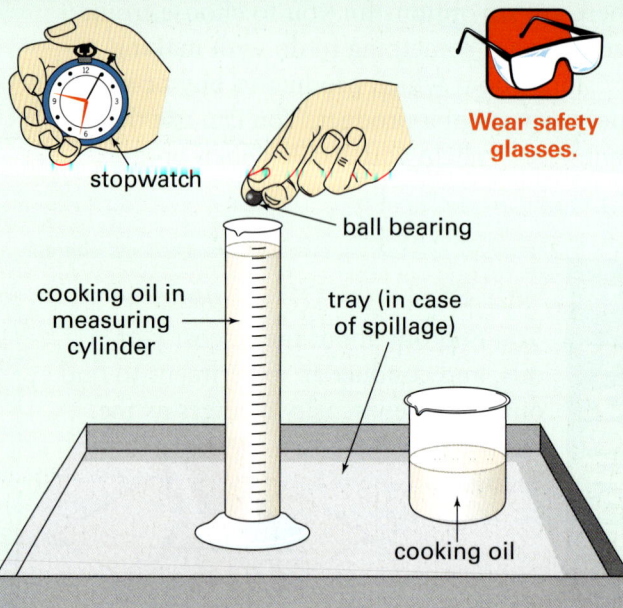

stopwatch

Wear safety glasses.

ball bearing

cooking oil in measuring cylinder

tray (in case of spillage)

cooking oil

You need to be very careful with the warm oil. Hold the beaker with a paper towel or a cloth when pouring, and take care not to splash it. In case of spillage, it is best to work on a tray. If you spill warm oil on yourself, wipe it off quickly with a paper towel or cloth, then wash well with cold water and detergent.

Discussion

1   Which is the independent variable in this experiment? Which is the dependent variable?

2   How does the fall time change as the temperature increases?

3   At which temperature is the oil most viscous? How do you know?

4   Use your graph to predict the viscosity of the oil at 35°C, 0°C and 60°C.

5   How accurate do you think your results are? Suggest ways of improving the experiment.

Conclusion

Is your hypothesis supported by the results? If not, rewrite it.

Thick and thin oils

Did you find in the experiment that cooking oil becomes less viscous (thinner) at higher temperatures? The oil used in the engine of a car behaves in much the same way.

Engine oil is a lubricant that reduces friction between the moving parts of a car's engine, especially on the pistons as they move up and down inside the cylinders. For good lubrication the oil must have the right **viscosity**. 'Thick' liquids like honey have a high viscosity, and flow slowly. 'Thin' liquids like water have a low viscosity, and flow quickly.

Oil must work over a wide range of temperatures. On a cold winter morning the temperature may be as low as 0°C, and when the engine is running its temperature will be between 90°C and 100°C. Technologists have developed special oils, called multigrade oils, by including special additives. The viscosity of a multigrade oil does not decrease much as the temperature rises. At low temperatures the oil is thin enough for the engine to start easily; and at high temperatures it is thick enough to lubricate the engine properly.

Look at a container of oil. The viscosity of the oil is usually given by an SAE number.

Fig 17 What do you know about engine oil? You probably know that it is usually changed when the car is serviced, and sometimes needs 'topping up'.

Single-grade oils have only one number, from 5 to 50. The higher the number the thicker the oil. Multigrade oils have two numbers, eg 20W/50. This means that the oil acts like 20 oil at low temperatures (the W stands for winter), and like 50 oil at higher temperatures.

Check!

1   What is meant by the viscosity of oil?

2   What happens to the viscosity of oil when it is heated? How can you explain this in terms of the forces between the long hydrocarbon molecules in oil?

3   Explain the differences between the following oils:

   SAE 20W/40   SAE 20W/50   SAE 40

4   Suggest why an engine is easier to start if you use a thinner oil.

5   Suggest why engines last longer if you use thicker oils.

6   Joe filled a burette with a liquid and put a cork in the top, leaving an air bubble. He then turned the burette upside down and measured how long the air bubble took to move up the burette. He did this for four different liquids, and recorded his results.

Liquid	Air bubble time (s)
A	12
B	20
C	16
D	5

a   In which liquid did the air bubble rise most quickly?

b   Which one of the four liquids is the most viscous?

c   If liquid C is heated, its viscosity will change. Which of the other liquids will it probably become most like in viscosity?

Experiment
TESTING GLUES

Aim

To do some consumer testing of glues, using the six steps from pages 26 and 28.

Planning hints

1 Some features of glues which you could investigate are:
   - the strength of the bond formed
   - the type of glue, eg paper, wood or plastic, one-part or two-part
   - the unit cost (how much does 1 g or 1 mL of glue cost?)
   - whether the instructions are simple and clear
   - whether the safety precautions are adequate.

2 You could investigate how well the glues bond to different materials, for example: wood to wood, paper to paper, plastic to plastic or plastic to metal?

3 You will need to work out a way of testing the strength of the bonds formed. Two possible methods are illustrated below.

4 You could also investigate how the strength of a bond increases with time.

5 **All glues must be handled with great care.** Avoid contact with skin and eyes, and use gloves if possible. Wipe any glue off your skin immediately with a clean cloth. Work in a well-ventilated area, and do not inhale the vapour. Before using a glue read the instructions carefully.

6 In your opinion, how easy is the glue to use? Are the nozzle and cap well designed? Does the container leak? Does it stand up to repeated use? You could use a rating scale here.

7 Consider the best way to display your findings. One way is to use a data table similar to the one below. The details will depend on which tests you do.

8 Once you have completed your tests, you need to interpret the results and write a report, advising consumers about the best types of glues to buy.

Method A

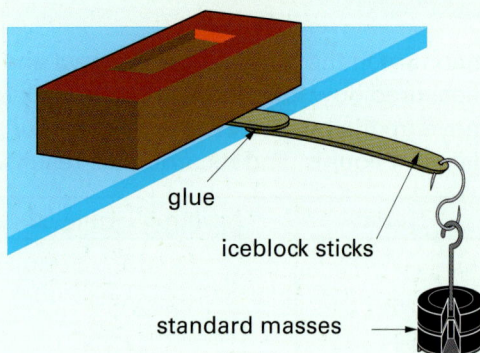

glue

iceblock sticks

standard masses

Method B

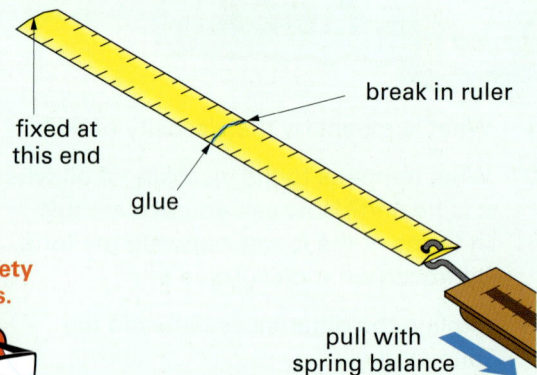

fixed at this end

glue

break in ruler

pull with spring balance

Wear safety glasses.

Glue brand	Price paid	Net contents	Cost per g or mL	Instructions	Safety labelling	Ease of use	Strength

Fire danger

The photo below shows scars on a young girl from burns received when her dress caught on fire. Most burns children suffer occur when clothing catches fire from heaters and open fires or from them playing with matches and flammable liquids such as petrol and kerosene. Scalding from boiling water is also common.

Some fabrics are more flammable than others. Some synthetic fabrics also melt when they burn, and the hot molten fabric can stick to the skin, causing severe burning. For these reasons most manufacturers of children's sleepwear now use fire-resistant materials or close-fitting styles (see Fig 21). When buying fabrics or clothes you can check whether they are fire-resistant or of low flammability by looking for the label LOW FIRE DANGER (Fig 22).

To make clothing fire resistant manufacturers use a *flame retardant*. One type of retardant is a mixture of chemicals in which the cloth is soaked.

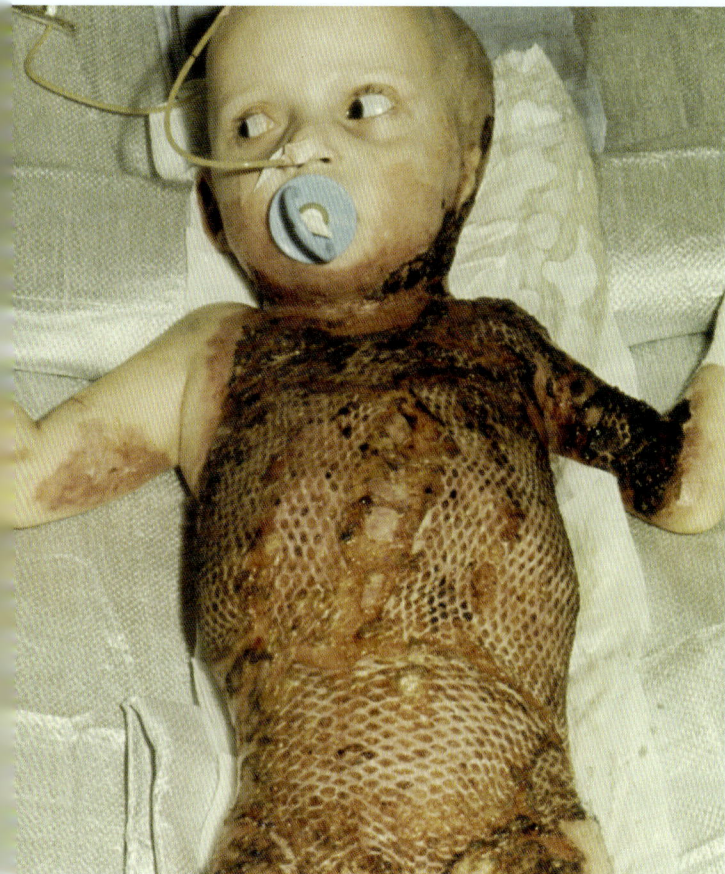

Fig 21 These tracksuit-style pyjamas are close-fitting so that the sleeves and legs are less likely to catch fire in heaters and open fires.

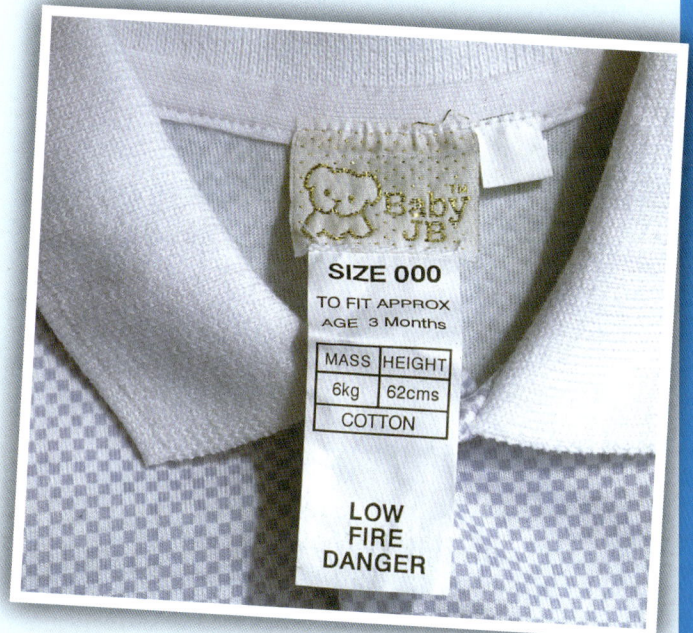

Fig 22 When buying children's nightwear look for the label LOW FIRE DANGER.

Investigate
5 FIRE-RESISTANT CLOTHING

Aim
To compare the flammability of fabric samples before and after treatment with a flame retardant.

Materials
- samples of two different fabrics, eg cotton or wool and a synthetic
- metal tongs
- heatproof mat or tray of sand
- Bunsen burner
- stopwatch
- metal can
- scissors
- alum
- borax
- boric (boracic) acid
- balance
- 250 mL beaker
- washing powder

Wear safety glasses.

Planning and Safety Check
- This investigation may take more than one day. So that you will know exactly what to do, and in what order, draw up a flowchart summarising the steps in the Method.
- Because some fabrics give off toxic fumes when they burn, it is best to do this investigation in a fume cupboard. Discuss this with your teacher.

Method
1. Cut out three 3 cm squares of each fabric.

2. Make the flame retardant solution using the following:

13 g alum	0.5 g boric acid
1.5 g borax	100 mL water

3. Saturate two samples of each fabric in this solution, then dry them thoroughly.

4. Wash one sample of each treated fabric using a small amount of washing powder in warm water, then dry it.

5. Using the metal tongs, hold one of the untreated fabric samples close to the burner flame until it ignites. Hold the burning fabric over the metal can.

   ✏ Measure the time taken for the sample to **a** catch alight and **b** burn completely.

   If the flame goes out before the burning has been completed, relight the sample immediately and keep it alight until it has all burnt.

6. Repeat the burning test for:
   - the other untreated sample
   - the two treated samples
   - the two treated and washed samples.

   Remember to control variables.

   📋 Record your results in a data table.

Discussion
1. Which is more flammable—the cotton or the synthetic fabric?

2. What effect did the flame retardant solution have on the flammability of the fabrics?

3. Does the flame retardant work better on the cotton or on the synthetic fabric?

4. Does the flame retardant work as well after the fabric has been washed?

5. What extra information would you need before you could write a full consumer report on flame retardants?

Note: Do this in a fume cupboard.

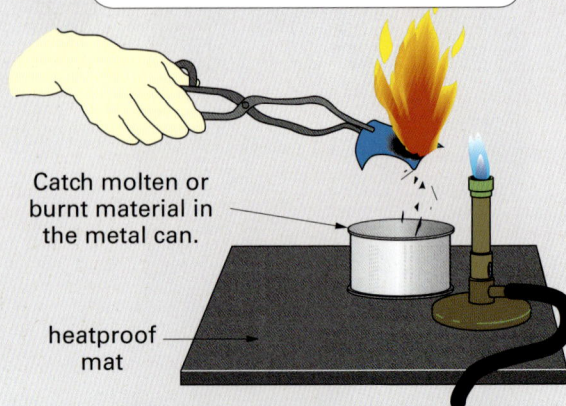

Catch molten or burnt material in the metal can.

heatproof mat

OPTION 4

Food additives

Some of the food we eat is fresh, like apples and tomatoes. But most of it has been *processed* in some way—to make it look better, to change its flavour, or to make it last longer. When food is processed, the chemicals in it are altered or extra chemicals, called *food additives*, are added to it. There are laws about the labelling of foods. Fresh food does not have to be labelled, but most processed food does. The illustration below shows the information the label must show.

Datemark

Most foods 'go off' eventually, but some last longer than others. The datemark helps consumers and shops make sure the food is in good condition.

Name

The name should give honest information about what the food actually contains. For example, a product called 'strawberry jam' must contain strawberries.

Ingredients

Most packaged food has to have a list of ingredients, showing what is in the food. The ingredients are listed in order of decreasing mass, that is, the main ingredients are listed first, and the additives at the end. The main ingredient must also be given as a percentage of the product. For example, the percentage of strawberries in the jam below is 40% of the total mass. The additives are food acid (to give it a 'tang'), preservatives (to stop it 'going off') and red colouring.

Additives have to be approved by the government, and most of them have a number. This number tells you what the additive is. For example, 160a is carotene, the colour found in carrots and pumpkins and often used to colour fruit drinks and margarine. The table on the next page lists the main types of food additives. For a more complete list, see the Australia New Zealand Food Authority website.

Most processed food is also required to have basic nutritional information about fat (including saturated fat), protein, carbohydrate (including sugars) and sodium (sodium chloride or salt).

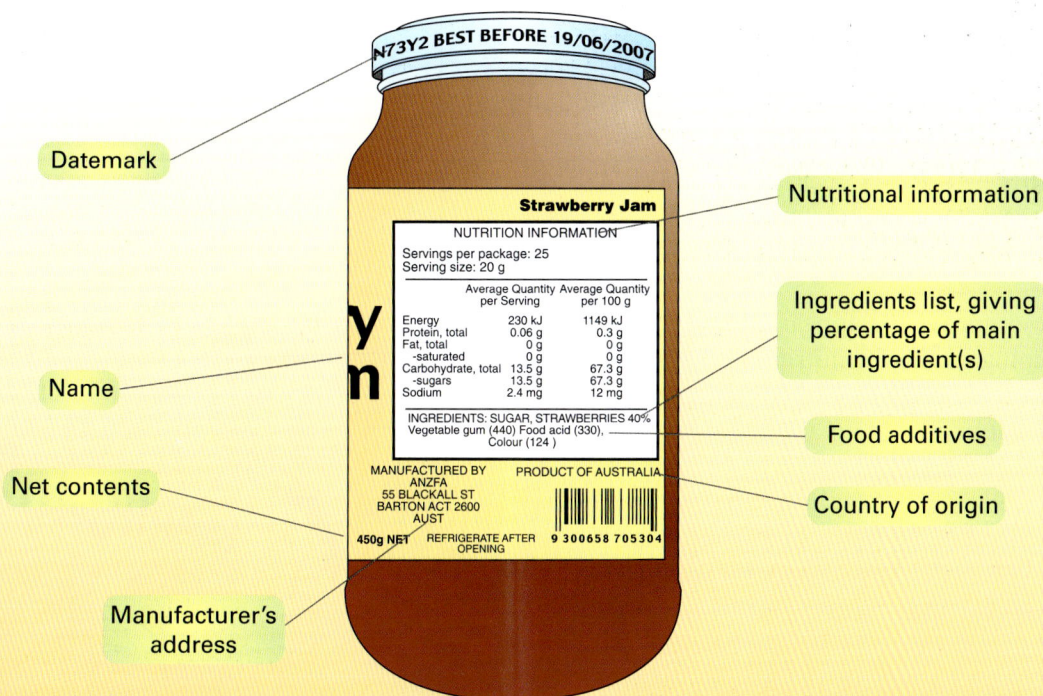

OPTION 4

Additive	Why it is added	Some examples	Code number	Found in . . .
flavours	to give food more taste	usually complex mixtures	no number	sweets, sauces, soups, soft drinks, cordials, potato crisps
colours	to make food more attractive	tartrazine 102 (yellow), cochineal 120 (red), chlorophyll 140 (green), carotene 160a (orange)	numbers beginning with 1	soft drinks, ice-cream, snack foods, soups, sauces, biscuits, cakes, margarine, sweets
preservatives	to stop bacteria and fungi growing in food and making it 'go off'	salt, sugar, sodium benzoate 211, sodium nitrite 250, sulfur dioxide 220	numbers beginning with 2	soft drinks, fruit drinks, wine, pickles, cheese spreads, sausage meat, ham, bacon, dried fruits
antioxidants	to help stop fats and oils going rancid (bad taste and smell)	ascorbic acid 300 (vitamin C), tocopherol 306–309 (vitamin E)	numbers beginning with 3	chewing gum, instant soups, cake mixes, potato crisps, margarine
flavour enhancers	to improve the flavour	monosodium glutamate 621 (MSG)	numbers beginning with 6	Asian food, potato crisps, biscuits
emulsifiers	so that oil and water mixtures do not separate into layers	lecithin (from soya beans)		salad dressings, mayonnaise, margarine, ice-cream, chocolate
food acids	to give food a 'tang' and keep acid level constant	acetic acid 260, citric acid 330	various numbers	lemon soft drink, canned tomatoes
vegetable gums	to thicken and set foods	alginates 400–405 (from seaweed)		ice-cream, flavoured milk drinks, desserts, pie fillings
humectants	to stop foods from drying out	glycerin 422		cakes, biscuits, muesli bars, pie fillings, some pet foods

Additives improve the appearance, texture, flavour, keeping quality or nutritional value of processed foods. On the other hand, some people are allergic to certain additives, especially preservatives and artificial colours, which may cause hay fever, skin rashes, headaches, stomach upsets or hyperactivity. It is also possible that some additives could cause cancer if eaten in large amounts for many years.

Food additives are tested before they can be used. These tests are usually done on animals. Any additives that are shown to cause health problems are banned.

I hope this sandwich doesn't contain any ah, ah....ah..... YAAHHCHOOO!

Investigate
6 SULFUR DIOXIDE IN FOOD

Aim
To test various foods to determine whether they contain sulfur dioxide preservative.

Materials
- selection of foods such as dried apricots, desiccated coconut, raisins, wine
- dilute **iodine–potassium iodide** solution (5 g iodine and 10 g potassium iodide per litre of water) **Toxic**
- mortar and pestle (or blender)
- beaker
- 1% starch suspension
- balance
- measuring cylinder

Method
1 Weigh out about 10 g of the food.

2 Mix the food with about 100 mL of water in a mortar or blender. Decant the solution into a beaker. With liquids you can omit this step. Simply use 100 mL of the liquid.

3 Add 10 mL of iodine–potassium iodide solution to the beaker.

If the food contains sulfur dioxide, it reacts with the iodine, removing it from the solution. So, when the starch suspension is added in the next step, no blue-black colour is seen. If the food does not contain sulfur dioxide, the iodine remains and reacts with the starch to produce a blue-black colour.

4 Add about 2 mL of starch suspension.
   Does the food contain sulfur dioxide?

5 Try other foods.
   Record your data in a data table.

Discussion
1 Which foods contained sulfur dioxide?

2 Can you tell which foods contained the *most* sulfur dioxide? How could you modify the investigation to find out?

Check!

1 Why do most foods have a datemark?

2 Why do you think it is important to know the percentage of fruit juice in a drink?

3 Look at the list of ingredients below.
   a Which is the main ingredient?
   b List the additives and say why you think each has been added.
   c What do you think the product is?
   CARBONATED WATER, SUGAR, LEMON JUICE (5%) FLAVOURS, FOOD ACID (330), PRESERVATIVE (211), COLOUR (102)

4 Use the table of food additives on the previous page to answer these questions.
   a A food item has an additive with the number 210. What would the purpose of this additive be?
   b What does an emulsifier do?
   c Why are vegetable gums added to some foods?
   d Why is citric acid added to some soft drinks and fruit drinks?
   e How are preservatives and antioxidants similar?
   f Which additives would you expect to find in margarine?

5 The jelly beans in a packet come in eight different colours, yet there are only five different colours in the ingredients list. How can this be?

6 Can you tell the difference between sugar and artificial sweetener? Design a fair test to find out.

7 What is hyperactivity? How is it related to what we eat? What can be done about it?

Experiment
DISPOSABLE NAPPIES

Aim

To apply the six steps on pages 26 and 28 to compare the effectiveness of different brands of disposable nappies.

A typical disposable nappy is shown below. It should have the following important features:

- absorbent—to soak up lots of liquid

- leakproof—so liquid cannot leak out around the legs and waistband

- comfortable for the baby to wear

- disposable—as much of the nappy as possible should be biodegradable.

Planning hints

This experiment is open-ended and you will need to decide what you are going to test and how you will do it. Before you start, read through the following suggestions.

1 You could test the absorbent padding to see how much liquid it will soak up. Note that most disposable nappies contain a special white powder called sodium polyacrylate. It is a polymer that swells to form a gel (a kind of jelly) on contact with water.

2 Most manufacturers claim that their nappies have one-way liners. This means they allow liquid to pass through them to the absorbent padding, but do not allow liquid to flow back the other way. This means the baby's skin stays reasonably dry. You could test some one-way liners to see if this claim is true.

3 How strong are the tapes used to fasten the nappy? Are they strong enough to hold the nappy on an active baby? Do they still work when the nappy is wet?

4 You could do a survey of nappy users to see which brands they use, how easy they are to use etc. You could interview neighbours, friends and relatives, or you could design a questionnaire.

5 Remember your tests must be fair, so make sure each brand of nappy is tested in the same way. Also, your findings must be reliable. If someone else repeats your tests, they should get the same results.

6 Write a detailed report describing what you did and what you found out. The intended audience for your report should be people who buy disposable nappies.

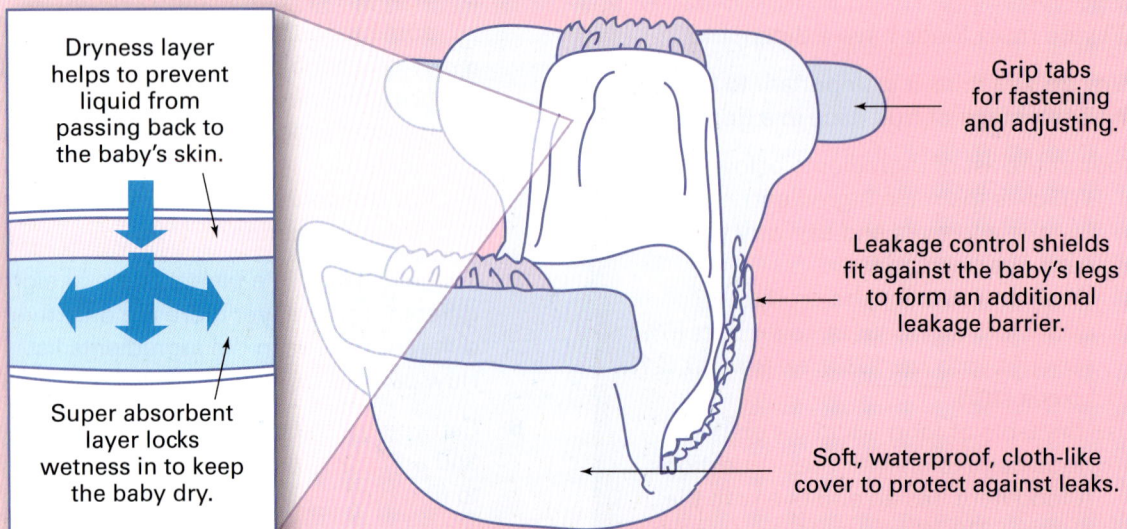

Dryness layer helps to prevent liquid from passing back to the baby's skin.

Super absorbent layer locks wetness in to keep the baby dry.

Grip tabs for fastening and adjusting.

Leakage control shields fit against the baby's legs to form an additional leakage barrier.

Soft, waterproof, cloth-like cover to protect against leaks.

Cosmetics

One of the most common cosmetics used today is cleansing cream. It moisturises as well as soothes the skin. It is also used to remove make-up and to clean the skin. The use of cleansing cream avoids having to use large amounts of soap that extract the natural oils from the skin and can have a damaging effect.

Cleansing cream is an emulsion consisting of tiny droplets of oil and wax suspended in water. Normally water and oil do not mix, because water molecules are polar (contain electric charges) and oil molecules are non-polar. Each prefers to stay with its own kind, rather than getting mixed up with the other.

If you mix oil with water, the oil floats on top as a separate layer. If you shake the mixture vigorously, the oil is broken up into tiny droplets. But when you let the mixture stand, the oil separates out again. What is needed is a 'go-between' to bring the two liquids together. These 'go-between' molecules are called **emulsifiers**. They have a polar end and a non-polar end and are therefore attracted to both oil and water molecules, as shown in Fig 28.

Cleansing cream is called an oil-in-water emulsion, and it can be rubbed onto your skin without leaving it feeling greasy. When it is applied to your skin, the water evaporates, producing a cooling effect. This is why it is sometimes called *cold* cream. The oily ingredients in the cream are left as a thin film on your skin. They can be washed off easily with water.

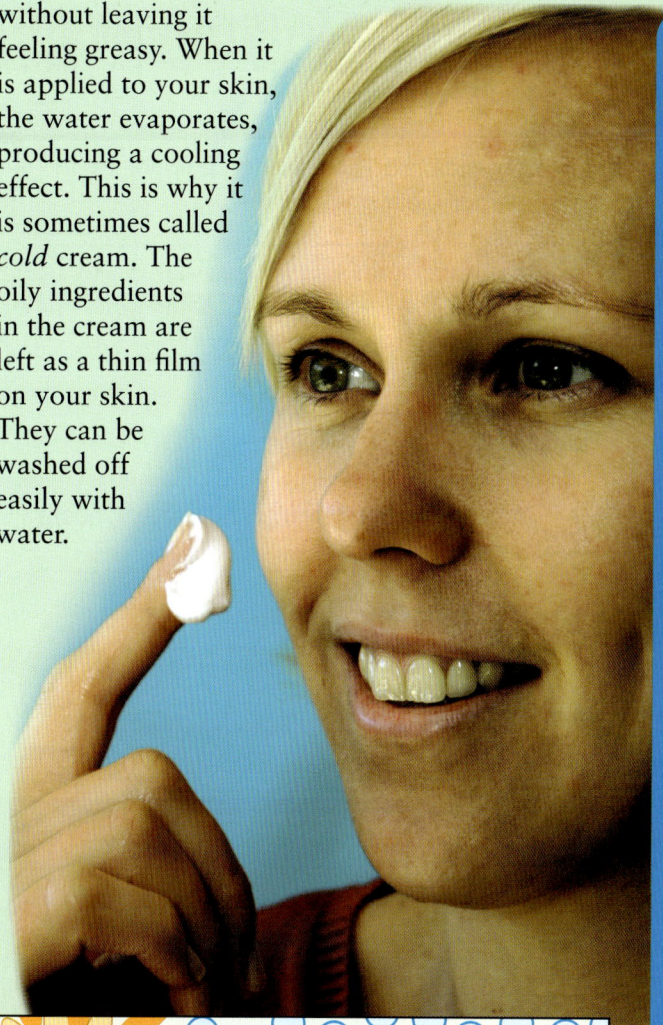

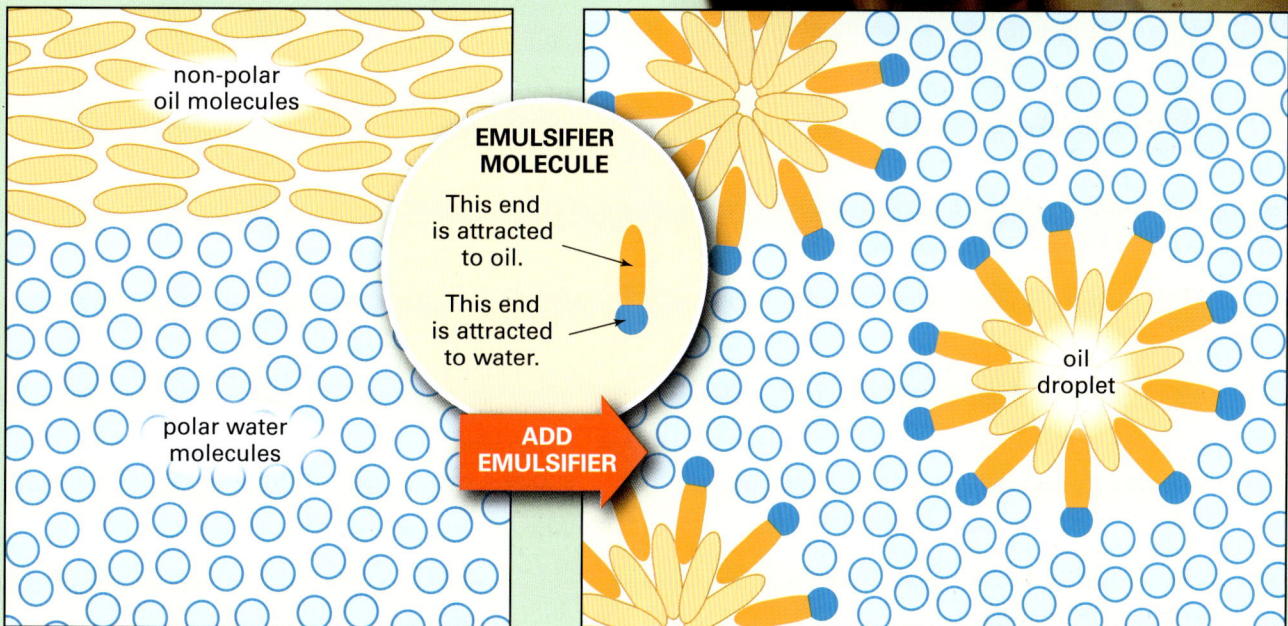

EMULSIFIER MOLECULE

This end is attracted to oil.

This end is attracted to water.

non-polar oil molecules

polar water molecules

ADD EMULSIFIER

oil droplet

Fig 28 How an emulsifier helps oil and water mix. Emulsifiers work in the same way as soaps and detergents.

Investigate

7 MAKING CLEANSING CREAM

Aim
To make cleansing cream and compare it with commercial cleansing creams.

Materials
- **liquid paraffin** (100 g)
- **white beeswax** (30 g)
- borax (2 g)
- 2 beakers (250 mL)
- measuring cylinder (100 mL)
- balance
- water bath (see Planning and Safety Check)
- heatproof mat
- 2 stirring rods
- 2 thermometers
- small storage bottle
- make-up
- several commercial cleansing creams
- soap

Flammable

Wear safety glasses.

water bath, beeswax and liquid paraffin, borax and water, hot water, hotplate

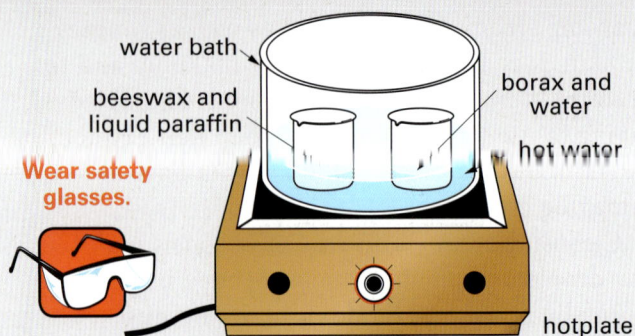

Planning and Safety Check
Read the Materials and Method carefully and note any safety hazards. The beakers and storage bottle you use must be perfectly clean, since you will be putting the cleansing cream you make on your skin.

Discuss with your teacher what you will use for a water bath and how you will lift the beakers out of it in Step 4. You could use a large beaker, flat tray or large aluminium pot on a hot plate. Alternatively you could use an electric frypan.

Method
1 Add water to your water bath and heat it until the water temperature is about 75°C.

2 Weigh out 30 g of white beeswax, break it into small pieces and put it in a small beaker. Then add 100 g of liquid paraffin while stirring gently. Place the beaker in the water bath.

3 Dissolve 2 g of borax in 70 mL of water in a second beaker and put it in the water bath too.

4 When both beakers have reached 75°C, remove them from the water bath and stand them on a heatproof mat.

5 Pour the borax solution slowly into the beaker of beeswax and paraffin, while stirring. Continue to stir until the mixture has cooled to 35°C.

6 Allow the cream to cool to room temperature, then put it in the storage bottle.

7 Apply some make-up to your hand, then use your cream to remove it.
Apply some make-up to your other hand and this time try to wash it off with soap and water.
Describe the results of your tests.

8 Compare the properties of your home-made cream with those of several commercial cleansing creams.
Record your results.

Discussion
1 What are the ingredients in your home-made cleansing cream? What are the ingredients in the commercial cleansing creams?

2 You used two different oils? What are they?

3 Suggest why beeswax dissolves in paraffin but not in water.

4 Using what you learnt on the previous page, suggest why borax was added to the mixture.

5 Why do you think you heated the ingredients to 75°C?

6 Suggest ways you could improve your cleansing cream.

Try doing the Chapter 2 crossword on the CD.

MAIN IDEAS

Copy and complete these statements to make a summary of this chapter. The missing words are on the right.

1 To test a consumer product you first identify the _____ you consider important, then design _____ for each of these.

2 Tests where you count or measure something are _____. Tests based on people's opinions are _____.

3 A _____ is a method of obtaining information when you can't do a fair test. You use a _____ from a larger group.

fair tests
features
objective
sample
subjective
survey

Working with technology

REVIEW

1 For each question below, decide whether the answer will be objective or subjective.
 a How much does the mobile phone weigh?
 b Are the yellow shopping bags as strong as the white ones?
 c Which potato chips are the crispiest?
 d Which brand of sunscreen blocks most UV radiation?
 e Which bed is the most comfortable?
 f Which stroller is the easiest to use?
 g Does this cot meet the Australian standard?

2 The manufacturer of a skin care lotion claims that its product 'holds its moisture longer'. A scientist decided to test this claim by placing a sample on a sensitive balance in a very dry atmosphere. Each day she recorded the mass of the sample.
 a How much mass did the lotion lose over 5 days?
 b Suggest a reason for this loss of mass.
 c Was the rate of moisture loss increasing or decreasing?
 d Does the experiment 'prove' anything about the claim made by the manufacturer? Explain.

Day	Mass(g)
0	15.006
1	14.562
2	14.189
3	13.873
4	13.587
5	13.330

3 Use the graph below to answer these questions.
 a How was the reliability of the cars measured?
 b Which was the most reliable make of car tested?
 c At what age are Holdens slightly more reliable than Toyotas?
 d For how many years is the reliability of Mazdas more than 70%?
 e What happens to the reliability of all three cars after about 12 years?

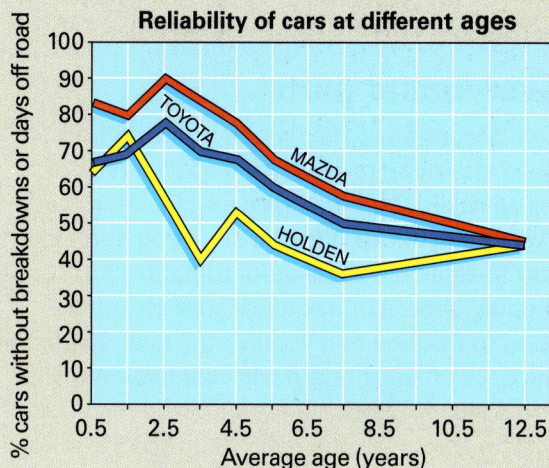
Reliability of cars at different ages

4 Some students conducted a survey by asking people the following question: *What do you think about the use of cigarettes, alcohol and marijuana by adults?* Here are their results.

	What people thought		
	acceptable	unacceptable	undecided
Cigarettes male %	14	45	41
female %	10	48	42
Alcohol male %	32	25	43
female %	20	38	42
Marijuana male %	15	81	4
female %	11	83	6

a What percentage of females thought smoking cigarettes was acceptable?

b What differences were there between the opinions of males and females on the drinking of alcohol?

c On which issue did people have the most definite opinion?

d Write a short paragraph summarising the students' results.

5 Read the following article from a sports magazine and answer the questions below.

Skateboard parts

The *deck* or *board* is the part you stand on. Most decks are made from a special type of wood called Canadian rock maple. Decks vary in size, so choose one that suits you and feels comfortable when skateboarding. Try out some friends' boards or ask to try some from the shop to find the one you like the best. Replacing the deck on your board will cost between $65 and $140.

The *trucks* are the parts that hold the wheels on. Basic skateboards have 'pressure cast' trucks, which cost about $25 each. (You need two of these of course.) The best trucks are 'sand cast' and can cost up to $50 each. They can be loosened for greater manoeuvrability, so you can turn more easily. You can also buy 'lappers' and 'copers'. These are plastic fittings which fit over the trucks to protect them if you ride over curbs and other obstacles.

Wheels are made from a special rubbery type of material. The best ones have what is called a 'high rebound factor'. One way to test for this is to put a clear plastic tube on the surface of the wheel and drop a marble into it as shown. The higher the marble bounces, the better the wheel. If the wheels wear out (or you don't like the colour), they cost between $25 and $70 for a set.

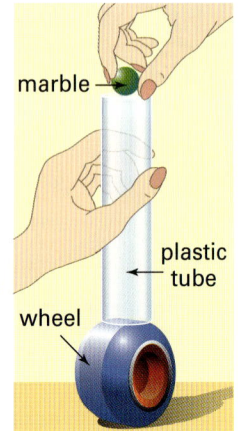
marble
plastic tube
wheel

Bearings are the tiny steel balls which fit inside the wheels to make them turn freely. If you look after your skateboard, you may not have to replace them. However, if they become worn or rusty, your skateboard won't run smoothly. A set of bearings for four wheels costs between $20 and $50.

Skidpads and *noseguards* are plastic fittings which can be attached to the front and back of the skateboard so you don't break or wear out the deck.

a What are the five main skateboard parts?

b What is the purpose of the bearings?

c Why are some wheels better than others? How can you test them?

d Which variables would you need to control in this wheel test?

e Suppose you built a skateboard from parts. What would be the cheapest board? What would be the most expensive?

6 Design an experiment to test which type of correcting fluid dries most quickly.

a Which is the independent variable in this experiment?

b Which is the dependent variable?

c Which variables will you need to control?

d Write down the steps in the experiment.

Check your answers on pages 331–332.

3 Light and sound

Getting Started

Work in a small group to discuss each of the following. Keep your answers for later on in this chapter.

- You are playing pool and you have to pocket the yellow ball by hitting it with the white ball. How does a knowledge of reflection help you pocket the yellow ball? Which pocket will you aim for? Why?

- When the sun shines onto a large crystal hanging in your bedroom window, you sometimes get a rainbow image on your wall. How is the rainbow of colours formed?

- How would you write the word SELF on paper so that when you hold it in front of a mirror you can see the reflection of the word written correctly?

- Two actors stand on a stage. One of them wears a white costume. When a spotlight with a coloured filter is turned on, one of the costumes looks red and the other looks black. What colour is the filter and what colour is the other costume?

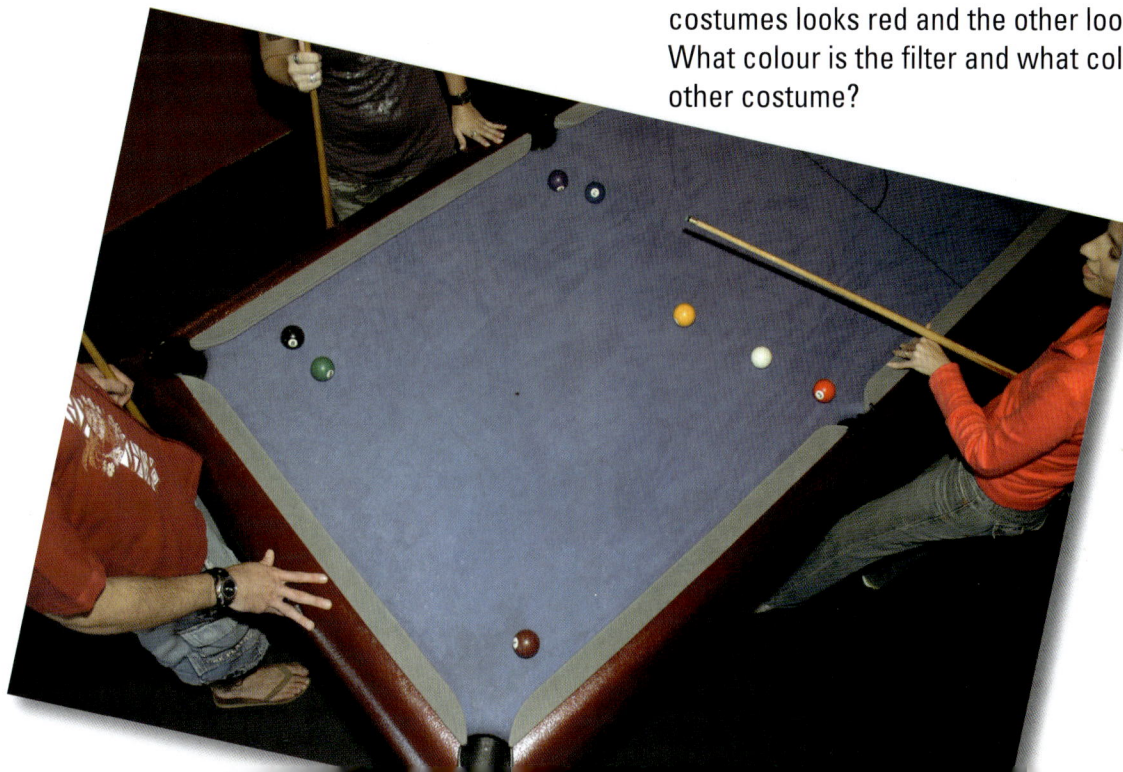

Activity

This is a revision activity. Form a small group and discuss each of the following questions. Be prepared to discuss your answers with the class.

1   Light and sound are forms of energy. All forms of energy have a starting point or source. Name two sources of light and two sources of sound.

2   Which of the following shapes can be seen as the letter K in a mirror?

What does this tell you about the images formed in a mirror?

3   When you hit a metal cymbal with a drumstick, it rings. If you put your hand on the cymbal and hit it again it does not ring. Explain why this happens.

4   Three rays of light shine onto a glass lens as in the diagram at right. What will happen to the light rays when they pass through the lens?

5   The diagram below shows four light rays reflecting from a plane mirror. Each light ray is coloured. There are five errors in the diagram. Can you find them?

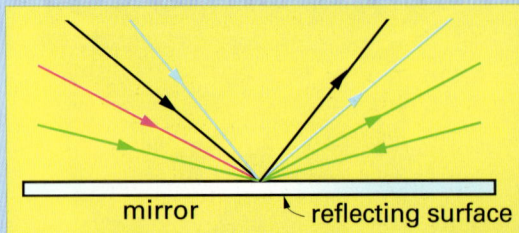

mirror   reflecting surface

3.1 Properties of light and sound

In the first Getting Started problem in which you had to pocket the yellow ball, you used the fact that the angle the ball strikes the cushion is equal to the angle at which it leaves the cushion. This is the same principle as the reflection of light. Reflection is one of the *properties* of light and sound.

Both light and sound are forms of energy and both can be transformed into other sorts of energy. For example, light can be transformed into chemical energy in a leaf during photosynthesis, or into electrical energy in a solar cell. Sound can be transformed into kinetic energy in a radio speaker. The transformation of energy is another property of light and sound.

Another property of light is that it can travel in straight lines. Surveyors rely on this property when they use their instruments to find boundary lines or take measurements for new roads.

Fig 5   Surveyors use the property that light travels in straight lines to find the depth of the trench on the other side of the road.

The law of reflection

When light strikes a mirror, the reflected light ray bounces off the mirror at the same angle as it strikes the mirror. This is the **law of reflection**.

When doing experiments on the law of reflection, scientists measure the angle between the light ray and an imaginary line, called the *normal*. This line is at right angles to the surface. The light ray coming towards the surface is called the *incident ray*, and the outgoing one is called the *reflected ray*. The angles formed between the rays and the normal are called the *angle of incidence* and the *angle of reflection*. These two angles are always equal no matter how the light rays strike the surface. This is the law of reflection.

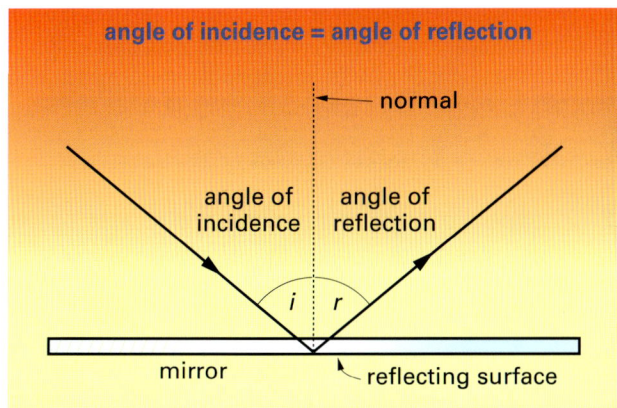

angle of incidence = angle of reflection

Reflection from curved mirrors

The law of reflection applies to curved mirrors as well as plane (flat) mirrors. In the diagram below two parallel light rays hit a concave mirror (concave means curved inwards like a cave). These rays reflect off the mirror and meet at a point called the **focus**. The focal length of the mirror is the distance of the focus from the mirror's reflecting surface.

Notice that the light rays reflect off the curved mirror surface and obey the law of reflection—the angle of incidence (i) is equal to the angle of reflection (r).

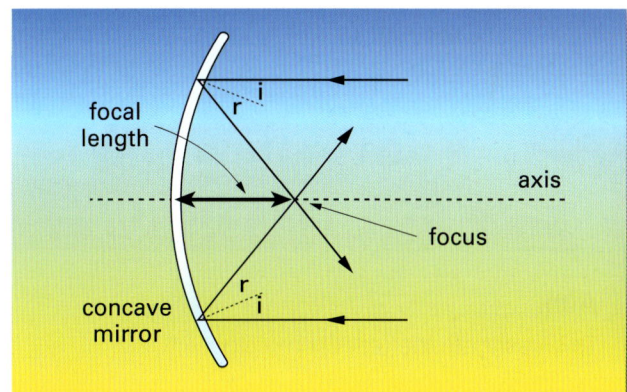

Fig 7 Parallel light rays reflect from a curved mirror and meet at a point called the focus.

science bits

The history of mirrors

Around 600 BC, the early Etruscans and Greeks used polished discs of thin bronze as mirrors. During the Roman Christian times, small metallic mirrors made of highly-polished silver or steel were worn by fashion-conscious men and women.

Mirrors made of glass with a very thin layer of metal were first used in the 1300s. However, it wasn't until 1564 when the mirror-makers of Venice formed a corporation, that glass mirrors gained popularity. These mirrors were made from highly polished glass with a very thin metal backing, usually made from an alloy of tin and mercury. In very expensive mirrors, silver metal was used as the reflective backing.

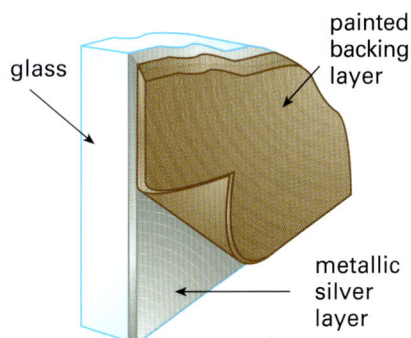

Today, mirrors have a silver or aluminium layer which is sealed by a painted or plastic outer layer to protect the metal.

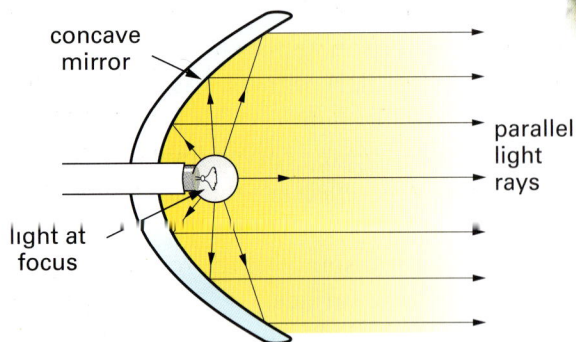

concave
mirror

parallel
light
rays

light at
focus

Fig 9 When a light source is placed at the focus of a concave mirror, a beam of parallel light rays is produced. This is why concave mirrors are used as reflectors in torches, car headlights and floodlights.

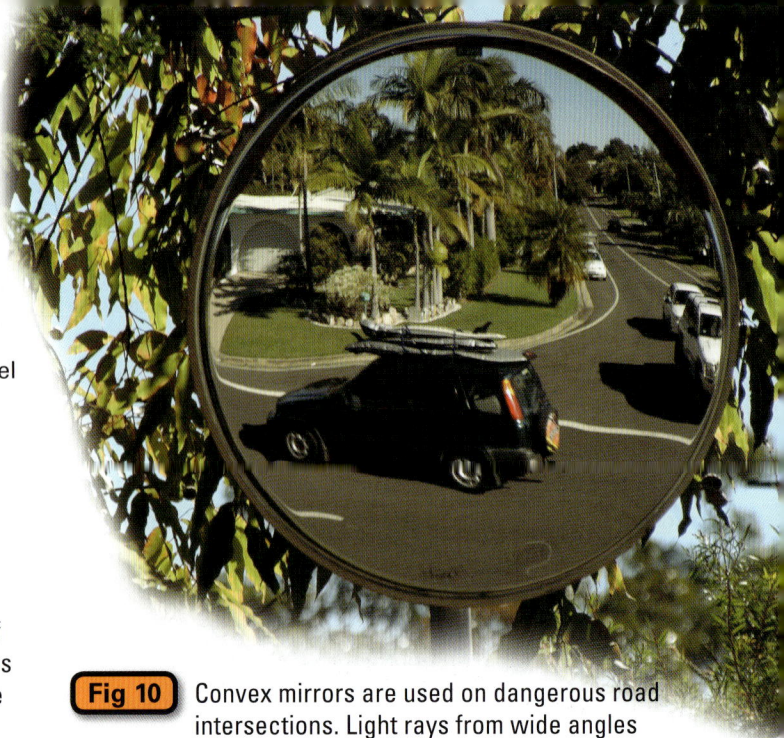

Fig 10 Convex mirrors are used on dangerous road intersections. Light rays from wide angles strike the mirror giving a wider-angle image than would be seen using a plane mirror.

Investigate

8 REFLECTION

Aim
To investigate the reflection of light.

Materials
- ray box kit and power pack
- pencil, ruler and protractor

Planning and Safety Check
- Your teacher will tell you how to set up the power pack and ray box kit correctly.
- Make sure you ask your teacher to check your set-up before you turn on the power.

Method

1 Use the diagram as a guide to set up the ray box and plane mirror on a clean page of your notebook. Draw a pencil line along the back of the mirror. Then draw pencil lines along the incident light ray and the reflected ray.

  Use a protractor to draw the normal, then measure the angle of incidence and angle of reflection. How do they compare?

2 Change the angle of the mirror and repeat Step 1. Measure at least three different angles.

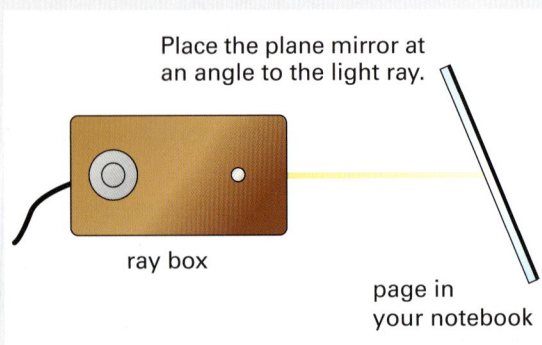

Place the plane mirror at an angle to the light ray.

ray box

page in your notebook

3 Replace the plane mirror with a concave mirror and shine parallel rays of light directly at it.

  Describe what happens. Draw a diagram of the set-up and mark on it the axis and focus (see Fig 7).

4 Use a ruler to find the focal length of the mirror.

  Record your results.

5 Try using a convex mirror.

  Draw a diagram of what happens when parallel light rays strike the mirror. Does this mirror have a focus?

Refraction of light

Air and water are *transparent* substances. This means that light passes through them. Substances such as paper, wood and brick do not allow light to pass through them and are called *opaque*. However, when light passes from one transparent substance to another, for example from air to water, strange things happen.

Activity

1   Put a coin in a coffee mug (or a beaker) and place it on a bench.

2   Hold a ruler vertically on the bench. Place your eye level with the zero mark on the ruler and have your partner position the mug until you can see only the far edge of the coin.

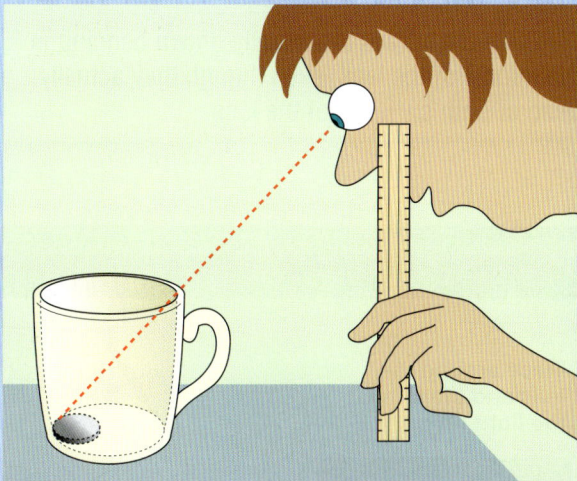

3   Have your partner slowly pour water into the mug until it is full.
    📝 What happens to the coin as the water is added?

4   Move your eye down the ruler until you see the edge of the coin again.
    📝 How far down the ruler did you move your eye?
    This effect shows another property of light—refraction.

The activity showed that when you put a coin in a mug and add some water, the coin seems to change position. This is caused by light bending when it passes through different transparent substances at an angle. This bending of light is called **refraction**. Refraction is another property of light.

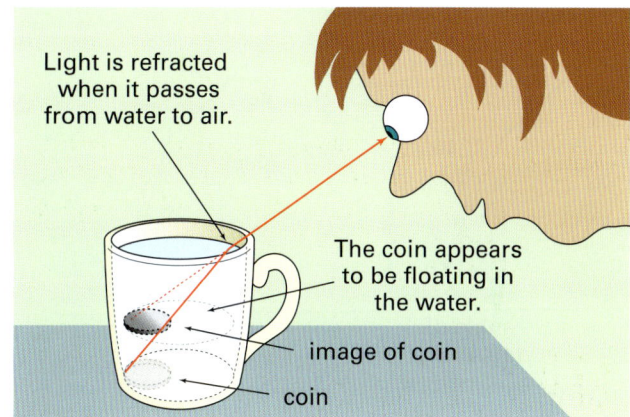

Light is refracted when it passes from water to air.

The coin appears to be floating in the water.

image of coin

coin

You can see how light refracts as it passes through the glass block in the photo below. Notice that the angle of refraction is less than the angle of incidence. This is because the refracted light ray bends towards the normal.

In general, when light passes from air to another transparent substance such as water, glass, plastic, diamond or alcohol, it bends towards the normal—the angle of refraction is always less than the angle of incidence.

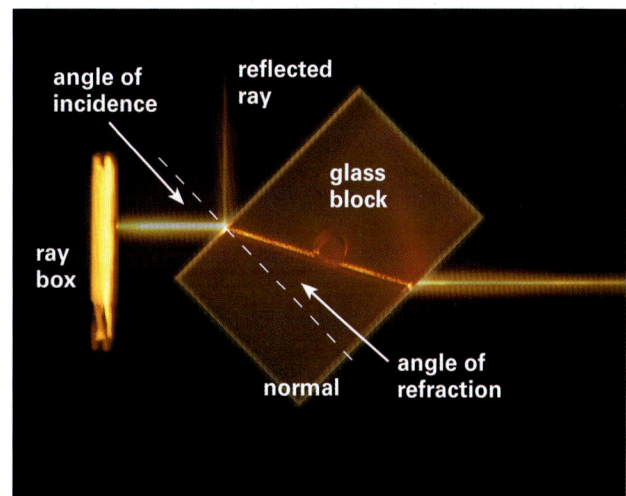

angle of incidence

reflected ray

glass block

ray box

normal

angle of refraction

Fig 14 Light is refracted as it passes through a glass block. Notice that some light is also reflected by the block.

The amount of refraction of a light ray depends on the type of substance. For example, light bends more when it passes from air to glass than it does when it passes from air to water.

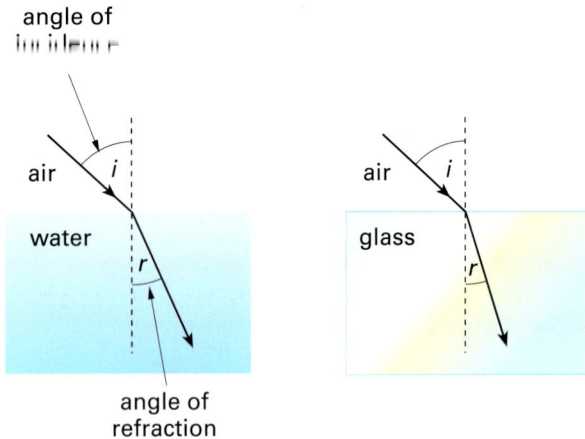

angle of incidence

air

water

angle of refraction

air

glass

focus

focal length

Converging lenses

Diverging lenses

Lenses are pieces of glass or plastic curved on one or both surfaces. They refract light in certain patterns; for example, lenses that refract light inwards are called *converging lenses*. *Diverging lenses* refract light outwards.

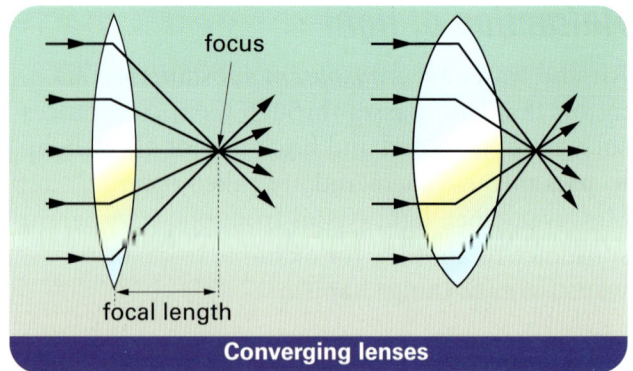

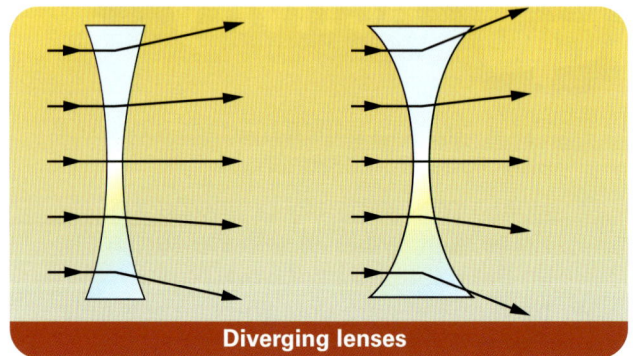

Note: The light rays are usually drawn bending in the middle of the lens, even though they actually bend at both surfaces of the lens.

Investigate
9 LENSES AND LIGHT

Aim
To observe how lenses refract light and form images on a screen.

PART A
Ray box lenses

Materials
• ray box kit

Method
1 Set up the ray box and a converging lens as shown in the diagram on the right.

2 Find the focal length of the lens.

Trace around the lens and draw in the light rays.

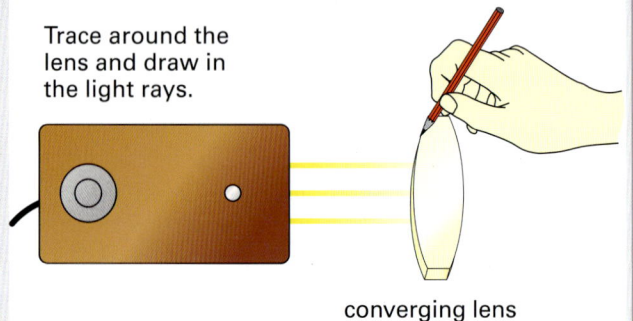

converging lens

3 Replace the lens with a different converging lens and find its focal length.

What happens when you use a diverging lens instead of a converging lens? Can you find the focal length of a diverging lens? Try it.

Discussion

1 Does a fatter converging lens refract light more or less than a thinner one? Suggest a reason for your answer.

2 Do diverging lenses have a focus? Explain your answer.

PART B
Images with lenses

Materials

- metre rule
- candle
- round glass converging lens and lens holder or plasticine
- screen (white hardboard or cardboard)
- ruler

Method

1 Hold the converging lens near a window and focus the image of a distant object on the screen. Measure the distance between the lens and the screen. This is the *focal length*.

round glass converging lens

screen

Record the focal length.

2 Light the candle. Then place the lens in a holder (or plasticine) and position it so that the distance from the lens to the candle is twice the focal length of the lens (2f).

3 Move the screen backwards and forwards until you get a clear image of the candle.

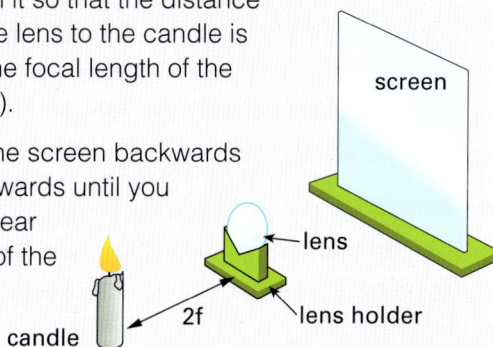

screen

lens

candle

2f

lens holder

Is the image bigger, smaller or about the same size as the candle flame? Is it right side up or upside down?

4 Move the lens further away from the candle and describe what happens to the image. Do this for two or three distances.

Record your observations.

5 Now move the lens closer to the candle but not up to the focus.

What happens to the image?

6 Move the lens inside the focus. Remove the screen and look through the lens at the candle flame.

Describe the image.

Conclusion

Summarise your results in a table. Put the distance between the lens and the candle in one column and the image description in another. The distances are:

- at twice the focal length (2f)
- further than 2f
- between 2f and f
- closer than f

PART C
Predicting images

Ray diagrams are scale models used to predict the position and size of the image. The ray diagram below uses a lens of focal length 20 cm. To find the image, draw one light ray straight through the centre of the lens, and another through the focus to the lens and then parallel to the axis. The image is where these two lines meet.

Take some measurements using your set-up from Part B, and then check the image distances with those predicted using ray diagrams.

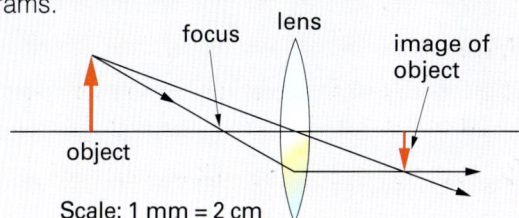

focus

lens

image of object

object

Scale: 1 mm = 2 cm

Optical fibres

The photo below shows a surgeon using an *endoscope* to examine a patient's stomach. The endoscope has a long flexible tube containing *optical fibres* which is inserted through the patient's mouth and oesophagus.

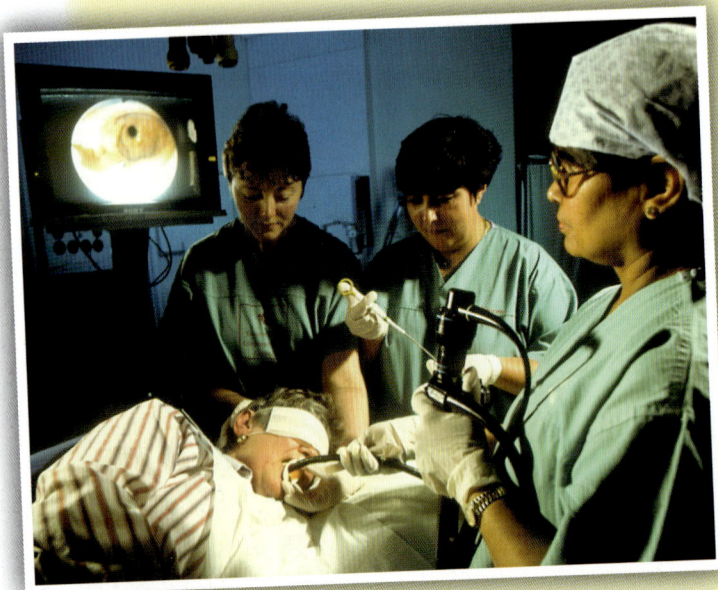

The endoscope contains bundles of optical fibres, each one about 10 micrometres in diameter. The optical fibres act like a flexible torch. Light shines through one end of the optical fibres in the endoscope and it comes out the other end no matter how much the tube is twisted or bent.

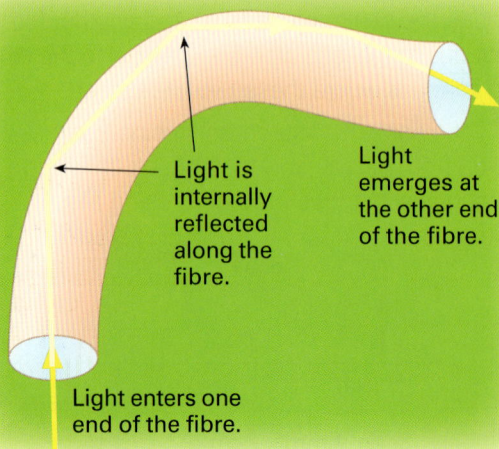

Light emerges at the other end of the fibre.

Light is internally reflected along the fibre.

Light enters one end of the fibre.

Activity

You will need a ray box kit and power pack for this activity.

1 Use the diagram below as a guide to set up the ray box and a triangular prism.
2 Shine one beam of light onto the side of the prism, and slowly rotate the prism until the light beam is totally internally reflected.

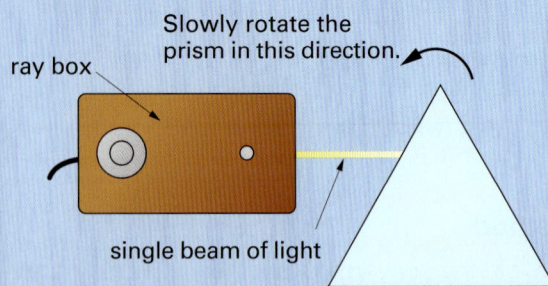

ray box

Slowly rotate the prism in this direction.

single beam of light

An optical fibre uses the principle of **total internal reflection** to transmit the light. The diagram bottom left shows how the light ray comes in from one end, hits the side of the fibre and is reflected back into it. None of the light escapes from the fibre. This is why it is called total internal reflection.

Endoscopes have two bundles of optical fibres inside the flexible tube, and each bundle consists of thousands of fibres. One bundle transmits the light from the surgeon's end to the patient so that the surgeon can see. The other bundle carries the image back to the surgeon via a microscope, video screen or computer.

Optical fibre communications

Optical fibres have replaced most metal cables used in communications. Electrical signals from computers, telephones, televisions and fax machines are converted to pulses of light using a laser. These light pulses are then sent along optical fibres which can transmit the signal over large distances.

Optical fibres are much lighter, and the same thickness of fibres can transmit thousands more messages than copper wire cables.

How the eye focuses light

Light enters the eye through the transparent cornea which covers the front of the eye. The coloured part in the front of the eye is called the iris. This is a ring of muscle which changes in size and thus controls the amount of light which enters the eye. The light passes through the pupil, the lens and the jelly-like substance inside the eye and finally hits the retina. The retina contains structures called *vision receptors* which detect light.

Both the cornea and the lens refract the light and focus it onto the retina. The lens is much better than a glass lens because it can change shape to focus near objects and distant objects. To focus on close objects, tiny muscles around the lens make it thicker and more sharply curved. When you focus on distant objects the lens becomes thinner and flatter.

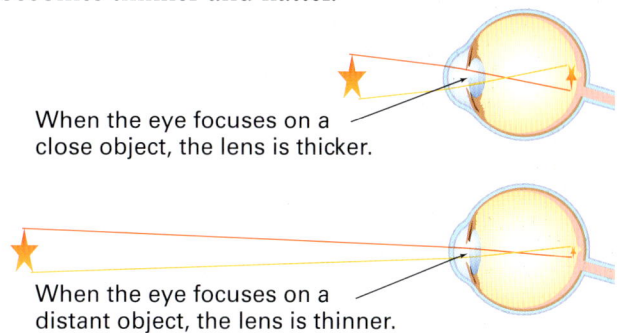

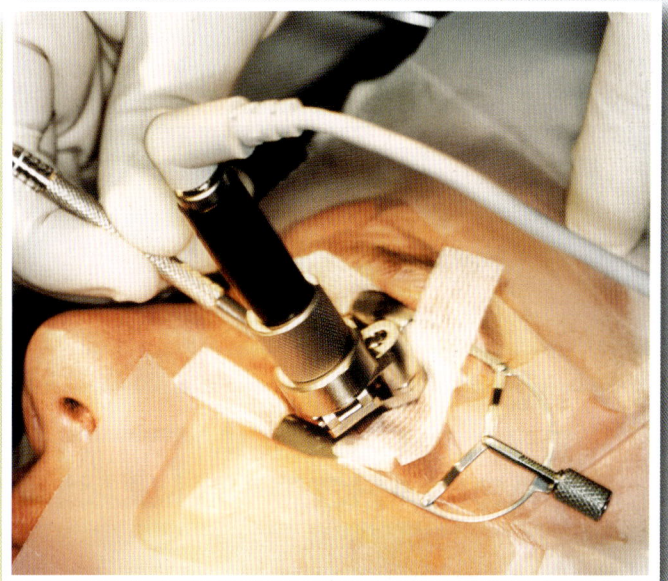

top eyelid

lens muscle

cornea

pupil

lens

iris

lower eyelid

retina

fovea

jelly-like substance inside the eye

optic nerve

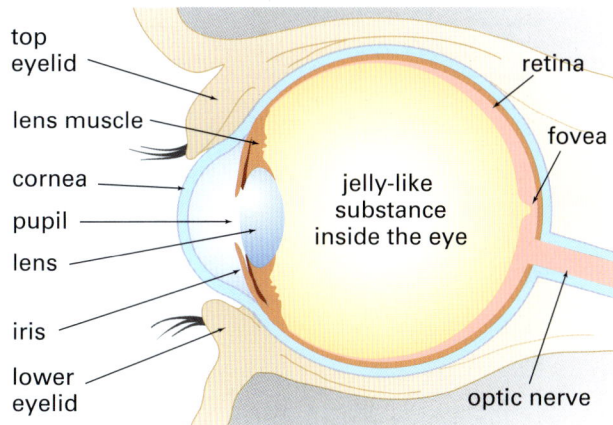

Fig 24 A cross-section of the human eye

When the eye focuses on a close object, the lens is thicker.

When the eye focuses on a distant object, the lens is thinner.

Science in action

Corneal transplants

When a person's cornea becomes cloudy as a result of disease, injury or infection, their vision is reduced, often making them blind. In a surgical operation called a *corneal transplant* a damaged cornea can be replaced by a donated healthy one.

In a corneal transplant, an eye surgeon, called an ophthalmologist (OFF-thal-MOL-o-gist), cuts a circular section of the damaged cornea using a tool that works in the same way as a round pastry cutter (see photo). The damaged section of cornea is removed and replaced with the same sized section of a healthy cornea. The new cornea is held in place by hair-like stitches.

Corneal transplants are the most succesful of the organ donation transplants. Over 90% of all patients have restored vision after the operation. The greatest risk with corneal transplants is tissue rejection. This is where the body of the patient rejects the donor's eye tissue. The eye swells and the two types of tissues never bind together.

WEBwatch

Use the internet to find out more information on corneal transplants and organ donation of eyes. Try entering the following words in the search engine: *corneal transplant* and *eye organ donor*.

Check!

1 Match each of the descriptions with the correct word from the list below.

image   reflection   incident ray
converging   plane mirror   refraction
focus   convex mirror   diverging

a a mirror that is flat and not curved
b when sound or light strikes a surface and bounces off
c the ingoing ray of light
d the point at which light rays meet after passing through a converging lens
e a picture of an object formed after light rays have been reflected or refracted
f light rays that come together.

2 a How could you demonstrate to someone that light and sound are forms of energy?
b Apart from the things mentioned on page 48, name some other things that convert light or sound into other forms of energy.

3 Why is the sign on this van written like this?

4 Explain the difference between the words reflection and refraction.

5 Some substances are transparent and some are opaque. Describe the differences between the two terms, giving two examples of each.

6 Copy the drawings below and show what happens to the light rays when they pass through the lenses. In each case label the focus.

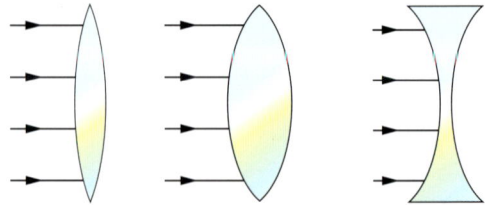

7 Two light beams strike a plane mirror as shown in the diagram below. Copy the diagram and show the normal and the reflected rays.

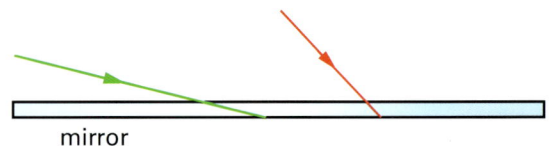

mirror

8 Two plane mirrors are placed at right angles to each other. A light ray is shone onto mirror 1 at 30° to the mirror.
a At what angle will the beam strike mirror 2?
b Will the reflected ray from mirror 2 be parallel to the original incident ray? Explain.

9 Reflection is a property of light. Briefly describe how you would demonstrate two other properties of light.

10 Describe what happens to light rays from when they enter the eye until they hit the retina.

11 When you read these words, the lens in each eye automatically adjusts to focus on the words. Now look out of a window. Immediately you focus on distant objects. Describe what happens to the lens in your eye when you do this.

12 Some substances are transparent, some are opaque, while others are translucent. Use a dictionary to find out what translucent means.

challenge

1 The diagram below shows a solar hot water heater using a semi-circular shiny, silvered reflector.

　a Explain how you think the heater works.

　b Where would you place the water tube to get the maximum heating efficiency?

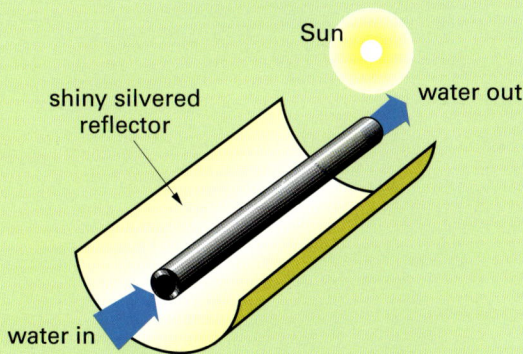

2 A pencil 15 cm long stands vertically on a bench 30 cm from a small spotlight. A screen is placed 1 m away from the spotlight and a shadow of the pencil forms on it.

　a Which property of light is being shown here?

　b How tall will the shadow be?

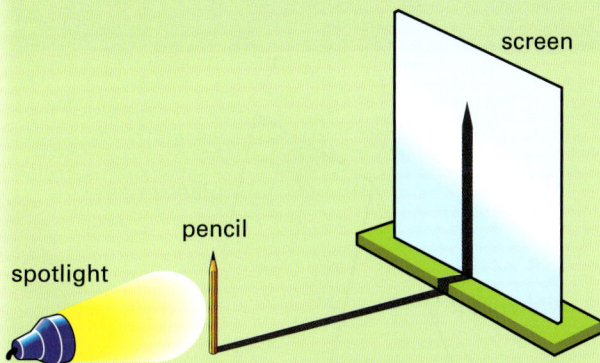

3 What type of mirror (plane, concave or convex) would be best to use as a rear-vision mirror with a wide field of view. Your teacher will give you the mirrors to help you with your decision.

4 A pencil 20 cm high was placed 60 cm in front of a concave mirror of focal length 20 cm. The ray diagram (top right) shows that the image of the pencil is upside down and smaller than the object.

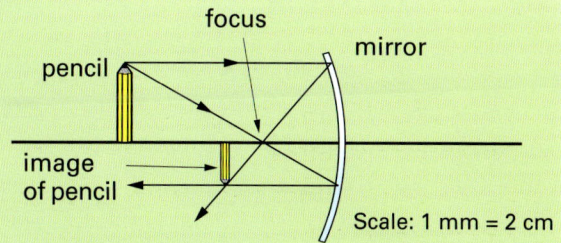

Scale: 1 mm = 2 cm

Do a similar drawing to find out what happens to the image if the pencil is placed 100 cm in front of the mirror.

5 A converging lens has a focal length of 20 cm. If an object 15 cm high is placed 40 cm from the lens, use a ray diagram to describe what the image will be like.

6 Design the following items using mirrors.

　a Make a periscope that can be used to see things around corners.

　b Use a concave mirror to make a solar cooker.

7 The diagram shows a light ray hitting the surface of a transparent substance. The light ray refracts at the surface and bends towards the normal.

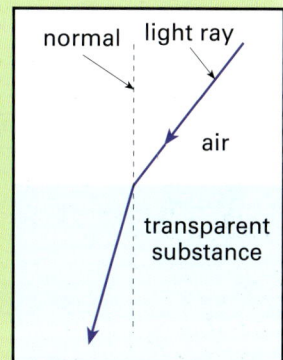

How much the refracted ray bends depends on the type of substance. The table below shows different substances and their refractive index. The higher the refractive index, the greater the refracted ray is bent.

Substance	Refractive index
air	1.00
water (at 25°C)	1.33
ethanol	1.36
glass	1.52
diamond	2.40

　a Does light bend more when it goes from air to water, or when it goes from air to glass? Justify your answer.

　b Glycerine has a refractive index of 1.47. Does glycerine bend light more or less than glass?

　c Predict what happens when a light ray passes from air to glass to water and out to air again. Draw a diagram of your prediction.

3.2 Light and colour

Rainbows make a ribbon of colours in the sky after rain. They form when sunlight passes through the raindrops. The drops split the white light from the sun into a **spectrum** of colours.

The colours that make up the spectrum are continuous and blend into each other, but for convenience we say there are seven colours—red, orange, yellow, green, blue, indigo and violet. The splitting up of white light into this spectrum of colours is called **dispersion**. This occurs because each colour is refracted slightly differently when it passes through a raindrop.

White light is also dispersed into separate colours when it passes through a glass prism.

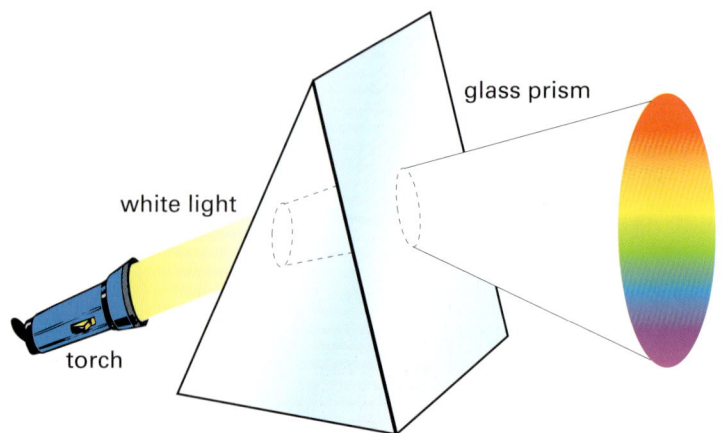

glass prism

white light

torch

Fig 35 A glass prism disperses white light into colours because each colour is refracted slightly differently. Violet light is refracted more than red light and so appears at the bottom of the spectrum.

Why are things coloured?

Why is a leaf green, milk white and a tomato red?

When white light hits a leaf, most of the colours in the white light are absorbed. Only the green light is reflected, and it is this colour that reaches your eye. So you see the leaf as a green colour.

Fig 36 A leaf reflects the green colour in white light and absorbs the others, so it appears green.

Fig 37 Milk reflects all the colours, so it appears white. A red tomato reflects only red light and absorbs the others.

Filters made of coloured glass or plastic can also change the colour of light. When white light hits a red glass filter, the glass allows the red light to pass through and absorbs all the other colours. The colour of the filter tells you what colours it transmits (allows to pass through).

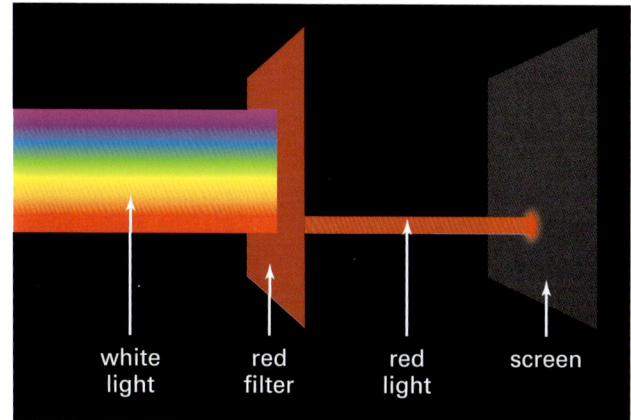

Fig 38 Coloured filters transmit their own colour and absorb the other colours.

What happens when you view a red tomato in green light? Since the tomato reflects only red light and absorbs all the others, green light is absorbed by the tomato. This means no light reaches your eyes, and the tomato therefore looks black.

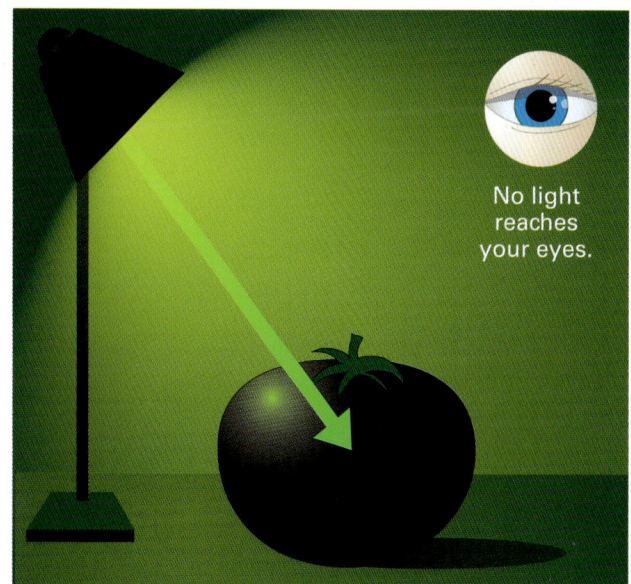

Fig 39 A red tomato will look black in green light because it absorbs all colours except red.

Investigate
10 COLOURS

Aim

To observe the effects of filters and coloured cards on white light.

Materials

- ray box kit with colour filters
- piece of white paper
- pieces of coloured card (red, green, yellow, blue)

Planning and Safety Check

This investigation is best done in a darkened room.

Make sure you ask your teacher to check your set-up before you turn on the power pack.

PART A
Coloured filters

1 Place the ray box on a sheet of white paper. Shine a full beam of light onto a triangular prism and turn the prism until the spectrum of colours is formed.

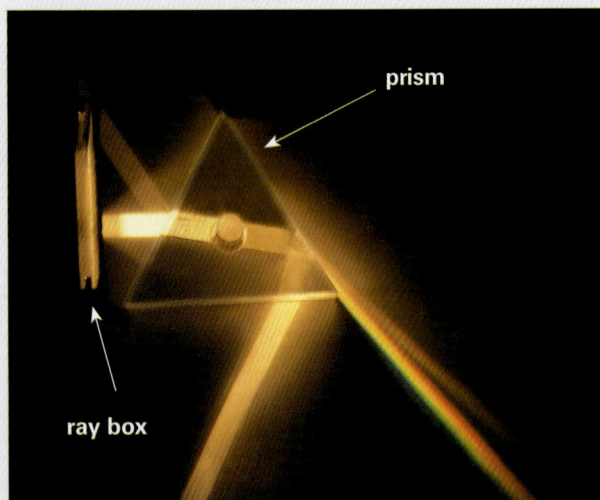

prism

ray box

2 Predict what will happen when you put a red filter between the light and the prism.

📋 Try it and record your observations.

3 Try other filters and record your observations.

PART B
Coloured objects

1 Shine a full beam of light from the ray box onto a piece of red card. Then place different coloured filters in the ray box and record the colour of the card in each light.

📋 Draw up a table and record your results in the table.

2 Repeat Step 1 with the other coloured cards.

Discussion

1 How do the results in Part A Step 1 help you decide which colour of the spectrum is refracted the most? Which one is refracted the least?

2 Which colours are transmitted and which are absorbed when white light is shone through a yellow filter?

3 Which colours of the spectrum would you see if white light was shone through a red filter and then a green filter? Explain your answer.

4 Explain using the words *absorb* and *reflect* why a blue card is blue in white light.

5 What would you see if you placed the blue card in red light? Explain your answer.

Making colours

There are two main ways of making colours. The first way is to shine different coloured lights together. The other way is to mix different coloured paints or pigments together.

Activity

Your teacher will set up three slide projectors (or light boxes) in a darkened room. Each projector will have a different coloured filter, red, green and blue, and the spots of colour will overlap on a white screen.

📋 What colour do you see when red light and green light overlap? As a challenge try to suggest why this happens.

📋 What colours would you see if the screen was red instead of white?

Addition

Making colours by adding different coloured lights together is called **addition**. White light can be made by shining red, green and blue lights together as shown below.

Subtraction

The method of making colours by mixing various paints together is called **subtraction**, because each paint colour subtracts or absorbs colours from white light. For example, blue paint reflects blue light and absorbs the rest.

Suppose 5-year-old Emily has seven pots of paints, and each one is a different colour of the spectrum. When she mixes them all together she ends up with a black mess. What happens is that each of the seven paints absorbs its colour from white light. When they are all mixed together, all the white light is absorbed and none is reflected. So the mixture looks black.

The diagram below shows how green is the only colour reflected when blue and yellow paints are mixed. All the other colours are absorbed.

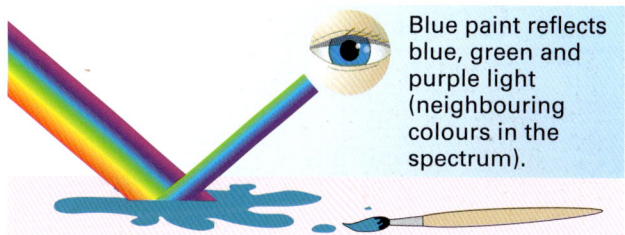

Blue paint reflects blue, green and purple light (neighbouring colours in the spectrum).

Yellow paint reflects orange, yellow and green light.

A mixture of the two paints reflects only green light.

Seeing colours

The retina that lines the inside of the human eye contains receptors that are sensitive to colours and give you colour vision. There are other receptors that are sensitive to shades of light and give you black-and-white vision.

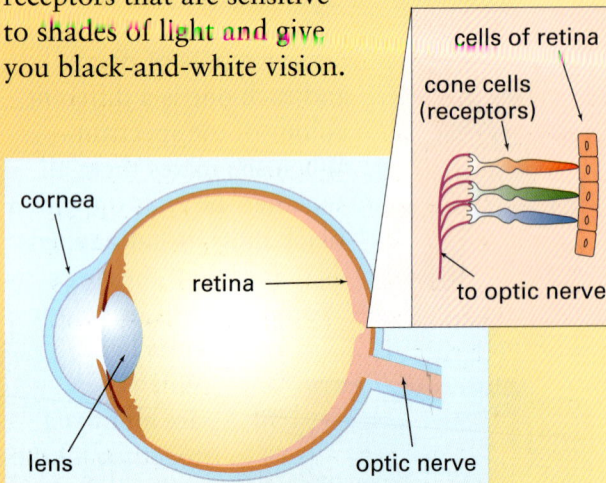

cells of retina
cone cells (receptors)
to optic nerve

cornea
retina
lens
optic nerve

The colour vision receptors are called *cone cells*. There are three types of cone cells—one type is sensitive to blue light, another to green light and the third to red light. The diagrams below show how you see colours.

Seeing red light

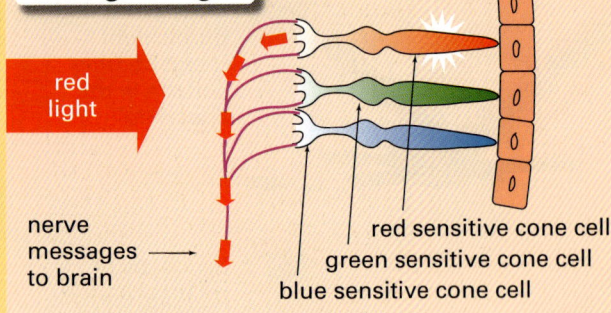

red light

nerve messages to brain

red sensitive cone cell
green sensitive cone cell
blue sensitive cone cell

Seeing white light

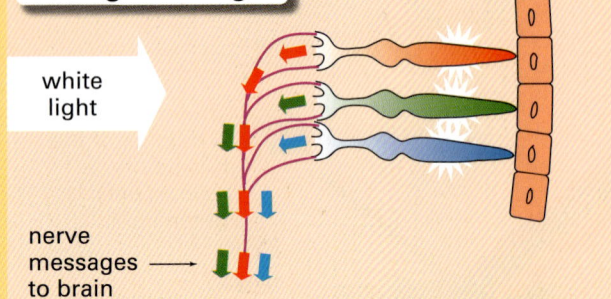

white light

nerve messages to brain

Colour blindness

Colour blindness is a condition which causes people to have trouble distinguishing between certain colours. The most common form of colour blindness is red/green colour blindness. People with this condition cannot see, or they confuse, shades of red, green and brown.

The condition is usually inherited, which means it is passed on from parents to children. In Australia, about 9% of males and about 0.4% of females have some form of colour blindness.

Causes of colour blindness

Each of the cone cells in the retina contains a type of light-sensitive pigment. One type of pigment is sensitive to blue light, another to green light and the third to red light.

In people with defective colour vision, one or more of the light-sensitive pigments functions poorly, or, in severe colour blindness, is absent altogether. Generally it is the red-sensitive and green-sensitive pigments in the cones that function poorly, giving rise to red/green colour blindness.

Questions

Use the websites below to answer the questions.
1 Does a colourblind person see only in black and white and shades of grey?
2 Is there a cure for colour blindness?
3 Describe three everyday frustrations for colourblind people.
4 Use the Ishihara colour charts to test your colour vision.

WEBwatch

Go to www.scienceworld.net.au and follow the links to the following websites.

Colours for the colourblind
This site describes colour blindness and lists some of the every day problems colourblind people put up with.

Ishihara tests for colour blindness
Contains the Ishihara colour charts to test for red/green colour blindness.

science bits

Why is the sky blue?

When a beam of light passes through smoke or dust, some of it bounces off the tiny particles and is reflected towards your eyes. This is why you can see the beam. This bouncing of light from particles such as smoke or dust is called **scattering**. You cannot see a beam of light in clean air because the particles of air are too small to scatter the light.

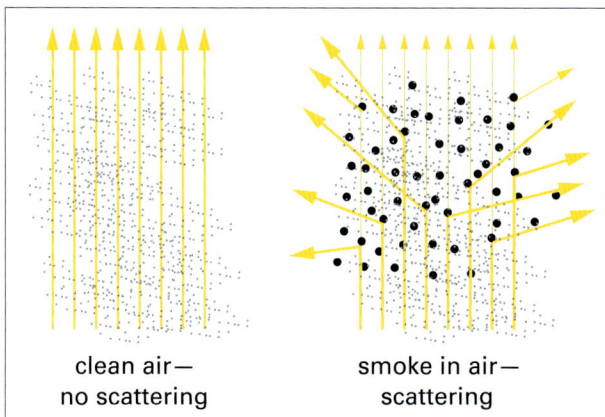

clean air—
no scattering

smoke in air—
scattering

The air around the Earth contains tiny bits of dust. These are too small to see, but they are big enough to scatter light. Blue light is scattered more by the dust than red light is. As the light from the Sun comes through the atmosphere, the blue light is scattered. This scattered blue light bounces from dust particle to dust particle, spreading blue light through the whole sky. This is why the sky normally appears blue.

Why are sunsets red?

When the Sun is low on the horizon, the light has more air to pass through as it travels through the atmosphere. Also the lower part of the atmosphere close to the horizon contains much more dust, so the blue light is scattered and the red light reaches your eyes. This is why sunsets are red. The dustier or smokier the atmosphere, the redder the sunset.

Questions

1 Why do suspensions scatter light but solutions do not?

2 a Why can you see the beam of light from a car's headlights when driving at night in fog?

   b Suggest why yellow lights are more effective than white lights when driving on foggy nights.

3 Suggest why sunsets are redder on cloudy or dusty days than on fine, clear days.

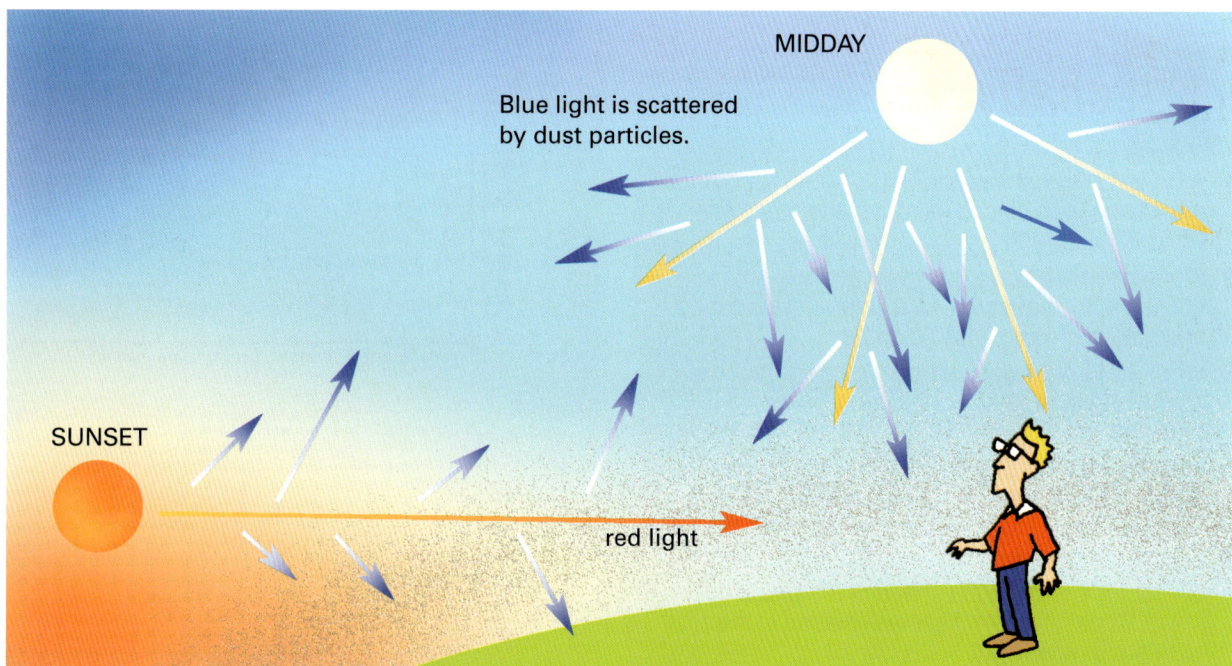

MIDDAY

Blue light is scattered by dust particles.

SUNSET

red light

Check!

1. Go back to your answer for the second question in Getting Started on page 47. Use the words *dispersion* and *spectrum* to explain why you see a rainbow of colours.

2. Use the words *absorbed* and *reflected* to explain why a banana looks yellow in white light.

3. What colour would a bunch of green grapes be in red light? Why?

4. A beam of white light shines through a blue filter. Use the words *transmitted* and *absorbed* to explain what happens to the colours in the white light.

5. A beam of white light passes through a filter and then through a prism. The prism disperses the light, and the different colours shine on a white screen. Use the information in the diagram below to work out the colour of the filter.

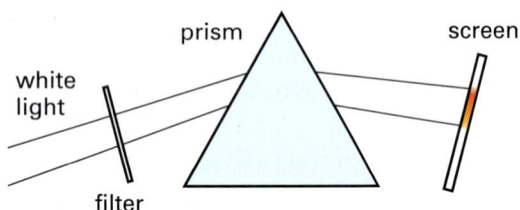

6. A combination beam of red and blue light hits a glass prism. On the other side of the prism, two separate beams of light are observed.
   a. Why did this happen?
   b. Which beam, A or B, on the diagram below is red? Give a reason for your answer.

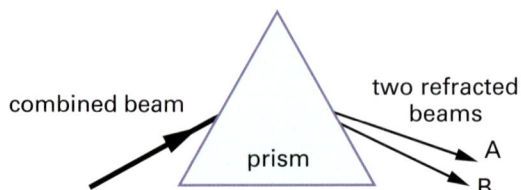

7. Why is the method of creating colours by mixing various coloured paints called subtraction?

8. Suppose green light is shone into your eyes.
   a. How do you see green light?
   b. Suppose a red light and a green light are shone together into your eyes. Predict what colour you would see. Which type of cone cells would not be detecting a colour?

challenge

1. A beam of light shines through a green filter. A red filter is then placed in front of the green filter. What will happen?

2. Some people believe that there are only six colours in the spectrum. Use library resources to find out which colour is in dispute.

3. When white light was detected by a light probe connected to a datalogger, Graph 1 was obtained. It shows that white light contains equal intensities of all the spectral colours.
   a. When a coloured filter was placed in the path of the light, Graph 2 was obtained. Infer the colour of the filter.
   b. Predict and draw the shape of the graph you would get if a violet filter was placed in the beam of white light.

Graph 1

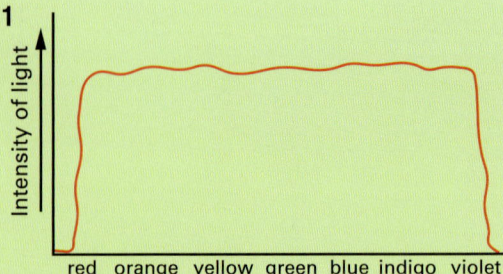

Graph 2

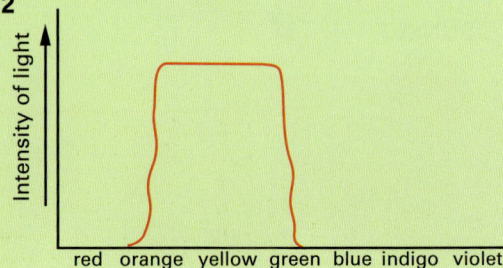

3.3 Light and sound waves

In the first section you learnt that sound and light are both forms of energy. How do these forms of energy travel from place to place?

Sound waves

Consider the following experiences.

*   If you put your ear to a metal railing, you can hear the sound of someone tapping on it a long way away.
*   When you are at the beach swimming underwater, you can hear the sound of a motorboat more than a kilometre away.
*   The photo below shows an electric bell inside a large jar. The bell is heard when the switch is pressed. However, if all the air is pumped out of the jar, you cannot hear the bell. (Your teacher may set this up for you.)

Sounds travel in solids, liquids and gases. This is why you can hear sounds in a metal railing, in water and in air. But when the air is pumped out of the jar, no sounds are heard.

Activity

To observe an effect of sound waves travelling through the air, your teacher will set up the following equipment, or you could set it up at home.

You will need a candle and a drum. (You could use a large can open at both ends with a rubber skin tied over one end.)

1 Make sure there is no wind in the room. Light the candle. Hold the open end of the drum close to the flame. Tap the skin on the drum and watch the flame.

2 For a more dramatic effect, hit the drum skin with a drumstick.

How do you think sound waves are responsible for the movement of the candle flame?

Sounds are made by vibrating objects. The vibrating strings on a guitar make sounds, as does the vibrating skin on a drum when it is struck. These vibrations are carried through the air as *sound waves*.

The activity showed that the sound from the drum travelled through the air. The air 'pushed' on the candle flame and made it flicker. These 'pushes', or sound waves, are the way sounds travel in air.

You may also have noticed that a soft tap on the drum made a soft sound and produced a small flicker in the flame. A harder hit on the drum made a louder sound and produced a larger flicker in the flame.

Sound waves are made up of bands of high and low air pressure. The energy from the vibrating source is transferred from one air particle to another as the sound waves travel.

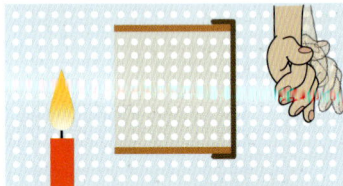

The air is made up of particles of various gases.

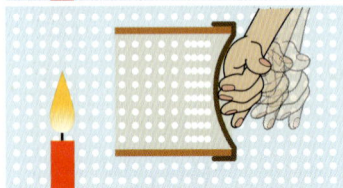

When the drum is struck, the particles are pushed together. This increases the air pressure.

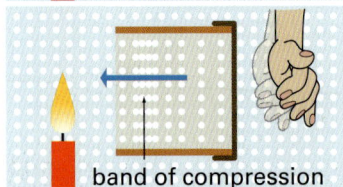

Each particle pushes on the next one as the wave moves through the drum, but the air as a whole does not move.

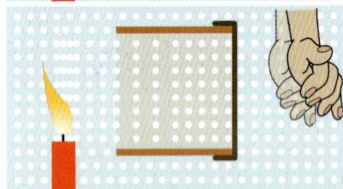

band of compression

The candle flame flickers when the wave of increased air pressure hits it.

Working with technology To see how sound waves are carried through the air, open the **Sound waves** animation on the CD.

Sound waves spread out in all directions through the air from the source of the sound. As they do this, the energy in the waves gradually decreases and the sounds become fainter.

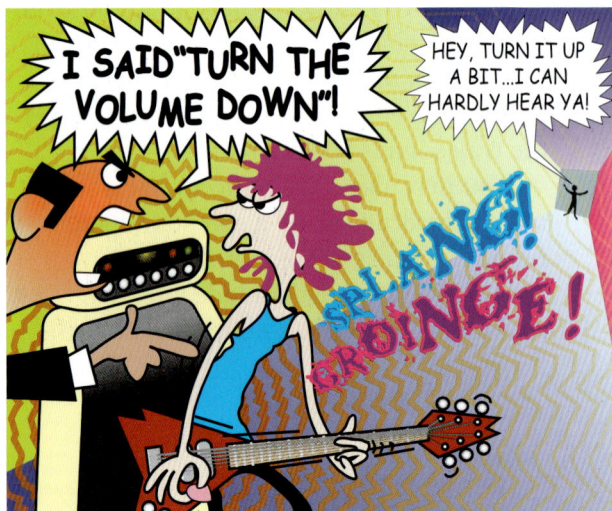

I SAID "TURN THE VOLUME DOWN"!

HEY, TURN IT UP A BIT...I CAN HARDLY HEAR YA!

SPLANG! GROINGE!

Activity

Your teacher may show you how you can model sound waves in a slinky spring. The waves travel through the spring as compressions.

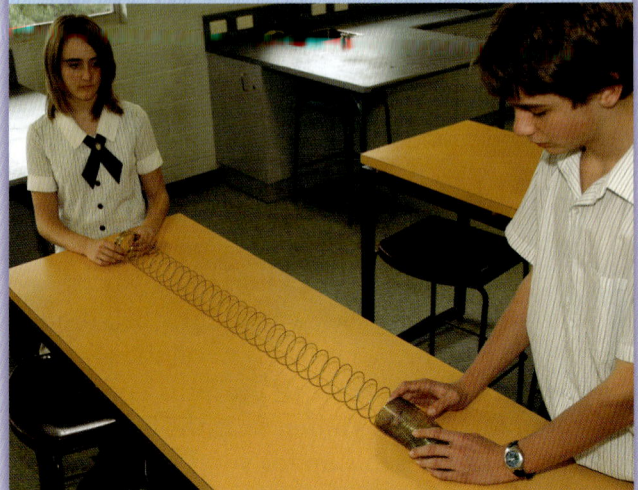

The speed of sound

When someone shouts at you from the far end of the schoolground, you hear the sound instantly. From this you can conclude that sound travels very rapidly in air.

Sound travels at 330 metres per second in air at 0°C. However, it travels even faster in other substances. The table below gives the speed of sound in various substances.

Substance	Speed of sound (m/s)	Speed of sound (km/h)
air (at 0°C)	330	1 188
air (at 15°C)	342	1 231
oxygen (at 0°C)	317	1 141
water (at 0°C)	1 410	5 076
water (at 15°C)	1 450	5 220
lead (at 20°C)	1 200	4 320
copper (at 20°C)	3 500	12 600
iron (at 20°C)	5 100	5 100
granite (at 20°C)	6 000	18 360
wood (at 20°C)	about 5 000	about 18 000

Light waves

Light from the Sun is a type of radiation that comes to us in the form of waves called *electromagnetic waves*. Unlike sound waves, light waves do not transfer their energy through the particles of gases, liquids or solids. Light waves can travel through the vacuum of space.

The various types of electromagnetic waves are different because they have different wavelengths.

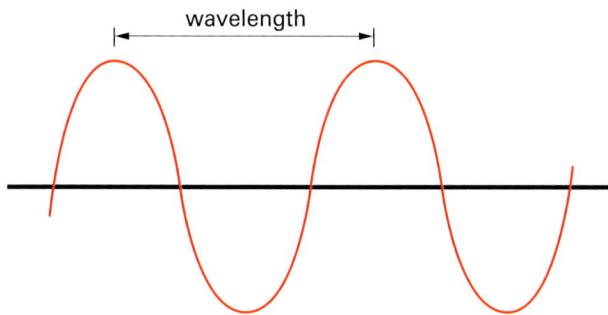

Light is just a small part of the **electromagnetic spectrum**. Microwaves, infra-red radiation and X-rays are other parts.

Visible light has a wavelength of about 0.000 000 5 m, while radio waves have very long wavelengths of about 10 m. The radiation with the shortest wavelength is gamma radiation, a very high-energy radiation which causes injury to the cells of living things. Generally, the shorter the wavelength of the radiation, the higher the energy of the waves.

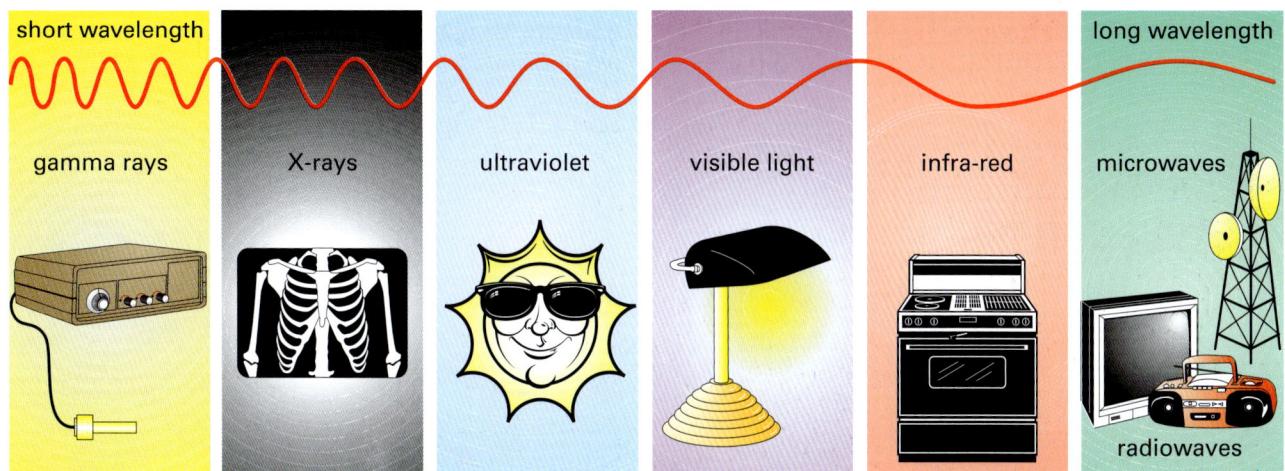

Activity

Models for light and sound

On page 66 you used two models to explain how sound behaves—a theoretical particle model and an actual spring model.

🖊 Suggest ways of making an actual particle model to show how sound travels. You might like to use marbles, or styrofoam balls attached to pieces of string.

🖊 Use your model to explain to other people the properties of sound.

🖊 Devise a second model to explain how light travels.

🖊 What are the limitations of your models?

Fig 62 The electromagnetic spectrum. The short wavelength waves carry more energy than long wavelength ones.

Light waves and refraction

In the first section of this chapter, you learnt that light refracts when it passes from one transparent substance to another. This is because light slows down as it passes from air to glass.

Light, like all types of electromagnetic radiation, travels at incredible speed—about 300 000 000 m/s or 3×10^8 m/s. This is about a million times faster than the speed of sound. No wonder you see the lightning before you hear the thunder of a distant thunderstorm!

The speed of light in glass is 1.98×10^8 m/s —about 1.5 times slower than in air. When light passes from air to glass at an angle, it slows down and bends towards the normal.

How far away is that thunderstorm?

You can use the fact that light travels nearly one million times faster in air than sound to calculate how far away a thunderstorm is.

It takes sound 3 seconds to travel 1 km in air. So when you see the lightning flash, count the seconds by saying 'one thousand, two thousand ...' etc, then calculate how far away the storm is.

WEBwatch

To find out more about lightning and thunder, go to www.scienceworld.net.au and follow the links to **Lightning and Thunder**.

science bits

How a rainbow forms

A drop of water has the same effect on light as a prism—it is dispersed into the spectrum of colours. But why is violet light refracted more than red light?

It has been found that different colours of light have slightly different speeds in the same substance. For example, the speed of red light in water is 2.280×10^8 m/s, while that of violet light is slower, at 2.255×10^8 m/s. This slight difference in speed means that violet light bends more than red light when it passes through a drop of water.

When sunlight hits a raindrop at a particular angle, the white light is dispersed into the spectral colours. These colours come out of the raindrop at different angles. Because of this, your eye only sees one colour from each drop (see the diagram on the left). The red light in the rainbow comes from the droplets highest in the sky and the violet light from the droplets lowest in the sky. So red should be on top of the rainbow and violet underneath. Check this in the rainbow photo on page 58.

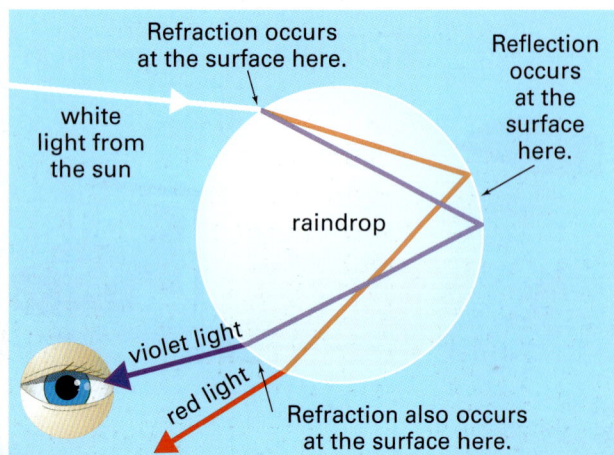

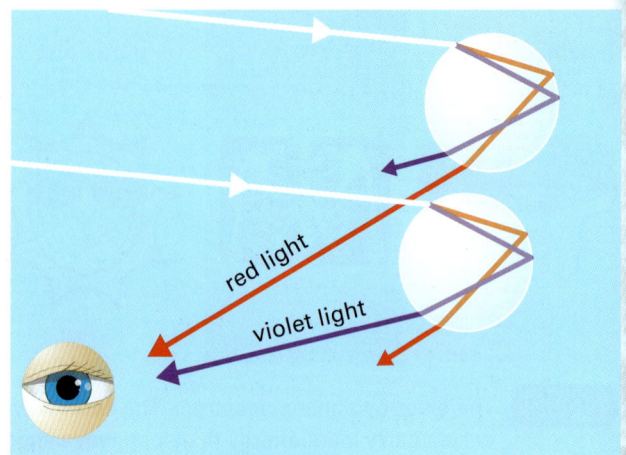

Check!

1 Sound cannot travel through:
   A wood
   B fresh water
   C outer space
   D the ocean
   E the Earth's crust
   Justify your answer.

2 Decide whether each of the statements below is true or false by referring to the table of speeds of sound on page 66. For each case, give reasons for your decision.
   a Sound travels faster through gases than through liquids.
   b Sound travels faster through warm air than through cold air.
   c Sound travels at the same speed through all gases.
   d Sound travels faster through metals than through non-metals.

3 Two waves were drawn on centimetre square graph paper.
   a Which wave has the longer wavelength?
   b What is the wavelength of wave A?

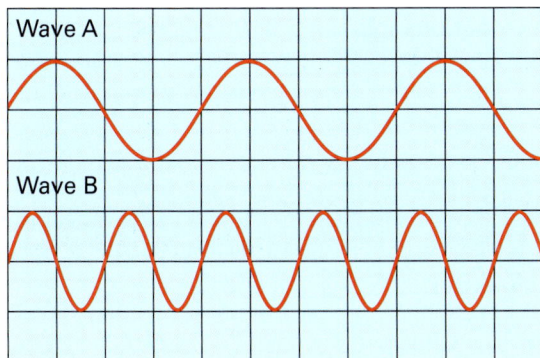

4 Why do you hear thunder after you see the lightning in a far-off storm?

5 Light is one type of electromagnetic radiation. Name three others.

6 Look at the electromagnetic spectrum at the bottom of page 67.
   a Which types of radiation can be detected by the human body?
   b Which receptors do you use to detect them?

c Which types of radiation can be used for communicating with other people?
d Which type of radiation is commonly referred to as heat?

7 Using your knowledge of sound and light, write a paragraph outlining the similarities and differences between them.

8 A combined beam of yellow and blue light was shone onto a prism. Two separate beams emerged from the other side. Use your knowledge of light waves to explain why beam B is blue.

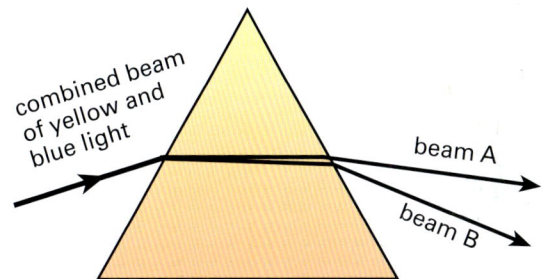

9 How does the candle and drum demonstration on page 65 show that sound is a form of energy?
   Use the particle model to explain why there is more energy in a loud sound than in a soft one.

10 Design an experiment to show that light, unlike sound, does not need a substance such as air in which to travel.

11 A string telephone can be made from two metal cans and some string. Suggest why:
   a the telephone works only when the string is stretched tight
   b the telephone does not work when a third person touches the string.

challenge

1 Sam is a long way away from you and he is trying to tell you something. He rolls up a piece of cardboard in the shape of a cone and speaks through it. You can now hear him. Explain in terms of sound waves why this happens.

2 Suggest why you can hear sounds better when the wind is blowing towards you than when it is blowing away from you.

3 In a science fiction movie, the goodies destroy an enemy spacecraft in deep space with laser guns, and they hear it explode as they fly past. What is wrong with this scene?

4 The diagrams below show two different sounds. Different sounds have different wavelengths. The wavelength of sound is the distance between the bands of compression of the particles.

Sound A

one wavelength

Sound B

a Which sound has the shorter wavelength?

b High pitched sounds have shorter wavelengths than low pitched sounds. Which sound has the higher pitch? A or B?

c Hold a ruler over a bench and flick it. It vibrates and makes a sound. Notice how the ruler vibrates. Increase the length of the ruler and flick it again. Look at the way it vibrates and listen to the pitch.

d How do you think the wavelength, the speed of vibration and the pitch of the sound are related?

5 The diagram below shows a ray of light passing from air through three different transparent substances.

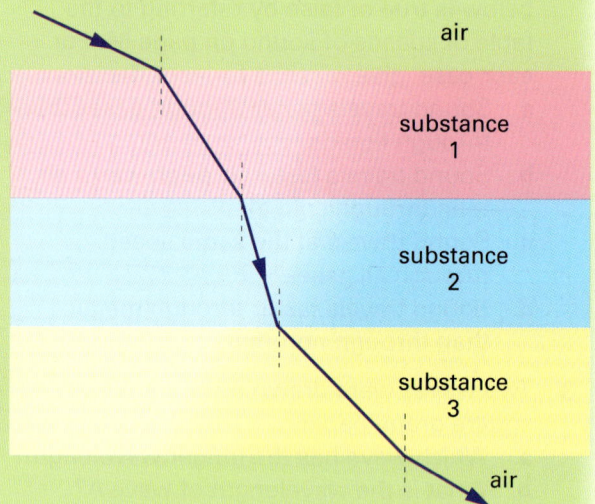

a Does light travel faster or slower in substance 1 than in air? Give a reason for your answer.

b In which substance is the speed of light closest to that in air?

6 On page 66 the particle model was used to explain how sound waves travel in air. Use the model to explain why sound travels faster in liquids than in gases, and even faster in solids.

7 A person fires a gun and hears an echo from a cliff after 5 seconds. If the temperature is 15°C, use the speed of sound on page 66 to calculate how far away the cliff is.

8 Suppose someone is talking about you in the next room. When you put your ear to the wall you can hear what the person is saying.

a Try to explain in terms of waves why you can hear sounds through the wall but cannot see light through it.

b Which types of radiation can pass through walls? (Hint: refer to the electromagnetic spectrum on page 67.)

MAIN IDEAS

Copy and complete these statements to make a summary of this chapter. The missing words are on the right.

1 Reflection is a _____ of light and sound. Another property of light is that it travels in _____.

2 The _____ states that the angle of _____ is equal to the angle of reflection.

3 _____ of light occurs when a beam of light passes from one _____ substance into another, eg from air to water. The amount of refraction depends on the substances.

4 White light can be _____ by a prism into the colours of the _____.

5 A coloured object reflects some colours and _____ the rest. The colour you see depends upon the colours that are reflected.

6 Different colours can be made by mixing different coloured lights (addition) or by mixing paints (_____).

7 Sound waves are produced by _____ objects and travel through gases, liquids and solids.

8 Light is a form of _____ radiation which can travel as waves through a _____. The speed of light is much greater than the speed of sound.

absorbs

dispersed

electromagnetic

incidence

law of reflection

property

refraction

spectrum

straight lines

subtraction

transparent

vacuum

vibrating

Try doing the Chapter 3 crossword on the CD.

Working with technology

REVIEW

1 A ray of light hits a mirror. The path of the light ray after it is reflected is shown by light ray:
   A AW
   B AX
   C AY
   D AZ

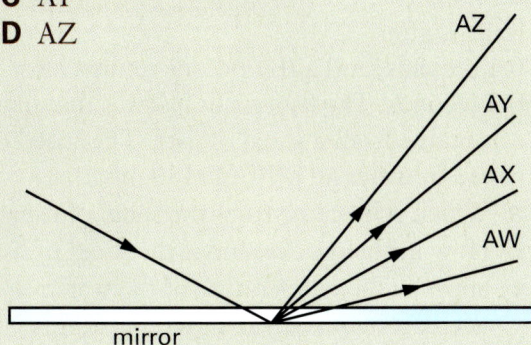

mirror

2 Ian is using a fine spray to water his seedlings. When he sprays the water into the air he sees the colours of a rainbow. The rainbow is caused by:
   A the reflection of light
   B the transmission of light
   C the absorption of light
   D the dispersion of light

3 Each of the drops of water in Question 2 is acting like a:
   A glass prism
   B lens
   C plane mirror
   D concave mirror

4 Three parallel light rays shine through a transparent object and are refracted as shown below. Which shaped object will cause this refraction?

A a rectangular glass block
B a converging lens
C a diverging lens
D a triangular glass prism

5 Three parallel light rays shine onto a converging lens. The scale drawing below shows the results. Each square of the grid is 5 cm × 5 cm.

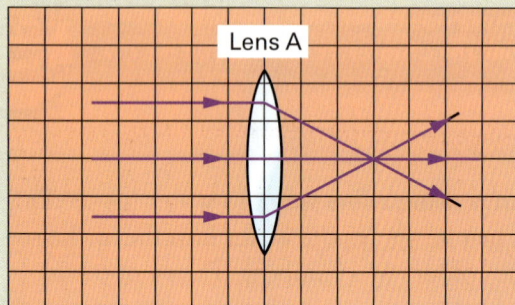

Lens A

a What is the focal length of the lens?
b Suppose lens A is replaced with another converging lens, B. This lens has a focal length of 25 cm. What is the shape of lens B compared with that of lens A?

6 A beam of light consisting of red, green and violet light shines on a white screen. A coloured filter is placed over the beam. Green light is seen on the screen.

a Which colours are being transmitted?
b Which colours are being absorbed?
c Infer the colour of the filter.

7 Which colour light is shining in your eye when all three types of receptors in your retina are sending messages to your brain? Explain your answer.

8 A combined beam of three different coloured lights is shone through a prism. Two of the coloured lights are green and red. The other coloured light is either yellow or blue. The diagram below shows the results. If beam C was green, work out which colour beams A and B are. Explain your answer.

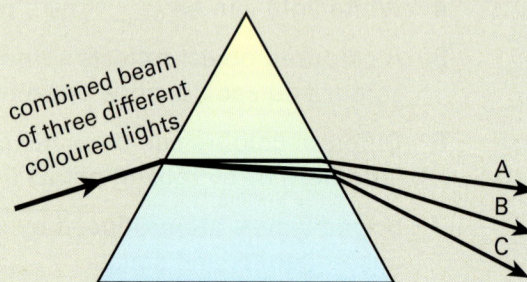

combined beam of three different coloured lights

A
B
C

9 Echo sounders send sound waves through water to determine its depth. They can also be used to find the depth of shoals of fish. Suppose a reflected sound wave returns after 0.1 seconds, and a second one returns after 0.2 seconds. The fisherman believes that one echo came from a shoal of fish. (The speed of sound in water at 15°C is 1450 m/s.)

a Which echo came from the shoal of fish?
b How far below the ship is the shoal of fish?
c Suppose the temperature of the water decreases with depth. How would this affect the calculations?

Check your answers on pages 332–333.

Communications technology

Getting Started

- Discuss ways in which technology such as broadband, mobile phones and digital TV is changing our lives.

- In the cartoon below you will see many different ways of communicating.
  Work in a small group and try to identify as many different examples as you can.

4.1 Communicating

Communication is the sending of a message (information) from one person to another. This message can be in written or spoken form, called *verbal communication*, or using gestures or symbols which are forms of *non-verbal communication*. However, communicating does not only occur between humans. In Getting Started you probably listed several examples of communication involving animals.

Communication involves the transmission of information from a sender to a receiver. The sender *encodes* this information into a message suitable for transmission. That is, the message is put into a *code*. The words that you are reading now are in a code which you have learnt over a number of years. These words form sentences which have meaning. Can you make any sense of this sentence? (See Check 2 on page 80.)

✳✳✳▲   ▲✳■▼✳■✳✳   ✳▲   ✳■   ✳□✳✳

To understand a message like the one above the receiver has to *decode* it—change it from this code to a code that you can understand.

The flow diagram below shows the steps in the process of communication. *Feedback* is an important part of this process because it tells the sender whether or not the message has been received and understood. *Noise* is something that might interfere with the transmission of the message: for example, someone playing loud music while you are trying to talk on the telephone. Noise can also be electronic.

Activity

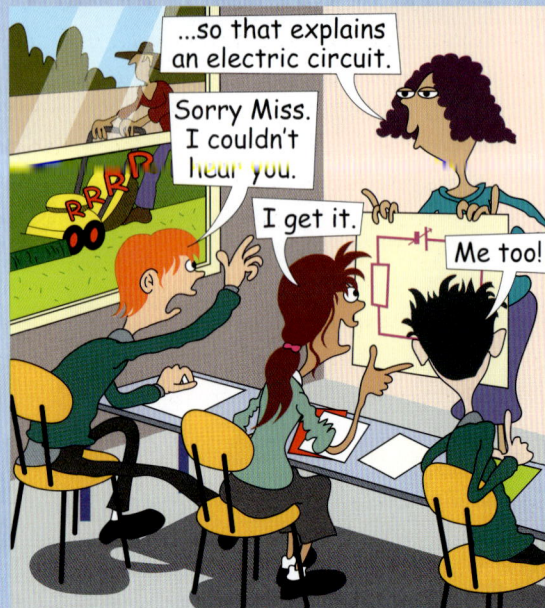

The teacher in the cartoon wants the students to set up an electric circuit.

✎ How does she know whether her message has been understood?

✎ What would you need to be able to do to decode her message?

✎ What is the effect of noise in this situation?

Fig 2 A model to show the steps in the process of communication

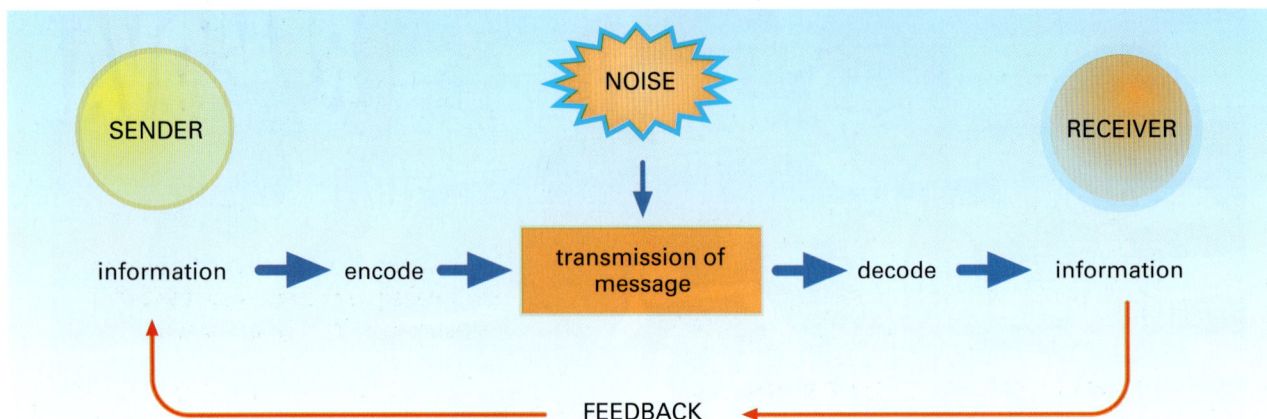

Communication devices

Communication devices such as a telephone require voice to be changed into electrical signals, radio waves or light pulses. These signals are transmitted over long distances and then changed back into voice which is heard by the receiver. Voice is changed into electrical signals by a *microphone* and the electrical signals are changed back to voice by a *loudspeaker*.

In previous studies you learnt that a magnet induces an electric current when it moves in a coil of wire. A microphone uses this principle. Sound waves make the diaphragm (DIE-a-fram) in the microphone vibrate. The coils of wire attached to the diaphragm vibrate near a magnet. This movement then creates a current in the wires which changes with the loudness of the voice. Soft sounds produce small currents and loud sounds produce larger currents. The pitch of the sound also affects the current.

A loudspeaker works in the opposite way to a microphone. The varying current in the wire passes through a coil near a magnet and this causes the coil to move. The coil is attached to a diaphragm which also moves. This movement causes the air next to the diaphragm to move and you hear a reproduction of the original sounds.

Digital and analog signals

In a microphone, the vibrating diaphragm produces a varying electrical signal like the one below. The size or **amplitude** of the signal determines the loudness of the sound.

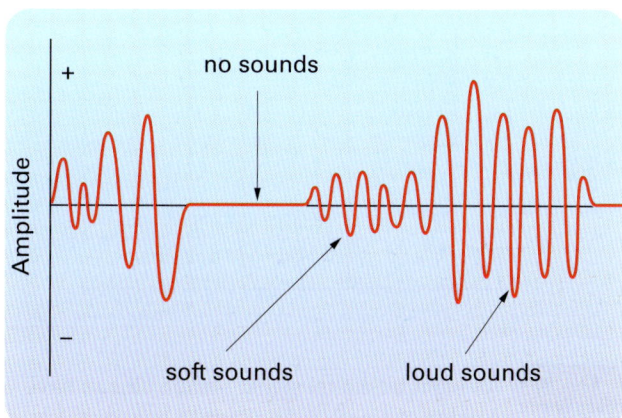

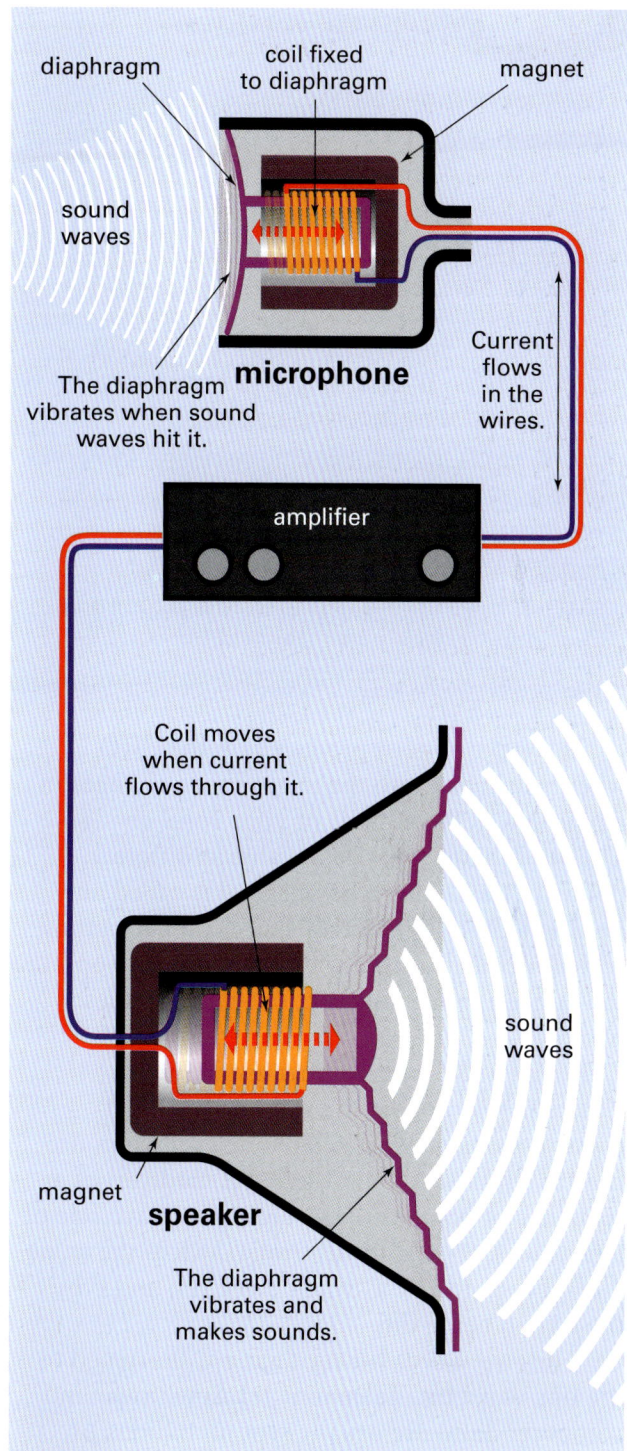

Fig 4 A microphone converts sound waves to electrical signals, and a loudspeaker converts electrical signals to sound.

To see an animation of this process, open **How a microphone works** on the CD.

Working with technology

Activity

Teacher demonstration

Your teacher will set up a microphone attached to a cathode ray oscilloscope (CRO). The electrical signals produced by the microphone can be seen on the screen of the CRO.

🖾 Observe a variety of different sound patterns on the CRO. For example, speak into the microphone, sing a note or use a tuning fork or musical instrument.

🖾 What is the relationship between the amplitude of the waves on the CRO and the volume of the sound made?

Instead of using a CRO you could use a sound probe connected to a datalogger and then print out the wave pattern.

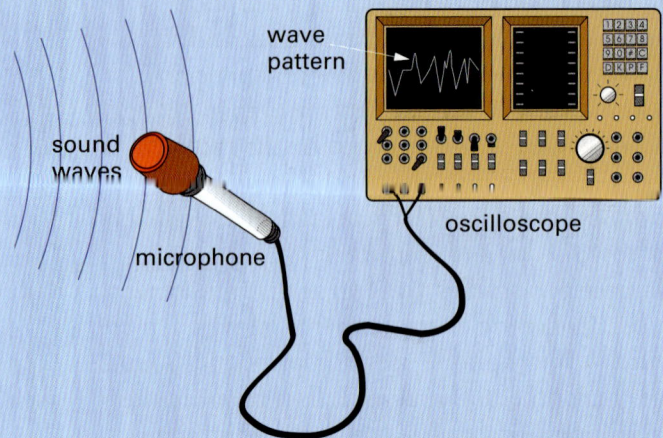

You could also connect a microphone to a galvanometer and observe the movement of the pointer as you speak into the microphone.

The wave pattern produced on the CRO when you speak into the microphone changes in amplitude as the volume of your voice changes. The wave pattern varies in value at different points in time. This type of signal is called an **analog** (AN-a-log) **signal**. The electrical signals which travel along the wires from the microphone in your telephone handset are similar to these waves.

Before 1980 telephone transmission in Australia was analog. Now, however, most transmissions between telephone exchanges use **digital signals**. A digital signal is made up of a sequence of *binary digits*—digits that have one of two values, 0 or 1. In electronic devices the value 1 is represented by a switch being on, and 0 by the switch being off.

The two words **b**inary dig**it** are shortened to the one word **bit**. Telephone transmissions (and computer data) are usually sent in millions of small units made up of eight bits which are called **bytes**. The digital signal to the right is a byte and has the value 10011010.

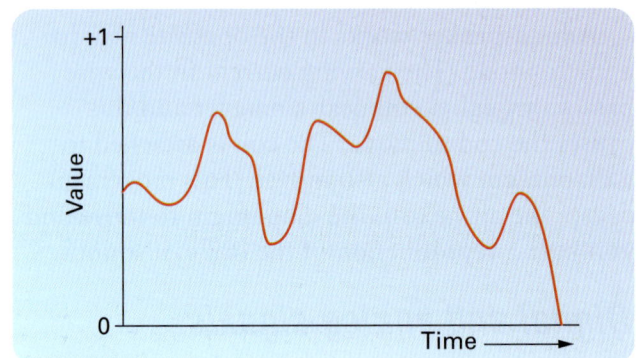

Fig 7 Analog signals vary continuously in value over time.

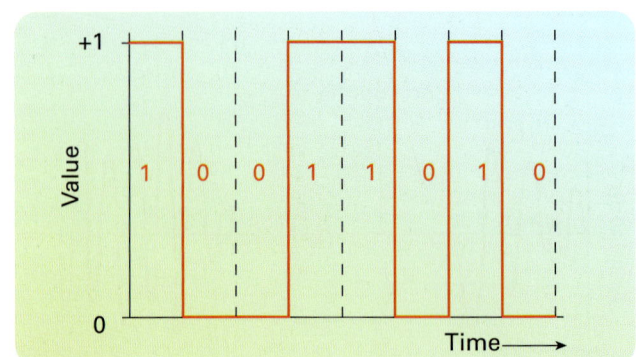

Fig 8 An eight bit digital signal—each bit can have a value of 1 or 0, but nothing in between.

The telephone network

Analog signals from your telephone are converted to digital signals at the telephone exchange. These digital signals then travel through cables to other telephone exchanges. Most of the cables that link major Australian cities are now **optical fibres** made of glass.

The diagram below shows how the telephone network encodes the information in sound waves to electrical signals and then to optical signals. At the receiver's end the information is decoded back again to sound waves. Instead of using cables, telephone signals can also be transmitted via microwave repeater stations or even satellites, especially in isolated areas.

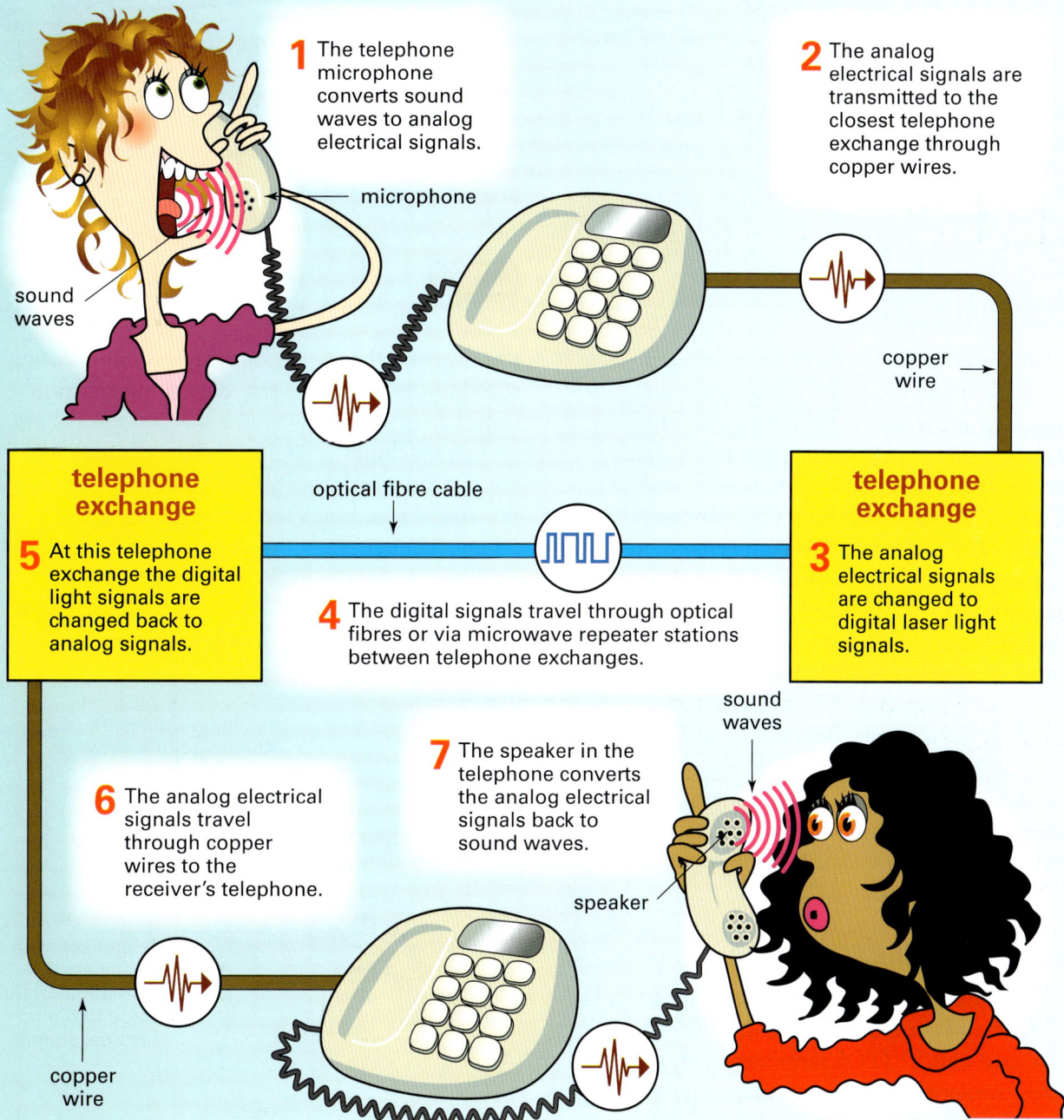

1 The telephone microphone converts sound waves to analog electrical signals.

microphone

sound waves

2 The analog electrical signals are transmitted to the closest telephone exchange through copper wires.

copper wire

telephone exchange

optical fibre cable

telephone exchange

5 At this telephone exchange the digital light signals are changed back to analog signals.

4 The digital signals travel through optical fibres or via microwave repeater stations between telephone exchanges.

3 The analog electrical signals are changed to digital laser light signals.

sound waves

7 The speaker in the telephone converts the analog electrical signals back to sound waves.

6 The analog electrical signals travel through copper wires to the receiver's telephone.

speaker

copper wire

Note: Digital phones use digital signals rather than analog signals.

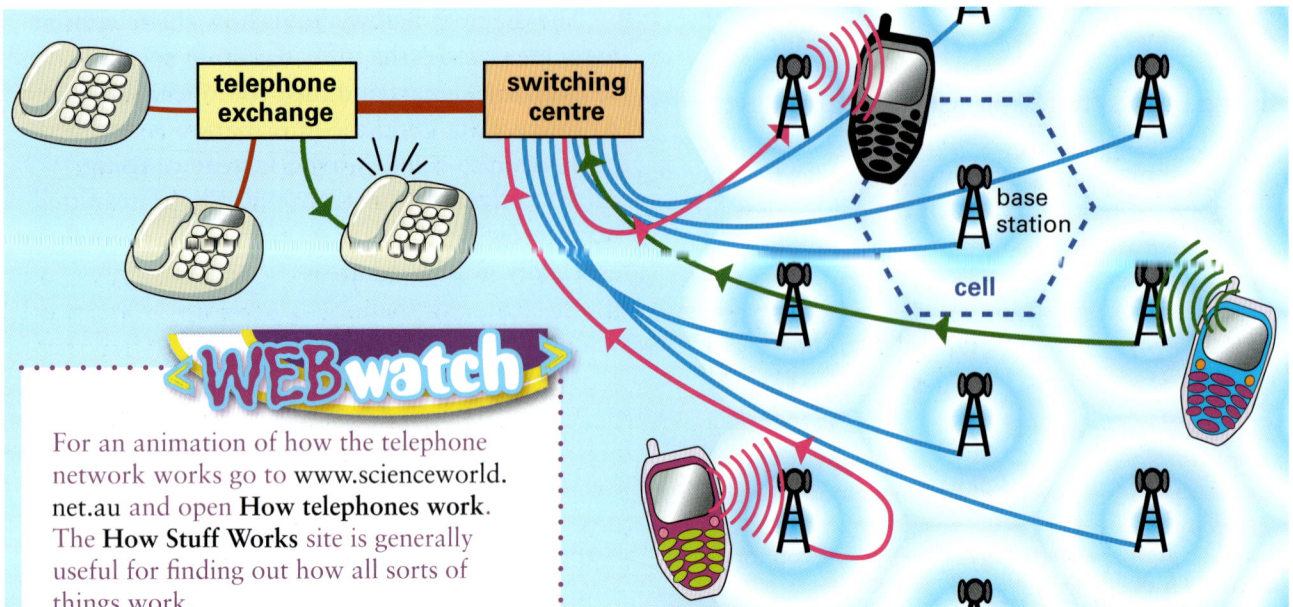

telephone exchange

switching centre

base station

cell

Fig 10 A mobile phone network

Mobile phones

Mobile phones don't need to be connected by wires. Instead they have a built-in radio transmitter and receiver. When you make a call the mobile phone sends out a radio signal. This signal is picked up by a base station that has several antennas on top of a tower or tall building. The base station is connected to a switching centre which switches the call to other base stations or to the fixed telephone network.

In the USA, mobile phones are called *cell phones*. This is because the base stations form a network of hexagonal cells, as shown above. The cells range in size from 100 metres across to more than 30 km. The base stations receive mobile phone calls from the cell around them. Each call is then passed from cell to cell until it reaches its destination. The base stations also return calls to the cell around them.

Faxes and modems

The telephone network also carries data from fax machines and computer modems, as well as from credit card and EFTPOS terminals in shops. Most of the data sent from these devices is digital. This means that the copper wires connecting these devices to the exchange have to be able to carry electrical digital signals as well as analog ones.

On the other hand, the optical fibres connecting telephone exchanges carry digital information only.

Fax machines send and receive documents containing words, graphics or photos. The document is fed into the fax machine where a light scanner reads the degree of lightness or darkness on the page. The scanned data is then encoded into digital signals which are sent through the telephone network.

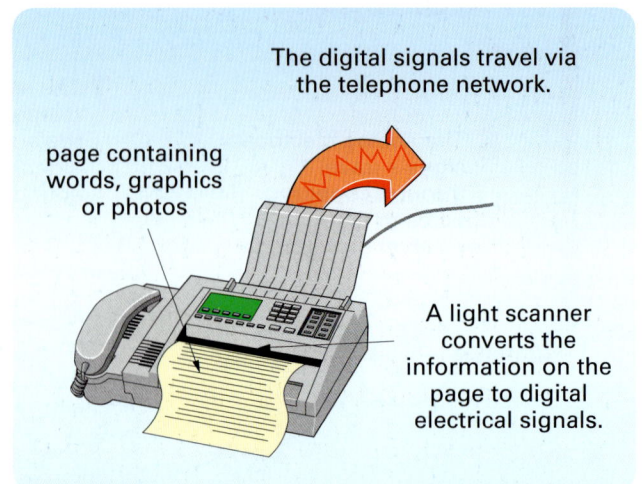

The digital signals travel via the telephone network.

page containing words, graphics or photos

A light scanner converts the information on the page to digital electrical signals.

Fig 11 Fax machines convert written information to digital electrical data.

Optical fibres

The optical fibres used in the telephone network are very thin pure glass fibres. Each fibre consists of a glass core, a glass cladding and a protective outer jacket, and the whole fibre is thinner than a human hair.

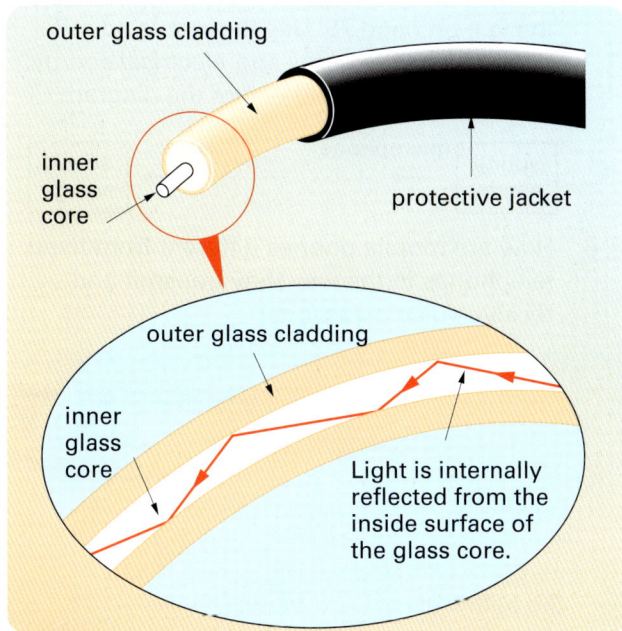

Fig 12 How light pulses travel through optical fibres

At telephone exchanges the electrical signals from local telephones are converted to pulses of laser light. These laser pulses are narrow high-intensity light beams of a single colour (wavelength). They are digital (on or off) and they travel through the optical fibre by *total internal reflection*. That is, the light can travel around bends and even loops by reflecting off the inside surface of the inner glass core. One optical fibre can carry up to 2 billion pulses of light per second.

The advantages of optical fibres are that they can carry much more information more quickly than copper wires do. They are lighter and cheaper to make, and they produce a better quality of communication with very low noise.

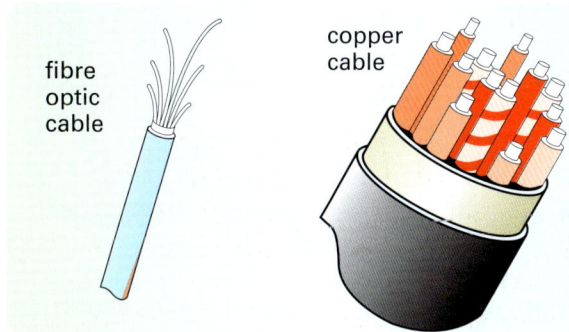

Fig 13 A copper cable which can carry 10 000 telephone calls is much larger and heavier than a fibre optic cable which carries the same number of calls.

Activity

1 Set up a binocular microscope and look at the end of an optical fibre.
   Sketch what you observe.
2 The diagram on the right shows the equipment you need to make a model which demonstrates how optical fibres work.
3 Use the diagram as a guide to make the model. You will need to test it in a darkened room, or test it at home at night.
4 Can you improve the design of the model? Discuss your design with your partners.

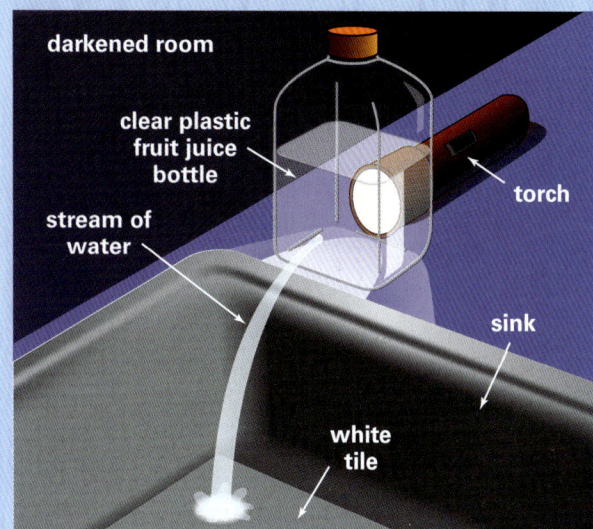

Check!

1 a The diagram below shows how a telephone network works. Select words from the following list to match the numbers in the diagram. You will need to use some words twice.

analog electrical signals   sound waves
digital light signals   microphone
telephone exchange   speaker

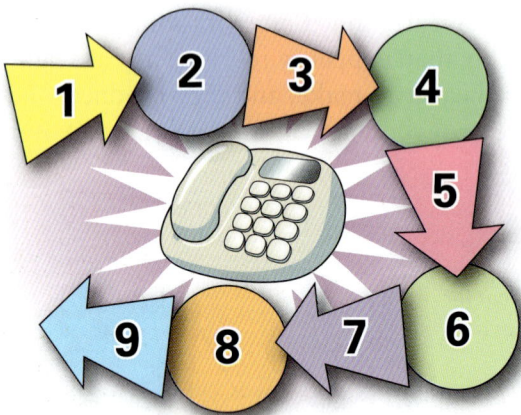

b Which of the numbered arrows could represent a distance of many thousands of kilometres? Explain your answer.

2 If you were given an incomplete code for the coded words on page 74, can you decipher the message?

✳ = T   ✳ = I   ▲ = S
✳ = E   ■ = N   ❑ = O

3 The CRO wave pattern below was made by sounds which were directed into a microphone.
a In which periods were there no sounds?
b Which sound was the the loudest?

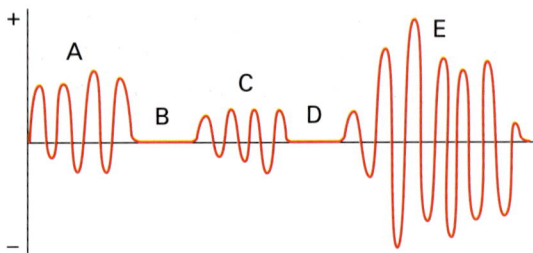

4 A speaker and a microphone work in opposite ways. Explain what this means. Use the words *sound waves*, *diaphragm*, *vibrate*, *coil*, *magnet* and *electric current* in your answer.

5 Construct an energy flow diagram that shows all the energy conversions that occur in Fig 4 on page 75. Use the words *sound energy*, *kinetic energy* and *electrical energy*. Below is the start and end of the diagram.

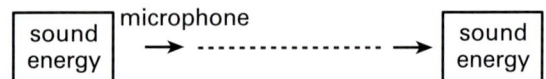

6 How are mobile phones different from fixed telephones in the way they transmit and receive voice messages?

WEBwatch

1 Use the internet to research whether mobile phones can cause cancer. A good way to start is to go to www.scienceworld.net.au and follow the links to **Mobile phones—communications on the go (NOVA)**.

2 Use the internet to find out other uses for optical fibres besides those in telephone networks.

3 How does SMS work? Go to www.scienceworld.net.au and follow the links to **How SMS works**.

challenge

1 a Why is feedback an important part of the communication process?

b During a conversation, the person listening might say 'Yes', 'I see' or OK'. Explain why these responses are forms of feedback.

c Give some examples of non-verbal feedback that might occur during a conversation.

2 Look at the telephone network diagram on page 77. Use this to construct an energy flow diagram that shows all the energy conversions that occur during a telephone conversation.

3 Use the code to decode the following message.

Code

```
A | D | G              K
B | E | H          J  X  L
C | F | I              M

N.| Q.| T.             X
O.| R.| U.         W .X. Y
P.| S.| V.             Z
```

Message

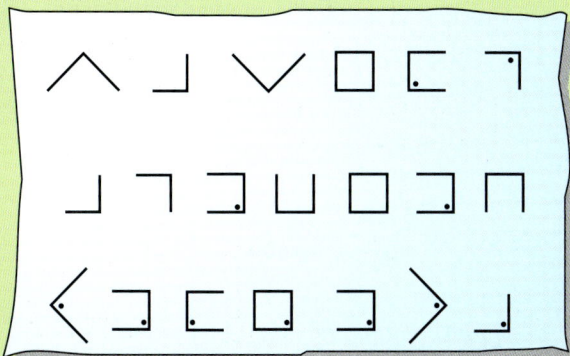

a What would happen if the message was turned upside down?

b Try to improve the code to overcome this problem.

c What other problems arise using this code?

4 A digital signal is made up of eight bits having the values 11001011. Using Fig 8 on page 76 as a guide, draw a graph of this signal.

5 The graph below shows the current produced by a microphone when a person speaks into it. The vertical axis has both positive and negative values. The horizontal axis is measured in units of time.

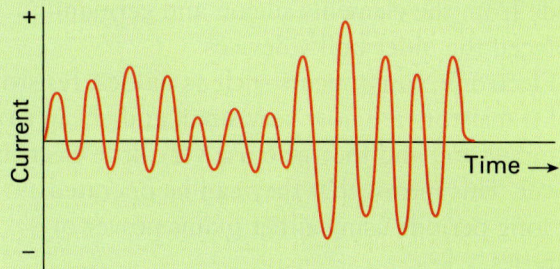

Using your knowledge of how a microphone works, explain:

a why the current has positive and negative values

b why the value of the current varies with time.

6 Encoding is changing one type of code to another. Decoding is the reverse process. Describe where signals are encoded during a telephone conversation and where they are decoded. In your description include the type of device used in the processes. (Use the telephone network diagram on page 77 as a guide.)

7 Study the data in the table below.

Colour of light	Speed of light (m/s)	
	in air	in glass
red	2.988×10^8	1.983×10^8
blue	2.998×10^8	1.958×10^8

a Describe the information in the table.

b In optical fibres, pulses of laser light are transmitted in the glass core. If white light is used, suggest why the pulses of light become stretched out or 'smeared' after travelling through a very long optical fibre.

c Suggest how the problem in **b** could be overcome.

4.2 Electronics

Communication devices such as mobile phones, computers and fax machines all have one thing in common—they need electricity to work. Before the 1950s most communication devices contained bulky parts which used a lot of electrical power. During the 1950s tiny electronic components made from the elements silicon and germanium replaced the older bulky devices.

Electronic components such as diodes, resistors and transistors are now very small and cheap to manufacture, and they also use very little electric power. This means that they can be operated for long periods using either mains power or batteries.

A great breakthrough in electronics has taken place with the development of the 'microchip' or *integrated circuit*. The microchip contains thousands of electronic components etched onto the silicon by a photographic process.

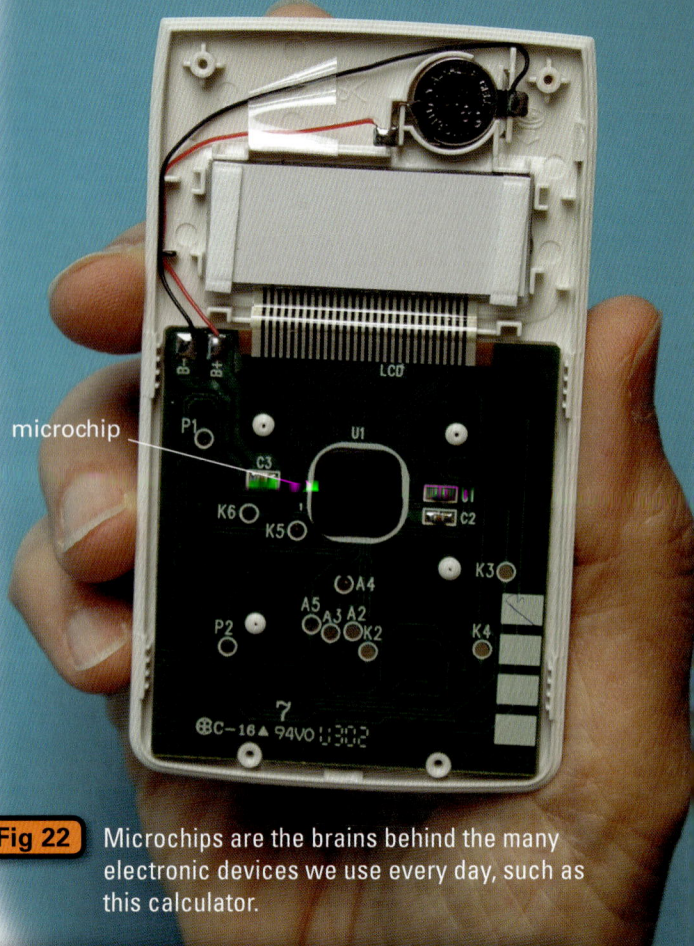

Fig 22 Microchips are the brains behind the many electronic devices we use every day, such as this calculator.

Resistors

Resistors control the amount of current in a circuit. The coloured stripes on the resistor indicate the size of the resistance. Resistance is measured in ohms (Ω).

Bands show size of resistance.

symbol

Light-dependent resistors (LDR) are light-sensitive resistors. The resistance of the resistor decreases with the intensity of the light. That is, more current flows in bright light.

symbol

Thermistors are heat-sensitive resistors. The amount of current flowing through the resistor usually increases with the temperature.

Diodes

Diodes allow current to flow in one direction only, making that part of the circuit a one-way street for the current. They are used in electronic circuits to stop current flowing in unwanted directions.

One end of a diode is marked with a band. This end should be connected to the negative side of the circuit.

Band shows negative side.

symbol

Light-emitting diodes (LED) are electronic light bulbs—they glow red, green, yellow, orange or blue when electricity is passed through them. They are widely used in digital displays, traffic lights and tail-lights on cars.

symbol

Transistors

Transistors are devices that can act like switches, turning the current in a circuit on and off. They can also increase the size of the current. In this way they act as amplifiers.

Transistors are made in different shapes, but each of them has three electrodes (legs), and the symbol remains the same.

Transistors have various shapes.

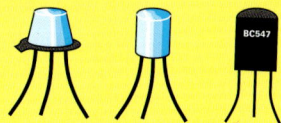

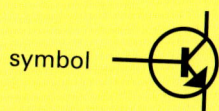

symbol

Capacitors

Capacitors are used in electronic circuits to store electric charge for a short time before allowing it to flow to other parts of the circuit. They are used to separate different parts of a circuit so that each can have a different current. They consist of two conducting plates separated by an insulating material called a dielectric.

The amount of charge that can be stored for each volt across a capacitor is called its *capacitance*. This is measured in farads (F), although microfarads (µF) are more commonly used in electronics.

Capacitors have various shapes.

symbol

Activity

In the next investigation you will be using resistors in circuits. For this you will need to know how to tell the value of a resistor by using the coloured bands on it.

Your teacher will give you some resistors. Use the information below to work out their values in ohms.

The resistors you will use have four coloured bands on them. The code for the coloured bands is shown in the table.

To read the code, hold the resistor with the gold or silver band on your *right*. Then start with the first colour on the *left*.

Colour	Value	Colour	Value
black	0	green	5
brown	1	blue	6
red	2	purple	7
orange	3	grey	8
yellow	4	white	9

This resistor has a resistance of 560 Ω.

The colour of Band 1 gives the value of the first digit.

The colour of Band 2 gives the value of the second digit.

The colour of Band 3 tells how many zeros follow the first two digits.

The colour of Band 4 tells how precise the value of the resistor is.

Investigate

11 ELECTRONIC CIRCUITS

Aim
To set up circuits using electronic components.

Materials
- resistors (1 watt) 10 Ω, 22 Ω, 56 Ω, 390 Ω, 10 000 Ω
- diode (1N4002 or similar)
- light-emitting diode
- light-dependent resistor (eg ORP12)
- switch
- ammeter (eg 1A range) or multimeter
- power pack
- 6 V torch bulb and socket
- 4 connecting wires with alligator clips
- two 10 cm x 10 cm pieces of cardboard, 5 drawing pins and some thin, bare wire
- adhesive tape

Planning and Safety Check
- Read through Part A and describe to your partner what you have to do. Swap roles and do the same for Part B (which itself has two parts).
- What precautions are necessary when using a power pack?

PART A
Resistors

Method
1 Use the clear tape to tape the four lower value resistors to one of the pieces of cardboard. (Alternatively you could use a 'breadboard'.) Write the value of each resistor next to it.

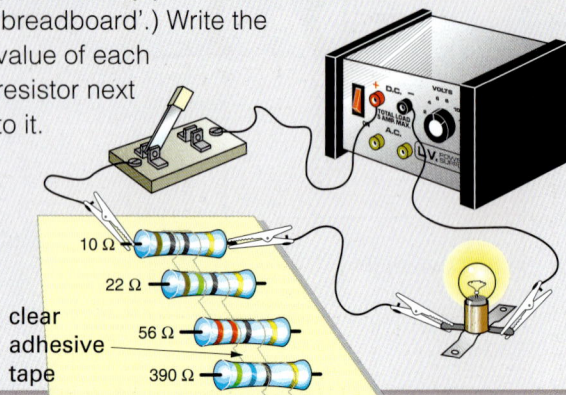

clear adhesive tape
10 Ω
22 Ω
56 Ω
390 Ω

2 Connect up the circuit as shown bottom left. Set the power pack on 6 V DC and connect each resistor in turn.

Observe the glow of the light bulb for each resistor. Record your observations.

3 Take the light bulb out of the circuit and replace it with an ammeter.
Note: Remember to connect the positive (red) terminal of the ammeter to the positive side of the power pack.

4 In turn, find the current flowing through each resistor.

Record your results in a table.

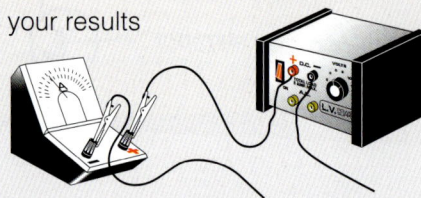

Discussion
1 Write a generalisation linking the resistance to the glow of the light bulb.

2 Write a generalisation linking the resistance to the current flowing in the circuit.

3 Predict the effect of a very large resistance (10 000 Ω) on the glow of the light bulb. Then test your prediction.

4 Why do the resistors heat up when you leave the power pack on for a while? Suggest why higher value resistors heat up more.

PART B
Diodes

1 Set up the circuit as shown. Make sure you connect the banded end of the diode to the *negative* side of the power supply.

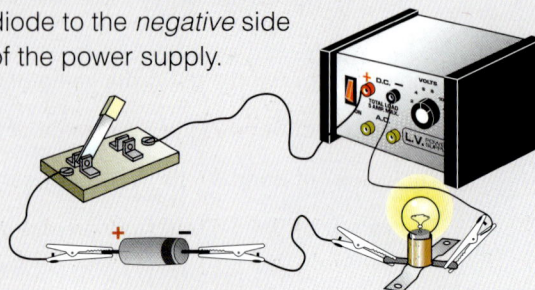

The circuit diagram for the set-up is shown below. In this circuit the banded end of the diode is shown by the vertical line in the symbol, and this is connected to the negative side of the power pack.

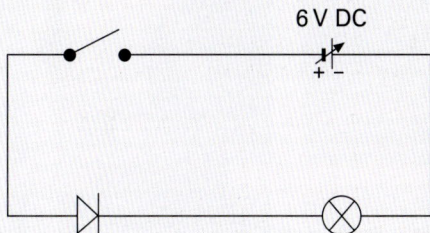

2   Set the power pack to 6 V DC.
    Record your observations when you close the switch.

3   Disconnect the diode and turn it around so that the banded side is connected to the *positive* side of the power supply.
    Record what happens this time.

4   To make a puzzle for your partner, push five drawing pins into the second piece of cardboard as shown. Connect a diode between two of the pins. Then connect some bare wire between the other pins.

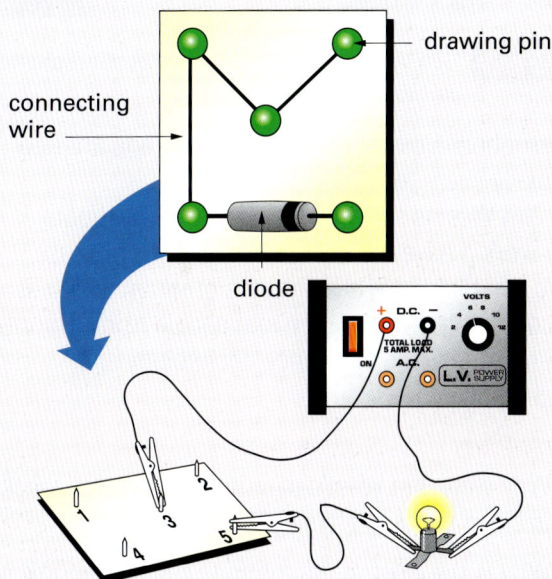

5   Turn the cardboard over and number each of the pins without your partner seeing. Now ask your partner to use the test circuit to find out where the diode is connected and which is the negative end.

    Ask your partner to explain how they solved the puzzle.

6   Set up the circuit below containing a light-emitting diode (LED). The 390 Ω resistor is used to reduce the current in the circuit so that the LED does not 'burn out'.

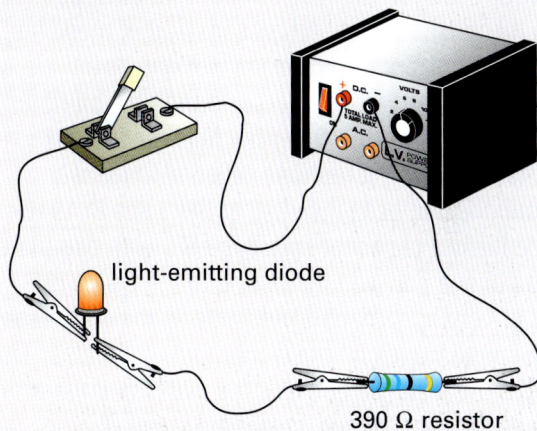

7   Experiment with the LED to find out:
    a   whether the LED allows current to flow in one direction only
    b   if the short leg of the LED is the positive or negative side
    c   if a current that lights an LED will light a torch bulb.
        Write a report of your findings.

Discussion

1   Draw circuit diagrams using the correct symbols for the circuits in Steps 3 and 6.

2   Does an LED look brighter when viewed from the top or from the side?

3   Look at the circuits below. Will the light bulbs glow?

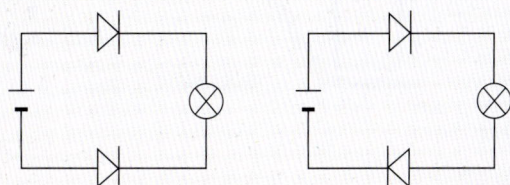

Science in action

Jim West and the electret microphone

Jim West was born in 1931 to African-American parents in Virginia, USA. Jim said that 'in those days in the South, the only professional jobs that seemed to be open to a black man were a teacher, a preacher, a doctor or a lawyer.' So his parents were disappointed when he chose to study physics instead of medicine. He went to university and began working as an intern at Bell Labs in New Jersey during his summer holidays. He joined the company full time in 1957.

A new type of microphone called a *condenser microphone* had been invented at Bell Labs in 1916. It is essentially a capacitor (see page 83) with two plates with a voltage between them. One of the plates is made of very light material and acts as the diaphragm. When sound waves hit the diaphragm, it vibrates. This changes the distance between the plates and therefore changes the capacitance, creating a small electric current. However, these microphones were not suitable for widespread use in telephones because they were expensive and required a large battery. So West and a colleague were given the task of inventing a new technology to produce a microphone that was small, high-quality and cheap to manufacture.

After several years of experimenting, West and his colleague patented an *electret microphone*. It uses a thin plastic film with a metallic coating. When exposed to a strong electric field the film retains its electric charge, and doesn't need a battery. These electret

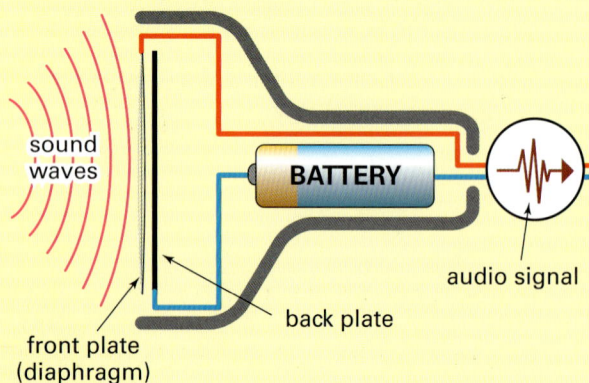

Fig 38 Jim West invented the electret microphone in 1962.

microphones can be made very small and are now in virtually every telephone in the world.

Jim West is still working and says 'My hobby is my work. I have the best of both worlds because I love what I do.' He is active in a program aimed at encouraging more women and people from minorities to enter the fields of science, technology and engineering.

Questions

1 Why were Jim West's parents disappointed when he decided to study physics?

2 Why is the electret microphone suitable for use in mobile phones?

3 How is an electret microphone different from a condenser microphone?

Fig 37 A condenser microphone

Semiconductors

Diodes and transistors are made from materials called **semiconductors**. These materials, which include the elements silicon and germanium, have properties in between conductors and insulators.

Silicon is the most important semiconductor material. It is made from sand (silicon dioxide), and it is cheap and easy to manufacture in pure form. In pure form silicon does not conduct electricity very well. But when very small amounts of another substance, such as arsenic or boron, are added (this process is called *doping*) the silicon conducts electricity.

An atom of silicon has four outermost electrons. An atom of arsenic has five electrons, one more than silicon. When silicon is doped with arsenic and wires from a battery are placed at each end of the crystal, a current flows. The fact that the extra electrons in the arsenic atoms are relatively free to move causes the doped crystal of silicon to conduct electricity. This type of doped semiconductor is called *n-type* or negative type because of the extra electrons.

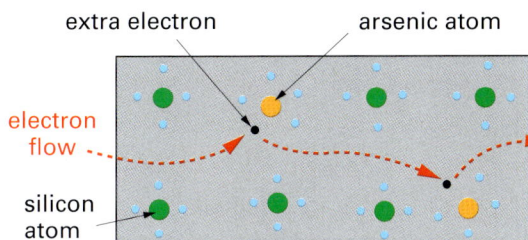

Fig 39 How an electric current is carried through an n-type semiconductor by mobile electrons

Boron has only three outermost electrons, one less than silicon. When silicon is doped with boron, the crystal also conducts electricity. It seems that the boron atom creates an electron space or 'hole' into which electrons from the silicon can flow, causing an electric current. This type of doped semiconductor is called *p-type* or positive type.

Diodes

A diode is made by placing an n-type crystal next to a p-type crystal. When this is connected in a circuit the 'extra' electrons in the n-type crystal can jump across to the holes in the p-type crystal. However, if the battery terminals are reversed, the electrons cannot jump back in the other direction. This is why diodes carry current in one direction only. (By convention, the arrow in the diode symbol points in a direction *opposite* to that in which the electrons flow.)

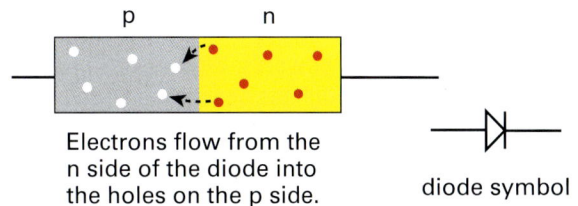

Electrons flow from the n side of the diode into the holes on the p side.   diode symbol

In the diagram above you will notice that the electrons flow in the opposite direction to the arrow in the symbol. When scientists first studied electricity they thought it was a flow of positive charge—from positive to negative. It was a long time before they discovered that it was, in fact, negatively charged electrons which were moving. By this time everyone had been thinking about current flowing from positive to negative for so long that it was impossible to change. This flow from positive to negative is called 'conventional current'.

Transistors

A transistor is made of three pieces of semiconductor crystal sandwiched together. This is why transistors have three legs (electrodes).

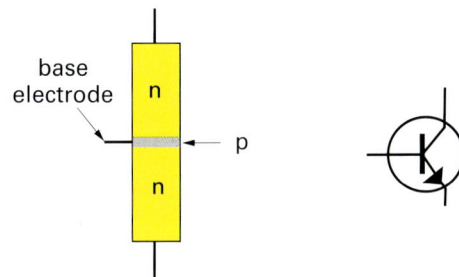

Fig 41 An n-p-n transistor and its symbol

A transistor can be used as a miniature switch, as shown on the next page. It works like a gate where one person can control the movement of thousands of people.

A small flow of electrons through the base ...

... turns on a large flow of electrons this way.

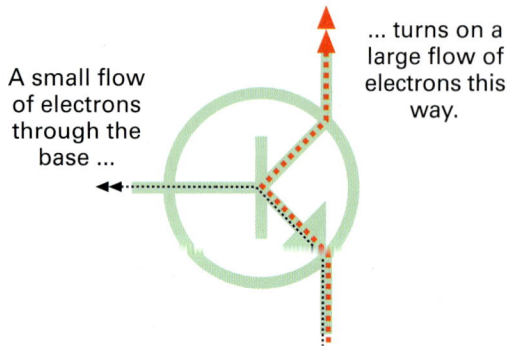

Fig 42 How a transistor works. When a small current is applied through the base leg, a large current can flow through the other two legs.

A transistor can also be used as an amplifier, as in the circuit below. When the microphone on the left is turned on the current it produces is not enough to power the loudspeaker. However, the small current flowing into the transistor is amplified, producing a larger copy of the original signal from the microphone. This amplified current is large enough to operate the loudspeaker.

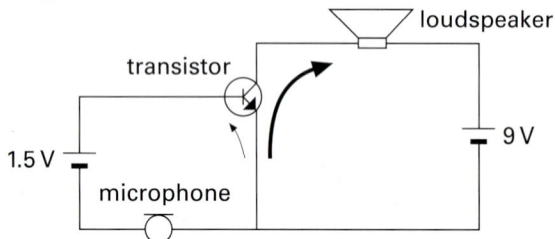

Fig 43 In this circuit a transistor amplifies a small microphone current to produce a large current in the loudspeaker.

Check!

1 What do the following symbols represent?

a

b

c

d

e

f

2 How is a resistor different from a diode? In what units is resistance measured?

3 Which one of the following circuits contains a battery, one resistor, one transistor, and two diodes?

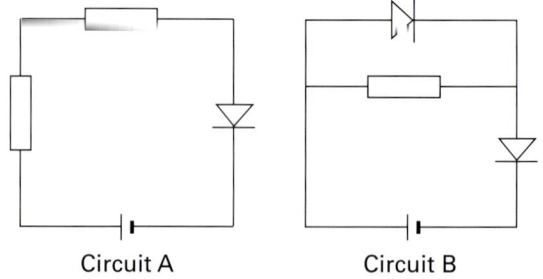

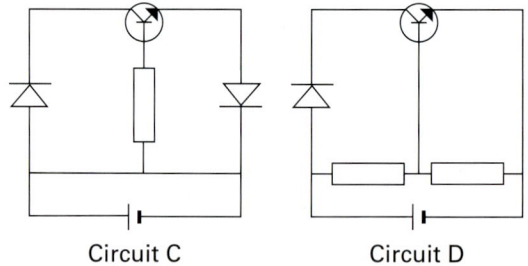

Circuit A

Circuit B

Circuit C

Circuit D

4 List the equipment you would need to build the following circuit.

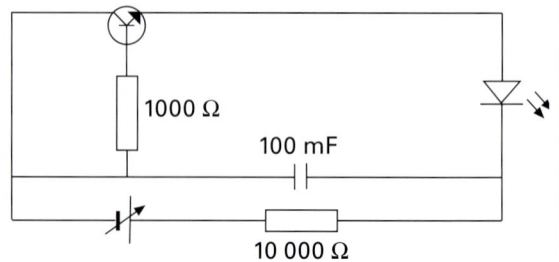

1000 Ω

100 mF

10 000 Ω

5 In which of the following circuits would you expect the light bulb to glow?

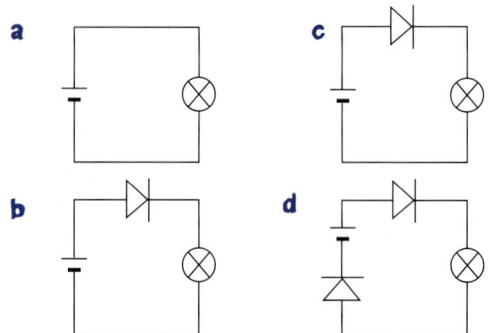

a

c

b

d

 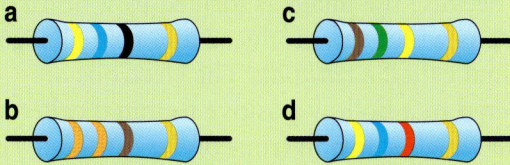

1 Use the resistor code table on page 83 to find the values of the following resistors.

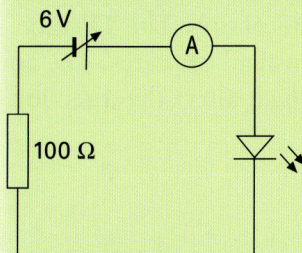

a   c

b   d

2 Why were very small portable radios not available in the 1930s?

3 Security beams in the doorways of shops sometimes use a light-dependent resistor. How do they work?

4 a In which of the two circuits below would the LED glow more brightly? Explain.

  b If the LED in the circuits below has a resistance of 50 Ω, find the current flowing in each circuit.

  c Suggest why LEDs, rather than light bulbs, are used in electrical appliances.

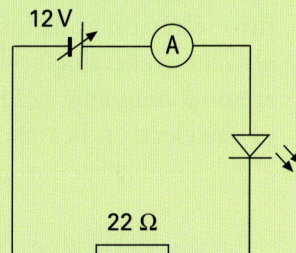

Circuit A   **Circuit B**

5 Suppose you are making an electronic fire alarm. Which electronic component could you use to detect the fire? Explain.

6 An undoped semiconductor like pure silicon will not conduct electricity at low temperatures. However, as the temperature rises the ability of the silicon to carry current increases. Suggest how electronic thermometers might use this material to measure temperature.

7 a Explain in terms of electrons how semiconductors differ from conductors and insulators.

  b Explain how an n-type semiconductor differs from a p-type.

8 The circuit below can be used to switch on a light when the Sun goes down.

  a Explain how a light-dependent resistor (LDR) works.

  b Explain what happens in the circuit during the day and when the Sun goes down.

  Hint: Consider the effect the two resistors and the LDR have on the electric current in the different parts of the circuit. During the day the resistance of the LDR is about 500 Ω and at night about 200 000 Ω.

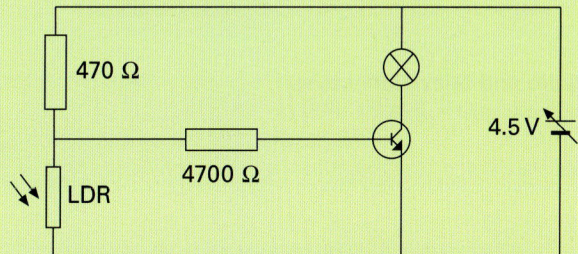

(You might like to build this circuit if your teacher can organise the components.)

➲ try this

1 Use library resources to find out what microchips or integrated circuits are. Where are they used?

2 Use an electronics kit, eg Dick Smith's *Funway*, to build a simple everyday device such as flashing lights, a siren, a radio or a Morse code sender. You simply follow the instructions to put the electronic components together to make the device.

4.3 Television and radio

In 1896 Guglielmo Marconi, an Italian inventor, patented the radio, or 'wireless' as it was known. The first television picture was produced by John Logie Baird, a Scotsman, in 1925. Black and white TV was introduced to Australia in 1956 and colour in 1975. We now have satellite, cable and digital TV.

The information sent by television and radio is transmitted via *electromagnetic waves* of long wavelength. These waves are received by a metal aerial or antenna which converts electromagnetic waves into electric current. This current is then decoded into pictures or sound.

visible light (red light)
wavelength = 4×10^{-6} m

microwaves
wavelength = 1×10^{-6} m

radio and television waves
wavelength = 1 m to 1000 m

How does television work?

The heart of a TV set is the picture tube. This is a type of **cathode ray tube** (CRT) which is also found in a cathode ray oscilloscope (see the activity on page 76). It is called a cathode ray tube because the image is formed by a beam of electrons which are produced at a heated negative terminal called a *cathode*. The electrons are attracted to a hollow positive terminal called the *anode* which is just in front of the cathode. The electrons pass through the anode in a narrow beam. They then strike the back of the screen which is coated with a special material that glows when electrons hit it.

The direction of the electron beam in the cathode ray tube is controlled by two sets of deflecting plates—one positioned horizontally, the other vertically. A changing electric current in the plates creates a changing electric field between the plates which, in turn, affects the direction of the electron beam.

The picture tube in a colour TV is similar to the cathode ray tube in a CRO except that it has three electron guns instead of one. The TV tube also has deflecting coils instead of plates. The coils create a magnetic field which alters the direction of the electron beams.

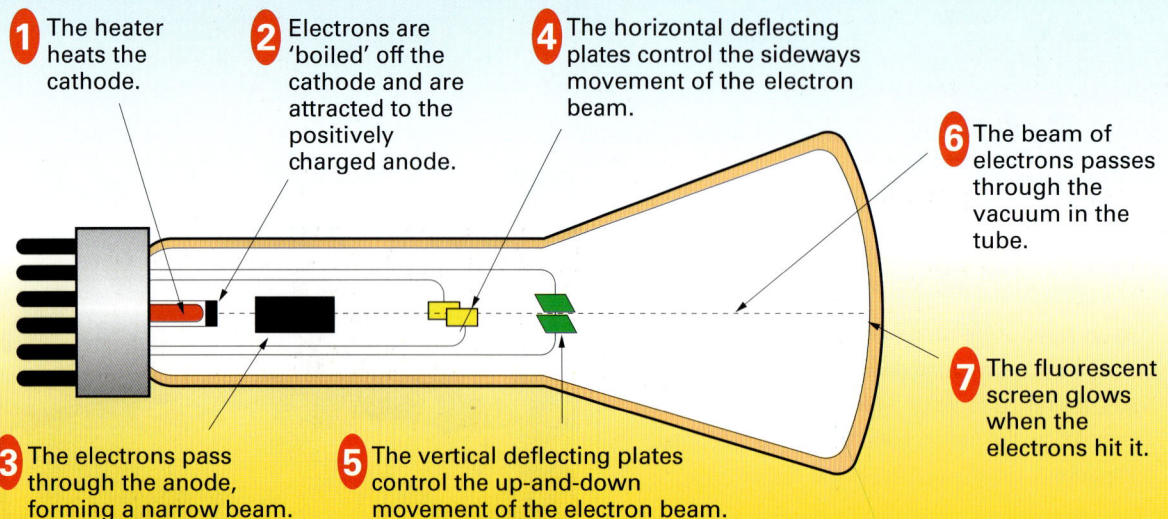

1 The heater heats the cathode.

2 Electrons are 'boiled' off the cathode and are attracted to the positively charged anode.

4 The horizontal deflecting plates control the sideways movement of the electron beam.

6 The beam of electrons passes through the vacuum in the tube.

3 The electrons pass through the anode, forming a narrow beam.

5 The vertical deflecting plates control the up-and-down movement of the electron beam.

7 The fluorescent screen glows when the electrons hit it.

Fig 53 A cutaway drawing of a cathode ray tube from a CRO

Activity

Your teacher will set up a CRO and adjust the controls to give a spot on the screen. When the *time sweep* control is on the largest setting, the spot moves very slowly across the screen. The *position* knobs control the vertical and horizontal deflecting plates.

1 Watch what happens to the spot when the position knobs are adjusted.

2 Hold a bar magnet near the spot on the screen.

📋 How does the magnet affect the position of the spot?

📋 What inference can you make about the way the deflecting plates work?

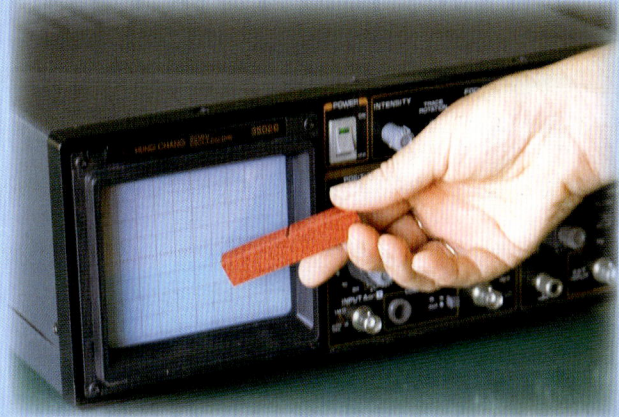

Warning: Do not hold a magnet near a colour TV set. You will do permanent damage to it.

Inside the TV picture tube, the electron guns fire electrons at the screen. The deflecting coils sweep the electron beams over the screen making a horizontal line. After the first horizontal sweep the deflecting coils move the electron beams down to sweep across a second line. Each complete picture on the TV screen is made up of 625 horizontal lines and each set of 625 lines is redone 25 times every second. These changes are far too fast for our eyes to detect, so we see a continuous picture on the screen.

The inside of the screen is coated with three different substances in very small strips or dots called *pixels*. These substances are called **phosphors** (FOS-fours). One phosphor glows red when struck by an electron beam, the other glows green and the third glows blue. The picture on the screen is built up of millions of red, green and blue strips or dots. The shadow mask positioned close to the screen makes sure the electron beams strike the correct phosphors.

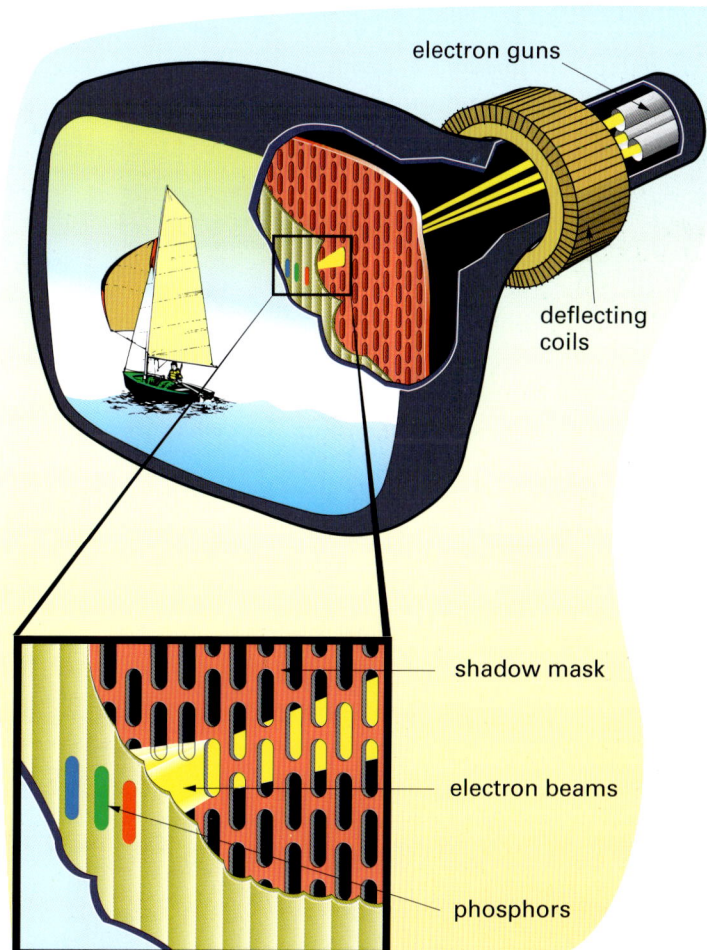

Fig 55 Inside a TV picture tube

Activity

A: Observing phosphors

A computer monitor is similar to a TV screen. Before you turn it on, use a magnifying glass or hand lens to look at the screen.

The vertical lines that you observe are the pixels, separated by thin black lines. Each pixel is made up of three individual phosphors that glow red, green and blue when struck by electrons.

B: Observing colours

1   Open a computer program such as *Word* or *Paintbrush* and find the colour palette. Alternatively you can make your own as shown below. You need the three primary colours (red, green and blue) and the three secondary colours (yellow, cyan and magenta), plus black and white.

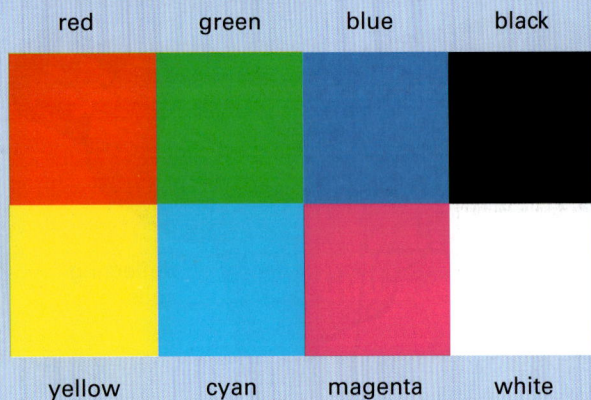

red	green	blue	black

yellow	cyan	magenta	white

2   Use the hand lens to look at a white patch on your palette. Notice the spots or strips of colours. Can you see the individual red, green and blue spots?

3   Predict what you will see if you look at the black patch. Give a reason for your prediction. Use the hand lens to check your prediction.

4   Use the hand lens to look at the red, green and blue patches on the screen. Record the colours of the phosphors in each patch.

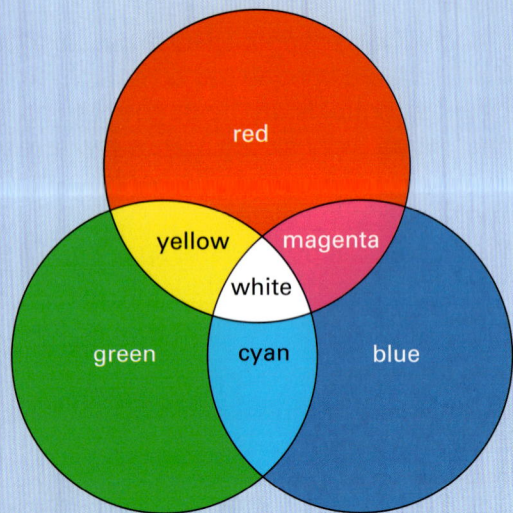

Fig 57   A colour mixing wheel

5   Use the colours in the colour mixing wheel to work out which two primary colours combine to give yellow. Then observe the yellow patch on the screen.

6   Repeat Step 5, but this time look at the cyan and then the magenta patches.

   Which phosphors combine to give yellow, cyan and magenta?

   How are other colours such as orange and purple formed?

Teacher note: The phosphors are easier to observe on a TV screen, but you will need to use a video on pause. You could video the test pattern on this page.

WEBwatch

Go to www.scienceworld.net.au and follow the links to this website.

How television works

A comprehensive site with links to digital TV, satellite TV, plasma displays, DVD players and VCRs.

LCD screens

The picture tubes used in the older CRT TV and computer screens are quite bulky. The flat screens now used in many computers and some TV screens use **liquid crystal displays (LCDs)**. A liquid crystal has the properties of both a liquid and a solid. The long molecules in a liquid crystal stay in position like those in a solid, but they also move around like the molecules in a liquid.

To make an LCD, two polarising filters (like those in polaroid sunglasses) are used. When these are arranged at right angles to each other, no light passes through them (see Fig 58 below). The liquid crystals are placed between the filters and arranged in a twisted pattern that allows light to pass through. However, when an electric field is passed through the liquid crystals, the twist disappears. This means that light can no longer pass through—that area of the screen appears dark.

LCDs do not give off light. Those in digital watches and calculators have a mirror behind them to reflect light. This is why they don't work in the dark. In flat screen TVs, each pixel is an LCD instead of a phosphor. The LCDs are lit from the back by tiny fluorescent tubes. They have red, green and blue filters above them to produce colours.

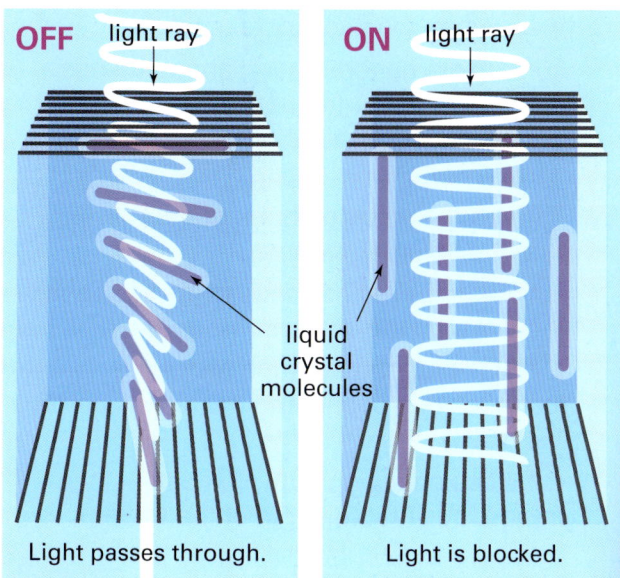

Plasma screens

Many people are now buying plasma TV screens. These are much larger than normal screens but are only about 15 cm thick. So they can be mounted on the wall in a home theatre. However, at this stage they are still very expensive.

In a *plasma* screen each pixel consists of three tiny fluorescent cells, like fluorescent lights. Inside each fluorescent cell is a mixture of xenon and neon gases. When a voltage is passed through this gas, high-speed electrons are produced. These electrons collide with the atoms in the gas, knocking out more electrons and creating positive ions. The resulting mixture of positive ions and electrons is a plasma. Particles speed rapidly in all directions, bumping into each other. These collisions excite the atoms in the plasma, causing them to release ultraviolet radiation. When this UV radiation hits the phosphors on the bottom of the cell, it produces red, green or blue light.

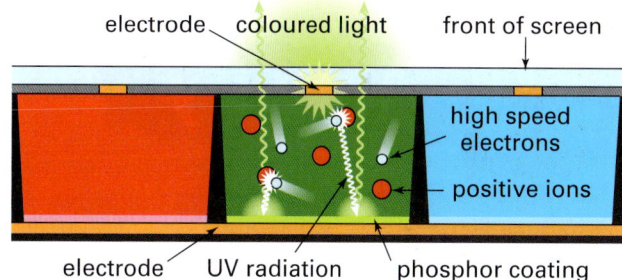

Fig 59 How a plasma screen works (above)

Fig 58 How a liquid crystal display (LCD) works

Radio and TV transmission

Your favourite radio station might have a call sign of 107.5. What does the 107.5 mean? And what is the difference between AM and FM?

Each commercial radio station in Australia has its own broadcast frequency which you can tune in to with your radio tuner. To understand what frequency means, your teacher may set up a CRO as in the activity below to show you different wave patterns.

A microphone converts sound waves into an electronic audio signal. These are low frequency waves and if broadcast would travel only a few metres through the air. To overcome this problem, radio stations mix this audio signal with a much higher frequency wave with more energy, which can travel hundreds of kilometres through the air. This wave is called a *carrier wave*, and the combined audio signal and carrier wave is called a *modulated wave*.

AM

There are two ways to combine an audio signal with a carrier wave. One way results in a wave that has its *amplitude modulated* or varied. Radio stations that broadcast in this form are called **AM** stations.

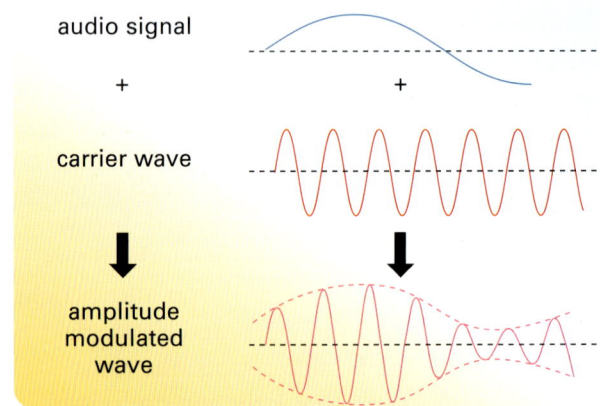

audio signal

+

carrier wave

amplitude modulated wave

Fig 61 Modulated waves from an AM station. The frequency is the same as the carrier wave but the amplitude varies.

Activity

Your teacher will connect an audio generator to a CRO.

1 Look at the wave pattern produced by the generator. What do you notice when the pitch of the sound is changed?

The **frequency** of a wave is the number of waves that pass a point in one second. Frequency is measured in hertz (Hz), where one hertz is one wave per second. The wave below has a frequency of 2 Hz. Two complete waves pass each point every second.

What happens to the frequency when the pitch of a sound increases?

What happens to the wavelength of the wave when the pitch increases?

Make a generalisation about the pitch of sound and the frequency. Make another generalisation about the frequency of a wave and its wavelength.

2 Turn up the volume on the generator. Now turn the volume down.

Record what happens to the shape of the wave on the screen.

Make a generalisation about the loudness of a sound and the amplitude of the waves.

Does changing the volume affect the frequency or wavelength of the waves?

FM

The second way of broadcasting is to combine an audio signal with a carrier wave to produce a wave whose frequency changes but whose amplitude stays the same. This type of radio wave is called *frequency modulated* or **FM** (see Fig 63 on the right).

FM stations broadcast on a much higher frequency than AM stations. AM stations broadcast at frequencies between 520 kHz and 1600 kHz (1 kHz = 1 kilohertz = 1000 Hz). FM stations broadcast at much higher frequencies, between 87 MHz and 108 MHz (1 MHz = 1 megahertz = 10^6 Hz).

The steps in sending and receiving radio signals are shown in the diagram below.

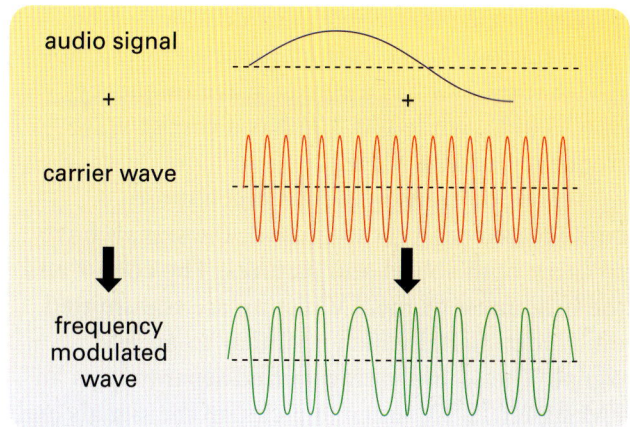

Fig 63 Modulated waves from an FM station. The amplitude is the same as the carrier wave but the frequency varies.

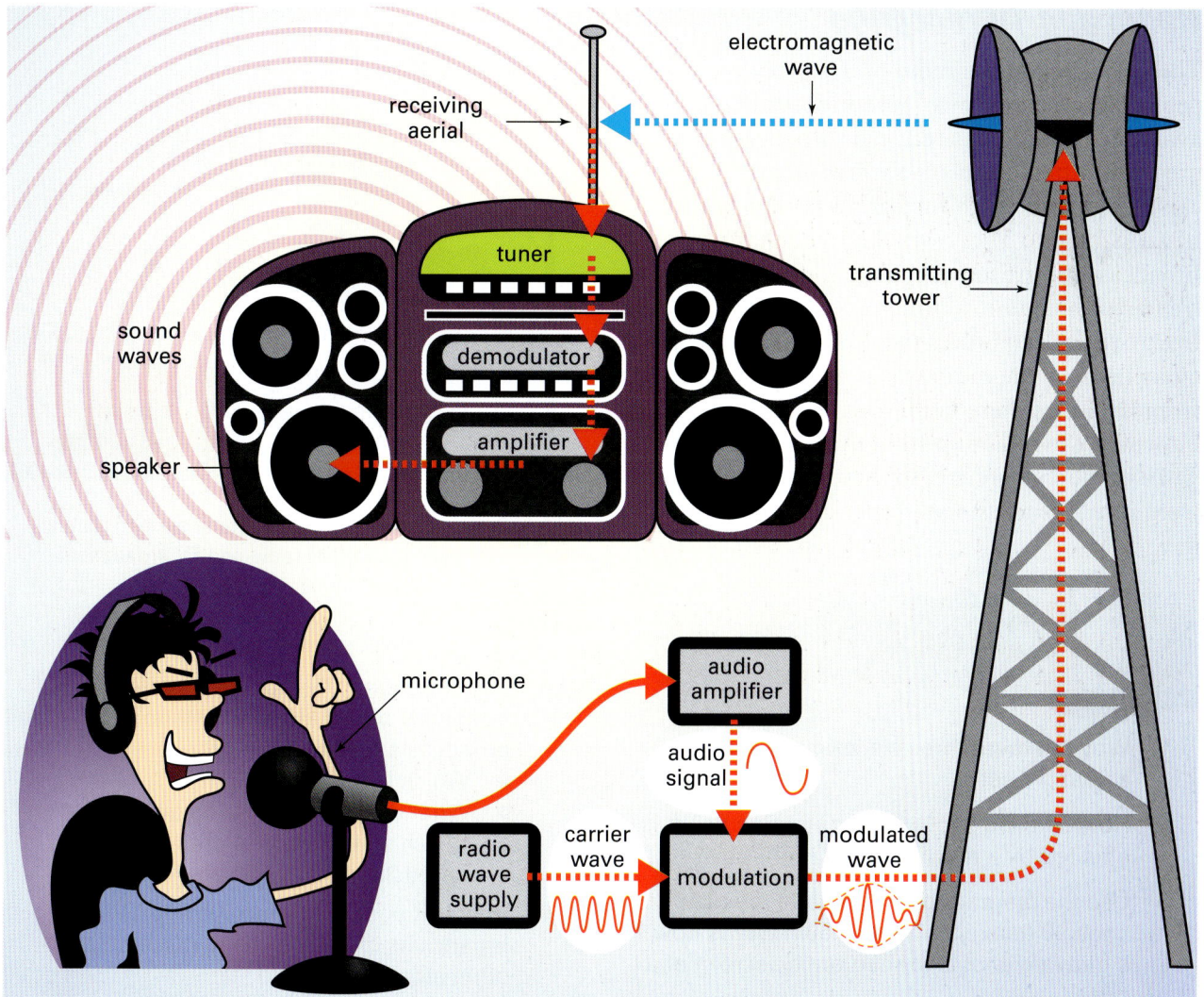

The carrier wave frequency determines the radio station's broadcast frequency. For example, AM station 873 has a carrier wave frequency of 873 kHz, while FM 104 has a carrier wave frequency of 104 MHz.

Television transmission is much more complicated than radio because the signals have to carry both sound and pictures. The colour and the brightness of the TV picture are transmitted on a video signal which is similar to an AM signal. The sound is transmitted separately as an FM signal. A TV antenna picks up the signals and relays them to the TV set where the picture signals and sound signals are synchronised.

With cable TV the signal travels directly to your TV without being transmitted.

Radio and TV reception

The frequency of the radio or TV broadcast determines the quality of reception and how far away the broadcast is received. Broadcasts that are transmitted on relatively low frequencies can be received much further away than higher frequency ones. The lower the frequency of broadcast the greater the range. For example, low frequency amateur radio broadcasts can be heard from overseas countries thousands of kilometres away because the radio waves are reflected from the ionosphere in the Earth's atmosphere. However, the radiation from the Sun affects the gases in the ionosphere, so these broadcasts suffer from interference (noise), especially during the day.

Local AM stations broadcast on a lower frequency than amateur radio. Their signals can travel many hundreds of kilometres from the transmitting tower and are less affected by interference from the Sun.

The very high frequency waves transmitted by FM radio and TV stations suffer less interference and the sound quality is usually far superior to AM stations. However, these waves travel only in straight lines and are not reflected by the atmosphere. So if your antenna is behind a hill or mountain, your radio and TV reception will be poor. Another disadvantage of FM radio and TV waves is that they normally have a range of only about 100 km. With satellite TV this problem is overcome by beaming the signal up to a satellite and then back down to your TV.

Fig 65 You have to be in the line of sight to receive good quality FM radio and TV broadcasts.

Check!

1 Why are there three electron guns in a colour TV set?

2 How can you show that an electron beam is affected by a magnetic field?

3 Use the diagram of the cathode ray tube on page 90 to explain in your own words how a glowing spot is formed on the screen of a CRO.

4 Radio station FUN broadcasts on a frequency of 690 kHz while station WIZ broadcasts on 94.5 MHz.
   a Which is the FM station?
   b What do kHz and MHz mean?
   c Which station do you predict could be heard 300 km away? Why?

5 How is it possible to receive live TV broadcasts of events taking place on the other side of the world?

6 Why do radio stations use a carrier wave to transmit their broadcasts? What is the difference between a carrier wave and a modulated wave?

7 Suppose you use a magnifying glass to look at the phosphors in a very small area of your TV screen. At 10 second intervals you record the colours of the phosphors that are glowing (0 = phosphor not glowing).

Use the colour wheel on page 92 to determine which colours you will see at the five recording times if you are standing back from the TV screen.

Interval number	Colours of phosphors
1	red, 0, 0
2	red, green, 0
3	0, green, blue
4	0, 0, 0
5	red, green, blue

challenge

1 If someone next door is using a power tool it may cause interference on your TV set. How?

2 Construct a flow chart to show how a free-to-air TV picture gets from a studio at the TV station to the TV set in your home.

3 Make inferences from the following observations.

  a The car radio goes crackly when you drive under high voltage power lines.

  b People living in valleys have to have very tall TV antennas.

  c TV and radio signals can be picked up by aerials inside houses.

  d AM radio fades when you drive through an underpass or tunnel but FM does not.

4 The diagram below shows modulated radio waves from four stations.

  a Which are FM stations? How do you know?

  b Which AM station broadcasts at a higher frequency?

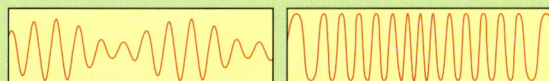

Station 1   Station 2

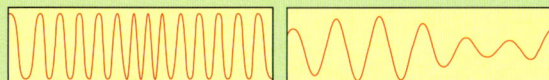

Station 3   Station 4

5 Suggest how feedback could be achieved with TV and radio transmissions to make them a true form of communication according to the flow diagram on page 74.

6 Most TV transmissions are digital. Screen colour information is transmitted in a three-bit binary code. The first bit codes for red, the second bit for green and the third bit for blue. For example, the binary code for the screen colour red is 1 0 0.

What are the digital codes for the screen colours black, green, cyan, yellow, blue, magenta and white?

7 Each of the numerals in a digital clock has seven segments, and each segment is a separate LED. When current flows through a particular combination of the seven terminals (marked 1 to 7 on the diagram), the LEDs glow and a number is formed.

  a Which terminals have current flowing through them when the numeral 3 is glowing?

  b Digital clocks have four seven-segment LEDs separated by a colon (:). Which terminals on each of the four segments are illuminated when the clock reads 12:45?

terminals   1 2 3   4   5 6 7

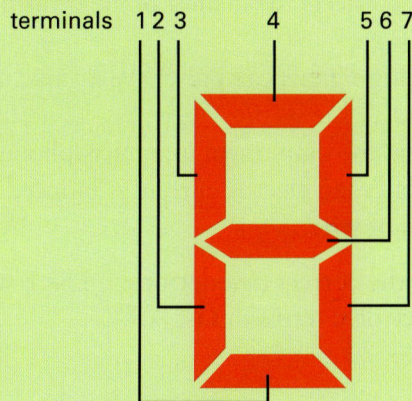

8 Find out what the difference is between analog and digital TV.

MAIN IDEAS

Copy and complete these statements to make a summary of this chapter. The missing words are on the right.

1   Communication occurs when information is encoded by a sender, _____, then _____ and understood by a receiver.

2   Electronic communication devices such as telephones, modems and fax machines encode messages into _____ signals or _____ pulses which are then sent over long distances.

3   Optical fibres transmit information in the form of _____ light pulses.

4   Diodes, transistors, _____ and capacitors are electronic components used in communication devices.

5   Diodes and transistors are made from _____. These are substances that conduct electricity when doped with small amounts of another element.

6   Television and radio signals are transmitted though the air as _____ waves of long wavelength.

7   In a cathode ray tube, _____ electron guns fire electrons which hit _____ and create tiny spots of colour on the TV screen. The newer flat screens use liquid crystal displays or _____.

8   Radio signals are made up of an audio signal mixed with a carrier wave. AM radio signals have a _____ frequency than FM radio signals.

decoded
digital
electrical
electromagnetic
light
lower
phosphors
plasma
resistors
semiconductors
three
transmitted

Try doing the Chapter 4 crossword on the CD.

Working with technology

REVIEW

1   Which of the following statements is *incorrect*?
   A A microphone converts sound energy into electrical energy.
   B Noise affects the quality of the transmitted message.
   C Analog signals can only have a value of 0 or 1.
   D When the diaphragm in a microphone vibrates, an electric current is induced in the coils of wire.

2   Match the correct descriptions in List B with the electronic terms in List A.

List A	List B
resistance	1 lets electric current pass in one direction only
transistor	2 an electronic light bulb
LED	3 stores charge
diode	4 can act as a switch or as an amplifier
capacitor	5 is measured in ohms
LDR	6 is measured in amps
current	7 its resistance changes with the intensity of the light

3 Match the pieces of television equipment with the functions listed below:

antenna	speaker
electron gun	phosphor
deflecting coil	brightness control

  a changes electrical energy into sound energy
  b gives off light when struck by electrons
  c alters the number of electrons hitting the TV screen
  d changes electrical signals into electron beams
  e alters the direction of the electron beam
  f changes electromagnetic waves into electric current

4 a In which of the following circuits will the light bulb glow? Explain your answer.
  b If the diodes and light bulbs each have a resistance of 50 Ω, which circuit has the largest current flowing through it?

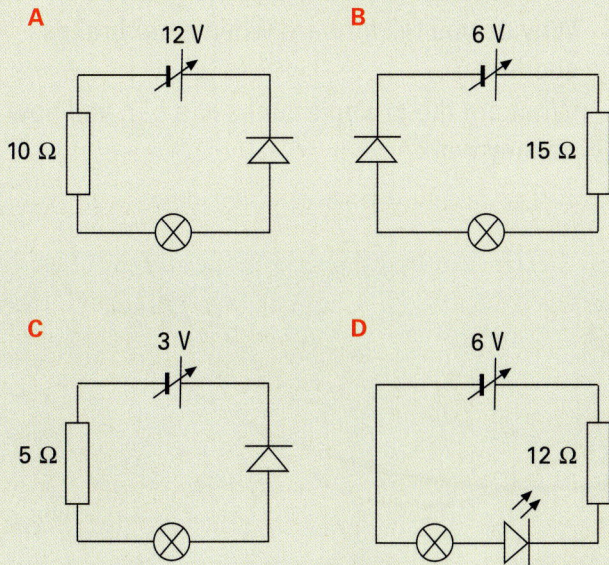

5 A fax machine is connected by wires to the telephone exchange which, in turn, is connected to other exchanges by optical fibres. Draw a flow diagram that shows all the energy changes that occur when you send a fax to your friend in another state.

6 Four wave patterns were produced on the screen of a CRO by a sound generator. Which sound:
  a is the loudest?
  b has the lowest pitch?
  c is quiet and has a high pitch?

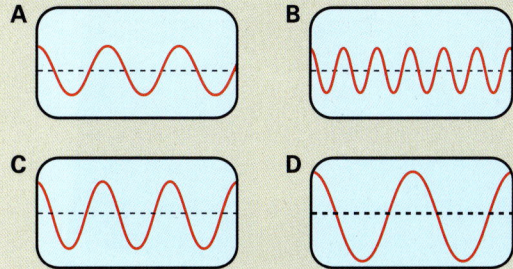

7 The wave below was produced on a CRO connected to an audio generator.

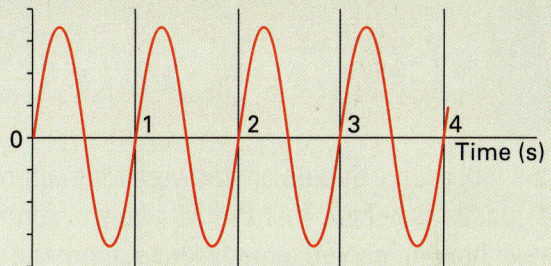

  a What is the frequency of the wave?
  b Sketch this wave in your notebook. On the same sketch, draw the wave produced by a sound of higher pitch but the same loudness.

8 Use the diagram below to explain how a loudspeaker works.

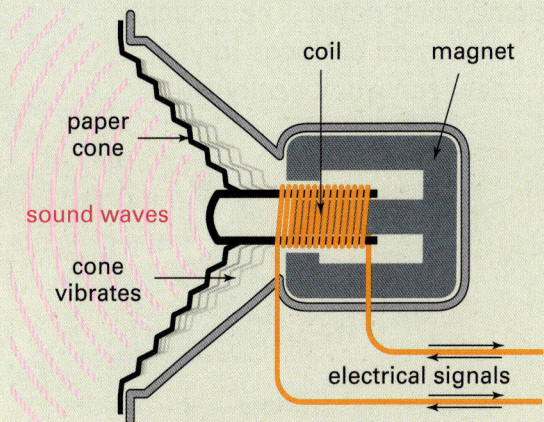

Check your answers on page 333.

5

Road science

Getting Started

In a small group, decide on answers for each of the questions below. This should give you some idea of how much you already know about the science involved in driving a car.

1 How do you calculate your average speed for a trip?

2 What is deceleration?

3 When you have to stop in an emergency, what is meant by the term 'reaction time'?

4 When you brake hard you sometimes lose control of the car. Why is this?

5 Why do you fall forward when a car brakes suddenly?

6 What are the crumple zones in a car, and how do they work?

Yeah, hi Dad. Er, I've got some good news. The crumple zones and air bags in your new car work really well.

5.1 Speed and acceleration

Activity

Three radio-controlled cars, A, B and C, were being raced against each other. They all crossed the starting line together. The motion of the three cars was recorded using a motion detector and datalogger. The graphs show the position of each car, measured from the starting line, for the first 10 seconds of the race. Use the graphs to answer these questions.

1 Which variable is measured on the horizontal axis of each graph?

2 What is measured on the vertical axis?

3 Which car moved at a constant speed throughout the 10 seconds? How do you know?

4 Which car stopped during the race? How do you know?

5 How far did each car travel in 10 seconds?

6 Which car was winning the race after 10 seconds? Explain your answer.

7 Which car was travelling the fastest:

 a at 4 seconds?

 b at 10 seconds?

 Give reasons for your answers.

8 At what speed did car A travel during the first 10 seconds?

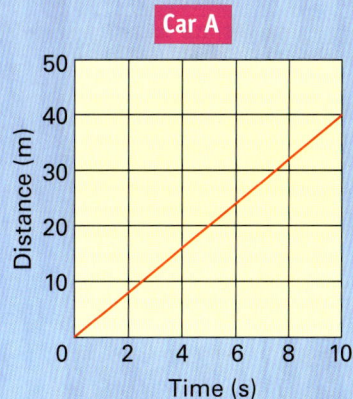

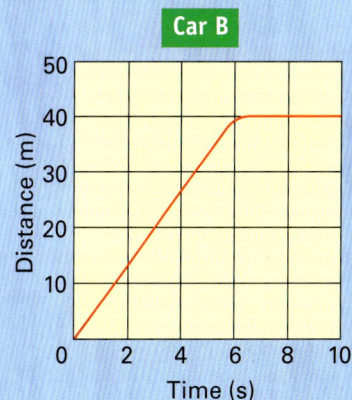

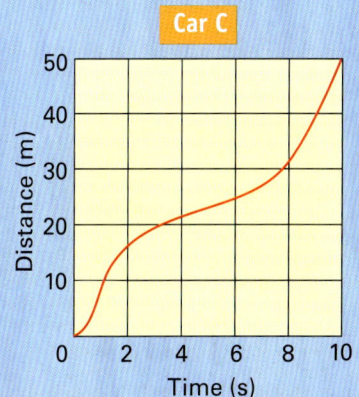

Car A

Car B

Car C

Speed

Look at the graph for car A. It travelled 40 metres in 10 seconds. To calculate its **average speed** you divide the distance travelled by the time it takes to travel that distance. The speed is usually measured in kilometres per hour (km/h) or, in this case, metres per second (m/s).

$$\text{average speed} = \frac{\text{distance travelled}}{\text{time taken}}$$
$$v_{av} = \frac{d}{t}$$
$$= \frac{40\ m}{10\ s}$$
$$= 4\ m/s$$

You can also find the average speed by calculating the slope of the distance–time graph.

$$v_{av} = \frac{d}{t} = \text{slope of graph}$$

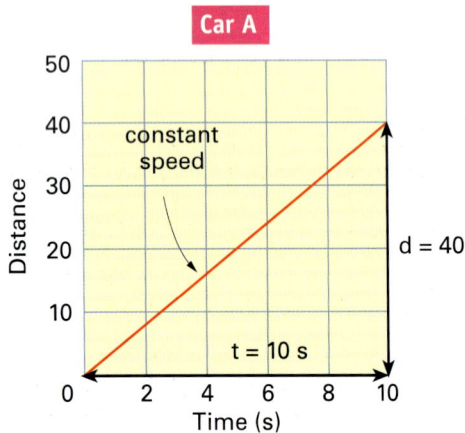

Car A

You can rearrange the equation using the triangle rule:

$$d = vt$$
$$t = \frac{d}{v}$$

You can also calculate the average speed in the same way you calculate any average:

$$v_{av} = \frac{v + u}{2}$$

where v is the final speed and u the initial speed.

Notes

1 To convert m/s to km/h you multiply by 3.6.

$$1\ m/s = \frac{1}{1000}\ km/s = \frac{60 \times 60}{1000}\ km/h = 3.6\ km/h$$

To convert km/h to m/s you divide by 3.6.

2 The symbol v is used for speed because v stands for *velocity*. Velocity is the same as speed except it includes a direction; for example, an aeroplane might have a velocity of 400 km/h *north*.

Now look at the graph for car B. For the first 6 seconds car B also travelled at a constant speed. You know this because the graph is a straight line. The graph is steeper than for car A, which means that for the first 6 seconds it travelled faster than car A. You can calculate the speed as before:

$$v = \frac{d}{t} = \frac{40\ m}{6\ s} = 6.7\ m/s$$

From 6 seconds to 10 seconds the graph is flat (zero slope). This means that the speed was zero, or the car had stopped.

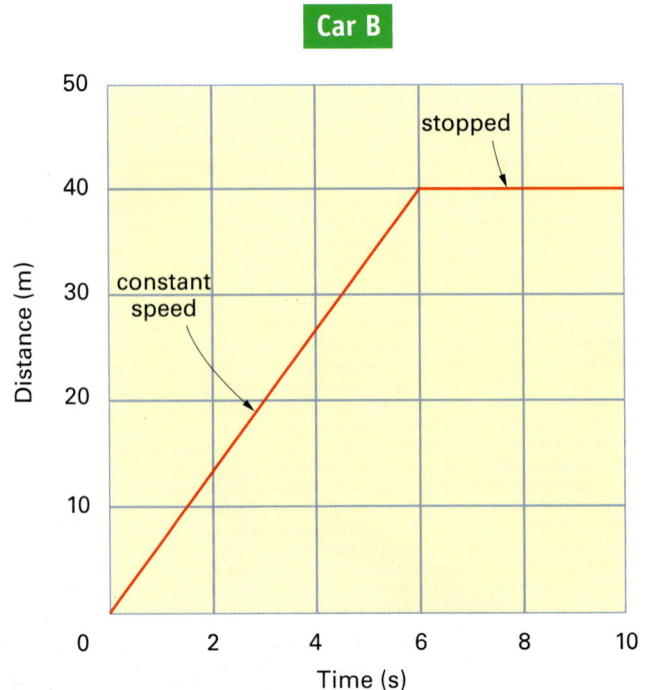

Car B

Finally, look at the graph for car C. The average speed can be calculated as usual:

$$v = \frac{50 \text{ m}}{10 \text{ s}} = 5 \text{ m/s}$$

From the slope of the graph, however, you can tell that the speed varied over the 10 seconds. After 1 second the car was moving very quickly (steep slope). Around 5 seconds it had slowed down (not so steep), and finally it sped up again.

Car C

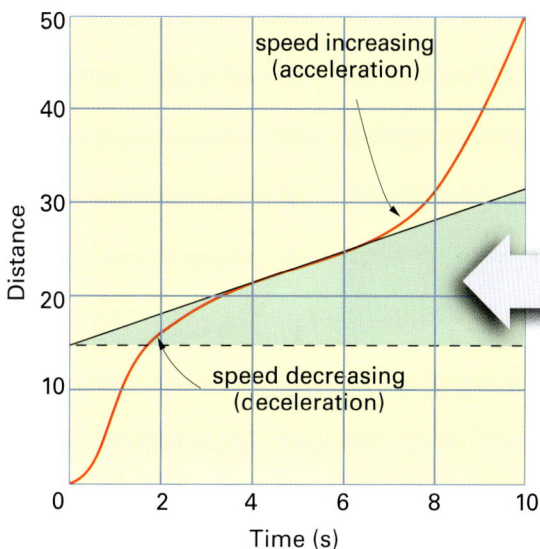

50
40
30
Distance
20
10

speed increasing (acceleration)

speed decreasing (deceleration)

0   2   4   6   8   10
Time (s)

You can find the speed at any particular time by drawing a tangent to the curve and calculating its slope. This is called the *instantaneous speed*. For example, at 5 seconds the slope (and the instantaneous speed) is about 1.7 m/s, and at 10 seconds it is about 11.1 m/s. (Check it yourself.)

The speedometer on a car measures your instantaneous speed. Suppose you go on a trip to the beach and it takes you an hour to travel 60 km. This means your average speed is 60 km/h, even though there were times when your instantaneous speed was greater than 60 km/h, and there were times when you were going slower than this or were even stopped.

$$\text{slope of tangent at 5 seconds} = \frac{32 \text{ m} - 15 \text{ m}}{10 \text{ s}}$$
$$= \frac{17 \text{ m}}{10 \text{ s}}$$
$$= 1.7 \text{ m/s}$$

Fig 6 The slope of the distance–time graph gives the instantaneous speed at a particular time.

Radar and laser guns

Police use radar and laser guns to find the instantaneous speed of cars. A radar gun emits high-frequency radio waves, which are reflected by the car. If the car is coming towards the gun, the reflected waves have a shorter wavelength than those sent out. If the car is moving away from the gun, the reflected waves are longer. The gun picks up the reflected waves and calculates the speed from the difference in wavelength.

A laser gun emits a very short pulse of infra-red light in a narrow beam. This beam is reflected back to the gun, which measures the time for the round trip. Multiplying this time by the speed of light and dividing by two (because of the round trip) gives the distance to the car. The gun measures the distance many times during an interval of about half a second, and from this the computer in the gun can calculate the speed. For more information go to www.scienceworld.net.au and follow the links to **How does a laser speed gun work?**

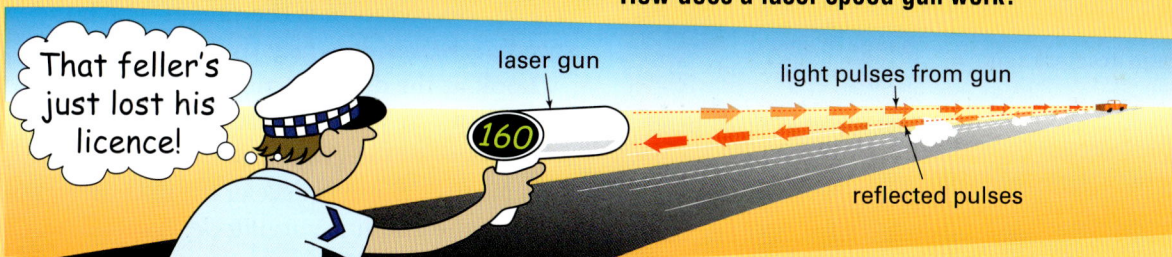

That feller's just lost his licence!

laser gun

160

light pulses from gun

reflected pulses

Acceleration

Time = 0
Speed = 0

Time = 1 second
Speed = 2 m/s

Time = 2 seconds
Speed = 4 m/s

Time = 3 seconds
Speed = 6 m/s

When an object gets faster we say that it accelerates. The diagram above shows the position of a cyclist each second, and his speed. The speed is increasing steadily, and we say that there is a constant **acceleration**. Acceleration is the rate at which the speed increases. In this case it is increasing at 2 metres per second each second. We write this as 2 m/s/s or 2 m/s^2.

Acceleration is important when considering the performance of cars. For example, Kartika wants to compare a Holden Astra with a Mazda RX-8 Turbo. She has found the following performance figures in a car magazine. The Astra takes 5.0 seconds to reach 60 km/h, whereas the RX-8 takes only 3.1 seconds.

Performance	Holden Astra	Mazda RX-8 Turbo
Standing start to ...		
60 km/h	5.0 s	3.1 s
80 km/h	8.0 s	4.4 s
100 km/h	11.4 s	5.7 s
120 km/h	16.0 s	7.5 s
from *Wheels*, September 2005		

To calculate the acceleration of each car, Kartika used this equation:

$$\text{average acceleration} = \frac{\text{change in speed}}{\text{time taken}}$$

$$= \frac{\text{final speed} - \text{initial speed}}{\text{time taken}}$$

$$\text{or } a_{av} = \frac{v - u}{t}$$

Fig 9 A dragster decelerating

For the Astra the speed increases from 0 to 60 km/h in 5.0 s (60 km/h = 60/3.6 = 16.7 m/s). So:

$$\text{acceleration} = \frac{16.7 - 0 \text{ m/s}}{5.0 \text{ s}} = 3.3 \text{ m/s}^2$$

For the RX-8:

$$\text{acceleration} = \frac{16.7 - 0 \text{ m/s}}{3.1 \text{ s}} = 5.4 \text{ m/s}^2$$

So the RX-8 accelerates much more quickly than the Astra.

When a car slows down it is said to *decelerate*; for example, a dragster at the end of its run (Fig 9). Deceleration is the rate at which the speed *decreases*. It is negative acceleration.

Look at the distance–time graph for radio-controlled Car C on the previous page. From 1 to 4 seconds the graph is curving downwards. This means the car is decelerating. From 6 to 10 seconds the graph is curving upwards—the car is now accelerating.

Investigate
12 INVESTIGATING MOTION

Aim

To use a ticker timer or a motion detector and datalogger to measure the distance, speed and acceleration of various objects and analyse this motion.

Planning and Safety Check

Discuss with your teacher how you will do this experiment. You will need to be able to work as a team, with different people doing different things.

Teacher note: Depending on your school situation you can do this experiment using ticker timers or a datalogger (Part B).

PART A
Using a ticker timer

The diagram below shows how a ticker timer works. The vibrating arm strikes the carbon paper and leaves dark marks on the paper tape. If the tape is attached to a moving object, a series of dots is left on the tape. Because the ticker timer vibrates 50 times per second, the dots are made $1/50$ of a second apart.

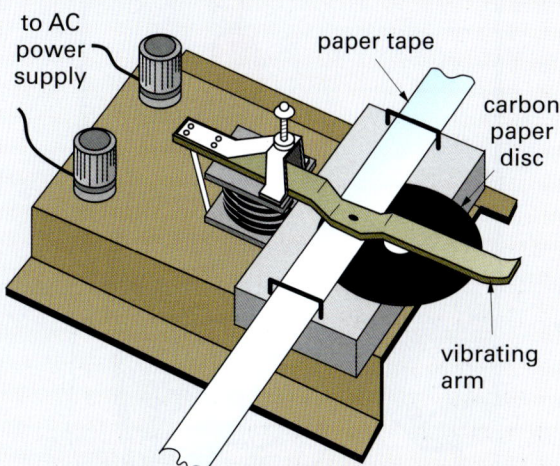

The further apart the dots are, the faster the object is moving. The closer the dots, the slower the object. If the dots are evenly spaced, then the object has a constant speed (tape 1). If the distance between the dots is increasing, the object is accelerating (tape 2). And if the dots are getting closer together, the object is decelerating (tape 3).

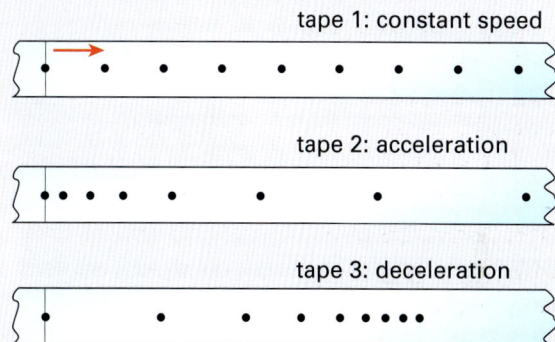

tape 1: constant speed

tape 2: acceleration

tape 3: deceleration

Materials

- ticker timer, complete with carbon disc
- ticker tape
- AC power supply and connecting wires
- dynamics trolley
- G-clamp
- pair of scissors
- adhesive tape
- board for ramp approx. 1.5 m long and 30 cm wide (eg old table top)

Method

1 Set up the ticker timer as shown on the left. Clamp it to the bench. Cut off several 1 m lengths of ticker tape.

2 Start the timer and pull a piece of tape through at a *constant speed* until about 60 cm of tape has gone through. Label the tape and show the direction of movement.

3 Repeat Step 2 for several different tapes, with a new piece of tape each time.

4 Examine the tapes.

   What do you notice about the spacing between the dots on each tape?

   Explain the differences between the tapes.

5 Select one of the tapes and mark a starting point. Count along the tape from the first dot, marking off every fifth dot, as shown below. Five dots represent 0.1 second.

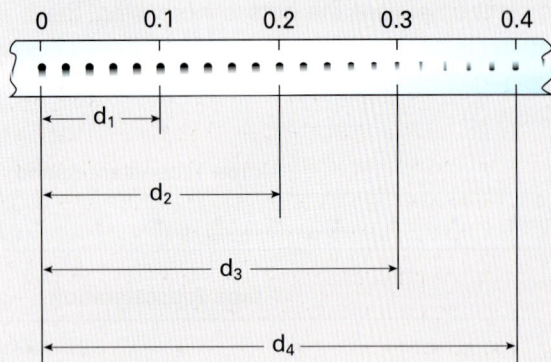

6 Measure the distances d_1, d_2, d_3, d_4, etc and record them in a data table.

7 Plot a graph of distance versus time and draw a line of best fit.

📋 Calculate the slope of the graph, which gives you the average speed of the trolley for this tape. (Give your answer in cm/s.)

8 Cut the tape at each 0.1 second mark. Then stick the strips onto graph paper in the correct order, as shown. (It is a good idea to number them.) Each strip represents the distance travelled in 0.1 seconds, so you have made a graph of speed against time.

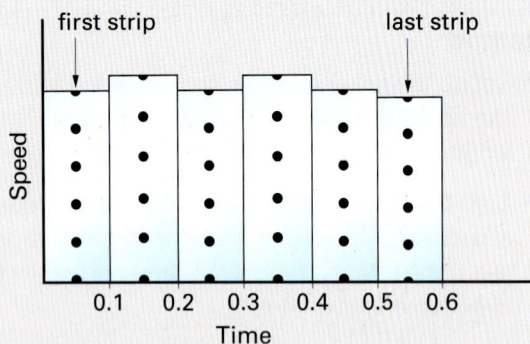

📋 Describe in your own words what you can infer from this graph.

📋 If the speed is not constant, suggest a reason for this.

📋 Estimate the average speed. Does this agree with what you calculated in Step 7?

9 If you have time, analyse the other tapes as well.

10 Repeat the experiment, but this time pull the tape through at *increasing* speed. (Give it a quick pull.) To get a steadily increasing speed you can attach the tape to a trolley that can run down a steep ramp. Another way is to set up the ticker timer vertically, attach the tape to a mass and let it fall.

11 Analyse the tape and draw a distance–time graph. Then cut up the tape to make a speed–time graph.

📋 How does this graph compare with those for constant speed?

📋 How do you know there was an acceleration? Was it constant?

12 Estimate the acceleration. This is the average increase in speed in each 0.1 second interval. Give your answer in cm/s^2.

PART B
Using a datalogger

A motion detector is similar to a police radar or laser gun (page 103), but it sends out ultrasound waves which are reflected back to it from the moving object. From these reflected waves the

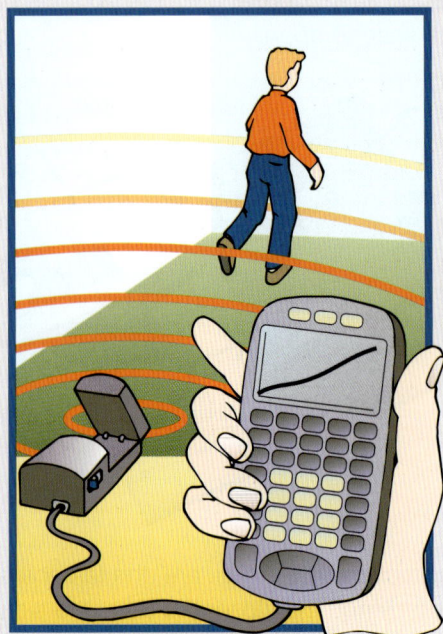

detector can calculate the distance of the object every tenth of a second, or other chosen time interval.

The data from the motion detector is sent either directly or via a datalogger to a computer or graphing calculator. The data can then be displayed in a table or as a graph, eg distance versus time or velocity versus time.

Materials

- datalogger and motion detector
- computer or graphing calculator

> **Working with technology**
>
> **For information on using dataloggers, open the ICT skillsheet on the CD.**
>
> **Detailed instructions on how to set up and operate dataloggers, as well as suggested experiments, are available from the suppliers. The output of the datalogger can be displayed on an overhead projector or computer screen.**

Method

1. Set up the motion detector with a clear space in front of it so that you can walk backwards and forwards. You can get as close as 0.5 m and as far away as 6 m.

2. Carefully connect the motion detector to the datalogger and computer or graphing calculator. Set up the datalogger to show a distance–time graph.

3. Move slowly away from the detector.

4. Look at the distance–time graph. Print it out and put it in your notebook.

   How can you explain the shape of the graph?

5. Repeat Step 3 to collect a new set of data, but move in a different way, eg slowly or quickly, away or towards the detector, speed up or slow down, stop. It is probably best to try only one or two things at a time and then see if you can make sense of each graph.

   Print out the graphs and label them, eg moving away, moving fast, slowing down, stopped.

6. To check that you understand what the graphs mean, you can record a distance–time graph and ask someone who didn't see how you moved to try to match it by moving in the same way.

7. Now that you understand the distance–time graphs, look at the velocity–time graphs.

   How can you explain the shapes of the graphs?

> **Working with technology**
>
> **To help you understand how the motion of an object can be represented by graphs, open the Motion graphs animation on the CD.**

try this

Choose a moving object to investigate using a datalogger. You could try:

- a trolley rolling down a ramp (see diagram)
- a falling object
- a bouncing ball
- a pendulum
- someone starting a sprint
- a radio-controlled car.

Analyse the distance, velocity and acceleration graphs, and write a report of your investigation.

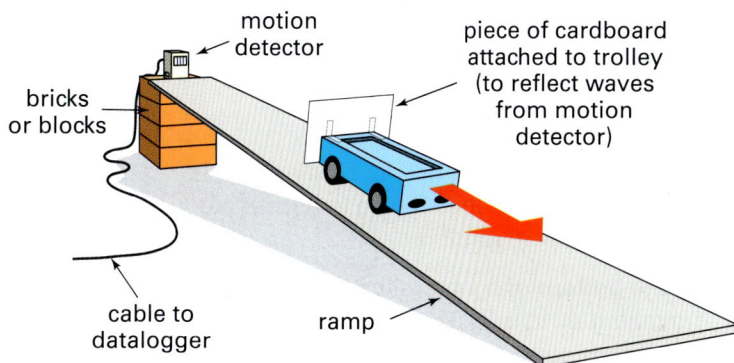

motion detector

piece of cardboard attached to trolley (to reflect waves from motion detector)

bricks or blocks

cable to datalogger

ramp

Hint: stop the trolley before it reaches the bottom of the ramp.

Check!

1 Use what you have learnt in this section to explain the cartoon below.

> Nar, I don't drive fast. We left home four hours ago. That means our average speed is only 80 kph.

> Fair go, Macca, you can't include a two hour lunch break in your calculation!

2 Find the average speed of a jet that flies 2700 km from Melbourne to Perth in 3.5 hours.

3 If the average speed of a spaceship is 32 000 km/h, how long would it take to travel the 80 million kilometres from Earth to Mars? (Give your answer in days.)

4 If you can run at an average speed of 7 m/s, how far can you run in 30 seconds?

5 A car started from rest and reached a speed of 30 m/s in 10 seconds.
   a What was its average speed?
   b How far did it travel in this time?

6 A train travelling at 10 m/s accelerates to 20 m/s in 5 seconds.
   a What is its acceleration?
   b What will its speed be after another three seconds if it continues to accelerate at the same rate?

7 A bike coasts down a hill. Its acceleration is 3 m/s². How long does it take to accelerate from 5 m/s to 16 m/s?

8 At the bottom of a waterslide Stacey is travelling at 10 m/s. She skids across the pool, coming to a stop after 2.5 seconds. What is her deceleration?

9 Draw a distance versus time graph for a car that stops at lights, then accelerates away.

10 Draw a velocity versus time graph for a person who is walking, stops briefly, then starts to run. (You could check your answers for 9 and 10 using a motion detector.)

11 Which of the speed–time graphs below could possibly represent the motion of:
   a a car coming to a stop?
   b a car travelling at constant speed?
   c a car moving from a stop at traffic lights?
   d a car accelerating?

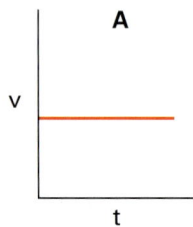

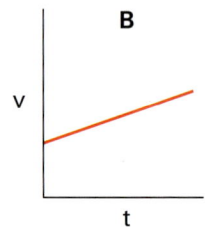

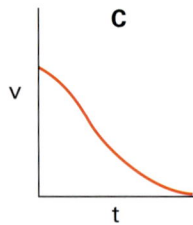

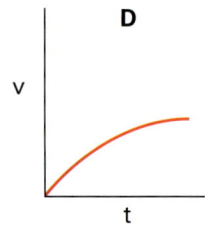

challenge

1 Two cars make the same trip, a distance of 160 kilometres. Both cars travel at a constant speed, but one averages 50 km/h, and the other 100 km/h. Represent these two trips on a single distance–time graph.

2 After 6 seconds of accelerating at 2.5 m/s², a car is moving at 50 m/s. What was the initial speed of the car if the acceleration was:
   a positive?
   b negative?

3 Use the internet to find answers to these questions about police radar and laser guns.
   a What is the Doppler effect?
   b What advantages do laser guns have over radar guns?
   c What is the range of laser guns?
   d How do speed cameras work?

4 The graph below shows the motion of two objects, X and Y. Use the graphs to answer these questions.

  a What was the speed of X after 4 seconds?

  b What was the maximum speed of Y?

  c What happened to X at 7 seconds?

  d When did X and Y have the same speed?

  e Calculate the acceleration of X.

  f What was the acceleration of Y between 6 seconds and 10 seconds?

  g At which time was Y travelling twice as fast as X?

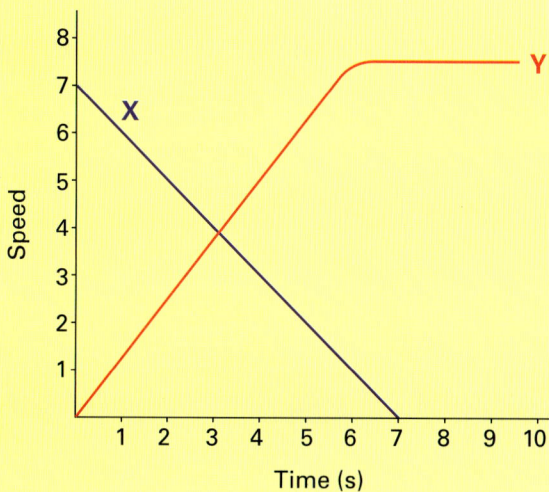

5 Hannah and Kirralee investigated the motion of a ball tossed into the air above a motion detector. They obtained these graphs from their datalogger. Explain the shape of each of the three graphs.

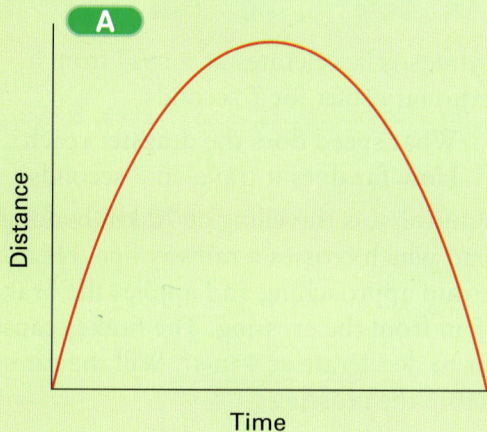

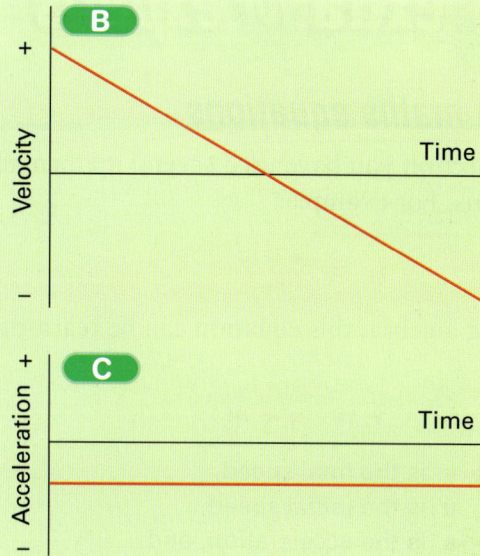

6 Look at the special photograph below of a golfer's swing. It was taken using a stroboscopic light that flashed 50 times per second (so that the time between flashes is 0.02 s).

  a What was the speed of the golf club just before and just after it struck the ball?

  b Suggest why these speeds are different.

  c What was the speed of the ball in the first 0.02 s and the second 0.02 s? What does this tell you about the motion of the ball?

Fig 21 Analyse the golfer's swing (scale = 1/30).

⭐ extra for experts

Using maths equations

In this section you have used several mathematical equations. For example:

$$a = \frac{v - u}{t}$$

Using algebra, this equation can be rearranged to give:

$$v = u + at$$

where **v** is the final speed,
   u is the initial speed,
   a is the acceleration, and
   t is the time.

From this equation you can obtain a second equation:

$$d = ut + \tfrac{1}{2}at^2$$

where **d** is the distance travelled.
You can use these two equations to solve various problems.

Sample problem 1

A car was travelling at 15 m/s. It then accelerated at 2 m/s^2 for 4 seconds. What was its final speed?

Step 1   List the things you know and what you want to find.

$$u = 15 \text{ m/s}$$
$$a = 2 \text{ m/s}^2$$
$$t = 4 \text{ s}$$
$$v = ?$$

Step 2   Write down the appropriate equation and substitute the values into it.

$$v = u + at$$
$$= 15 + (2 \times 4)$$
$$= 15 + 8$$
$$= 23 \text{ m/s}$$

Sample problem 2

A car and a semitrailer are travelling at 90 km/h (25 m/s). To overtake the semitrailer the car accelerates at 1.6 m/s^2 for 5 seconds. How far does the car travel in this time?

$$u = 25 \text{ m/s}$$
$$a = 1.6 \text{ m/s}^2$$
$$t = 5 \text{ s}$$
$$d = ?$$

$$d = ut + \tfrac{1}{2}at^2$$
$$= (25 \times 5) + \tfrac{1}{2}(1.6 \times 25)$$
$$= 125 + 20$$
$$= 145 \text{ m}$$

Questions

1   A car was stopped at traffic lights. When the lights changed it accelerated at 3 m/s^2 for 6 seconds.
   a   What was the car's initial speed?
   b   What was its speed after 6 seconds (in km/h)?

2   A spacecraft is moving at 250 m/s when it fires its retro-rockets for 6 seconds to slow it down. This causes it to decelerate at 10 m/s^2. What is the spacecraft's speed after the 6 seconds?

3   Owen drops a stone from the top of a mountain pass. If it takes 12 seconds to reach the valley below, how high is the pass. (Hint: the acceleration due to gravity is 9.8 m/s^2.)

4   A dragster accelerates at 9 m/s^2 from a stationary start for 7 seconds.
   a   What speed does the dragster reach?
   b   How far does it travel in 7 seconds?

5   A motorist is travelling at 70 km/h along a road which crosses a railway line. He notices a train approaching and applies the brakes 55 m from the crossing. The brakes cause the car to decelerate at 4 m/s^2. Will the car stop before the crossing?

5.2 Stopping

Imagine you are driving along a road and a child suddenly runs onto the road in front of you. You apply the brakes, and the car stops just in time.

Here is an action replay. The child runs onto the road. Your eyes record the scene. This information passes to your brain, which sends a signal to your right leg to push hard on the brake pedal. All this takes about a second. This time is called your **reaction time**. The distance the car travels in this time is called the *reaction distance*.

Under test conditions, reaction time is usually about 0.75 seconds. In real driving situations it is about one second, but may be much longer, depending on the individual and their alertness. The faster you are going, the further the car travels during this reaction time. For example, at 60 km/h (16.7 m/s):

reaction distance = vt = 16.7 m/s × 1 s = 16.7 m

When you put your foot on the brake pedal the car takes a certain distance to stop. This is called the *braking distance*. Good brakes and good tyres can slow a car about 23 km/h every second (about –6 m/s²) on a good road. If you double

your speed, the braking distance is four times as far! And on gravel or wet bitumen, the braking distance is even longer.

The distance it takes your car to stop is made up of the reaction distance plus the braking distance. This is called the *stopping distance*. The chart below shows the stopping distances when travelling at various speeds in a car.

In the experiment on the next page you can investigate the variables that affect stopping distance.

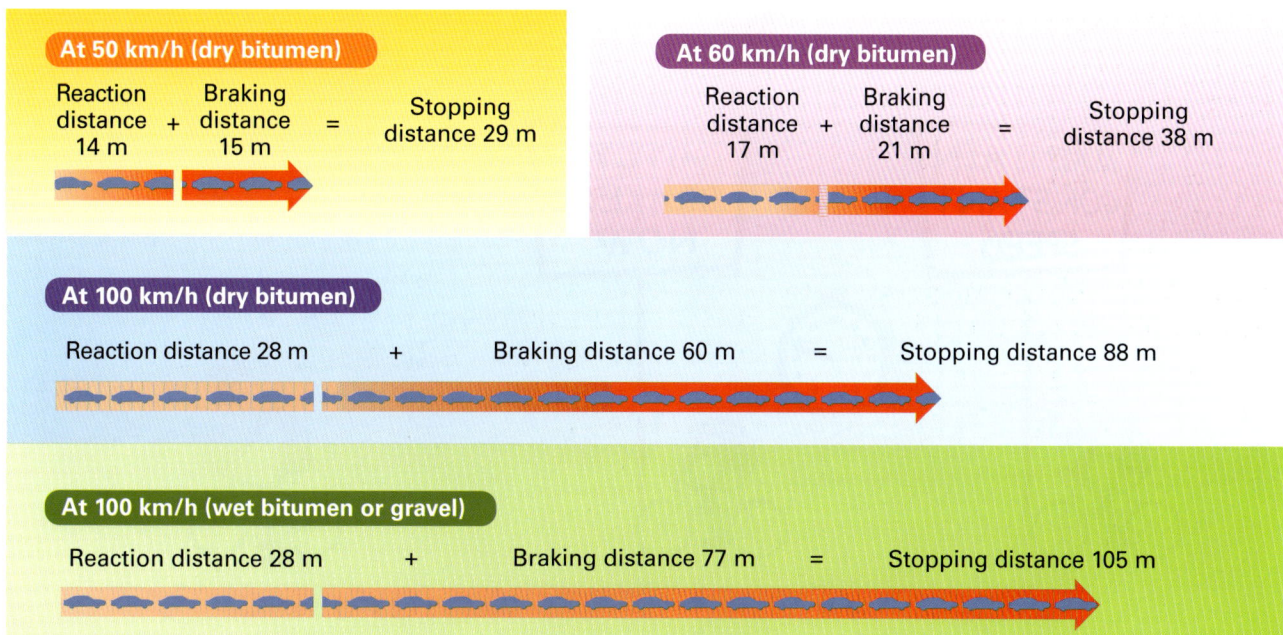

At 50 km/h (dry bitumen)
Reaction distance 14 m + Braking distance 15 m = Stopping distance 29 m

At 60 km/h (dry bitumen)
Reaction distance 17 m + Braking distance 21 m = Stopping distance 38 m

At 100 km/h (dry bitumen)
Reaction distance 28 m + Braking distance 60 m = Stopping distance 88 m

At 100 km/h (wet bitumen or gravel)
Reaction distance 28 m + Braking distance 77 m = Stopping distance 105 m

Fig 24 Stopping distance = reaction distance + braking distance

Experiment
STOPPING DISTANCES

Problem to be solved

What is the relationship between speed and stopping distance?

Planning the experiment

In a group, use the questions below to help you design an experiment to solve the problem above. Then carry out your experiment and write a report.

- How are you going to do the experiment? If you work outside you could use a bicycle. If you work in the laboratory you could let a trolley run down a ramp and vary the slope of the ramp.

Whichever method you use you will need to answer these questions:

- How will you measure the speed of the bicycle or trolley?

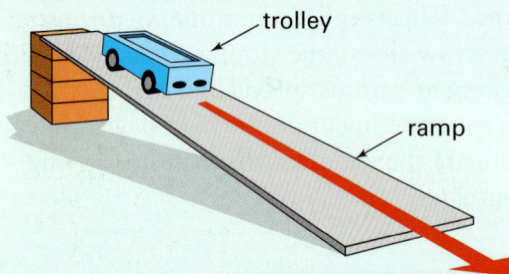

- What variables will you need to control?
- How can you make your measurements more reliable?

Processing the data

- How will you record your data? For example, can you put them into a spreadsheet such as *Excel*?
- How will you work out the relationship between stopping distance and speed? Will you need to draw a graph? Will the spreadsheet do this for you?

Evaluating the experiment

- How well did your method work?
- Do you think your results are reliable?
- Is your conclusion valid?

❷ try this

What other variables affect the stopping distance? Choose one of these variables and then investigate how it affects the stopping distance.

MAINTAIN CONSTANT SPEED — APPLY BRAKES NOW — 10 m — Measure braking distance.

Friction

After the accident Teresa said: *When I saw the other car coming I slammed on the brakes, but I didn't seem to have control. The car just kept skidding until it hit the pole.* What happened here was that Teresa had put the brakes on too hard, stopping the wheels from turning. The brakes had 'locked'.

Tyres grip the road by **friction**, and this is what allows a driver to control the car. There has to be enough friction between the tyres and the road to enable the tyres to grip the road. Then, when the engine turns the wheels, the car will go forward. When you turn the steering wheel, the car will turn. And when you put on the brakes, the car will stop.

If the friction between the tyres and the road is reduced, driving can become dangerous. That is why you have to take extra care driving on wet roads. The water acts as a lubricant between the tyres and the road, reducing the friction and increasing the braking distance considerably.

There are two types of friction—**static friction** and **sliding friction**. Static friction holds the tyre on the road. As the wheel rolls, another part of the tread comes into contact with a different part of the road, as shown below. The wheel does not slide.

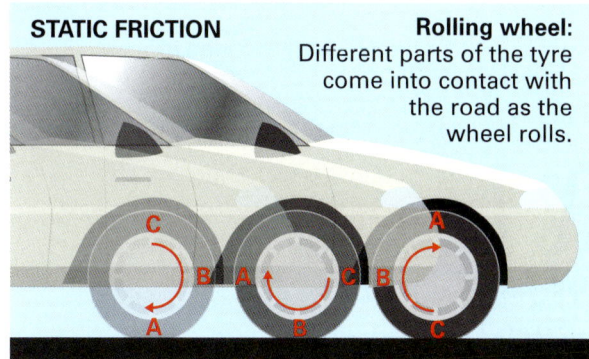

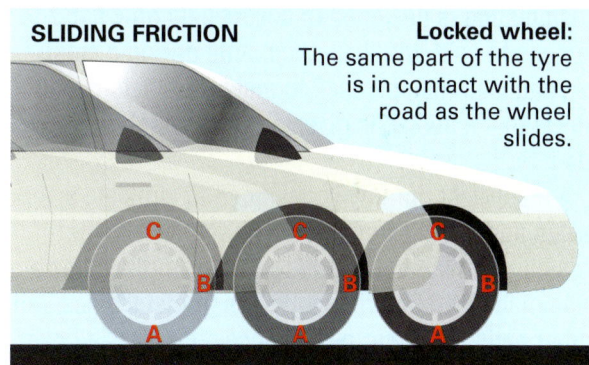

Fig 27 A tyre photographed at high speed through a wet glass roadway

STATIC FRICTION — **Rolling wheel:** Different parts of the tyre come into contact with the road as the wheel rolls.

SLIDING FRICTION — **Locked wheel:** The same part of the tyre is in contact with the road as the wheel slides.

When a wheel locks or slides sideways, the same part of the tyre tread slides along the road. The gripping force in this case is sliding friction, which is less than static friction (see the activity on the next page). Hence the tyres have considerably less grip on the road in a skid than when the wheels are rolling.

A skilled driver knows just how hard to brake without locking the wheels. However, most new cars are equipped with an antilock braking system (ABS). It senses that a wheel is about to lock up or skid and pumps the brake off and on rapidly. When the brakes are released the wheels start rolling again, and when the brakes are reapplied the larger static friction forces help stop the car. The 'brains' behind ABS is a computer chip, which can detect whether one wheel is turning more slowly than the others.

Activity

Use the set-up below to investigate the difference between static friction and sliding friction.

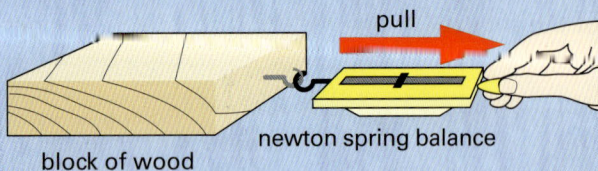

pull

block of wood

newton spring balance

1 Pull gently on the spring balance, without moving the block.
   Which type of friction is operating?

2 Gradually increase the pull until the block starts to slide. Watch carefully the reading on the spring balance.
   What happens to the frictional force when the block slides?
   Which type of friction is operating now?

Science in action

Crash tests

Crash testing is designed to collect data on what happens to cars and their occupants during a crash. This data can then be used to make cars safer. Each vehicle that is tested is given a rating to indicate how safe it is.

A crash-test dummy is designed to simulate a person and is built from materials that mimic the physiology of the human body. For example, it has a spine made from alternating layers of metal discs and rubber pads. The dummy has accelerometers all over it to measure the acceleration in all directions. For example, the sudden deceleration of the driver's head during the crash is measured. There are load sensors to measure the amount of force on different parts of the body. For example, the force on the thigh bone is measured to determine the probability of it breaking. There are also movement sensors in the dummy's chest to measure how much it is pushed in during a crash. The dummy's knees, face and parts of the head are painted different colours. In the photo you can see that blue paint from the dummy's face is smeared on the airbag and that its left knee (painted red) hit the steering column. Each crash-test dummy costs about $250 000.

Ballast is added to the car to give it the correct weight. There are calibration marks on the car to help the testers analyse the slow-motion replays. The area is well lit and there are 15 or so high-speed cameras. The car is mounted on a track and propelled into a solid concrete barrier at about 60 km/h. A huge amount of data is temporarily stored in the dummy's chest and then downloaded to a computer. Side-impact tests are also carried out, in which a trolley is crashed into the side of the car.

WEB watch

For more information on crash tests go to www.scienceworld.net.au and follow the links to **How crash testing works**. This site has an excellent video of a crash test.

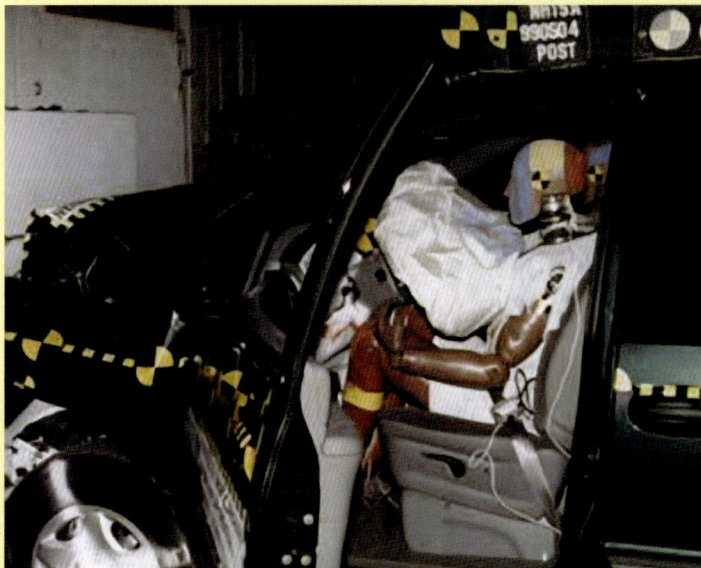

Check!

1 **Fred is on a pleasant Sunday drive.** (0.0 seconds)
2 **A kangaroo hops out from behind a bush.** (1.0 seconds)
3 **Fred sees the kangaroo.** (1.2 seconds)
4 **What will he do?** (1.3 seconds)
5 **Fred steps on the brake pedal.** (2.0 seconds)
6 **The car decelerates ...** (2.5 seconds)
7 **... and skids sideways!** (3.0 seconds)
8 **The car stops. Phew!** (5.1 seconds)

1 The cartoon strip above shows what happened to Fred while driving in the country.
   a What is Fred's reaction time?
   b What is his braking time?
   c What is his stopping time?

2 Use the chart on the right to answer these questions.
   a You are travelling at 50 km/h. What speed is this in metres per second?
   b What is your reaction distance at this speed?
   c What happens to the braking distance and stopping distance when the speed doubles from 40 km/h to 80 km/h?
   d The chart assumes a reaction time. What is it? How do you know?
   e Two identical cars side by side on the freeway brake at the same time. If one is travelling at 80 km/h and the other at 100 km/h, how far apart will they be when they stop?

f You are 50 m from a pedestrian crossing when an elderly person starts to cross. If you are travelling at 60 km/h, will you stop in time? What if the road is wet?

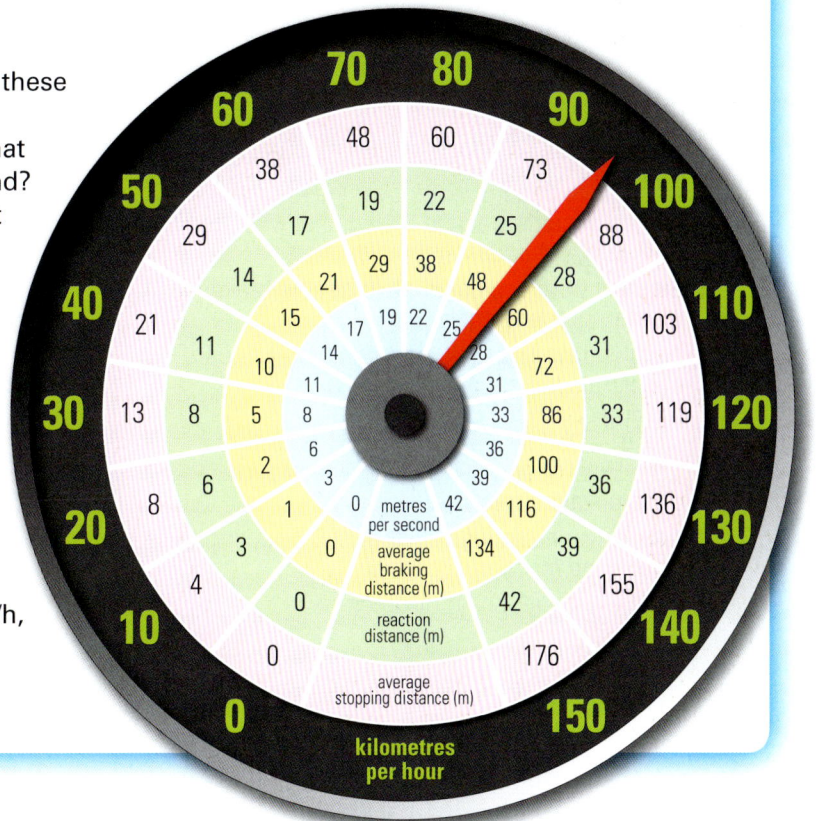

3 Why is the braking distance greater on a wet road than on a dry one?

4 The stopping distances on the chart on the previous page are for an alert driver in a car with good brakes and tyres, on a dry road. What difference would each of the following make to the stopping distance?
   a rain   **c** drunk driver
   b tired driver   **d** fog

5 Gayle wants to move a heavy cupboard. She pushes harder and harder, then suddenly it moves with a jerk. Try to explain why this happens.

6 What is ABS in a car and how does it work?

7 Why is it that the reaction distance increases with speed while the reaction time stays the same?

challenge

1 It is often recommended that, under good conditions, you should drive at least two seconds behind the car in front. (This means that it should take your car at least 2 seconds to reach the present position of the car in front.)
   a How far behind should you be when travelling at 60 km/h? At 100 km/h?
   b Try to explain why a time of 2 seconds is recommended.

2 a Use the chart on the previous page to draw a graph of average braking distance versus speed. Plot reaction distance versus speed on the same graph.
   b Use your graph to find the reaction distance, braking distance and stopping distance at 65 km/h.

3 a Use the diagram on the right to write a paragraph explaining how disc brakes work.
   b If you drive through water over the road, the brakes become wet and they do not work as well. Suggest a reason for this.
   c Suggest what you could do to get the brakes working properly again.

4 a A car is travelling at 60 km/h. If its brakes can decelerate the car at 6 m/s², what is its braking distance? Use the formula $v^2 = u^2 + 2ad$, where v is the final speed, u the initial speed, a the acceleration and d the distance travelled.
   b If the driver has a reaction time of 0.8 seconds, what is the reaction distance?
   c What will the stopping distance be?

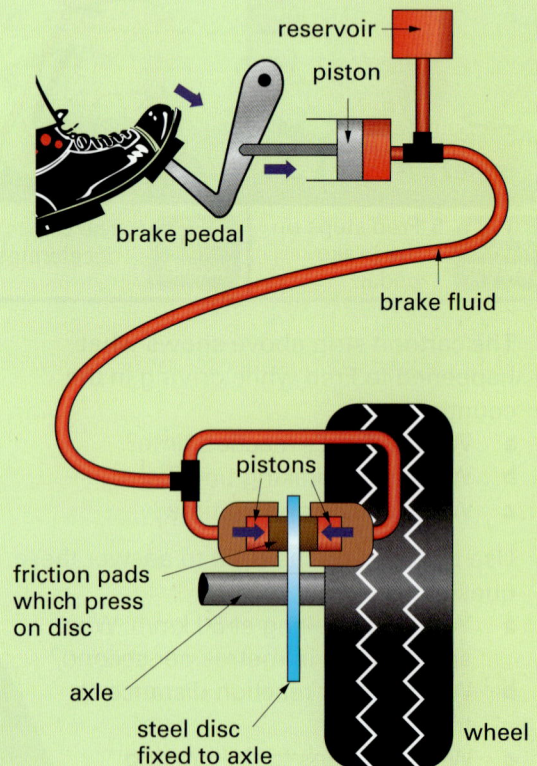

reservoir
piston
brake pedal
brake fluid
pistons
friction pads which press on disc
axle
steel disc fixed to axle
wheel

try this

1 Design and carry out an experiment to test whether wider tyres give you better grip than narrow ones.

2 Does it make any difference whether the front wheels, the back wheels or all four wheels are locked up during braking? Design and carry out an experiment to test this.

5.3 Collisions

Inertia

Suppose you are in a car travelling at 60 km/h. Your body is also moving at 60 km/h. If the driver brakes suddenly the car slows down, but because your body is not attached to the car it tends to keep moving at the same speed of 60 km/h. This is why you feel as though you are falling forwards. A seatbelt holds you so that you do not crash into the dashboard, windscreen or front seats.

Similarly, if you are standing in a bus or a train you may be thrown off balance when it starts to move. Your body tends to stay at rest as the bus begins to move. If the bus suddenly speeds up, you may fall backwards. And if the bus turns a sharp corner you may be thrown to the other side.

The train's sudden acceleration was about to cause Mikie a few embarrassing moments.

An object will stay at rest, or will not change its speed or direction, unless acted on by a force. The object is said to have **inertia** (in-ER-sha). This inertia depends on the mass of the object— the greater the mass, the greater the inertia. For example, a bus has more mass than a car. Therefore it has more inertia. A bus is harder to start or stop than a car. That is, it takes a larger force to change its motion.

To sum up, if an object is at rest, it tends to remain at rest; and if it is moving, it tends to keep on moving at the same speed and in the same

Activity

Here is a fun way to illustrate inertia. Place a 20 cent coin on a piece of cardboard on top of a glass as shown. Then flick the card.

Explain what happens in terms of inertia.

direction. This is called *Newton's first law of motion*, even though it was first proposed by the Italian Galileo in 1612. The Englishman Sir Isaac Newton was born in the year Galileo died, and he used Galileo's idea and developed it further.

Momentum

A heavy truck is harder to stop than a car travelling at the same speed. This is because the truck has more momentum. The **momentum** of an object depends on its mass and its speed. It can be calculated using the formula:

> **M = m v**
> where **M** is the momentum, **m** is the mass in kilograms and **v** is the speed of the object in m/s

Momentum increases as either the mass or the speed increases. A truck has more momentum than a car moving at the same speed. The larger mass of the truck gives it more momentum. For this reason it will do more damage if it collides with something. Also, a fast-moving car has more momentum than a slow-moving one. Its greater speed gives it more momentum.

In Investigate 13 you can investigate the effects of inertia and momentum in car accidents.

Investigate
13 CAR ACCIDENTS

Aim

To use trolleys and dummies as a model for car accidents.

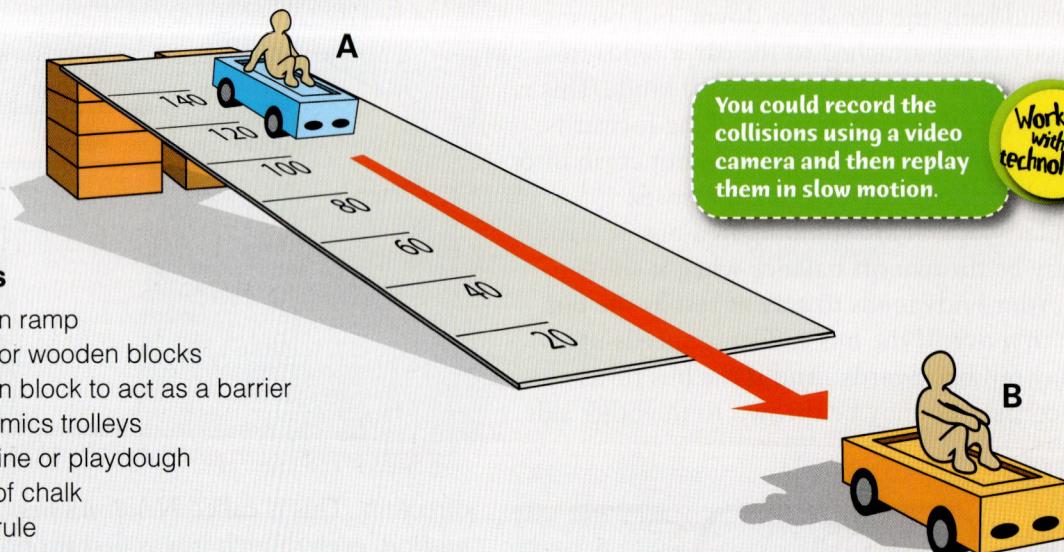

You could record the collisions using a video camera and then replay them in slow motion.

Working with technology

Materials

- wooden ramp
- bricks or wooden blocks
- wooden block to act as a barrier
- 2 dynamics trolleys
- plasticine or playdough
- piece of chalk
- metre rule
- masking tape
- talcum or graphite powder
- graph paper

Planning and Safety Check

Read both parts of the investigation carefully.
- What is the aim of each part?
- Design a data table for Part B.

PART A

Method

1. Make two plasticine dummies to represent people in car accidents.

2. Put a dummy on the front of each trolley. (You should powder the bottoms of the dummies to reduce their stickiness.)

3. Mark 20 cm intervals on the ramp, starting from the bottom, as shown.

4. Place trolley B about 40 centimetres in front of the ramp. Place trolley A at the top of the ramp, directly in line with trolley B.

5. Release trolley A so that it collides with trolley B.

    Observe carefully what happens to the dummies in the collision.

6. Repeat Step 5 two or three times.

Discussion

1. What happened to the dummy on trolley A during the collision? Explain *why* this happened.

2. What happens to the occupants of a moving car when it collides with a stationary car?

3. What design features of cars reduce the risk of injury in this type of collision?

4. What happened to the dummy on trolley B? Explain why this happened.

5. What happens to the occupants of a stationary car hit from behind by another car?

6. What design features reduce the risk of injury in this type of collision?

PART B

Method

1 Tape a wooden block firmly to the bench or floor 30 to 40 cm in front of the ramp.

2 Put the plasticine dummy on the trolley and line it up on the 20 cm mark. Release it so that it crashes into the wooden block and observe what happens to the dummy.

📋 Measure the distance from the dummy to the impact side of the wooden block. Measure to the nearest centimetre, and record the result in a data table.

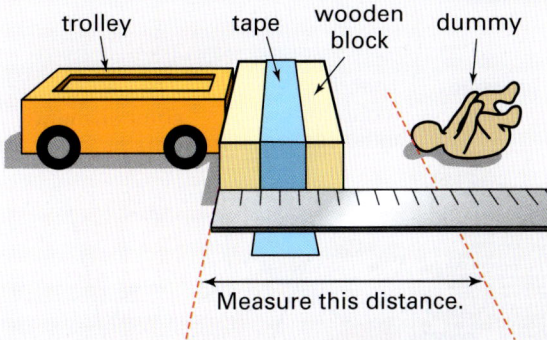

trolley   tape   wooden block   dummy

Measure this distance.

3 Repeat Step 2 at least three times, exactly the same way each time. You will probably get a different result each time. This is because there are variables that are difficult to control. For instance, the trolley may hit the block differently because of small changes in the way it rolls down the ramp.

📋 Find the average of the measurements.

4 Repeat Steps 2 and 3 by placing the trolley at higher positions on the ramp. Record all results.

5 Plot your results on a graph. Try to draw a line of best fit.

Discussion

1 What happens to the impact speed of the trolley as it is released from higher up the ramp?

2 What is the relationship between the impact speed and the distance that the dummy was thrown?

3 Use your graph to predict how far the dummy would be thrown if you released the trolley from one of the marks you have not used. Try it and check your prediction.

4 Could you modify the experiment to get more reliable results? How?

☉ try this

1 Redesign Part A to model what happens in a head-on collision.

2 Experiment with a crumple zone for the trolley, eg a cylinder of paper as shown below. You could also experiment with a seatbelt or airbag for the dummy.

paper cylinder taped to front of trolley

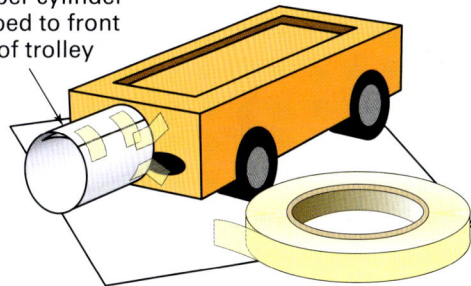

The second and third collisions

How can one person walk away from a major collision and another person die in a minor collision? The following true story will help you answer this.

A farmer loaded his truck with eggs and headed for the markets. On the way he lost control of the truck and crashed into a tree beside the road. The truck was travelling at 60 km/h when it was stopped by the tree. However, due to inertia, the farmer's body continued moving until it collided with the steering wheel and windscreen. There was also a third collision when the farmer's internal organs were slammed against each other and against his skeleton. It was these second and third collisions that seriously injured the farmer.

The eggs in the back of the truck were packed in soft cardboard cartons and stacked in crates.

The crates were also tied down. Some of the crates were thrown from the truck and the eggs smashed, but most of the crates remained in the truck and the eggs were undamaged!

Why was the farmer injured while most of the eggs were safe? Obviously the eggs were carefully packaged, but the farmer was not. Because he was not wearing a seatbelt he smashed into the steering wheel and was seriously injured. At 60 km/h, the impact of the second collision is like landing face first on the ground after falling from the fifth floor of a building. Worse, it is like falling on a steering wheel sticking up from the ground, or on a glass windscreen or a dashboard!

Inertia and car design

Seatbelts hold car occupants securely in place during a crash and reduce the chance of serious injury and death by about 60%. This is why the wearing of seatbelts is law. Also, babies and young children who are too small for seatbelts must have specially designed child restraints.

Some deaths and serious injuries have been caused when car occupants, whether wearing seatbelts or not, have been struck by loose objects flying forward from the rear seat or parcel shelf. If you and the car come to a complete stop from even a moderate speed, say 40 km/h, loose items will continue travelling at that speed. Imagine being struck in the back of the head by a portable radio or something similar travelling at 40 km/h! Even small light objects can kill at that speed.

Head restraints help to prevent neck damage to occupants, particularly in rear-end collisions. Look at the top part of Fig 39, where there is no head restraint. When the car is struck from behind, the person's body is moved forward by the seat, but the head is left behind because of its inertia. The effect is like that of cracking a whip, and the person can suffer a serious neck injury called whiplash. If the head is supported by a head restraint, both body and head move together.

Modern cars are designed to help you survive serious crashes. In a head-on collision, the engine compartment is designed to crumple and absorb as much energy as possible. The engine is forced

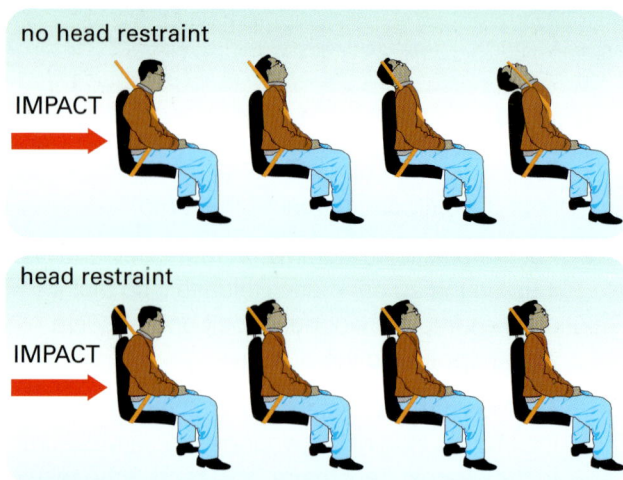

Fig 39 How head restraints work

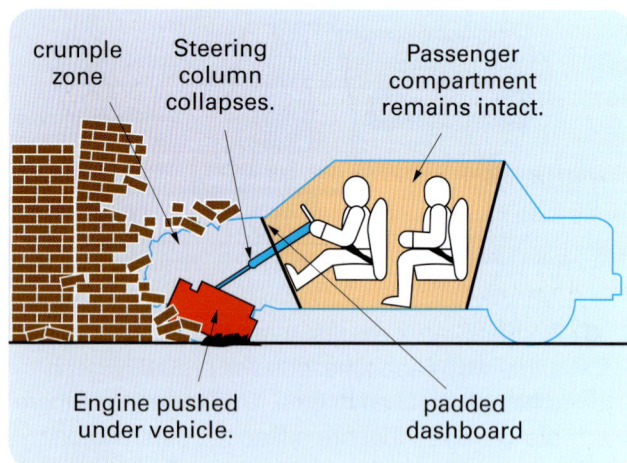

Fig 40 Safety features in a car

under the rigid passenger compartment, and the steering column collapses so that the driver is not speared.

Many new cars are now fitted with *airbags*. These do not replace seatbelts, but are an additional safety device. In a serious crash, belted front occupants may still move forward enough to hit the steering wheel or windscreen. Airbags are designed to inflate in frontal collisions that are comparable to hitting a solid wall at about 25 km/h. Most sensors contain a micromachined accelerometer which produces an electronic signal when jolted. This sends an electric current to the igniter in the inflator. This causes the chemical

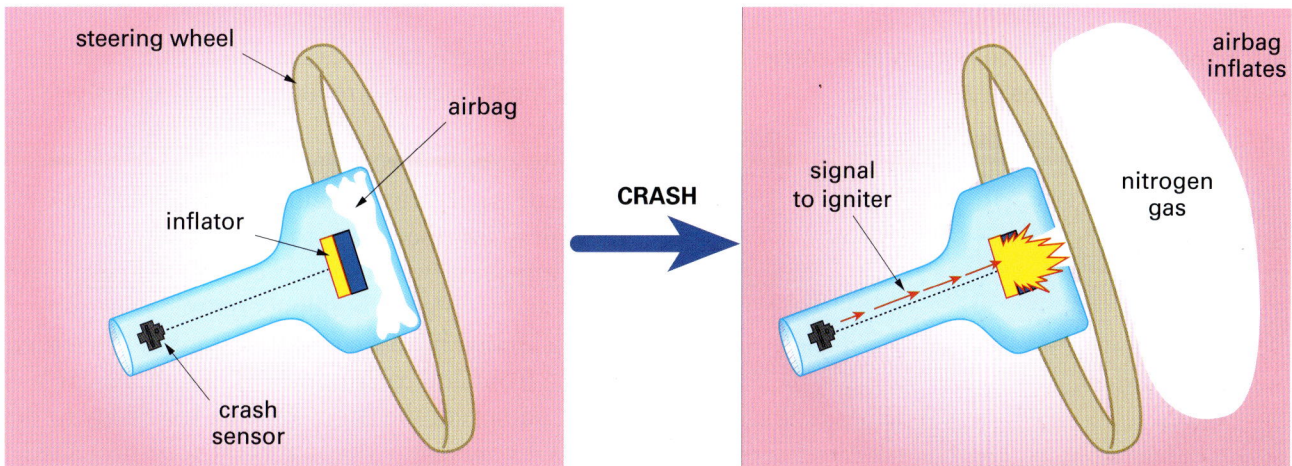

propellant (usually sodium azide) that is sealed in the module to undergo a rapid chemical reaction which produces nitrogen gas that inflates the bag in about 0.3 seconds. A second later the gas quickly escapes through tiny holes, thus deflating the bag so you can move.

Force, mass and acceleration

We know that force causes acceleration, but Sir Isaac Newton was the first to work out the relationship between the size of a force and the acceleration it causes.

Firstly, the larger the force, the larger the acceleration it causes. For example, if you push an empty shopping trolley very gently it only moves slowly. If you apply a large force by pushing hard it moves rapidly. This means that the force and the acceleration produced by the force are directly proportional. To double the acceleration of the trolley you need twice the force. And half the force will produce only half the acceleration.

WEBwatch

To find out more about airbags go to www.scienceworld.net.au and follow the links to **How air bags work.**

Secondly, a force will give a greater acceleration to an object with a small mass than it will to an object with a large mass. If you push an empty shopping trolley with a large force, it will accelerate rapidly. But when you use the same force to push the same trolley filled with groceries, the acceleration is less. What this means is that for a constant force the acceleration is inversely proportional to the mass of the object being accelerated. In other words, if you double the mass, you halve the acceleration. And if you halve the mass you double the acceleration.

Fig 42 A small push gives an empty shopping trolley a small acceleration.

A bigger push gives the empty trolley a large acceleration.

But this same push gives a full trolley only a small acceleration.

These two relationships between acceleration, force and mass can be combined as a single mathematical equation:

$$a = \frac{F}{m}$$

where **a** is the acceleration in m/s², **F** is the force in newtons and **m** is the mass in kilograms.

The equation can then be rearranged as shown:

$$F = m\,a$$

This equation is known as Newton's second law of motion.

Crumple zones

Newton's second law of motion is useful in analysing collisions. Using the equation for acceleration you can rearrange the equation F = ma as follows:

$$F = m\,a = m\left(\frac{v-u}{t}\right) = \frac{mv - mu}{t}$$

The quantity mv is the momentum of the object, so you can rewrite F = ma as:

$$\text{force} = \frac{\text{final momentum} - \text{initial momentum}}{\text{time taken}}$$

$$= \frac{\text{change in momentum}}{\text{time taken}}$$

Suppose a car has a mass of 600 kg. It is travelling at 90 km/h (25 m/s) when it collides with a tree and comes to a stop in 0.1 seconds. We can calculate the force exerted on the car as follows. Because the car comes to a stop its final speed is zero.

$$F = \frac{mv - mu}{t}$$
$$= \frac{(600 \times 0) - (600 \times 25)}{0.1}$$
$$= \frac{-15\,000}{0.1}$$
$$= -150\,000 \text{ N}$$

The negative sign means that the force is decelerating the car. Because it is such a large force, the occupants are likely to be seriously injured.

How can the forces during a collision be reduced? Apart from driving more slowly, the most practical method is to lengthen the time from impact to when the car comes to a stop. This can be done by building crumple zones into a vehicle. In a head-on collision it takes some time for the front end to crumple. Although the car is badly damaged, the occupants are less likely to be hurt. Of course, the occupants must be protected in a rigid passenger compartment (see Fig 40) so that they are not crushed. And they must wear seatbelts to stop them colliding with the interior of the car.

Suppose the car in the previous example had a crumple zone so that it stopped in 0.3 seconds instead of 0.1 seconds. The force now would be 50 000 N, only a third of what it was without the crumple zone. If the car had hit a pile of hay bales it would have stopped in about 1 second. In this case the force on the car would have been only 15 000 N, a tenth of the force when it hit the tree. This is why some roads have energy-absorbing barriers, to increase the collision time and decrease the force on the car.

Fig 43 These energy-absorbing wire ropes prevent vehicles crossing the median strip into the path of oncoming vehicles.

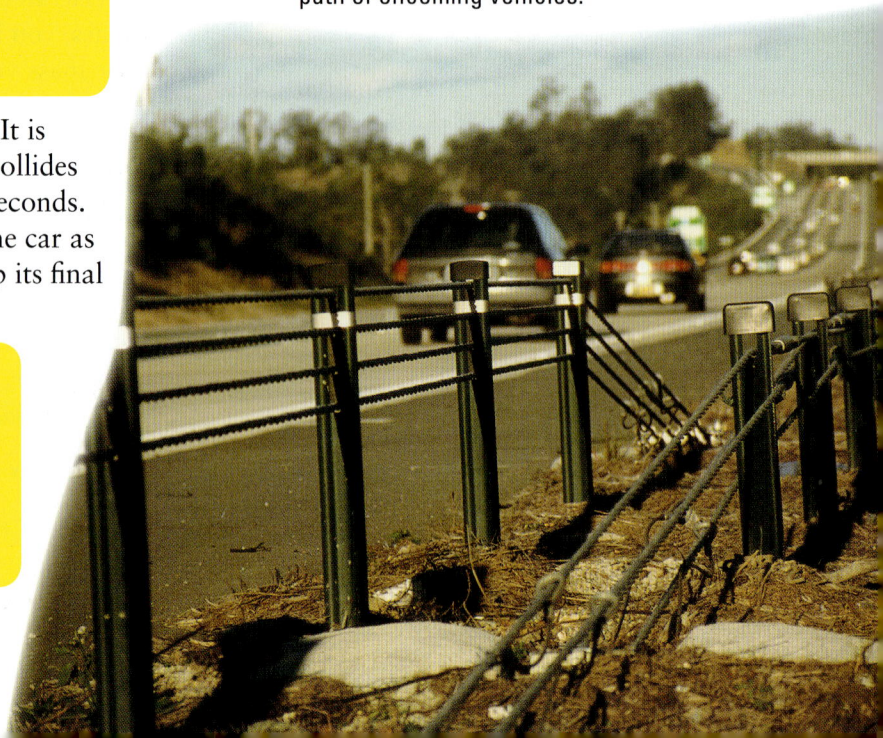

Drink driving

It is illegal to drive a motor vehicle if your blood alcohol concentration is more than 0.05, or zero if you are a learner driver or P-plater. *Blood alcohol concentration* is the amount of alcohol per 100 mL of blood in your body at a particular time. It is measured in g/100 mL. So 0.05% means that there is 0.05 g of alcohol in each 100 mL of blood.

On average, a person reaches a blood alcohol concentration of 0.05 after consuming three *standard drinks* in an hour (Fig 44). However, this can vary considerably from person to person. It depends on your weight, whether you are male or female, and whether or not you eat food with the alcohol. As part of its normal functions, the body processes alcohol and gets rid of it. Each hour, blood alcohol concentration falls by about 0.015, equivalent to one standard drink.

Drinking and driving are a deadly combination. The alcohol slows down your reaction time and therefore increases braking distance. As well, your powers of judgment and decision-making are reduced, and you take foolish risks. The more alcohol you consume, the greater the risk of having an accident, as shown in Fig 45. In fact, with a level of 0.05 you are more than twice as likely to have an accident as normal.

Questions

1   What does a blood alcohol concentration of 0.05 mean?
2   Use the graph to calculate the risk of having a crash when the driver has a blood alcohol concentration of 0.08, 0.10 and 0.14.
3   How many 375 mL cans of full-strength beer could an average person drink in an hour before reaching the 0.05 limit? How many cans of light beer?
4   Andrew drank three 375 mL cans of beer. How long will it be before all the alcohol is removed from his body?
5   Lauren, Ben, Stephanie and Michael got together for a few drinks one evening. This is what they drank in three hours.
Lauren: 4 glasses of beer and a vodka and tonic
Ben: a can of light beer and a rum and coke
Stephanie: a glass of wine and 3 glasses of orange juice
Michael: 5 pots of beer
   a   How many standard drinks did each have?
   b   Who is legally fit to drive home? (All have full licences.)

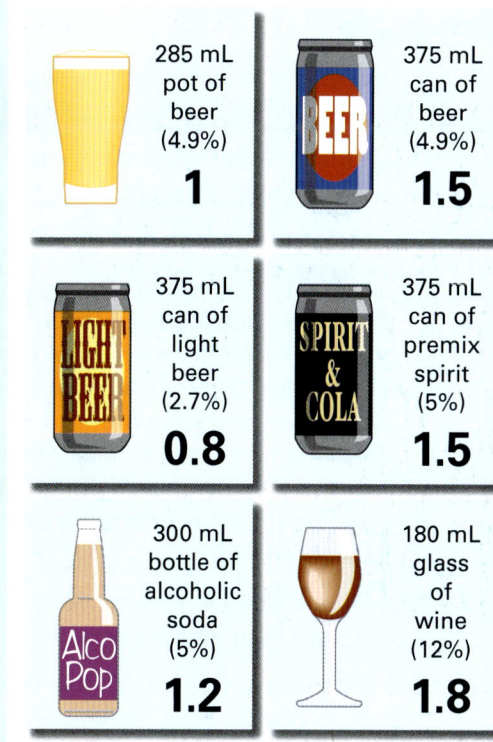

Fig 44   How many standard drinks?

285 mL pot of beer (4.9%) **1**	375 mL can of beer (4.9%) **1.5**
375 mL can of light beer (2.7%) **0.8**	375 mL can of premix spirit (5%) **1.5**
300 mL bottle of alcoholic soda (5%) **1.2**	180 mL glass of wine (12%) **1.8**

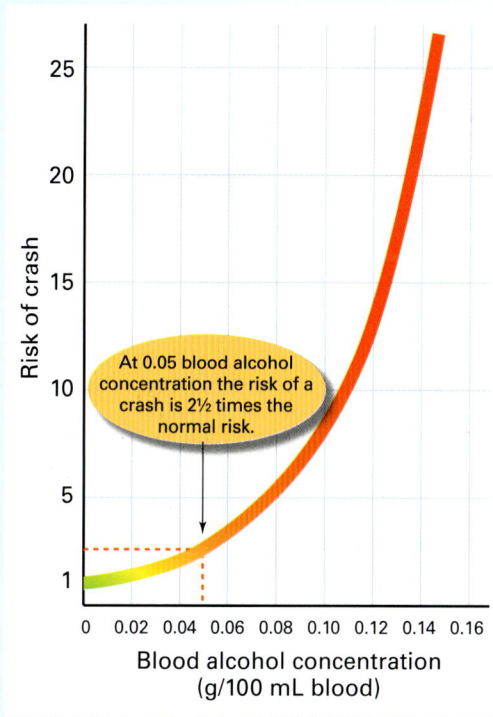

At 0.05 blood alcohol concentration the risk of a crash is 2½ times the normal risk.

Fig 45   Relative probability of crashing at various blood alcohol concentrations

Check!

1 A sports car and a semitrailer are both stationary. Which one has more inertia?

2 Most small trucks have a sturdy wall behind the driver's cabin. Why is this?

3 List at least five design features that have increased the safety of cars.

4 **a** Two cars have the same mass but one has an engine three times as powerful as the other. How would the acceleration of the two cars compare?

   b Two cars have the same engine but one has a mass one-quarter of the other. How would the acceleration of the two cars compare?

5 Why does a slowly-moving train have more momentum than a speeding bullet?

6 Use what you have learnt in this chapter to explain what is likely to happen to a standing train traveller when the train:
   a accelerates rapidly
   b stops suddenly.

7 Copy and complete the following table.

Force acting	Mass of vehicle	Acceleration
?	1000 kg	2 m/s^2
2000 N	500 kg	?
5000 N	?	5 m/s^2
10 N	?	26 m/s^2
?	1500 g	3.5 m/s^2
5 N	200 g	?

8 Put these four objects in order, starting with the one with the most momentum.
   • a 600 kg car travelling at 100 km/h
   • a 5 tonne truck travelling at 15 km/h
   • a 45 gram golfball in flight at 100 km/h
   • a 100 kg person cycling at 40 km/h

9 Suppose you are travelling at 60 km/h. Which of the following accidents is likely to be most serious? Least serious? Explain your answers.
   a hitting a wooden fence
   b hitting a large tree
   c hitting an oncoming vehicle

challenge

1 When the Space Shuttle takes off, its acceleration increases as it rises. Suggest why this happens.

2 Four-wheel drive vehicles are often fitted with bullbars. What is the purpose of bullbars? Do they protect the occupants of the vehicle in a head-on collision? Explain.

3 How fast would a 25 kg rocket be going if it started from rest and accelerated under the influence of a 350 N force for 6.5 seconds?

4 A spacecraft of mass 2000 kg is moving away from a space station with a speed of 100 m/s. It fires its main engines for 20 seconds. Its speed when it stops accelerating is 400 m/s.
   a What is its acceleration?
   b What is the force of the rocket engines?

5 What force must your seat belt be able to withstand if you hit a tree at 60 km/h and stop in 0.08 seconds? (Assume your mass is 70 kg.)

6 A football of mass 0.5 kg reaches a speed of 25 m/s as a result of a kick with an impact time of 0.22 seconds. Find:
   a the final momentum of the ball
   b the average force on the ball
   c the acceleration of the ball

7 A 5 kg trolley rests on a table. A horizontal force of 10 N acts on the trolley for 5 seconds. (Hint: use the equations in Extra for Experts on page 110, and assume there is no friction.)
   a What is the speed at the end of the 5 seconds?
   b How far does the trolley move in the 5 seconds?
   c If the force ceased to act after 5 seconds, how fast would the trolley be moving after 6 seconds?

8 A 30 tonne semitrailer travelling at 70 km/h brakes suddenly to avoid a collision. What force must the brakes of the semitrailer exert to stop it in 150 m?

Copy and complete these statements to make a summary of this chapter. The missing words are on the right.

acceleration
airbags
divide
force
equation
inertia
inversely
mass
reaction time
skid
slope
speed

MAIN IDEAS

1 To find average speed, _____ the distance travelled by the time taken:

$$\text{average speed} = \frac{\text{distance travelled}}{\text{time taken}}$$

2 The _____ of a distance–time graph gives the instantaneous speed.

3 Acceleration occurs when an object changes _____.

$$\text{average acceleration} = \frac{\text{change in speed}}{\text{time taken}}$$

4 Stopping distance depends on your _____, the speed of your vehicle, and the condition of the brakes, tyres and road surface.

5 Tyres grip the road by friction. When the wheels _____ the friction is less.

6 Inertia is the tendency of an object to stay at rest or continue its present motion, unless acted on by a _____. The inertia of an object depends on its _____.

7 The momentum of an object depends on its mass (m) and its speed (v). Momentum (M) can be calculated by using the _____ M = mv.

8 In a collision a car stops but the occupants have _____ and continue moving until they collide with some solid object. Seat belts, head restraints and _____ are designed to protect people in collisions.

9 The _____ of an object is directly proportional to the force acting on it, and _____ proportional to its mass.

$$a = \frac{F}{m} \quad \text{or} \quad F = ma$$

Try doing the Chapter 5 crossword on the CD.

Working with technology

REVIEW

1 The acceleration of a car moving at a constant speed of 30 m/s is:
A 30 m   C 15 m/s^2
B 30 m/s   D 0

2 A bus driver has a trip of 280 km to complete. If the average speed of the bus is 80 km/h, how long will the trip take?

3 Study the velocity–time graphs on the right. Which was made by an object:
a travelling at constant speed?
b accelerating?
c slowing down?
d speeding up and then slowing down?

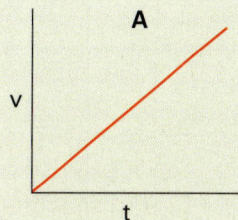

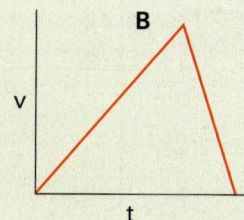

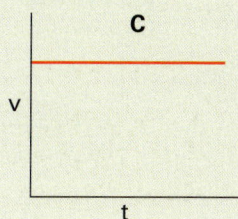

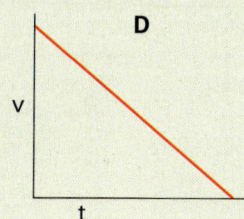

A, B, C, D velocity–time graphs

4 A sports car and a furniture van are both travelling at a speed of 60 kilometres per hour. Which vehicle would require more force to stop it? Why?

5 Scott was driving to the golf course. He braked to avoid a cat. Explain why the golf clubs hit Scott on the head.

6 The same person drives a motorbike, a car and a semitrailer at 100 km/h. Compare his reaction distances and braking distances for the three vehicles if he has to stop suddenly.

7 A car stopped at traffic lights is hit from behind by another car. Describe what happens to the people in:
 a the stationary car
 b the car that hit the stationary car.

8 a What is meant when we say 'the car's brakes locked'?
 b What happens to the car when this occurs?
 c What have car designers done to solve the problem of brakes locking?

Yeah, Sarge, it's a mystery. The victim appears to have been knocked out by a wood and a nine iron from inside the car. Witnesses say nobody left the scene.

9 Tim is riding his bicycle at a uniform speed of 15 m/s. He brakes and comes to a stop in 3 seconds. If he and the bike have a total mass of 80 kg, what force did the brakes apply?

10 The graph below shows the change in speed of a lift as it travels from the ground to the top floor.
 a Explain the shape of the graph.
 b At what rate does the lift accelerate?
 c At what rate does it decelerate?

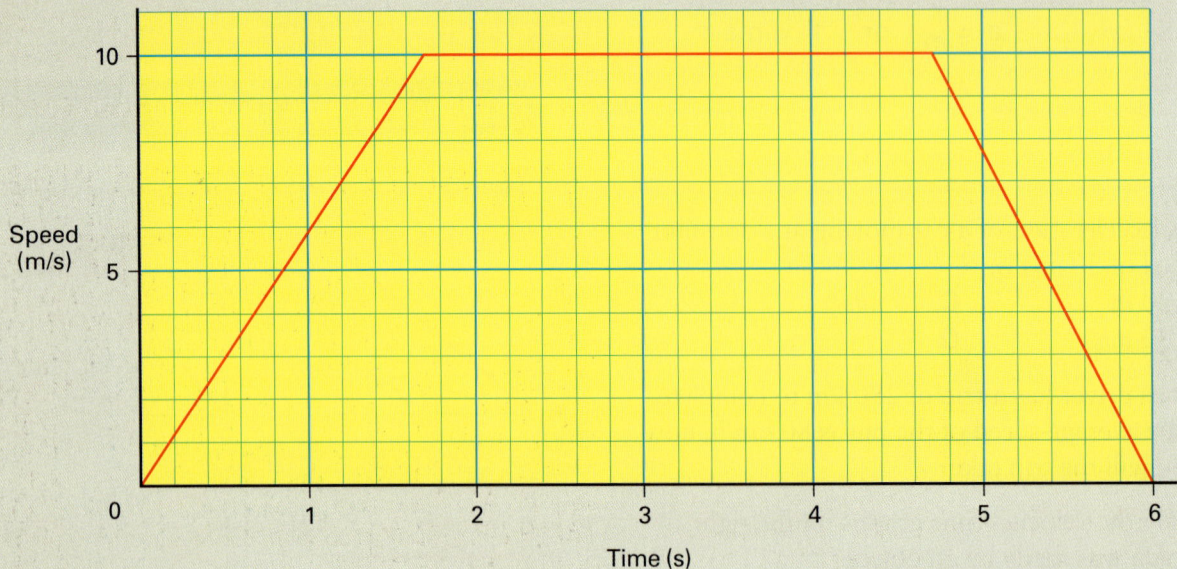

Speed (m/s) vs Time (s)

Check your answers on pages 333–334.

6

Our energy future

Getting Started

Working in small groups, decide whether each of the following is true or false. Afterwards you may be able to hold a class forum to discuss any questions where groups did not agree on the answers.

1 Coal, oil and natural gas are renewable resources.
2 Australia's coal reserves are predicted to last hundreds of years.
3 The Middle East has about two-thirds of the world's oil reserves.
4 Developing countries have about 50% of the world's population, but consume only about 10% of the world's energy.
5 Nuclear power stations do not produce greenhouse gases.
6 The reason there are no nuclear power stations in Australia is because we have no reserves of uranium.
7 Solar cells are almost 100% efficient.
8 Solar cells are 100 times cheaper than they were 25 years ago.
9 There are many wind generators connected to state electricity grids.
10 It is possible to generate electricity from the methane produced at rubbish dumps.
11 A small car uses less energy per person per kilometre than walking.
12 Electric cars are not as efficient as normal cars.
13 Fluorescent tubes use more energy than ordinary light bulbs.
14 Building a house with the living areas facing north can reduce heating costs.
15 It is possible for cars to run on hydrogen gas.

6.1 Energy today

How much energy do we use?

Imagine how much electrical energy you would use if you ran three 1000 watt bar heaters continuously throughout the year. The energy used would be about 94 thousand million joules $(94 \times 10^9$ J). This might seem an enormous amount, but it is the average energy each person in Australia uses each year. It is almost four times the world average, and 12 times more than our neighbours in Indonesia use.

How do we use energy?

In Australia we use 32% of our energy in industry, 41% in transport, 20% in homes and shops, and 7% in mines and farms. Much of this is in the form of electricity, but we also use large amounts of petrol and diesel for transport and industry, and gas for heating in our homes.

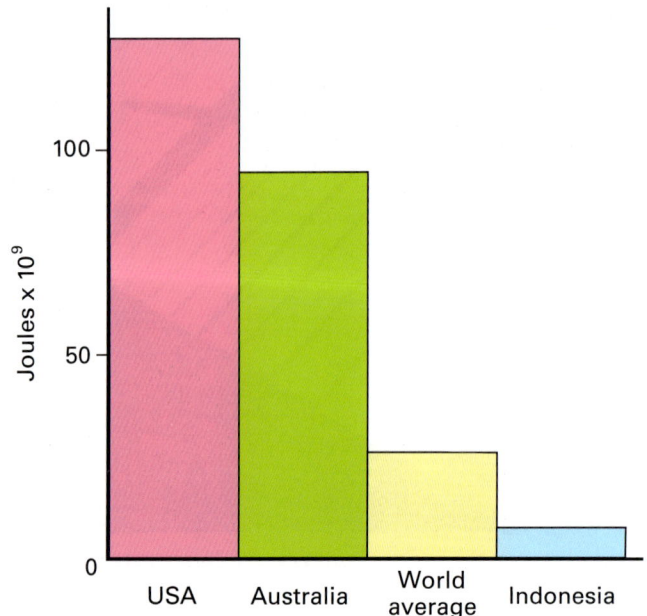

Fig 2 Energy used per person per year in selected countries, based on data from *BP Statistical Review of World Energy*, June 2006

Activity

The diagram below shows how much energy is used to make a loaf of bread.

What percentage of the energy needed to produce a loaf of bread is used to produce the wheat?

What percentage of the energy needed to produce the loaf is used in transport?

Do you think the amount of energy used to produce the loaf of bread could be reduced? How?

RETAIL 27% — 9% Shop heat & light — 18% Transport

BAKERY 49% — 9% Other ingredients — 24% Baking fuel — 8% Packaging — 8% Transport

MILL 14% — 2% Packaging — 7% Milling fuel — 3% Transport — 2% Other

FARM 10% — 7% Tractor fuel — 2% Fertiliser — 1% Other

Activity

Energy reserves	'Lifetimes' of world reserves from 2005 (in years)	Known Australian reserves in 2005 ($\times 10^{18}$ joules)	Annual Australian production ($\times 10^{18}$ joules)
oil	41	8	0.4
natural gas	65	96	0.5
coal	155	632	3.3
uranium	70	366	5 (all exported)

Source: *BP Statistical Review of World Energy*, June 2006, and data from Australian Uranium Association

Use the data in the table above to answer the questions below.

1 Which is Australia's largest energy reserve?

2 Use the equation below to calculate how long Australia's oil, gas, coal and uranium reserves will last at their present rate of use.

$$\text{lifetime} = \frac{\text{proven reserves}}{\text{annual production}}$$

Australia's production and consumption of oil (in thousands of barrels per day)		
Year	Production	Consumption
1981	449	624
1984	568	611
1987	628	625
1990	651	694
1993	572	720
1996	619	794
1999	625	843
2002	731	846
2005	554	884

Source: *BP Statistical Review of World Energy*, June 2006

3 Compare the lifetimes for the Australian reserves with the lifetimes of the world reserves. What do you notice?

4 Use the data in the table bottom left to plot a graph showing how Australia's production and consumption of oil have changed between 1981 and 2005.

 a Summarise in one or two sentences what the graph tells you.

 b Is Australia a net importer or exporter of oil?

 c Has our consumption of oil ever fallen? When?

 d Was Australia ever self-sufficient (relying on its own oil without importing any)? When?

 e Suggest reasons for the rises and falls in production.

 f In which year did we import most oil? How much?

 g If Australia's population was 20.3 million in 2005, how many litres of oil did each person use each day in that year, on average? (1 barrel = 159 L)

5 Oil makes up less than 1% of our energy reserves but 37% of our energy consumption. What does this mean for our future?

6 Why are we not using our reserves of uranium?

Problems with fossil fuels

From Fig 4 you can see that in Australia we obtain 94% of our energy from fossil fuels—coal, oil and gas. These are **non-renewable energy** sources. Once used they are not replaced, or replaced only very slowly, by natural processes. On the other hand, hydro-electricity, solar, wind, tides and waves are **renewable energy** sources. 'Renewable' means that they are always available or can be replaced as they are used. Provided they are properly managed, they should not run out.

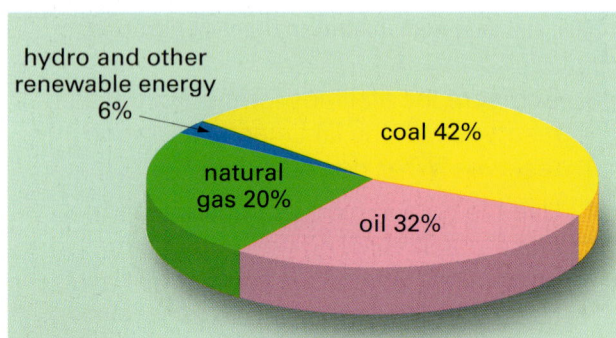

Fig 4   Australia's energy consumption (2005)

Oil is widely used in industry and transport, but Australia has limited reserves of it. The pie chart below shows that some countries have more oil reserves than others. In 2005 Australia produced less than 70% of its own oil, and this percentage will decrease as our reserves are used up. Much of our oil will have to be imported from the Middle East, an area of the world that has been politically unstable.

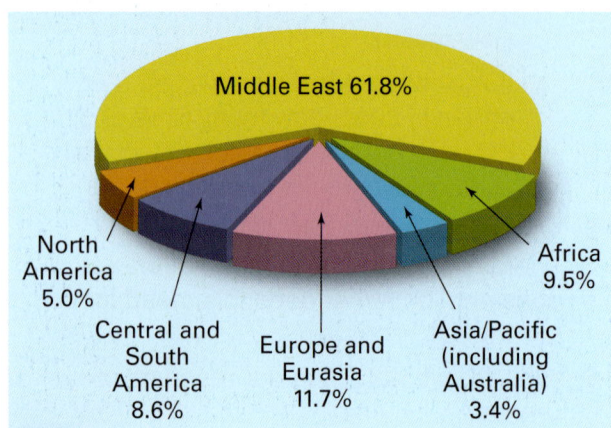

Fig 5   World oil reserves in 2005

The other problem is that the burning of fossil fuels releases gases into our atmosphere. Increasing levels of carbon dioxide are likely to lead to global warming and climate change; and other gases can lead to pollution problems such as acid rain and photochemical smog.

We use almost all our oil as a fuel, but it may be wiser to use more of it to make other materials. For example, you might be surprised to learn that the oil needed to make 100 litres of petrol (about two tankfuls) could provide the raw materials and energy to make a large number of useful items: for example about 20 polyester shirts, 6 garbage bags, 20 acrylic jumpers, a car tyre, 20 bicycle tubes and 500 pairs of pantihose!

The nuclear alternative

In contrast to fossil fuel power stations, nuclear power stations do not usually cause air pollution. The use of nuclear fuel not only conserves valuable fossil fuels, but also reduces greenhouse gas emissions and reduces the problem of acid rain. However, there are two major problems with the use of nuclear power: the disposal of highly radioactive wastes, and the risk of serious accidents occurring in nuclear reactors.

A nuclear power station uses the process of **nuclear fission**, and typically produces 25 tonnes of spent fuel each year (Stage 5 of the nuclear fuel cycle on the next page). Most of this spent fuel is uranium and plutonium which can be recycled (Stage 7), but there is almost 1 tonne of unused, highly radioactive material produced each year. These wastes can be solids, liquids or gases.

The first step in handling radioactive wastes is simply to let them sit for several months in shielded containers. The **half-life** of a radioactive substance is the time it takes for its radioactivity to halve. Substances with short half-lives decay enough to become safe during that time. However, substances with longer half-lives must be stored for hundreds, perhaps thousands of years and not allowed to escape into the environment.

For many years low-level wastes were cast into concrete, put into drums and then dumped at sea. This method of disposal has now been banned, because some drums started to leak. High-level wastes are at present stored in large concrete ponds. The water stops radiation escaping and removes the heat produced by the radioactivity (Stage 6 below).

Scientists are investigating various methods for long-term storage of nuclear wastes. One idea is to solidify the wastes in glass and seal them in stainless steel canisters. These canisters would be stored in deep underground caverns such as old salt mines (Stages 8–9). An Australian scientist,

Professor Ted Ringwood, invented an alternative rock-like material called *Synroc* for storing wastes, but this method is still being trialled.

The area where radioactive waste is buried must be free from earthquakes. Also, there are a number of questions about long-term storage which we simply cannot answer. For example, can we be absolutely sure of what will happen to the wastes over the next thousand years?

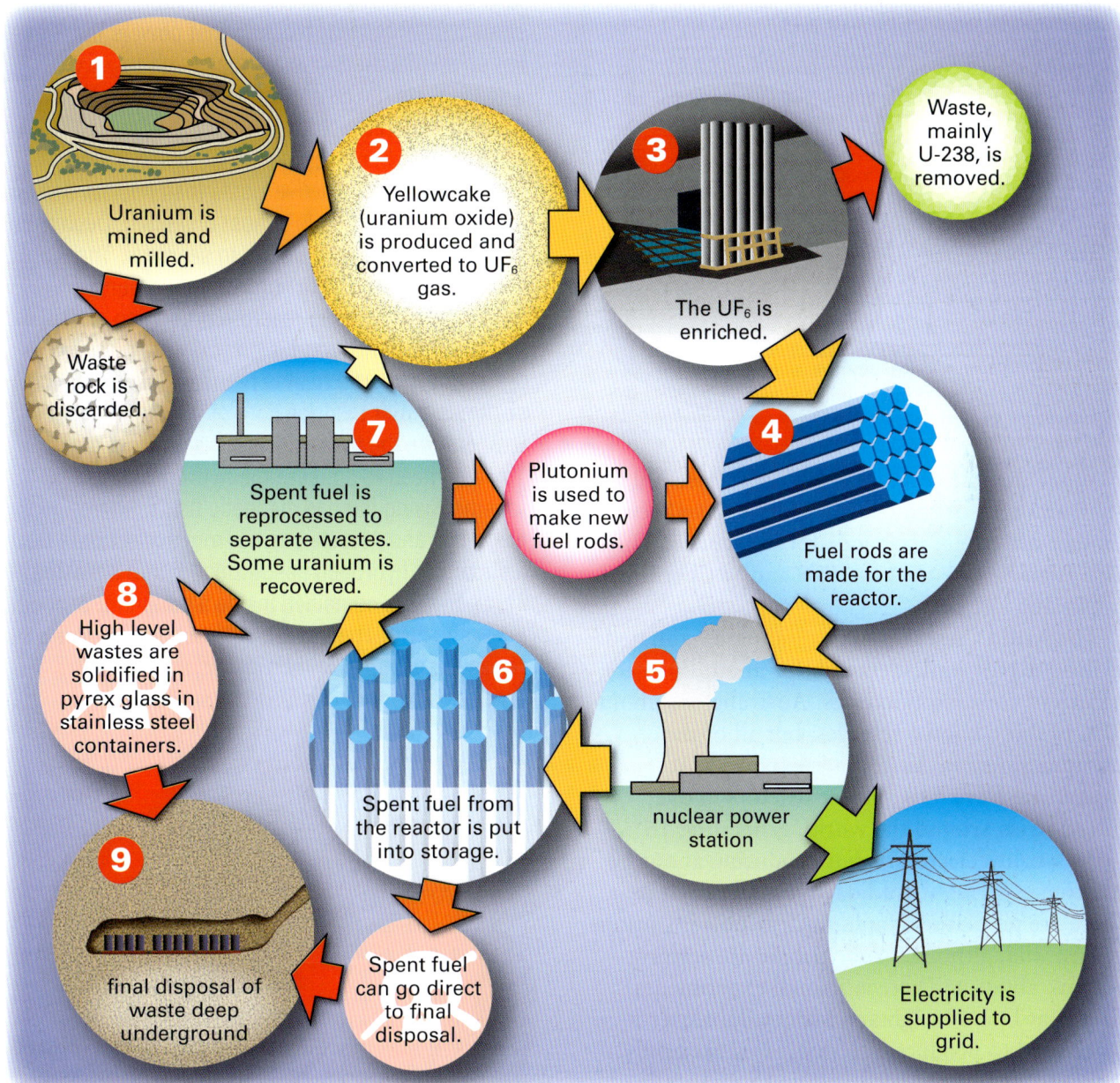

Fig 6 The nuclear fuel cycle

extra for experts

The half-life of a radioactive substance is the time it takes for its radioactivity to halve, or the time taken for half the atoms in a sample to decay. Suppose a substance has a half-life of 30 years. If the radioactivity is 200 counts per minute to start with, then in 30 years time it will be only 100 counts per minute. After 60 years it will be 50, and after 90 years it will be 25 counts/min. This information can be displayed on a graph.

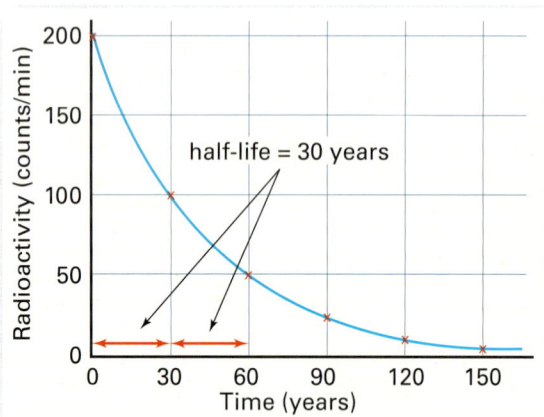

While nuclear reactors normally release only small amounts of radioactivity, there have been a number of serious accidents: for example at Three Mile Island in the USA in 1979 and at Chernobyl in Ukraine in 1986.

The world's reserves of uranium are estimated at 1800×10^{18} joules, enough for about 70 years at current consumption rates. Australia has about 30% of these known reserves, but all of the uranium mined in Australia is exported. At present there are 440 nuclear reactors in over 31 countries around the world, generating 16% of the world's electricity, but producing about 400 tonnes of highly radioactive waste each year. There are no plans to build nuclear power stations in Australia, although some people are starting to think about it. There is a small experimental reactor at Lucas Heights in Sydney. However it is not used to produce electricity. It is used only for research and the production of radioactive substances such as technetium-99 for use in medicine.

Science in action

Nuclear fusion

Current nuclear reactors use nuclear fission where you split large atoms of uranium to produce large amounts of energy. In **nuclear fusion** you produce energy when two small atoms join together to form a larger atom. For example, hydrogen atoms fuse to form helium atoms and neutrons. It's the same type of nuclear reaction that powers the Sun. For an animation of nuclear fusion, go to www.scienceworld.net.au and follow the links to **How nuclear fusion reactors work**.

The good thing about nuclear fusion is that it produces less radioactive waste than nuclear fission. Also, the fuel needed is almost unlimited. Deuterium, a form of hydrogen, is found in seawater. There are several experimental fusion reactors around the world, but no working reactors producing electricity.

To produce nuclear fusion you need a temperature of 100 million degrees Celsius—about six times hotter than the core of the Sun! At that temperature the hydrogen is a plasma, not a gas. You also need to squeeze the hydrogen atoms together using intense magnetic fields. Microwaves, electricity and particle beams from accelerators heat a stream of hydrogen gas, turning it into a plasma. This plasma is contained inside a doughnut-shaped magnetic field. The fast-moving neutrons that are released heat up a liquid which is then used to produce steam.

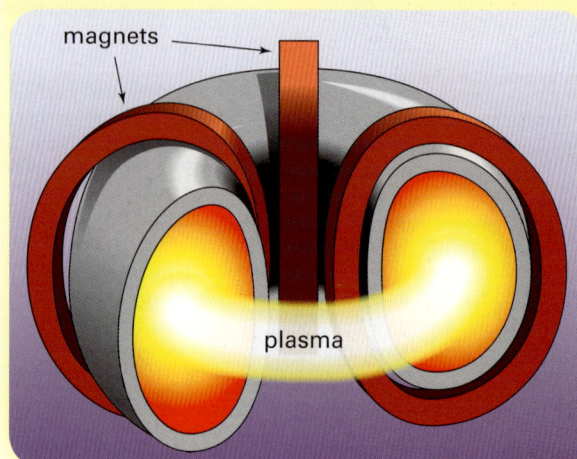

Activity

The world is running out of coal and oil and Australia has large reserves of uranium which can provide vast amounts of energy.

Nuclear power plants have leaked and dangerous radioactivity has escaped into the environment. In 1986 there was a major accident at a nuclear power station at Chernobyl in Ukraine, spreading harmful radiation across Europe.

Nuclear power stations provide plutonium which can be used to make nuclear weapons.

Nuclear power stations are cleaner than coal-burning power stations which produce dangerous gases that can add to the greenhouse effect.

There's enough coal for hundreds of years and there are energy alternatives that are safer than nuclear power.

Nuclear waste must be stored for thousands of years, and at present there is no proven way of doing this.

Mining of uranium is safer than coal mining. The nuclear power industry has strict safety regulations.

The debate about nuclear power has been going on for years. Since nuclear power stations were first built many people have vigorously opposed them. Others are just as strongly in favour of them. The main arguments for and against uranium mining and the use of nuclear power are summarised in the cartoon.

Postbox activity

On your own, answer each of the six questions opposite. Write each answer on a separate piece of paper and put them in the numbered boxes.

Form groups of about four, go through all the answers in one of the boxes and decide what is the correct answer. Report your answer to the class.

For extra information go to www. scienceworld.net.au and follow the links to these two websites. One is pro-nuclear and one anti-nuclear.

Uranium Information Centre

ANAWA Anti-Nuclear Alliance

1 What are the details of the nuclear accident at Chernobyl in 1986?

2 How many nuclear power stations are there in other countries? What percentage of the total electricity produced in these countries is nuclear?

3 Which produces cheaper electricity—a coal-burning power station or a nuclear power station?

4 Where in Australia is uranium mined? To which countries is it exported?

5 How does exposure to radioactivity affect people?

6 What is presently done with radioactive wastes? What future plans are there?

Here are some other things you could do:

- Have a debate for and against nuclear power.

- Role play an inquiry which has been set up to decide whether or not a nuclear power station should be built near your home.

- Write a letter to the editor of a newspaper in favour of or against nuclear power.

Check!

1 What is the difference between a non-renewable and a renewable energy source? Give an example of each.

2 **a** List reasons for looking for energy alternatives other than fossil fuels.
   b Why is finding a replacement for oil and gas more urgent than finding a replacement for coal?

3 Compare and contrast nuclear power stations and coal-burning power stations.

4 About 100 years ago the Russian chemist Dmitri Mendeleev said that burning petroleum 'would be akin to firing up a kitchen stove with banknotes'. Why do you think he believed petroleum was too valuable to burn?

5 Energy is used to produce the many foods we take for granted—for example, a loaf of bread (page 128). Think of a food and list the ways in which energy is used to provide the finished wrapped product ready for you to eat.

6 Suppose there is a leak in a nuclear reactor and highly reactive strontium-90 is released into the surrounding countryside which is used for dairy farming. Two months later breastfed babies are found to have small amounts of strontium-90 in their bodies. Explain how this could have happened.

7 Use the internet to find out what oil shale is, where it is found in Australia, and how it can be converted to oil.

challenge

1 The table shows the total nuclear energy produced in the world from 1981 to 2005.
   a Display the data on a line graph. (You will be predicting up to the year 2020, so think carefully about the units for the axes.)
   b Do you think nuclear energy production was affected by the Chernobyl disaster in 1986? Explain.
   c Use your graph to predict the nuclear energy production in 2010 and 2020.
   d Which one of your predictions is likely to be more accurate? Explain.
   e Compare your predictions with those of other people. How much variation is there? Mark the range of predictions for 2020 on your graph.
   f List factors which you think may increase the use of nuclear energy over the next 20 years. Also list factors which may decrease its use.

2 Use the nuclear fuel cycle on page 131 to answer these questions.
   a Which stages in the cycle produce wastes?
   b What happens at Stage 7?
   c Which is the longest stage?

3 You have 64 g of a radioactive substance with a half-life of 5 days. How much will be left after 5 days? After 10 days? How many days will it take for the mass to decrease to 1 g? Show this information on a graph.

4 Given that we are so short of oil, do you think that oil exploration should be allowed in environmentally sensitive areas such as the Great Barrier Reef? You could have a debate.

5 Use the internet to find answers to these questions:
   a What is the enhanced greenhouse effect?
   b What is the Kyoto Protocol?
   c What is carbon emissions trading?

Year	Nuclear energy production (million tonnes of oil equivalent)
1981	189
1984	282
1987	393
1990	453
1993	495
1996	545
1999	571
2002	611
2005	627

6.2 Renewable energy

At present we obtain about 94% of our energy from fossil fuels. However, some time in the near future these *non-renewable* resources will run out. We will then have to rely on *renewable* energy sources.

The largest energy source available to us is the Sun, and most of the renewable energy sources described in this section involve the Sun's energy—either directly, for example in solar water heaters, or indirectly, for example in plants grown by photosynthesis using the Sun's energy. Not all the renewable energy sources described are economically viable at present. However, as the prices of existing fossil fuels increase, the use of renewable resources will become more economical.

It is important that you have some knowledge of the range of energy alternatives described on the following pages.

Solar energy

The solar energy striking the Earth every minute is enough to supply the world's energy needs for a year! Most of this solar energy is transformed to heat on the Earth's surface, where it produces winds and waves. A smaller amount of solar energy is absorbed by plants during photosynthesis.

Solar energy can be harnessed in two main ways: for the production of electricity and for heating, for example in solar water heaters.

Solar cells

The Mars *Pathfinder* rover that landed on Mars in July 1997 was powered by *photovoltaic cells* or **solar cells**, which can convert light energy into electricity. The first solar cells were only 6% efficient, but efficiencies more than 30% are now possible.

Fig 10 Which of these energy resources are renewable and which are non-renewable?

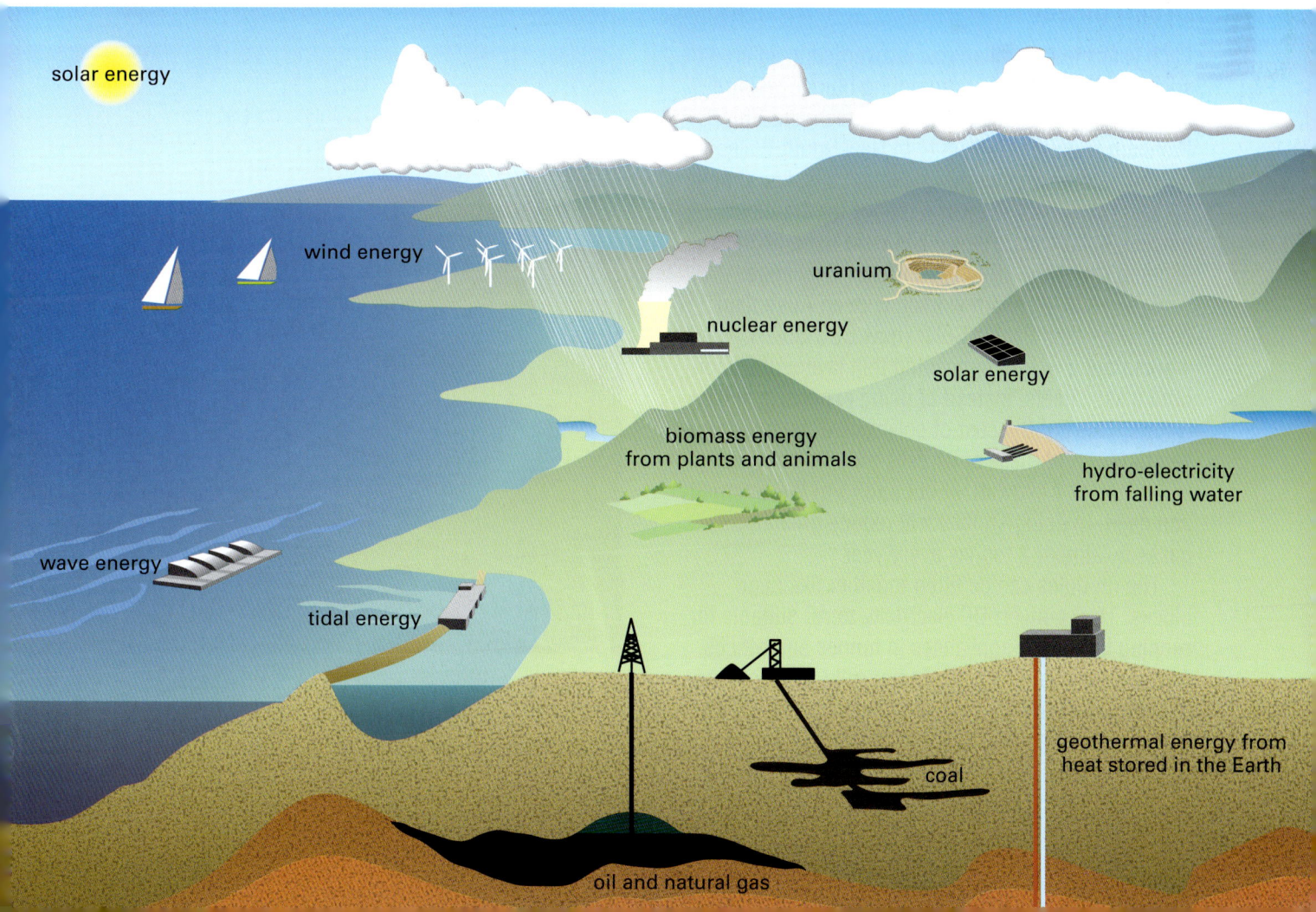

solar energy

wind energy

uranium

nuclear energy

solar energy

biomass energy from plants and animals

hydro-electricity from falling water

wave energy

tidal energy

coal

geothermal energy from heat stored in the Earth

oil and natural gas

The use of solar cells has become widespread in devices such as watches and calculators. They are also used to provide power to homes in remote areas, to pump water, and to operate roadside signs and street lighting systems.

There are three disadvantages of generating electricity using solar cells. Firstly, they are expensive. Secondly, they are less effective in cloudy weather and do not operate at night. Thirdly, large areas of land are needed for collection areas due to their relatively low efficiency. However, as the cost of solar cells decreases and their efficiency increases, they will almost certainly become more widely used. They are already 100 times cheaper than they were 25 years ago!

solar cells

Fig 11 The Mars *Pathfinder* rover

Science in action

For an animation of how a solar cell works, go to www.scienceworld.net.au and follow the links to **Photovoltaic energy**.

Working with technology

Green power

Each year the Australia Prize is awarded in an area of science and technology promoting human welfare. In 1999 it was awarded to Martin Green and Stuart Wenham from the University of New South Wales for their pioneering work with solar cells. For almost 20 years they held the world record for the most efficient solar cells. These cells were used by the winning car in the 1999 World Solar Challenge.

Green and Wenham worked with an Australian company called Pacific Solar (now CSG Solar). They worked out a way of depositing thin layers of silicon onto glass sheets, instead of using expensive silicon wafers. This cut the cost of solar power by two-thirds. Ten modules of these solar cells mounted on your roof will generate 1 kilowatt, about a third of the electricity you need. In doing so they will reduce greenhouse gases by almost 2 tonnes every year.

The modules can be fitted together like Lego blocks. They convert DC electricity to AC suitable for running lights and appliances in homes and offices. Any surplus electricity is automatically fed back into the electricity grid through the meter box, giving the owner a credit on their bill.

Fig 12 These solar panels generate electricity directly from sunlight.

Investigate
14 SOLAR CELLS

Aim
To investigate the efficiency of a solar cell or solar panel.

Materials
- solar cell or panel of solar cells
- small electric motor plus propeller
- variable resistor or a range of resistors
- milliammeter or multimeter
- voltmeter or multimeter
- connecting wires

Planning and Safety Check
Read through both parts of the investigation and design a data table for Part B.

Method
1. Connect the solar cell or panel to a small electric motor (preferably fitted with a propeller). Put the cell in bright sunlight and observe how fast the motor turns.

   📋 What is the effect of placing your hand over the cell?

   📋 Is the angle of the cell in relation to the Sun important? Which angle is best?

2. Set up the electrical circuit as shown in the diagram.

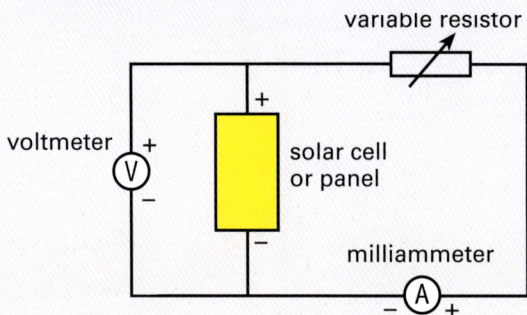

3. Place the solar cell or panel so that sunlight falls directly onto it.

4. Set the variable resistor to zero resistance and measure the current and voltage.

   📋 Record these values in your data table.

5. Increase the resistance in steps, recording the voltage and current each time. Stop when further increases in resistance have little effect on the current or voltage.

Discussion
1. For each value of the resistance, calculate the power output of the cell or panel using the following formula:

   power (watts) = voltage (volts) × current (amps)

   or   P = VI

   📋 Add the power values to the data table.

2. Draw a graph of power versus resistance.

   📋 What is the maximum power of your cell or panel? At what resistance does this occur?

3. How many solar cells like yours would be needed to power a 60 watt light bulb?

4. If the maximum power required by a household during the day is 3000 watts, calculate the number of solar cells like yours you would need, assuming sunny conditions.

5. What is the efficiency of the solar cell, assuming the average available power of sunlight is about 1000 watts per square metre?

   You will need to measure the surface area of the solar cell to find the maximum power *per square metre*.

   $$\text{efficiency} = \frac{\text{power of cell}}{\text{power of sunlight}} \times 100$$

⊙try this
- How does the angle at which the cell or panel is positioned affect its output?
- How does the light intensity affect the power output? (Use a light meter.)
- How does cloud cover affect the output? (To simulate cloud cover you could hold sheets of translucent material over the cell.)

Solar power stations

At Liddell Power Station near Muswellbrook in NSW a solar power system is being built beside the coal-burning power station. It consists of a giant array of flat mirrors which will eventually cover an area the size of four football fields. The mirrors track the Sun and concentrate its heat onto what is in effect a huge solar hot water system. The heated water is pumped into the power station where it is heated further to produce high-pressure steam to drive turbines and generate electricity. This solar power system will cut down on the amount of coal needed to produce our electricity.

Wind energy

Windmills have been used in Australia for many years to pump water. Only recently have wind generators been used to produce electricity.

A small wind generator can produce 40–50 kilowatts, enough electricity for a single house. A huge generator whose blades sweep a circle 80 metres in diameter can produce 1.65 megawatts of electricity. A normal coal-burning power station generates about 2000 megawatts, so you need 1200 wind generators to produce the same amount of electricity as a single power station!

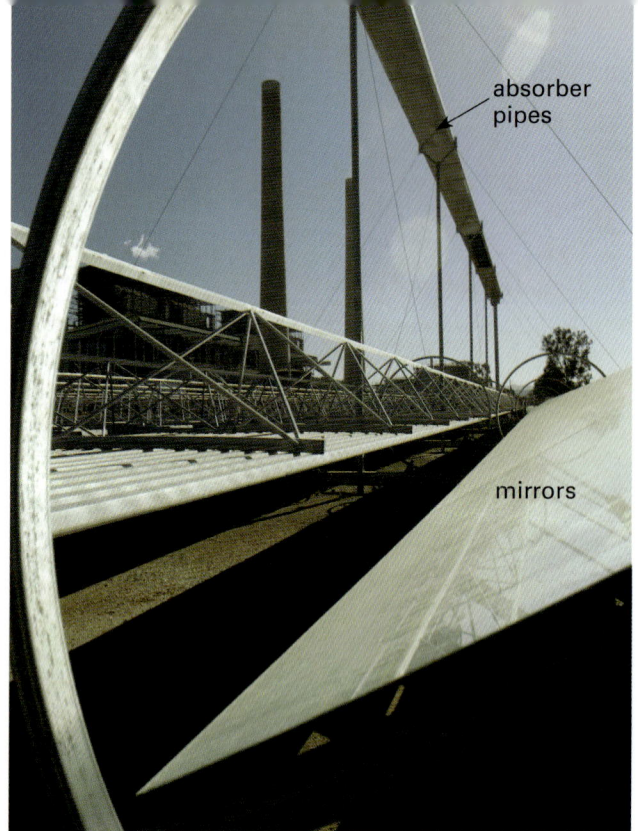

Fig 14 The Solar System at Liddell Power Station

Australia's largest wind farm is at Wattle Point on the Yorke Peninsula in South Australia (see Fig 16 on the next page). It has 55 wind turbines and generates enough electricity to supply more than 55 000 homes. Each turbine is 68 metres tall and the blades are 41 metres long. The largest wind farm in Queensland is at Windy Hill on the Atherton Tablelands.

Solar power tower

A Melbourne-based renewable energy company called EnviroMission is planning to build a solar power tower near Wentworth in south-west NSW. The proposed tower would be a kilometre high—the world's tallest structure. Around the base of the tower there would be a circular 'greenhouse' canopy of transparent plastic, about 5 km in diameter. The air under the canopy would heat up and rise up the central tower at 35–50 km/h. This rising air would spin 32 turbines mounted 40 m above ground level, generating 200 megawatts of electricity—day and night. This would be enough electricity to supply 200 000 homes.

A recent report written by CSIRO scientists estimates that a 35 square kilometre area with plenty of sunlight and little cloud could produce all Australia's electricity using solar power systems like this and the one at Liddell.

extra for experts

Wind generators

The power output of two different-sized wind generators was measured at different wind speeds, and the results recorded.

Wind speed (m/s)	Power output (watts)	
	Rotor blade diameter 3 m	Rotor blade diameter 6 m
2	15	60
4	120	475
7	400	1 600
9	950	3 600
11	1 840	7 360
13	3 180	12 760

1 Plot two line graphs on the same axes to show how power output varies with wind strength. Label the graphs carefully.
2 Write two generalisations about the power output of wind generators.
3 Use the data to work out what happens to the power output when the wind speed doubles.

4 A phone company wants to power outback telecommunication equipment that needs 1.5 kW to operate. Wind speeds in the area vary from 7 m/s to 11 m/s.
   a Which generator would be more suitable— the one with 3 m blades or the more expensive one with 6 m blades?
   b Would the generator you chose still be suitable in an area where the wind speed varies from 6 to 10 m/s? Explain.
5 The power that can be obtained from a wind generator operating at 50% efficiency can be calculated as follows:

$$\text{power (watts)} = 0.3 \times A \times v^3$$

   where A = area in m^2 swept by the blades and v = wind speed in m/s.

   a Calculate the power produced by a wind generator with 10 m diameter blades operating in a 10 m/s wind.
   b Use the equation to work out what happens to the power when:
   • the wind speed doubles
   • the diameter of the blades is doubled.
   c Are the wind generators in the table operating at 50% efficiency? Explain.

Fig 16 Wattle Point wind farm in South Australia

Biomass

Biomass is plant and animal material used as a source of renewable energy. It may be wood from forests, residues from agriculture and industry, or human and animal wastes.

In Australia we throw away over 10 million tonnes of household rubbish every year. Much of this is biomass and contains about the same energy as 3 million tonnes of coal. This rubbish can be used to produce electricity, as shown in Fig 17. When it is dumped and covered with soil, the breakdown of biodegradable materials produces *biogas*, which is mainly methane. PVC pipes that have a porous outer surface are partly buried in the rubbish, and pumps draw the biogas into these pipes. The gas is then burnt and used to generate electricity.

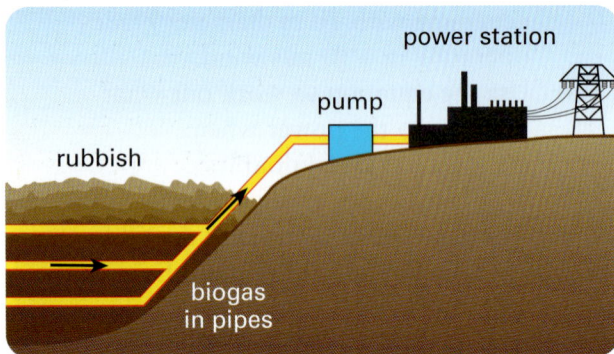

Fig 17 How a biogas power station works

Some processed food manufacturers are using waste peelings to produce biogas. This solves a waste disposal problem as well as producing useful heat energy for the factory. Some sewage treatment plants, eg the one at Luggage Point in Brisbane, use biogas to produce electricity to power the plant. As well as using a renewable energy source, such power plants use up methane, which is one of the gases thought to be contributing to global warming.

Hydro-electricity

In Australia about 3% of our total electricity is produced from falling water in hydro-electric power stations. However, hydro-electric power stations can only be built in mountainous areas, and there are few suitable sites remaining. Also, the building of storage dams can cause serious damage to the environment by flooding unique habitats. This is why a dam proposed for the Gordon River downstream from the Franklin River in Tasmania was never built.

An advantage of hydro-electric power generation is the ease with which generators can be started up and shut down. It thus provides a convenient and cheap way to supply the additional power needed during peak periods of use. Look at Fig 18. Water from the upper reservoir can be used to produce power during the day when demand is high, and at night when demand is low, the water can be pumped back into the upper reservoir for re-use.

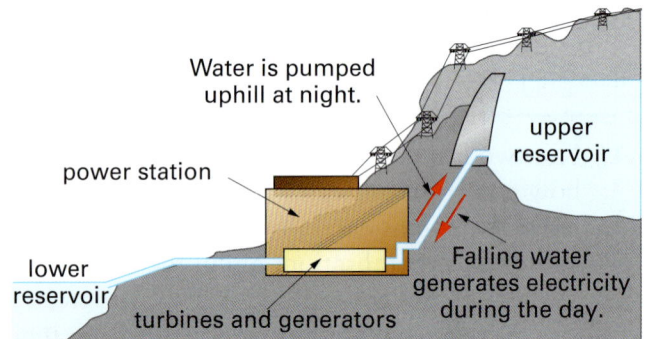

Fig 18 A pumped storage hydro-electric system

Tidal and wave energy

The tides contain vast amounts of energy, if only we could harness it. To harness the tides, you need to dam off a bay. As the tide comes in, water flows into a reservoir, driving turbines which generate electricity. As the tide goes out, water flows through the turbines in the opposite direction, generating more electricity. However, for this process to work effectively, you need large tides and these occur only in a few places.

The northwest coast of Australia is ideal for power generation because of the large tidal range there. A tidal power station is proposed near Derby, with dams across two arms of a tidal creek and a canal between them. With this design it is possible to generate electricity continuously. However, some people feel that damming the creek will damage the local environment.

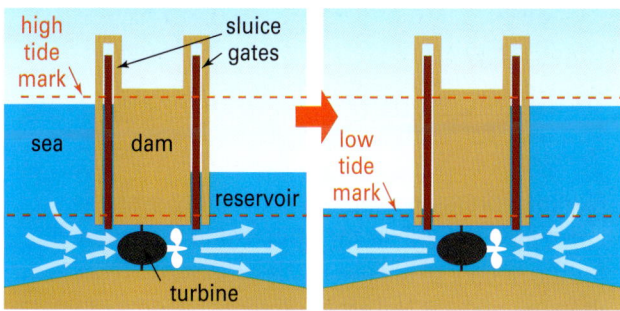

Fig 19 In a tidal power station the turbine can be driven by water flowing either way—from the sea to the reservoir as the tide comes in, and from the reservoir to the sea as the tide goes out.

Ocean waves also have a large amount of energy, as you will know if you have been 'dumped' by a wave. It is possible to use the up and down movement of waves to generate electricity, and scientists have suggested several different ways of doing this. One idea which has been shown to work is shown below. Another idea is to use floats which bob up and down on the waves. These floats would be expensive to build, but may be a possibility in the future. For an animation of these floats, go to www.scienceworld.net.au and follow the links to **The Salter duck**.

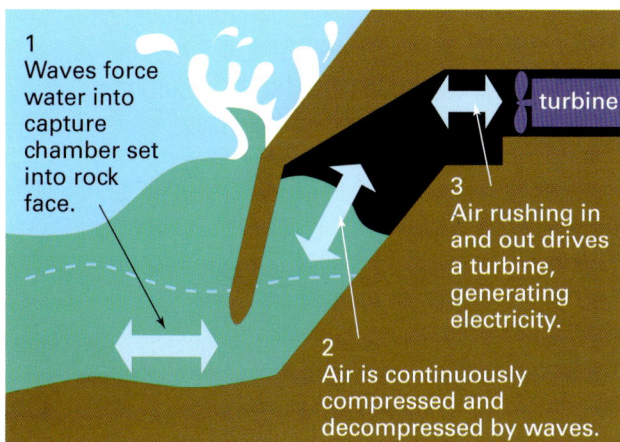

Fig 20 One design for a wave power station

Geothermal energy

Geothermal power stations make use of the heat inside the Earth. In some parts of the world there is a great deal of volcanic action and

hot water and steam reaches the surface. New Zealand, Italy, Iceland and the USA have all built geothermal power stations that use this steam to turn turbines and generate electricity. There are no such areas in Australia. However, if holes are drilled down several kilometres, hot granite rocks are found.

This granite contains radioactive elements like uranium and thorium which release heat as they decay. Suitable hot rocks have been found near Innamincka in north-eastern South Australia. The rocks are at a temperature of around 250°C and extend over an area of 1000 square kilometres. The sedimentary rocks on top of the granite act like a blanket, keeping in the heat. There is another smaller region of hot rock near Muswellbrook in New South Wales.

Water is injected into the central borehole and circulated through the hot cracked granite. The heated water is returned to the surface through the outside boreholes. It can then be passed through a heat exchanger where most of its heat can be removed and used to generate electricity. The water can then be returned to the first borehole and used again.

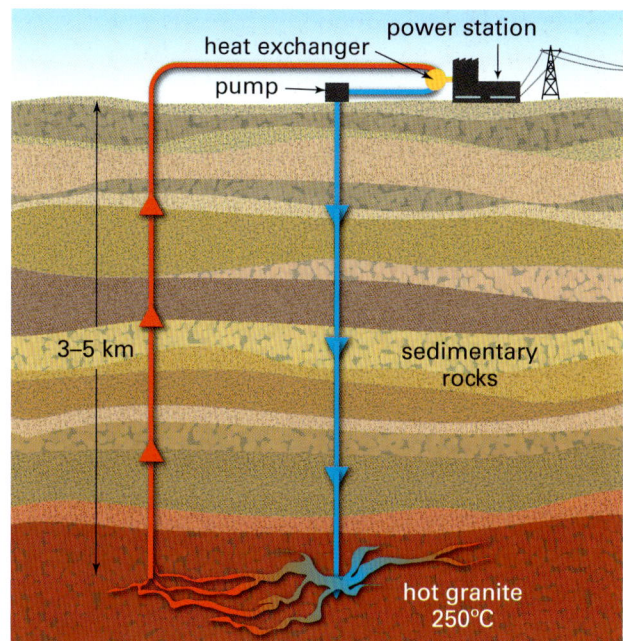

Fig 21 How electricity can be generated from hot rocks. For an animation go to www.scienceworld.net.au and follow the links to **HDR geothermal energy**.

Activity

Energy supply proposal

Suppose a mine is to be developed on the Nullarbor Plain in South Australia. Your task is to prepare a proposal for the supply of energy. You will work in small groups, each group representing a different company responding to the notice on the right.

Step 1: Select an energy system
Research all the energy alternatives available. Use the information on pages 135–141, but look for more detailed information by going to www.scienceworld.net.au and following the links to these websites.

Renewable energy (AGO)

Sustainability Victoria

Renewable energy (NSW)

To summarise your findings, draw up a table giving advantages, disadvantages and notes for each source.

Step 2: Collect information
Collect detailed information on your chosen energy system. Identify the strengths and weaknesses of your energy system, and suggest ways of overcoming any problems (as part of your proposal).

Step 3: Prepare proposal
Decide on a name for your energy supply company, and a title for your proposal. Then prepare the proposal for presentation to the group.

Step 4: Presentation
Present your proposal (5–10 minutes) on your energy supply system, including arguments for its use. You could prepare a *PowerPoint* presentation. Other students will ask questions about your proposal and try to identify weaknesses in your arguments.

Step 5: Discussion
To finish up, have a general discussion of the difficulties of energy supply systems on the Nullarbor Plain. Compare the Nullarbor with your local situation.

Nullarbor Mine

Tender for Supply of Energy System
Manufacturers and suppliers of energy systems are invited to register their interest in tendering for the supply of energy to the proposed uranium mine at Nullarbor. Potential suppliers will be required to provide a general description of their proposed method of energy supply. The proposed method should be cost-effective and suited to the area. The estimated energy requirement for the mine and settlement is 500 megawatts. All proposals must include an environmental impact study.

The Nullarbor mine is approximately 650 km west of Adelaide. The settlement is close to the main highway and about 125 km south of the railway, but it is very expensive to bring in fuel by road, rail or air.

No coal, oil or gas has been found in the area. It hardly ever rains and there are few cloudy days. There are no trees and no streams, but water can be obtained from underground bores.

Nullarbor is close to the ocean, at the top of 80-metre high cliffs. The average difference between high tide and low tide is 1.5 metres. The average wind speed is 8 km/h in summer and 25 km/h in winter, from the west.

Check!

1 What energy change takes place in:
   a a solar cell?
   b a solar water heater?

2 What is biogas? What can it be used for?

3 An experimental wave generator can extract 50% of the energy carried in waves. If many similar generators were placed along a 25 km front in waves with a power of 80 kW per metre, what would the total power output be?

4 What are the similarities and differences between a hydro-electric power station and a tidal power station?

5 A solar water heater costs about $2500 more than an electric or gas hot water system. However, there is a government rebate of $1000. If a solar heater saves 70% of water heating bills, calculate how long it would take for the solar heater to pay for itself. (Assume electric or gas water heating costs are about $350 per year.)

6 Draw a diagram to show how you could generate and collect biogas from household rubbish. What kinds of rubbish would work best?

challenge

1 Use the diagram below to answer these questions about solar heaters.

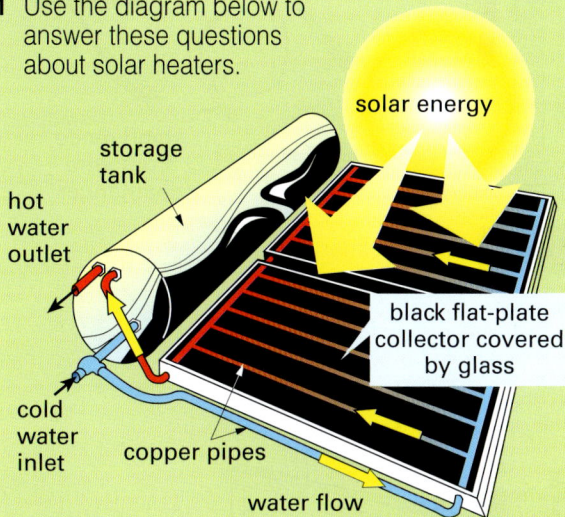

a Why is the collector covered with a glass plate?

b Would there be any advantage in using a plastic cover instead of a glass one?

c Why is the collector black?

d Why does the water move in a cycle from the storage tank to the collector and back to the storage tank?

e Why is the storage tank insulated?

f What advantage would there be in having the storage tank inside the house instead of on the roof?

g Why is the solar heater positioned on the roof so as to face in a northerly direction?

2 A coal-burning power station has a maximum generating capacity of 2640 MW. The average daily rate at which this area receives solar energy is 1000 W/m².

a What area of solar cells, operating at 15% efficiency, would produce the same amount of power as the power station?

b If a typical residential block of land in the city has an area of 750 m², how many of these blocks does your answer in a represent?

3 In 2005 Australia used 140 million litres of oil per day. Crude oil contains about 12% petrol.

a Calculate the quantity of petrol used every day in Australia in 2005.

b Alcohol is an excellent fuel which can be produced from sugarcane and other plants. Petrol containing up to 10% ethanol (gasohol) can be used in cars without making any engine modifications. Find the quantity of crude oil that could be saved if all the petrol in Australia was converted to gasohol.

c If we were to use gasohol instead of petrol we would need to use half our present farmland to grow energy crops like sugarcane. This means new farmland would have to be made by clearing forests. Discuss the pros and cons of this course of action.

d Suggest why alcohol is not used as a fuel in Australia at present.

4 Explain why the energy in wind and waves is sometimes called 'second-hand solar energy'.

5 We presently pay about 15 cents per kWh for electricity that is produced mainly in coal-burning power stations. Create a table of costs between now and the year 2020, assuming this cost increases by 5% per year. Then create a table of costs for electricity from solar cells, assuming it costs 50 cents per kWh now and decreases by 10% each year.

   Plot the two sets of data on the same graph, and predict when solar electricity will be cheaper than power station electricity.

6 Use what you have learnt in this section to decide which type of power generation would be most suitable for a small town of 500 people in each of the following locations. In each case explain your choice.
a an Antarctic base
b a small Pacific Island
c a valley in the mountains of Nepal
7 Is there any energy source that can be used without any environmental impact? Discuss this in a group.

→ try this

Your task is to design and construct one of the following:

- a solar water heater that will increase the temperature of about 4 litres of cold water by at least 20°C after standing in sunlight for one hour, or
- a wind or wave generator that will generate a small electric current.

Use these steps in your construction:

1 Use the diagrams on the right for ideas. Search for other ideas in the library or on the internet, and discuss the task with other people.
2 Draw a plan of your device before you start. List the materials and equipment you will need. You may need to ask your teacher for help.
3 Build a *prototype*—your first experimental model.
4 Test your prototype and make any necessary modifications. Then test your modified model.
5 Demonstrate your design to the rest of the class. Then prepare a written report, saying what you did, how successful your model was, and giving suggestions for improvements. (Your model may be good enough to enter in a science contest.)

Teacher note: You will need to do this outdoors.

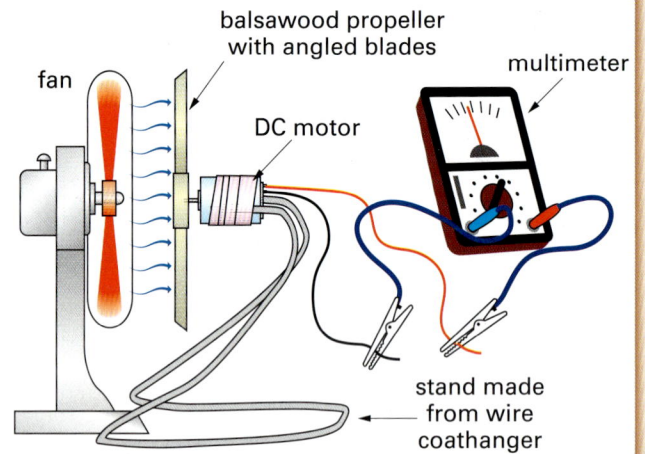
Fig 24 A wind generator

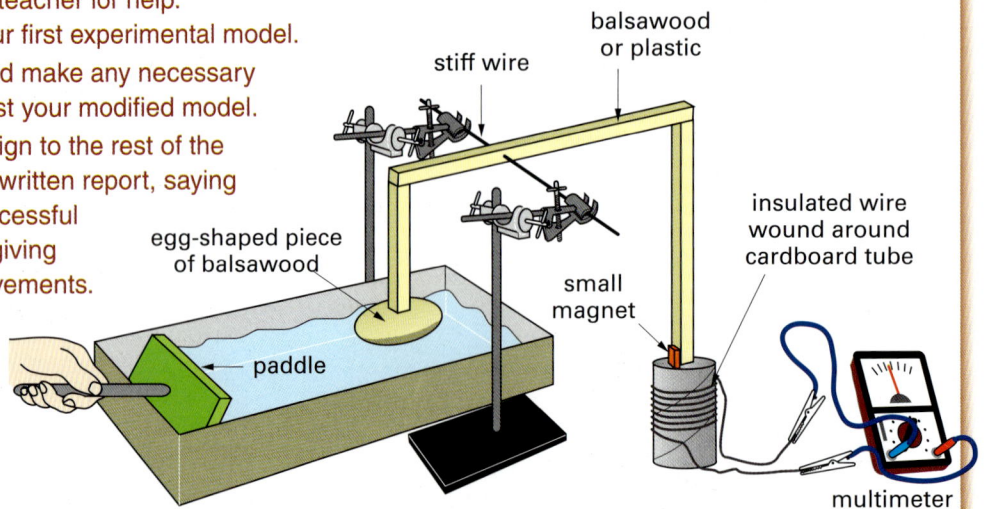
Fig 25 A wave generator

6.3 Managing energy

As the graph below shows, the world's use of energy has changed greatly over time. Combustion of wood was the main method of obtaining energy before 1900. Wood supplies once seemed inexhaustible and, like fossil fuels, satisfied most of the demands of the time. The clearing of forests and an increasing demand for a cheaper and more convenient fuel to operate machines led to the change from wood to coal and oil as sources of energy.

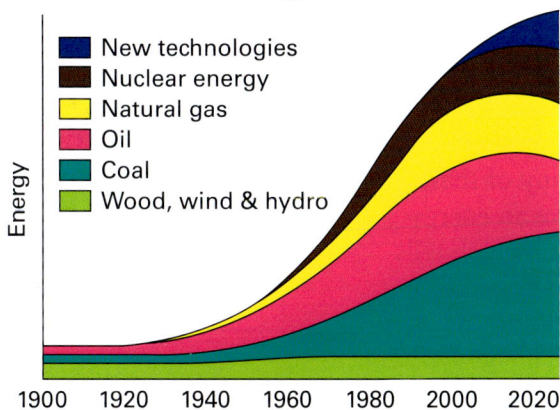

Non-renewable fossil fuels are our *energy capital*—like money in the bank waiting to be used. But once used, these resources are gone forever. On the other hand, the Sun's energy is supplied continuously. So is the energy of the wind and tides. These renewable resources will always be available. They are our *energy income*—like money from a permanent job.

Almost half of the world's energy needs are presently met by oil, but world oil supplies are predicted to run out in about 40 years time. This is like having a large tank of fuel which you keep

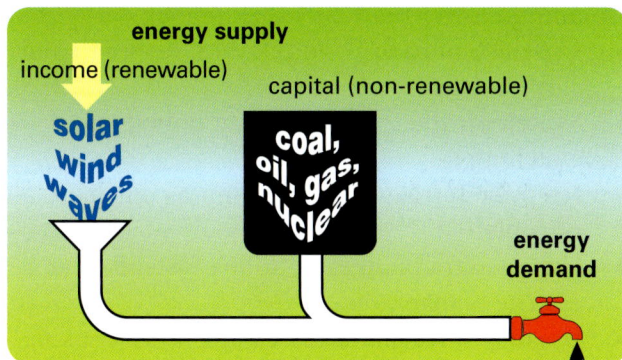

using. Eventually the tank will be empty! Demand cannot be greater than supply for any great length of time. Our energy capital is shrinking and cannot be renewed. However, we can decrease our energy demand by using less of our energy capital, and we can use more of our renewable energy income. At present most of this renewable energy is not used.

We do not yet know the best mix of energy resources for the future. However, it is clear that to slow down global warming and to reduce air pollution, there must be a significant reduction in fossil fuel combustion. Obviously we need to save energy where possible, and use energy more efficiently. We also need to make greater use of renewable energy sources.

Saving energy

There are many ways in which you as an individual can cut down on energy wastage. Below are a few ideas. For more ideas go to www.scienceworld.net.au and follow the links to **Global Warming—Cool It**.

Transport

About 40% of the energy used in Australia is used for transportation. So if we are to cut down on our usage of energy, we must cut down on the use of petrol for cars, diesel for trucks and kerosene for aircraft.

To get from one place to another requires energy. The table lists the amounts of energy needed for various methods of transport. Cycling and walking are by far the most efficient ways of travelling; travelling by car or by plane is very inefficient in terms of energy use.

Energy needed per person per kilometre (10^6 joules)	
cycling	39
walking	54
by train	390
by bus	480
by car	1350
by plane	1890

Many people prefer to travel to work or school by car. However, large numbers of cars in cities use huge amounts of petrol and also cause air pollution. For this reason people are being encouraged to use public transport. For example, you can travel by car or bicycle to the nearest railway station, and then travel into the city by train.

Our present petrol cars are only about 25% efficient. In other words, for every 100 joules of petrol you put in the tank, you get only about 25 joules of kinetic energy (Fig 28). However, there are other ways of powering cars. One of the most likely possibilities so far is the electric car. It is quiet, produces very little pollution, and has an efficiency of about 70%. The electricity for electric cars would probably come from coal, thus cutting down our use of oil.

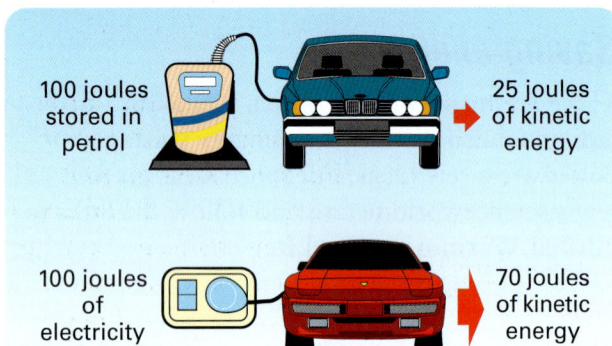

Fig 28 Battery-powered electric cars are more efficient than petrol-powered cars.

At present electric vehicles have a limited range. This means you cannot go far without recharging the batteries. What is needed is a better battery than the present lead storage battery, and much research is being done on this. However, hybrid electric vehicles are already available in Australia, eg Honda's Civic and Toyota's Prius. They have a petrol engine *and* an electric motor.

There are things which can be done to conserve petrol. Here are some of them.

- If possible, use a small car.
- Reduce your cruising speed. Reducing speed from 110 km/h to 90 km/h cuts fuel consumption by up to 25%.
- Share a car with a friend.
- Keep the engine properly tuned, eg check spark plugs regularly.
- Use good tyres, properly inflated.
- Keep well behind other cars, so that you do not need to brake when they do.

Electrical appliances

In prehistoric times the only energy available to humans came from the stored energy in the food they ate, and from their fires. We now have many electrical appliances to make life easier. Many of these have an energy label which tells you how efficient they are and how much energy they use.

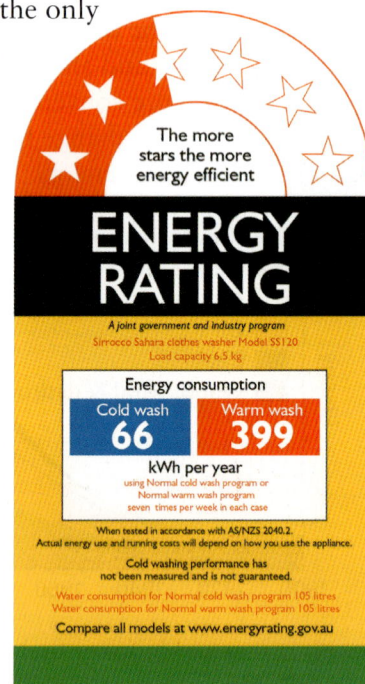

You could probably do without some electrical appliances. There are also many things you can do to cut down on the energy used by the appliances you do have. Here are some suggestions:

- Turn lights off when you don't need them.
- Fluorescent tubes are more economical than ordinary light bulbs, except when they are turned on and off frequently.
- If you have an airconditioner, set the thermostat no higher than 21°C during winter and no lower than 23°C in summer.
- Use the Sun to dry your clothes, rather than a clothes drier.
- Switch off the television when nobody is watching it.
- Keep the refrigerator door shut as much as possible.
- Use an extra blanket or doona instead of an electric blanket.
- Use only small amounts of water when cooking.

- Fix dripping hot-water taps quickly.
- Do not iron sheets and other items which do not really need it.

Activity

In a group discuss the suggestions on this page and the previous page for saving energy at home and when travelling.

✐ Which of the things suggested are you already doing?

✐ Brainstorm other things you could do to save energy.

✐ What factors might prevent you from implementing some of these energy-saving ideas? (For example, why don't you change to a solar hot water system?)

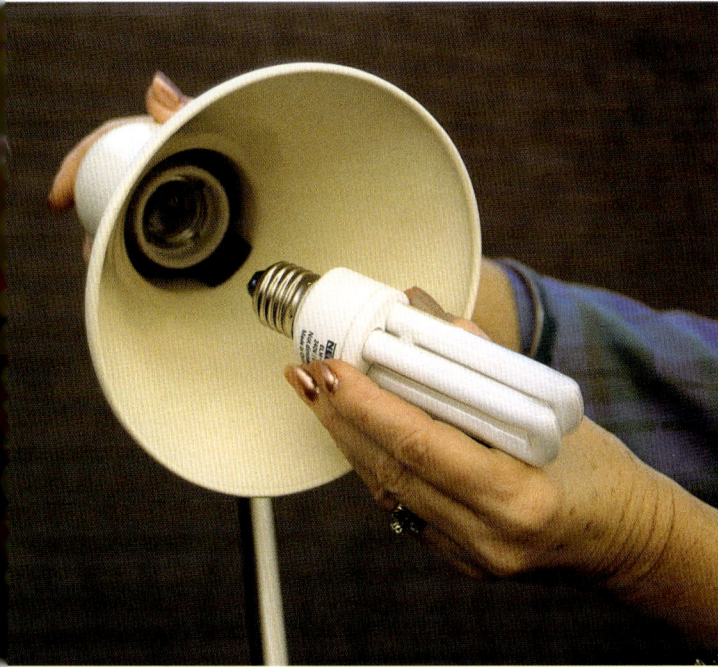

Fig 30 Low-energy light bulbs cost more but use less energy and last longer.

House design

In Australia about 15% of our total energy use is in the home. The amount of energy used for lighting, cooking and appliances is much the same throughout Australia, but the amount used for heating and cooling varies with the climate. Water heating costs can be reduced by using a solar water heater. Heating and cooling costs can be reduced by the design of the house and by insulation.

In Australia the Sun moves across the northern sky and is lower in winter than in summer. For this reason it is suggested that homes be built with the living areas facing north, so that the Sun will warm them in winter, thus reducing heating costs. Shading devices are needed in summer to stop the sunlight from reaching the windows. Deciduous trees planted close to the house also block the heat from the Sun in summer.

Insulation in the walls reduces heat loss during winter and heat gain during summer.

Fig 31 A house designed to reduce heating and cooling costs

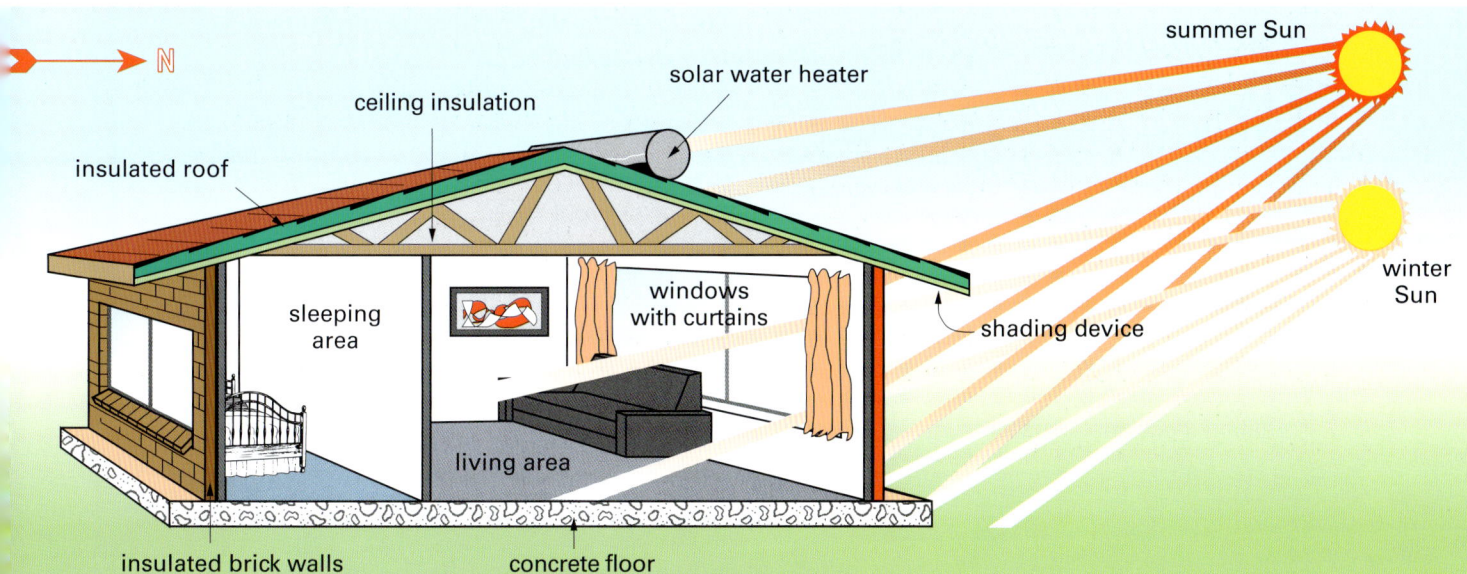

Experiment
A MODEL HOUSE

Your task

To design a model house to test the effectiveness of insulation

Planning and Safety Check

Read through the Method ideas and work out a plan for your experiment. If you are going to do it over 24 hours you will need a safe place to leave the equipment set up.

Materials

- shoebox or similar box with lid
- scissors
- clear plastic (for windows)
- 2 thermometers or temperature probes and datalogger
- insulation materials, eg corrugated cardboard, styrofoam, aluminium foil, woollen cloth

Method ideas

1 Use the shoebox (or other box) to make a model house similar to the one in the diagram. Make sure the house has:

- a window covered in clear plastic in each wall, and a door
- a well-fitting roof
- one thermometer on the outside and one on the inside that can be read without removing the roof.

2 To heat the house, place it in the sun or near an electric heater or high-wattage light bulb.

    How often should you record temperatures?

3 To test the effectiveness of insulation you will need to do the experiment with and without insulation and compare the results.

Discussion

1 Which are the independent and dependent variables in this experiment? Which variables did you control?

2 Write a brief report on the effectiveness of insulating the model house.

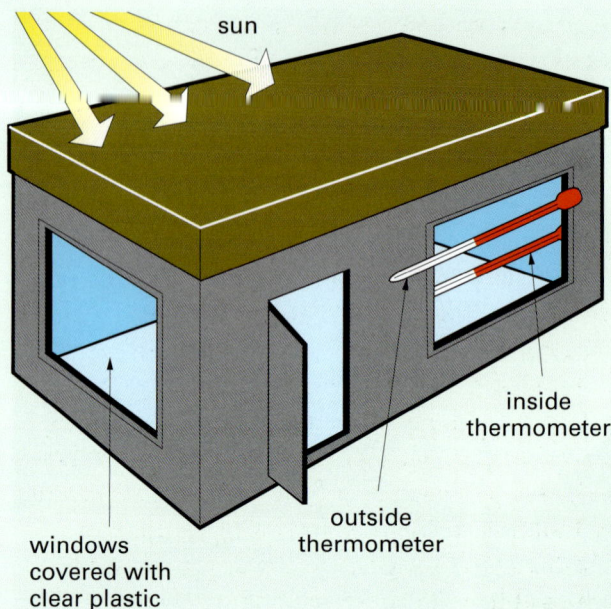

sun

inside thermometer

outside thermometer

windows covered with clear plastic

3 Compare your results with those of other groups. Which is the best insulating material?

4 Suggest reasons for any unusual results.

5 Evaluate your experiment and suggest ways of improving it.

try this

You could extend your experiment into a project by investigating some of these questions:

- How quickly does the house cool after the Sun sets?
- Does the thickness of the insulation make any difference?
- Do curtains on the windows make any difference?
- What effect does an overhang (eaves) on the roof have?
- What difference does altering the number of windows and their position have?
- Does the type of roofing material make any difference?

The electricity grid

Electricity is a convenient form of energy because it can be transmitted from one place to another, it can be switched on and off, and it can be used as a source of power for many different appliances. In Australia and in most countries our lifestyle has come to depend on electricity.

Power stations produce this electricity, which is transmitted to our homes and to industry via a vast network of mostly overhead cables called the *electricity grid*. All the power stations in the state are inter-connected, and if there is not enough electricity in one part of the grid it can be obtained from another part. Similarly, excess electricity can be fed into the grid and used elsewhere. Electricity generated using renewable energy sources such as solar cells, wind generators and biomass can also be fed into the grid.

Instead of connecting to the electricity grid, it is possible to be energy self-sufficient using a system called Remote Area Power Supply (RAPS). In a typical RAPS system, electricity is generated by solar cells and a wind generator. There is also a backup generator and batteries to store electricity.

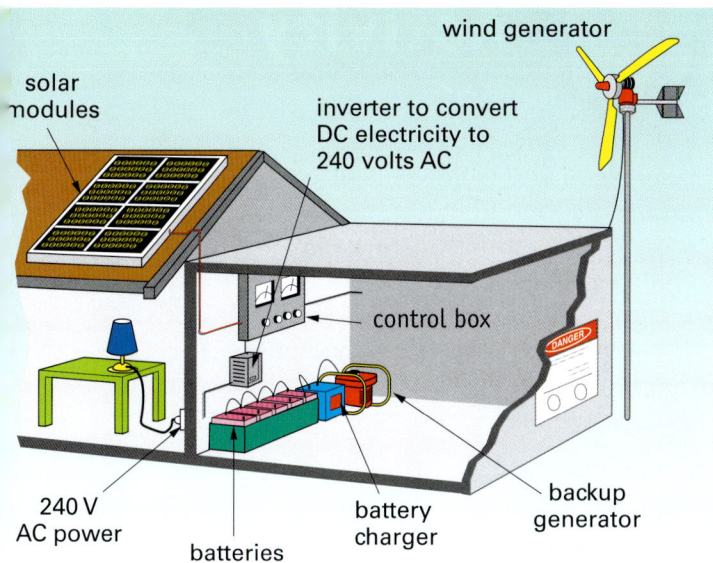

Fig 33 A Remote Area Power Supply (RAPS) can be used in towns and cities, as well as in remote areas where it is not possible to be connected to the electricity grid.

Hydrogen—fuel of the future

Take an imaginary journey into the future.

It is the year 2100, in the middle of a busy city. The traffic is remarkably quiet and there are no smelly exhaust fumes. Most of the cars, trucks and buses are using hydrogen fuel and produce little more than harmless water vapour. There are no electric power lines and no chimneys spewing tonnes of harmful gases into the atmosphere. As you move into the industrial area you notice a row of large storage tanks. These store liquid hydrogen which is piped into the city and used for transportation, heating, cooling and electricity. You travel to the country and find huge solar panels and wind farms generating electricity to produce the hydrogen.

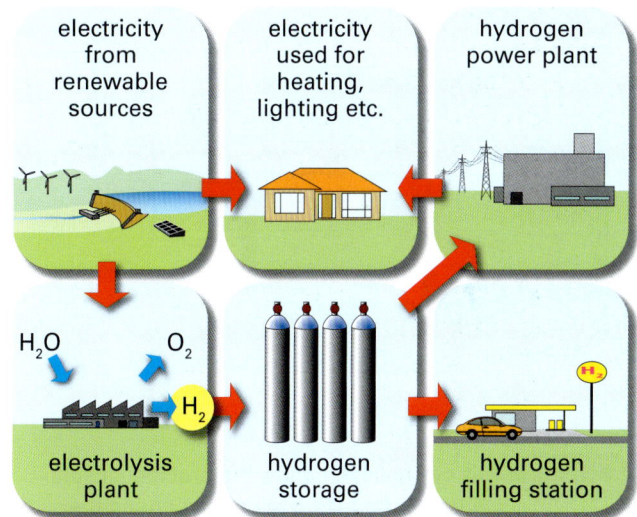

Fig 34 A possible hydrogen energy system—for an animation of this, go to www.scienceworld.net.au and follow the links to **miniHydrogen**.

This science fiction may come true in the future. Most of the technology already exists, but there are many obstacles to be overcome—mainly cost. Hydrogen is an ideal fuel. It can be made from water by electrolysis—passing an electric current through it.

$$2H_2O + \text{ENERGY} \rightarrow 2H_2 + O_2$$

Making hydrogen this way uses up more energy than the gas gives up when it burns in oxygen. However, this problem could be overcome by making the hydrogen using renewable energy sources such as solar cells. Scientists are also experimenting with other ways of making hydrogen. For example, certain photosynthetic microbes produce hydrogen using light energy. The hydrogen can be used directly as a fuel or it can be used to generate electricity using **fuel cells**.

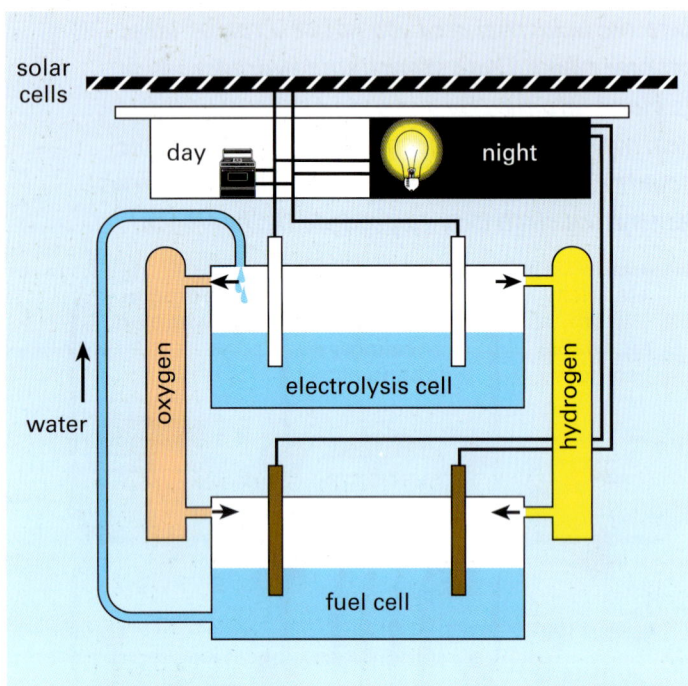

$$2H_2 + O_2 \rightarrow 2H_2O + \text{ENERGY}$$

Fig 35 This system overcomes the problem of solar cells only producing electricity during the day. Some of the electricity generated during the day by solar cells is used to electrolyse water into hydrogen and oxygen. At night the hydrogen and oxygen are recombined in a fuel cell to produce electricity.

Two big advantages of hydrogen are that it can store energy and it is easily transportable. It can be liquefied and used as a motor fuel in the same way that LPG is used now. One problem with hydrogen is that it is flammable. This problem, however, can be overcome using a storage tank containing fine particles of a metal alloy that absorbs hydrogen like a sponge, forming a compound known as a metal hydride. Heating the tank releases the hydrogen gas slowly and safely.

Our energy future

We seem to use energy as though it were unlimited. We buy more and more electrical gadgets: high-rise office blocks are airconditioned all year round, with windows that do not open; city lights blaze all night; we drive to the corner shop instead of walking; and so on. We just seem to take energy for granted. However, our energy reserves are very limited—especially oil, from which we get petrol for our cars. Fossil fuels will one day be exhausted, and alternative energy sources will have to be developed to replace them.

Many alternative sources such as wind and solar are being used to supplement our power needs, and scientists and engineers will no doubt develop new ways of harnessing energy. But *science cannot provide all the answers*. Before we use new energy sources we must consider any possible environmental problems they might cause. Different sources of energy have different problems, and no energy source is trouble free. We must choose wisely from the alternatives. Energy is a very valuable resource. Without it we could not live as we do now.

Activity

Electricity from renewable sources such as solar, wind and biomass is at present more expensive than from non-renewable sources such as coal-burning power stations. Most energy supply companies will buy renewable energy if you pay them $3–4 extra per week. This not only conserves our reserves of non-renewable energy but also cuts down on greenhouse gas emissions.

✎ Suggest why energy from renewable sources is called *green power*.

✎ Do you think you would pay extra for green power? Explain.

✎ At present only 1% of people are paying extra for green power. What would need to be done to get more people to switch to green power?

Science in action

Light up the world

Dave Irving-Halliday is an electrical engineer at the University of Calgary in Canada. In 1997 he was trekking in Nepal when he saw a sign outside a schoolhouse in a small village inviting people to stop and help teach the children. He went inside and was shocked to find the students working in semi-darkness. His first thought was *Gosh, it's dark in here*, followed by *I wonder if I can help them?*

As Dave travelled back to Canada he was thinking about the challenge of lighting homes in remote villages around the world. He realised that he would have to come up with a system that was extremely cheap and reliable. He had an important thought— *Why light a whole house, when you only need light in certain areas?* He decided to investigate light-emitting diodes (see page 82). These were invented in the 1960s and were gradually becoming brighter and more efficient. They could also last for 30 or 40 years. However, because they emitted only coloured light, they were unsuitable for domestic lighting.

After a year trying to develop his own white LEDs, Dave was surfing the web when he found that a Japanese company called Nichia had already solved the problem. When he got hold of one of these new white LEDs, he exclaimed to his assistant *Good God, John. A child could read by the light of a single diode!* So he set up a foundation called 'Light up the World' and began developing a multi-diode lamp to light homes in Nepal. He also developed a simple pedal generator and a small wind turbine to power the lamps. He returned to Nepal in 2000, where he teamed up with another engineer, Stewart Craine, from the University of Melbourne, who had been working with Australian Volunteers International.

Today Dave's lamps can provide limited lighting for a Nepalese village of 60 households for the same amount of energy as a single 100-watt lightbulb in one room of an Australian home. The lamps have also spread to India, Sri Lanka, Africa and South America. A father of five in a Sri Lankan village said, *This is the first time in the lives of my children that they have been able to read at night.*

Fig 36 Dave Irving-Halliday with his lamps, outside a village in Sri Lanka

Dave set up a company called Pico Power Nepal in Kathmandu. It manufactures lighting systems and sells them at affordable prices to the villagers. Nepalese households spend half their $330 annual income on batteries for torches and kerosene for lamps. So with the new lamps, they don't need as much kerosene, and the use of rechargeable batteries means fewer used batteries are thrown away.

For the first five years the Light up the World Foundation was funded entirely by Dave and his wife, but lately people around the world have supported the foundation with donations.

Questions

1 Why can't normal lights be used in Nepalese villages?
2 What was the scientific breakthrough that enabled Dave to fulfil his dream to 'light up the world'?
3 What provided the power for Dave's white LED lamps?
4 In what way is the white LED lamp good for the environment of developing countries like Nepal?
5 What lessons can we in Australia learn from this story?

Check!

1 Answer the true–false questions in the Getting Started on page 127 again. Have any of your answers changed?

2 How do the following help conserve energy and reduce greenhouse gas emissions?
  a wearing a jumper inside the house on cool nights
  b using lids on pots when cooking vegetables
  c using public transport instead of your own car
  d recycling cans, bottles and paper
  e using only small amounts of water when cooking
  f repairing things that break down instead of replacing them

3 In a group discuss the advantages and disadvantages of the RAPS system in Fig 33 on page 149.

4 This sign was painted on the side of an experimental vehicle which used an alternative fuel: $2H_2 + O_2 = No\ Smog$
  a Suggest what the fuel was.
  b Explain what you think the sign means.

5 Write down a list of electrical appliances that you use which you feel are:
  a essential to your present lifestyle
  b not essential to your present lifestyle.

6 Assuming that each kilowatt-hour of electricity produces about 1.2 kg of CO_2, check your family's electricity bills and determine how much carbon dioxide your family produces each year.

7 Use the internet to research fuel cells and hydrogen cars.

challenge

1 Use the graph on page 145 to answer these questions.
  a Calculate the proportion that each energy source contributes to the world's present energy use.
  b How are these proportions expected to change by the year 2020?
  c Which energy source would you expect to make up the greatest proportion in the year 2050? Explain your answer.
  d Use the graph to predict when the world reserves of oil will run out.

2 Write a story describing what could happen if we don't manage our energy resources wisely.

3 The graph on the right relates quality of life to the amount of energy used by different countries.
  a What does 'quality of life' on the vertical axis mean?
  b Give an example of a developing country.
  c Would you say that Australia is an 'over-developed' country? Explain.
  d Explain what the graph tells you.

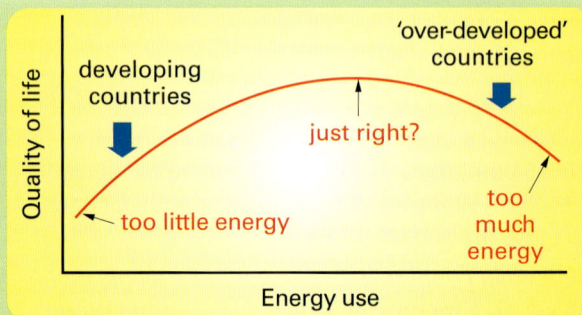

4 You are trying to decide which type of lights to put in your new home. The table gives technical data for five different types of household lights which produce about the same amount of light.

Type of lighting	Unit cost	Lifetime (hours)	Power (watts)
incandescent globe	$1	1000	60
fluorescent tube	$4	5000	40
compact fluorescent	$10	8000	15

If the cost of electricity is 15 cents per kWh, which type of lighting would be the cheapest to run over 8000 hours? (Hint: take into account the running costs and cost of replacement bulbs/tubes.)

![Main Ideas lightbulb logo]

Copy and complete these statements to make a summary of this chapter. The missing words are on the right.

1 Most of our present energy sources (coal, _____ and natural gas) are _____ and will be used up in the near future.

2 Nuclear reactors do not cause air pollution, but have two major problems: the possibility of reactor _____ and the disposal of _____ wastes.

3 Solar energy can be converted to electricity in solar cells and to _____ in solar water heaters and solar power stations.

4 Some _____ sources of energy are solar, hydro-electricity, wind, tides, waves, geothermal and _____.

5 Renewable energy sources will have to be used more widely to keep up with the world demand for energy and to reduce _____ emissions.

6 Some ways in which we can save energy are:
- use smaller cars or share cars,
- use _____ rather than private cars,
- _____ our homes
- reduce our use of _____ wherever possible.

accidents
biomass
electricity
greenhouse gases
heat
insulate
non-renewable
oil
public transport
radioactive
renewable

Try doing the Chapter 6 crossword on the CD. *Working with technology*

REVIEW

1 Which one of the following is a non-renewable energy source?
A solar energy
B tidal energy
C coal
D wood

2 The main advantage of solar energy over other energy sources is that it:
A is unlimited.
B can be converted into heat energy.
C can be converted into electrical energy.
D can be used only during the day.

3 At a particular place at midday the power of the sunlight is about 500 watts per square metre. This energy can be converted to electricity using solar cells which are about 10% efficient.

To run a one kilowatt electric motor, the area of solar cells required (square metres) would be:
A 2   C 50
B 20   D 500

4 The devices listed below all generate electricity from a source of energy.
a solar cell
b coal-burning power station
c wind generator
d hydro-electric power station
e geothermal power station

For each device, select the appropriate source from the following:

heat energy   potential energy
chemical energy   light energy
kinetic energy   nuclear energy

REVIEW

5 The graph on the right shows world usage of energy from 1989 to 2005.

  a How much energy was used per day during 1995?

  b In which year did energy use first exceed 10×10^9 tonnes of oil equivalent per day?

  c Why is it difficult to use this graph to predict our energy use in 2015?

6 The Australian government's greenhouse program suggests we try to cut down our use of energy. How would this reduce global warming?

7 The graph below is a forecast of energy supply and demand for Bananaland.

  a What is meant by 'energy demand'? What is 'energy supply'?

  b Suggest how the energy gap on the left of the graph was filled.

  c The middle of the graph shows an energy surplus. What is meant by this?

  d When does the graph predict the surplus will end?

  e How big is the energy gap predicted to be in 2015?

  f Suggest at least three ways of filling Bananaland's future energy gap.

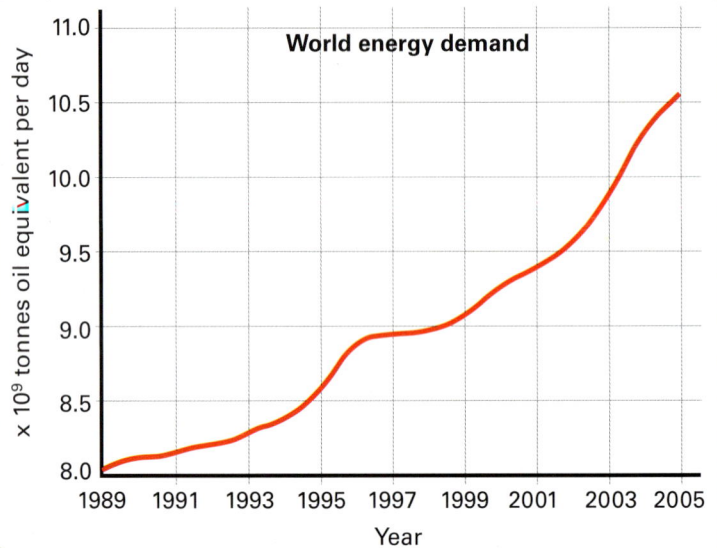

8 A nuclear power company placed the cartoon advertisement below in a magazine. What is the advertisement trying to say? Do you agree with it?

9 Why can energy sources such as wind power, geothermal and tidal power contribute only a small amount to our energy needs in the future?

10 Imagine that you are an architect designing a holiday home. The home is to be built in the mountains where you cannot connect to the electricity grid. Describe how you would supply the home with electricity, hot water and heating.

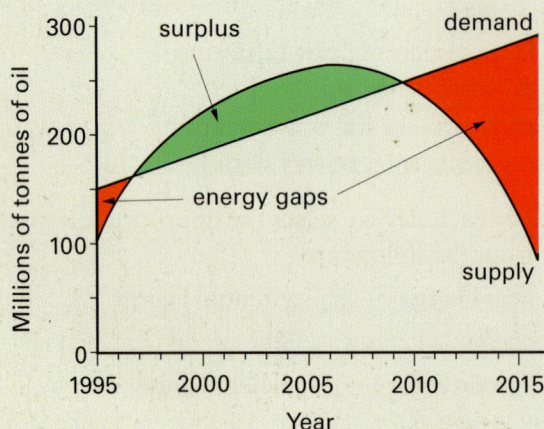

Check your answers on pages 334–335.

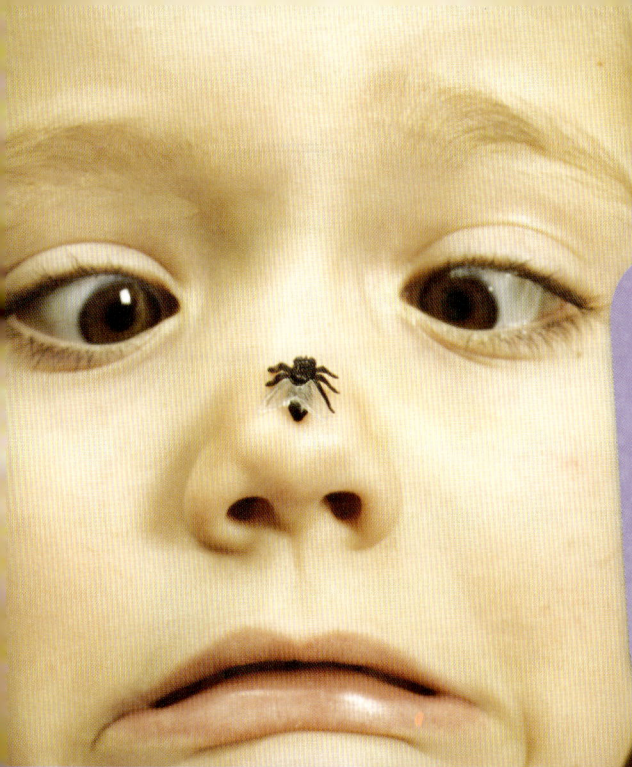

7 Responding

Getting Started

Work in small groups and discuss the following.

- Lucy is driving her car towards an intersection. The traffic lights turn amber and Lucy immediately takes her foot off the accelerator and applies the brakes. The car stops.

  📋 Which parts of Lucy's body are involved in this series of events?

  📋 On a piece of paper, draw a flow diagram showing the events, starting from the receptor that detects the amber light to the car stopping.

- Ruby's aunt gave her a pot plant for her room. She placed it near a window. After two weeks the stem had bent towards the window. Ruby rotated the plant 180°. After a week the plant had straightened up, and after another week it was again bending towards the window.

  📋 What stimulus made the plant bend?

  📋 Design an experiment to test your idea.

  📋 Given that plants have neither bones or muscles, suggest how they bend towards the light.

Oh-oh, amber light!

Foot off accelerator

Foot on brake

7.1 Nerves and hormones

You are walking along a path with a friend, eating an apple. Have you ever wondered how you can move, digest food, breathe, think, talk and keep your blood flowing all at the same time without even having to think about it?

All the systems in your body are controlled and coordinated by two other systems—the **nervous system** and the **endocrine system**. The **brain** is the main organ of the nervous system and controls the actions of the nerves and the endocrine system.

The nervous system consists of the brain, the spinal cord and nerves which run to all parts of your body. Messages called nerve impulses travel very quickly along nerves.

The endocrine system consists of a number of endocrine glands throughout your body, which produce chemical messages called **hormones**. These are sent out by the blood, so they take longer to act than nerves, but their effects generally last longer.

The nervous system

The brain is the control centre of your body, and has nerve connections to all parts of the body. At any one time, a huge number of signals are travelling to and from the 10 000 million nerve cells that make up your brain.

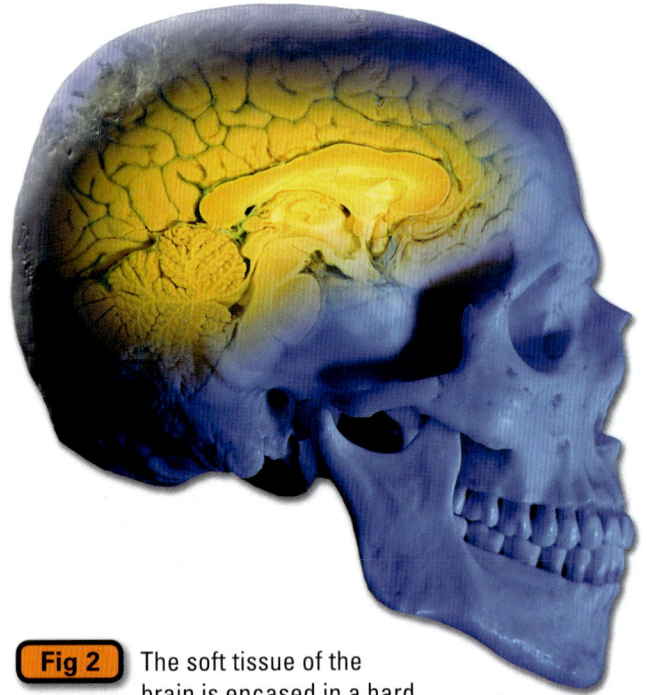

Fig 2 The soft tissue of the brain is encased in a hard, bony skull for protection.

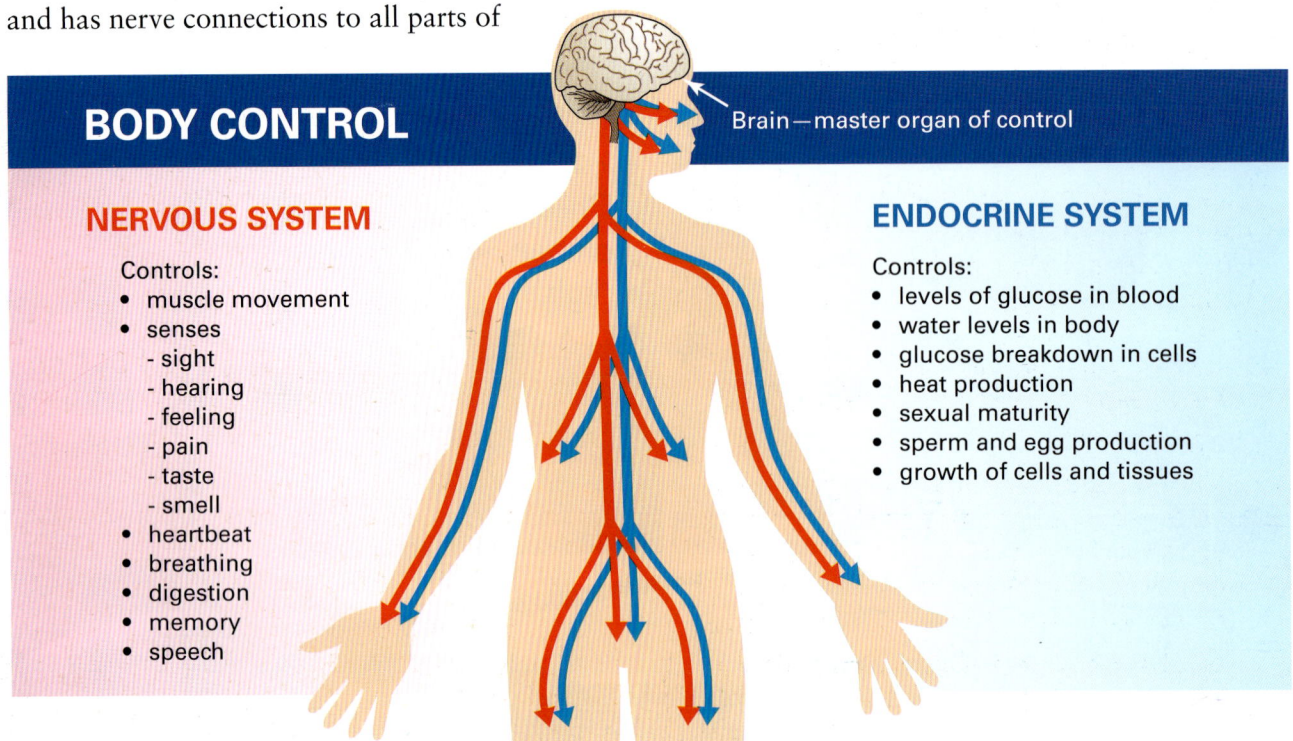

BODY CONTROL

Brain—master organ of control

NERVOUS SYSTEM

Controls:
- muscle movement
- senses
  - sight
  - hearing
  - feeling
  - pain
  - taste
  - smell
- heartbeat
- breathing
- digestion
- memory
- speech

ENDOCRINE SYSTEM

Controls:
- levels of glucose in blood
- water levels in body
- glucose breakdown in cells
- heat production
- sexual maturity
- sperm and egg production
- growth of cells and tissues

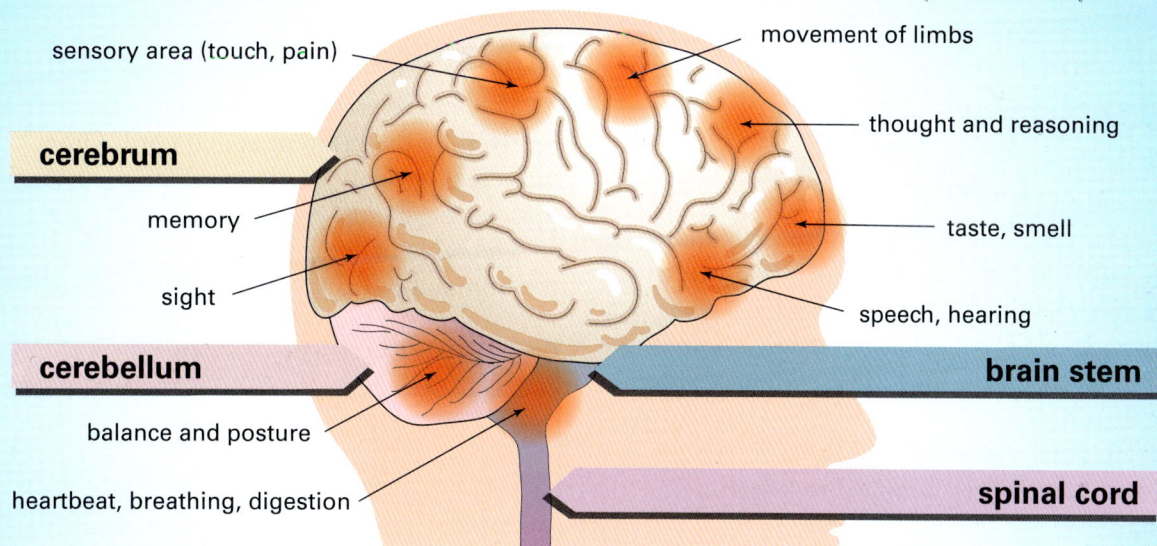

sensory area (touch, pain)

movement of limbs

thought and reasoning

cerebrum

memory

taste, smell

sight

speech, hearing

cerebellum

brain stem

balance and posture

heartbeat, breathing, digestion

spinal cord

There are three main parts to the brain.

Cerebrum

The **cerebrum** (ser-EE-brum) is the largest part and controls memory, speech and conscious thought. It receives information from sense receptors to give you the sensations of taste, sight, touch, hearing and smell. The cerebrum also controls actions such as walking, running and jumping. All of these actions are called *voluntary actions* because you control them by thinking about them.

Cerebellum

The small part of the brain behind the cerebrum is the **cerebellum** (ser-a-BELL-um). This coordinates muscular activity without you having to think about it (*involuntary actions*). It helps you balance when you ride your bike, surfboard or rollerblades, and it coordinates all your muscles when you walk, run and jump so that you do not fall over.

Brain stem

The **brain stem** at the base of the brain is responsible for other *involuntary actions* such as heartbeat, pulse, digestion and breathing.

 **Activity**

Dissection of a sheep's brain

You will need a sheep's brain, scalpel, cutting board, disposable gloves and newspaper.

Your teacher may show you the features of a brain by using a videoflex microscope camera before you start.

1 Identify the cerebrum, cerebellum and brain stem. Describe their colour and appearance.

2 Notice that the cerebrum consists of two parts called hemispheres. Use the scalpel to separate the two hemispheres, then cut one of the hemispheres in half lengthways to see a cross-section of the cerebrum.

Draw a cross-section of the brain and label the parts.

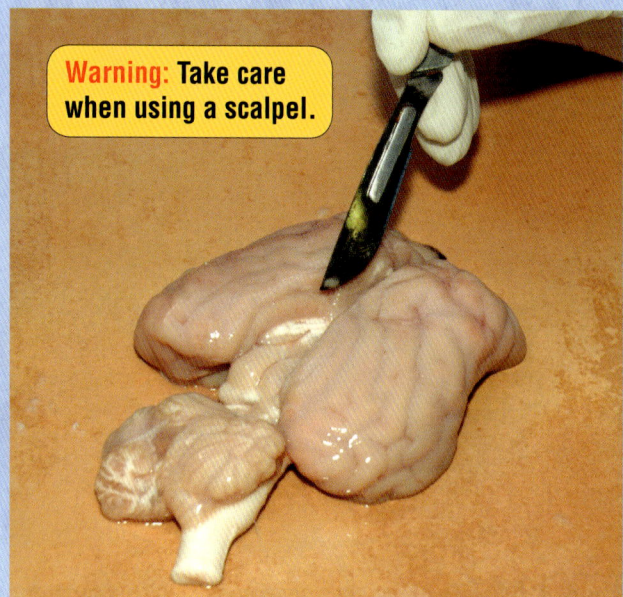

Warning: Take care when using a scalpel.

Types of nerves

The basic unit in the nervous system is a nerve cell or **neuron** (NEW-ron). Neuron is sometimes spelled *neurone*. This is a specialised cell and it is different from other body cells in two ways. Firstly, it is the longest cell in the body, with a long branch or fibre. Secondly, electrical impulses travel along the nerve fibre. These impulses travel in one direction only.

The main nerves in the body contain many individual nerve fibres wrapped together in a sheath.

There are two types of neurons—*sensory neurons* and *motor neurons*. Sensory neurons send nerve impulses to the brain from the body's receptors. These receptors are attached to one end of the neuron, and detect external stimuli such as light and sound, or internal stimuli such as the level of carbon dioxide in the blood or the fullness of your bladder.

The impulses from the sensory neurons are received by the brain or spinal cord. Other impulses are sent out along the motor neurons to muscles or glands.

The table below lists the sensory receptors in the human body and the stimuli they detect.

Receptor	Stimuli detected
rods and cones in eye	light
cells in cochlear (inner ear)	sounds
skin (many receptors)	touch, tissue damage (pain), vibration, pressure, hot and cold
around hairs in skin	touching the hair
taste buds in tongue	chemicals in food
olfactory cells in nose	chemicals in air

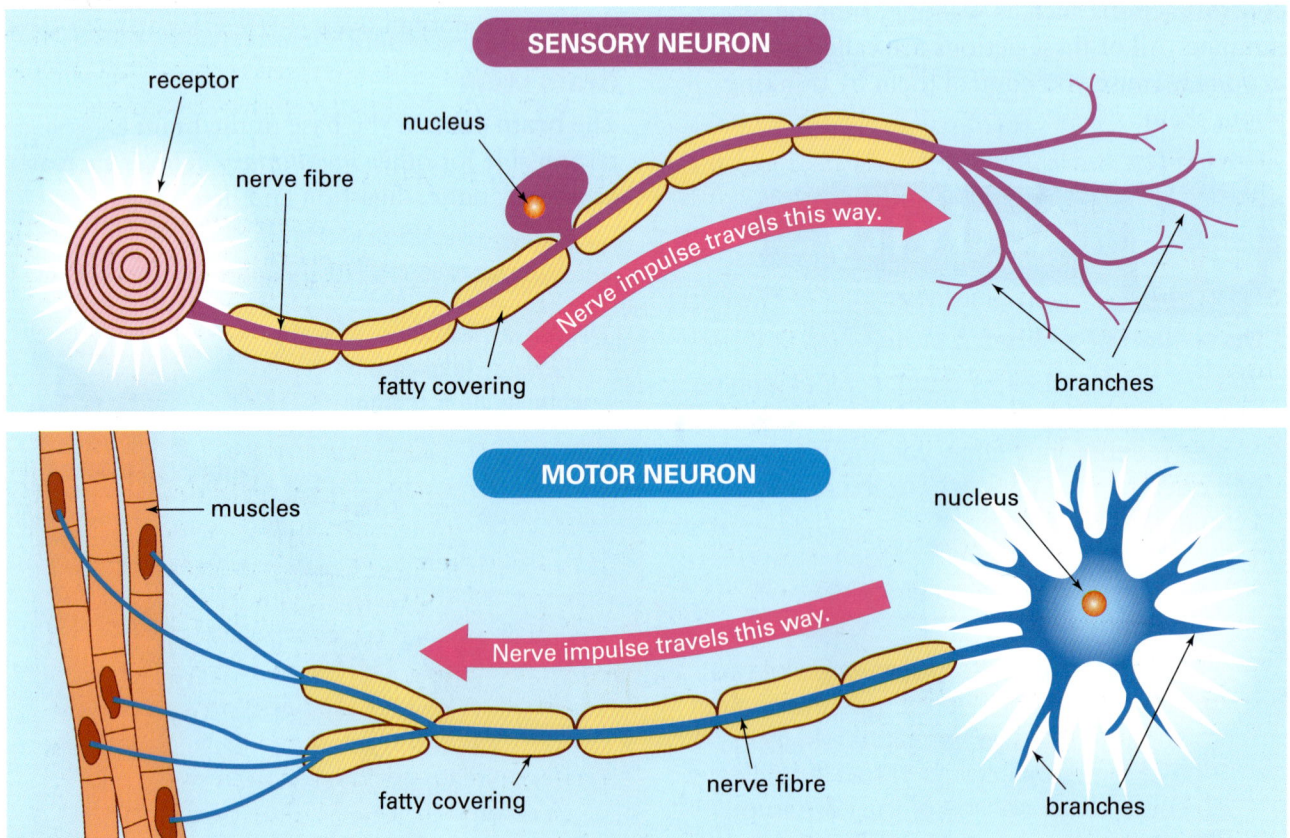

Fig 6 Sensory nerve cells send impulses from receptors to the brain, and motor nerve cells send impulses from the brain to muscles or glands.

science bits

Diseases of the nervous system

There are three major diseases of the nervous system—polio, multiple sclerosis and motor neuron disease.

Polio

Polio, or more correctly poliomyelitis, is a viral disease. The polio virus can be found in faeces and enters the body when a person ingests contaminated food or drink. The virus spreads to the gut and infects the motor neurons in the spinal cord, which control the movement of the trunk, limbs and rib muscles.

When a person is exposed to the disease, it can take from 3 to 35 days for them to first show symptoms. Thus the disease can spread quickly before the person realises they have it. The first symptoms are fatigue, fever, vomiting and pain, but about 90% of the people infected with the polio virus fully recover after the first symptoms.

In severe cases, muscle paralysis occurs in the legs and the ribs, making breathing difficult. People suffering from paralytic polio have to use a ventilator or an 'iron lung' to help them breathe.

Multiple sclerosis (MS)

MS is a disease that attacks the neurons in the brain and spinal cord. It is an unpredictable disease because the symptoms can occur at any time and be mild or severe. MS symptoms range from blurred vision to complete blindness, and from tingling and numbness to paralysis.

MS affects more women than men, and occurs more commonly in people with northern European ancestry. In 2002 there were 2.5 million people worldwide affected with MS, and 15 000 of those were in Australia.

MS is not contagious or directly inherited and the actual cause is at present not known. The disease occurs when the body's own immune system attacks the fatty substance (called myelin) around the neurons, causing a disruption to nerve transmission.

Motor neuron disease (MND)

MND is a group of diseases that affect the motor neurons which control the muscles that enable you to use your arms and legs, breathe, talk and swallow. It does not affect your intellect or your memory.

The cause of MND is not known. In almost all MND sufferers there is no family history of the disease. The disease is often fatal within 2 to 5 years after diagnosis. One well-known exception is Stephen Hawking, the Cambridge University physicist and cosmologist (see photo), who has had MND for over 40 years.

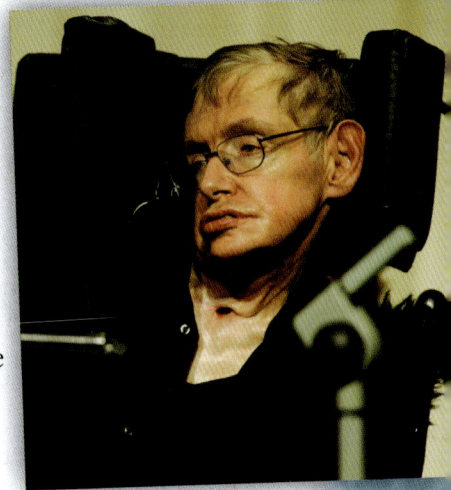

Symptoms of MND usually occur in people aged 50 to 70. They start with muscle weakness in the arms and legs, which gets progressively worse. Muscles tend to wither and speech becomes slurred.

At present there is no cure for MND.

WEB watch

Use the internet to find out more about the three diseases on this page.

Questions and research

1 Draw up a table listing the causes, symptoms and treatment of the three diseases.
2 Use the table to write a 'compare and contrast' paragraph about MS and MND.
3 Use the table in Question 1 to write a short feature article for a science magazine on one or all of the diseases. Include a fictitous interview in your article.
4 Between 1946 and 1955 there were 10 000 cases of polio and 1013 deaths. In 2006 there were 309 cases worldwide and none in Australia. Use information from the web to write an inference explaining this.

Reflex action

Not all the information from the receptors is coordinated by the brain. Sometimes a nerve impulse takes a short cut to the spinal cord and back. This is called **reflex action**. A reflex action is a very fast response to a stimulus, and is generally a response to danger. For example, you blink to protect your eyes when an object approaches your face, and you move your arm away quickly from a frying pan that is burning hot to avoid damaging your skin. Coughing is also a reflex action.

In a reflex action the nerve impulse travels from a receptor along a sensory neuron to the spinal cord and then back along a motor neuron to a muscle. The whole action takes place very quickly because the brain does not coordinate the action.

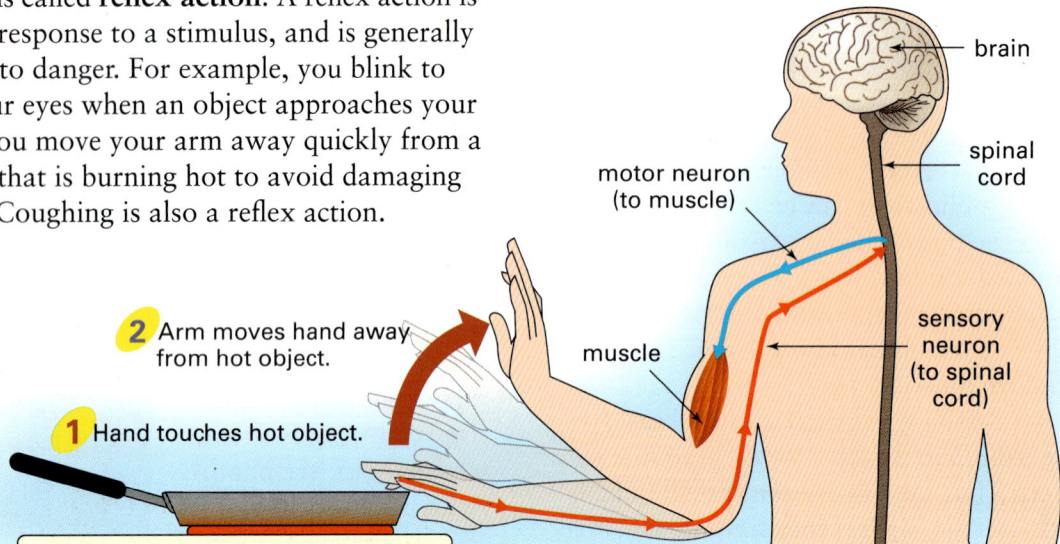

2 Arm moves hand away from hot object.

1 Hand touches hot object.

brain

spinal cord

motor neuron (to muscle)

muscle

sensory neuron (to spinal cord)

Reflex action flow diagram

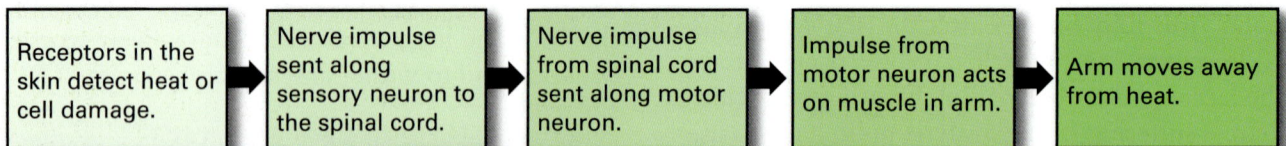

| Receptors in the skin detect heat or cell damage. | → | Nerve impulse sent along sensory neuron to the spinal cord. | → | Nerve impulse from spinal cord sent along motor neuron. | → | Impulse from motor neuron acts on muscle in arm. | → | Arm moves away from heat. |

Activities

Reflex actions

There are a number of reflex actions that you can observe in humans.

A Have your partner sit on a chair with one leg crossed over the other. With the side of your hand, gently tap their knee just below the knee cap.

✎ Describe this reflex action. What type of receptor detects the stimulus?

✎ Draw a flow diagram like the one above to show the reflex action.

B Stand behind a window or a glass door or hold a piece of clear plastic in front of your face. Have your partner throw a crumpled-up piece of paper at the glass.

✎ Why do you blink every time the paper ball is thrown, even though you are protected by the glass?

✎ Which receptor is used in this reflex action?

✎ Draw a flow diagram to show the reflex action.

C Cover one eye with your hand for at least 30 seconds. After this time have your partner look at your eye when you take your hand away.

✎ What happens to the size of the pupil?

✎ What was the stimulus that caused this response?

✎ Draw a flow diagram to show the reflex action.

Science in action

Nerves, poisons and drugs

The neurons in your nervous system do not touch each other—there is a tiny gap between them. When a nerve impulse reaches the end of one neuron, it cannot jump to the next neuron. Instead, the impulse releases a chemical called a *neurotransmitter* which travels over the tiny gap and stimulates the other neuron to send a nerve impulse.

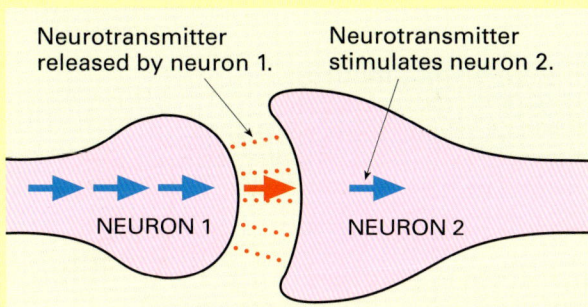

Neurotransmitter released by neuron 1.

Neurotransmitter stimulates neuron 2.

NEURON 1

NEURON 2

When the neurotransmitter has stimulated the other neuron, it is quickly broken down so the neuron can be stimulated again by more neurotransmitter.

Scientists have found more than 50 types of neurotransmitters in the human body.

Poisons

There are a number of poisons which react with neurotransmitters causing paralysis and even death. For example, curare (coo-RAR-ray) is a poison extracted from plants in South American forests. Animals that are hunted and hit by arrows dipped in curare become paralysed. The poisons given off by bacteria that cause food poisoning and those that cause tetanus also stop neurotransmitters working.

Insecticides

When the neurotransmitter is released and stimulates the other neuron, an enzyme destroys it so that it cannot keep acting and stimulating the other neuron. This process also occurs in insect nerves. The active ingredient in some insecticides reacts with the enzyme and destroys it. This means that nerve impulses fire continuously, causing the insect's muscles to move rapidly and uncontrollably, resulting in death.

Drugs

Nicotine, found in tobacco, is a stimulant because it acts like a neurotransmitter in the brain, giving a pleasurable effect (making the body more active or alert). However, it is addictive and very toxic in large amounts.

Amphetamines ('speed') and cocaine are also stimulants because they increase the release of neurotransmitters. This results in heightened emotions and an increased feeling of alertness and confidence. But later this can lead to anxiety, panic, depression and hostility.

Some other drugs such as alcohol and heroin decrease the release of neurotransmitters, making the person inactive or drowsy. These drugs belong to a group called depressants (the opposite effect of stimulants).

Fig 10 Long term use of depressants such as alcohol leads to liver and heart damage as well as memory loss and brain damage.

Questions and research

1 Compare the action of drugs (stimulants and depressants) on nerve transmission with the action of poisons such as curare.
2 Suppose you want to use the internet to find out more about what is on this page. What search words would you use? How could you guarantee that the information was genuine and accurate?
3 Invite a drug and alcohol consultant to discuss with the class the use and misuse of stimulants and depressants. Prepare some questions to present to the consultant well before the discussion.

Hormones—chemical controllers

Hormones are produced in **endocrine glands**. The difference between these glands and others in your body, such as sweat glands and glands in the stomach lining, is that the hormones made by endocrine glands pass directly into the blood.

There are many different hormones and each one acts on specific target cells. For example, a hormone released by certain cells in the lining of the first part of the small intestine acts only on cells in the pancreas that make digestive juices. On the other hand, insulin, which is produced in specialised cells in the pancreas, has a broader action. It makes the liver cells store glucose and helps muscle cells throughout the body absorb more glucose from the blood.

Hormones are different from nerves in that they can act on the whole body, on body systems or on individual organs. Nerves act only on muscles and glands.

The diagram below shows some of the major endocrine glands and the effects the hormones produced have on the body.

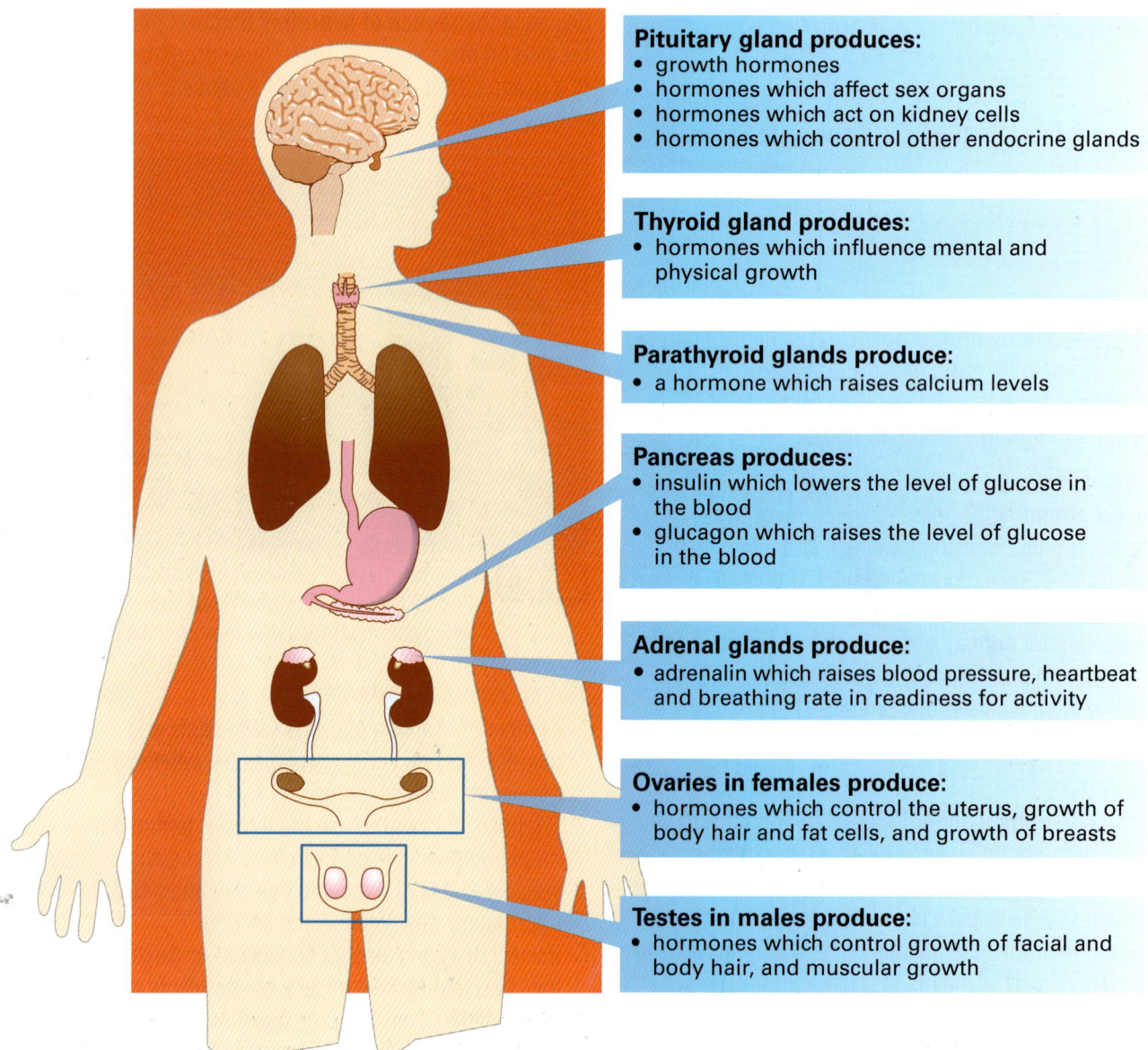

Pituitary gland produces:
- growth hormones
- hormones which affect sex organs
- hormones which act on kidney cells
- hormones which control other endocrine glands

Thyroid gland produces:
- hormones which influence mental and physical growth

Parathyroid glands produce:
- a hormone which raises calcium levels

Pancreas produces:
- insulin which lowers the level of glucose in the blood
- glucagon which raises the level of glucose in the blood

Adrenal glands produce:
- adrenalin which raises blood pressure, heartbeat and breathing rate in readiness for activity

Ovaries in females produce:
- hormones which control the uterus, growth of body hair and fat cells, and growth of breasts

Testes in males produce:
- hormones which control growth of facial and body hair, and muscular growth

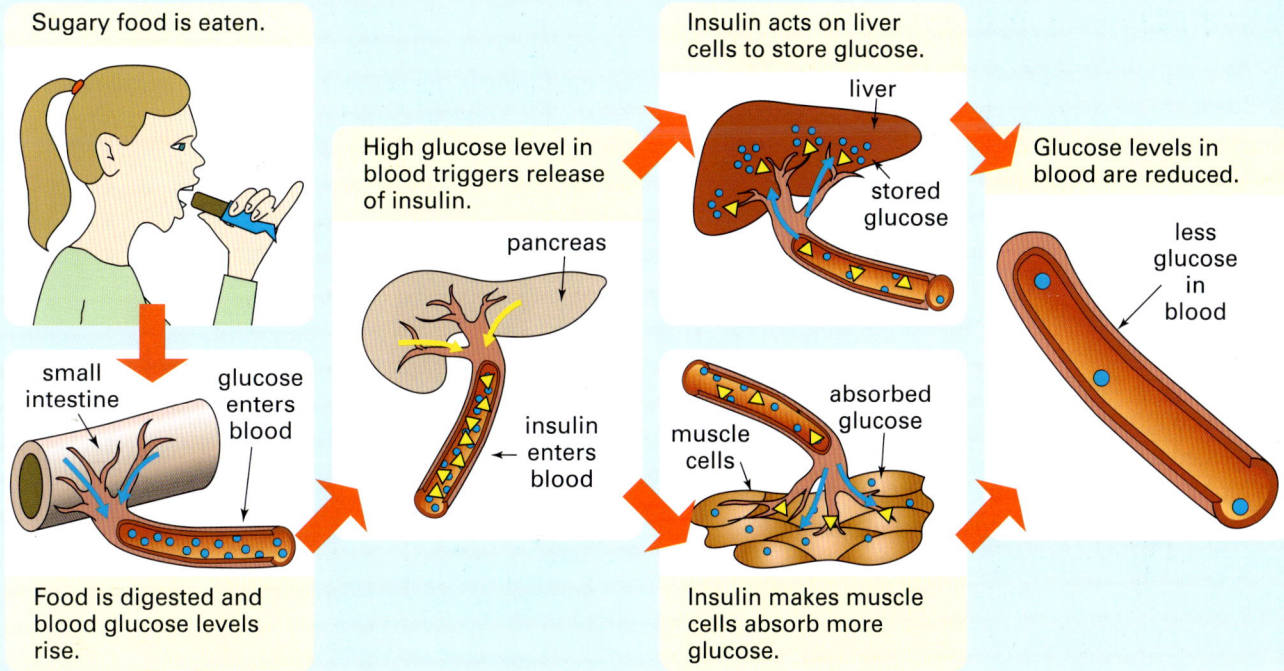

Sugary food is eaten.

Food is digested and blood glucose levels rise.

small intestine

glucose enters blood

High glucose level in blood triggers release of insulin.

pancreas

insulin enters blood

Insulin acts on liver cells to store glucose.

liver

stored glucose

Insulin makes muscle cells absorb more glucose.

muscle cells

absorbed glucose

Glucose levels in blood are reduced.

less glucose in blood

Fig 12 How insulin reduces blood glucose levels

The pituitary—the master gland

The **pituitary** (pit-YOU-it-tree) **gland**, located on the underside of the brain, is the master gland that controls other endocrine glands. For example, the release of the hormone from the thyroid gland in your neck is controlled by a thyroid-stimulating hormone from the pituitary.

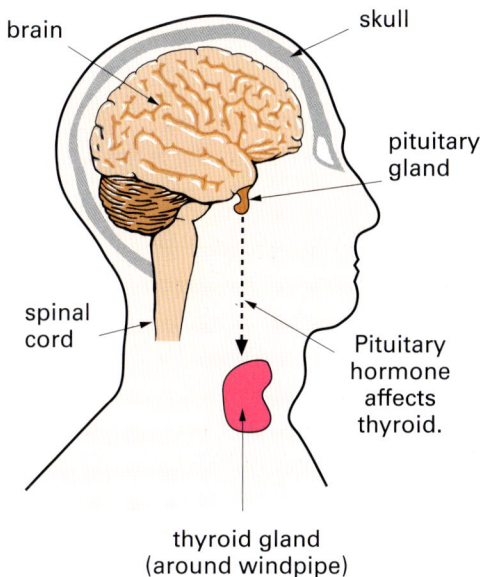

brain

skull

pituitary gland

spinal cord

Pituitary hormone affects thyroid.

thyroid gland (around windpipe)

Growth and development in humans

The pituitary gland also releases hormones which affect the reproductive organs. Before puberty the main physical growth of a person is under the control of the pituitary, which releases growth hormones.

Between 10 to 15 years after birth, the pituitary begins to release hormones which affect the reproductive organs. This causes major changes to the body and is the beginning of puberty.

In males, one pituitary hormone acts on the cells in the testes, which make sperm. Another acts on the testes to make the hormone testosterone. Testosterone stimulates the growth of facial and body hair and is also responsible for rapid muscular growth.

In females, one pituitary hormone leads to egg production in the ovaries and also to the manufacture of the hormone estrogen. Estrogen causes an increase in body hair growth, the growth of fat cells under the skin and the development of breasts. Another pituitary hormone acts on the ovaries and is responsible for the start of the menstrual cycle.

Science in action

Diabetes

Diabetes is a fairly common disorder. Its main symptoms are glucose in the urine, extreme thirst, hunger and loss of weight. Before the 1930s fewer than 20% of people lived more than 10 years after developing diabetes.

Diabetes is caused by the body not producing any or enough of the hormone insulin. After a meal is digested a large amount of glucose is absorbed by the blood and the level of blood glucose rises. Insulin makes liver cells store glucose, and makes muscle cells absorb more glucose from the blood. The net effect is to reduce the amount of glucose in the blood. In people with diabetes, the pancreas does not produce enough insulin, or in other cases none at all, hence the high levels of glucose in their blood.

Types of diabetes

There are two main types of diabetes.

- **Type 1 diabetes** occurs when the body stops making insulin. This type is found in only 10 to 15% of all diabetes sufferers, and it occurs mainly in younger people. It cannot be prevented and is treated by daily insulin injections.
- **Type 2 diabetes** is the most common type and it occurs mainly in people over 40 who are overweight and inactive, have high blood pressure or heart disease, or in women who develop diabetes in pregnancy.

Diabetes is a serious illness for which there is no cure at present. *You cannot cure diabetes but you can control it.*

Parts of the body affected by diabetes

The high levels of glucose in the blood cause serious problems in the body. The blood vessels and nerves are the most affected. The walls of the small blood vessels thicken and block the blood supply. This causes problems in your eyes, kidneys, legs and heart.

WEBwatch

Go to www.scienceworld.net.au and follow the links to the websites below.

Diabetes Australia
International Diabetes Home Page

Working with diabetes

Susan Mylne is a podiatrist (a person who examines feet) who works in Community Health and is very interested in diabetes.

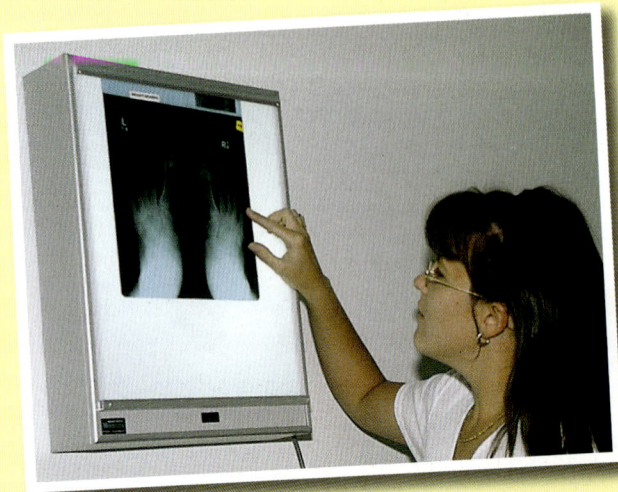

Why is Susan interested in diabetes? Type 2 diabetes sufferers often have nerve damage in their feet. This causes 'pins and needles', a burning sensation and numbness. These people also suffer blood vessel damage which leads to poor blood circulation, and causes cramps, ulcers and pains in the legs.

Many of Susan's patients who have these symptoms often do not know they have diabetes. She can test for the complications of diabetes in their feet, help them in their treatment, and help educate them about their illness.

Questions and research

For this section you may use the websites on the left or surf the web for further information.

1 What is the importance of insulin in the body?
2 What is the difference between Type 1 and Type 2 diabetes? Which type would you class as a 'lifestyle illness'? Why?
3 There has been a rapid increase in the number of people contracting Type 2 diabetes in the last 5 years. Suggest reasons for this.
4 Suppose you are in charge of preparing a diabetes brochure. What information will you include to inform people about the affects of diabetes and its prevention? Prepare a draft design for the brochure.

Check!

1 Some of the following statements are false. Find the false ones and rewrite them to make them correct.
   a The endocrine system controls muscle movement, speech and the senses.
   b The cerebrum controls involuntary actions like heartbeat and breathing.
   c The spinal cord is protected from injury by the skull.
   d Motor nerves carry impulses from receptors to the brain.
   e Hormones are released directly into the bloodstream.

2 Suggest why reflex actions might be useful for an organism's survival.

3 What are the differences between a sensory nerve and a motor nerve?

4 The knee jerk reflex that occurs when the knee is tapped is an example of a simple reflex action. Copy the drawing top right and replace the letters with a description of what occurs at each stage.

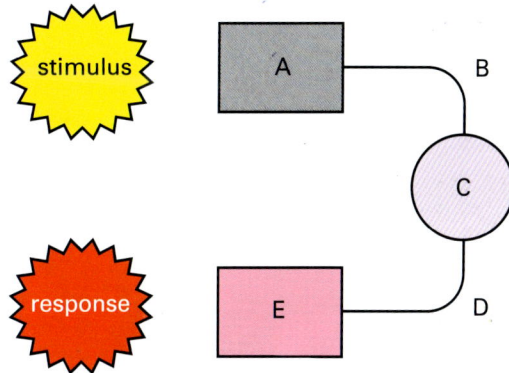

5 Describe how hormones control the growth and development of the human body.

6 How are the actions of nerves different from those of hormones? Give examples.

7 What is the role of the pituitary gland in the functioning of your body?

8 Suppose you hear a sudden, extremely loud noise. What type of responses might occur to this stimulus? Would these responses be caused by nerves or by hormones? Explain.

challenge

1 A way to test a person's reaction to a stimulus is to drop a ruler between their thumb and fingers. The reaction distance is how far the ruler falls before they catch it.
   a Ruby tested Ben's reaction by dropping a ruler seven times. The table shows his results. Suggest an inference to explain the results.

Trial	1	2	3	4	5	6	7
Reaction distance (cm)	28	21	17	13	11	10	9

   b Ruby then tested Mia's reactions. The ruler fell an average of 16 cm before she caught it with her right hand, and 18 cm with her left hand. Suggest a reason for the different results.
   c Use the formula below to find Mia's reaction time.

   $$\text{reaction time (s)} = \sqrt{\frac{\text{reaction distance (cm)}}{500}}$$

2 A person who suffers a fractured neck is often paralysed below the fracture. Why is this?

3 The graph below shows the amount of glucose in someone's blood over a 24-hour period.
   a Explain the reason for the peaks in the graph.
   b At what times during the 24 hours did the amount of insulin being released from the pancreas increase? Suggest what caused this increase. What was the effect of the increase in insulin in the blood?
   c Suggest why the level of blood glucose decreases slightly during sleep.

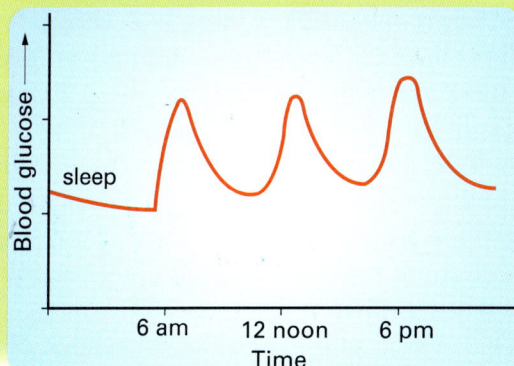

daytime

night-time

7.2 Responses in plants

Why do some plants, like the one in the photos above, close the their leaves at night?

The plant closes its leaves in response to light and darkness. In the morning, the sunlight acts as a stimulus for the leaves to open. Plants also respond to other external stimuli such as gravity, temperature, moisture and, in some plants, touch.

Plants have no nervous system, muscles or specialised glands, so how do they detect stimuli and how do they react to these stimuli?

Plant hormones

The internal control of activities in a plant are due to hormones. These chemical compounds are made by certain cells and are distributed throughout the plant from cell to cell or by the microscopic tubes that run through the plant. Plant hormones are quite different chemically from those in animals. But, like in animals, very small amounts of the hormones have a large effect on the target cells and the plant as a whole.

Plants have far fewer hormones than animals, and, unlike animals, have no specialised glands such as those in the endocrine system.

Plant hormones are responsible for controlling the growth of stems and roots, the ripening of fruit and the loss of leaves during autumn. Hormones also determine when a plant will flower and when seeds will germinate.

When a seed germinates, the young root of the

Fig 19 Deciduous plants lose their leaves in autumn. As the weather becomes warmer in spring, hormones are produced which stimulate the growth of new leaves.

plant grows downwards. If the seedling is turned upside down, the root will bend and continue to grow downwards. This response to gravity is caused by a number of hormones which are produced in the root cells. You can investigate the response to gravity on the next page.

Investigate
15 RESPONSES OF PLANT ROOTS

Aim
To investigate the responses of roots to gravity.

Materials
- 8 small bean seeds, eg mung beans (see Planning and Safety Check below)
- glass jar
- petri dish (11 cm diameter)
- filling, eg rubber carpet underlay, cotton wool, newspaper or cardboard
- 2 filter papers (to fit petri dish)
- Blu-Tack
- adhesive tape

Planning and Safety Check
Prepare the bean seeds in advance. Soak them in a jar of water until they start to germinate. Tip out the water and leave the jar in a cupboard until the roots grow to about 1 cm long. Rinse the sprouts with fresh water each day.

Method
1 Place some filling (cotton wool, rubber underlay, cardboard) in the bottom of the petri dish. Then place two filter papers on top of the filling.

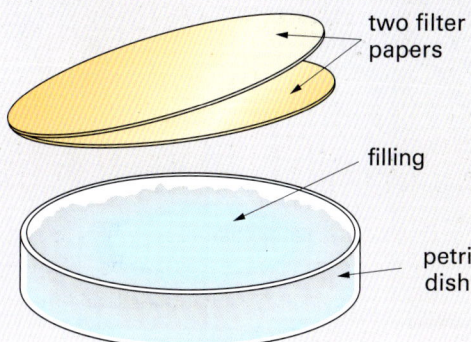

two filter papers

filling

petri dish

2 Place two bean sprouts on the filter paper with their roots pointing outwards, as shown in the diagram at the top of the next column. Place another two sprouts at the 90°, 180° and 270° positions.

Position the pairs of seeds as shown.

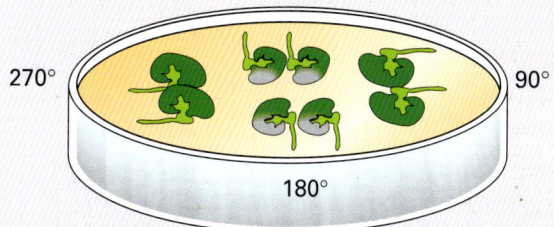

0°
270°   90°
180°

3 Moisten the filter paper with some water. Put the lid on, and tape it securely. Make sure the seeds are jammed in by the thickness of the filling and filter papers. If the seeds move, add more layers of filter paper.

4 Place the petri dish on a piece of Blu-Tack in a vertical position, as shown. Use a marking pen to mark the position of the roots.

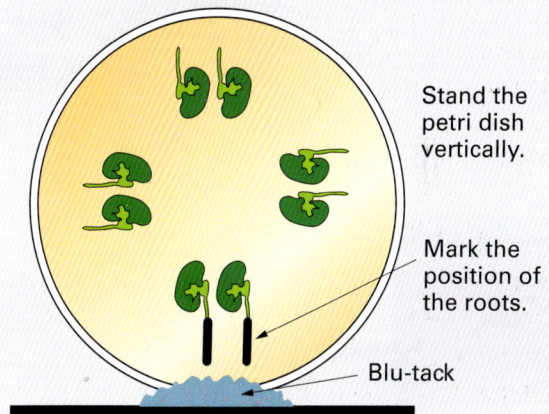

Stand the petri dish vertically.

Mark the position of the roots.

Blu-tack

5 Leave the petri dish in this position for a day. Then rotate the dish 90°.
   📋 Record what happens to the direction of growth of the roots.

6 Repeat for another position and again record your observations.

Discussion
1 Write a report of your findings.

2 Suggest what might happen to the roots if the petri dish was taken into space.

Growth hormones

A group of hormones called **auxins** (ORK-sins) are responsible for controlling the growth of stems and roots. They also make plants bend towards the light.

Response to light

One type of auxin is made in the cells in the growing tips of plants. This hormone moves through the cells away from the light.

The hormone passes downwards until it reaches the cells in the growth region just below the tip. It acts on these cells and makes them divide and grow in length. Hence the plant grows taller. The cells in the growing region of the plant are the target cells for auxin. Cells outside this region do not respond to the hormone. (See Fig 24.)

When light comes from one side, more auxin is found on the side away from the light. This causes the growth of cells on the darker side, which bends the plant towards the light. (See Fig 25.)

Auxin is made here.

growth region of shoot

Cells divide and grow longer.

Fig 24 Auxin moves to the cells in the growth region where it makes them divide and grow longer.

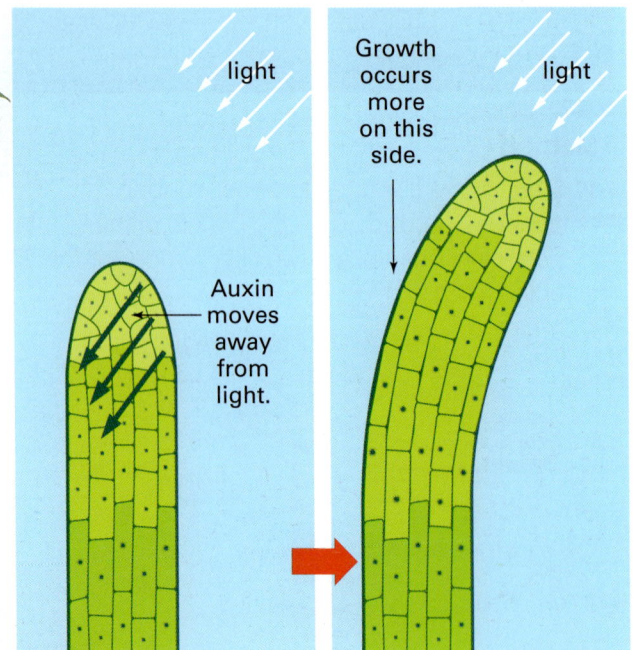

Fig 23 This tomato plant was placed on its side two days before the photo was taken.

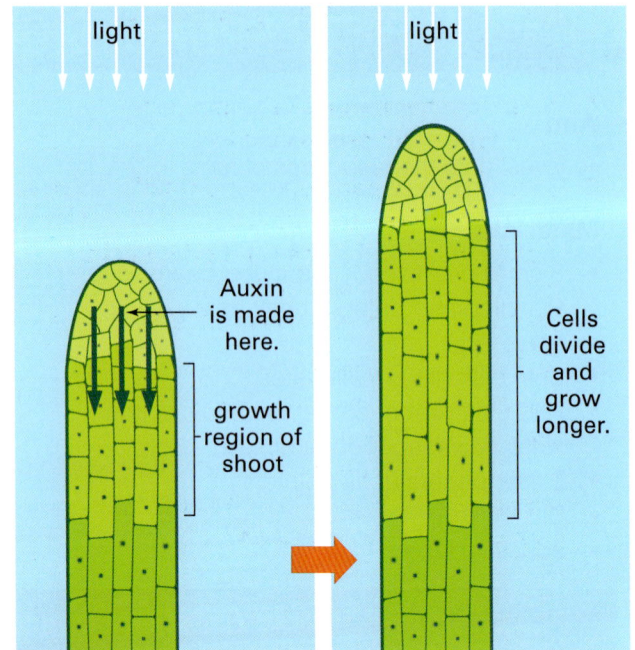

light

Growth occurs more on this side.

light

Auxin moves away from light.

Fig 25 When light comes from one side, cells on the darker side divide and grow more than the ones on the other side.

Weedkiller

The weedkiller *glyphosate* is a compound with a similar structure to the auxin produced in a plant's growing tip. (*Roundup* is a brand name of the weedkiller which contains this compound.) When glyphosate is applied in very dilute solutions it will promote plant growth. However, in stronger solutions, plants grow uncontrollably and eventually die.

Check!

1 Describe the changes in plants that hormones are responsible for.

2 Most animals, particularly mammals, show rapid responses to certain stimuli such as hot objects, loud noises and bright light. Plants, however, respond very slowly to stimuli. Suggest reasons for this difference.

3 A pot plant has been growing near a window for a number of weeks and all the leaves face the window.

   The plant is turned around 180°. After a few weeks the leaves of the plant have moved around to face the window again.

a What external stimulus is the plant responding to?

b What is the advantage of such a response to the survival of the plant?

4 A bean seed was germinated and left to grow for a number of days. It was then turned sideways as shown.

a Draw what you would expect to happen to the seedling.

b What stimulus is the seedling responding to?

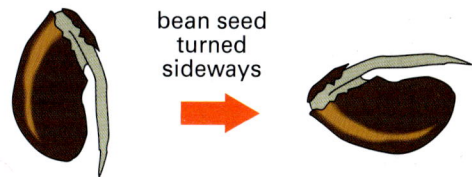

bean seed turned sideways

challenge

1 Biologists believe that another hormone besides auxin is produced in root tips. They think that this hormone stops the action of auxin. Suggest how the two hormones might be responsible for the growth of the bean shoot in Check 4 above.

2 The diagrams below show the results of four tests in an experiment using oat seedlings. Use the diagrams to answer the following questions.

a Suggest a title for the experiment.

b Look at the results of C and D. Write an inference to explain the differences.

c Which were the control seedlings? Explain.

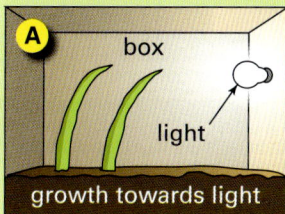

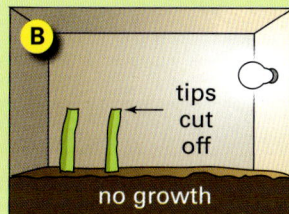

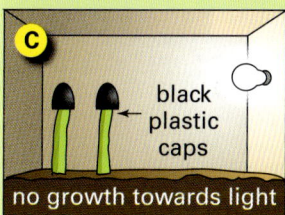

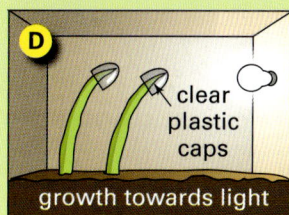

3 Plant fertilisers promote the growth of plants. In which ways are fertilisers different from plant hormones?

4 The root of a one-day-old bean seedling was marked with equally spaced lines. The root was observed on the second day.

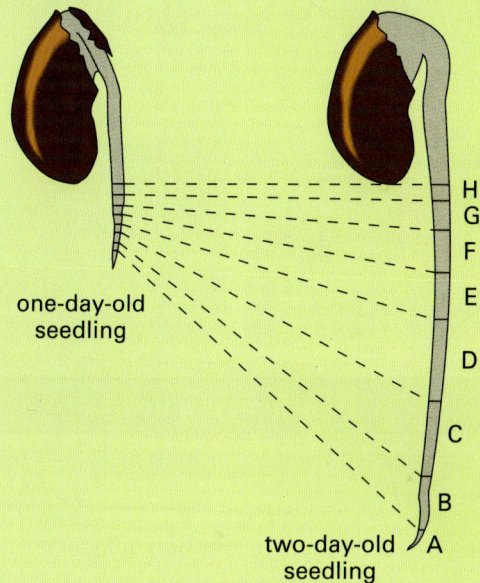

a Which sections showed most growth?

b Suggest what would have happened if the lower four sections had been cut off after day one.

7.3 Body balance

In Section 1 you learnt how the glucose level in the blood is controlled by the hormone insulin. Now let's look at the control of heat and water in the body.

Heat balance

Your body temperature stays at about 37°C. This is the set-point temperature for humans. The chemical reactions in the cells of your body work best at this temperature. All mammals and birds have a constant body temperature, although the set-point temperature varies between groups of these animals. For example, the set-point temperature for a magpie is about 39°C, while for echidnas it is about 31°C.

Most of the heat needed to maintain the set-point temperature is generated during the respiration of glucose in your body cells,

particularly in the liver, kidney and brain. On the other hand, most of your body's heat loss is by radiation from your skin surface and by evaporation of sweat from your skin. The table at the bottom of the page summarises the ways in which heat is gained and lost by your body.

Control of heat balance

During exercise, your muscles generate heat, which increases the temperature of the blood. A receptor in the brain just above the pituitary gland is sensitive to changes in the temperature of the blood and sends out nerve impulses to the skin and sweat glands.

Fig 29 The heat receptors in your brain are sensitive to changes in blood temperature and send impulses to the skin.

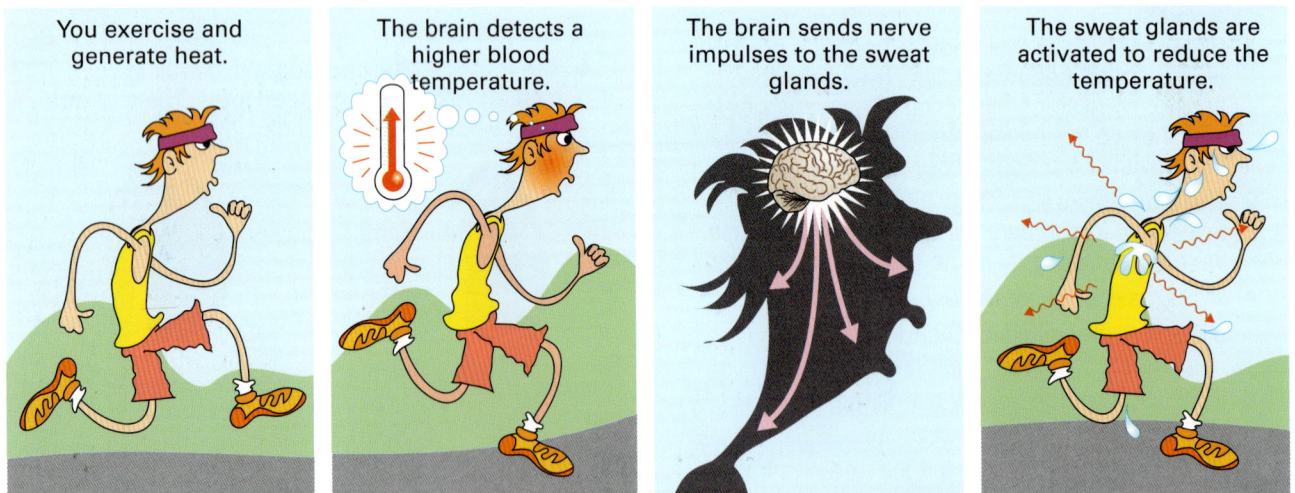

You exercise and generate heat.

The brain detects a higher blood temperature.

The brain sends nerve impulses to the sweat glands.

The sweat glands are activated to reduce the temperature.

How heat is gained	How heat is lost
• heat released from respiration in all cells in the body • heat released from respiration in muscle cells during exercise • absorption of heat from the Sun and atmosphere	• radiation of heat from blood flowing beneath the skin (The heat loss increases as the outside temperature decreases.) • evaporation of sweat from the skin • heat lost when breathing out • heat lost in urine and faeces

By sweating and radiating heat, your body temperature falls. But when the temperature falls below the set-point temperature, the heat receptors in the brain detect a lower blood temperature and send nerve impulses to the skin and sweat glands to reduce heat loss, and the body temperature gradually rises. All of these actions cause the body temperature to fluctuate between 36°C and 38°C.

This system of control is called a **negative feedback system** because the response acts as a stimulus to oppose (negative action) the change caused by the original stimulus.

In the example, the original stimulus is the higher body temperature. The body's response is to activate the skin and sweat glands to lower the body temperature. Following this, the lower body temperature acts as a stimulus for the brain to oppose the original action caused by the high body temperature.

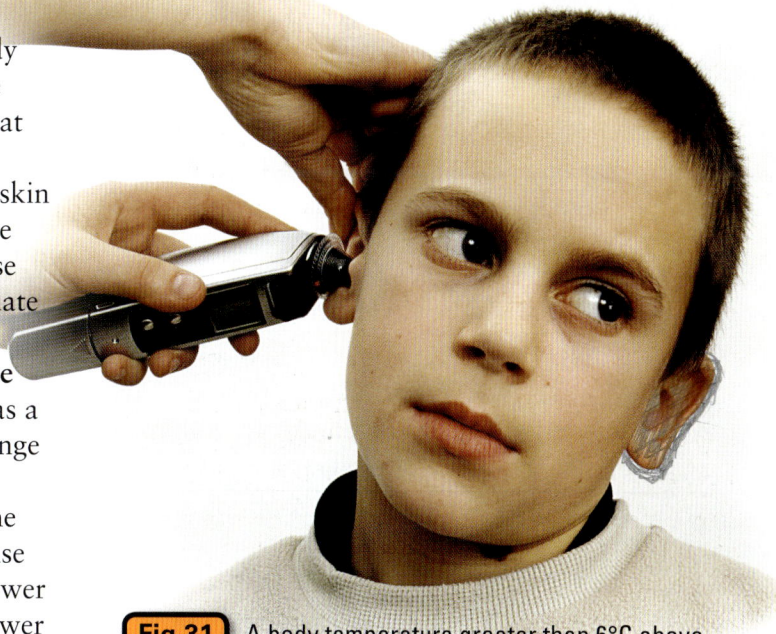

Fig 31 A body temperature greater than 6°C above set point can lead to death. This is why the temperature of patients suffering from fever is closely monitored.

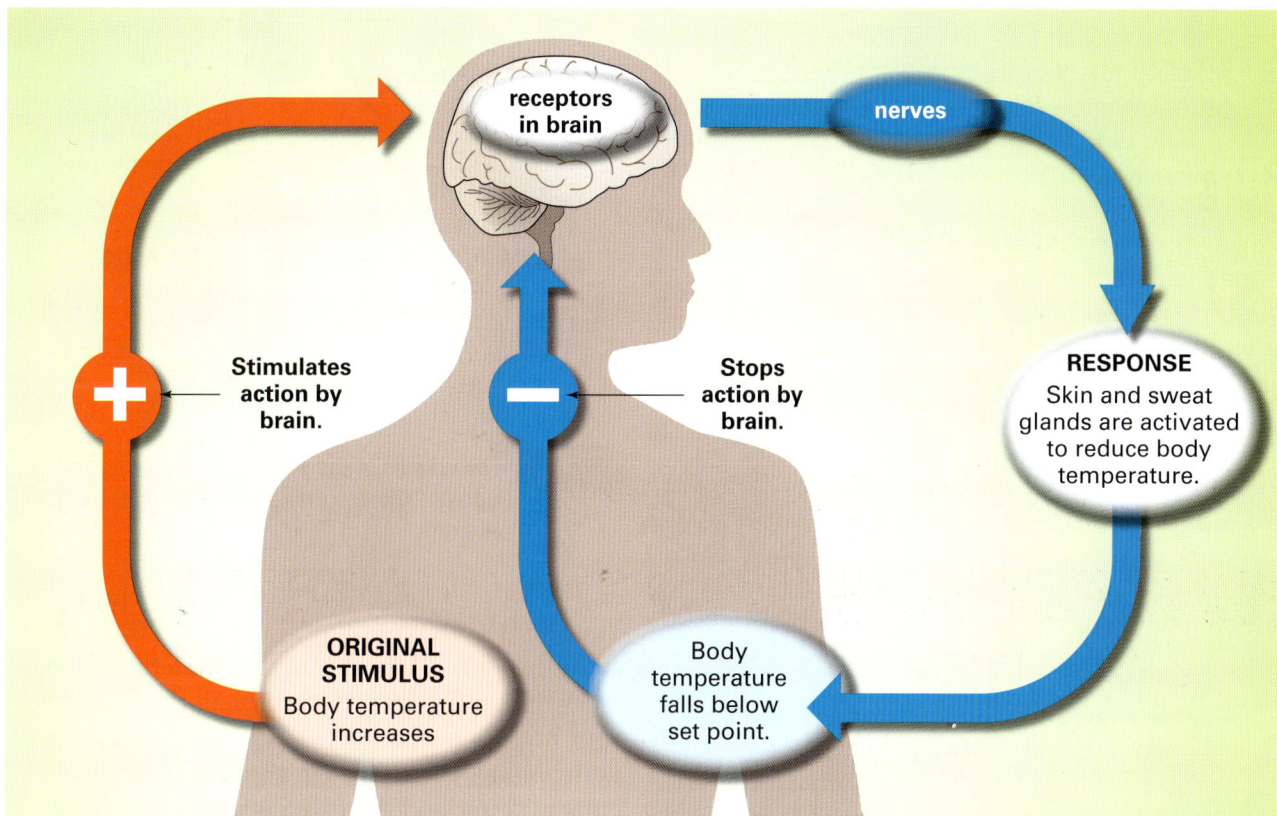

Fig 30 The negative feedback system involved in the control of body temperature

To see how the body controls temperature, open the **Negative feedback** animation on the CD.

Working with technology

Activities

Evaporation and cooling

When your body gets hot, you sweat to reduce your temperature. How does sweating affect body temperature?

1   Place a small drop of water on your arm. Blow on it to evaporate the drop.

📋 What do you feel? Blow on your other (dry) arm to compare the sensation.

2   Repeat Step 1 using a drop of methylated spirits.

📋 Suggest a reason for the different sensation with the methylated spirits.

📋 Your arm feels cooler when the liquids evaporate. Why? Use the particle model and your knowledge of change of state to help you answer this.

📋 Write an inference to explain why sweating lowers your body temperature.

📋 Design an experiment to measure the cooling effect of evaporation. (You can use a thermometer or a datalogger with a temperature sensor for this.)

Air conditioners

Like your body's control of temperature, air conditioners also use negative feedback to control temperature.

Use the points below to design a negative feedback flow diagram for an air conditioner, like the flow diagram on the previous page.

- You set the temperature on the control panel to, say, 23°C. This is the set-point temperature.

- There is a temperature sensor in the air conditioner unit.

📋 Draw the flow diagram showing how the air conditioner works.

📋 A sensitive thermometer will show that the temperature in the room fluctuates around 23°C. Why is this? Sketch a graph that shows the temperature in the room over a few hours. Mark on it when you think the air conditioner switches on, and when it switches off.

Water balance

Water is a very important substance in the body since just over 70% of your body mass is water.

You constantly lose water by evaporation from your skin (sweat), in your breath and in liquid and solid wastes. However, water is replaced by drinking liquids and by eating foods. Many cell reactions also produce water.

The kidneys are responsible for water balance in your body. These two bean-shaped organs lie close to your backbone behind the small intestine. They have a rich blood supply from a branch of the large artery that runs from the heart to the lower part of your body.

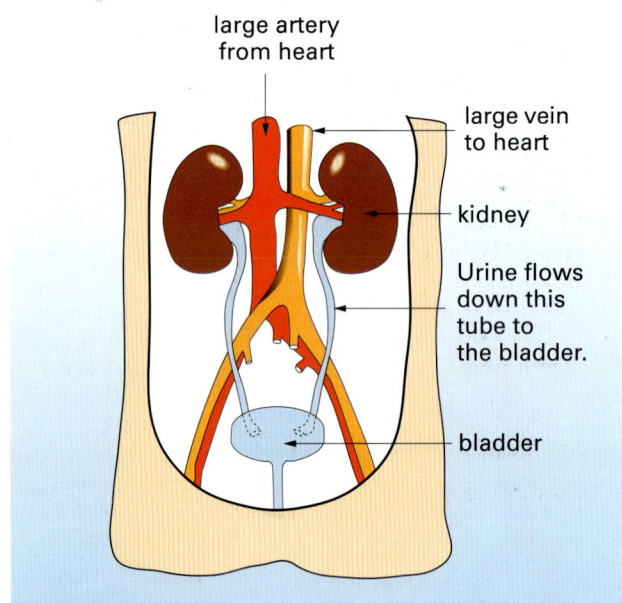

large artery from heart

large vein to heart

kidney

Urine flows down this tube to the bladder.

bladder

Fig 32 The wastes in the blood are filtered by the kidneys and are then eliminated by the body as urine.

The kidneys filter wastes from your blood. Your body contains about 5 litres of blood, and about one litre of this passes through the kidneys every minute. So in five minutes all the blood in your body is filtered. The filtering process occurs as the blood flows through capillaries in the kidney. Water and dissolved wastes pass out of the blood into tiny collecting tubes. A lot of the water is reabsorbed, and a concentrated solution called urine flows into the bladder for storage until it is eliminated.

Investigate
16 KIDNEY DISSECTION

Aim
To examine a sheep's kidney.

Materials
- sheep's kidney
- scalpel, scissors and tweezers (forceps)
- dissecting board
- disposable gloves and lab coat
- newspaper
- microscope and slides
- disinfectant and towel

Wear safety glasses.

Planning and Safety Check
- Read through the investigation so that you know exactly what to do.
- What safety precautions will you take when handling the kidney? How will you dispose of the kidney when you have finished with it?

PART A

1 Lay a few pages of a newspaper on the bench and put the dissecting board on them.

2 If the kidney has fat around it peel it off. Then look for the blood vessels attached to the concave side of the kidney.

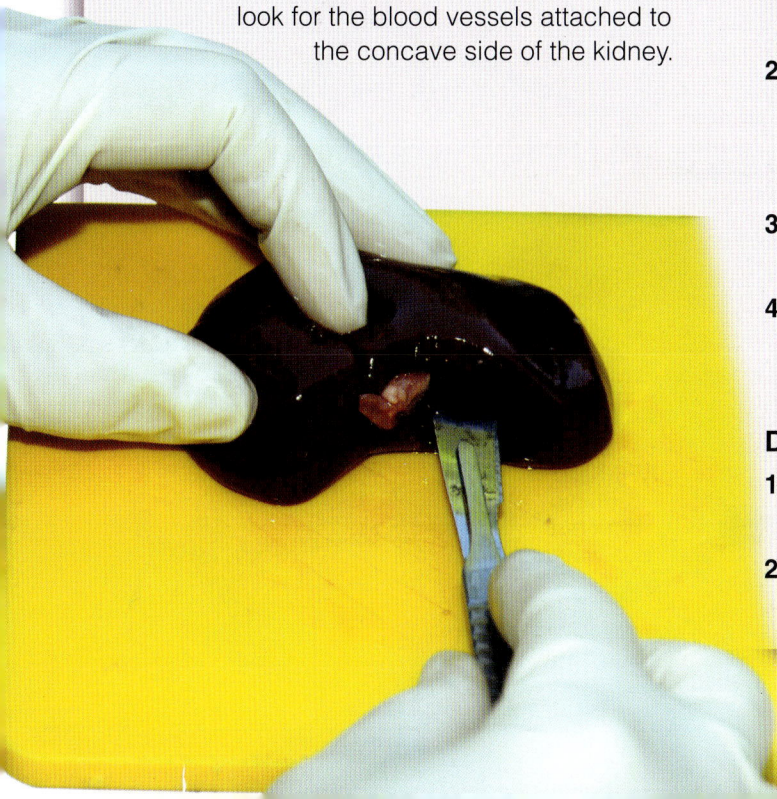

3 Use the scalpel to cut the kidney in half. Then use the diagram to identify the various parts.

Warning: Take care when using a scalpel.

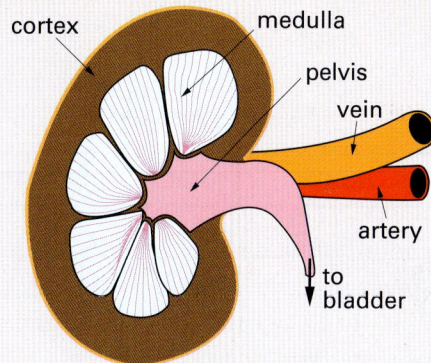

The cortex is where the wastes are filtered out of the blood into tiny collecting tubes. The dark red colour of the cortex is due to blood capillaries. The medulla contains the collecting tubes. There are about a million of these tubes in a kidney. Urine trickles down the collecting tubes into the pelvis and then into the bladder.

PART B

1 Use a scalpel to cut a very thin piece of kidney tissue from the cortex region.

2 Place the thin section on a microscope slide and look at it under low power on a microscope.
Record what you see.

3 Take a thin section of the medulla and look at it under a microscope.

4 When you have finished, dispose of the kidney and scraps, disinfect the dissecting board and wash your hands thoroughly.

Discussion
1 Suggest why there is usually a thick layer of fat around the kidneys.

2 Suggest the advantages in having two kidneys and not just one.

The table below shows the water inputs and outputs that might occur in a person on a mild day. The outputs and inputs are generally balanced.

Water outputs (mL)		Water inputs (mL)	
urine	1500	drinking	1500
sweat	600	food	800
breath	400	from cell reactions	300
faeces	100		
total	**2600**	**total**	**2600**

The amount of water that is filtered out of the blood changes with the heat and humidity of the day, the amount of sweat you produce and the amount of water you drink.

How much water is lost from the kidneys is controlled by nerves and hormones. Receptors in the brain are sensitive to changes in the amount of water in the blood. For example, on a hot day a lot of water is lost in sweat. This means that the water content of body fluids, including blood, drops. The brain detects a lower water content in the blood and sends a nerve impulse to the pituitary gland. A hormone called ADH is released which acts on the tiny tubes in the kidney. These tiny tubes filter out less water and the volume of water lost decreases.

Water balance and negative feedback

Water balance in the body operates by a negative feedback system (see diagram below). When the kidneys reduce the amount of water in the urine (because of the water lost by sweating), the water content of the blood gradually increases. This increase is detected by the receptors in the brain which in turn stimulate the pituitary gland to release less hormone, and so the reverse of the original action occurs.

Fig 35 The amount of water lost by the body through the kidneys operates by negative feedback.

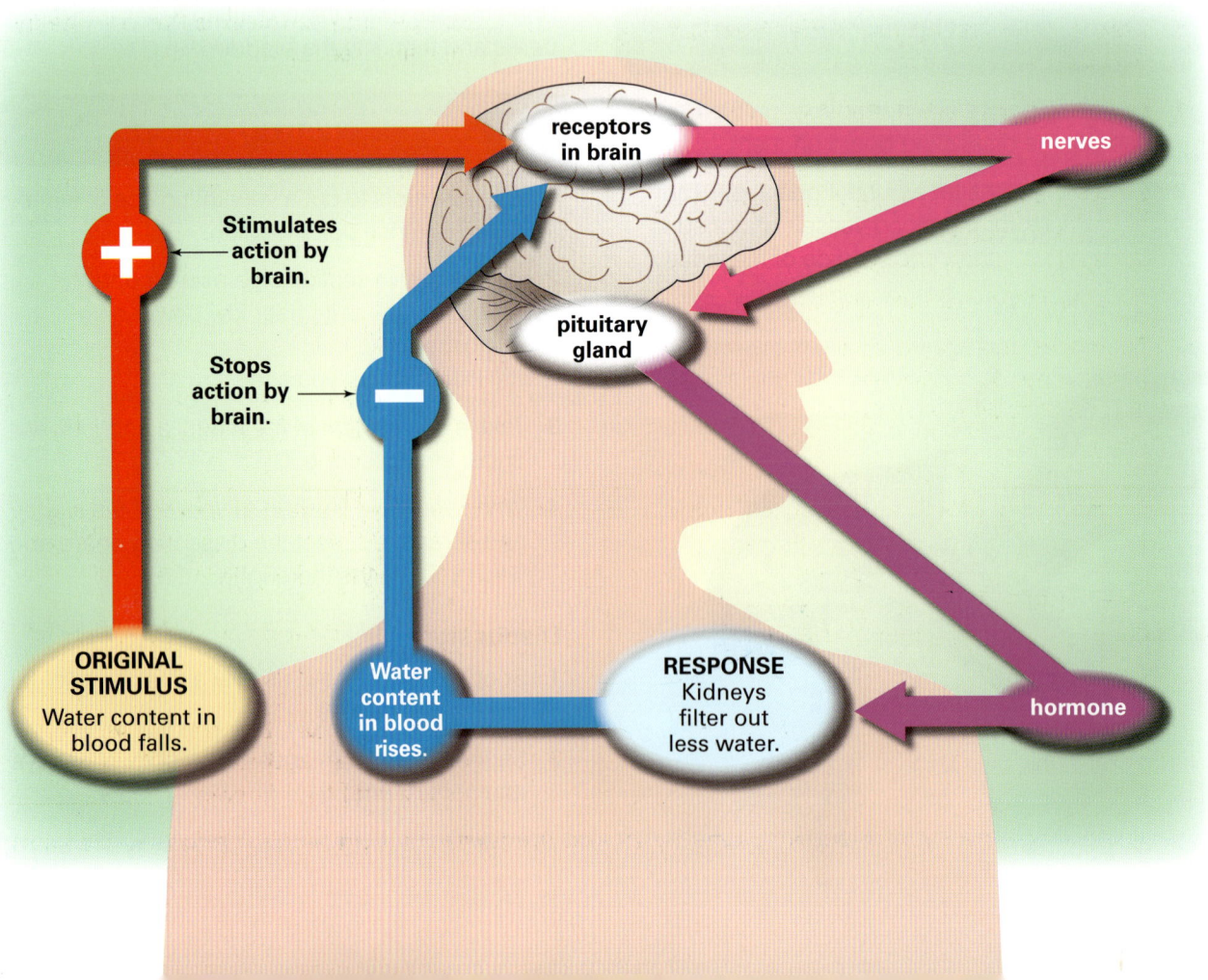

Check!

1 How is heat lost from the human body? In which ways can this loss be reduced?

2 a What is a set-point temperature?
  b Which groups of organisms have a constant body temperature?
  c What is the advantage to organisms that have a constant body temperature?

3 Some of the sentences below are false. Select the false ones and rewrite them to make them correct.
  a Most water is lost from the body as sweat.
  b Body heat is lost only by evaporation of water from the skin.
  c Heat energy is released during cell respiration.
  d Urine is made in the bladder and stored in the kidneys.
  e The pituitary gland detects changes in body temperature and sends hormones to the skin and sweat glands.

4 How is water lost by your body? How is it replaced?

5 Use the table of water inputs and outputs on page 174 to infer the changes that would occur if:
  a the measurements had been taken on a very cold day.
  b the measurements had been taken over a period which included exercise.

6 The boxes and arrows below represent the negative feedback system involved in the control of body temperature in Fig 30 on page 171.
    Use the labels on the diagram in Fig 30 to replace the letters in the diagram below.

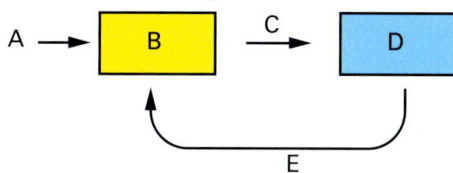

7 The diagram shows the parts of a heating unit that controls the temperature in a house.

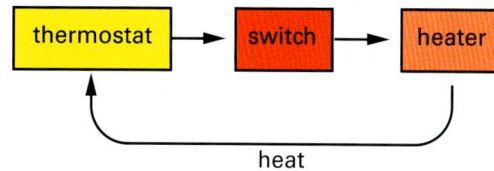

  a What is the function of the thermostat?
  b What is the function of the switch?
  c Why is this an example of a negative feedback system?

8 The graph below refers to the information in Question 7. It shows the temperature inside the house over a 2-hour period.
  a What is the set-point temperature?
  b At what time did the heater turn on? When did it turn off?
  c By how many degrees did the house temperature vary?
  d Why do you get small rises and falls of temperature in systems that operate by negative feedback?

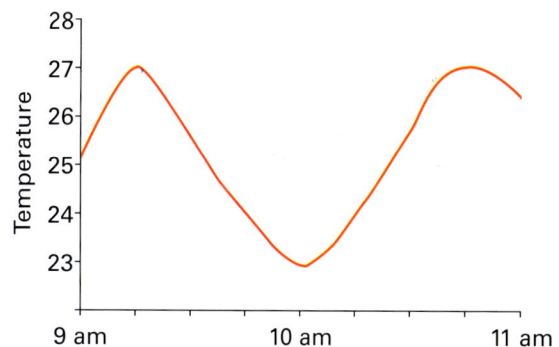

9 Your body contains about 5 L of blood.
  a If the kidneys filter one litre of blood per minute, how much blood is filtered in one day?
  b How many times is the total volume of blood filtered in a day?
  c Suppose your body produced 1500 mL of urine in a day. Express this volume of urine as a percentage of the total volume of blood filtered in a day.

challenge

1 Sweat contains about 99% water and 1% salt, mainly sodium chloride. It is made in the sweat glands in the dermis of the skin and is released over the surface of the skin through the sweat pores. There are about 2 million sweat glands in the human skin.

   a Use your knowledge of change of state of matter to explain in terms of the particle model how sweat reduces the temperature of the skin.

   b Some other mammals such as dogs have very few sweat glands. During exercise or hot weather dogs pant. Suggest how they might lose heat by this action.

   c Why do you think that athletes, after a very vigorous workout, drink liquids containing salts and minerals?

2 To lose heat, the capillaries in your skin dilate (become much larger in diameter) and carry more blood. To retain heat, the capillaries constrict (become smaller in diameter).

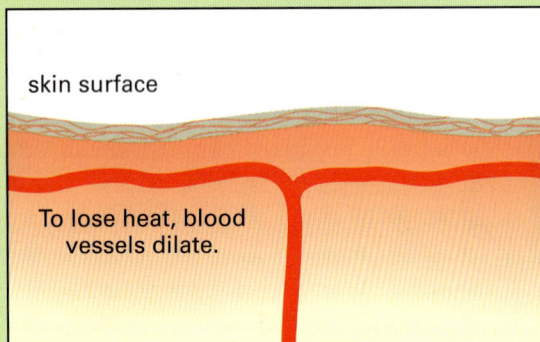

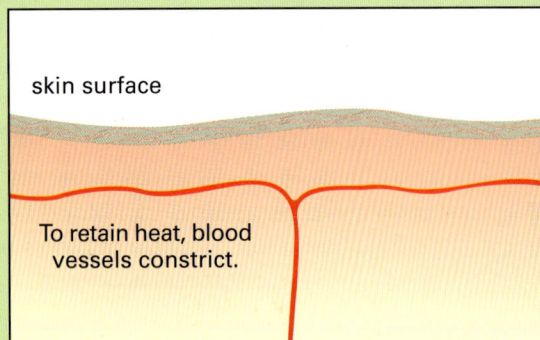

skin surface

To lose heat, blood vessels dilate.

skin surface

To retain heat, blood vessels constrict.

   a Suggest how the actions of the blood capillaries can increase and decrease heat loss from the body.

   b Why does your skin look much redder during or just after exercise?

   c Suggest how a wet suit helps divers reduce heat loss when they are under water.

3 A car is being driven at 60 km/h, the speed limit around town. The car goes up a hill and starts to slow down. The driver presses harder on the accelerator pedal. As the car goes over the top of the hill, it speeds up.

   Draw a flow diagram to explain how keeping a car at 60 km/h in this story is controlled by negative feedback.

4 Your breathing rate at rest is about 18 breaths per minute, but when you breathe into and out of a paper bag, your breathing rate increases.

   To find out whether it is the lack of oxygen or the rise in carbon dioxide that acts as the stimulus to increase breathing rate, an experiment was carried out. The tables below show the results.

% of O_2 in air breathed in	10	15	20	25	30
breathing rate (breaths/min)	18	19	18	18	19

% of CO_2 in air breathed in	1	3	6	9	12
breathing rate (breaths/min)	18	19	25	35	50

   a Which gas seems to affect the rate of breathing?

   b A receptor at the base of the brain is sensitive to levels of CO_2 in the blood. Suggest how negative feedback might control your breathing rate. Draw a flow diagram to help your explanation.

Copy and complete these statements to make a summary of this chapter. The missing words are on the right.

1 All of the body's functions are controlled and coordinated by the _____ system and _____ system.

2 The _____ is the main organ of the nervous system and consists of three main parts; the _____ controls voluntary actions, while the cerebellum and brain stem control _____ actions.

3 Sensory neurons relay _____ from _____ to the brain, while _____ neurons relay impulses from the brain to muscles or glands.

4 A _____ is an automatic response which occurs when an impulse travels to the spinal cord then straight back to a muscle.

5 Hormones are _____ which are made in endocrine glands and are released directly into the blood.

6 _____ are responsible for controlling growth, ripening of fruit and the timing of flowering.

7 Many of the body's processes such as water and _____ balance are controlled by _____.

brain
cerebrum
chemical controllers
endocrine
heat
impulses
involuntary
motor
negative feedback
nervous
plant hormones
receptors
reflex action

Try doing the Chapter 7 crossword on the CD.

Working with technology

REVIEW

1 In a darkened room, Joel felt a sticky cobweb suddenly cover his face, and he immediately pulled away.
 Which type of receptor was used for this action?
 A vision
 B taste
 C touch
 D sound

2 The action of Joel pulling away from the cobweb was probably:
 A caused by muscles activated by hormones
 B a reflex action
 C the stimulus to the response
 D caused by a negative feedback system

3 Parts of the body are under voluntary control and others are under involuntary control.
 a Which body actions are involuntary?

 b Which parts of the nervous system coordinate involuntary actions?

4 The flow diagram below shows a typical reflex action after a bright light has been shone in your eye. Match the letters in the diagram with the words in the following list.

receptors in eye   pupil
flash of light   motor neuron
spinal cord   pupil decreases
sensory neuron

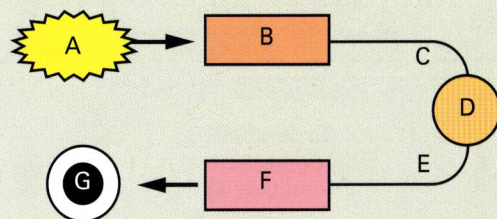

REVIEW

5 Nerves and hormones are both used by the body to relay messages from one point to another. How does the action of nerves differ from that of hormones?

6 The body temperatures of four animals were recorded over a 12-hour period. The results are shown in the graph below.

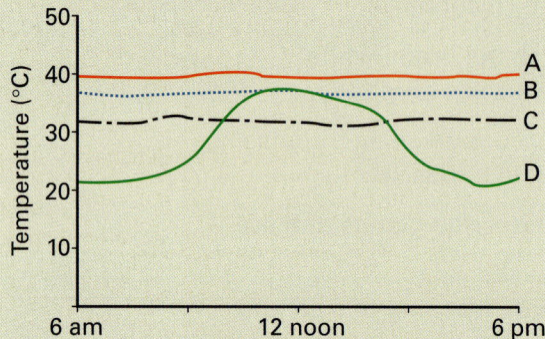

a Which of the animals are likely to be mammals or birds. Explain.

b What is the set-point temperature for animal A?

c Which animal is probably a human?

d Suggest an inference to explain the shape of the graph for animal D.

7 The following three experiments on plant hormones were done with oat seedlings.

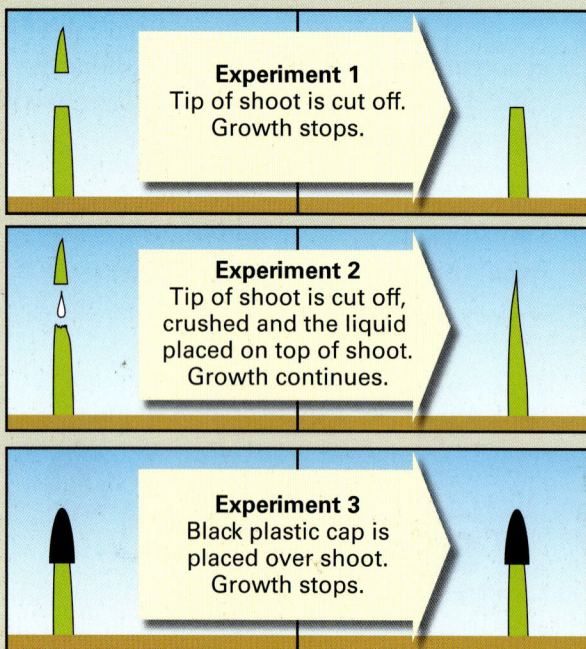

Experiment 1
Tip of shoot is cut off. Growth stops.

Experiment 2
Tip of shoot is cut off, crushed and the liquid placed on top of shoot. Growth continues.

Experiment 3
Black plastic cap is placed over shoot. Growth stops.

a Write an inference to explain the results of each of the three experiments.

b Design an experiment to show that the plant hormone will act only on cells just below the tip of the seedling and not on cells further down.

8 Read the following about a hormone which controls the sodium levels in your body.

The adrenal glands are situated on top of each kidney and produce a hormone (we will call this hormone X) which regulates the amount of sodium in the blood. It does this by acting on the kidney to reduce the amount of sodium that is filtered out into the urine.

The adrenal glands are under the control of the brain and the pituitary gland. Receptors in the brain detect a low blood sodium level. Nerve impulses from the brain are sent to the pituitary gland which releases a hormone (called hormone Y) which stimulates the adrenal glands to release hormone X.

a What happens to the blood when hormone X is released from the adrenal glands?

b Which part of your body is sensitive to levels of sodium in the blood?

c Negative feedback is used to control the amount of sodium in the blood. Use the information above to replace each of the letters in the flow diagram below.

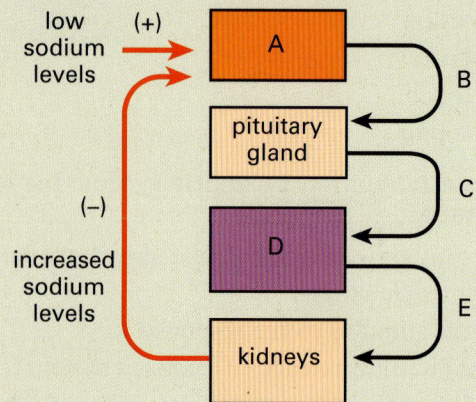

Check your answers on page 335.

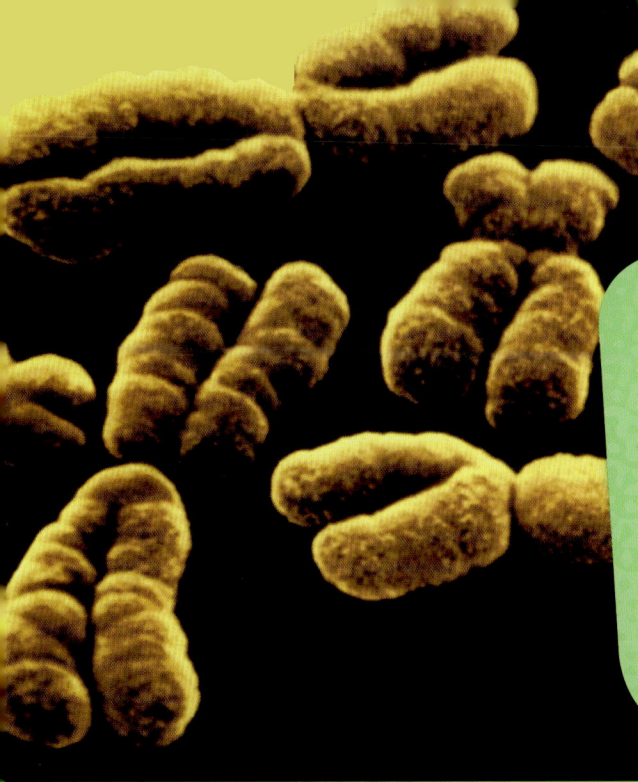

8

Inheritance

Getting Started

Work in a group of 3 or 4 and discuss the following questions. Keep your answers for later in the chapter.

The forensic scientists in the photo are investigating a crime scene. They are looking for sources of DNA from the victim and also from the suspect.

1 What is DNA and where is it in your body?
2 What would be good sources of DNA at this crime scene?
3 Suggest how a suspect could be convicted using DNA.
4 If you were a forensic scientist what other evidence would you gather to help convict the suspect?

8.1 Chromosomes

Long ago the Ancient Egyptians recognised that the racing characteristics of greyhounds were inherited. It is believed that they selected parent dogs that were strong and fast runners, and bred them to produce young dogs with these characteristics. By selectively breeding they produced dogs that were highly valued in Egyptian society.

Greyhounds reproduce sexually. That is, the male produces sperm and the female produces eggs. A new individual forms when the nuclei of the sperm and egg join together. After fertilisation, the egg divides and the new organism gradually grows in size.

It is reasonable to assume that the sperm and the egg must contain all the instructions for the cells to make the new organism.

Chromosomes and inheritance

At the turn of the 20th century, many scientists wanted to find out what part of an organism's cell was responsible for passing on characteristics from one generation to another. An American biologist, Walter Sutton, provided one of the earliest clues to the problem. He wondered about the importance of sausage-shaped objects that had been observed in cells undergoing division. He noticed that the rounded nucleus in a cell seemed to change into these sausage-shaped objects just prior to cell division, and each of the new cells contained these objects. These objects we now call **chromosomes**.

Sutton also observed that a particular species of organism always had the same number of chromosomes, and that the number of chromosomes was different for different organisms.

Sutton chose fruit flies for his experiments because they had only 8 chromosomes in their cells and they bred very quickly. On the basis of his experiments, Sutton inferred that the chromosomes carry the inherited characteristics and that each organism has a particular number of chromosomes.

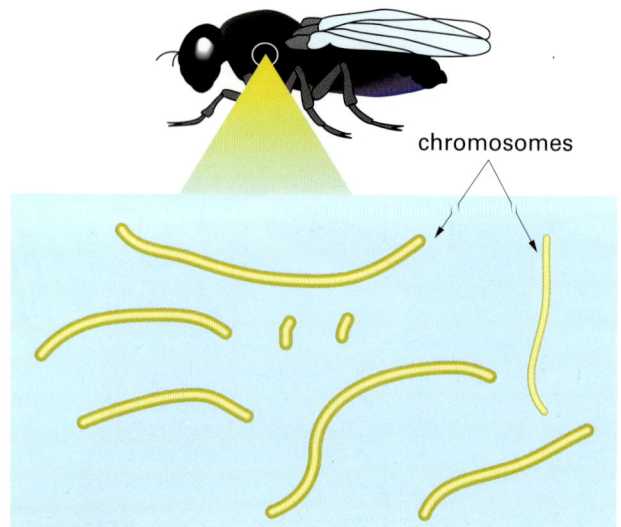

Fig 2 The chromosomes in the cells of a fruit fly carry all of its inherited characteristics.

Chromosomes in cells

In *Science World 2* you learnt that chromosomes can be seen only during cell division, and the two new cells that are formed each get one of every chromosome. This means that the new cells contain *exactly* the same number of chromosomes as the original cell.

Chromosomes are usually in pairs. This is why the numbers in the table below are even numbers. For example, humans have 23 pairs, a fruit fly has 4 pairs and corn has 10 pairs.

In the diagram on the next page, the 46 chromosomes in a human have been placed in pairs from largest to smallest (except the X chromosomes). Notice that each chromosome is roughly **H** shape. This is because each chromosome strand is duplicated and the strands are joined at one place.

Organism	Number of chromosomes
human	46
mouse	40
fox	34
fruit fly	8
pea	14
corn	20
chicken	78
algae	148

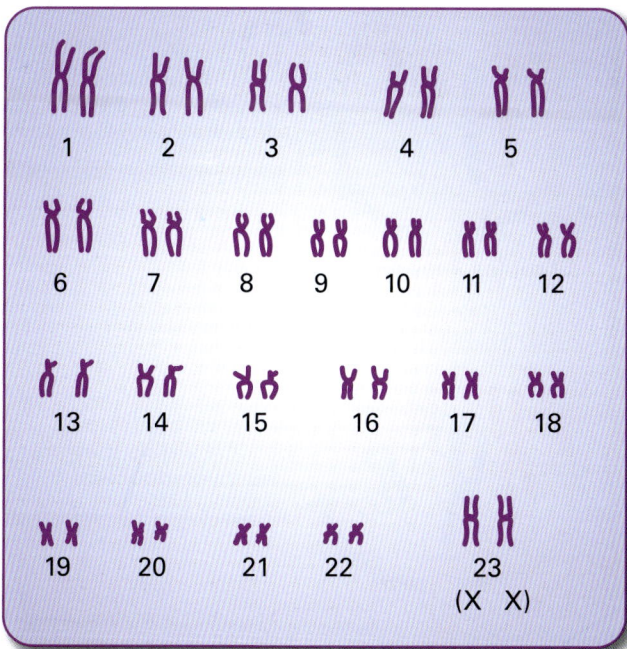

Fig 3 The 46 chromosomes in a human female are arranged in pairs based on size. The pair numbered 23 contains the sex-determining genes.

The nuclei of sex cells (sperm and eggs) contain only *half* as many chromosomes as the nuclei of all other cells. Why is this? The formation of sperm and ova occurs by a special type of cell division during which the chromosome pairs separate. This means that each sex cell receives 23 *single* chromosomes. When the nuclei of the sperm and egg join during fertilisation, the new cell then contains 23 *pairs* of chromosomes.

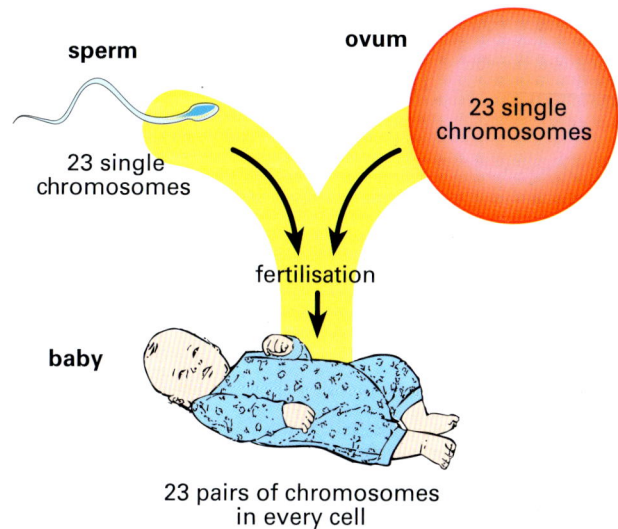

23 pairs of chromosomes in every cell

Activity

Chromosomes in sex cells

In this activity pipe cleaners will represent chromosomes. You will need 3 pairs of pipe cleaners, each pair a different length. One of each pair is white and the other is coloured.

1. Place the pipe cleaners in pairs so that you have a white one and a coloured one in each of the pairs.

2. Draw a circle at the top of the sheet of paper and lie the 3 pairs of chromosomes in it. This represents a body cell containing 3 pairs of chromosomes.

3. Your task is to make sex cells. For this you select one long chromosome, one medium one and one short one. One selection has been done for you.

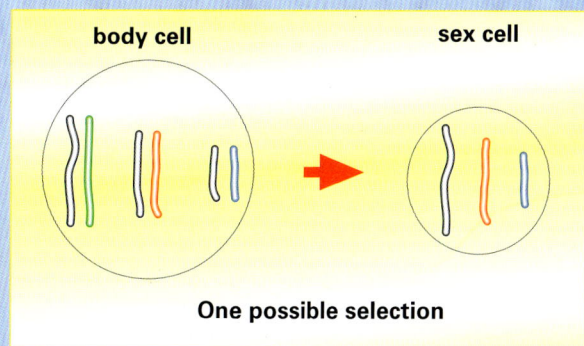

One possible selection

4. How many different sex cells can you make?

   Use coloured pencils to draw the three single chromosomes in each of the sex cells.

⭐ extra *for* experts

Formation of sex cells

When your body cells divide, each new cell has the same number of chromosome pairs as the parent cells. In humans this is 23 pairs. These cells are referred to as *diploid* cells: *di* means two and *ploid* refers to the chromosome number. So in your body most of the cells are diploid and have two copies of each chromosome. In *Science World 2* you learnt that this type of cell division is called *mitosis*.

When sex cells are formed they have only one chromosome of each pair. These cells are called *haploid* cells. This means the cell division process has to be different from mitosis. The process of sex cell formation is called **meiosis** (my-OH-sis). Meiosis occurs only in special cells in the testes and ovaries in animals, and in the anthers and ovaries in plants.

In mitosis two daughter cells are produced in each division. However, in meiosis four different sex cells are produced, as shown the diagram on the right and the animation.

Questions

1   Meiosis can be thought of as having two cell divisions. Describe how the first division is different from the second division.

2   There is another way the chromosomes can be arranged in line 3 of the diagram. Using red and blue pens, draw this arrangement. Draw the sex cells this arrangement will produce. How is it different from those in the diagram?

3   Imagine the blue chromosomes originally came from the organism's mother. What is the chance that a sex cell could carry all of the mother's chromosomes? Justify your answer.

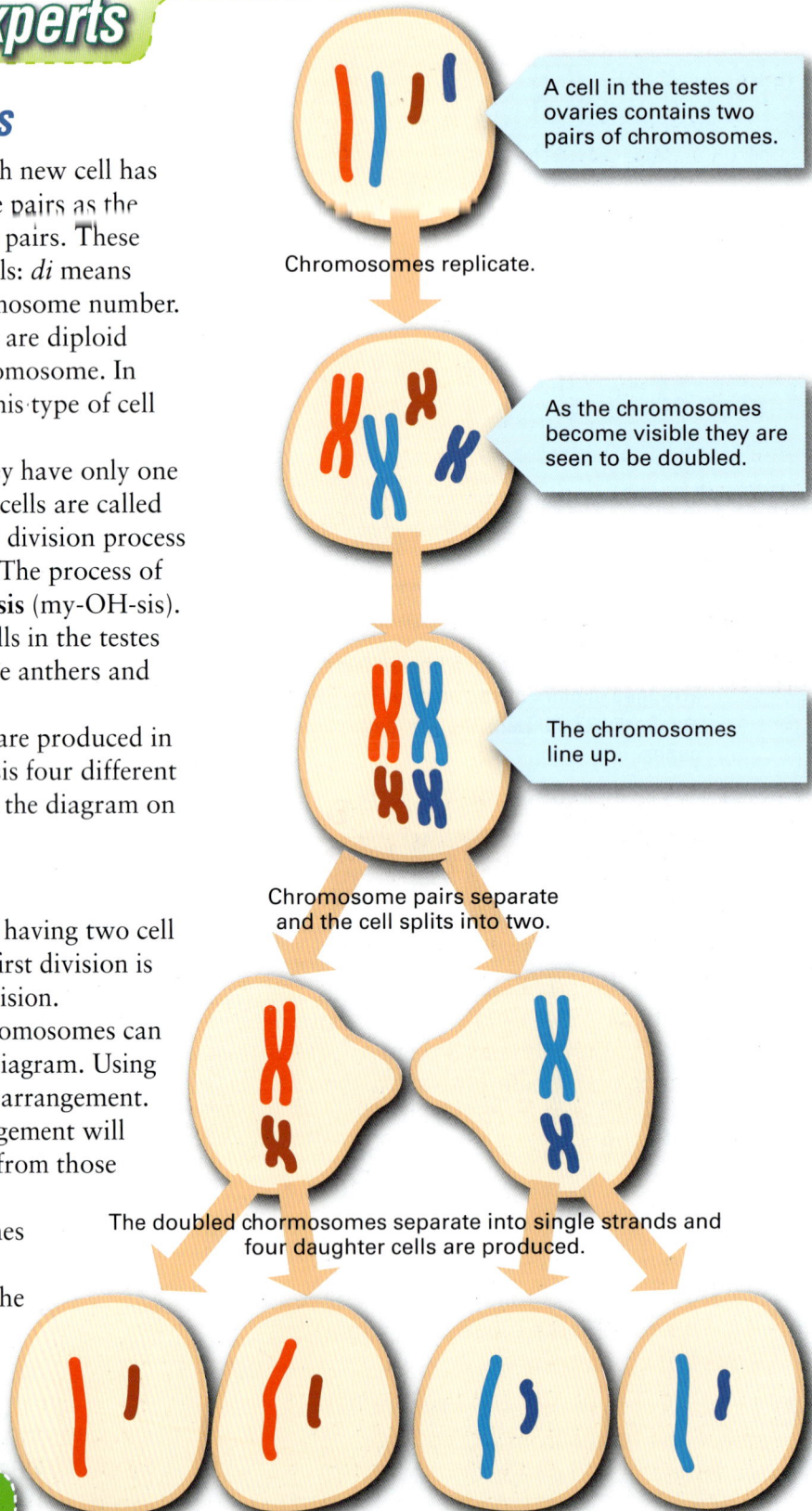

Working with technology To see an animation of this, open the animation **Making sex cells** on the CD.

A cell in the testes or ovaries contains two pairs of chromosomes.

Chromosomes replicate.

As the chromosomes become visible they are seen to be doubled.

The chromosomes line up.

Chromosome pairs separate and the cell splits into two.

The doubled chormosomes separate into single strands and four daughter cells are produced.

Fig 6 The process of meiosis produces sex cells with half the number of chromosomes of a body cell.

Determining sex

The chromosomes on the right are from a human male. How are they different from the chromosomes in a female in Fig 3 on page 181?

Notice that chromosome pair 23 in the male is different from that in the female—the male has two quite different chromosomes. The larger one is called the X chromosome and the smaller one is the Y chromosome. These chromosomes are called *sex chromosomes* because their genes determine the sex of the offspring.

Sperm cells, which are made in the testes, contain either an X chromosome or a Y chromosome, and 22 other chromosomes. On the other hand, ova, which are made in the ovaries, contain an X chromosome and 22 others.

If you are a boy, you would have received a Y chromosome from your father and an X chromosome from your mother. And if you are a girl, you would have received an X chromosome from each of your parents.

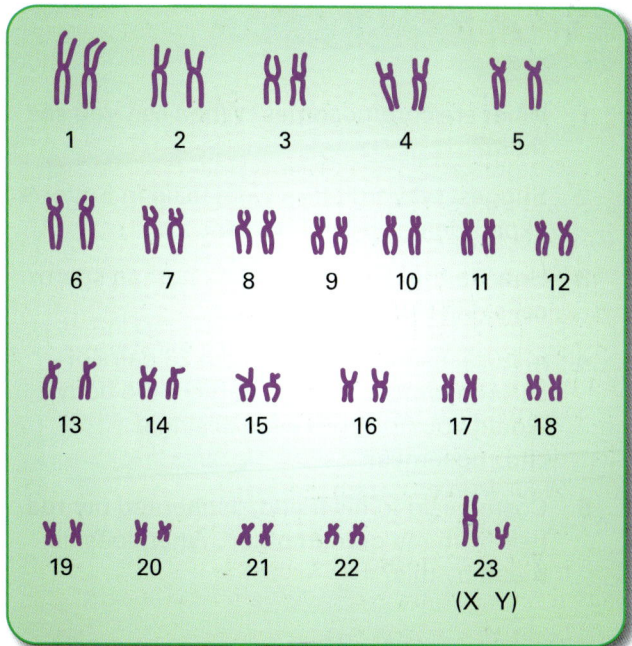

Fig 7 The chromosomes from a human male

Activity

If a couple are having a baby, what are the chances of having a boy? A girl? You can use a model to find out.

You will need eleven small plastic disks for this activity.

1 Use a felt pen to write X on five disks and Y on five others. These disks represent sperm.

2 Place all ten disks in a box or bag.

3 Mark the eleventh disk with an X. This represents an ovum.

4 Place the X disk on a piece of paper on the table.

5 Then, without looking, select a sperm disk and place it on the table next to the ovum.
   🖊 Record whether the result is a boy or a girl.

6 Replace the disk and repeat for a total of 10 draws.
   🖊 Calculate the percentage of boys and girls.

7 Repeat the procedure for a total of 100 draws.
   🖊 Calculate the percentages of boys and girls. Suggest why these results are different from the result in Step 6.
   🖊 Pool all the class results. Are the results the same as your results?
   🖊 In 1 mL of male semen there are about 40 million sperm. How many would be carrying the Y chromosome? What is the chance that a sperm carrying an X chromosome will be the first to fertilise the ovum?
   🖊 A couple have five daughters. What is the chance that their next child will be a son?

Check!

1 What are chromosomes? When can you see them?

2 Suggest why fruit flies were used in Sutton's experiments and not humans.

3 How do the chromosomes in human sperm cells differ from those in ova?

4 In humans most cells contain 23 pairs of chromosomes. In which parts of the body would you find cells with 23 single chromosomes?

5 Cosmo said to his friend, 'I inherited my red hair from my grandmother'. What does he mean by this?

6 The Smiths have three sons. Mrs Smith is pregnant and believes she is having another son. Mr Smith disagrees and says that because they have three sons the next child has a greater chance of being a daughter. Who is correct? Explain your answer.

7 Use the table on page 180 to work out how many chromosomes there are in:
   a a fox's ovum.
   b the pollen of a corn plant.

8 The father's sperm determines the sex of the child. Is this statement true or false? Give a reason for your answer.

9 Look at the table of the number of chromosomes in different organisms on page 180. Notice that they are all even numbers. What is the reason for this?

challenge

1 The diagram below shows the chromosomes of a human female. The chromosomes circled are a pair.
   Could both of these chromosomes have come from only one of the parents? Explain.

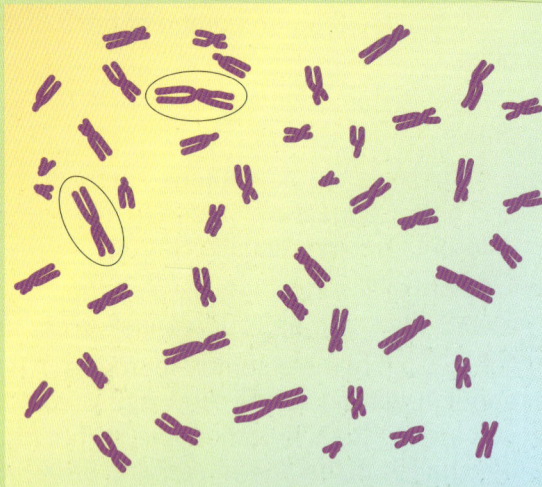

2 Is it true to say that the most complex organisms have the greatest number of chromosomes? Use the table on page 180 to justify your answer.

3 There are two types of twins in humans— identical twins and fraternal twins.

Fig 8 Identical twins (top) and fraternal twins (bottom)

Identical twins form when an ovum splits into two just after a sperm fertilises it. Fraternal twins form when two ova are fertilised by two different sperm.

a Explain in terms of chromosomes why identical twins are always the same sex, yet fraternal twins can be the same or different sex.

b Explain why one member of fraternal twins can have blue eyes while the other has brown eyes, yet identical twins both have the same eye colour.

4 In the formation of sex cells in the testes or ovaries (meiosis), the pairs of chromosomes line up in the middle of the cell. Then each member of the pair separates and moves apart. A new cell membrane forms down the middle and separates the two daughter cells.

Sometimes a pair of chromosomes may not separate, resulting in one sex cell with too many chromosomes and the other with too few. Using X and Y chromosomes only, explain, using diagrams, how a person's cells could contain three sex chromosomes, XXY.

5 The person in the photo below has Down syndrome, a genetic disorder affecting about one in every 600 births. Children born with this disorder often have a lower than normal immunity to disease. Before antibiotics and other treatments became available, many of these children died when they were very young. People with Down syndrome have one extra chromosome in their cells.

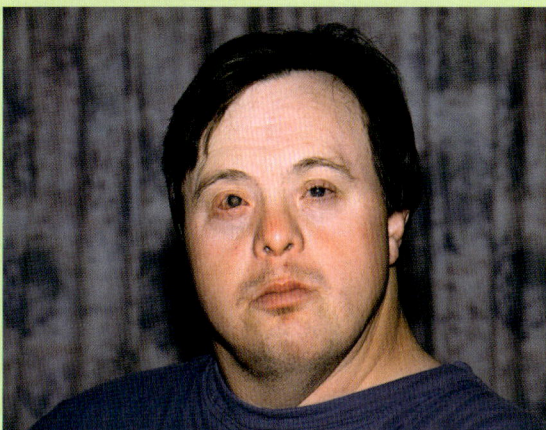

Use the diagram in Fig 11 at the top of the next column and the ones on pages 181 and 183 to work out:

a which chromosome pair is affected.

b whether the person whose chromosomes are shown in Fig 11 is a male or a female.

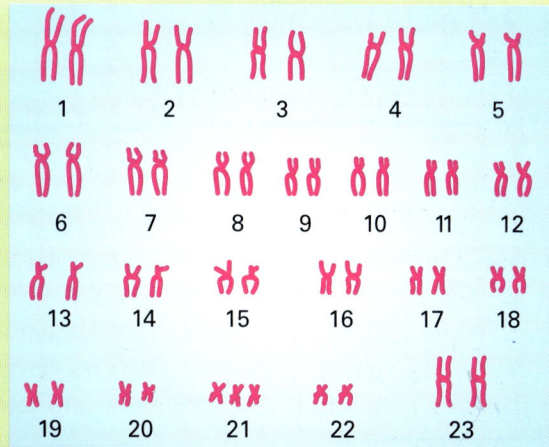

Fig 11 Chromosome map for Challenge 5

6 Use the information above and in Challenge 5 to suggest how a person could be born with Down syndrome.

7 Not all the features of organisms are controlled by genes. Some are influenced by factors in the environment experienced when the young organism is growing.

a What environmental factors might affect the features of humans?

b During which part of a human's life would these environmental factors have most influence?

c The blue flowers in the photo below were from a hydrangea plant grown in acidic soil. The red flowers were produced from a cutting of the same plant grown in basic soil.

What other environmental factors might affect the features of a plant?

Fig 12 Hydrangea flowers grown in acidic soil (blue) and basic soil (red)

8.2 DNA

Chromosomes contain a substance called **deoxyribonucleic acid** or **DNA** for short. It is the DNA in the chromosomes that determines your characteristics.

The chemical composition of DNA was first investigated in 1869 when the German chemist Friedrich Miescher found that a substance from cell nuclei was acidic and contained the element phosphorus. Because it was found in the nucleus, this substance was initially called *nuclein* and later called deoxyribonucleic acid.

In the 1950s, Watson, Crick and Wilkins proposed that the DNA molecule is shaped like a *double helix*—something like the lookout in King's Park, Perth (see the photo below).

The DNA contains sugars (deoxyribose), phosphates and nitrogen-containing substances called *bases*. There are four types of bases: adenine (A), guanine (G), thymine (T) and cytosine (C). In the DNA molecule, base A on one strand will bond only with T, and C will bond only with G. For this reason A – T, and C – G are called *base pairs*.

The DNA molecule is double stranded with each base on one strand weakly bonded to its base pair on the other strand. This bonding makes the two strands lock together to form the double helix shape.

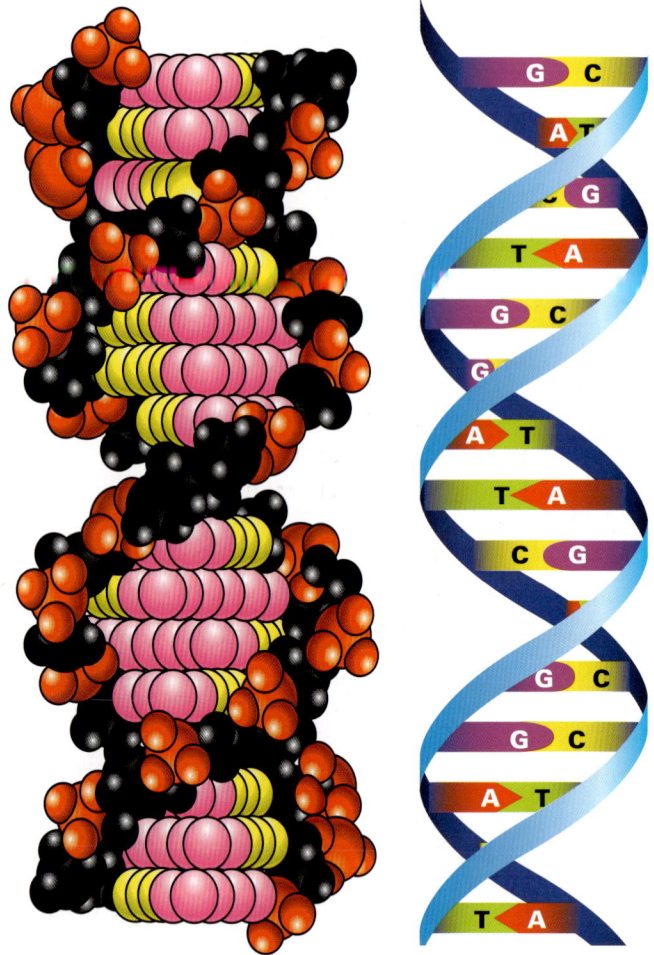

Fig 14 A model of DNA and a simplified structure on the right. The weak bonds between the matching base pairs on each strand hold the DNA molecule in its helical shape.

Genes

Organisms are different because the proteins in their cells are different. It is the DNA that provides information about the types of amino acids that make up proteins. The arrangement of the four different bases along a DNA strand will determine what type of protein will eventually be made. These sections on the DNA containing the bases are called **genes**. A gene is the portion of a chromosome that tells the body what type of protein to make.

Many of the substances in cells are made with the aid of enzymes, and all enzymes are proteins. So by determining the types of enzymes that are produced, the DNA code determines the organism's characteristics.

science bits

DNA replication

During cell division the DNA in the chromomosomes copies itself. This process is called **replication** because the DNA copy is an exact *replica* of the original DNA.

The DNA is made up of building blocks called *nucleotides* (see Fig 15). The nucleotides are made of three molecules—sugar, phosphate and a base molecule. The nucleotides are linked together in the DNA to form strands.

The two twisted strands of DNA in the double helix are held together by weak bonds between the base pairs on each strand. When replication begins the weak bonds break and the DNA 'untwists', as shown below.

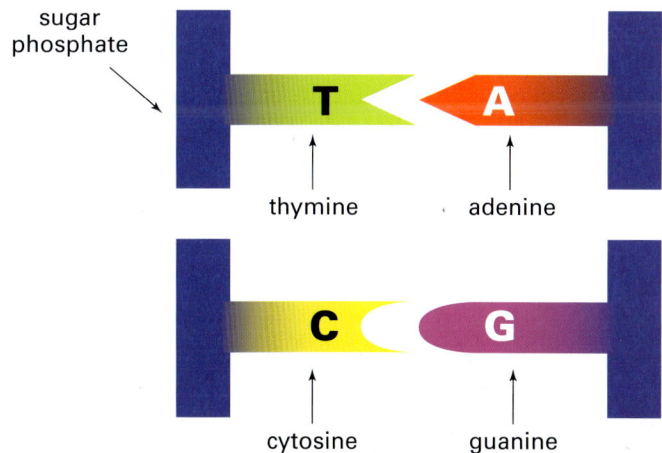

sugar phosphate

thymine   adenine

cytosine   guanine

Fig 15 Nucleotides are the building blocks of DNA. They consist of sugar, phosphate and base molecules.

To see an animation of DNA replication, open **DNA replication** on the CD.

Working with technology

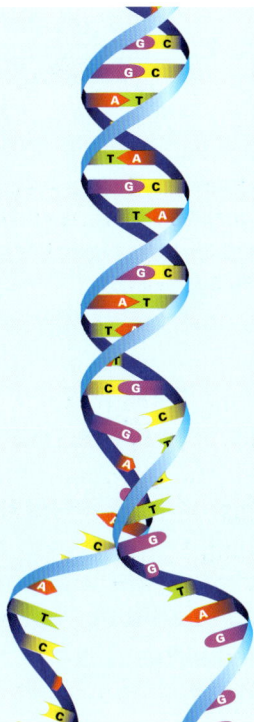

Replication begins as the DNA helix 'untwists'. The strands unzip as the weak bonds between the bases break.

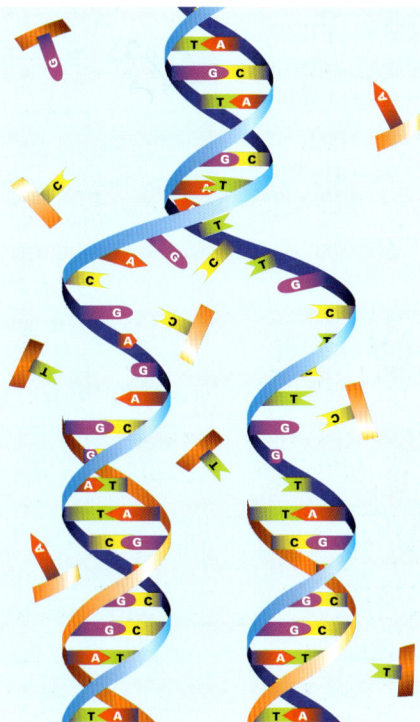

The new strands begin to be built on each strand of the original DNA, using spare nucleotides.

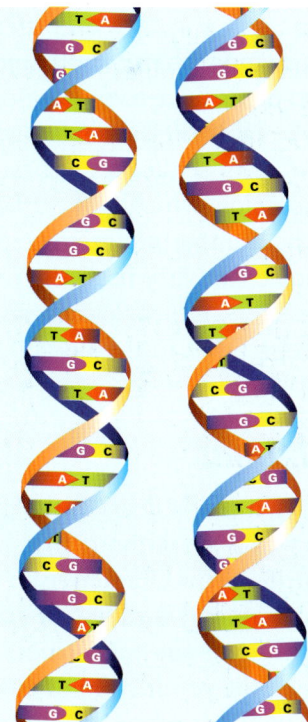

Finally an identical copy of the original DNA is made.

The DNA code

If the two strands in the molecule of DNA separated, part of a single strand would look like the structure in the diagram below. It is the sequence of the bases along the DNA that forms the code.

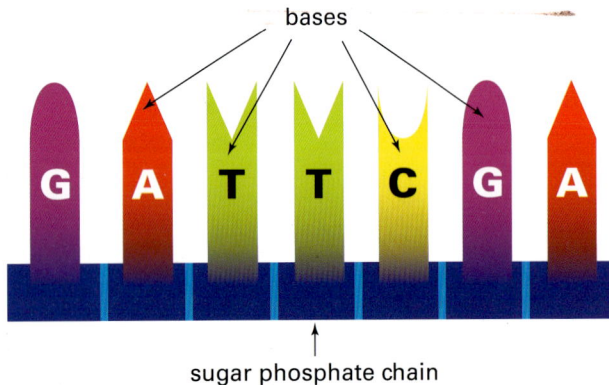

bases

G A T T C G A

sugar phosphate chain

Any *three* of these bases form a triplet code for one amino acid. For example, GAT will code for one type of amino acid and TCG will code for another. However, with four types of bases you can make 4 × 4 × 4 = 64 different triplets. This is many more than the 20 amino acids, so some amino acids have two or more alternative codes (see the table on the next page).

Different sequences of bases code for different amino acids, which make up different proteins; and the number of amino acids in a protein molecule can vary between 50 and 50 000 or more. DNA molecules contain millions of bases. Hence, a DNA molecule can code for thousands of proteins.

Mutations

The fawn (baby deer) in the photo on the next page was born without any skin colouring or hair colouring. This characteristic is called *albinism* and the animal is called an *albino*.

This fawn has a gene in its cells that has stopped the production of any pigment. There has been an alteration in the original gene that codes for normal colouring. Alterations to genes are called **mutations**. (See Science Bits on page 190 to learn more about the chemical basis of albinism.)

Some mutations can be detrimental to the organism, and most are fatal causing death. Other

Activity

Model DNA
You will need some coloured paper clips and a small sheet of cardboard.
1 Choose four colours from the pile of paper clips, and assign a base to each colour. For example, blue = A, red = T, etc.
2 Cut a 12 mm wide strip from the sheet of cardboard. Make it between 20 and 30 cm long. The strip represents the sugar phosphate chain of the DNA molecule.
3 Place 18 paper clips (in any order) along the strip of cardboard. For convenience, group them into threes with a small gap in between.

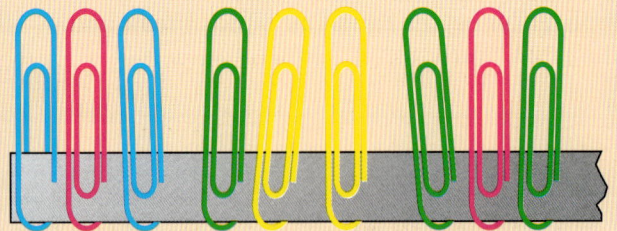

The table on the next page shows the code for the 20 amino acids that are found in the body. Notice that most amino acids have two or more alternative triplet codes. Notice there are also codes for STOP and START.
4 Use the table on the next page to find the code for STOP. This indicates the end of the amino acid chain of the protein that is to be made. Add this triplet to the end of your chain.

Use the table to work out the amino acid sequence on your model DNA.

Swap strips with your partner and work out their amino acid sequence.
Keep your model for the next activity.

mutations can be beneficial. For example, humans have benefited from a mutation in seeded grapes which produced seedless grapes.

How do mutations cause changes to characteristics? Suppose a small part of a DNA

DNA code	amino acid	DNA code	amino acid	DNA code	amino acid	DNA code	amino acid
AAA AAG	phenylalanine	GAA GAG	leucine	TAA TAG	isoleucine	CAA CAG	valine
AAT AAC	leucine	GAT GAC		TAT		CAT CAC	
AGA AGG AGT AGC	serine	GGA GGG GGT GGC	proline	TAC	methionine/ START	CGA CGG CGT CGC	alanine
				TGA TGG TGT TGC	threonine		
ATA ATG	tyrosine	GTA GTG	histidine	TTA TTG	asparagine	CTA CTG	aspartic acid
ATT ATC ACT	STOP	GTT GTC	glutamine	TTT TTC	lysine	CTT CTC	glutamic acid
		GCA GCG GCT GCC	arginine	TCA TCG	serine	CCA CCG CCT CCC	glycine
ACA ACG	cysteine						
ACC	tryptophan			TCT TCC	arginine		

Fig 19 The triplet codes on DNA and the amino acids they code for—notice that there are alternative triplet codes for almost all of the 20 amino acids, as well as codes for STOP and START.

strand had the following sequence of bases:

AATCAACCTTCA

For convenience, let's separate the triplets.

AAT CAA CCT TCA

Using the table above this would code for the following amino acids:

leucine valine glycine serine

If there was a change to one of the bases:

AAT CCA CCT TCA

the new sequence of amino acids would be:

leucine glycine glycine serine

This change could produce quite a different protein from the one that was made originally.

Mutations occur naturally, and it has been estimated that 1 in 1 000 000 cells contains a mutation in its DNA. However, the rate of mutations can be increased by exposure to

Fig 20 An albino fawn (baby deer)

high energy radiation from X-rays and nuclear reactors, as well as exposure to chemicals such as formalin and certain pesticides.

The UV part of sunlight can also increase mutations in organisms. These mutations can lead to cancer, particularly in skin cells. This is why over-exposure to the Sun is dangerous, especially for people with light coloured skin.

Why didn't I slip, slop, slap like Mum told me to?

Activity

DNA and mutations

You will need the model strand of DNA that you made in the activity on page 188.

Simulate a mutation by selecting one paper clip at random and replacing it with another colour.

📋 Find the new sequence of amino acids.

📋 Sometimes a mutation will not change an amino acid in a protein. Work out how you can change a base in your sequence but not change the original amino acid sequence.

science bits

Why there are albinos

The colour of your skin, eyes and hair is due mainly to a chemical compound called *melanin*. Melanin is made in special cells called *melanocytes* found at the bottom of the epidermis in your skin. The colour of your skin and hair depend upon the size of the melanin granules in the melanocytes. In black skins, the granules are larger and in white skins they are less obvious.

Melanin is made from tyrosine, a colourless amino acid. Tyrosine is converted to melanin by an enzyme called *tyrosinase*. If a mutation occurs in the gene that codes for the production of tyrosinase, the enzyme is not produced and melanin is not made. This results in an albino with whitish-pink skin, white hair and red eyes.

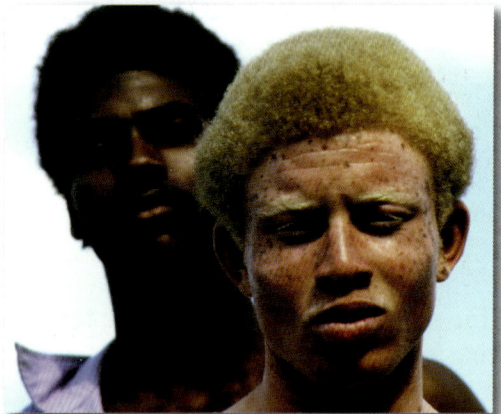

Fig 23 An albino Papuan boy

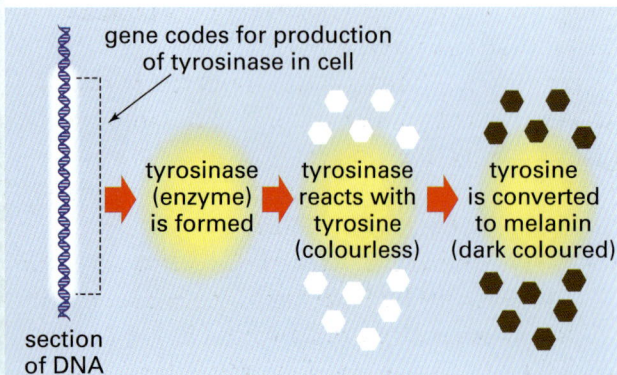

gene codes for production of tyrosinase in cell

tyrosinase (enzyme) is formed ➡ tyrosinase reacts with tyrosine (colourless) ➡ tyrosine is converted to melanin (dark coloured)

section of DNA

WEBwatch

Use your internet browser to find more information about albinism. Search using the following words: *melanin, melanocytes, albino, skin colour*.

Find out why albinos cannot tan in the sun and why an albino's eyes are red. Also try to find out why albino wild budgerigars are yellow.

Genomes

In 1916, after years of experimenting, Walter Sutton inferred that the inherited characteristics of fruit flies were carried on the chromosomes in the cell. In March 2004, scientists who had been experimenting collaboratively for five years found there were 250 million bases in the DNA in each fruit fly cell. They also determined the order in which the bases are arranged on the DNA.

The whole of the fruit fly's genetic information is found in these 250 million bases, and is called its **genome**.

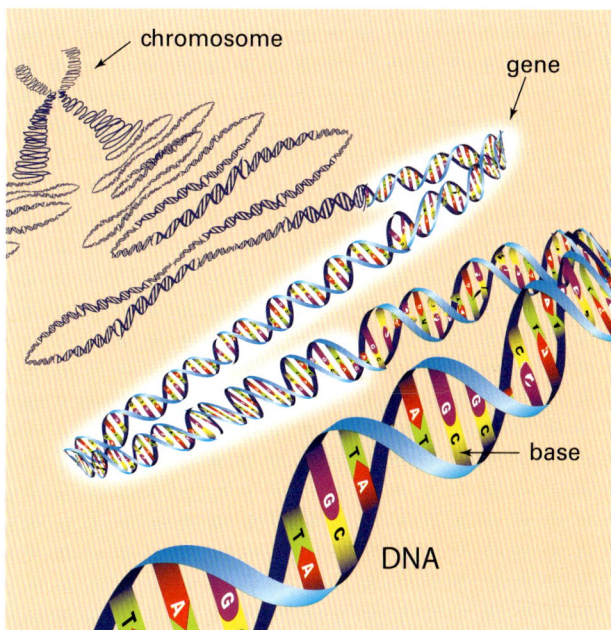

Fig 24 A gene is a section of DNA containing a particular sequence of bases

What makes up a genome?

The researchers working on the fruit fly genome have also identified 13 601 genes on the DNA. These genes are made up of thousands of bases. The average gene contains about 2000 bases. If you multiply the number of genes by the number of bases an average gene contains, you find that the genes make up less than 20% of the genome.

The larger part of the genome contains sections that control how genes are turned on and off. There are also long sections of bases that are called 'junk' or nonsense DNA because scientists are uncertain of their function.

The Human Genome Project

The Human Genome Project (HGP) which ran from 1990 to 2003 mapped the position of the genes in the human genome. This massive task was co-ordinated by the US National Institutes of Health and involved hundreds of scientists from at least 18 countries, including Australia. By the time the HGP had finished it had:

- identified 20,000 protein-coding genes in human DNA, and another 2000 DNA segments which are predicted to be genes
- determined the sequence of the 3 billion bases on human DNA
- stored the information on databases
- addressed ethical, legal and social issues that arose from the project.

The expected benefits of the Human Genome Project are:

- improved diagnosis of disease
- treatment of genetic diseases such as cystic fibrosis
- manufacture of custom drugs
- replacement of defective genes
- reduced risk of inheritable mutations
- improved techniques for DNA identification in legal and criminal cases.

HGP–the future?

Although the HGP was coordinated by government departments, one of the project's aims was to transfer all the technologies to private companies. Now almost all of the HGP follow-up research is being done by private commercial companies, particularly multi-national US-based companies, who expect to earn billions of dollars through sales of new drugs, equipment, technologies and information.

However, will the knowledge of the human genome benefit all humankind? Here are some problems that might arise:

- Will treatment and diagnosis be so expensive that only the rich will benefit?
- Will an individual's genetic file be private and secure, or will it be available to banks, health funds, insurance companies etc?
- Will the large companies patent their drugs so that they control certain treatments?

Activity

Work in a group of 3 or 4 people and discuss some of the issues in the statements and questions below. Use the internet, or find material from library books, magazines and newspapers.

1 Getting a man on the moon in 1969 was a massive project involving many scientists. How was this different from the scientific collaboration in the Human Genome Project?

2 Collect as much information as you can on new discoveries, techniques or inventions resulting from the Human Genome Project. Compile a scrapbook or information file and share this with the other groups in the class.

3 Suppose you have no family history of genetic diseases, and are thinking about having children. Should you ask your partner to have a DNA test done to make sure that their genome is disease-free?

4 Some life insurance companies are suggesting that a person's genetic file be submitted when they apply for life insurance, so that the company can assess whether that person is a high-risk case. What do you think? Give reasons for your answer.

WEBwatch

Go to www.scienceworld.com.au and follow the links to the websites below.

Student Guide to the Human Genome Project
Extensive and easy-to-read information on HGP and links to a large number of other sites.

Frequently asked questions—Human Genome Project
Answers to questions about the HGP.

Educational Resources (HGP)
The education section of the National Human Genome Project Institute has links to facts sheets and information about the HGP.

DNA detective work

With the completion of the Human Genome Project and advances in computer technology, large segments of DNA or even the whole genome will allow precise identification of an individual. This is important in the following situations:

- matching donor organs with recipients in transplant operations
- identifying suspects whose DNA matches evidence left at a crime scene
- exonerating people who are wrongly accused
- identifying victims in major accidents, catastrophes or natural disasters
- establishing paternity of a child.

How is DNA used to identify people?

Detectives and forensic scientists have to gather a number of pieces of evidence together in order to convict a person of a crime. For example, a suspect's blood type and fingerprints are compared with those found at the crime scene, as are pieces of hair or fabric from their clothes and the tread of their shoes. All these pieces of evidence have to prove 'beyond reasonable doubt' that the suspect is the guilty person.

When using DNA to convict people, forensic scientists have to match the sequence of bases in a number of regions of the DNA of the suspect with those of the DNA samples found at the crime scene. Since only 0.1% of your DNA is different from anybody else's, scientists have to match base sequences of the DNA in those regions which are different.

A court will not convict a person when only one or two of the DNA base sequences match. This is too little evidence. However, when at least five DNA base sequences match, a jury can be confident 'beyond reasonable doubt' that the suspect is the guilty person.

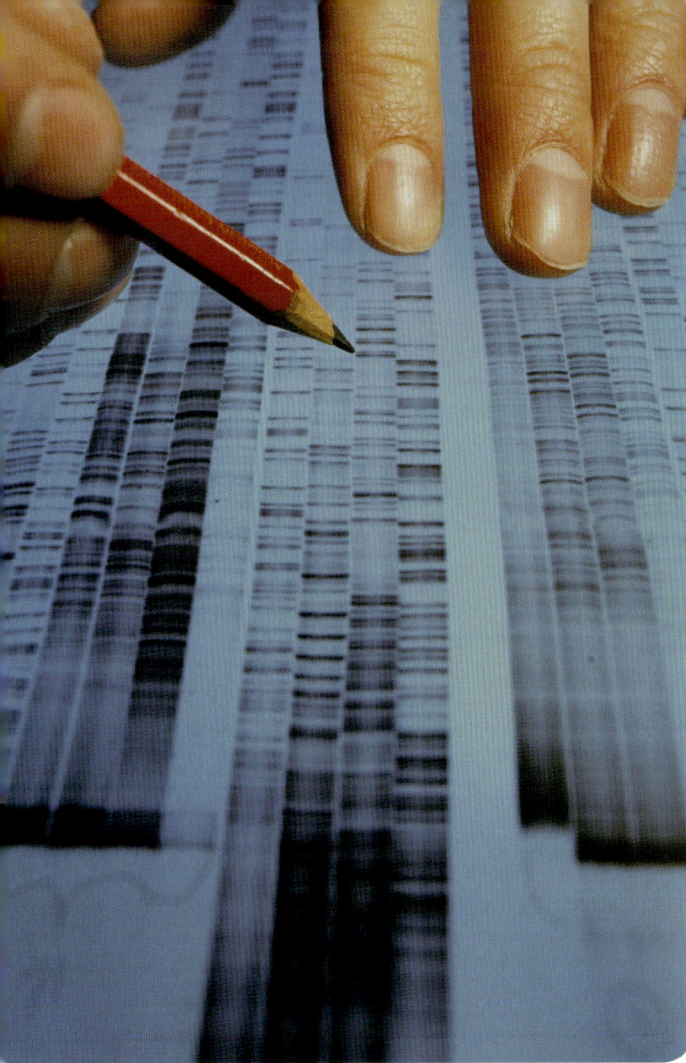

Fig 25 A forensic scientist examines the sequence of bases in sections of DNA.

Solving the French royal mystery

In 1795 Louis-Charles, the young son of King Louis XVI and Marie-Antoinette, supposedly died in a Paris prison. But many people believed he had escaped the brutality and executions of the French revolution and fled to England.

In April 2000, scientists used DNA matching technology to try to solve one of history's greatest mysteries. They used some tissue from the young prince's suspected remains and compared the DNA in it with the DNA in hair from his mother, as well as other samples from living and dead members of the royal family.

The DNA matching tests showed that the tissues were from the young prince, but many people are still not convinced. Go to www.scienceworld.net.au and follow the links to **Louis-Charles** for more information about this mysterious case.

Science in action

Testing the foetus

If parents-to-be know that one or both of them has a family history of genetic disorders, doctors may suggest that the pregnant woman have one or more tests. Doctors also know that children born to women more than 37 years old have a greater chance than normal of having genetic disorders such as Down syndrome.

Doctors will first suggest an *ultrasound* test when the woman is about 11–13 weeks pregnant. In this test reflected sound waves generate a picture of the foetus. If doctors suspect an abnormality, they may recommend other tests.

In a test called *genetic amniocentesis* (AM-nee-oh-sen-TEE-sus), a fine hollow needle is passed through the abdomen of the pregnant woman and into the amnion. This is a fluid-filled sac surrounding and protecting the foetus. A tiny amount of amniotic fluid is withdrawn and tested.

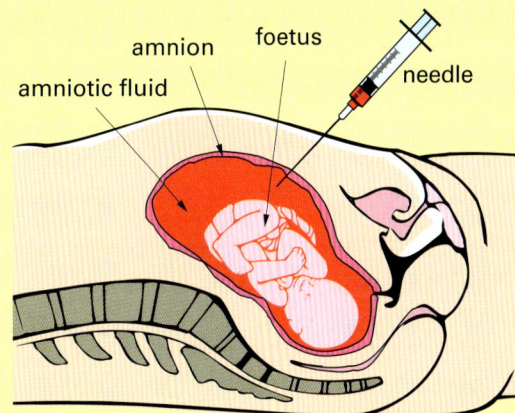

High levels of protein in the fluid may indicate diseases such as spina bifida. DNA in the foetal cells that are found in the fluid are tested to check for the presence of Down syndrome and other genetic abnormalities. However, because amniocentesis is an invasive test there are certain risks. About one in every 200 tests results in a miscarriage.

If the woman is found to be carrying an abnormal foetus she may be given choices of action. She may continue with the pregnancy or she may terminate the pregnancy before the legal limit (28 weeks in most states of Australia).

Check!

1 What is DNA, and where is it found in the body?

2 What is a base pair? How do the bases help form the double helix shape?

3 a What is the genetic code?
   b What materials does the genetic code eventually produce?
   c Why are these materials so important in organisms?

4 A small part of a DNA strand contains the following bases: GGATAGCTTAGCG
What are the matching bases on the other strand of DNA?

5 Insulin is a relatively small protein, having a total of 51 amino acids in its structure. What is the smallest number of bases on a DNA strand needed to code for insulin?

6 A small segment of DNA has the following sequence of bases:

ACA GGT TAA CAA CCT TCA GGG

Use the table on page 189 to work out the amino acid sequence.

7 Explain, by using the base sequence in the question above and the table on page 189, how mutations alter proteins.

8 Which environmental factors can increase the rate of mutations in organisms?

9 Make a list of the benefits that might be gained and the problems that might arise from the Human Genome Project.

10 The Human Genome Organisation has allocated 3–5% of its budget for the study of the project's ethical, legal and social issues. Make a list of some of these issues. You may want to discuss this with others.

challenge

1 Biologists estimate that 99.9% of all your genes are similar to the genes of other people. The 0.1% makes you different. However, about 80% of your genes are the same as those in a cat or dog, and about 60% are the same as in an earthworm. What can you infer from this information?

2 The following amino acids are from a small section of a protein.

leucine–glycine–tyrosine–lysine–lysine–glycine

a Work out *one* base sequence on the DNA strand that would code for this section of protein.

b Compare your base sequence with others in the class. How many different sequences did the class make for this section of protein?

c What is the base sequence on the other strand of the double-stranded DNA?

3 Suppose a mutation occurs in a sperm cell of an animal and a gene is altered. This sex cell fertilises an ovum and an offspring is produced. However, many mutations are fatal and the offspring dies.
Use your knowledge of the materials genes make to suggest why this occurs.

4 A forensic scientist matches the DNA from the suspect with a sample from the crime scene. Explain to someone who doesn't know what DNA or forensic science is how this works. Use the terms *base sequence*, *DNA regions* and *beyond reasonable doubt* in your answer.

5 Man A believes he is the father of a child. The mother believes that man B is the father. How would you use DNA technology to go about solving this problem?

6 Use the internet to find out about other ways to test the health of a foetus. Try looking for Chorionic Villus Sampling (CVS) and the Maternal Serum Test.

WEBwatch

Watson and Crick were awarded the Nobel Prize in Physiology and Medicine in 1962 for their work on DNA structure.

Use the internet to find out more about their work. Also find out about the work of Rosalind Franklin and why she might have shared the Nobel Prize with Watson and Crick.

Then write a feature story about the discovery of the structure of DNA.

8.3 Dominant and recessive

Suppose you have set up an aquarium with two black fish—one male and the other a female. One day, a few months later, you notice 8 baby fish. Your two parent fish have bred and had offspring. However, the puzzling thing about the baby fish is there are six black fish and two red ones!

The colour of the fish is controlled by a particular gene. This gene comes in two forms—one that codes for black colour and the other that codes for red colour. Different versions of the same gene are called **alleles** (a-LEELs).

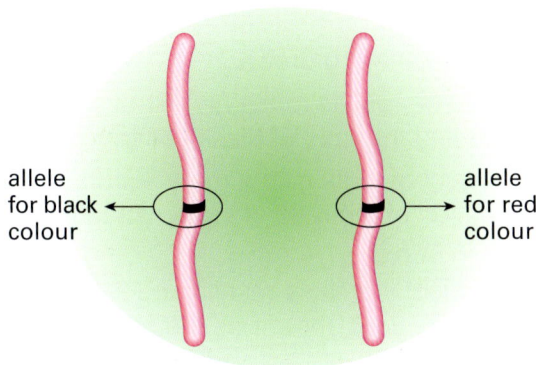

| Fig 28 | The colour of the fish's skin is controlled by two alleles of the same gene. Each allele is found at the same location on each of the chromosomes in the pair. |

allele for black colour

allele for red colour

However, if the parents have the genes for black colour as well as red colour, why don't you see any red colour in the parents? This is because the gene for black colour completely masks the gene for red colour. The gene for black colour is said to be the **dominant gene**. The gene for red colour, which is masked by the dominant gene, is called the **recessive gene**.

It is usual to represent the genes by the first letter of the dominant gene. A capital letter is used for the dominant gene, and the lower case of that letter for the recessive gene. In this case, the allele for black colour is **B**, and the allele for red colour is **b** (not **r**).

Fish carrying the genes **BB** will be black, and those carrying the genes **bb** will be red. Those fish carrying **Bb** will also be black because **B** is the dominant gene. (The dominant gene is usually written first, ie **Bb** and not **bB**.)

If the parents have a gene for black colour and one for red colour, they can produce some baby fish with black colour and some with red colour.

BB = black colour
Bb = black colour
bb = red colour

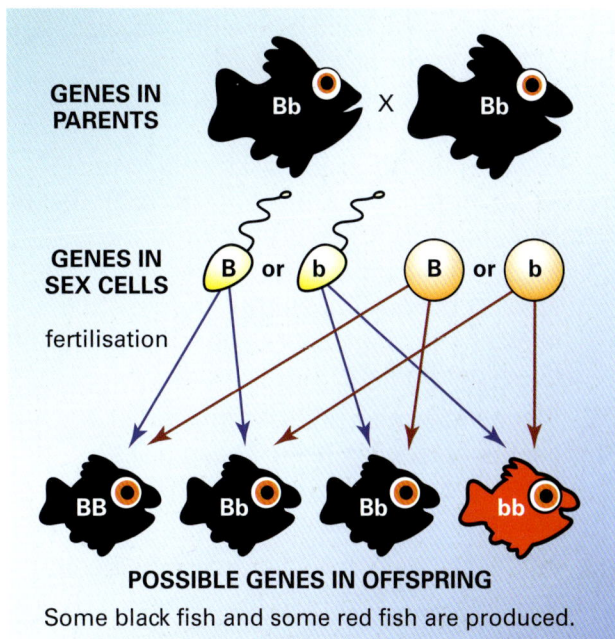

GENES IN PARENTS

Bb X Bb

GENES IN SEX CELLS

B or b   B or b

fertilisation

BB   Bb   Bb   bb

POSSIBLE GENES IN OFFSPRING
Some black fish and some red fish are produced.

If only one of the parents has the gene for red colour then none of the offspring will be red, as shown in the diagram below.

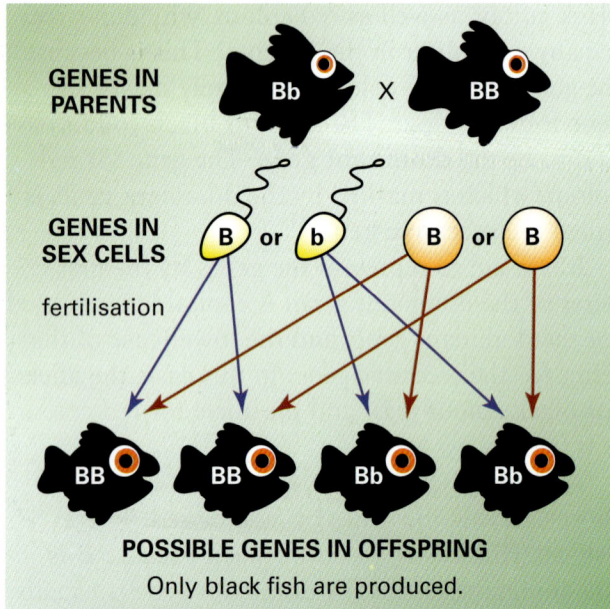

GENES IN PARENTS
GENES IN SEX CELLS
fertilisation

POSSIBLE GENES IN OFFSPRING
Only black fish are produced.

WEBwatch

Gregor Mendel was a monk and science teacher in a monastery in Austria. In 1866 he published his results of breeding experiments with peas. His meticulous and accurate records showed how characteristics could be passed from generation to generation. Mendel is often called the father of genetics.

Use the internet to answer the following questions. Remember to record the websites where you found the information.

1 What characteristics in peas did Mendel first study? What were his conclusions?

2 Why is Gregor Mendel called the father of genetics?

3 How did Mendel try to explain how characteristics were passed on from generation to generation?

4 It is said that Mendel's work was poorly understood and largely forgotten until after his death. Suggest a reason for this.

Activity

Fish genes model

In the example on page 195, you found that if both parent fish have genes Bb, they will have some black offspring and some red offspring. Let's investigate how many of each colour are produced.

You will need 20 black disks and 20 red disks for this activity. (You can use other colours, or coins, if you wish.)

1 Place 10 black disks and 10 red disks in a small container. These disks represent the ova carrying the colour genes. Label this container Female.

2 Place the remaining disks in another container labelled Male. These disks represent the sperm carrying the colour genes.

3 Without looking, select a disk from the first container and one from the second.

Record the genes and the colour of the offspring. (Remember the gene for black colour is the dominant gene.)

4 Replace the disks and make another selection. Do this 10 times.

Calculate the ratio of black fish to red fish.

5 Make another 10 draws.

Add these results to the first results and again find the ratio of black fish to red fish.

Which results give a more accurate indication of the ratio of black fish to red fish? Why?

Collect the class results and find the ratio. Give your answer as the nearest whole number.

6 Repeat this activity to confirm that parent fish with genes Bb and BB will produce only black fish.

Some genetics terms

The two fish below look the same but have different genes. Biologists use special terms to describe this situation.

black fish
genes = **BB**

black fish
genes = **Bb**

The type of genes in an organism is called its **genotype** (JEE-no-type). What the organism looks like or its physical characteristics is called its **phenotype** (FEE-no-type).

In this example, both fish have the same phenotype but different genotypes.

The fish with genotype **BB** is said to be **homozygous** (HO-mo-ZYE-gus), or a pure breeder, because both the alleles for the skin colour gene are the same. The other fish is said to be **heterozygous** (HET-er-o-ZYE-gus), or *hybrid*, because its two alleles for skin colour gene are different.

So the first fish in the diagram could be described as being a homozygous black fish, while the other one is heterozygous black.

Predicting crosses

In the previous activity you should have found that the ratio of black fish to red fish was about 3:1. It is possible to predict the type of offspring produced when two organisms mate. This mating is called a *cross*. One of the easiest ways of predicting crosses is to use a *Punnett square*.

In the Punnett square below two heterozygous black fish have been crossed.

Using a Punnett square you can predict on average that, for each red baby fish, three black baby fish will be produced.

You also found that when a homozygous black fish (**BB**) crosses with a heterozygous black fish (**Bb**), all the offspring are black. Let's use a Punnett square to check this.

Parents = **Bb** x **Bb**

Expected ratio of phenotypes = 3 black : 1 red

Parents = **BB** x **Bb**

Expected ratio of phenotypes = all black

Pedigrees

Earlobe attachment is an inherited characteristic. The gene for attached earlobes is dominant over the gene for unattached earlobes.

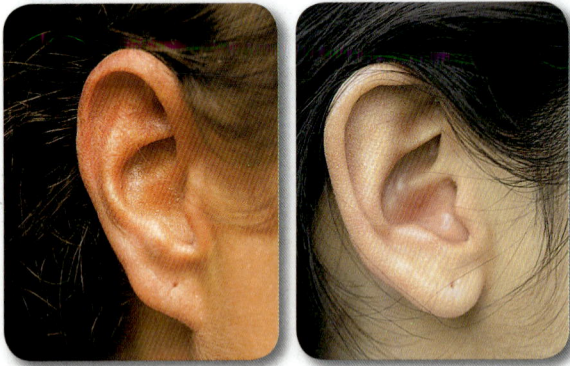

Fig 34   Attached earlobes (left) and unattached earlobes (right)

By studying family histories, biologists can build up a pattern of inherited characteristics. This pattern can be seen on diagrams called family trees or **pedigrees**. Pedigrees can show the phenotypes of related individuals over a number of generations.

No way am I gonna grow up to be like my father

Look at the pedigree at the top of the page. It traces the history of earlobe attachment through three generations. The circles ◯ represent females and the squares ☐ represent males. The shaded circles ● represent females with attached earlobes, and the shaded squares ■ represent males with attached earlobes.

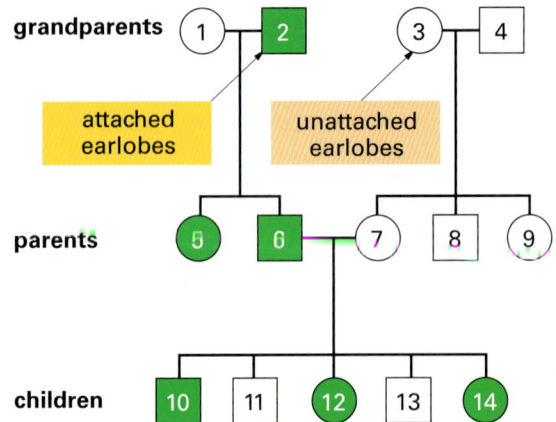

Pedigrees can be used to work out the genotypes of the individuals. For example, biologists know that the gene for attached earlobes is dominant over the gene for unattached earlobes. Let's call the gene for attached earlobes **A**, and the gene for unattached earlobes **a**. Using these symbols you can deduce that:
- grandparents 1, 3 and 4 will be **aa**
- individuals 7, 8, 9, 11 and 13 will be **aa**
- grandparent 2 could be **AA** or **Aa**
- individuals 5, 6, 10, 12 and 14 will be **Aa.**

The pedigree can be rewritten to show the phenotypes and genotypes of the individuals.

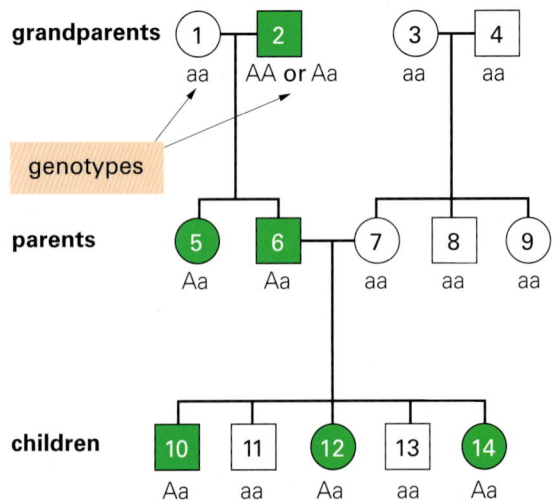

Fig 37   Pedigrees can show the genotypes as well as the phenotypes of individuals

Not so simple inheritance

Gregor Mendel delivered his scientific paper detailing the results of his breeding experiments with garden peas in 1866. His experiments were well designed and well recorded, and he tested more than 28 000 plants to reduce experimental errors. His success was largely due to the great care he took with his experimental methods. His knowledge of mathematics also helped him interpret his results.

However, Mendel was also very lucky. The seven characteristics he studied in peas were each determined by a single gene. For example, the gene that determines seed pod colour has two alleles. The dominant one codes for green pods, while the recessive one codes for yellow pods.

Single gene inheritance

There are very few characteristics in organisms that are controlled by a single gene. The following are two humans characteristics determined by a single gene:

- Earlobe attachment is determined by the presence of the dominant allele.
- *Cystic fibrosis* is a severe disease of the lungs and intestines caused by a recessive gene. A person inheriting the two affected alleles would develop cystic fibrosis. A person with only one affected allele would not develop cystic fibrosis, but would be a 'carrier' for the disease.

Human eye colour

For many years eye colour in humans was thought to have been controlled by a single gene. The allele for brown eyes was dominant over the allele for blue eyes. However, this idea did not explain green eyes or grey eyes or the variation of colours in between.

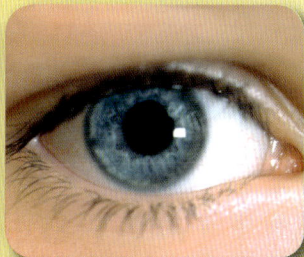

Biologists currently think that eye colour is controlled by at least three genes and probably others that may control how the coloured pigment is distributed over the iris causing flecks and rings. Eye colour is thought to be controlled by:

- a gene found on chromosome pair 15 which controls brown–blue colours,
- a gene found on chromosome pair 19 which controls green–blue colours, and
- another gene located on chromosome pair 15 that may affect the other two genes.

Eye colour

The colour of eyes is primarily determined by the amount of melanin in them. This dark brown pigment is deposited in the cells on the front surface of the iris. If a lot of melanin is present, your eyes will be brown. If very little or no melanin is present your eyes will be blue.

There is also a brownish-yellow pigment found in people with green eyes. It may also determine whether you have dark brown or light brown eyes.

There is no blue pigment in humans. Blue eyes is the absence of melanin. The cells in the front of the iris scatter the blue light in sunlight more than the red light. So your eyes appear blue just like the sky appears blue.

Blended genes

Budgerigars are native birds that live naturally in woodlands and grasslands throughout inland Australia. There are two purebred forms—yellow birds and blue birds.

Fig 40 The green budgerigar (right) is the offspring of one parent with blue feathers and the other with yellow feathers.

When a homozygous blue bird mates with a homozygous yellow bird, the offspring are green, not blue or yellow. In this case, the two alleles for feather colour are not dominant or recessive over each other, but instead result in a mixture or blend of characteristics. This is said to be **incomplete dominance.**

There are many examples of incomplete dominance. A red shorthorn bull mates with a white shorthorn cow to produce red and white calves, and red carnations cross with white ones to produce plants with pink flowers.

Suppose a blue male budgerigar mates with a yellow female. All the offspring have green feathers. Let's call the allele for blue feathers **B**. The allele for yellow colour cannot be **b** because it is not recessive. In this case we will call it **Y**, because offspring with alleles **BY** will be green.

The Punnett square at the top of the page shows the results of the cross between a blue budgerigar and a yellow one. When the green offspring are crossed, birds with blue, yellow and green feathers are produced.

Parents = **BB** x **YY**

Expected ratio of phenotypes = all green

Human blood types

There are four main blood types in humans—A, B, AB and O type. ABO blood type is controlled by a gene found on chromosome number 1, and biologists have found that there are three alleles of this gene—**A**, **B** and **o**. A person can have only two of the three alleles, one on one chromosome and the other on its pair. Allele **o** is recessive, while both alleles **A** and **B** are dominant. Therefore, if a person inherits allele **A** from one parent and allele **o** from the other, they will carry **Ao** alleles and will have **A** type blood.

But if a person inherits allele **A** from one parent and allele **B** from the other, the resulting blood type is **AB**. This blood type has features of both **A** type blood and **B** type blood, and not a blend of the two as you would get with incomplete dominance. This type of gene action is called **co-dominance.** The table below shows the relationship between the phenotypes and the genotypes.

Alleles (genotype)	Blood type (phenotype)
AA or Ao	A
BB or Bo	B
AB	AB
oo	O

Activity

There are two parts to this activity. For each part, work in a group of 3 or 4 people.

Part A: Determining blood groups
Because there are three different alleles for blood type it is possible for children of a couple to:

- all have one blood type
- have two different blood types
- have three different blood types
- have four different blood types.

Use the table on the previous page to help you work out the genotypes of the parents and the children in each of the four situations above.

A woman of blood type B claims that a man of blood type A is the father of her two children, who have blood types AB and O. Explain whether her claim is true or false. Does your explanation prove that he is the father of the children?

Part B: Blood transfusions
Carefully read the following extract.

A person requiring a blood transfusion has to be carefully matched to the donor's blood.

The structure of certain molecules on the surface of the cell membrane of a red blood cell determines blood type. There are two types of surface molecules, called A and B, which are controlled by genes. For example, a person with allele A will have red blood cells with A type molecules. A person with allele B produces B type molecules, while alleles A and B together produce both A and B type molecules, and gene o produces no surface molecules. Thus, there are four main blood types in humans.

Now if a person with A type blood is given B type blood, a reaction occurs resulting in a blood clot. These blood clots can block blood vessels in the heart, brain and other organs, and can be fatal.

The reason the clot forms is due to molecules called antibodies in the blood plasma (the clear part). Antibodies are produced when the body recognises that the surface molecules on cells are foreign. They destroy them by joining to them. This also happens to bacteria and 'foreign' blood.

People with A type blood produce anti-B antibodies. If this person is given B type blood, anti-B antibodies will be produced and will react with the type B blood cells forming a clot.

The table below shows the types of red blood cells and the antibodies that can be produced in the four different blood types.

What are antibodies? Why are they important in the human body?

Draw up a table showing a patient's four possible blood types. Then in another column show the possible blood types that could be given to each patient in a transfusion.

Explain why blood type O can be given to people with any blood type.

Which blood type can receive all the other types of blood?

Blood type	Type of surface molecules on red blood cells	Antibodies found in plasma
A	A	anti-B
B	B	anti-A
AB	A and B	neither
O	neither	both anti-A and anti-B

X-linked genes

In humans, there are a number of genes on the X chromosome that have no equivalent on the smaller Y chromosome. This is because the X is much larger than the Y chromosome. These genes are said to be **X-linked** and the characteristic is said to be sex-linked. Colour vision and blood clotting are two examples.

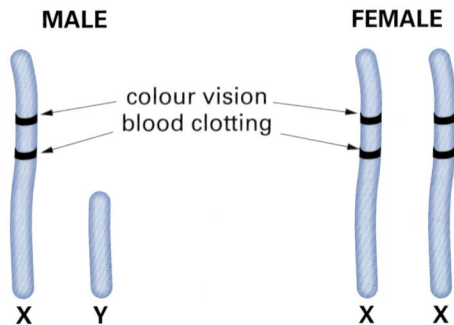

MALE   **FEMALE**

colour vision
blood clotting

X   Y   X   X

Fig 42   The genes for colour vision and blood clotting are found on the X chromosome. Females have two alleles for each characteristic but males have only one because there are none on the Y chromosome.

The allele for normal colour vision is dominant in humans (as you would expect). Now suppose a male is colour deficient (incorrectly called colour blind). He has an affected gene for colour vision on the X chromosome, but there is no matching allele on the Y chromosome. On the other hand, a female who has an allele for colour-deficient vision on one X chromosome and an allele for normal colour vision on the other, will have normal colour vision. However, she is called a *carrier* because she carries the affected gene for colour-deficient vision.

The pedigree below shows the inheritance of the gene for colour vision.

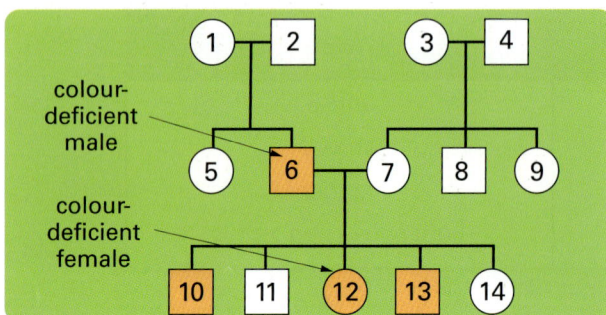

Male 6 is colour deficient and must have inherited the gene on the X chromosome from female 1 who is a carrier. Males 10 and 13 inherited their genes from female 7, while their colour-deficient sister, 12, got her genes from both her mother, 7, and her father, 6.

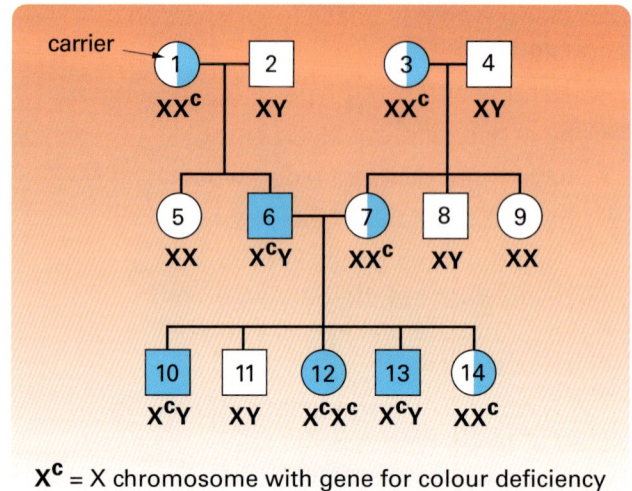

X^c = X chromosome with gene for colour deficiency

Check!

1 Explain the differences between these terms:
   a dominant and recessive genes
   b heterozygous and homozygous
   c genotype and phenotype.

2 Suppose a characteristic in humans is represented by the alleles **G** and **g**.
   a Which one is recessive?
   b Show two genotypes that produce the same phenotype.

3 If you get half your genes from your mother and half from your father, why don't you have half your mother's features and half your father's?

4 Toby crossed a brown mouse with a white mouse. He discovered that all of the baby mice were brown. What can you infer about the genotypes of the parent mice?

5 Explain the difference between genes which show incomplete dominance and those that are co-dominant.

6 A farmer breeds a black rooster with a white hen. She finds that all the chickens have grey feathers.

  a Use appropriate symbols to show how this happens.

  b What colour feathers should the off-spring have if two of the grey-feathered chickens are crossed?

7 Explain in simple language what the following statements mean:

  a The gene for blood clotting is an X-linked gene.

  b Females can be carriers for X-linked genes but males cannot.

8 What would happen if a person with A type blood was injected with B type blood?

challenge

1 Suppose that the allele that controls right-handedness is dominant over the one for left-handedness. A heterozygous right-handed male and a left-handed female have four children, three who are left-handed and one right-handed

  a If the allele for right-handedness is called R, use a Punnett square to calculate the proportion of children that should be right-handed.

  b Suggest a reason for the difference between your result in **a** and the actual proportion of children with this characteristic in this family.

2 When a homozygous hen with black eyes mates with a rooster with red eyes, all the chickens have black eyes.

  a Which allele for eye colour is dominant?

  b What is the genotype of the chickens?

  c Suppose two of the chickens mated when they matured. Use a Punnett square to find the genotypes and phenotypes of the chickens in the next generation.

3 In guinea pigs short hair is dominant over long hair. Explain how you could get some long-haired baby guinea pigs if you had a short-haired female and you had to buy a male guinea pig.

4 Muscular dystrophy is an inherited disease caused by an X-linked recessive gene. A man and a woman without the disease have a son with muscular dystrophy.

  a What are the genotypes of the parents?

  b What are the chances that their next son will have the disease?

  c What are the chances that their next female child will have the disease?

5 In humans, the allele for long eyelashes is dominant over the allele for short eyelashes. In the pedigree in the next column the shaded circles and squares show people with long eyelashes.

  a Use appropriate symbols to work out the genotypes of the members in the pedigree.

  b List the individuals who are definitely heterozygous and those who are definitely homozygous. Which ones are in doubt?

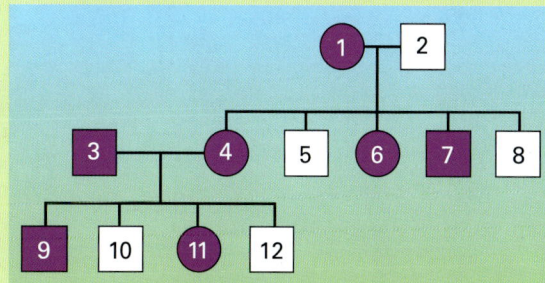

6 The ability to roll your tongue into a tube is an inherited characteristic in humans. In the pedigree below, the shaded individuals can roll their tongues. Work out if tongue-rolling is dominant or recessive. Then deduce the genotypes of the individuals.

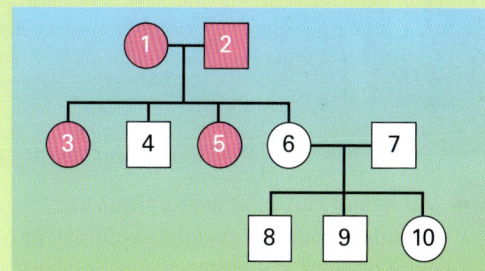

7 You are a genetic counsellor advising a couple who wish to have a baby. The man tells you that his only sister has had a son and a daughter; the daughter died from Gaucher's disease, a non-X-linked recessive disease of the blood. The woman has no family history of the disease.

  a Use a pedigree to find the chance of the man being a carrier for the disease.

  b What are the chances that the man's children will have the disease?

Science in action

Genetic counselling

Mrs Van Tronk has just given birth to a baby boy. A few days later she and her husband are asked whether they will permit their baby boy to be tested for the presence of Duchenne muscular dystrophy, or DMD, an X-linked disease which develops mainly in boys and occasionally in girls. It causes the muscles of the lower limbs to weaken and waste away, and eventually control of all muscle movement is lost.

Fig 45 Duchenne muscular dystrophy is an inherited disease caused by a defective gene on the X chromosome.

After careful consideration, the Van Tronks give permission for the test to be done. Doctors first test the blood for the presence of a particular enzyme which indicates muscle damage, but this is not a conclusive test for DMD. They find the enzyme in the baby's blood, so a DNA test is done to see whether the baby has the DMD gene.

The results of the DNA test show that baby Van Tronk has the gene for DMD. The parents are then counselled by medical and social experts and are made aware of the difficulties of raising a DMD child, and also of the help that is available.

Two years later, Mrs Van Tronk becomes pregnant once more. The Van Tronks know that there is a chance that this baby might also develop DMD. Because the baby is an 'at risk' baby, they make an appointment to see a genetic counsellor. The genetic counsellor explains to them about chromosomes and X-linked genes. They are told that the disease is caused by a gene on one of Mrs Van Tronk's X chromosomes, so that if the developing baby is a boy, he has a 50:50 chance of suffering DMD. The counsellors also discuss how X-linked genetic diseases run in families, and trace her family history with the aid of a pedigree. The counsellors suggest two possible courses of action.

- Test the developing baby's chromosomes to determine the sex of the child and whether it carries the DMD gene. The mother can continue with the pregnancy or terminate it within 28 weeks.
- Have no tests, but be aware that the child may have DMD if it is a boy, and be prepared to care for him.

Questions

1. Work with two or three other people and draw up a list of options that are available to the Van Tronks.
   a. Make a decision on what you would do if you were a Van Tronk. Give reasons for your decision.
   b. Suggest what help and support may be necessary for the Van Tronks with each of the options.
2. Should it be compulsory to test all pregnant women to find out if their offspring have genetic abnormalities? Give reasons for your opinion.
3. Under United States law, discrimination based on genetics is banned. At present, this is not so in Australia. How do you think Mrs Van Tronk could be discriminated against if her gene file was known?
4. Go to www.scienceworld.net.au and follow the links to **Gene Testing**. You will find information about gene testing, the pros and cons of the procedures and the current regulations.

MAIN IDEAS

Copy and complete these statements to make a summary of this chapter. The missing words are on the right.

1 _____ are found in the nuclei of cells. They carry _____ which determine what an organism looks like and how it functions.

2 Body cells contain pairs of chromosomes while _____ contain only single chromosomes. When fertilisation occurs, the single chromosomes form pairs in the cells of the new organism.

3 Sex in humans is determined by sex chromosomes—females have a pair of _____ and males have an X and a _____.

4 Chromosomes are made of _____. The sequence of the _____ on the DNA determines which types of proteins will be made.

5 _____ alter the sequence of bases in cells, and occur spontaneously or from exposure to _____ or certain chemicals.

6 The whole of an organism's genetic information found in its DNA is called its _____.

7 Different versions of a gene, called _____, are found at the same location on a pair of chromosomes.

8 For an inherited characteristic, the _____ form of the gene masks the recessive one.

9 The _____ of an organism is the types of genes it contains, whereas its physical characteristics are called its _____.

alleles
bases
chromosomes
DNA
dominant
genes
genome
genotype
mutations
phenotype
radiation
sex cells
X chromosomes
Y chromosome

Try doing the Chapter 8 crossword on the CD.

Working with technology

REVIEW

1 Chromosomes are found in:
A sex cells only
B all cells
C fertilised eggs only
D animal cells only

2 A gene is:
A a chromosome
B a molecule of DNA
C part of a chromosome that carries a single instruction
D one base on a molecule of DNA

3 Tongue rolling in humans is controlled by a single gene. Which one of the following statements is correct?
A Both genes for tongue rolling came from the male parent.

B Both genes came from the female parent.
C One gene came from each parent.
D Two genes came from each parent.

4 Horses have a total of 64 chromosomes in each of their body cells. Male horses have an X and a Y chromosome in their cells.
a How many pairs of chromosomes are found in the body cells of horses?
b How many chromosomes are found in the sperm of a horse?
c Which chromosomes do sperm carry?

5 A strand of DNA contains the bases AAGTC.
a What is the sequence of bases on the other matching strand of DNA?
b How are the two strands of DNA held together in the double helix?

6 A small section of DNA has the following sequence of bases.

TTAAGACTCAAGGGGTCCTCA

a How many amino acids does this section code for?

b Use the table on page 189 to work out the sequence of amino acids in the section of DNA.

c A mutation changes the triplet AAG to GAG. How will this affect your answer to **b**?

d Suppose the section of DNA is part of the gene in humans that makes your blood clot when blood vessels have been damaged. Suggest what might happen if this mutation did occur.

7 The Sloans have just had a baby boy. They also have another son and a daughter. Mrs Sloan is blood type O while her husband is blood type A.

a Which parent is definitely homozygous for blood type?

b If the daughter has O type blood, what blood genotype does Mr Sloan have?

c What are the chances that baby Sloan will have A type blood?

8 In corn plants, there are two types of seeds. The gene for smooth seeds (S) is dominant over the gene for wrinkled seeds (s).

a If a plant is homozygous and has smooth seeds, what are its alleles?

b What is the phenotype of a plant with the alleles Ss? Explain.

c What is the genotype of a plant with wrinkled seeds?

d Why would a plant with wrinkled seeds have to be homozygous?

9 The gene for height in pea plants has two alleles. The allele for tallness is dominant over the one for shortness. Joshua used a Punnett square to predict the results of a cross between two pea plants. Unfortunately, he spilt some ink over his notebook. From his ink-stained calculations:

a work out the genotypes and phenotypes of the parent plants.

b calculate the ratio of phenotypes in the offspring plants.

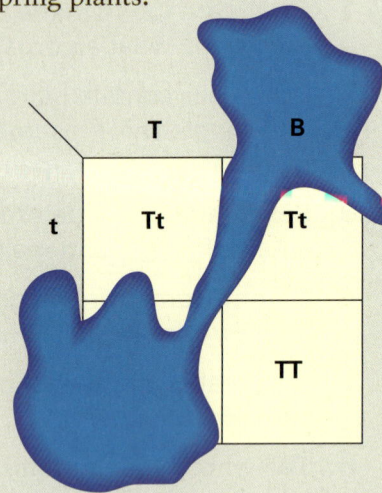

10 A couple have four children—three girls and a boy. The father, mother and two of the daughters can roll their tongue, while the other daughter and son cannot. Tongue-rolling is controlled by a single gene. If the allele for tongue-rolling is dominant, use a pedigree to work out the possible genotypes and phenotypes of all the members in the family.

11 Colour-deficiency is an X-linked characteristic. Use pedigrees and the symbols X, X^c and Y to explain why males are much more likely to be colour deficient than females.

12 The people in the pink-shaded shapes in the pedigree below have a particular characteristic. Use the information in the pedigree to work out whether the allele for the characteristic is dominant or recessive.

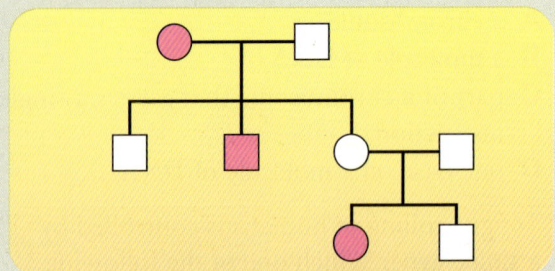

Check your answers on pages 335–336.

9

Species survival

Getting Started

What does *endangered species* mean? Why do you think the population of the possum is now very small?

Form into a small group and discuss the following questions.

- Two orange trees were grown from cuttings so are genetically identical. The trees were planted in different areas many kilometres apart. One tree produced many kilograms of sweet oranges, the other tree produced a small number of small-sized fruit.
  If the trees have the same genes, why are they so different?

- Charles Darwin was a naturalist (biologist) on board the ship HMS *Beagle*. Between 1831 and 1836 the ship sailed along the coastline of South America and then across the Pacific. It docked in Sydney on 12 January 1836. Why is Darwin famous?

- The photo shows a Leadbeater's possum. It is a highly endangered species and the small population of possums is protected by law. It is found only in the Victorian central highlands, where it lives in hollow parts of trees in old growth forests.

9.1 Variations in organisms

You found out in the last chapter that genes control many of the characteristics in humans. Earlobe attachment, the ability to roll your tongue into a tube, and the colour of your hair, eyes and skin are some of these characteristics.

Earlobe attachment is controlled by one pair of genes. Therefore, this characteristic has two phenotypes—you have attached earlobes ot unattached earlobes.

Most other human characteristics such as height, weight, hair colour and skin colour are controlled by more than one pair of genes. This produces a range of phenotypes. For example, the colour of your eyes is controlled by at least three pairs of genes on different pairs of chromosomes. Some other genes may turn these genes off and on. So it is the way all of these genes combine that determines the exact colour of your eyes. And it is this combination that creates the wide range of variation in human eye colour.

Variation in hair colour and skin colour, and such characteristics as head and face shape, are also due to the interaction of many genes.

Fig 3 Hair colour is controlled by many genes.

Activity

In this activity you will need data from all the members of your class.

1 Find out how many people in the class can roll their tongue, and how many cannot.

  ✐ Record your results.

2 Measure the hand span of your right hand to the nearest 1 cm. To do this stretch your fingers out as wide as you can. Then place the tip of your thumb on the zero mark of a ruler and measure to the tip of your little finger.

  ✐ Record your results.

3 Draw up a table to record the hand span data for the class. It is best to group the results in 5 cm intervals.

  First, find out who in the class has the smallest hand span and who has the largest. Use these measurements to work out the range of your 5 cm intervals.

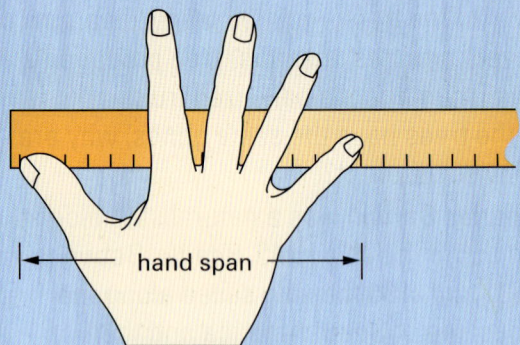

hand span

For example, if 160 cm is the smallest hand span and 219 cm is the largest, the first 5 cm interval will be 160–164, and the last will be 215–219 cm.

  ✐ Draw a bar graph of the class data for tongue rolling. Then draw a bar graph for hand spans.

  ✐ Suggest why the two bar graphs are different.

The source of variations

The horticulturist in the photo below is taking cuttings from a geranium that produces good flowers. She knows that the cuttings from this plant will produce plants that produce exactly the same quality of flowers as the parent plant. This is an example of asexual reproduction. It does not produce variation in the offspring.

Fig 5   A horticulturist takes cuttings from the parent plant. These cuttings will grow into plants identical to the parent plant.

As you have seen in the last chapter, organisms that reproduce sexually produce variations in the offspring. There are three main ways that this occurs:

- *independent assortment* of chromosomes during cell division in the reproductive organs
- *recombination* of genes in chromosome pairs during sex cell division
- *mutations* in the DNA in the cells in the testes and ovaries.

1 Independent assortment

You found out earlier that a cell with three pairs of chromosomes could produce sex cells with eight different combinations of chromosomes.

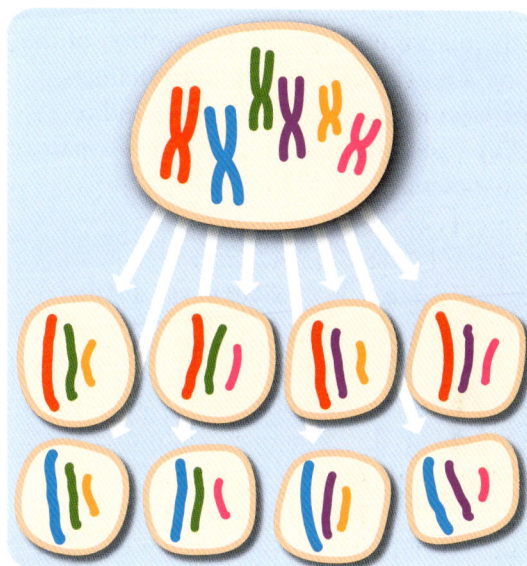

Fig 6   An organism with three pairs of chromosomes can produce eight different types of sex cells.

In humans with 23 pairs of chromosomes, there are about 8 million different possible combinations of chromosomes in the sex cells. This is why siblings look similar but not identical to each other and to their parents! The production of different arrangements of chromosomes in sex cells is called *independent assortment*.

extra for experts

The numbers game

A cell with two pairs of chromosomes can produce sex cells with four different arrangements of chromosomes. A cell with three pairs of chromosomes can produce sex cells with eight different arrangements of chromosomes. How many different types of sex cells can a fruit fly whose cells contain four pairs of chromosomes produce?

Use the data to work out a formula to calculate this. Then calculate the different types of sex cells an organism that has seven pairs of chromosomes can produce.

2   Recombination

During the production of sex cells in the testes or ovaries, the pairs of chromosomes sometimes swap bits of each other, resulting in a different arrangement of genes on the chromosomes.

In the diagram below, the top section of the DNA on a pair of chromosomes exchanges. This process is called *crossing-over*, and it results in a **recombination** of genes in a pair of chromosomes.

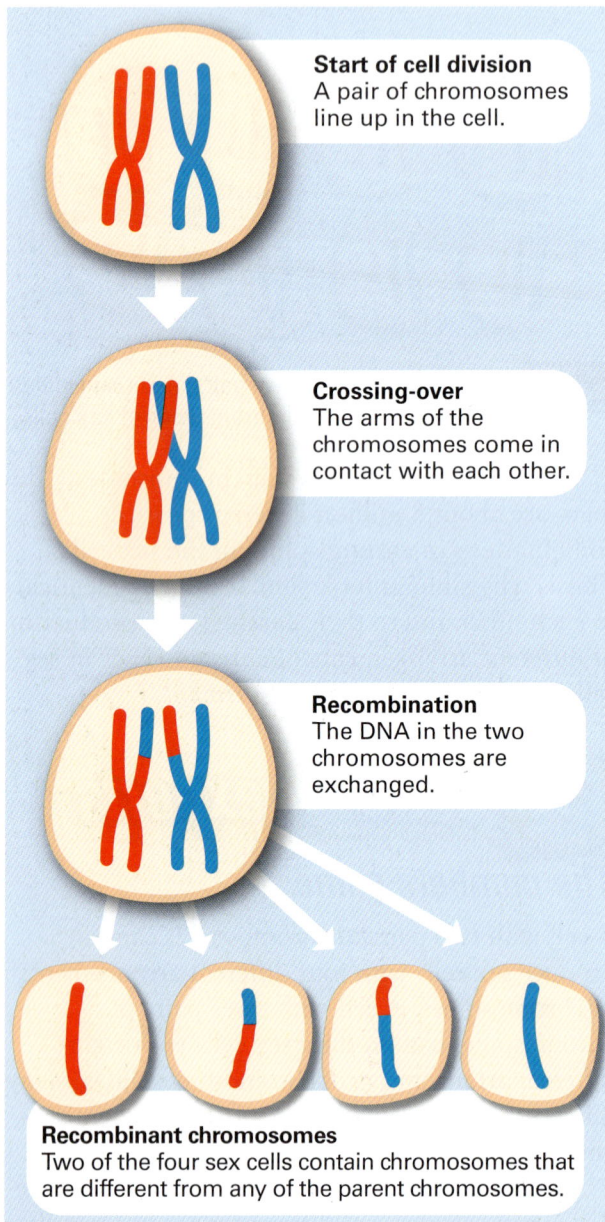

Start of cell division
A pair of chromosomes line up in the cell.

Crossing-over
The arms of the chromosomes come in contact with each other.

Recombination
The DNA in the two chromosomes are exchanged.

Recombinant chromosomes
Two of the four sex cells contain chromosomes that are different from any of the parent chromosomes.

Fig 7   Crossing-over produces a different combination of genes in the chromosomes in the sex cells.

Activity

Recombining DNA
You will need two different colours of playdough for this activity. This is a simple hands-on activity to show you how chromosomes cross-over and result in a recombination of genes.

1 Using one colour of playdough, make two chromosomes the size of a pencil.
2 Lie them side by side and squeeze them together about halfway along their length so that they make a H shape.
3 Repeat Steps 1 and 2 using the other colour of playdough.
4 Use Fig 7 as a guide to show how the two chromosomes can cross-over and recombine.

Challenge: Use your model to show that if two genes are a long way apart on a chromosome, they have a greater chance of recombining by crossing-over.

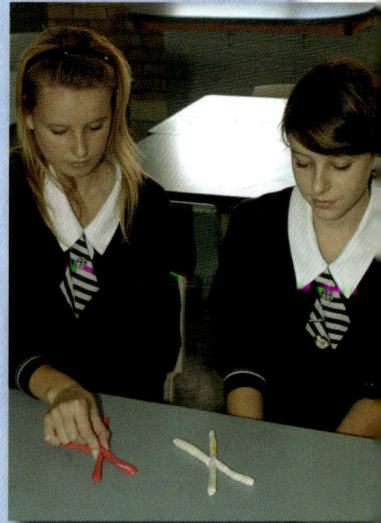

To see how crossing-over creates a new assortment of genes on chromosomes, open the **Recombining chromosomes** animation on the CD.

Working with technology

3   Mutations

When the base sequence in a gene is changed, it is highly likely that the proteins that are produced by this gene will be different from the original. The random changes to the DNA are called mutations.

Mutations in body cells cause little or no change to the organism, although cancerous tumours can develop from these mutations. However, if mutations occur in a sex cell, the changed DNA may be passed to the next generation when fertilisation occurs.

It is the combination of genetic and environmental factors that determines the characteristics of a population of organisms. The genes determine the potential phenotype of an organism, while a combination of the genes and the environment determines its actual phenotype.

Effects of the environment

This mandarin tree is loaded with sweet, juicy mandarins. About 100 km away, mandarin trees bear very few, fairly dry fruit. Why is this, when all the mandarin trees came from the same stock? The juicy mandarins are grown in an area that has had good autumn rain; the other area has had very low rainfall. Cold weather occurred at the start of winter, which increased the sugar in the juicy mandarins. The other area has had unusually warm weather.

Even though the mandarin trees have the same genotype, the environmental conditions have produced different phenotypes. The trees have the same alleles, but they are expressed differently because of the different environments they are in.

The young boy in the photo below has grown up in a country ravaged by malnutrition and disease. His growth is stunted, his immunity to disease is poor and his mental development may be limited—all because of environmental conditions.

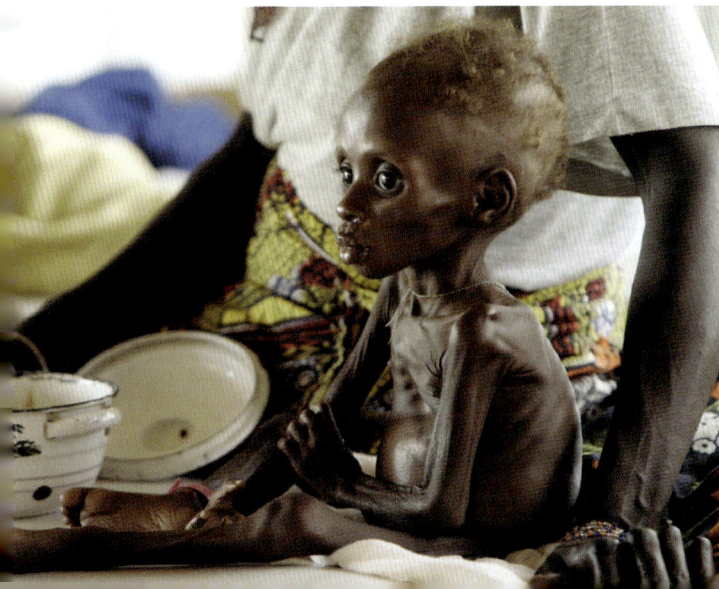

Fig 11 The characteristics of a population of organisms are determined by the environment as well as by the organism's genes.

Check!

1 How do you account for the fact that some people have attached earlobes and others have unattached earlobes, while there is a wide range in the shapes and sizes of ears?

2 **a** Where does independent assortment occur in the body?
   b What is the importance of the word *independent* in this process?
   c Explain how this process produces variations in organisms.

3 What is crossing-over? Use a diagram to show how it is a source of variations in organisms.

4 Explain why a mutation in the cells in the skin does not affect the variation in future generations, whereas a mutation in the sex cells may.

5 Explain how variations in a population are caused by genetic factors as well as by environmental factors.

6 Explain, giving an example, how a particular environmental factor can affect the phenotype of an organism. (Do not use the examples in this book.)

challenge

1 The particular type of Siamese cat in the photo has light fur on its body except on its face, ears, tail and legs. This cat carries a gene that makes a heat-sensitive version of the enzyme involved in making the dark colour (melanin) in the fur.

   a Suggest why the extremities of the cat's body have darker fur.
   b Do you think that the enzyme is turned off or turned on by high temperatures? Give a reason for your answer.
   c When the cat was a kitten, a patch of fur from its back was removed and the skin kept warm until new fur grew. Would you expect this fur to be dark or light? Explain.

2 In biology books you often see the term *gene expression*.

   a Suggest what this term means.
   b Use biology books or the internet to find a definition of the term. In what ways is this definition different from yours?
   c Use the example in Challenge 1 to explain how the environment can affect gene expression.

3 Hydrangea plants produce pink flowers and blue flowers depending on the acidity of the soil, as shown in the graph.

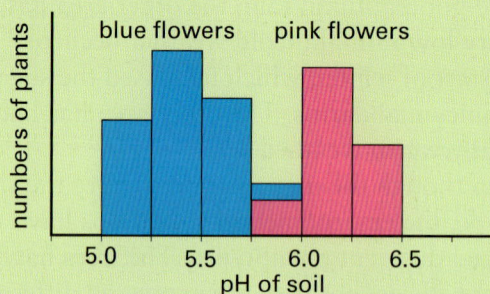

   a Write a generalisation about the colour of flowers and the pH of the soil.
   b What is the best soil pH for growing blue flowers? For growing pink flowers?

4 The colour of skin is controlled by three genes, each found on different chromosomes. The alleles for dark skin are M_1, M_2 and M_3, and they are dominant over the alleles for pale skin— m_1, m_2 and m_3. For example, a person with the darkest skin would have the alleles M_1M_1, M_2M_2 and M_3M_3.

   a What genes would a person with the palest skin carry?
   b How many combinations of skin colour are possible with these genes?
   c Predict the shade of skin colour a person with the alleles M_1m_1, M_2m_2 and M_3m_3 might have.
   d Is your prediction in **c** accurate? What other factors might affect the phenotype of this person?

9.2 Natural selection

Most organisms produce many more offspring than their habitat can support. If these offspring are produced by sexual reproduction, they will show variations of characteristics. Some of these characteristics will give the offspring a better chance of survival than others. Individuals with these particular characteristics are said to be better *adapted* to the environment. Individuals with unfavourable characteristics will usually die before they are able to reproduce.

Biologists say that the environment has selected certain characteristics for survival. This process is called **natural selection**, and is sometimes refered to as *survival of the fittest*. This means that the best adapted individuals will survive in a particular environment. It does not always mean that the largest, most muscular and physically fit individuals survive. In some cases smaller or slower organisms may be better suited to a particular environment. For example, shrubs that grow close to the ground and have small leaves will be better suited to a windy environment than tall, large-leaved trees.

Selection agents in the environment

The factors in an organism's environment which affect its survival are called *selection agents*. These agents can be divided into two groups:

- biotic agents, including predators, disease, competition between members of the same species, and availability of food

- abiotic agents, including heat, cold and wind, availability of oxygen and water, pH of soil and water, and availability of living space.

The 'fittest' organisms are those which can reduce the effects of these selection agents.

In the investigation on the next page you can use a model to help you understand how natural selection works.

Fig 15 The plants that grow successfully on sand dunes can survive on very little water and withstand the damaging effects of salt spray, strong sunlight and strong winds.

Fig 14 The flowers on this plant will produce more seeds than can survive. The seeds have slightly different genotypes and only the ones best adapted to this environment will survive.

Fig 16 Male antelopes often compete for the breeding females in a herd at mating time. The male that wins passes his favourable genes to the offspring in the next generation.

Investigate
17 FROG SELECTION

Aim

To use a model to show how natural selection affects two populations of frogs.

Materials

- three different colours of frog cards—20 red, 20 green and 20 yellow (for preparation see the Teacher note)
- a dice

Teacher note: You will need A4 sheets of red, green and yellow card (about 120 gsm) which are available in newsagents. To prepare the frog cards, photocopy the frogs below so that you have 24 frogs on a sheet of white paper. Photocopy enough frogs on red card for the whole class—these are the red frogs. Do the same for the green and yellow frogs. There are also frog templates in the Teacher Resource Book.

Planning and Safety Check

- It is important you know exactly what to do before you proceed. Carefully read through the investigation. Then test your knowledge by telling your partner what you have to do and what you have to record.
- Prepare data tables for your results for the POND and the FOREST before you start.

Background

You will be investigating the process of natural selection in two different and separate environments—a pond and a rainforest. The pond is surrounded by reeds and rushes which are yellowish in colour, while the forest has much leafy green vegetation.

You will look at only two organisms in these environments—a frog which occurs in three colours, red, green and yellow, and a snake which is a predator of the frog.

In this model, for simplicity, assume that each pair of frogs produces one offspring each year, and that snakes eat 15 frogs each year.

PART A
The frog population

Method

1 Write POND on a sticky label and FOREST on another. Then stick them apart on a table. These labels represent the location of the two environments.

2 Count out 10 red frogs, 10 green frogs and 10 yellow frogs and place them in one of the two environments. Shuffle the cards thoroughly and place them at *random* into 15 pairs.

3 Repeat Step 2 for the other environment.

4 Each pair of frogs produces *one* offspring a year. To work out the colour of the offspring use Table 1 and Table 2. Then add the correct coloured frog to each pair.

Notes

1 The three different colours of frogs are the same species and can interbreed and produce different coloured offspring.

2 If the parents in Table 1 produce more than one colour of offspring, throw a dice and use Table 2 to work out the colour.

Table 1

Colour of parents		Colour of offspring
red x red	=	red
yellow x yellow	=	yellow
red x yellow	=	green
red x green	=	some red, some green—see Table 2
green x green	=	some red, some green, some yellow—see Table 2
green x yellow	=	some green, some yellow—see Table 2

Table 2

Number on dice	Colour of offspring		
	red x green parents	green x green parents	green x yellow parents
1	red	red	green
2	red	red	green
3	red	green	green
4	green	green	yellow
5	green	yellow	yellow
6	green	yellow	yellow

Table 3

Number on dice	Pond	Forest
1	red	yellow
2	red	yellow
3	red	yellow
4	green	red
5	green	red
6	yellow	green

Results: Pond

Year	Red frogs	Green frogs	Yellow frogs
1	10	10	10
2			
3			
4			
5			

PART B
Predation by snakes

Method

1 Around the pond, the red frogs are the most likely to be eaten and the yellow frogs the least. In the forest the yellow frogs are most likely to be eaten and the green frogs the least.

2 Mix all the frog cards for the POND, throw a dice and use Table 3 to decide which 15 frogs are eaten. Remove an appropriately coloured frog each throw. (Note: If there are no frogs of a particular colour left, roll the dice again.) Do the same for the FOREST.

3 After the 15th frog has been removed from each environment, tally the numbers. Record the numbers in the Year 2 row in the data tables you have prepared. (The POND data table is shown as an example.)

4 Repeat Parts A and B for 10 years or until all the frogs are the same colour.

Discussion

1 Suggest why the red frogs around the pond are most likely to be eaten by snakes. Why are the yellow frogs most likely to be eaten in the forest?

2 Draw a fully labelled line graph of the changes in the numbers of the different coloured frogs around the pond over 10 years. Do the same for the forest.

3 Compare your results with those from other groups. Why are the results similar? Why are there some differences?

4 Write a conclusion for this experiment. Use the words *model* and *natural selection*.

Science in action

Sickle cell anaemia

Sickle cell anaemia is a blood condition caused by a mutated gene. The allele produces an abnormal type of haemoglobin (the red pigment found in red blood cells) which turns the normally concave disc-shaped red blood cells into sickle shaped cells.

The abnormal haemoglobin allele is recessive to the allele that codes for normal haemoglobin.

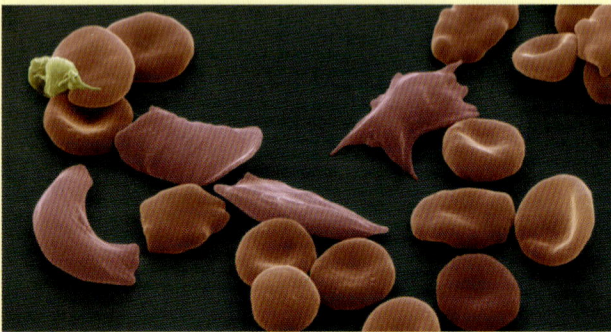

Fig 19 Normal red blood cells are rounded, in contrast with the distorted sickle-shaped cells (pink).

The sickle red blood cells are much less efficient at carrying oxygen than the normal cells. They also have a 'sticky' surface and the cells tend to stick together, causing blockages in blood vessels. This causes painful and sometimes fatal conditions such as heart attacks.

Fig 20 The percentage of people carrying the sickle cell allele

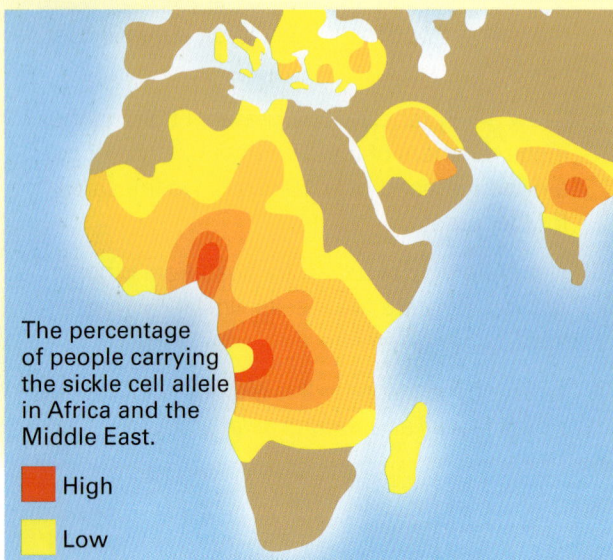

The percentage of people carrying the sickle cell allele in Africa and the Middle East.

■ High
■ Low

Most people who carry both abnormal haemoglobin alleles die in childhood. However, because the alleles are *co-dominant* (like human blood types on page 200) some of the blood cells of heterozygous people contain abnormal haemoglobin.

If sickle cell anaemia is fatal why then does the allele still exist in the human population?

Sickle cell anaemia and malaria

Sickle cell anaemia is much more common in Africa, India and parts of the Middle East than elsewhere in the world. Fig 20 shows the percentage of people in the population with the allele for abnormal haemoglobin.

Fig 21 shows the areas affected by malaria. The parasite that causes malaria lives in red blood cells and eventually destroys them, causing the death of the infected person. The parasite for some reason cannot live in cells that contain abnormal haemoglobin.

Questions

1 What does co-dominance mean?
2 What alleles would a person carry if they were homozygous for normal haemoglobin?
3 If sickle cell anaemia is fatal how does the allele stay in the population?
4 Why is it an advantage for people who are heterozygous for sickle cell anaemia to live in areas where malaria is common?
5 Suggest how *survival of the fittest* might apply to people with sickle cell anaemia.
6 Suggest how sickle cell anaemia might have originated in the human population.

Fig 21 Areas in Africa, India and the Middle East where malaria is prevalent

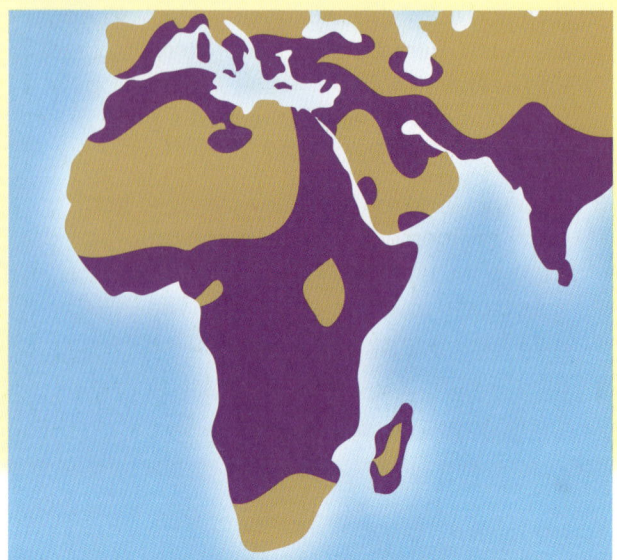

Check!

1 In your own words describe what is meant by the term *natural selection*.

2 A spider has spun a large web between two trees. Describe the selection agents which might affect the spider's survival.

3 What does *survival of the fittest* mean? Give two examples of where this could apply.

4 How does 'survival of the fittest' apply to the people in the malaria regions of West Africa? Describe the selection agents in this case.

5 The albino kookaburra in the photo is in a wildlife sanctuary. Why do you think that an animal with this phenotype would have little chance of survival in the wild?

challenge

1 Explain why natural selection works only if:
a there is variation of characteristics within the species
b characteristics are inherited.

2 About 65 million years ago, the Earth was inhabited by many species of dinosaurs. Some of them were herbivores but others were very efficient predators. Why did these enormously strong animals become extinct if they were such powerful and efficient predators?

3 The dodo was a flightless bird found on the island of Mauritius in the Indian Ocean off the coast of Africa. It laid one large egg in a nest on the ground. The dodo has been extinct since about 1680. Europeans who came to the island 100 years before this brought cats which ate the young chicks and pigs which ate the eggs.
a Suggest why the dodo survived for so long prior to European settlement, and then became extinct so quickly.
b Describe the selection agents in this case.

4 The graph is for a population of fruit flies that was sprayed with an insecticide.
a How many times were the fruit flies sprayed with insecticide?
b Why didn't all the fruit flies die after the first spraying?
c How many fruit flies died after each spraying? Suggest reasons for the difference in the numbers.

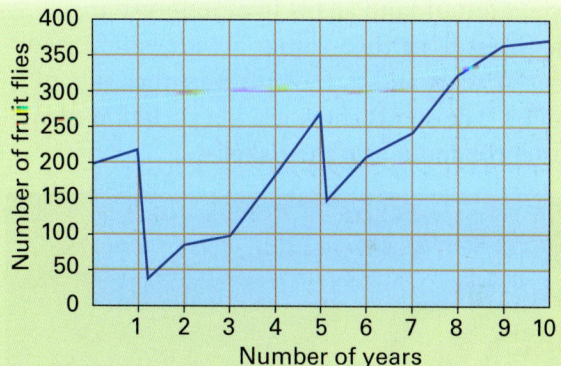

d What is the selection agent in this study?
e Predict what might happen if the fruit flies were sprayed with a different insecticide after 10 years.

5 The butterfly in the photo has eye spots on its wings. When the butterfly rests on plants, it folds its wings so that the eye spots are not visible. However, when disturbed by a predator the butterfly opens its wings and displays the large eye spots.
a How do the eye spots help the survival of this type of butterfly?
b Can you think of any situations where this characteristic might be a problem for the butterfly?

9.3 Evolution

The best adapted organisms are those that survive environmental changes and pass on favourable characteristics to their offspring. But changes to the environment also affect the types of organisms that live there.

- Changed weather patterns cause short-term effects such as droughts, floods or cyclones, or long-term effects such as atmospheric warming and a rise in sea levels.
- Forces inside the Earth cause earthquakes and volcanoes, and the movement of Earth plates causes changes over millions of years.

Formation of new species

A population of land snails lives in moist areas on the forest floor throughout a wide valley many kilometres wide and in the hills on either side of the valley. The snails show a wide variation of colour and banding on their shells.

Over thousands of years the climate changes. The creeks and wet areas in the valley dry up and the snails are no longer able to travel from one side of the valley to the other. The forest on the eastern side of the valley becomes drier than the forest on the western side. The eastern forest also contains lizards which eat snails. These predators are not found on the western side.

The two populations of snails become isolated and as a result they cannot mix and interbreed. Because of the different conditions in the two habitats, the phenotypes of the two snail populations eventually become distinctly different. The eastern snail is generally smaller and has a thicker shell with many bands. These features help the snail to avoid water loss, and protect and camouflage it against predators. The western snail, on the other hand, is generally larger and has few bands on its relatively thin shell.

A **species** is defined as a population of organisms that normally interbreed. The eastern and western snails are said to be different species because they have different mating seasons and behaviours, and do not interbreed.

Fig 27 After many years of dry weather the creek and vegetation in the valley disappear.

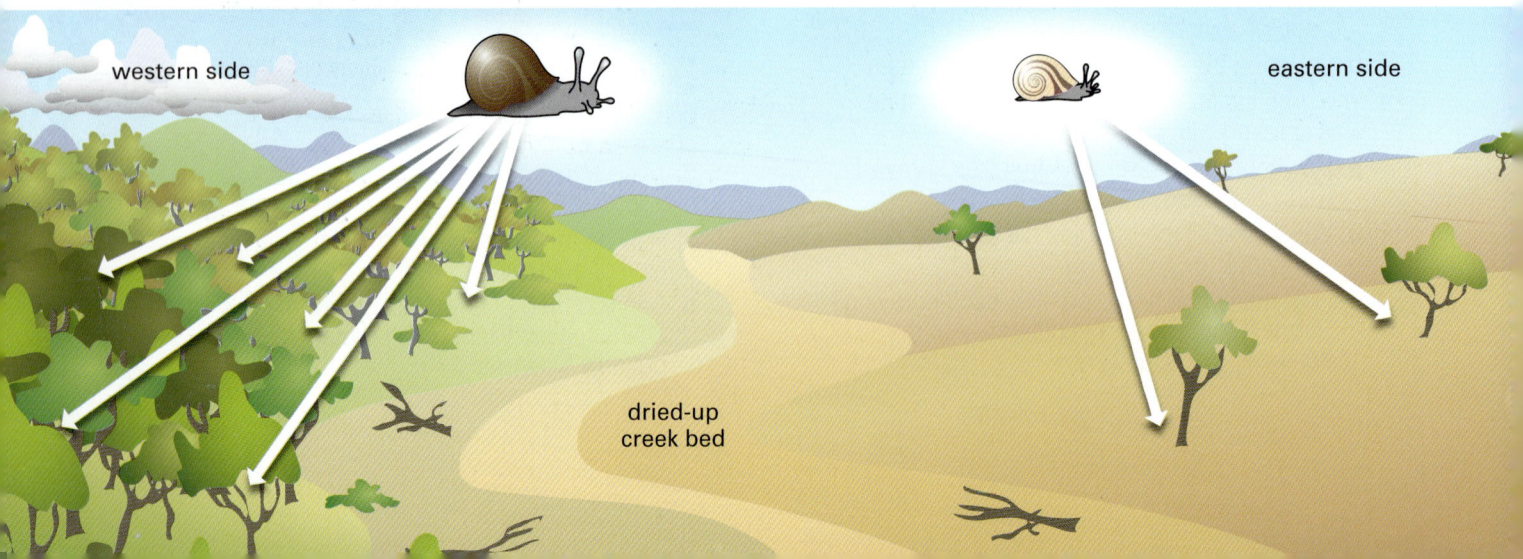

Gene pools

A population of any organism contains all the genes that produce the variations of characteristics in its individuals. The sum of all these genes is called the **gene pool**. For example, the gene pool of the original snail population contained all the genes that produced the range of shell patterns and colours.

The gene pool of a population can change by mutations and by natural selection. Mutations add new genes to the gene pool, and selection removes genes. For example, the eastern snail population has a thick shell which is an advantage against predators and water loss. The gene for this characteristic may have been added to the gene pool from a mutation in the snails' chromosomes. The gene for thin shells may have been removed from the gene pool because all snails with thin shells were eaten or dried out and died.

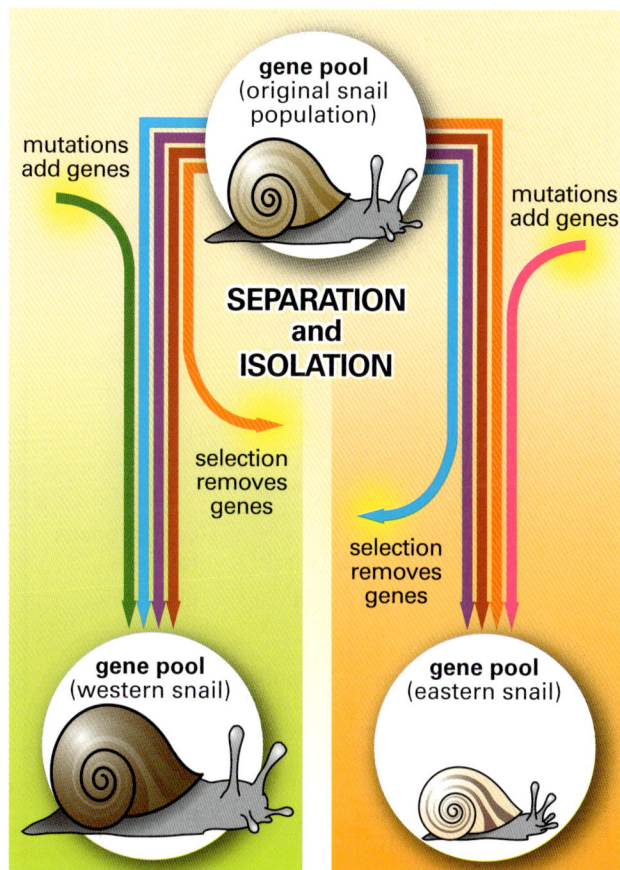

Fig 28 New species can be formed by separation and isolation of the gene pool.

Evolution—inferences and theories

In his famous book called *The Origin of Species*, published in 1859, Charles Darwin suggested that natural selection was the process in which species change over time and develop into new species. This process is now called **evolution**. His ideas created a lot of controversy because they conflicted with the accepted Biblical belief that all organisms were created at the same time.

Although Darwin was not the first person to suggest that currently living organisms evolved from earlier types of organisms, he was the first to argue that the change was brought about by the process of natural selection or 'survival of the fittest'. Darwin and his contemporaries had no knowledge of genetics and could not explain the cause of the variations and the way they are inherited.

To construct a theory explaining how species form, biologists made inferences from data obtained from the relationships between currently living species and those species that were previously living (fossils). These inferences were used to construct the *theory of evolution*. Biologists believe that this theory is useful for explaining how different species can form from a common ancestor. The changes to organisms usually occur over a very long period of time, very much longer than one human lifetime. Consequently, it is usually impossible for biologists to directly observe species formation and to test their inferences.

The evidence that is used to make inferences about evolution is gathered by many different people using many different techniques. As new discoveries and inferences are made the theory of evolution is modified accordingly. Only the future will show whether the current ideas about evolution are correct.

Evidence for evolution

Fossil evidence

Fossils are the remains of once-living organisms, and are important pieces of evidence for the theory that life has evolved on Earth. The fact that many of these fossils are not like present-day organisms suggests that major changes have taken place on the Earth.

You learnt in your previous studies that most fossils form in sedimentary rock, and that usually only the hard parts of organisms become fossilised. Scientists can use various radioactive dating techniques to find the age of the surrounding rocks and then make inferences about the age of the fossils. It appears that not all fossils lived on Earth at the same time. Because of this it is likely that the various species evolved from earlier ones, and that many living organisms have common ancestors.

Even though the fossil record shows only a very small fraction of the organisms that have lived on the Earth, biologists have been able to suggest possible evolutionary changes that have taken place.

Fig 30 Dinosaur fossils are evidence that the types of organisms on Earth have changed over a long period of time.

Activity

The fossil record below shows the types of organisms that were alive at various times over the last 600 million years. Use this to answer the following questions.

- How long ago did the first fish appear?
- When did coal deposits form? What does this suggest about the environmental conditions at that time?
- How long have mammals been on Earth?
- What age are the oldest winged insects?
- Suggest inferences about how different organisms have appeared and disappeared on Earth at different times.

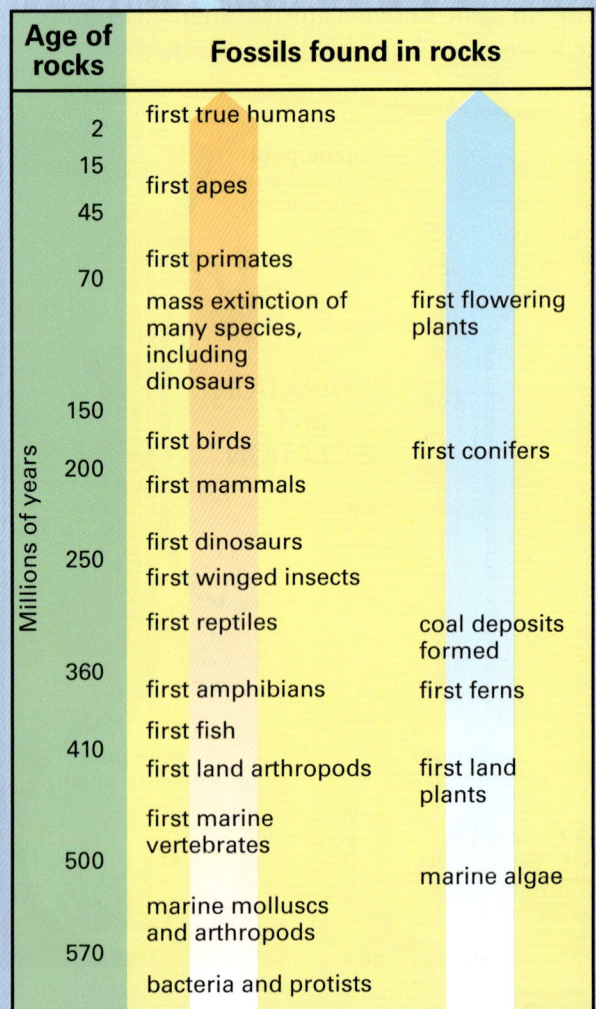

Age of rocks	Fossils found in rocks	
2	first true humans	
15		
45	first apes	
70	first primates	
	mass extinction of many species, including dinosaurs	first flowering plants
150		
200	first birds	first conifers
	first mammals	
250	first dinosaurs	
	first winged insects	
	first reptiles	coal deposits formed
360		
	first amphibians	first ferns
	first fish	
410	first land arthropods	first land plants
	first marine vertebrates	
500		marine algae
	marine molluscs and arthropods	
570		
	bacteria and protists	

(Millions of years)

Biogeography

Biogeography is the study of the distribution of organisms. For example, marsupials are mainly found in Australia and include kangaroos, wallabies, koalas, wombats, possums and bandicoots. These mammals have pouches and give birth to immature young. Only two other types of marsupials live outside Australia—the possums and pouched shrews from South America. Fossil marsupials have been found in North America, South America and Australia, but none has ever been found in Africa or Europe. The present distribution of these animals gives clues to their evolution.

Scientists have inferred that millions of years ago Australia, Antarctica, South America and Africa formed the supercontinent Gondwana. Africa separated from this land mass about 100 million years ago and left the other continents joined. Marsupials were distributed widely over this remaining land mass. Then the plates that contain these continents started to separate. The South American plate separated first, and then about 55 million years ago, Australia separated from Antarctica, and drifted northwards towards the equator.

During the slow drift northwards the climate of Australia became progressively drier. Fossil records show that during this time marsupials became even more numerous and many different types evolved. In South America, however, the marsupials decreased in number and diversity, probably due to the competition from placental mammals such as the ancestors of jaguars. The very long period of isolation of Australia from other land masses has meant that many different marsupial species evolved.

By studying the distribution of the different types of living organisms and fossils, inferences have been made to show how the various types of organisms may have evolved.

Comparing embryos

When the embryos of different animals are studied, similarities can be seen. This is particularly evident when studying the embryos of vertebrates. The similarities, particularly in the very early stages, suggest that the genes that control the early growth of vertebrates may have come from common ancestors. The differences the embryos show as they develop further are due to other genes which are unique to each type of vertebrate.

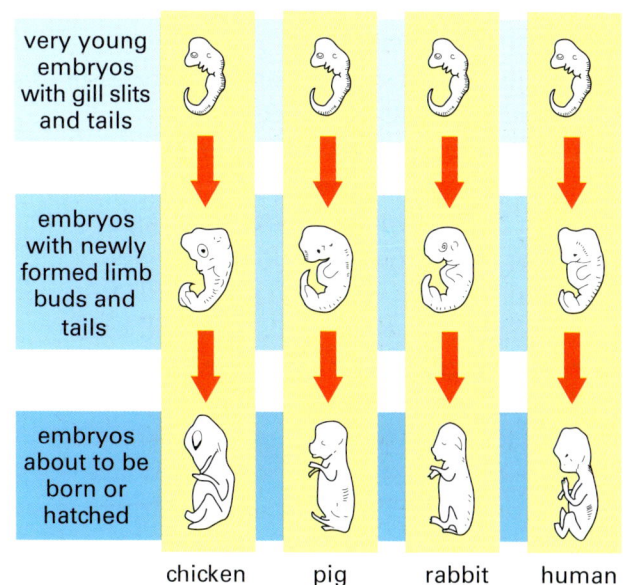

Fig 32 Part of the supercontinent Gondwana about 85 million years ago, which allowed organisms to spread over the now separated continents.

Fig 33 These vertebrate embryos are very similar at an early stage, suggesting that they might share a common ancestor.

Activity

The forelimbs shown below are from six different vertebrates. They show a number of similarities. This suggests that they share a common ancestor. However, they are each modified to suit a particular type of environment.

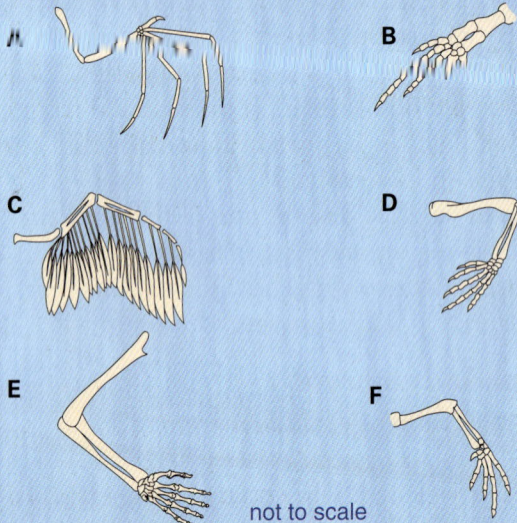

A

B

C

D

E

F

not to scale

1   Match the name of the vertebrate in the list to its forelimb in the diagram.

    bat   whale   bird
    frog   human   lizard

    Discuss how you arrived at your answers.

2   Make a list of the similarities of the forelimbs.

3   Suggest the specific function of each forelimb.

4   The study of the shapes and sizes of the bodies of different organisms is called comparative anatomy. Apart from forelimbs, which other parts of vertebrates could be useful for comparison?

Comparative DNA studies

Until the last 30 years, most of the studies that show evolutionary links between organisms relied on *comparative anatomy* (used in the activity above), and evidence from fossils and biogeographical distribution. Now, however, the DNA in living species and that found in fossils can be analysed and compared.

A particular species is different from another species in the number and types of genes it contains. In comparative DNA tests, single strands of DNA from two different species are mixed together. If the two pieces of DNA are similar, the bases on each strand will bind strongly. The greater the difference between the DNA, the less tightly the strands will bind.

DNA studies have shown that the percentage similarity of DNA strands from humans and chimpanzees is 98.5%, while the similarity between humans and orang-utans is 96.5%. This shows that there is a close evolutionary link between these animals.

Using DNA tests we can establish evolutionary links between various organisms and construct an evolutionary tree to show these links.

Fig 35 Strands of DNA from humans, apes and chimpanzees show a great degree of similarity, suggesting that these animals may have a common ancestor.

Science in action

How theories change

If Charles Darwin was alive today and studied modern evolutionary theory he would see many differences from the theory he proposed in 1859.

Scientific models and theories are constantly modified as new discoveries are made. For example, the platypus is an egg-laying mammal called a monotreme. Together with its relative the echidna, these mammals are the only living monotremes. No ancestral forms had been found, and this led biologists to believe that these families of monotremes evolved separately from a common ancestor in Australia. However, in 1991 fossilised teeth found in sediments in South America were identified as very similar to fossil platypus teeth found in Australia. As a result of this discovery, biologists may have to modify their ideas about the ancestor of the platypus and its distribution.

Fig 36 The platypus was once thought to have lived in Australia only. Recent fossil evidence suggests that it may have lived in other continents as well.

Theories develop as inferences are suggested and evidence is collected to support or dispute them. This is why theories have to be treated as tentative—likely to change. In the future, new fossil discoveries and advanced technology will undoubtedly change some of the ideas that form the current theory of evolution.

Check!

1 **a** What is a gene pool?
   b How do gene pools change over time?

2 Parrot A lives in forests and feeds on nectar and pollen. It has a repeating, high-pitched call, and breeds between May and August each year. Parrot B lives in the same habitat as Parrot A and also feeds on nectar and pollen. It has a similar call to Parrot A but breeds between September and November. Would you consider Parrot A and Parrot B to be the same species? Explain.

3 **a** What do you understand by the term evolution?
   b Use the snail story on page 218 and explain how it is an example of the process of evolution.
   c List the selection agents that acted on the snail populations over the period of time in the story.

4 What is the fossil record? How is it used as evidence for the evolution of organisms?

5 A particular type of tree called the Antarctic beech grows in small areas of Papua New Guinea, Australia's east coast, New Zealand and the far south of South America. Fossil beech trees have been found in these countries as well as in Antarctica. How do you account for the distribution of the Antarctic beech?

6 Apart from fossils and the distribution of organisms, what other evidence is used by biologists to support the theory that organisms have evolved on Earth?

7 Suggest why evolutionary changes to organisms that reproduce many times a year are more rapid than those in organisms that reproduce only once a year.

8 The theory of evolution has changed since the time of Charles Darwin. Give reasons why this might have occurred.

9 Suggest why comparing DNA is a more powerful tool in establishing evolutionary links than comparing embryos.

challenge

1 The shark is a fish and the dolphin is a mammal, but these two animals have the same basic body shape and structure. Suggest how natural selection might have caused this similarity.

2 The Tasmanian tiger (thylacine) was last seen in the wild in 1932. However, fossils show that it lived throughout Tasmania and mainland Australia. Biologists now think that this marsupial is extinct.

   a What does extinct mean? Use the term *gene pool* in your answer.

   b Some people think that endangered species should be protected and breeding programs established. Others think that it is simply natural selection at work and that the fittest species will survive. Outline your views on this and then discuss your views with others.

3 The map shows the distribution of Fletcher's frog. It is found in rainforests and breeds in small pools and creeks.

   a Suggest why this species of frog is found in two locations that are widely separated.

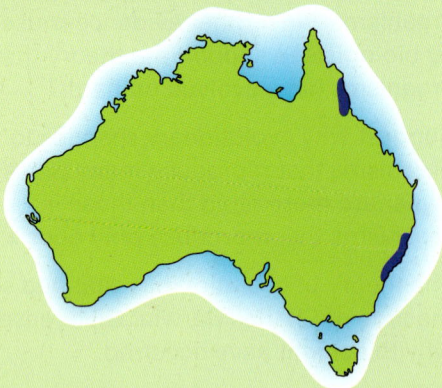

   b Suggest what could happen to the frog populations in the two different locations over a period of time.

c Biologists say that distribution maps like this are only tentative and may change in years to come. Suggest factors which you think may cause this map to change.

4 Do you think that organisms stop evolving in environments that change very little over long periods of time? Explain your answer.

5 The models below show two ways in which the gene pools of an original species can be separated and isolated over a long period of time.

   In Model 2 only a very small number of organisms are isolated from the larger population. Biologists suggest that this model accounts for those species that change very quickly from the original one. Give reasons why biologists suggest this.

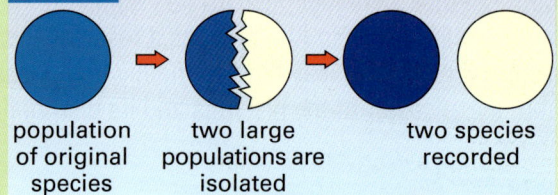

Model 1 — population of original species → two large populations are isolated → two species recorded

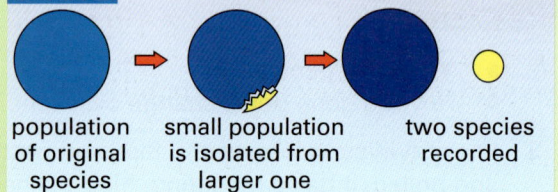

Model 2 — population of original species → small population is isolated from larger one → two species recorded

WEBwatch

Use the internet to find out how the work and theories of Jean Baptiste Lamarck and Alfred Wallace contributed to the modern theory of evolution. Compare and contrast the theories of both of these biologists to that put forward by Darwin.

   Suggest why Darwin is more well-known than Lamarck or Wallace.

9.4 Selecting genes

The fantail goldfish in the photo cannot swim very well, has vision problems and probably will not live as long as those in the wild. However, to a collector of fish it is worth hundreds of times the value of a wild form of goldfish.

Fig 40 A selectively bred fantail

Artificial selection

Artificial selection or *selective breeding* is the process in which *humans* select those phenotypes in organisms that have a value or serve a purpose.

For example, the particular features of the goldfish are valued by certain people, so fish breeders select fish with unusual phenotypes and try to produce offspring with the same features.

Dogs are the oldest domestic animals and may have been selectively bred by humans for more than 10 000 years. At the time Europeans landed in North America, the indigenous American people had selectively bred more than 20 breeds of dogs.

The grey wolf is thought to be the ancestor of the dog, and many of the characteristics of the wolf are present in some dog breeds. For example, wolves tend to guard the den which houses their young. This feature has been selected in certain breeds of dogs, namely German shepherds and Doberman pinschers, which are used as guard or watch dogs. The hunting characteristic in the wolf has been selected in such breeds as the hounds and spaniels (for trailing after prey), retrievers (for finding and retrieving prey), and terriers (for attacking prey).

However, the selective breeding of dogs has also brought with it some genetic problems. For example, German shepherds have hip problems and suffer endocrine gland problems. Pugs and bulldogs suffer from breathing and teeth problems due to the odd shape of their jaws.

Fig 41 The pug, like the bulldog, was bred for its sporting and fighting ability but has inherited breathing and teeth problems due to the shape of its jaws.

Fig 42 Cocker spaniels have been bred for their ability to find prey. However, they often suffer ear infections because of their large floppy ears.

Biotechnology

Biotechnology is a field of science that uses organisms to produce materials for people to use, for example food, clothing and medicines. Most of the work in modern biotechnology is at the molecular level and involves the manipulation of genes in organisms. This is commonly called **genetic engineering** or *recombinant DNA technology* and is the technique of inserting desired genes from one species into the chromosomes of another species.

The photo above shows the caterpillar of the moth (cotton bollworm) that causes severe damage to cotton crops. Traditionally, farmers have used pesticides to control the caterpillars and to stop damage to crops. However, over the years the insect has become resistant to the pesticides. Consequently farmers have to use more concentrated pesticide solutions to have any effect on the caterpillars.

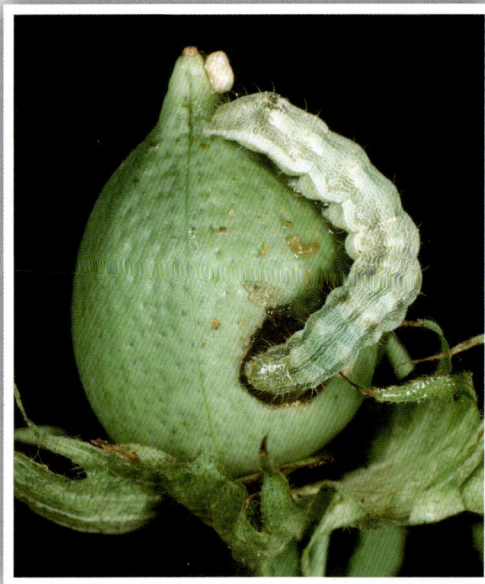

A particular species of bacterium called *Bacillus thuringiensis* or Bt naturally produces a protein that kills caterpillars. In plant nurseries you can buy packets of Bt which you mix with water and spray onto vegetable crops. The bacteria infect the caterpillars on the plants and cause them to die.

Scientists have found that a gene in the Bt chromosome is responsible for making the protein that kills caterpillars. They have inserted this gene into the chromosomes of cotton cells, so that as the cotton plant grows it makes the special protein. When the caterpillar eats the plant, it takes in the protein and dies. Using this technology the farmers enjoy a double benefit—they are able to reduce quite dramatically the amount of pesticide used and also increase their yields of cotton from the crop.

Transferring a gene between two unrelated species, like the bacterium and the cotton plant, produces a transgenic organism.

Fig 44 Transferring a gene from a bacterium to a chromosome in a cotton plant

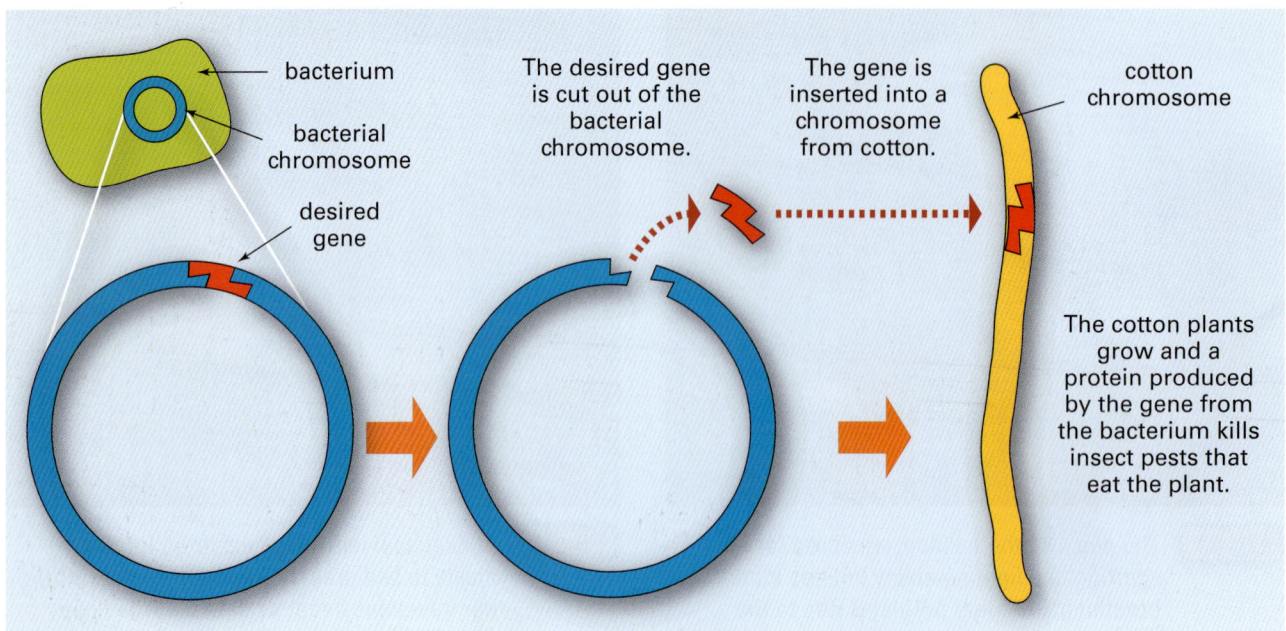

Cutting and recombining genes

DNA normally consists of two strands and is called double-stranded DNA. Each base on one strand is paired to a *complementary base* on the other strand. You can see in the diagram below that A bonds only to T, and G only to C. So A is the complementary base to T.

To cut DNA, biologists use special enzymes called restriction enzymes. These cut the DNA at particular places along the sequence of bases. There are several hundred restriction enzymes, each able to cut the DNA at a particular place. For example, the restriction enzyme *Eco*RI recognises the base sequence GAATTC and cuts the DNA after the G in this sequence, leaving a tail or 'sticky end'. In the diagram below the *Eco*RI enzyme has found and cut two GAATTC sequences out of the piece of DNA.

To join the fragments of DNA, other enzymes called *ligases* (LYE-gay-zes) are used. These enzymes occur in the cells of most organisms and are used to repair pieces of DNA that have been broken or damaged. In the laboratory, ligases are used to recombine the fragments of DNA that have been cut.

Using gene technology to make insulin

People suffering from diabetes have low blood levels of the hormone insulin. Diabetics can lead normal lives by having daily injections of insulin. The insulin was traditionally obtained from pigs and cattle. However, it differs slightly from human insulin, and can contain impurities that cause an allergic reaction in some people.

To overcome this problem, biologists have added the human insulin gene to a bacterial chromosome using a process similar to the one below. Bacteria are used because they reproduce very quickly and can make large quantities of pure insulin.

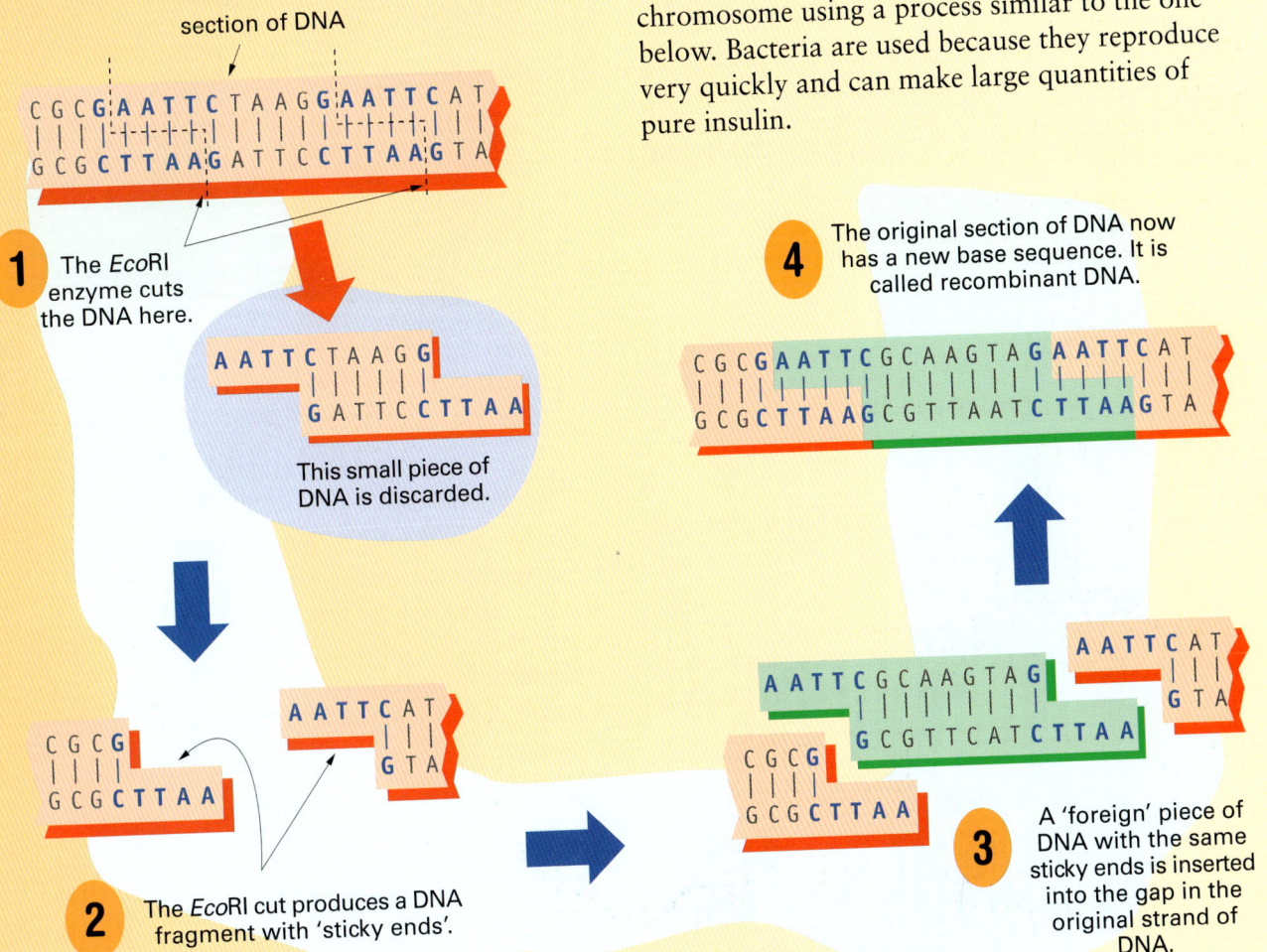

section of DNA

C G C G A A T T C T A A G G A A T T C A T
G C G C T T A A G A T T C C T T A A G T A

1 The *Eco*RI enzyme cuts the DNA here.

A A T T C T A A G G
G A T T C C T T A A

This small piece of DNA is discarded.

C G C G
G C G C T T A A

A A T T C A T
G T A

2 The *Eco*RI cut produces a DNA fragment with 'sticky ends'.

4 The original section of DNA now has a new base sequence. It is called recombinant DNA.

C G C G A A T T C G C A A G T A G A A T T C A T
G C G C T T A A G C G T T A A T C T T A A G T A

A A T T C G C A A G T A G
G C G T T C A T C T T A A

A A T T C A T
G T A

C G C G
G C G C T T A A

3 A 'foreign' piece of DNA with the same sticky ends is inserted into the gap in the original strand of DNA.

Huno!

Investigate
18 GENE TECHNOLOGY MODEL

Aim

To use a model to show how genes are cut from chromosomes and recombined into other chromosomes.

Materials

- about 100 coloured paper clips (4 colours —red, green, yellow and blue)
- strip of cardboard 7 cm x 50 cm
- scissors

Planning and Safety Check

- In the activity on page 116 you made a model DNA using coloured paper clips. The same model is used in this investigation. The four colours of the paper clips represent the four types of bases in DNA. Blue = A, red = T, yellow = G and green = C.
- Read through the Method carefully. You will need to refer to the table on page 117 to work out your amino acid sequence.

Method

1   On one side of the strip of cardboard place about 50 paper clips in random order side by side. Make sure the total number can be divided by three. Label this Strand 1.

2   Make sure you have two sets of the base sequence GAATTC somewhere along the chain of paper clips.

3   On the other side of the cardboard strip place paper clips which represent the complementary bases to those on Strand 1.

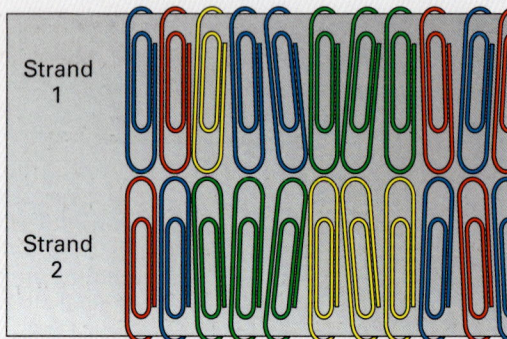

Remember, A bonds only to T, and G only to C. So if the first five bases on Strand 1 are ATGAA, the complementary bases in Strand 2 will be TACTT. This is your model of double-stranded DNA.

Use the code for amino acids in the table on page 189 to work out the sequence of amino acids that is coded by Strand 1.

4   Look for the first base sequence GAATTC in Strand 1 and cut through both strands as shown in the diagram on the previous page.

5   Locate the second sequence GAATTC and cut through both strands. You should now have three fragments of double-stranded DNA.

6   Keep the two end fragments of the double-stranded DNA and swap the middle fragment with another group.

7   Join the new middle fragment between the end fragments. Does it fit? Why?
    Work out the amino acid sequence on your recombinant piece of DNA. Compare this one to the original sequence in Step 3.

Discussion

1   Write a conclusion for this experiment. Use the term *recombinant DNA technology*.

2   What is the complementary base sequence to the sequence CTTAAG? Read the complementary sequence back-to-front. What do you notice? What is the importance of this in the DNA molecule?

science bits

Genetically modified foods

Transgenic organisms are being bred to produce foods or ingredients for foods. These foods are called *genetically modified foods* or *GM foods*.

GM foods are usually defined as those foods that contain genetically modified ingredients. Sometimes the whole of the food is genetically modified, for example soybeans and corn. Other foods that are considered GM foods contain varying amounts of GM ingredients. For example, 10% of the mass of a doughnut may be GM soybean meal. Other foods might contain smaller amounts of GM ingredients such as food preservatives or additives.

What are the advantages of GM foods?

The GM foods currently available in Australia contain mostly soybeans, canola, corn, potato or sugar beet. In the USA, more than 70% of the foods in supermarkets contain some GM foods.

Some of the GM crops have been modified to protect them against either insect or virus attack. This means that farmers can reduce the amount of pesticides they spray on their crops. Other GM crops such as soybeans can withstand the effect of herbicides, which means that they can be sprayed with herbicides that kill weeds but not the crop.

Currently, scientists are experimenting to produce GM foods with greater amounts of vitamins and proteins, and ones that are free from the proteins which cause allergic reactions in some people.

Animals are also used to produce GM foods. Transgenic technology is being used to produce faster-growing and leaner pigs that use food more efficiently and are resistant to common diseases. This technique is also used to breed fish, sheep and poultry.

Concerns about GM foods

In 1992 scientists working for a multinational seed company produced a transgenic soybean containing a gene from a Brazil nut. The gene produces a protein rich in a particular amino acid which is found in small amounts in normal soybeans. Before being released the soybean was given to a test group of people. Some of the people allergic to Brazil nuts became allergic to the soybeans. Because of this the GM soybeans were withdrawn and never released.

Some scientists are concerned about the use of GM crop plants. It has been estimated that 20% of crop plants escape from farms and establish wild populations. It is likely that the wild crops could crossbreed with weeds to produce plants that are herbicide and pesticide resistant, or drought, cold or salt tolerant. Also GM plants which are poisonous to insects kill both the 'pest' as well as beneficial insects. Then the insects may become resistant to the GM plants and farmers will again have to spray the crops with poisons.

Discussion and debate

The questions below deal with a number of GM food issues. To help in your discussion, search the internet under *genetically modified foods*, *transgenic animals* or *biotechnology*.

1 The Food Standard 1.5.2, which came into effect in December 2001, requires labelling of GM foods. Go to www.scienceworld.net.au and follow the links to the **ANZFA** website to find out more about this requirement.

2 Do a supermarket survey to find out how many products contain GM foods.

3 Prepare a questionnaire to find out how much people in your neighbourhood know about the benefits and risks of GM foods.

4 The genes of some animals, for example pigs, have been added to plants that are grown for food. Should genes be allowed to be swapped between animals and plants? What are some of the consequences for people of certain religions or for vegetarians if this occurs?

5 What are the benefits of using GM crops that are resistant to pests and certain climatic conditions? What are the possible problems?

6 Prepare for and against cases about GM foods and transgenics. Your teacher might organise you into groups for a class debate.

Science in action

Cloning

In 1997, the world's first cloned mammal was born. 'Dolly' the lamb was developed from the single body cell of a ewe (female sheep). In this process the cell developed without being fertilised by a sperm.

Since Dolly, many improvements have been made to this cloning technique which is often called *nuclear transfer*. The diagram shows the technique used to produce Australia's first cloned pigs in 2001.

The nuclear transfer technique allows the production of a large number of identical animals, called **clones**, all from the one cell grown in a culture. This could mean that herds of identical farm animals could be produced. For example, the best milk-producing cows could be cloned, and then smaller herds could produce large quantities of milk for less food and lower production costs.

Cloning is also important for future human organ transplants. For example, cloned pigs could be used as a source of transplant organs, namely the heart, lungs, liver and kidneys.

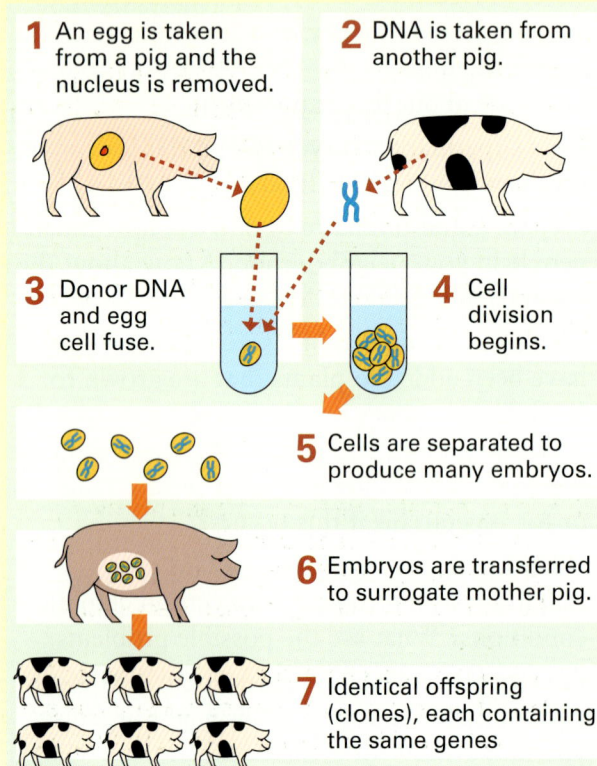

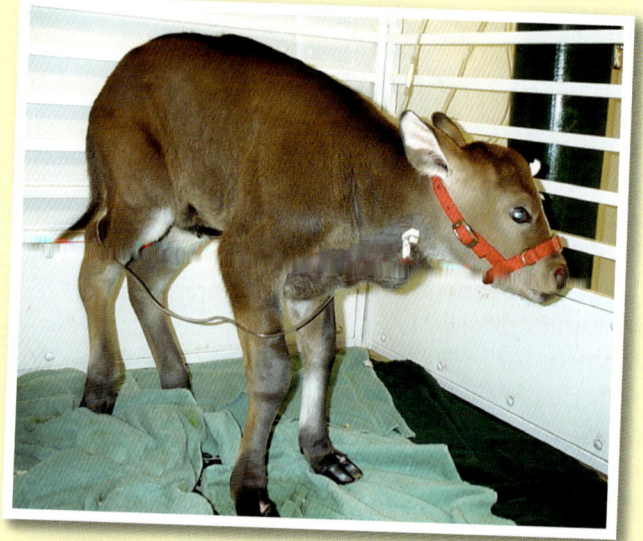

Fig 49 This baby gaur, a wild ox from India, was born in 2001 and was the first endangered animal to be cloned. The baby gaur, called Noah, died from an infection (unrelated to the procedure) two days after its birth.

1 An egg is taken from a pig and the nucleus is removed.

2 DNA is taken from another pig.

3 Donor DNA and egg cell fuse.

4 Cell division begins.

5 Cells are separated to produce many embryos.

6 Embryos are transferred to surrogate mother pig.

7 Identical offspring (clones), each containing the same genes

Goodbye Dolly

Dolly the sheep died in February 2003, six years after her birth was headlined in newspapers around the world.

Dolly died from a lung infection which is fairly common in sheep. She also had arthritis in her back legs. However scientists are uncertain if her premature death was a result of the cloning procedure or just a natural occurrence.

Before developing arthritis, Dolly had given birth to six healthy lambs as a result of natural mating.

WEBwatch

For more information on cloning go to www.scienceworld.net.au and follow the links to the websites below.

Cloning fact sheet

How cloning works

Science in action

Human gene therapy

Human gene therapy is an experimental area of biotechnology which treats people with genetic diseases. It involves introducing a piece of DNA which carries a 'normal' dominant gene into a person who has a genetic disease. The 'normal' gene replaces the disease-causing gene in the body cells of the sick person. Currently only diseases that are caused by a single recessive gene are treatable. These include cystic fibrosis and thalassaemia.

How does the new gene get into body cells?

At present the most successful way to insert a gene into a person's chromosomes is to use another organism—a virus. When viruses infect people they insert their genetic material into the person's chromosomes. Scientists render the virus's own genes harmless, and insert the human gene into the chromosome. The viruses are then injected or inhaled and invade the body cells, inserting the dominant gene into the affected person's chromosomes. This gene masks the recessive gene which is causing the disease.

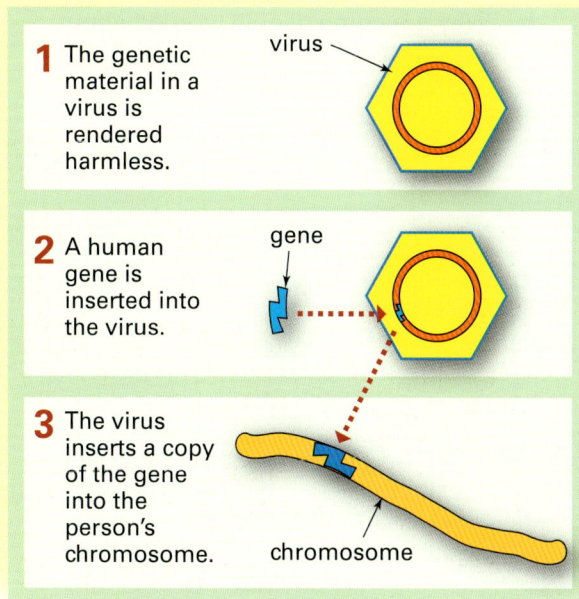

Germ-line gene therapy—creating designer people?

Instead of inserting the gene into a person's body cells, it is possible to insert it into the cells of an embryo and allow the normal cell division and growth to occur. This is called *germ-line therapy* and is currently prohibited in Australia and in most other countries.

The main concern with this technology is that it could be used to create designer babies. For example, a woman could have an egg fertilised by sperm and cultured in the laboratory. Before it is placed into her uterus, the embryo's genes could be scanned for potential diseases and replaced if necessary. However, other 'selected' genes could also be inserted in the embryo at this stage.

1 The genetic material in a virus is rendered harmless.
virus

2 A human gene is inserted into the virus.
gene

3 The virus inserts a copy of the gene into the person's chromosome.
chromosome

Questions

1 Draw a simple flow chart to show how a virus can be used to insert a gene into chromosomes in a lung cell of a person suffering from cystic fibrosis.
2 Why do you think germ-line therapy is prohibited by most governments?
3 Use the internet to search under *human gene therapy* and *germ-line therapy*. Use the information to prepare a for and against discussion.

Check!

1 How does artificial selection differ from natural selection?

2 Genetic engineering is called recombinant DNA technology. Explain in simple language why these terms are interchangeable. (Hint: refer to page 226.)

3 The greatest advantage of gene technology is that it can be used to make large amounts of substances needed by humans (eg hormones) by placing human genes into bacteria.
   a Why are bacteria used in this process?
   b At present many of these substances are extracted from other mammals. Suggest why there are problems with this.

4 Restriction enzymes have sometimes been called gene shears. What does the word 'shears' mean? If you are unsure find the meaning in a dictionary. Why do you think this term describes the role of restriction enzymes?

5 **a** Describe what a clone is.
  b Why is cloning called nuclear transfer?
  c Suppose a farmer had a herd of 30 cloned sheep. What would be the advantages and disadvantages of a cloned herd compared with a normal herd?

6 The diagram on the right shows foreign DNA being placed into a bacterial chromosome.
  a Copy the diagram in your notebook and add these labels: bacterial chromosome containing donor DNA, deleted section of bacterial DNA, donor DNA, bacterial chromosome.
  b In which steps are restriction enzymes and ligase enzymes used? Explain your answer.

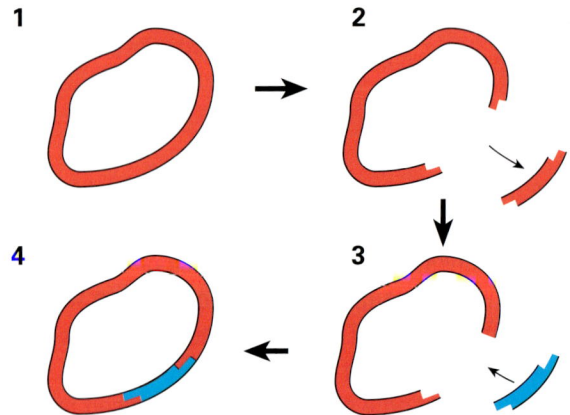

  c Why is the same type of restriction enzyme used for the bacterial DNA as for the donor DNA?

7 The cotton plant in the photo on page 226 is called a transgenic organism.
  a What does the word transgenic mean?
  b Why are some people worried about the effect of GM crops like this cotton on the environment?

challenge

1 The diagram below shows an ear of modern corn and an ancestor of modern corn.

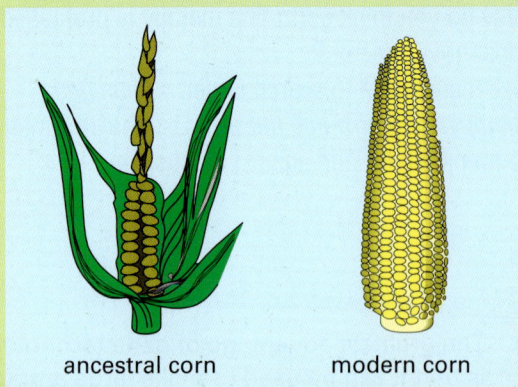

ancestral corn   modern corn

  a Unlike the ancestral corn, the seeds (or kernels) of modern corn cannot come away from the stem and therefore cannot self seed. Suggest why this characteristic would have been selectively bred in corn. Could modern corn survive in the wild?

  b Many biologists argue that the wild forms of plants like corn should not be allowed to become extinct. Suggest why.

2 Consider the following cloning scenario. Suppose a woman suffers from a severe genetic disorder. She and her husband want a child and are opposed to abortion and egg donation from another woman. Doctors say that the husband's DNA can be fused into one of his wife's eggs whose nucleus has been removed.

  a Use the diagram on page 230 as a guide to explain how this might be done.
  b What other technique in biotechnology could possibly be used in this case?

3 A CSIRO researcher found a gene which makes plants destroy their own seeds. Discuss the pros and cons of adding this gene to plants that supply our fruit and vegetables.

4 Selective breeding is just one technique used in what is now called traditional biotechnology. Find out about other techniques. Then make a list of the techniques in traditional and modern biotechnology. Beside each technique list its benefits and risks to our society.

MAIN IDEAS

Copy and complete these statements to make a summary of this chapter. The missing words are on the right.

1 There are three ways in which variations in a genotype occurs: _____ of chromosomes as well as recombination of DNA during sex cell division, and _____ in the chromosomes in sex cells.

2 The _____ of phenotypes in a population occur as a result of genetic factors and _____ factors such as nutrition and health.

3 _____ is the process in which individuals with favourable _____ have a better chance of surviving in a particular environment than other individuals.

4 The factors in an organism's environment which affect its survival are called _____. These include _____ and predation from other organisms, heat and cold, and the availability of soil and water.

5 A _____ is the sum of all the genes in a particular _____ of organisms.

6 _____ is the process in which species change over time and may develop into new species.

7 _____ or selective breeding by humans has changed the phenotypes of many types of organisms.

8 _____ describes the process in which _____ from one organism are inserted into the DNA of another organism.

artificial selection

competition

environmental

evolution

gene pool

genes

genetic engineeering

independent assortment

mutations

natural selection

phenotypes

population

selection agents

variations

Try doing the Chapter 9 crossword on the CD.

Working with technology

REVIEW

1 Which is the best definition of a gene pool?
  A the type of gene in a population
  B the sum of all the genes in a population
  C the number of combinations of genes possible
  D the genes carried by the parents of a particular offspring

2 Which of the following factors would least influence natural selection?
  A natural death
  B competition from other species
  C mutation
  D interbreeding

3 Which statement about natural selection is *incorrect*?

  A It indicates how new species may form.
  B It relies upon the fact that characteristics are inherited.
  C It suggests that only the largest and most physically fit organisms survive.
  D It suggests that the biotic and abiotic factors may favour some individuals and not others.

4 The domestic dog has over 100 different breeds, yet wild dogs have very few variations (eg jackal, wolf, dingo). How can you explain this?

5 An organism's genotype is not the only factor that determines its characteristics (phenotype). The environment also plays an important part in how the organism's genes are expressed. Explain, giving an example, what this statement means.

REVIEW

6 The diagram below shows a fruit fly with normal wings and one with curly wings. Flies with curly wings cannot fly. The gene for this characteristic occurs as a natural mutation. Suggest why very few adult fruit flies with this phenotype are found in nature.

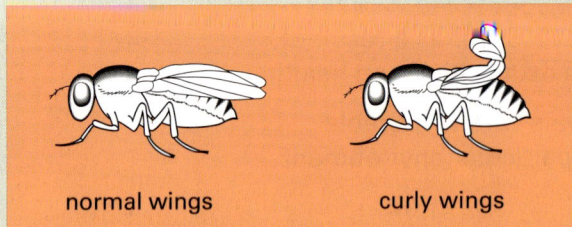

normal wings   curly wings

7 In which of the following activities are humans least likely to influence the evolution of other organisms? Justify your answer.
A spraying gardens with pesticides
B breeding frost-resistant oranges
C recycling wastes from cities
D using antibiotics in the control of bacteria

8 The diagram below shows the five species of finches that Charles Darwin observed when he visited the Galapagos Islands. It also shows the finch that lived on the mainland of South America, which Darwin inferred was the ancestor of the Galapagos Islands finches. Suggest how modern DNA testing techniques could be used to support Darwin's inference.

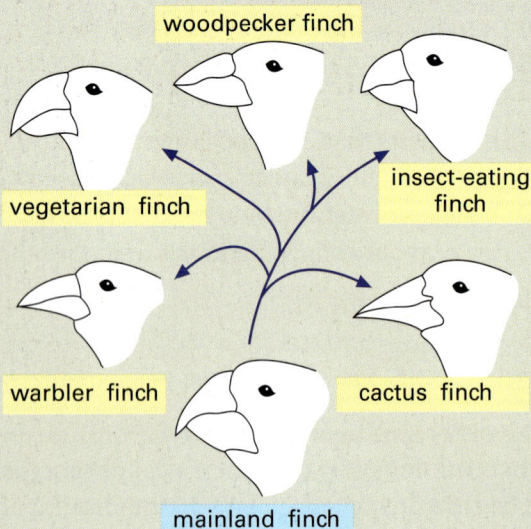

woodpecker finch

vegetarian finch

insect-eating finch

warbler finch

cactus finch

mainland finch

9 A human gene that is responsible for the manufacture of a growth hormone in humans can be produced in the laboratory by genetically modified bacteria. Using simple labelled diagrams explain how this procedure works.

10 A particular species of moth exists in two forms, a light-coloured form and a dark-coloured form. These moths rest on the bark of trees in the daytime. When a bird catches a moth, it swallows the body and rejects the wings.

Suppose you had 100 of each type of moth. Design a test to show that birds are selection agents of this moth.

11 A species of forest tree has spread over a mountain from the dry side to the moist side. The three populations show different characteristics: the trees at X are drought-resistant, those at Y are frost-resistant, while those at Z need high humidity.

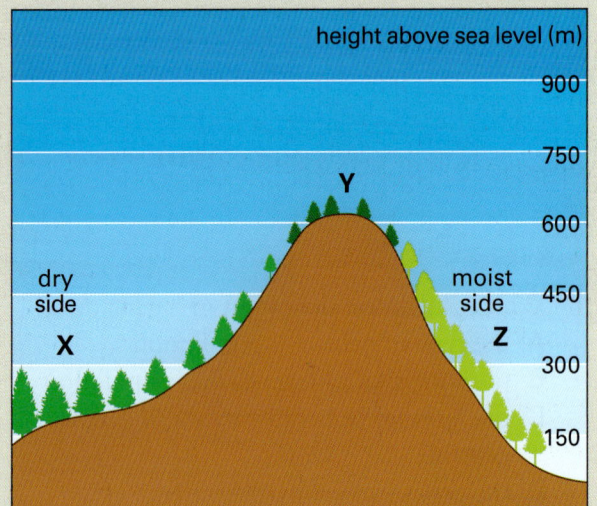

height above sea level (m)
900
750
600
Y
dry side
moist side
450
X
Z
300
150

a List the selection agents in this situation.
b Explain why the populations of trees in each location are different.
c Suggest why the trees at X are more likely than the trees at Y to form a different species from the trees at Z.

Check your answers on page 337.

Explaining reactions

$$2Mg\,(s) + O_2\,(g) \rightarrow 2MgO\,(s)$$

Getting Started

The photo shows what happened when the teacher mixed two colourless liquids.

- Describe what happened.
- Has there been a chemical reaction? How do you know?
- How could you explain what has happened in terms of atoms?
- Why is it important to understand what happens when chemicals are mixed?

In this chapter you will be able to investigate this reaction for yourself. You will also learn how to explain chemical reactions in terms of atoms, molecules and ions.

10.1 Chemical bonds

Ions

Why is it that salt solution conducts electricity yet sugar solution does not? You can explain this in terms of the particles they contain. Salt solution contains sodium **ions** and chloride ions, which can carry an electric current. On the other hand, sugar solution contains uncharged sugar molecules which cannot carry an electric current.

As you know from previous studies, atoms consist of a nucleus containing positive protons and neutral neutrons, surrounded by negative electrons. The number of electrons is the same as the number of protons, so the atom has no charge. In chemical reactions it is only the outermost electrons that are involved.

Atoms of metals tend to lose electrons. You will find out the reason for this in the next chapter. For example, a sodium atom can lose one electron to form an ion with a single positive charge Na^+, as shown below. Copper atoms lose two electrons to form Cu^{2+} ions with two positive charges, and aluminium loses three electrons to form Al^{3+}.

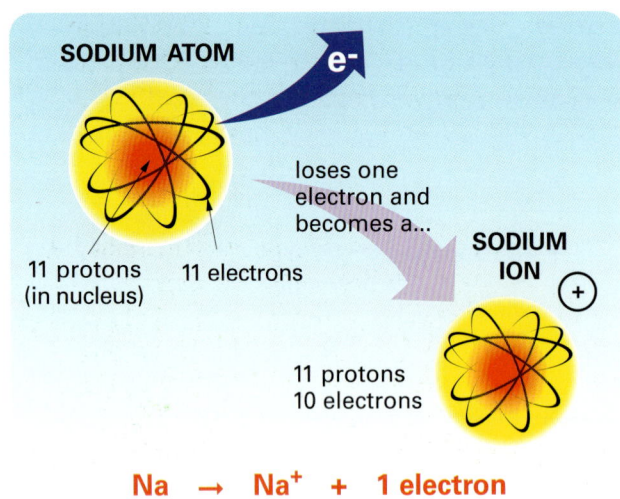

SODIUM ATOM — e⁻

loses one electron and becomes a...

SODIUM ION (+)

11 protons (in nucleus)   11 electrons

11 protons
10 electrons

$$Na \rightarrow Na^+ + 1 \text{ electron}$$

Fig 2 How sodium ions are formed

In contrast to metals, atoms of non-metals tend to form ions by gaining extra electrons. For example, chlorine atoms form negative *chloride* ions Cl^-.

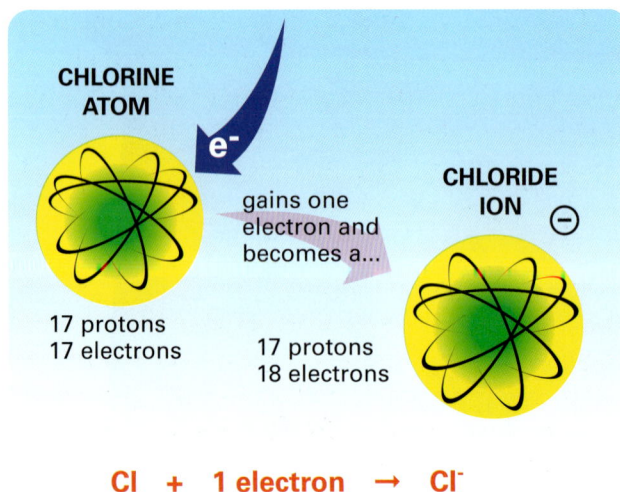

CHLORINE ATOM e⁻

gains one electron and becomes a...

CHLORIDE ION ⊖

17 protons
17 electrons

17 protons
18 electrons

$$Cl + 1 \text{ electron} \rightarrow Cl^-$$

Fig 3 How chloride ions are formed

We can summarise what we have learnt about ions as follows.

| METAL ATOMS LOSE ELECTRONS | TO BECOME | POSITIVE IONS |

For example:

sodium ($Na \rightarrow Na^+ + 1$ electron)

copper ($Cu \rightarrow Cu^{2+} + 2$ electrons)

aluminium ($Al \rightarrow Al^{3+} + 3$ electrons)

Note: Hydrogen behaves like a metal and loses an electron to form H^+ ions.

| NON-METAL ATOMS GAIN ELECTRONS | TO BECOME | NEGATIVE IONS |

For example:

chlorine ($Cl + 1$ electron $\rightarrow Cl^-$)

bromine ($Br + 1$ electron $\rightarrow Br^-$)

iodine ($I + 1$ electron $\rightarrow I^-$)

Atoms are not usually found on their own. Rather, atoms join together to form molecules such as water H_2O. The atoms in these molecules are held together by the attractive forces of **chemical bonds**.

There are two main types of chemical bonds—ionic and covalent. Both kinds of bonds result from the behaviour of the outermost electrons in atoms. Some of these electrons may be lost, some may be gained, or they may be shared. It depends on the kinds of atoms.

Ionic bonds

Metals tend to lose electrons, and non-metals tend to gain electrons. So when a metal reacts with a non-metal, electrons are transferred from the metal to the non-metal, forming positive metal ions and negative non-metal ions.

IONIC BOND   Ions formed

Ordinary table salt has the chemical name sodium chloride and has the formula NaCl. It is made from the metal sodium and the non-metal chlorine. When sodium and chlorine react, each sodium atom loses one electron to form a positive sodium ion Na^+, and each chlorine atom gains an electron to form a negative chloride ion Cl^-. Opposite charges always attract each other, so the positive sodium ions and the negative chloride ions attract each other. This mutual attraction holds the ions together in what is called an **ionic bond**. See the diagram below.

A salt crystal contains millions and millions of sodium ions and chloride ions, and each ion attracts the oppositely charged ions around it. It is not possible to identify a molecule of sodium chloride because every ion belongs to every other ion surrounding it. There is a regular pattern of positive and negative ions called a *crystal lattice*, as shown in Fig 6 on the next page. If your school has a model of the sodium chloride lattice, notice how the sodium and chloride ions are arranged.

Sodium chloride is called an *ionic compound*. This is because it is made of ions held together by ionic bonds. In solid form, it will not conduct an electric current because the ions are locked into the crystal lattice and cannot move. However, when you dissolve sodium chloride in water, the sodium ions and the chloride ions break apart and spread throughout the water. These ions are free to move and conduct an electric current. The ions carry the electric current through the solution. This is why a salt solution conducts electricity. All ionic compounds conduct electricity when dissolved in water. See Fig 7 on the next page.

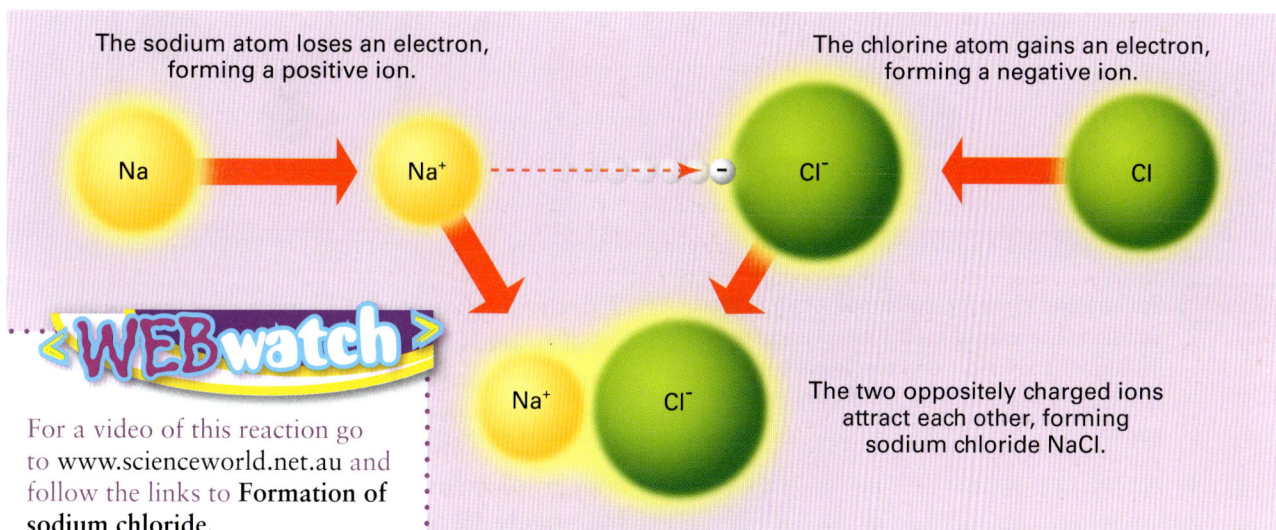

The sodium atom loses an electron, forming a positive ion.

The chlorine atom gains an electron, forming a negative ion.

Na   Na⁺   Cl⁻   Cl

The two oppositely charged ions attract each other, forming sodium chloride NaCl.

Na⁺   Cl⁻

WEBwatch

For a video of this reaction go to www.scienceworld.net.au and follow the links to **Formation of sodium chloride.**

chloride ion
Cl⁻

sodium ion
Na⁺

Fig 6 Sodium chloride crystals and their lattice of sodium chloride ions. The positive and negative charges balance each other, so there is no overall charge.

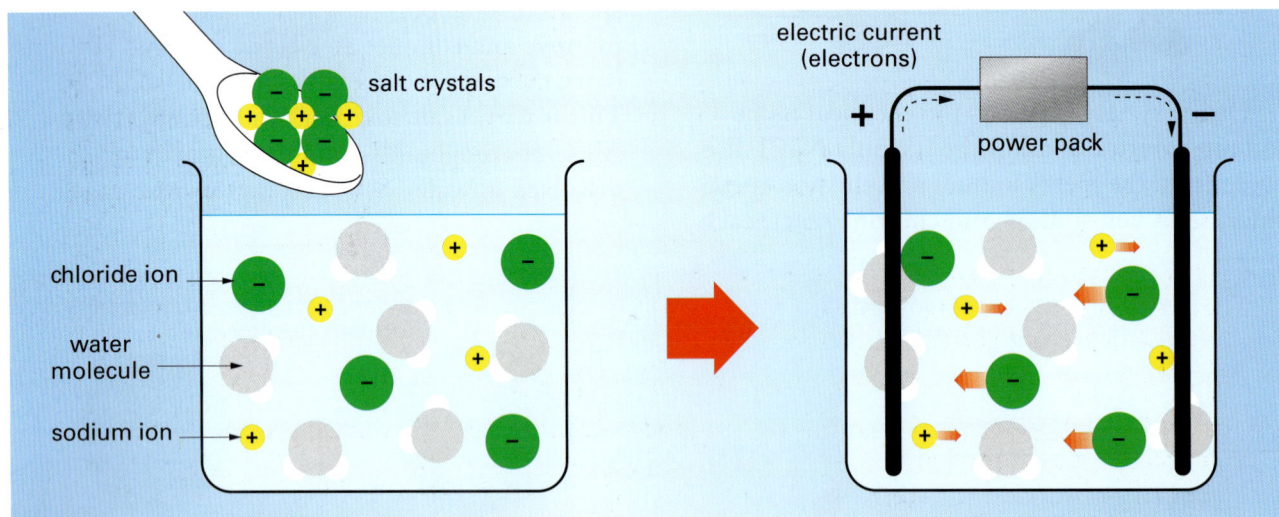

salt crystals

electric current (electrons)

power pack

+   −

chloride ion

water molecule

sodium ion

Fig 7 Sodium and chloride ions break apart in the solution. The ions carry the electric current through the solution, and electrons carry it through the wires to and from the power pack.

Individual atoms and ions are of course too small to see. However, you can observe them when there are millions and millions of them together, say in a piece of copper metal. When these copper atoms lose electrons to become copper ions, you can see the results, as in Investigate 19 on the next page.

Investigate
19 OBSERVING COPPER IONS

Aim

To observe the formation of copper ions in a solution.

Materials

- clean copper strip, approximately 4 cm × 1 cm
- clean strip of copper, brass or bronze mesh, approx 2 cm × 1 cm
- 10 mL of ammonium nitrate solution (40 g of NH_4NO_3 in 450 mL water and 50 mL concentrated ammonia)
- petri dish
- 2 connecting wires, with alligator clips
- power pack

Planning and Safety Check

- Your teacher may set up this investigation on an overhead projector so that you can see what happens on a large screen.
- To explain your observations you need to answer the Discussion.

Method

1 Set up the copper strip and copper mesh in a petri dish on a sheet of white paper, as shown. The copper mesh should be about 5 cm from the copper strip. Use clean alligator clips to attach the strip and mesh to the side of the dish.

2 Connect the set-up to the power pack, making sure the copper mesh is connected to the positive (+) DC terminal of the power pack.

3 Half fill the petri dish with the ammonium nitrate solution. Then turn on the power pack to 6 volts DC.

   📋 Record your observations of what happens in the next few minutes.

Discussion

1 Towards which terminal (positive or negative) did the blue colour move?

2 Suppose the blue colour is due to copper ions. Which charge would these ions have—positive or negative? Why?

3 Infer where the copper ions came from.

4 In forming ions, did the copper atoms lose electrons or gain electrons? Write an equation for this (see page 236).

5 Although some blue colour was formed on the other side of the copper mesh, it didn't form streaks. Try to explain this.

6 Suppose you added a second copper strip on the other side of the mesh, and then connected both it and the other strip to the negative terminal of the power pack. What do you predict would happen? Explain.

7 Predict what would happen if you reversed the connections to the power pack. (You may be able to try this, with a new solution.)

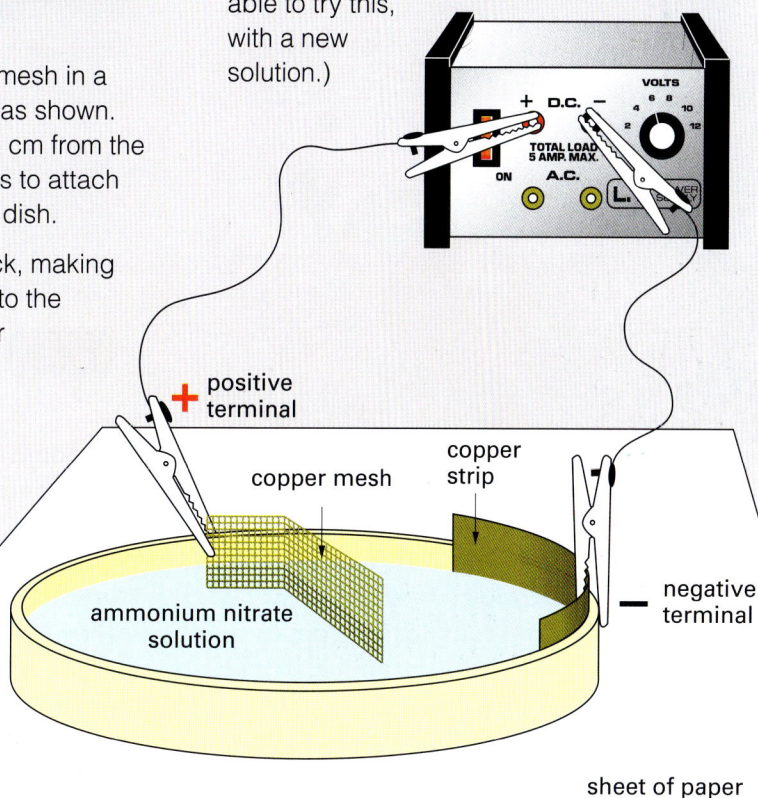

positive terminal

copper mesh

copper strip

ammonium nitrate solution

negative terminal

sheet of paper

Metallic bonds

Pure metals such as copper, gold and iron are elements and contain only one type of atom. The outermost electrons around these atoms are very weakly held, and they are easily lost. As a result, inside any piece of metal there are a lot of positively charged metal ions that have lost one or more electrons. These positive metal ions are surrounded by a 'sea' of electrons that belong to no particular atom and are juggled about rapidly.

The positively charged metal ions and the negatively charged electrons attract each other, and this mutual attraction is called a *metallic bond*. It is because of these freely moving electrons that metals are such good conductors of electricity and heat.

METALLIC BOND
Free electrons

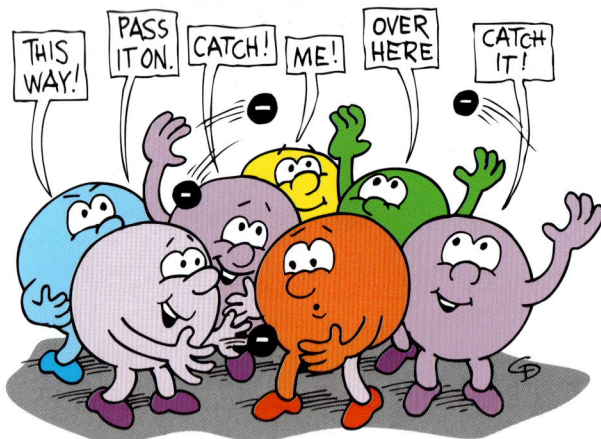

Questions

1   Copper atoms have two weakly held electrons. Draw a two-dimensional diagram of a tiny piece of copper that contains ten copper atoms. How many free electrons are there?
2   Use your diagram to explain why metals are such good conductors of electricity.

Covalent bonds

Non-metal atoms tend to gain electrons. So when two non-metal atoms come together they will both tend to gain electrons, without either of them losing electrons. They can do this by *sharing* electrons to form a **covalent bond**.

When two hydrogen atoms form a molecule of hydrogen H_2, one electron from each atom is shared by the other. Similarly, two chlorine atoms share an electron pair to form a molecule of chlorine gas Cl_2. So, a covalent bond is a shared electron pair holding two atoms together.

COVALENT BOND
Electrons shared

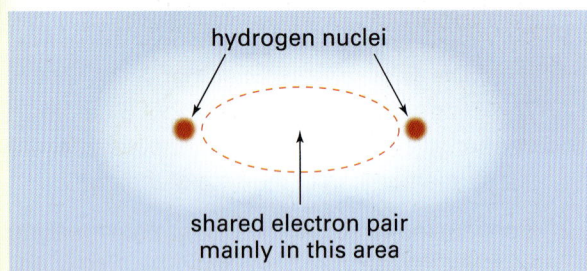

hydrogen nuclei

shared electron pair
mainly in this area

Fig 10   In a hydrogen molecule the hydrogen atoms share electrons equally.

Some non-metal atoms can form more than one bond. For example, oxygen can form bonds with two hydrogen atoms to form water H_2O. Nitrogen can form bonds with three hydrogen atoms to form ammonia NH_3. And carbon can form bonds with four hydrogen atoms to form methane CH_4. It can also form bonds with other carbon atoms (see Fig 12 on page 241). Compounds containing covalent bonds are called *covalent compounds*.

Sugar is a covalent compound containing carbon, hydrogen and oxygen. It consists of large molecules with the formula $C_{12}H_{22}O_{11}$. When you dissolve sugar in water, these molecules separate and spread throughout the solution. However, because the molecules do not form ions, the solution does not conduct an electric current. Similarly all covalent compounds are non-conductors of electricity.

Sometimes non-metals don't share their electrons equally. For example, in the covalent bonds between hydrogen and oxygen in water molecules, the oxygen atom tends to get more than its share of electrons because it is 'greedier' for electrons than hydrogen is. As a result the oxygen atom has a slight negative charge and the hydrogen atoms have a slight positive charge. So the molecule has one positive end or pole, and two negative ends or poles. For this reason the bond is called a *polar* covalent bond.

POLAR COVALENT BOND
Unequal sharing of electrons

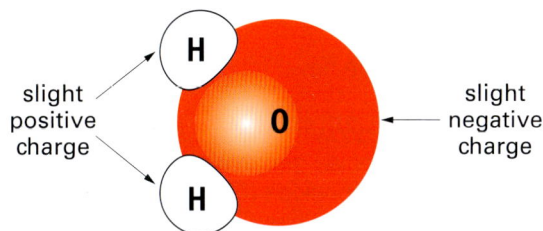

Fig 11 Water molecules are polar because the bonding electrons are pulled slightly towards the oxygen atom. The positive and negative charges balance each other, so the molecule has no overall charge.

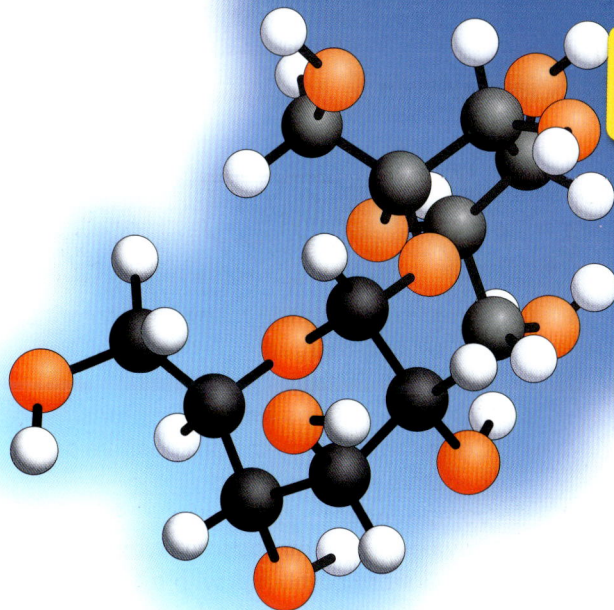

Fig 12 Sucrose (cane sugar) is a covalent compound with the formula $C_{12}H_{22}O_{11}$. In this model carbon atoms are black, hydrogen white and oxygen red.

Bonds between different non-metals are always polar, since no two non-metals are equally greedy for electrons. On the other hand, bonds between atoms of the same non-metal are non-polar: for example the two oxygen atoms in an oxygen molecule. In this case there is equal sharing of the electrons.

Activity

You can demonstrate the polarity of water by bringing a charged rod near a trickle of water as shown.

Use your knowledge of electric charges to explain what happens.

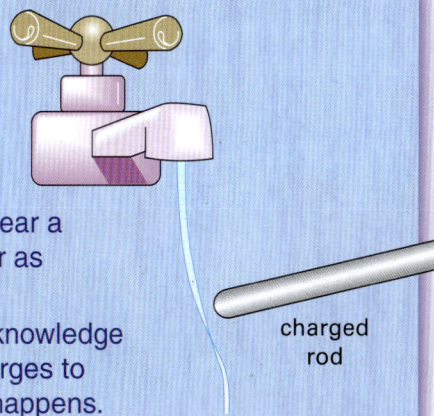

charged rod

WEBwatch

For a summary of the different types of bonds, go to www.scienceworld.net.au and follow the links to **Dog bone bonds**.

Check!

1 Copy and complete the following sentences
   a An ion is a charged _____.
   b Metal atoms form _____ ions.
   c Non-metal atoms form _____ ions.
   d Compounds formed from positive and negative ions are called _____ compounds.
   e Covalent compounds form when a non-metal atom combines with a _____ atom.
   f Covalent bonds occur when electrons are _____ between atoms.

2 A magnesium atom has 12 protons in its nucleus. It loses two electrons to form a magnesium ion.
   a How many electrons does a magnesium atom have?
   b How many electrons does a magnesium ion have?
   c How many protons are there in the nucleus of a magnesium ion?
   d What charge does an electron have?
   e What charge does a proton have?
   f What charge does a magnesium ion have?
   g Explain why a magnesium ion has this charge.

3 The symbol for a silver ion is Ag^+. How many electrons does a silver atom lose to become a silver ion?

4 An aluminium atom Al can lose three electrons. What is the symbol for an aluminium ion?

5 Bromine is a non-metal similar to chlorine. Predict whether bromine atoms tend to lose electrons or gain them. Explain your answer.

6 Magnesium burns in air to form the compound magnesium oxide.
   a Would you expect this compound to be ionic or covalent?
   b Which atoms would be positive and which would be negative?

7 Electricity is passed through a zinc sulfate solution containing zinc ions and sulfate ions.

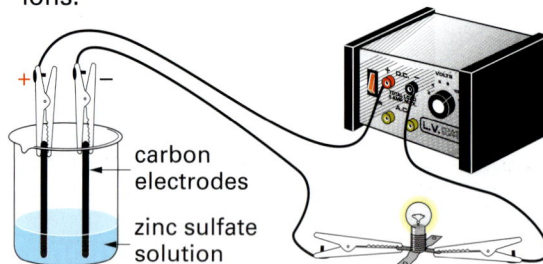

carbon electrodes

zinc sulfate solution

   a Draw a simple diagram showing what you predict will happen to the zinc and sulfate ions.
   b Predict what will happen if the connections to the power pack are reversed.

challenge

1 What would need to happen for an oxide ion O^{2-} to become an oxygen atom?

2 Copy and complete this summary of chemical bonding.

Type of bond	Kinds of atoms	Electrons are …	Result
	non-metals		molecules
		lost and gained	

3 Explain why ionic compounds, which consist of electrically charged ions packed together, are electrically neutral. Use sodium chloride as an example.

4 Copper ions are never found on their own. Why is this?

5 Which of the following molecules would you expect to be polar: ammonia (NH_3), chlorine (Cl_2), carbon monoxide (CO), hydrogen bromide (HBr), hydrogen sulfide (H_2S) and nitrogen (N_2)?

6 The red colour of blood is due to iron. Would this colour be due to iron atoms or iron ions? Explain your answer.

7 Why is it wrong to speak of *molecules* of sodium chloride? What should you say instead?

10.2 Chemical shorthand

Chemical formulas

Covalent compounds are formed when atoms join to form molecules; and ionic compounds form when positive and negative ions join together in a crystal lattice. A shorthand way of representing a compound is to use a chemical formula made up from the symbols of the elements in it. For example, the formula for carbon dioxide is CO_2. The 2 after the oxygen shows that there are two atoms of oxygen in a molecule of carbon dioxide. (Note that the 2 is written as a subscript, a little below the line.) There is only one atom of carbon, but the 1 is never written in the formula. Similarly, the formula for water is H_2O (two atoms of hydrogen bonded to one atom of oxygen). Ammonia (NH_3) has three atoms of hydrogen bonded to one atom of nitrogen.

Sodium chloride is an ionic compound consisting of sodium and chloride ions held together by ionic bonds. Its formula is NaCl, which means that the ratio of sodium ions to chloride ions is 1:1. But how do we know that the formula is NaCl, rather than $NaCl_2$ or Na_2Cl or Na_2Cl_3? The answer is that you can tell from the combining powers of the atoms.

An atom's combining power or **valency** predicts how it will combine with other atoms through the loss, gain or sharing of electrons. For ionic compounds the valency is the same as the charge on the ion. For example, sodium atoms lose one electron to form Na^+ ions—so sodium has a valency of 1+. Oxygen atoms gain two electrons to form oxide ions O^{2-}—so oxygen has a valency of 2-.

A sodium ion Na^+ can combine with one negative ion that has a valency of 1-, eg Cl^-, to form NaCl. Sodium ions can also combine with oxide ions. However, two Na^+ ions are needed for each O^{2-} ion. Hence the formula for sodium oxide is Na_2O.

> sodium Na^+ + chlorine Cl^- → sodium chloride NaCl
>
> sodium Na^+ + oxygen O^{2-} → sodium oxide Na_2O

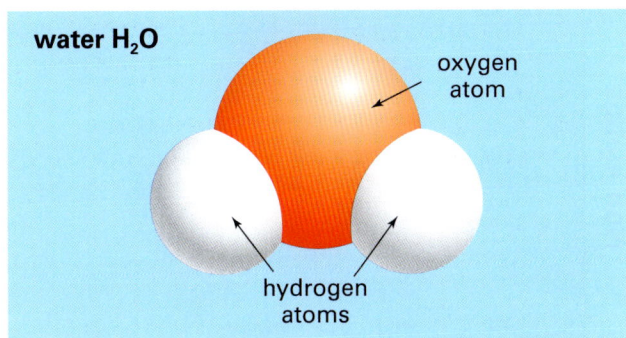

water H_2O — oxygen atom, hydrogen atoms

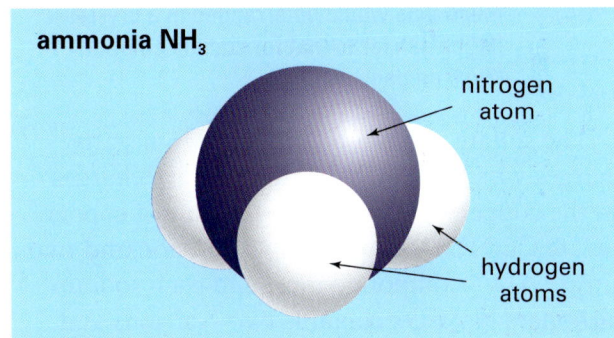

ammonia NH_3 — nitrogen atom, hydrogen atoms

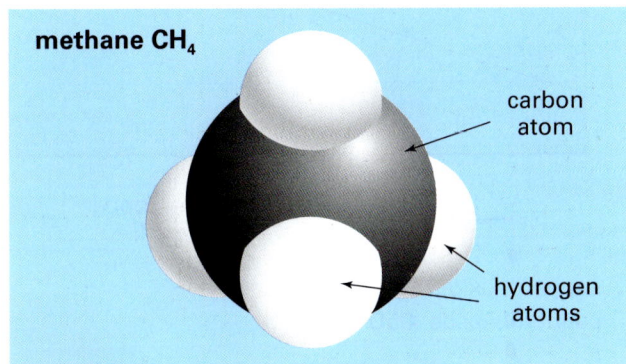

methane CH_4 — carbon atom, hydrogen atoms

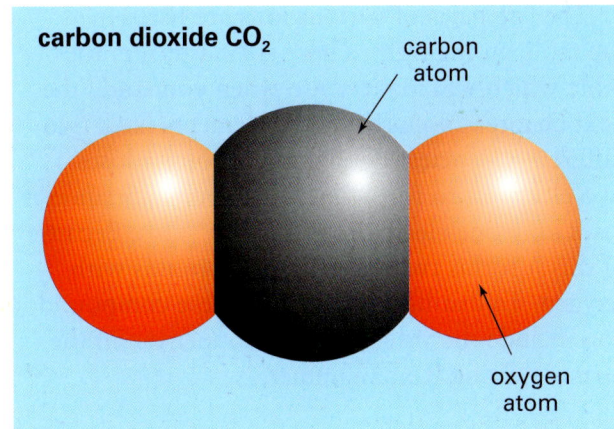

carbon dioxide CO_2 — carbon atom, oxygen atom

Fig 15 Some common molecules and their formulas

Sometimes the ions consist of groups of atoms called *compound ions*. For example, copper sulfate is made up of copper ions and sulfate ions. Each copper ion (Cu^{2+}) has two positive charges. Each sulfate compound ion (SO_4^{2-}) consists of one sulfur atom covalently bonded to four oxygen atoms, as shown. The five atoms of the sulfate ion usually stay together in chemical reactions.

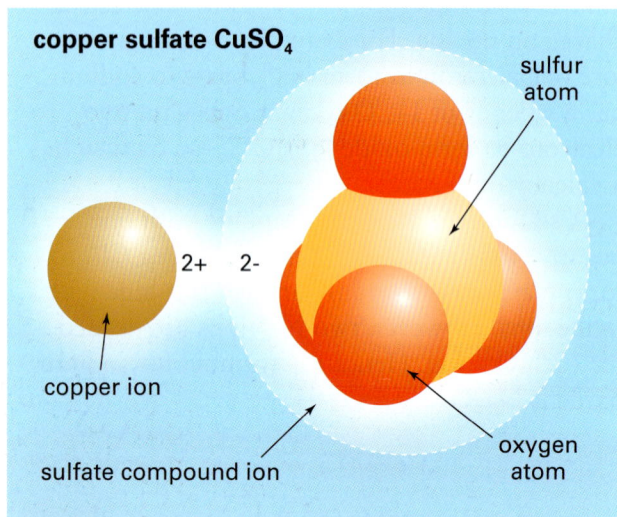

copper sulfate CuSO₄

sulfur atom

2+ 2-

copper ion

sulfate compound ion

oxygen atom

Fig 16 A model of copper sulfate CuSO₄. Note that these ions would be arranged in a crystal lattice similar to that for sodium chloride (Fig 6 on page 238).

The sulfate compound ion has two negative charges which balance the two positive charges on the copper ion. Similarly each unit of copper nitrate $Cu(NO_3)_2$ contains one Cu^{2+} ion and two nitrate NO^{3-} compound ions; and each sodium carbonate Na_2CO_3 contains two Na^+ ions and one carbonate CO_3^{2-} compound ion.

The valencies of various ions are listed in the table on the right. There is a pattern in the table which will make sense when you study the next chapter. Note that some elements have two different valencies. For example, copper loses two electrons to form Cu^{2+} ions; but sometimes it loses only one electron to form Cu^+ ions. Because of this it forms two different compounds with oxygen. To distinguish between these compounds you include the valency of the copper ion in the formula, using Roman numerals.

Ion	Symbol	Valency
ammonium	NH_4^+	1+
hydrogen	H^+	1+
potassium	K^+	1+
silver	Ag^+	1+
sodium	Na^+	1+
calcium	Ca^{2+}	2+
copper	Cu^{2+}	2+ (or 1+)
lead	Pb^{2+}	2+ (or 1+)
magnesium	Mg^{2+}	2+
zinc	Zn^{2+}	2+
aluminium	Al^{3+}	3+
iron	Fe^{3+}	3+ (or 2+)
bromide	Br^-	1-
chloride	Cl^-	1-
hydrogen carbonate	HCO_3^-	1-
hydroxide	OH^-	1-
iodide	I^-	1-
nitrate	NO_3^-	1-
carbonate	CO_3^{2-}	2-
oxide	O^{2-}	2-
sulfate	SO_4^{2-}	2-
sulfide	S^{2-}	2-
sulfite	SO_3^{2-}	2-
phosphate	PO_4^{3-}	3-

Metals / Non-metals

This means the copper has a valency of 1.

copper(I) oxide Cu_2O
copper(II) oxide CuO

This means the copper has a valency of 2.

Writing ionic formulas

To write the formula for an ionic compound, follow these rules.

Example 1

1 Write down the symbols of the ions. Note that the positive ion (usually a metal) goes first. Write the valencies above the symbols.

silver   sulfide

1+   2–

Ag   S

2 Crisscross the valencies to get correct subscripts. Leave out the + and – signs.

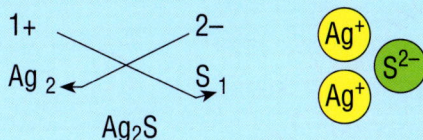

$1+$ $2-$

Ag_2 S_1

Ag_2S

Ag^+ S^{2-} Ag^+

3 Write the correct formula with subscripts, leaving out the 1. Note that the charges are balanced. You need two Ag^+ ions to balance one S^{2-} ion.

Example 2

magnesium   oxide

$2+$ $2-$

Mg_2 O_2

MgO

Mg^{2+} O^{2-}

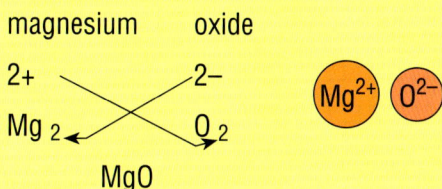

In this example you simplify Mg_2O_2 to MgO since the magnesium and oxygen are in the ratio 1:1.

Example 3

calcium   hydroxide

$2+$ $1-$

Ca_1 $(OH)_2$

$Ca(OH)_2$

Ca^{2+} OH^- OH^-

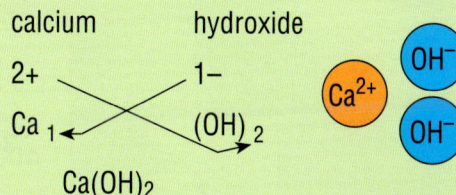

In this example you put the compound ion in brackets to indicate that it acts as a single unit. The subscript 2 refers to everything inside the brackets. In other words, there are two oxygen atoms and two hydrogen atoms. Where there is only one unit of the compound ion you can drop the brackets, eg NaOH rather than Na(OH).

Example 4

aluminium   sulfate

$+3$ -2

Al_2 $(SO_4)_3$

$Al_2(SO_4)_3$

Al^{3+} SO_4^{2-} Al^{3+} SO_4^{2-} SO_4^{2-} SO_4^{2-}

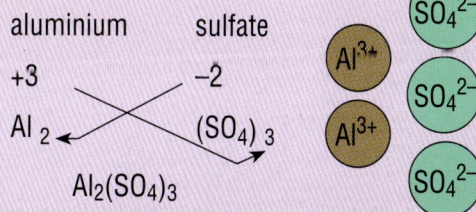

Two 3+ charges balance three 2– charges.

What do you reckon the symbol would be for banana?

That's easy —$Ba(Na)_2$!

Did you know that the formula for water is HIJKLMNO?

That doesn't sound right to me.

Yes it is—our teacher told us—it's H to O.

Activity

Na^+ Mg^2 Al^{3+} Cl CO_3^2 PO_4^3

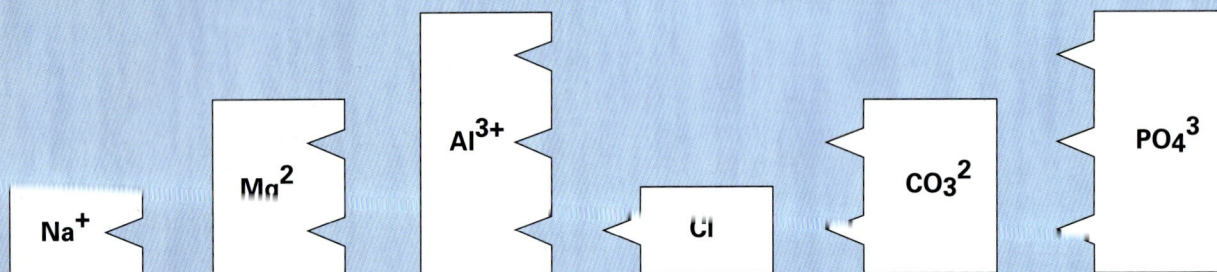

You can use paper or cardboard cut-outs to make models of various compounds. Look at the models above for various ions. Notches represent electrons lost to form positive ions. One notch indicates one positive charge or a valency of 1, two notches indicate a valency of 2, and three notches a valency of 3. Similarly, spikes represent electrons gained to form negative ions. Work in a group so you can share the work.

1 Your teacher will give you copies of the models—six of each. Colour each type of ion a different colour, eg sodium ions yellow, chloride ions green etc.

2 Use scissors to cut out the models.

3 Use your cut-outs to make a model of sodium chloride. Glue the model

compound into your notebook and write its formula under it.

4 Make models of the following compounds:
sodium carbonate
sodium phosphate
magnesium chloride
magnesium carbonate
magnesium phosphate
aluminium chloride
aluminium carbonate
aluminium phosphate

5 For each compound you make, count the number of positive charges and the number of negative charges to make sure they are equal. Then write the formula under the model.

Covalent compounds

You can also use valencies to write the formulas for covalent compounds. For example:

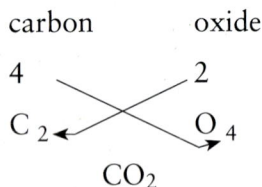

carbon   oxide
4   2
C_2 O_4
CO_2

Instead of calling this compound carbon oxide, it is usually called carbon dioxide. The *di* comes from the Greek word for 'two' since two oxygen atoms bond to one carbon atom. Similarly, CO is carbon monoxide, and SO_3 is sulfur trioxide.

Some elements form molecules containing a pair of atoms. These are called *diatomic*

Erk! Some H_2O has permeated the NaCl.

molecules, eg hydrogen H_2, oxygen O_2, nitrogen N_2, chlorine Cl_2 and iodine I_2. It is best to remember these formulas.

Chemical equations

A chemical equation is a shorthand way of writing down what happens in a chemical reaction. To write an equation you must know the names of the reactants and the products. If you don't know these you cannot write the equation. Sometimes, however, you can predict what the products might be, if you know the reactants.

Work through the following three examples step by step.

Equation 1

Zinc metal reacts with hydrochloric acid to produce hydrogen gas and a solution of an ionic compound called zinc chloride.

Step 1: Writing the word equation

zinc + hydrochloric acid → zinc chloride + hydrogen

Step 2: Writing down the formulas

You next write down the formulas of the reactants and products. For most elements the atoms exist on their own, so you simply write the symbol for the element, in this case zinc Zn. It is best to remember that the formula for hydrochloric acid is HCl. For zinc chloride you can work it out using valencies from the table on page 244. In hydrogen gas, however, the molecules are diatomic (H_2).

$$Zn + HCl \rightarrow ZnCl_2 + H_2$$

Step 3: Balancing the equation

In a chemical reaction the atoms are rearranged, but you end up with the same number of atoms as you started with. (This is the law of conservation of mass.) So the final step in writing an equation is to make sure that the numbers of atoms of each element are the same on both sides of the equation. This is called *balancing the equation*.

In this case, there is one zinc atom on each side of the equation. So the zinc atoms are balanced. There are two hydrogen atoms on the right-hand side, but only one on the left. So you can balance the hydrogen atoms by putting a 2 in front of the HCl on the left-hand side. This means 2 molecules of HCl.

$$Zn + 2HCl \rightarrow ZnCl_2 + H_2$$

The 2 refers to every atom in the formula. So 2HCl means that there are two atoms of H and two atoms of Cl. So the chlorine atoms are balanced. *Never change the number in a formula to balance an equation.* The balancing numbers always go in front of the formulas.

Symbols are usually added to tell you whether the reactants are solids (s), liquids (l), gases (g) or dissolved in water (aq—short for aqueous). For example:

$$Zn(s) + 2HCl(aq) \rightarrow ZnCl_2(aq) + H_2(g)$$

$$Zn(s) + 2HCl(aq) \rightarrow ZnCl_2(aq) + H_2(g)$$

Equation 2

Ammonia is a very important gas used in industry to make nitric acid, fertilisers, drugs, dyes and plastics. It is made by reacting the gases nitrogen and hydrogen at a high temperature in the presence of a catalyst.

$$nitrogen \ + \ hydrogen \ \rightarrow \ ammonia$$

You need to know the formulas for nitrogen, hydrogen and ammonia.

$$N_2 \ + \ H_2 \ \rightarrow \ NH_3$$

To balance the nitrogen atoms you have to add a 2 in front of NH_3.

$$N_2 \ + \ H_2 \ \rightarrow \ 2NH_3$$

This makes 6 atoms of hydrogen on the right-hand side. So to balance the hydrogens you have to add a 3 in front of H_2 on the left-hand side.

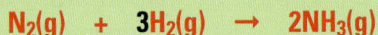

$$N_2(g) \ + \ 3H_2(g) \ \rightarrow \ 2NH_3(g)$$

As a final check on the balancing you can write down the numbers of atoms on each side of the equation, as shown.

LEFT	RIGHT
N 2	N 2
H $3 \times 2 = 6$	H $2 \times 3 = 6$

Equation 3

Iron rusts when it reacts with oxygen in the air to produce iron(III) oxide.

$$iron \ + \ oxygen \ \rightarrow \ iron \ oxide$$
$$Fe \ + \ O_2 \ \rightarrow \ Fe_2O_3$$

To balance the iron atoms, put a 2 in front of Fe.

$$2Fe \ + \ O_2 \ \rightarrow \ Fe_2O_3$$

To balance the oxygen atoms you need a 3 in front of O_2 and a 2 in front of Fe_2O_3. You may need to work this out by trial and error.

$$2Fe \ + \ 3O_2 \ \rightarrow \ 2Fe_2O_3$$

Finally, you need to balance the iron atoms again.

$$4Fe(s) \ + \ 3O_2(g) \ \rightarrow \ 2Fe_2O_3(s)$$

LEFT	RIGHT
Fe 4	Fe $2 \times 2 = 4$
O $3 \times 2 = 6$	H $2 \times 3 = 6$

Note that the balancing numbers you use should be the smallest possible. For instance, the equation $8Fe + 6O_2 \rightarrow 4Fe_2O_3$ is balanced, but can be simplified to $4Fe + 3O_2 \rightarrow 2Fe_2O_3$.

Fig 22 The iron in this old car is slowly turning to rust (iron oxide) and crumbling away.

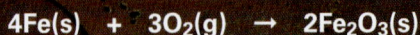

$$4Fe(s) \ + \ 3O_2(g) \ \rightarrow \ 2Fe_2O_3(s)$$

Activity

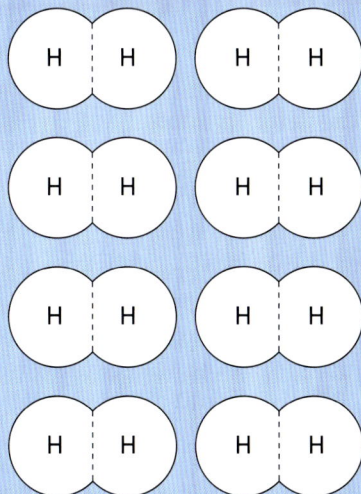

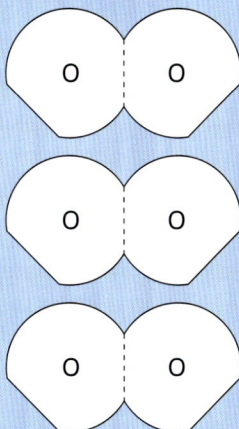

hydrogen (valency = 1)	oxygen (valency = 2)	nitrogen (valency = 3)	chlorine (valency = 1)

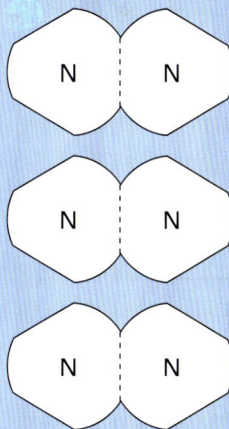

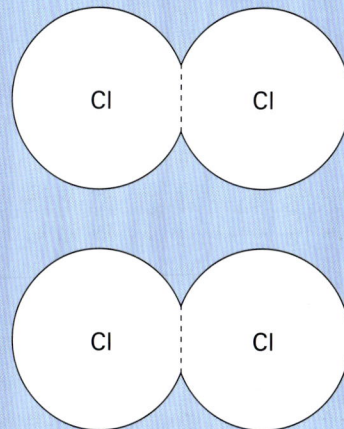

You can use paper or cardboard cut-outs to make models of chemical reactions. The cutouts above represent some diatomic molecules.

1 Photocopy or trace the molecular models above and label the atoms. Colour the atoms different colours, eg white for hydrogen, red for oxygen, blue for nitrogen and green for chlorine.

2 The example below shows how the models can be used to represent the reaction between hydrogen and oxygen to form water.

3 Use the models to represent the following reactions:

hydrogen + chlorine → hydrogen chloride

nitrogen + hydrogen → ammonia

nitrogen + oxygen → nitrogen dioxide

You will need to break the molecules into their atoms by cutting along the dotted lines. Unless you do this the 'reaction' cannot occur.

4 Glue the models into your notebook and write the balanced equations under them.

5 If you have a molecular models kit you can make three-dimensional models.

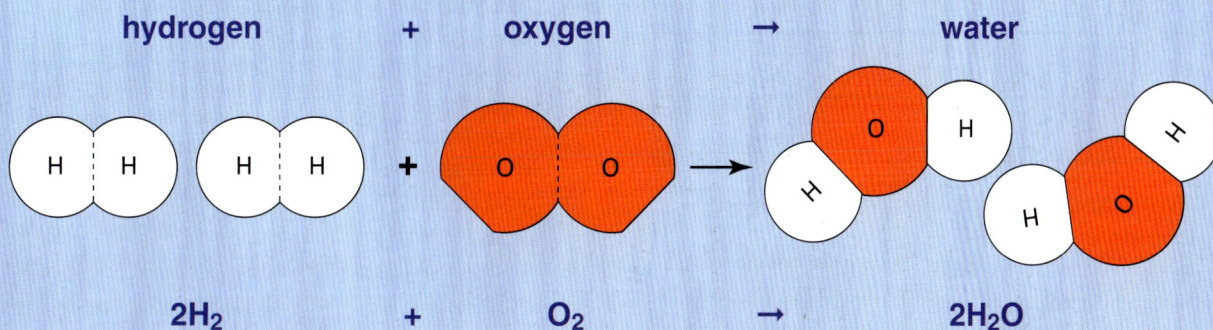

hydrogen	+	**oxygen**	→	**water**

$2H_2$	+	O_2	→	$2H_2O$

Check!

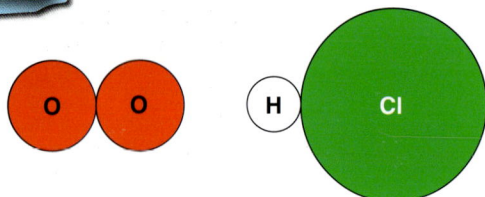

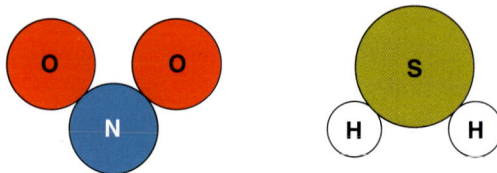

1 Look at the models of the four molecules above, and write the chemical formula for each of them.

2 Sulfuric acid contains hydrogen, sulfur and oxygen in the ratio 2:1:4. What is its formula?

3 One of the substances in superphosphate fertiliser has the formula $Ca(H_2PO_4)_2$. How many atoms of calcium, hydrogen, phosphorus and oxygen are represented by this formula?

4 Use the table on page 244 to write the correct formula (with its electric charge) for each of the following compound ions:
  a ammonium
  b carbonate
  c hydrogen carbonate
  d hydroxide
  e nitrate
  f phosphate
  g sulfate
  h sulfite

5 Name the following compounds:
  a KCl
  b $NaNO_3$
  c MgO
  d $FeCl_3$
  e $Al(OH)_3$
  f $(NH_4)_3PO_4$
  g HCl
  h $NaHCO_3$

6 Copy this table and complete the formulas.

	chloride	sulfate	phosphate
calcium			
iron (III)			
sodium			

7 Write down the formulas of the following compounds:
  a sodium hydroxide
  b ammonium sulfate
  c hydrogen sulfide
  d sodium sulfite

e calcium hydrogen carbonate
f magnesium sulfate
g calcium phosphate
h copper(II) hydroxide
i iron(II) oxide

8 Carlos heated some blue copper(II) nitrate in a test tube. A brown gas (nitrogen dioxide) and a colourless gas (oxygen) were produced and black copper(II) oxide was left in the test tube.
  a List the reactants and products.
  b Write a word equation for the reaction.

9 Copy these equations into your notebook and balance them where necessary. The formulas are all correct and must not be changed.
  a $NaBr + Cl_2 \rightarrow NaCl + Br_2$
  b $Fe + Cl_2 \rightarrow FeCl_3$
  c $Ba(NO_3)_2 + H_2SO_4 \rightarrow BaSO_4 + HNO_3$
  d $CaCO_3 \rightarrow CaO + CO_2$
  e $H_2 + I_2 \rightarrow HI$
  f $Zn + H_2SO_4 \rightarrow ZnSO_4 + H_2$
  g $NaOH + H_2SO_4 \rightarrow Na_2SO_4 + H_2O$
  h $P_4 + O_2 \rightarrow P_2O_5$
  i $CH_4 + Cl_2 \rightarrow CCl_4 + HCl$
  j $Pb(NO_3)_2 \rightarrow PbO + NO_2 + O_2$

10 Michael can't see the point of learning about chemical formulas and equations. In a group discuss how you could answer him.

What's the point of learning about all these formulas and equations? Will it be any use once we leave school?

challenge

1 Look at this balanced equation:
$$Mg + O_2 \rightarrow 2MgO$$

  a How many atoms of magnesium react with one molecule of oxygen?

  b How many atoms of magnesium react with 5 million molecules of oxygen?

2 Each of the following equations is incorrect. Rewrite them correctly and balance them.

  a $H + Cl \rightarrow HCl$

  b $H_2O_2 \rightarrow H_2O + O$

  c $Cu + O_2 \rightarrow CuO_2$

  d $Pb(NO_3)_2 + KI \rightarrow PbI + K(NO_3)_2$

  e $Na + H_2O \rightarrow NaOH + H$

3 Write balanced equations for the following reactions.

  a Zinc reacts with hydrochloric acid to produce zinc chloride and hydrogen.

  b Sulfur dioxide (SO_2) burns in oxygen to produce sulfur trioxide (SO_3).

  c Copper(II) carbonate reacts with hydrochloric acid to produce copper(II) chloride, water and carbon dioxide.

  d During cooking, sodium hydrogen carbonate (baking soda) decomposes to sodium carbonate, carbon dioxide and oxygen.

  e When heated, cane sugar ($C_{12}H_{22}O_{11}$) decomposes to give carbon and water.

  f During respiration, glucose ($C_6H_{12}O_6$) reacts with oxygen to give carbon dioxide and water.

4 Elements X and Y form compounds with carbon with the formulas CX_4 and CY_2. Predict the formula of a compound of X and Y. Explain how you worked it out.

5 A metal M forms a sulfate with the formula $M_2(SO_4)_3$. Given this information, which of the following formulas are correct?

  a M_2O **d** M_2Cl_3

  b $M_2(CO_3)_3$ **e** MPO_4

  c $M(OH)_3$ **f** M_3S_2

6 Challenge yourself by trying to balance these three equations:

  a $Al(NO_3)_3 + K_2Cr_2O_7 \rightarrow Al_2(Cr_2O_7)_3 + KNO_3$

  b $FeCl_2 + HNO_3 + HCl \rightarrow FeCl_3 + NO + H_2O$

  c $Cu + HNO_3 \rightarrow Cu(NO_3)_2 + H_2O + NO$

➡ try this

For this activity you will need playing cards with the names and valencies of positive and negative ions. Use all the ions listed on page 244 and make four identical cards for each one. You will need a total of 96 cards. (Use the 2+ valency for Cu, Fe and Pb.)

Play the game in a group of four or five. The aim of the game is to combine cards to make compounds with correct formulas; for example, one magnesium Mg^{2+} card goes with two chloride Cl^- cards to give $MgCl_2$.

The dealer shuffles the cards and gives each player seven cards. When it is your turn you try to make a compound using the cards in your hand. If you use two cards to make the compound then you pick up two cards to replace them, and so on. If you can't make a compound you pick up another card. You can also choose to pick up another card instead of making a compound.

The game continues until all the cards are used up. The winner is the player who has made the most compounds with the correct formula.

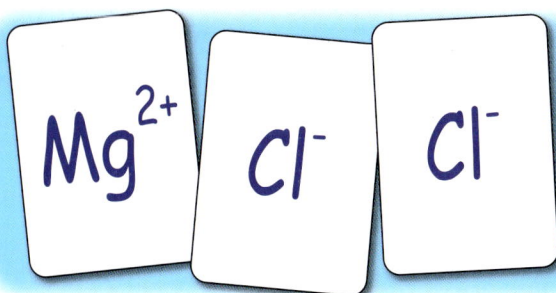

10.3 *Predicting a reaction*

In a chemical reaction substances react to form new substances. But what happens to the atoms, molecules and ions in the reactants? To answer this, consider the reaction between potassium iodide and lead nitrate solutions.

Potassium iodide is an ionic compound with the formula KI. It consists of K^+ ions and I^- ions. In solid potassium iodide, the ions are packed closely in a crystal lattice, like the sodium chloride lattice (Fig 6 on page 238). When the solid dissolves in water, the positive and negative ions break apart and spread throughout the solution.

$$KI \rightarrow K^+ + I^-$$

Similarly, lead nitrate $Pb(NO_3)_2$ breaks up to form lead ions Pb^{2+} and nitrate ions NO_3^- in solution.

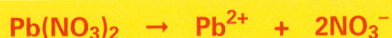

$$Pb(NO_3)_2 \rightarrow Pb^{2+} + 2NO_3^-$$

You can now try to predict what might happen when potassium iodide and lead nitrate solutions react. You can use spheres of different sizes and colours, as shown on the right, to represent the various ions.

When the two solutions are mixed, the four ions also mix. (This is like putting all the spheres in a box and shaking it.) The ions are constantly moving, and there is a good chance that they will bump into each other and possibly combine.

Lead ions can bump into nitrate ions or iodide ions, but are not likely to bump into potassium ions. This is because lead ions and potassium ions both have the same charge, and like charges repel. Similarly, potassium ions can bump into nitrate ions and iodide ions.

So, there is a possibility that the ions could change partners. Lead ions could combine with iodide ions to form lead iodide. Similarly, potassium ions could combine with nitrate ions to form potassium nitrate.

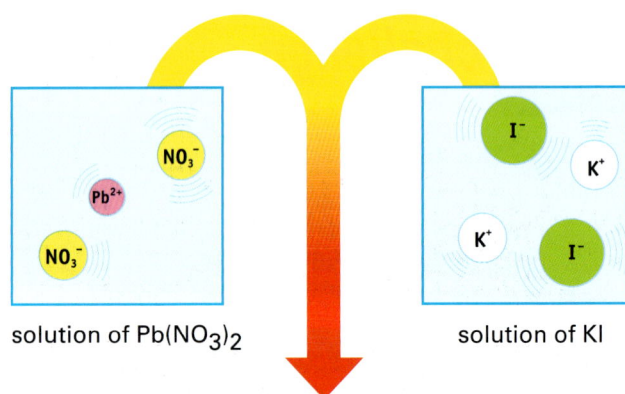

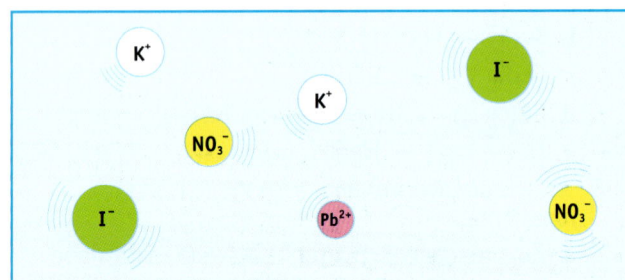

solution of $Pb(NO_3)_2$ solution of KI

The solutions are mixed.

Prediction: the ions can change partners and form new substances.

So, you can predict that when lead nitrate and potassium iodide are mixed, two new substances (lead iodide and potassium nitrate) could be formed. The word equation for the reaction is shown below. You can test this prediction in Investigate 20.

lead nitrate + potassium iodide → lead iodide + potassium nitrate

Investigate
20 WHAT IS THE PRECIPITATE?

Aim
To investigate the precipitate that forms when lead nitrate and potassium iodide solutions are mixed.

PART A
Forming the precipitate

Materials
- 2 test tubes
- test tube rack
- **lead nitrate** solution (0.1M)
- **potassium iodide** solution (0.1M)
- piece of filter paper
- filter funnel
- stand and ring clamp
- small beaker
- wash bottle containing water
- watch glass
- disposable gloves (optional)

Toxic

Wear safety glasses.

Planning and Safety Check
Read both parts of the investigation carefully.
- What is the aim of Part B?

Lead and all lead compounds are toxic. So be very careful not to get them on your hands or clothing. **Wash your hands well after using these chemicals.** You must follow the method and safety precautions closely.
- How will you dispose of the lead and lead compounds?

Since iodine fumes are produced in Part B, Step 2 should be done in a fume cupboard.

Method
1. Quarter fill one test tube with lead nitrate solution, and the other with potassium iodide solution.

2. Pour the potassium iodide solution into the lead nitrate solution.
   - Describe in your own words what happens.

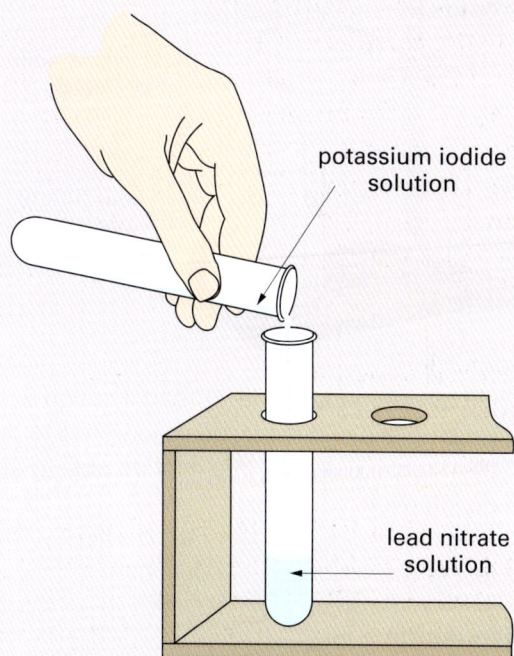

potassium iodide solution

lead nitrate solution

1 Fold here.
2 Then fold here.
3 Pull this single flap away from the other three.
4 This forms a cone.

3. Fold a filter paper and open it out into a cone, as shown. You can also use fluted filter paper.

4. Place the cone into the filter funnel and use the wash bottle to wet the paper to hold it in place. Carefully pour the contents of the test tube into the funnel and collect the filtrate in the beaker. Pour this into a special waste container.

Keep yellow solid for Part B.

Pour filtrate into waste container.

Method

1   Light a burner in the fume cupboard and adjust it so that you have a very small blue flame.

2   Use the spatula to put about half of the yellow solid into a test tube. Place a loose plug of cotton wool in the mouth of the tube (to prevent iodine fumes from escaping). Heat the test tube over the burner flame. If the solid produces purple iodine gas it contains iodide ions.

3   Light a match and let it burn briefly. The black, charred end is mainly carbon.

4   Dip the charred end into water, then into some of the yellow solid. (The water is to help the yellow solid stick to the match.)

Wear safety glasses.

water

yellow solid

Remember to wash your hands when you have finished.

5   Lift out the paper cone, spread it out on a watch glass and leave the yellow solid to dry, overnight if possible. You may be able to use a drying oven.
Keep the yellow solid for Part B where you will test to see which ions it contains.

Discussion

1   The yellow solid is called a precipitate. Could it be lead nitrate or potassium iodide? Explain.

2   According to the equation at the bottom of page 252, which two substances could the precipitate be?

3   How could you test that the filtrate contains something besides water?

PART B
Testing the precipitate

Materials

Toxic

*   **yellow solid** from Part A
*   2 small test tubes
*   test tube holder
*   spatula (narrow type)
*   burner and heatproof mat
*   matches
*   cotton wool
*   white tile

5   Hold the tip of the match just in the burner flame for a few seconds. Watch carefully what happens. If tiny drops of silvery lead form, then the yellow solid contains lead ions. Put the match on a white tile and look for any signs of lead. A simple test is to rub it on paper. Lead leaves a black mark.

6   Place any remaining yellow solid (and the test tube from Step 2) in a special waste container.

Discussion

1 Which ions does the yellow solid contain?

2 Suggest a name for the yellow solid. Write down its chemical formula.

3 Write a balanced equation for the reaction that occurred in Part A.

4 The yellow solid was once used as a paint pigment, but it is not used any more. Suggest a reason for this.

5 When you heated lead iodide in Part B, the products were iodine gas (I_2) and lead. Write a balanced equation for this reaction.

6 When you heated lead iodide on a charred match, it reacted with oxygen in the air to form lead(II) oxide and iodine gas. The lead oxide then reacted with the carbon in the match to form lead and carbon dioxide. Write balanced equations for these two reactions.

Explaining the reaction

When lead nitrate and potassium iodide are mixed there are four different ions in the solution. See the diagram on page 252. The reason the lead ions combine with the iodide ions is that lead iodide is very insoluble in water. Each lead ion Pb^{2+} combines with two iodide ions I^- to form a precipitate of lead iodide PbI_2. Hence the equation for the reaction is as follows. (Check the equation you wrote in Discussion question 3 above.)

$$Pb(NO_3)_2\,(aq) + 2KI\,(aq) \rightarrow PbI_2\,(s) + 2KNO_3\,(aq)$$

This equation can be written more simply by showing only the ions which form the precipitate. This is called an *ionic equation*. Because the K^+ and NO_3^- ions do not take part in the reaction they are called *spectator ions*.

$$Pb^{2+} + 2I^- \rightarrow PbI_2$$

Fig 33 When lead nitrate and potassium iodide are mixed, the lead ions are more strongly attracted to iodide ions than they are to nitrate ions. So the ions change partners.

To see an animation of the formation of lead iodide, open **Changing partners** on the CD.

Check!

1 Imagine you are agent 006 and have been captured by havoc agents. They have left you at a site in the desert formerly used to manufacture poisons. They have left two identical containers—one containing water and the other a colourless, odourless solution of toxic lead nitrate. You must drink soon or die of thirst. How could you find out which container holds the water? (There is a chemistry laboratory on the site.)

Hmm… Only scientific deduction will tell me which is safe to drink. Let's see now—eenie, meenie, minie, moe…

2 The table below gives the solubilities of various ionic compounds. The lower the solubility the more likely it is that the substance will form a precipitate. Silver chloride, which has a solubility of 0.0002 g/100 mL, is virtually insoluble and forms a precipitate, whereas magnesium nitrate, which has a solubility of 70 g/100 mL, is very soluble and would not form a precipitate.

a What is the solubility of:
  • lead nitrate?
  • magnesium carbonate?

Solubilities in g/100 mL water

	lead	magnesium	silver
carbonate	0.0002	0.01	0.002
chloride	1.0	55	0.0002
iodide	0.07	140	0.0000002
nitrate	55	70	220
sulfate	0.004	33	0.8

b Which of the compounds in the table is the most soluble in water? Which is the least soluble?

c Which group of compounds is the most soluble—the carbonates, chlorides, iodides, nitrates or sulfates?

d Which metal—lead, magnesium or silver—forms the most soluble compounds?

e Use the table to predict what will happen when you mix the following:
  • lead nitrate and magnesium sulfate
  • silver nitrate and magnesium iodide
  • magnesium chloride and sodium carbonate.
  Write a balanced equation for each reaction.

f Which compounds would you need to mix to form a precipitate of silver chloride?

3 Write ionic equations to show what happens when the following ionic compounds dissolve in water. (See page 255.)

a sodium chloride
b copper sulfate
c magnesium nitrate
d sodium phosphate

challenge

1 Lead nitrate and potassium iodide will not react unless they are dissolved in water. Write an inference to explain this.

2 In the reaction $PbI_2 \rightarrow Pb + I_2$ one element gains electrons and the other loses electrons. Explain how this happens.

3 Write a correctly balanced equation for each of the following reactions.

a Magnesium carbonate powder reacts with hydrochloric acid to produce a solution of magnesium chloride, carbon dioxide and water.

b Copper reacts with concentrated sulfuric acid (H_2SO_4) to produce a solution of copper(II) sulfate, sulfur dioxide and water.

c Lead(II) nitrate solution reacts with potassium chromate K_2CrO_4 to produce a yellow precipitate of lead chromate.

MAIN IDEAS

Copy and complete these statements to make a summary of this chapter. The missing words are on the right.

1 Atoms have no net charge. However, if they lose or gain _____ they become charged. They are then called _____.

2 Metals tend to _____ electrons to form positively charged ions. Non-metals tend to gain electrons to form _____ charged ions.

3 _____ bonds result from the attraction between _____ charged ions when metallic atoms transfer electrons to non-metallic atoms.

4 When an ionic compound _____ in water, the ions in the crystal lattice break apart and spread throughout the solution.

5 _____ bonds result from the sharing of electrons between non-metallic atoms.

6 The _____ or combining power of an atom tells you how it will combine with other atoms by losing, gaining or sharing electrons.

7 Chemical formulas can be used to write equations which represent reactions. These equations have to be _____ to give equal numbers of each type of atom on each side of the equation.

8 Atoms, molecules and ions are rearranged in chemical _____ to form new substances.

balanced
covalent
dissolves
electrons
ionic
ions
lose
negatively
oppositely
reactions
valency

Try doing the Chapter 10 crossword on the CD.

Working with technology

REVIEW

1 What is the charge on an atom if it:
  a loses one electron?
  b gains two electrons?

2 a Which of the following are elements? How do you know?
  A C_2H_6O
  B NH_3
  C Cu
  D F^-
  E H_2
  F NO^{3-}
  b Which represent compounds?
  c Which represent ions?
  d Which represent molecules?

3 What is the formula for a substance containing magnesium ions Mg^{2+} and hydroxide ions OH^-?
  A $MgOH_2$
  B $Mg(OH)_2$
  C $MgOH$
  D Mg_2OH

4 The formula for copper sulfate is $CuSO_4$.
  a How many different elements are there in copper sulfate?
  b What ions are formed when copper sulfate dissolves in water?
  c Is copper sulfate an ionic or a covalent compound?

REVIEW

5 What holds atoms together in:
  a an ionic compound?
  b a covalent compound?

6 Balance the following equations.
  a $C + Br_2 \rightarrow CBr_4$
  b $Fe_2O_3 + C \rightarrow Fe + CO$
  c $P_4 + H_2 \rightarrow PH_3$
  d $C_4H_8 + O_2 \rightarrow CO_2 + H_2O$
  e $Al_2(SO_4)_3 + Pb(NO_3)_2 \rightarrow$
$$PbSO_4 + Al(NO_3)_3$$

7 Magnesium sulfate solution $MgSO_4$ is mixed with potassium hydroxide KOH.
  a What ions would be in the mixture?
  b Predict what new substances would be formed.
  c Write a balanced equation for the reaction you predict.

8 Why is it that copper sulfate solution conducts electricity but distilled water does not?

9 The elements X, Y, Z and H form the following compounds: HX, YX_2 and YZ. Assuming H has a valency of 1+, what are the valencies of X, Y and Z?

10 a When nitric acid (HNO_3) is added to copper a reaction occurs and a blue solution is formed. Why is this so?
  b A brown gas called nitrogen dioxide is also formed. Infer whether the atoms in this gas come from the copper or the nitric acid. Explain your answer.

11 Kai placed an iron nail in some blue copper sulfate solution. The next day she noticed that the nail was partly dissolved and there were grains of copper on the bottom of the beaker. The solution had lost some of its blue colour. (See the photo below.)
  a Write an inference to explain why the solution lost some of its blue colour.
  b Use what you have learnt in Section 10.3 about ions changing partners to write a balanced equation for the reaction that occurred.

Fig 35 An iron nail in copper sulfate solution

Check your answers on pages 337–338.

11

Metals and non-metals

Getting Started

Use the table below to answer these questions about the physical properties of metals.

1 Which is the strongest metal?
2 Which is more dense—iron or copper?
3 Which are the two rarest metals listed in the table?
4 Which metals do not melt until the temperature is above 1000°C?

5 Is there a relationship between percentage abundance and cost? Explain your answer.
6 Suggest why bridges are made from steel (iron) rather than aluminium.
7 Which would be the best metal to make a spacecraft to explore the surface of Venus, where the temperature varies from 450°C to 1000°C?

Metal	Symbol	Percentage abundance in Earth's crust	Approximate cost ($/kg)	Density (g/cm^3)	Melting point (°C)	Strength (× 10^6 N/m^2)
aluminium	Al	8.1	3	2.7	660	80
copper	Cu	0.007	10	8.9	1083	150
gold	Au	0.000 000 5	27 000	19.3	1063	120
iron	Fe	5.0	0.6	7.9	1535	300
lead	Pb	0.002	1	11.3	327	15
silver	Ag	0.000 004	500	10.5	961	150
tin	Sn	0.000 4	11	7.3	232	30
titanium	Ti	0.6	16	4.5	1668	620
zinc	Zn	0.013	5	7.1	420	150

Periodic table of the elements

1
H
Hydrogen

Key

6
C
Carbon

— atomic number

— symbol

— name of element

The colour of the name for each element indicates its state at room temperature:

black—solid
blue—liquid
pink—gas
red—synthetic

I	II							
3 Li Lithium	4 Be Beryllium							
11 Na Sodium	12 Mg Magnesium							
19 K Potassium	20 Ca Calcium	21 Sc Scandium	22 Ti Titanium	23 V Vanadium	24 Cr Chromium	25 Mn Manganese	26 Fe Iron	27 Co Cobalt
37 Rb Rubidium	38 Sr Strontium	39 Y Yttrium	40 Zr Zirconium	41 Nb Niobium	42 Mo Molybdenum	43 Tc Technetium	44 Ru Ruthenium	45 Rh Rhodium
55 Cs Caesium	56 Ba Barium		72 Hf Hafnium	73 Ta Tantalum	74 W Tungsten	75 Re Rhenium	76 Os Osmium	77 Ir Iridium
87 Fr Francium	88 Ra Radium		104 Rf Rutherfordium	105 Db Dubnium	106 Sg Seaborgium	107 Bh Bohrium	108 Hs Hassium	109 Mt Meitnerium

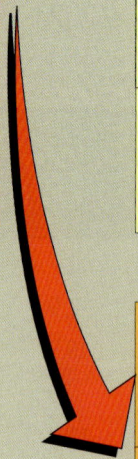

57 La Lanthanum	58 Ce Cerium	59 Pr Praseodymium	60 Nd Neodymium	61 Pm Promethium	62 Sm Samarium
89 Ac Actinium	90 Th Thorium	91 Pa Protactinium	92 U Uranium	93 Np Neptunium	94 Pu Plutonium

WEBwatch

For a lighthearted look at the periodic table go to www.scienceworld.net.au and follow the links to **The elements**.

Chemical families

- ■ Alkali metals
- ■ Alkaline earth metals
- ■ Transition metals
- ■ Rare earth metals
- ■ Other metals
- ■ Metalloids
- ■ Other non-metals
- ■ Halogens
- ■ Noble gases

	III	IV	V	VI	VII	VIII
						2 He Helium
	5 B Boron	6 C Carbon	7 N Nitrogen	8 O Oxygen	9 F Fluorine	10 Ne Neon
	13 Al Aluminium	14 Si Silicon	15 P Phosphorus	16 S Sulfur	17 Cl Chlorine	18 Ar Argon

28 Ni Nickel	29 Cu Copper	30 Zn Zinc	31 Ga Gallium	32 Ge Germanium	33 As Arsenic	34 Se Selenium	35 Br Bromine	36 Kr Krypton
46 Pd Palladium	47 Ag Silver	48 Cd Cadmium	49 In Indium	50 Sn Tin	51 Sb Antimony	52 Te Tellurium	53 I Iodine	54 Xe Xenon
78 Pt Platinum	79 Au Gold	80 Hg Mercury	81 Tl Thallium	82 Pb Lead	83 Bi Bismuth	84 Po Polonium	85 At Astatine	86 Rn Radon
110 Ds Darmstadtium	111 Rg Roentgenium							

63 Eu Europium	64 Gd Gadolinium	65 Tb Terbium	66 Dy Dysprosium	67 Ho Holmium	68 Er Erbium	69 Tm Thulium	70 Yb Ytterbium	71 Lu Lutetium
95 Am Americium	96 Cm Curium	97 Bk Berkelium	98 Cf Californium	99 Es Einsteinium	100 Fm Fermium	101 Md Mendelevium	102 No Nobelium	103 Lr Lawrencium

11.1 The periodic table

Imagine searching through piles of unsorted CDs looking for the latest album of your favourite artist. Such a task could take days. Fortunately music shops arrange their CDs in separate sections. They then divide each of these groups into smaller groups according to the type of music, eg rock, popular, jazz and classical. Artists within each group are then arranged alphabetically.

Scientists have a similar problem to the music store owner. There are over 100 different elements, each with different physical and chemical properties. However, some of these elements have similar properties. For example, fluorine, chlorine, bromine and iodine all react very easily with metals. Groups of elements with similar properties are called *families*. Fluorine, chlorine, bromine and iodine are all in the same family.

Mendeleev's table

Over the years chemists have tried many different ways of classifying the elements. In 1869 Dmitri Mendeleev (MEN-del-LAY-if), a Russian chemist, devised a classification system that, with some changes, is still used today. He made a card for each element, with its name, atomic mass and properties. He placed the cards in a row in order of increasing atomic mass. Hydrogen has the

lightest atoms, so it was first. He then took from the row of cards those elements whose properties were similar to others before them in the row and placed these cards in columns under the ones they were similar to. In this way he built up a table like a calendar. On a calendar the days of the month are in order, but the dates for the same day of the week are in the same vertical column. For example, on the calendar below, April 4, 11, 18 and 25 are all Mondays. In Mendeleev's table, elements in the same family were in the same column.

APRIL						
S	**M**	**T**	**W**	**T**	**F**	**S**
					1	2
3	4	5	6	7	8	9
10	11	12	13	14	15	16
17	18	19	20	21	22	23
24	25	26	27	28	29	30

Look at the left-hand blue column in the table on page 260. This column contains lithium, sodium and potassium, which all have similar properties. The number above each element is its **atomic number**—the number of protons in the nucleus, or the number of electrons surrounding the nucleus. If you begin with lithium Li (atomic number 3) and count eight elements to the right you come back to sodium Na (atomic number 11). Count another eight elements and you come to potassium K. Mendeleev's chart is called the **periodic table** because it shows a periodic (occurring at regular intervals) pattern in the elements.

Mendeleev was so convinced of the periodic properties of the elements that he left a few empty spaces in his table. He felt that none of the elements known at that time had the right properties to belong in those spaces. Instead he predicted the existence of new elements with the correct properties to fit the empty spaces. Years later his predictions were found to be correct when these new elements were discovered.

The modern periodic table

Elements that have similar properties appear in the same part of the periodic table. Families of elements are in the same vertical column, called a *group*. For example, lithium, sodium and potassium belong to Group I. The horizontal rows are called *periods*. The bottom two rows are so long that elements 57 to 71 and 89 to 103 are normally taken out and placed at the bottom so that the table fits on one page.

The elements fall into two main groups—metals and non-metals. Towards the right of the periodic table you will see a red zig-zag line. The elements above and to the right of this line are non-metals. The rest of the elements (about 80% of them) are metals.

The metals on the left become more reactive as you go down a group, and less reactive as you go from left to right across the periods. So the most reactive metal of all is francium (Fr) in the bottom left-hand corner of the table. The non-metals become less reactive as you go down a group, and more reactive as you go from left to right across the periods, except for the noble gases in Group VIII. So the most reactive non-metal is fluorine (F) in Group VII.

Elements next to the zig-zag line are neither metals nor non-metals. They are called *metalloids* or *semiconductors*, because they are neither good conductors of electricity nor good insulators. Examples are boron, silicon, germanium and arsenic, which are used to make diodes, transistors and microchips for the electronics industry.

You will notice that hydrogen is shown by itself. This is because it behaves like a Group I metal in some situations and like a Group VII non-metal in other situations.

Electron shells

The electrons moving around the nucleus of an atom are not all the same. They have different amounts of energy. The electrons nearest the nucleus have least energy, while those furthest away have most. Around the nucleus are several different *energy levels* or *electron shells*. The

WEBwatch

Use the internet to search for *periodic table*. You will find many different periodic tables. With most of these you can click on a particular element to obtain information about it. For one suitable website go to www.scienceworld.net.au and follow the links to:

The Visual Elements Periodic Table

Choose an element and find information on it; for example—

- when and how it was discovered
- its physical and chemical properties
- what it is used for
- how it was named
- what chemical family it belongs to.

electrons can be anywhere on the surface of these spherical shells. In the smallest atoms, hydrogen and helium, there is just one small shell close to the nucleus. Hydrogen (below) has one electron and helium has two.

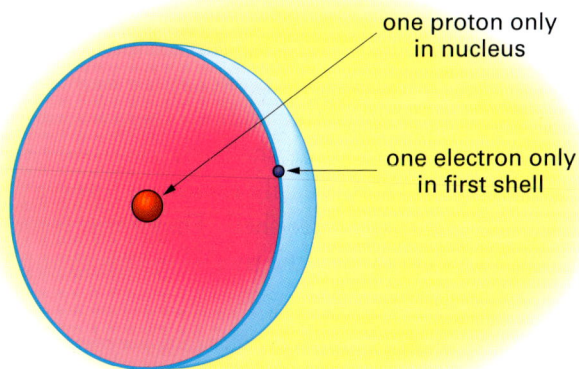

one proton only in nucleus

one electron only in first shell

Fig 4 A cutaway view of a hydrogen atom (atomic number = 1), showing its nucleus and spherical electron shell

There is a limit to the number of electrons each shell can hold. In the inner shell there is room for only two, so if the atom has any more electrons they occupy a second shell, further from the nucleus. This second shell can hold up to eight electrons. The third shell can hold up to eighteen electrons.

The electrons in the outer shell of an atom are called the **valence electrons**. These electrons are the most easily removed, and they determine the chemical reactions of the element. Atoms like neon (below), with a full outer shell, are very stable and rarely react with other elements. This is because it takes a lot of energy to add an extra electron or take one away. They form Group VIII in the periodic table—the noble gases.

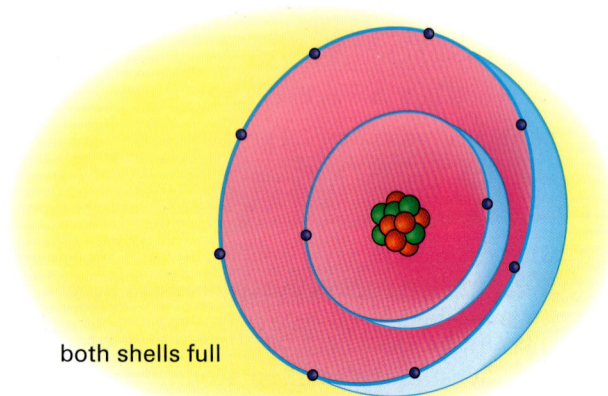

both shells full

Fig 5 A neon atom (atomic number = 10)

Note that *the periodic table group number is the number of electrons in the outer shell*. For example, Group VIII elements have eight electrons in their outer shell, except for helium, which has two. Atoms like sodium (below), with one electron in their outer shell, are very reactive because this electron is easily removed, leaving the atom with a full outer shell. They form Group I—the alkali metals. All the metals in this group have a valency of 1+.

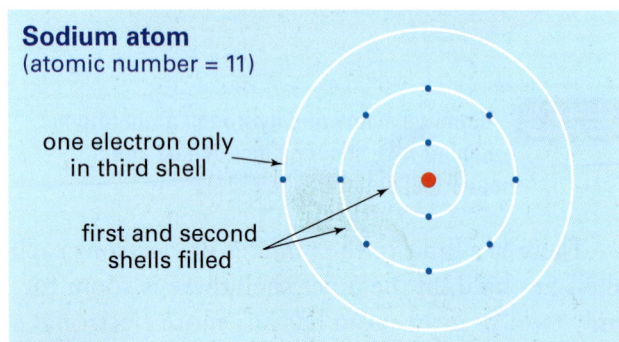

Sodium atom
(atomic number = 11)

one electron only
in third shell

first and second
shells filled

Fig 6 In chemical reactions a sodium atom tends to lose its outer electron to form a Na$^+$ ion. For simplicity the electron shells have been drawn in two dimensions.

Atoms like chlorine, which are one electron short of a full outer shell, are also very reactive because they readily accept another electron to fill their outer shell. They form Group VII—the halogens. All the non-metals have a valency of 1–.

When sodium reacts with chlorine to form sodium chloride, the sodium atoms lose an electron to form Na$^+$ ions, and the chlorine atoms gain an electron to form Cl$^-$ ions. In this way both sodium and chlorine have full outer shells. The mutual attractive force between the positive and negative ions is an ionic bond.

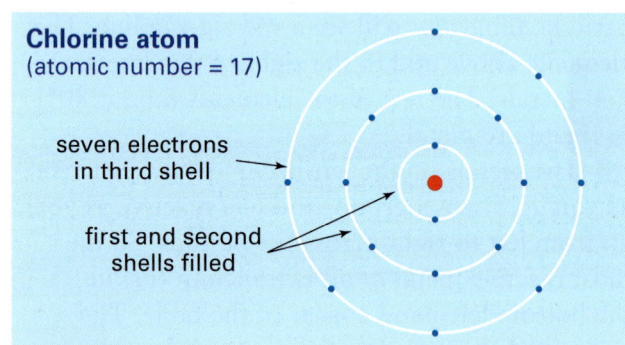

Chlorine atom
(atomic number = 17)

seven electrons
in third shell

first and second
shells filled

Fig 7 A chlorine atom tends to gain an electron to form a Cl$^-$ ion with a full outer shell.

Carbon (below) has four electrons in its outer shell and therefore has a valency of 4. Rather than losing or gaining electrons to form ions, it *shares* electrons to form covalent bonds. When it reacts with hydrogen it can form four of these bonds, giving it a full outer shell of eight electrons. Hence the compound CH_4 (methane) is formed.

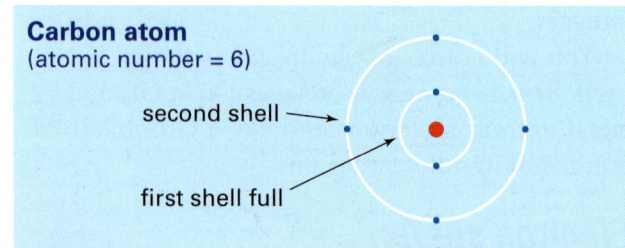

Carbon atom
(atomic number = 6)

second shell

first shell full

Fig 8 Carbon has 4 electrons in its outer shell and can therefore form 4 covalent bonds.

To see an animation of ionic and covalent bonds, open **Chemical bonds** on the CD.

Working with technology

Check!

For most of these exercises you will need to refer to the periodic table on pages 260 and 261.

1 What does the atomic number of an element tell you?

2 What is the atomic number of these elements?
   a hydrogen   **c** copper
   b carbon   **d** uranium

3 Roughly sketch the periodic table. On it show where you would find:
   a metals and non-metals
   b the noble gases, the alkali metals, the halogens and the transition metals.

4 Which of the following elements are metals?
   carbon   helium   radium   silicon
   sodium   sulfur   titanium tungsten

5 Use the periodic table to find at least three elements named after countries and at least three named after scientists.

6 Find calcium (atomic number 20) in the periodic table. Name three elements that are in the same family as calcium.

7 At room temperature, which of the non-metals are gases? Which are solids and which are liquids?

8 List the elements from Group IV in order of atomic number, and state whether each is a metal, non-metal or metalloid.

9 Use the periodic table to decide which three of the following elements have similar properties: aluminium, barium, calcium, chlorine, iron, magnesium, xenon.

10 Explain the difference between a period and a group in the periodic table.

11 What are valence electrons? How can they explain the different chemical properties of the elements?

challenge

1 Which would be more reactive:
   a magnesium or barium?   **c** carbon or oxygen?
   b sodium or magnesium?   **d** fluorine or chlorine?

2 Write a paragraph explaining how the periodic table is useful to scientists.

3 In 1996 scientists in Germany made a new element with atomic number 112. Predict which elements it is similar to.

4 Imagine that you have to learn the names of the first 10 or 20 elements. Design a jingle to help you remember. (A jingle is a sentence, sentences or rhyme to help you remember facts: for example My Very Educated Mother Just Served Us Nachos for the eight planets in the solar system.)

5 Copy and complete the table on the right for the first 20 elements in the periodic table, showing how the electrons are arranged. For each atom draw the electron shells as on page 264.

   a Which of the first 20 elements have one electron only in their outer shell? Which group is this in the periodic table?

Elements	Atomic number	Number of electrons...			
		first shell	second shell	third shell	fourth shell
hydrogen	1	1			
helium	2	2			
lithium	3	2	1		

   b Which elements need only one electron to fill their outer shell? Which group is this? What is their valency?

   c Which elements have full outer shells? Which group do they belong to?

   d How many hydrogen atoms does oxygen need to react with to give it a full outer shell? Write the formula for the compound formed.

   e When nitrogen reacts with hydrogen, predict the formula of the compound formed.

   f Which two elements have properties similar to beryllium? How do you know?

   g Magnesium reacts with chlorine to form magnesium chloride. What is the formula for this compound?

11.2 Chemical families

Metals

Metals have many properties in common. They are all good conductors of heat and electricity. They are *malleable*, meaning they can be pressed or bent into different shapes. For example, silver bars can be hammered into jewellery. Most metals also have what is called a *metallic lustre* or shine. These properties of metals can be explained in terms of their structure.

Metals conduct heat and electricity

The atoms in a metal are packed in a regular three-dimensional pattern called a *lattice*. The electrons are not firmly bound to the nuclei and can move freely in the spaces between the atoms. This is why metals conduct heat and electricity.

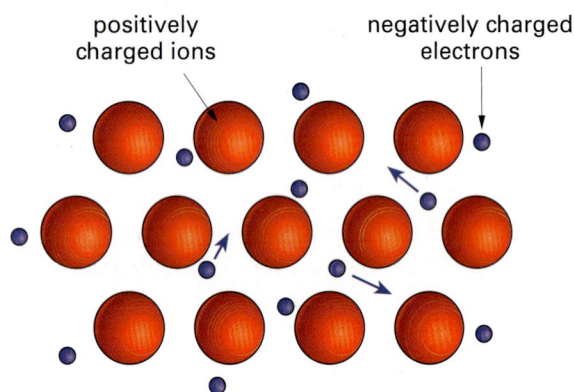

Metals are malleable

Metals can be rolled into thin sheets. This is because the layers of atoms can slide over each other and the free electrons can easily move into new positions.

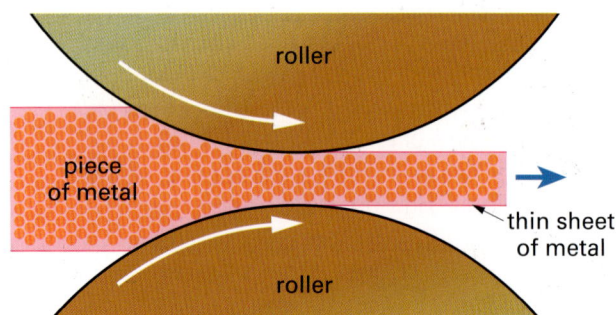

Alloys

An alloy is a mixture of two or more different metals made by mixing the molten metals together then allowing them to cool and solidify. For example, 'silver' coins are made from an alloy containing 75% copper and 25% nickel. Brass is an alloy of copper (70%) and zinc (30%). Because the zinc atoms are similar in size to the copper atoms they can take the place of copper atoms in the lattice.

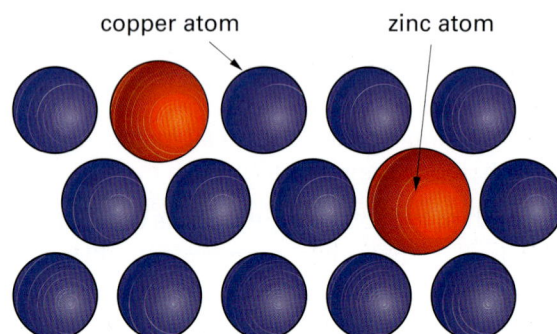

In some alloys the atoms are different sizes. For example, steel is an alloy of iron and traces of carbon. In this case the carbon atoms are much smaller than the iron atoms and they fit into the gaps in the lattice.

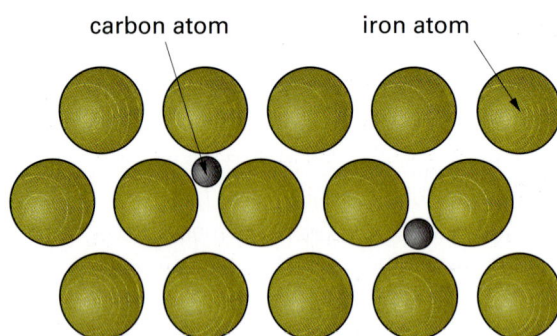

Because gold is a soft metal, other metals such as silver and copper are added to it to make it harder; and the addition of copper produces a more orange colour (rose gold). The proportion of gold is expressed in terms of carats. Most rings and bracelets are 18 carat or 9 carat gold.

carats	24	22	18	14	9
percentage gold	100	91.7	75	58.5	37.5

Investigate
21 METAL PROPERTIES

Aim

To test the chemical properties of metals and arrange them in the order of their chemical activity.

Materials

- small samples of various metals, eg

aluminium	magnesium	lead
copper	tin	zinc
iron	silver	

- steel wool or emery paper **Corrosive**
- dilute **hydrochloric acid** (1M) in a dropper bottle
- test tubes (in test tube rack)
- **zinc sulfate** solution (saturated)
- **copper sulfate** solution (saturated) **Toxic**
- ammeter or multimeter • power pack
- 4 connecting wires • switch

Planning and Safety Check

- Do a risk assessment for this investigation. What safety precautions will be necessary?
- Prepare a data table to record all your observations.

Method

Wear safety glasses.

Part A: Reactions with acid

1 Observe each of the metal samples. Which are tarnished (not shiny)?

2 Clean each sample with steel wool. Then put the samples in labelled test tubes.

3 Add 5 drops of dilute hydrochloric acid to each metal.

   Record the rate at which bubbles of gas are formed: for example *fast*, *medium*, *slow* or *no reaction*.

4 Clean out the test tubes and wash the remaining metal samples in water. Keep them for Part C.

Part B: Reactions with metal solutions

1 Put about 5 mL of zinc sulfate in each tube.

2 Add a metal sample to each and leave for 3–5 minutes.

   Record any reactions that occur. A reaction may be indicated by a dark deposit on the metal. If the metal remains shiny you can infer there has been no reaction.

3 Wash and clean the metal samples. Then repeat Steps 1 and 2 using *copper sulfate*.

   Again record your results.

Discussion

1 What usually happens when you add dilute hydrochloric acid to a metal?

2 Which metals reacted with:
   a all three test solutions (hydrochloric acid, zinc sulfate and copper sulfate)?
   b two solutions only?
   c one solution only?
   d none of the solutions?

3 Put the metals in order from the most reactive to the least reactive.

4 Suppose you wanted to make a metal tank to hold copper sulfate soultion. Which would be the best metal to use? Why?

Part C: Conductivity

1 To test the electrical conductivity of the samples, set up the electrical circuit shown. Set the power pack on 6 volts DC.

2 For each sample, record the electric current that flows.

   Which metal would be best to use in electrical wiring?

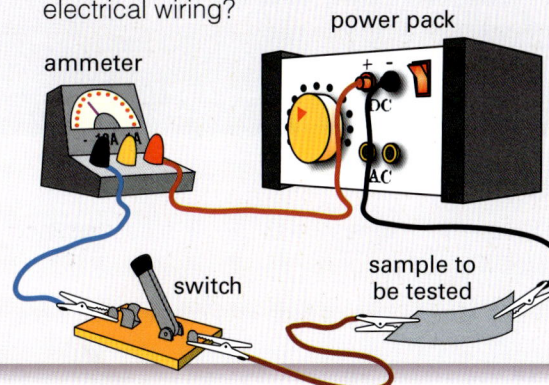

power pack

ammeter

switch

sample to be tested

Reactive metals

The elements in Group I of the periodic table (lithium, sodium, potassium, rubidium, caesium and francium) are metals with similar properties. Because they have a single electron in their outer shell they are very reactive and are never found in nature as elements, only as ionic compounds. They are called **alkali metals** because they react with water to form alkaline solutions. For example, sodium reacts violently with water to form sodium hydroxide and hydrogen.

The **alkaline earth metals** in Group II have two electrons in their outer shell. They are reactive, but not as reactive as the alkali metals. They contain two of the most biologically important metals: magnesium is found in chlorophyll, and calcium is found in bones and teeth.

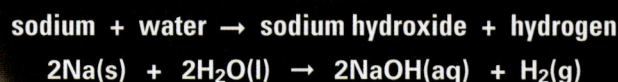

sodium + water → sodium hydroxide + hydrogen

$$2Na(s) + 2H_2O(l) \rightarrow 2NaOH(aq) + H_2(g)$$

Fig 14 Sodium reacts violently with water. Your teacher may demonstrate this.

Investigate

22 ALKALINE EARTH METALS WITH WATER

Aim

To investigate the reactions of magnesium and calcium with water.

Materials

- 2 test tubes, test tube holder and rack
- Bunsen burner and heatproof mat
- 5 cm strip of magnesium
- small sample of calcium
- phenolphthalein
- steel wool or emery paper

Planning and Safety Check

- Do a risk assessment for this investigation. What safety precautions will be necessary?

Method

1 Clean the magnesium strip with steel wool and coil it around a pen.

2 Put the coil in a test tube and cover it with water.

3 Watch carefully over the next 5 minutes for any sign of a chemical reaction. If nothing happens, heat the tube gently over a small flame.

4 What happens when you add a drop of phenolphthalein to the test tube?

5 Add a small piece of calcium to the second test tube and cover it with water. Test the gas given off with a lit match. Add a drop of phenolphthalein.

Record your observations.

Discussion

1 Which is more reactive? Magnesium or calcium?

2 What was the gas produced when magnesium and calcium reacted with water?

3 Why did the phenolphthalein change colour?

4 Write balanced equations for the reactions of magnesium and calcium with water. See the sodium reaction above.

Transition metals

The metals in the middle of the periodic table are called **transition metals**. They are hard and have high melting points. The properties of transition metals that are close together in the periodic table are often very similar. This is why they can be mixed to form alloys. Iron, cobalt and nickel, which are in the same period, have similar properties. For example, they are all magnetic. Copper, silver and gold, which are in the same group, also have similar properties. Metals near the top of the table (eg aluminium and zinc) are generally more reactive than those towards the bottom of the table (eg silver, gold and lead).

Many of the compounds that transition metals form with non-metals are coloured. For example, copper sulfate is blue and iron(II) chloride is green. This is why these compounds are used to colour glass. Copper ions give a blue colour, iron gives a green colour and gold gives a red colour. Hair colour is also determined by the presence of minute amounts of transition metal compounds. Blond hair contains titanium compounds, red hair contains iron compounds, and dark hair contains a mixture of iron, copper and cobalt compounds.

Metals give a characteristic colour to a flame, as you can see in Investigate 23.

Investigate 23 FLAME COLOURS

Aim

To observe the characteristic flame colours produced by metal salts.

Materials

- petri dish
- piece of nichrome wire, about 10 cm long
- wooden peg or test tube holder
- Bunsen burner
- saturated solutions of chlorides or carbonates of the following metals: barium, calcium, copper, potassium, sodium, strontium

Toxic

Planning and Safety Check

- Read the investigation carefully and do a risk assessment. Because the metal solutions are toxic you should wash your hands thoroughly after doing the investigation.
- Your teacher may set up six different 'stations' around the laboratory with the above materials and a different metal salt at each station.
- If the solutions are available in atomiser bottles you simply spray them into the flame.
- For Step 6 you will need an *unknown* metal salt to test.

Method

1. Bend the end of the nichrome wire to form a small loop. Hold the other end with a peg.
2. Light the burner and adjust to a hot flame.
3. Dip the wire into the solution of the metal salt in a petri dish.
4. Place the wire in the edge of the flame and observe the colour.

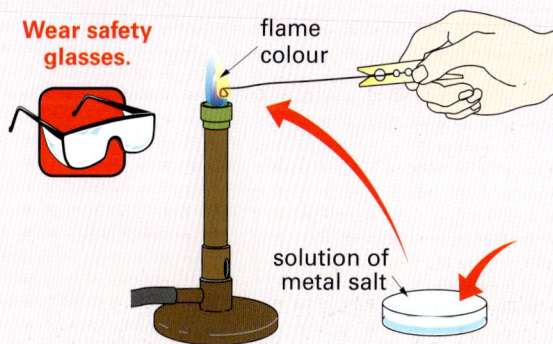

Wear safety glasses.

5. Move to a new 'station' and repeat the procedure with a different metal salt.
   Record the flame colours for the different metals in a data table.
6. Now that you know the colour each metal produces in a flame, your teacher will give you an unknown metal salt. Test it and infer which metal it contains.

Fig 16 The colours of fireworks are due to transition metal compounds.

Non-metals

The non-metals are on the right of the periodic table. Many are gases at room temperature. The elements in Group VII (fluorine, chlorine, bromine, iodine and astatine) are called the **halogens**. Because they have a vacancy of one in their outer shell they have a valency of 1–. They are very reactive and form salts when they combine with metals. (The word 'halogen' means 'salt former'.) For example, chlorine reacts with sodium metal to form sodium chloride.

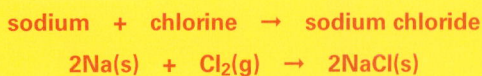

sodium + chlorine → sodium chloride

$$2Na(s) + Cl_2(g) \rightarrow 2NaCl(s)$$

The elements in Group VIII have a full outer electron shell. They are called the *inert gases* or **noble gases** because they do not react with other 'common' elements. Helium is used to fill balloons and as a mixture with oxygen for divers. Neon is used in neon signs and lasers because it gives a coloured light. Argon is used in light bulbs and in welding to provide an unreactive environment.

The noble gases are so unreactive that they do not even react with themselves. They are said to be *monatomic* because they consist of single atoms. The other non-metal gases form *diatomic* molecules, each consisting of a pair of atoms linked by a covalent bond; for example hydrogen H_2, nitrogen N_2, oxygen O_2, chlorine Cl_2 and fluorine F_2.

Fig 17 The red tubes in this sign contain the noble gas neon. The green, yellow and blue tubes contain argon.

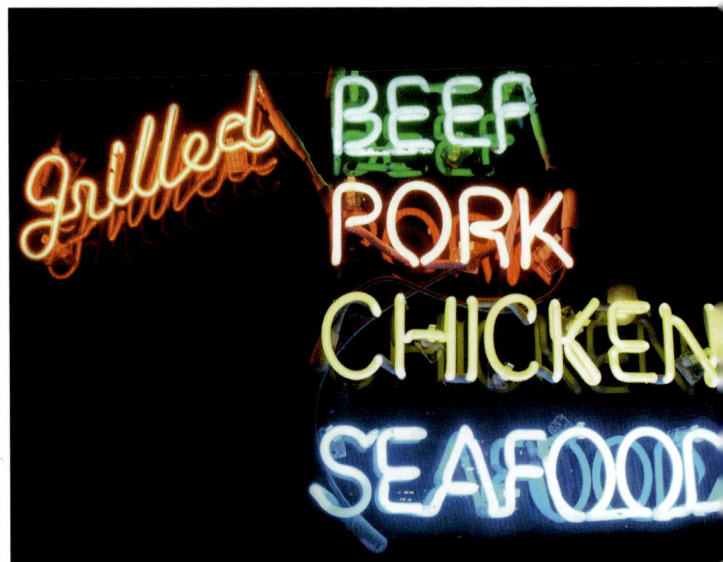

As you move to the left in the periodic table, the non-metals tend to form a greater number of covalent bonds. For example, molecules of white phosphorus (P_4) consist of four phosphorus atoms at the corners of a tetrahedron; and sulfur molecules (S_8) consist of eight atoms in a chair-shaped ring.

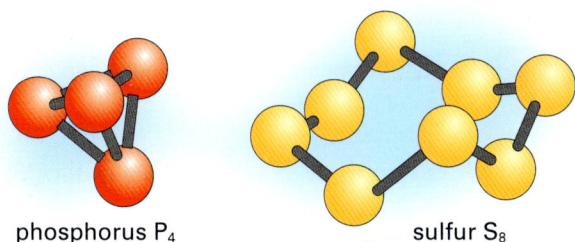

phosphorus P_4 sulfur S_8

Fig 18 As you move to the left in the periodic table, the non-metals form a greater number of covalent bonds.

Some non-metals exist in different forms called **allotropes**. For example, oxygen can exist as O_2 or as O_3 (ozone), whose properties are quite different from those of O_2. Similarly, carbon can exist as diamond, graphite or charcoal (soot). Diamond is the world's hardest substance—tough, brilliantly clear and sparkling, and unaffected by heat below 700°C. On the other hand, graphite

Fig 19 Diamond's unique properties are due to its structure of tetrahedrally bonded carbon atoms (top right).

is a soft, grey, flaky material with a greasy feel. It is used as the 'lead' in pencils. Diamond and graphite are both made of carbon atoms, but their structures are different.

There are no individual molecules in diamond or graphite. Instead they both consist of atoms covalently bonded to each other in a network lattice. In the diamond network each atom is linked to four others in an infinitely interlocking tetrahedral structure. It is this tight structure that makes diamond so hard.

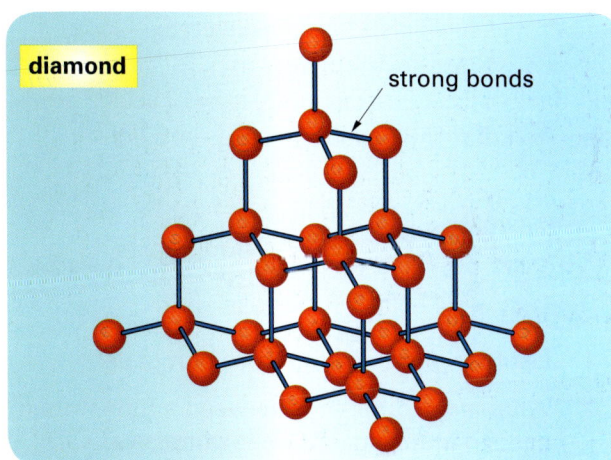

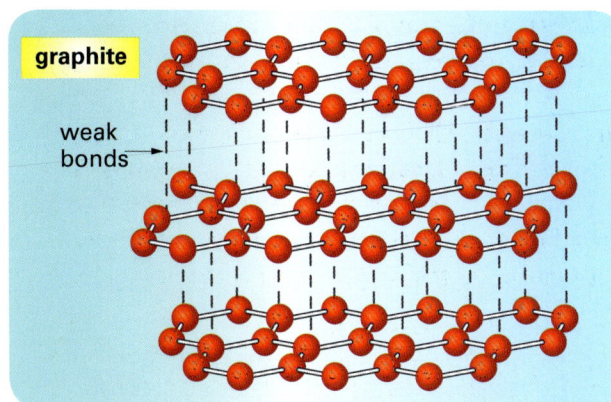

diamond   strong bonds

graphite

weak bonds

Note: these diagrams show only part of the structure of diamond and graphite.

In graphite, however, the atoms are arranged in layers, like sheets of hexagonal tiles. Each atom links with only three other atoms, not four as in diamond, and there are therefore electrons left over. These unattached electrons drift freely between the layers like the free electrons in a metal. This is why graphite is a conductor of electricity and tends to look metallic.

Graphite can be turned into diamond by squeezing it to push the layers of atoms closer together until they interlock and make diamond. But the pressure needed to make this happen is enormous, and so far only small artificial diamonds have been made this way.

Recently scientists have discovered another allotrope of carbon called *buckyballs* in which the carbon atoms are linked to form single molecules rather than a giant network. The first buckyball to be found contained 60 carbon atoms and is shaped like a soccer ball. Other shapes such as buckytubes have also been discovered.

Scientists are searching for uses for buckyballs and buckytubes. For example, it has been suggested that they could be used to make

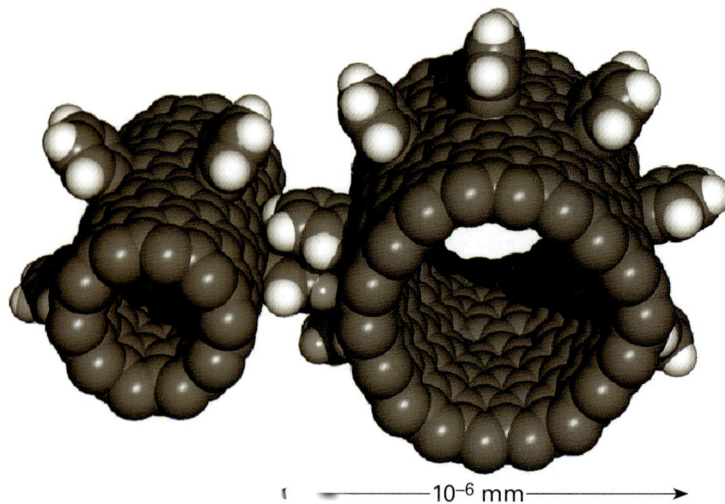

← —————10⁻⁶ mm————— →

Fig 22 Buckytubes could be used to make gears in nanomachines.

nanomachines like these gears, about a millionth of a millimetre in size. You can find out more about this by going to www.scienceworld.net.au and following the links to **Buckyballs**.

Check!

1 List four physical properties of metals.

2 What is the difference between a monatomic and a diatomic gas? Give examples of each.

3 What is an allotrope? What are the names of the four allotropes of carbon?

4 Explain in terms of its structure why graphite is flaky and feels greasy.

5 Toni tested a piece of eggshell, a marble chip and some garden lime. She dissolved each in hydrochloric acid and used the solution for a flame test. In each case she observed the same orange-red flame. What can she conclude from her observations?

challenge

1 Suggest how buckyballs might be useful as lubricants.

2 Alloying iron with carbon makes it harder. Explain this in terms of the structure of alloys.

3 Explain the following properties of metals in terms of their structure:
   a high melting point
   b high density
   c malleable (can be rolled into sheets)

4 The graph on the right shows how the melting point of solder (a tin–lead mixture) changes as its composition changes. A 60% tin mixture gives the lowest melting point. If the percentage of tin is lower or higher than this, the solder has a higher melting point.

a What would be the approximate melting point of an alloy of composition 25% tin and 75% lead?

b What are the possible compositions for a solder with a melting point of 200°C?

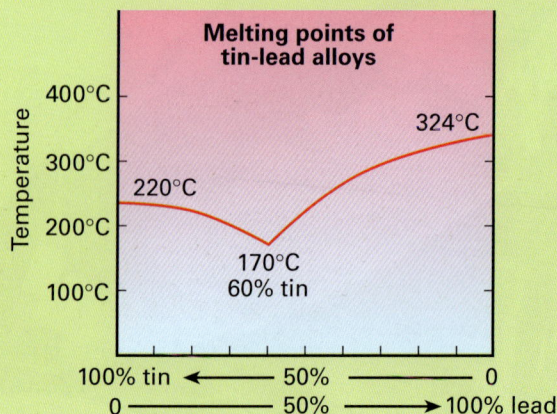

Melting points of tin-lead alloys

324°C

220°C

170°C
60% tin

Temperature: 400°C, 300°C, 200°C, 100°C

100% tin ← 50% → 0
0 ————— 50% ————→ 100% lead

11.3 Extracting metals

The pie chart below shows the main elements found in the Earth's crust. As you can see, the most common elements are the non-metals oxygen and silicon. These two elements are often combined as the compound silicon dioxide (SiO_2), found in sand and in rocks (as quartz).

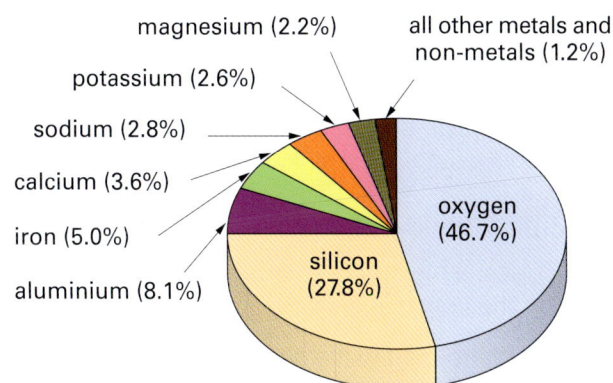

Fig 25 The composition of the Earth's crust

Fig 26 Gold is usually found in its uncombined state. This is the Poseidon Nugget found in central Victoria in 1906. It weighed 27 kilograms.

The metals are usually found as compounds with non-metals, although the unreactive metals such as gold can be found as elements (see Fig 26). Compounds of the reactive metals are fairly abundant: for example sodium chloride (common salt) and calcium carbonate (limestone). However, compounds of the less reactive metals such as copper, zinc, silver, tin and lead are quite rare. This is why mining companies spend so much money on exploration.

Metal compounds are called **minerals** when found in large amounts in rocks. If these rocks contain enough minerals to make it economical to mine them, they are called **ores**. The table below gives examples of ores commonly mined in Australia.

Ore	Chemical composition	Metal extracted
bauxite	aluminium oxide (Al_2O_3)	aluminium
chalcopyrite	copper iron sulfide ($CuFeS_2$)	copper
galena	lead sulfide (PbS)	lead
gold	found as element (Au)	gold
haematite	iron oxide (Fe_2O_3)	iron
pitchblende	uranium oxide (U_3O_8)	uranium
rutile	titanium oxide (TiO_2)	titanium
sphalerite	zinc sulfide (ZnS)	zinc

Before a metal can be extracted from its mineral, the impurities in the ore must be removed. One way to do this is by a process called *froth flotation*, which was developed at Broken Hill in Australia. (To see an animation of this, open the **Froth flotation** animation on the CD.) The ore is crushed and added to water in a tank. A frothing agent is added and air is bubbled through the mixture. The frothing agent attaches itself to the bits of mineral and rises to the surface as a froth. The froth containing the mineral is then scraped off and the mineral is dried, ready for the next step in the extraction process.

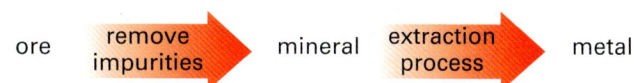

ore → remove impurities → mineral → extraction process → metal

Investigate
24 FROTH FLOTATION

Aim

To model on a small scale the process of froth flotation.

Materials

- fine sand
- kerosene
- spatula
- liquid detergent
- watch glass
- large test tube with stopper
- powdered **chalcopyrite**, **galena** or **haematite**

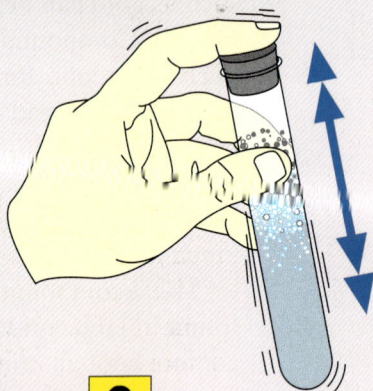

Toxic

Method

1 Mix a spatula of powdered mineral with the same amount of sand in a large test tube. Then half-fill the test tube with water.

2 Put the stopper in the test tube and shake it.

Do the sand and the mineral separate?

3 Add 2 mL of detergent and a few drops of kerosene.

4 Shake the test tube again.

5 Use the spatula to scoop off the froth into a watch glass and check that it contains the mineral.

6 Dispose of the sand and mineral in a waste bucket at the front of the class—not down the sink.

Discussion

1 Suggest a method of obtaining dry mineral from the froth in the watch glass.

2 What happened to the sand initially mixed with the mineral?

3 Suggest ways of improving the process.

Smelting

Thousands of years ago humans managed to extract metals without any idea of the chemical reactions involved. The metals were probably first extracted by accident, when rocks containing the ore were thrown on a fire and the new metal was observed the following day. From this, early humans worked out that two things were needed—heat and charcoal (carbon). Many metal ores are oxides, and we now know that when a metal oxide is heated with carbon, the oxide is converted to the metal. At the same time the carbon combines with the oxygen from the oxide to form carbon dioxide. For example, lead is extracted from lead oxide.

$$2PbO(s) \ + \ C(s) \ \rightarrow \ 2Pb(s) \ + \ CO_2(g)$$

This process is called **smelting** and the metal in the ore is said to be *reduced*, because it gains electrons. Hence the extraction of a metal from its ore is called *reduction*. The equation for the reduction of lead ore is:

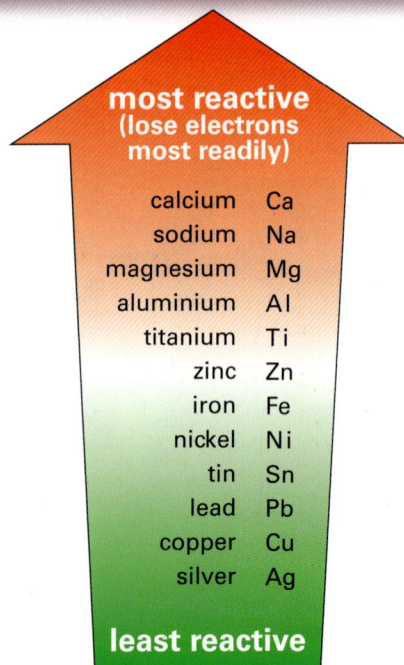

$$Pb^{2+}(s) \ + \ 2e^- \ \rightarrow \ Pb(s)$$

most reactive
(lose electrons most readily)

calcium	Ca
sodium	Na
magnesium	Mg
aluminium	Al
titanium	Ti
zinc	Zn
iron	Fe
nickel	Ni
tin	Sn
lead	Pb
copper	Cu
silver	Ag

least reactive

Fig 29 The metals can be listed from the most reactive to the least reactive. This is called the *activity series*. The metals at the top are harder to extract than the ones at the bottom. Do your results from Investigate 21 on page 267 agree with this?

The ore of iron is iron oxide (Fe_2O_3). The iron can be extracted in a *blast furnace*. In Australia there are blast furnaces at Port Kembla in New South Wales, Whyalla in South Australia and Kwinana in Western Australia. A mixture of iron oxide, coke (made from coal), and limestone is fed into the top of the furnace. Very hot air is blasted in near the bottom, causing the coke to burn and form the gas carbon monoxide. The carbon monoxide then reacts with the iron oxide, reducing it to iron.

$$2C(s) + O_2(g) \rightarrow 2CO(g)$$

$$Fe_2O_3(s) + 3CO(g) \rightarrow 2Fe(s) + 3CO_2(g)$$

The molten iron collects in the bottom of the furnace, where it is tapped off from time to time, as shown in Fig 30 below. Impurities in the ore combine with the limestone to form slag, which floats on the molten metal. The slag is used as a road-surfacing material or in cement manufacture. The molten iron is converted to steel in another furnace.

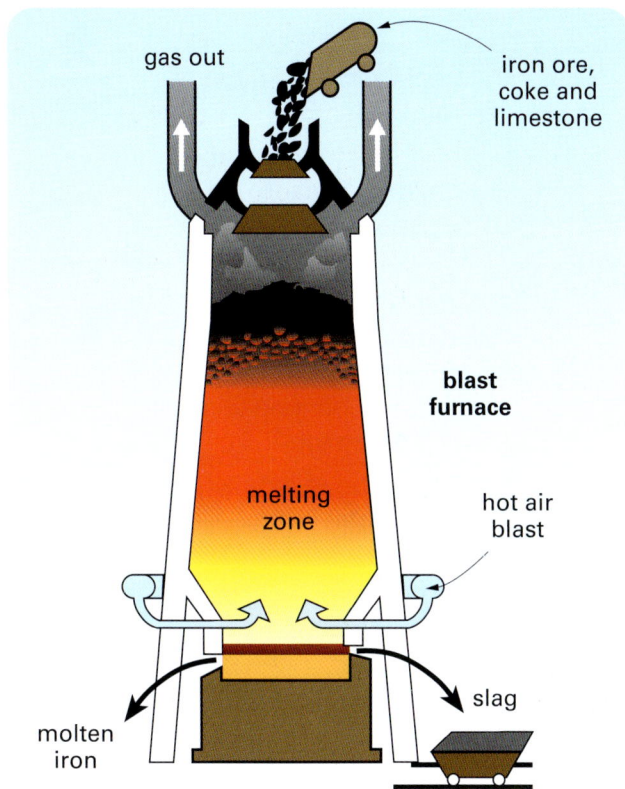

Fig 32 The molten steel is rolled into flat sheets and cut into sheets or rolled up as in the photo.

Copper can be extracted from its ore by 'roasting'. The chalcopyrite $CuFeS_2$ is converted to copper sulfide Cu_2S which then reacts with oxygen, forming copper metal and the gas sulfur dioxide.

$$Cu_2S(s) + O_2(g) \rightarrow 2Cu(s) + SO_2(g)$$

In the past copper producers built high chimneys to release the poisonous sulfur dioxide into the atmosphere. The high chimneys were used to avoid producing dangerous levels of the gas at ground level where people could be affected. However, high levels of sulfur dioxide in the atmosphere can cause acid rain. For this reason environmental laws now require producers to collect the sulfur dioxide and use it to make sulfuric acid or fertiliser.

Fig 30 Smelting in a blast furnace

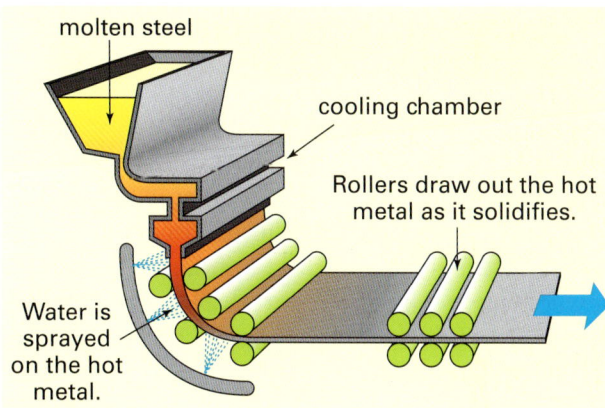

Electrolysis

The copper from a copper smelter is only about 98% pure, but it can be made 99.9% pure by the process of **electrolysis** (ee-lek-TROL-e-sis), where electricity is used to produce chemical reactions. The impure copper is made into a thick plate which is connected to the positive terminal of a power source. A thin plate of pure copper is connected to the negative terminal. Both plates are then placed in a bath of copper sulfate solution and sulfuric acid. As the current flows through this solution, the impure copper dissolves and pure copper is deposited on the thin plate in a reduction reaction.

$$Cu^{2+}(aq) + 2e^- \rightarrow Cu(s)$$

The 'mud' that falls to the bottom of the bath contains less reactive metals such as silver and gold which can be recovered. The process uses considerable electricity, so the copper refinery must be close to a source of abundant, cheap power. This is why copper produced in the smelter at Mt Isa in Queensland is shipped to Townsville for refining.

More reactive metals such as aluminium and magnesium cannot be extracted by smelting, but can be obtained by electrolysis. For example, to produce aluminium, the ore (aluminium oxide) is melted and electricity passed through it.

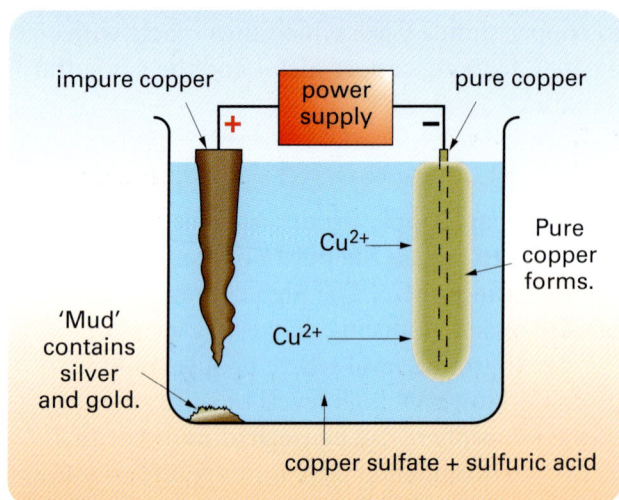

impure copper   power supply   pure copper

Cu^{2+} Pure copper forms.

'Mud' contains silver and gold. Cu^{2+}

copper sulfate + sulfuric acid

Fig 33 Purifying copper by electrolysis

Displacement

In Investigate 21 Part B (page 267) you put magnesium in copper sulfate solution. Did you find that copper fell to the bottom of the test tube? This reaction is called *displacement*, because the more reactive magnesium displaced (pushed out) the less reactive copper from the copper sulfate solution. This method is used to extract some metals. For example, titanium is displaced from titanium chloride solution by adding magnesium.

$$TiCl_4(aq) + 2Mg(s) \rightarrow Ti(s) + 2MgCl_2(aq)$$

The titanium and the magnesium swap places. The magnesium metal goes into solution as magnesium chloride, and the titanium comes out of the solution as the metal.

Activity

You will need a test tube and rack, silver nitrate solution, 15–20 cm of copper wire and a pen.

Toxic

1 Three-quarters fill the test tube with silver nitrate solution. **Be very careful not to spill any as it stains hands, clothing and benches.**

2 Twist the copper wire around a pen to make a spiral, with a bit left over to make a hook. Put it in the test tube, hooking it over the lip of the tube.

3 Leave the test tube in a dark cupboard overnight. In the morning observe what has happened.

🔖 What new substances have been formed?

🔖 Write a word equation for the reaction that has occurred, then a balanced symbol equation.

Investigate
25 COPPER METAL FROM COPPER ORE

Aim
To extract copper sulfate and copper metal from a simulated ore.

Materials
- copper ore made by mixing copper sulfate, sand and plaster of Paris, adding water and allowing to set
- balance
- mortar and pestle
- 2 beakers or conical flasks
- filter funnel and stand
- filter paper
- burner, tripod and gauze
- watch glass
- hand lens
- spatula
- sodium chloride
- stirring rod
- power pack
- strips of lead and copper
- 2 connecting wires
- steel wool

Wear safety glasses.

Wear a lab coat or apron.

Planning and Safety Check
This is a complex investigation which will take several days. You will need to work carefully so that you don't lose any copper.
- In a group, describe what you will be doing in each of the six steps shown in the flow diagram on the right.
- When will you need to weigh things?
- What safety precautions will be necessary?

Method
1 CRUSH
a Use a balance to find the mass of the ore to start with.
b Crush the ore thoroughly in a mortar using a pestle (PES-el) until it is a powder.

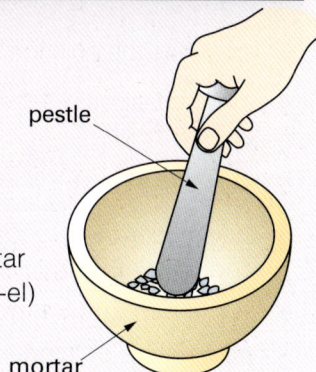

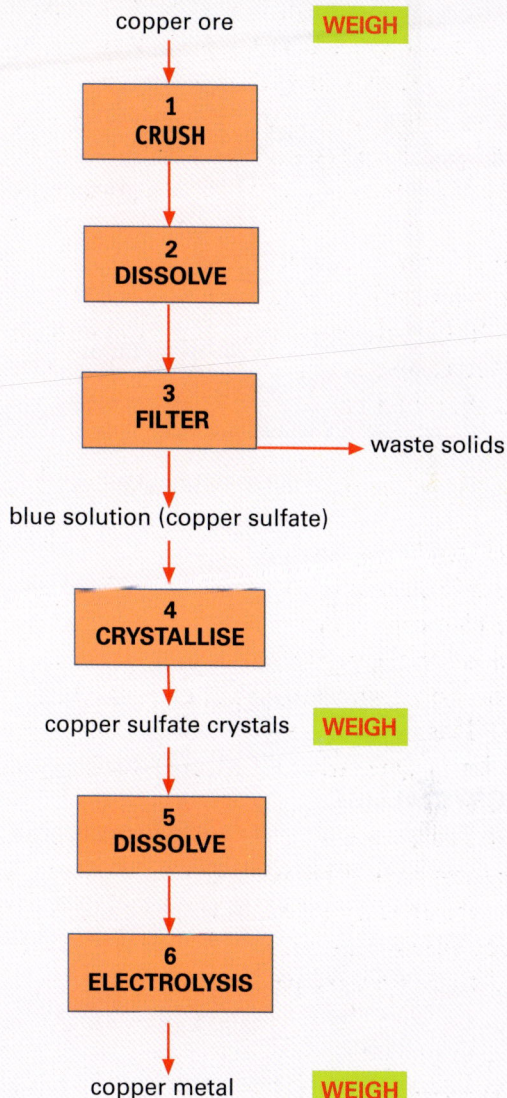

pestle

mortar

copper ore   **WEIGH**

1 CRUSH

2 DISSOLVE

3 FILTER → waste solids

blue solution (copper sulfate)

4 CRYSTALLISE

copper sulfate crystals   **WEIGH**

5 DISSOLVE

6 ELECTROLYSIS

copper metal   **WEIGH**

2 DISSOLVE
Put the crushed ore in a beaker. Add enough water to dissolve it when you heat it for 5 minutes.
What is the colour of the mixture?

3 FILTER
a Let the mixture cool for a few minutes while the solid settles.
b Decant the mixture through filter paper in a filter funnel. Keep as much of the solid as possible in the beaker because it may clog the filter paper. (Fluted filter paper is faster.)

waste solids
filtrate

c Set up the electrolysis apparatus as shown below, with the lead connected to positive and the copper to negative.

d Set the power pack to 4 volts DC and turn it on.

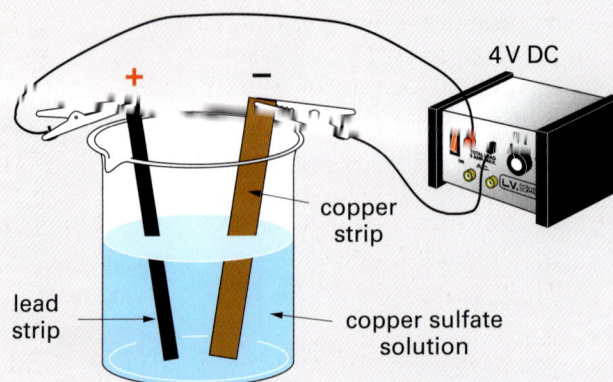
4 V DC
copper strip
lead strip
copper sulfate solution

c Rinse the solid left in the beaker with a further 10 mL of water, and filter this rinse water as well.

🖊 What is the colour of the filtrate? What is it?

🖊 What are the solids left in the filter paper? (Discard the filter paper and waste solids into a bin.)

4 CRYSTALLISE

a Boil the copper sulfate filtrate until only a few millilitres remain. Turn off the burner and leave the beaker until the crystals that form are dry.

b Scrape all the crystals onto a watch glass and weigh them.

🖊 Describe the copper sulfate crystals. (Use a hand lens.)

c Calculate your percentage yield as follows:

$$\% \text{ yield} = \frac{\text{mass of copper sulfate}}{\text{mass of ore}} \times 100$$

5 DISSOLVE

a Dissolve the copper sulfate in water. Stir to make sure it is completely dissolved.

b Add a spatula of sodium chloride. This is to help the solution conduct electricity in the next step.

6 ELECTROLYSIS

a Thoroughly clean a strip of lead and a strip of copper with steel wool.

b Weigh the copper strip.

🖊 At which electrode is copper deposited?

🖊 What happens at the other electrode?

🖊 What happens to the solution?

e When the solution is clear, or after 15 minutes, switch the power pack off.

f Remove the copper strip, wash it and leave it to dry. Then weigh it again.

🖊 Calculate the mass of copper deposited. (If there is any copper in the bottom of the beaker you need to collect and weigh it too.)

🖊 Calculate the percentage of copper in the copper ore you started with.

Discussion

1 Suggest why the ore had to be crushed before any processing was done.

2 Describe how the copper mineral was separated from the worthless material in Steps 2 and 3.

3 Why was the solution boiled in Step 4?

4 In which steps did the process need an input of energy?

5 Suggest a use for the waste solids from Step 3.

6 How accurate do you think your percentage of copper is? Explain.

7 Could you improve your method to get a higher percentage of copper? How?

Check!

1   Use the table below to answer these questions.
   a   How is copper extracted from its ore?
   b   Which elements are in bauxite? Chalcopyrite?
   c   Which metal is found as an element rather than as a compound?
   d   Why is there a blank space for the method of extracting gold?
   e   Which is the most reactive element in the table? (See Fig 29 on page 274.)
   f   Infer which is the most difficult metal to extract.
   g   Suggest reasons for the order in which the four metals were first extracted.

Fig 39   Pouring molten steel in a steelworks

Metal	Main ore	Method of extraction	First extracted
aluminium	aluminium oxide (bauxite)	electrolysis	19th century
iron	iron oxide (haematite)	smelt with coke (carbon)	1500 BC
copper	copper iron sulfide (chalcopyrite)	heat ore in air	3000 BC
gold	found uncombined		5000 BC or earlier

2   Use the pie chart on page 273 to answer these questions.
   a   Which is the most common non-metal in the Earth's crust?
   b   Which is the most common metal?
   c   What does the pie chart tell you about commonly used metals such as copper, lead, zinc and silver?

3   Aluminium is the most abundant metal in the Earth's crust, but it is not the cheapest. Suggest why.

4   Write a chemical equation for the smelting of copper oxide using carbon. (See page 274.)

5   Would you expect miners to find nuggets (lumps) of magnesium metal? Explain your answer.

6   Four minerals—A, B, C and D—have the following properties:
   A   is soluble in acid
   B   is insoluble in acid, and floats in a water frothing agent mixture
   C   is insoluble in water and in acid
   D   is magnetic
   Use this information to work out how you could separate each mineral from a mixture containing all four.

7   Why is it that one Cu^{2+} ion combines with two electrons?

8   Write down at least three uses for copper.

9   In what ways do the mining of metal ores and the extraction of metals affect the environment?

challenge

1000 kg of rock containing copper ore → **mining** → metal ore → **concentrating** → copper mineral → **smelting** → copper

500 kg waste   492 kg waste   6 kg waste

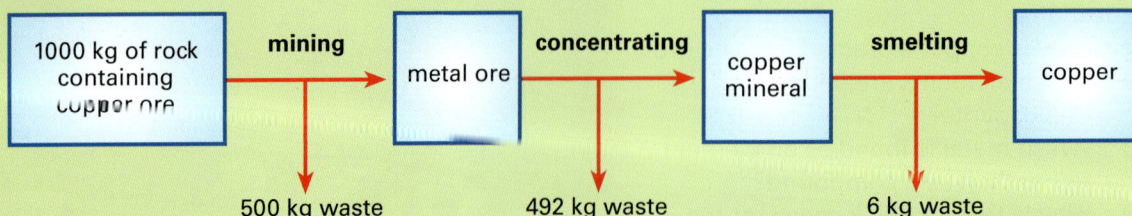

1 The flow chart above shows the extraction of pure copper from rock containing copper ore.

   a From each tonne (1000 kg) of rock from the mine, how much of the following do you obtain:
   - metal ore?
   - copper mineral?
   - copper?

   b From each tonne of rock mined, how much is waste?

   c How would this waste be disposed of?

   d What is the average percentage of copper in the mined rock?

   e The average percentage of copper in the Earth's crust is 0.005%. Suggest why copper cannot be extracted from ordinary rocks.

2 Which non-metals are commonly found combined with metals in metal ores?

3 When a metal oxide is heated with carbon, a metal is produced. What happens to the oxygen from the oxide? Explain using an example and write an equation.

4 a Which ions were present in the blue solution in Step 6 of Investigate 25? Which ions were attracted towards the negative copper strip?

   b Write an equation for the reaction that occurred at the copper strip.

   c When you add an iron nail to copper sulfate solution a displacement reaction occurs (see page 276) and the blue colour disappears. Explain what displacement is and write an equation for the reaction.

   d Objects made of iron exposed to water seeping from copper mines become coated with copper. Explain why this happens.

5 The diagram below shows how iron was extracted from its ore by people in Africa thousands of years ago. How is this similar to the blast furnaces used today? How is it different?

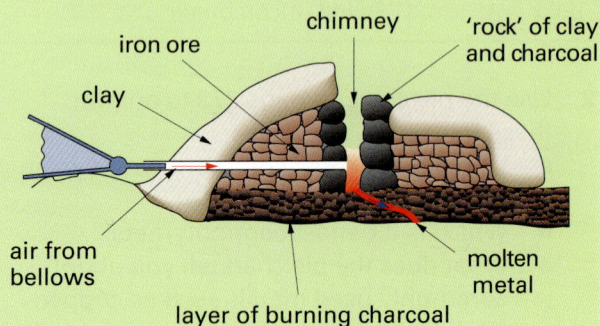

try this

1 Use library resources to research a metal of your choice. Make sure you find out:
   - where in Australia the metal is found
   - what the metal is used for
   - the ore from which the metal is extracted
   - how and where the metal is refined
   - its possible impact on the environment.
   Display your findings, for example on a poster.

2 See if you can design a process to extract copper from a mixture of sand and copper oxide, which is insoluble in water.

   Check your plan with your teacher, then try it. Record what you do and what happens.

MAIN IDEAS

Copy and complete these statements to make a summary of this chapter. The missing words are on the right.

1 Elements can be divided into two groups: metals and _____.

2 The _____ is a way of classifying elements according to their _____. Elements with similar properties are grouped together. It is extremely useful in explaining and predicting the _____ and reactions of elements.

3 The electrons in an atom are arranged in shells around the nucleus. The number of _____ in the outer shell determines the chemical properties of the element.

4 The number of electrons lost or gained by an element determines its _____. For example, alkali metals have a valency of 1+ and _____ have a valency of 1–.

5 All metals conduct heat and are malleable. Some are more _____ than others.

6 Metals can be extracted from their ____ by smelting, _____ or displacement.

7 During the extraction of a metal the positive ions in the mineral _____ electrons to form metal atoms.

atomic number
electrons
electrolysis
gain
halogens
non-metals
ores
periodic table
properties
reactive
valency

Try doing the Chapter 11 crossword on the CD.

Working with technology

REVIEW

1 In the periodic table, all the gases except hydrogen are:
   A in the first period
   B in the first group
   C in the same family
   D on the right-hand side

2 Use the periodic table on pages 260 and 261 to predict which one of the following elements has properties different from the other three.
   A aluminium   C calcium
   B barium   D radium

3 A sample of lead could be obtained in the laboratory by:
   A heating lead oxide very strongly
   B heating lead oxide with carbon
   C adding gold to lead nitrate solution
   D adding dilute sulfuric acid to lead carbonate

4 Air Pollution Control finds that a smelter is producing excessive levels of poisonous sulfur dioxide gas. What would you suggest be done?
   A Shut down the smelter.
   B Convert the sulfur dioxide into useful substances.
   C Shift the smelter into the desert.
   D Cut down production in the smelter so that less sulfur dioxide is produced.
   E Increase the height of the smelter's chimneys.
   Say why you rejected the other alternatives.

5 An impure copper sample contains a silver impurity. During electrolytic refining of this sample:
   a what happens to the copper?
   b what happens to the silver?

REVIEW

	A														B		C
		D														E	
				F													
															G		
						H											

6 In the periodic table above some elements have been replaced by letters. Use the letters to answer these questions. Find:
  a the two elements that are in the same group
  b two elements that are in the same period
  c the two elements that are gases at room temperature
  d the elements that are metals
  e the two transition metals
  f the element that is a noble gas
  g the element that is an alkali metal
  h the element that is a halogen
  i two elements that are likely to react.

7 Platinum exists as an uncombined element in nature. Copper can exist uncombined but more commonly occurs as a compound. Zinc is always found as a compound.
  a Arrange the three metals in order from most reactive to least reactive.
  b Which metal would be the best to polish and use as a mirror? Why?

8 Imagine that you are searching for two undiscovered elements with atomic numbers 117 and 118. Use the periodic table on pages 260 and 261 to predict the chemical properties of each of these elements.

9 Prepare a flow chart showing the sequence of processes used to convert copper ore (chalcopyrite) to copper metal suitable for electrical wiring.

10 Explain in terms of their chemical structures why copper is a good conductor of electricity and diamond is an insulator.

11 a Copy and complete the table below using the information on pages 263 and 264.
  b Which element has six protons in its nucleus?
  c Which element has all its electron shells full?
  d How many valence electrons does sodium have?
  e Which elements are likely to gain or lose one electron?

Element	Symbol	Atomic number	Number of electrons in		
			first shell	second shell	third shell
hydrogen carbon neon sodium chlorine					

Check your answers on pages 338–339.

Electrochemistry

Getting Started

You can make a simple electrical cell from a lemon, a thick piece of copper wire and a strip of magnesium.

1   Clean the copper wire and the magnesium strip with steel wool.
2   Push the wire and the strip into the lemon, about 2 cm apart, making sure they do not touch.

3   Connect the copper wire to the positive terminal of a sensitive voltmeter or multimeter as shown, and the magnesium to the negative terminal.
    ✎ What voltage is produced? Does the voltage stay the same? How many lemon cells would you need to make a 12 volt battery?
4   Does it make any difference how far apart the copper wire and the magnesium strip are, or how far you push them into the lemon?
5   What happens if you use different metals or different fruits?

12.1 Cells and batteries

What is an electric cell?

Do you have any grey amalgam fillings in your teeth? If so, have you ever bitten on a piece of metal foil and felt a tingle? This is caused by a small electric current in your mouth. All that is needed to produce this current is two different metals and a conducting solution.

When two different metals are placed in a conducting solution and connected together, an *electrochemical cell* is made. It is called an **electric cell** or voltaic cell. The conducting solution is called an **electrolyte** (ee-LEK-tro-lite). It conducts electricity because it contains ions. The metal strips are called **electrodes**.

In Getting Started the lemon, the copper wire and the magnesium strip form an electric cell. At the magnesium electrode a chemical reaction produces electrons which flow through the wire and voltmeter to the copper electrode where another chemical reaction uses up these electrons. Ions carry the electric current through the electrolyte in the lemon to complete the circuit.

The voltage produced by an electric cell depends on a number of variables. In Investigate 26 you can investigate what happens when you use different metals as the electrodes.

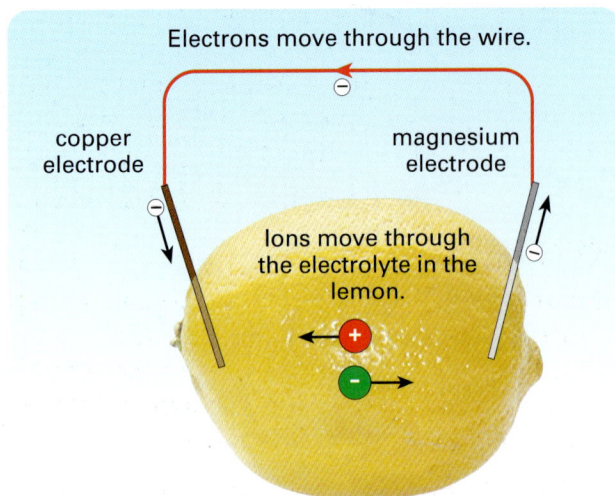

Electrons move through the wire.

copper electrode

magnesium electrode

Ions move through the electrolyte in the lemon.

Fig 2 An electric cell is a device which uses chemical reactions to produce an electric current.

Luigi Galvani

In the late 1700s Luigi Galvani, an Italian biologist, made a great discovery. While dissecting a frog, he noticed that its leg twitched when he held the knife and probe in a certain way. He inferred that the twitch was due to 'animal electricity' generated in the tissues of the frog's leg. Many people accepted this inference, but Alessandro Volta, a young Italian physicist, did not. He said that the source of electricity was not the frog but the two different metals in Galvani's dissecting instruments.

Galvani still believed he was right and eventually managed to get the same effect with two pieces of the *same* metal. But Volta wasn't convinced, saying that the metals must be somehow different. So Galvani got rid of the metals altogether and produced the twitch by tying the nerve of the frog's leg to the other end of the muscle. To answer this, Volta produced an electric current using two different metals and an electrolyte, and no frog at all! He then went on to make the first battery, a pile of silver and zinc disks with pieces of cloth soaked in salty water between the disks. He took his 'pile' to France where Napoleon Bonaparte was so impressed with it he made Volta a count. Science later honoured Volta by naming the volt after him.

Galvani was shattered by Volta's discovery and died soon after. However, his animal electricity wasn't all wrong. We now know that electricity is generated by the nerve cells in our body. It regulates the beating of our heart and the operation of our brain and muscles.

Investigate
26 VOLTAGES OF ELECTRIC CELLS

Aim

To investigate how the voltage of an electric cell varies, depending on the electrodes used.

Materials

- large test tubes and test tube rack
- strips of metal, eg aluminium, copper, iron, lead, magnesium, zinc
- strips of filter paper (about as wide as and slightly longer than the test tubes)
- voltmeter (2 V–20 V) or multimeter
- connecting wires
- dilute **sulfuric acid** (0.1M)   **Toxic**
- steel wool or emery paper

Planning and Safety Check

- Read the investigation carefully and design a suitable data table to record your results.
- What safety precautions will be necessary?

Method

1. Clean the metal strips by rubbing them with sandpaper or steel wool.

2. Select a pair of different metal strips and place them in a test tube. Bend the tops of the strips over the edge of the test tube, as shown.

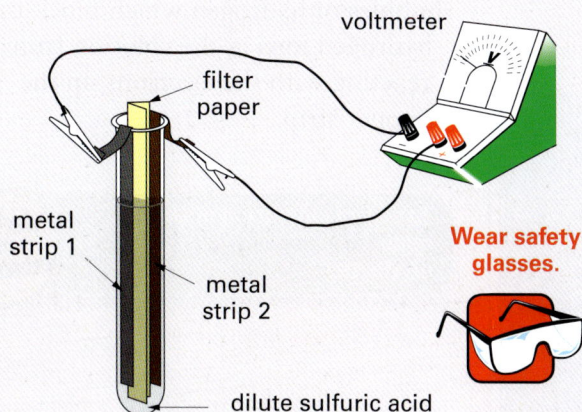

3. Fold a strip of filter paper and push it down between the metal strips. This is to prevent the strips from touching.

4. Two-thirds fill the test tube with dilute sulfuric acid.

5. Attach the connecting wires from the metal strips to the voltmeter. If there is no reading, reverse the connections so that you have the positive electrode connected to the positive terminal of the voltmeter. This is how you tell which metal strip is positive and which is negative.

    Record the reading on the voltmeter, and which metal is positive and which is negative.

    Did the voltage remain constant or did it change?

6. Repeat, using other combinations of metal strips. Include at least one with both metals the same.

    For each pair of metals, record the voltage, which metal was positive and which was negative.

Discussion

1. Which pair of metals produced the largest voltage?

2. Did a particular metal always have the same charge? For example, was the zinc electrode always negative?

3. What happened when you used two strips of the same metal? Why is this?

4. If you wanted to light a small bulb or LED using one of your cells, which metals would you use, and why? (You could try this.)

⊙ try this

1. Investigate whether it makes any difference what the electrolyte is. Instead of dilute sulfuric acid you could use dilute hydrochloric acid, sodium chloride solution, copper sulfate solution or dilute sodium hydroxide.

2. What happens when you connect two or more cells together? Does it matter which way they are connected?

How an electric cell works

If you made an electric cell using zinc and copper strips in dilute sulfuric acid in Investigate 26, you should have made several observations.

- When the negative terminal of the voltmeter is connected to the zinc and the positive terminal to the copper, the cell produces about 1 volt (to start with).
- The copper is the positive electrode, and bubbles of gas are produced there.
- The zinc is the negative electrode and slowly dissolves in the acid.

We can explain these observations as follows. The dilute sulfuric acid contains H^+ ions and SO_4^{2-} ions ($H_2SO_4 \rightarrow 2H^+ + SO_4^{2-}$). These ions allow the solution to conduct an electric current.

The zinc strip is more reactive than the copper strip. As a result the zinc atoms lose electrons to become positive ions Zn^{2+}. This loss of electrons is called *oxidation*. The ionic equation for this reaction is:

$$Zn \rightarrow Zn^{2+} + 2e^-$$

The Zn^{2+} ions move into the electrolyte, leaving the electrons behind.

When the zinc strip is connected to the copper strip, the electrons from the zinc strip flow through the wire from the zinc to the copper. Positive H^+ ions from the electrolyte around the copper electrode use these electrons to form hydrogen atoms. The hydrogen atoms then combine with each other to form molecules of hydrogen gas. This gain of electrons by the hydrogen ions is called *reduction*.

$$2H^+ + 2e^- \rightarrow 2H \rightarrow H_2$$

Notice that oxidation occurs at one electrode and reduction at the other. The electrons produced at the negative electrode are used up at the positive electrode. There is now a continuous flow of electrons through the wire, and a continuous flow of positive and negative ions in the electrolyte.

Zinc ions are produced, and hydrogen ions are used up. In theory, the cell will continue to produce electricity until all the zinc or all the H^+ ions from the electrolyte are used up. The solution remaining will contain zinc ions and sulfate ions (zinc sulfate).

You may have noticed in Investigate 26, however, that the voltage produced by the cell drops fairly rapidly. This is because the positive electrode becomes covered with bubbles of hydrogen which block the hydrogen ions in the solution from reacting with the electrons on the copper strip.

To see an animation of this, open **How an electric cell works** on the CD.

Working with technology

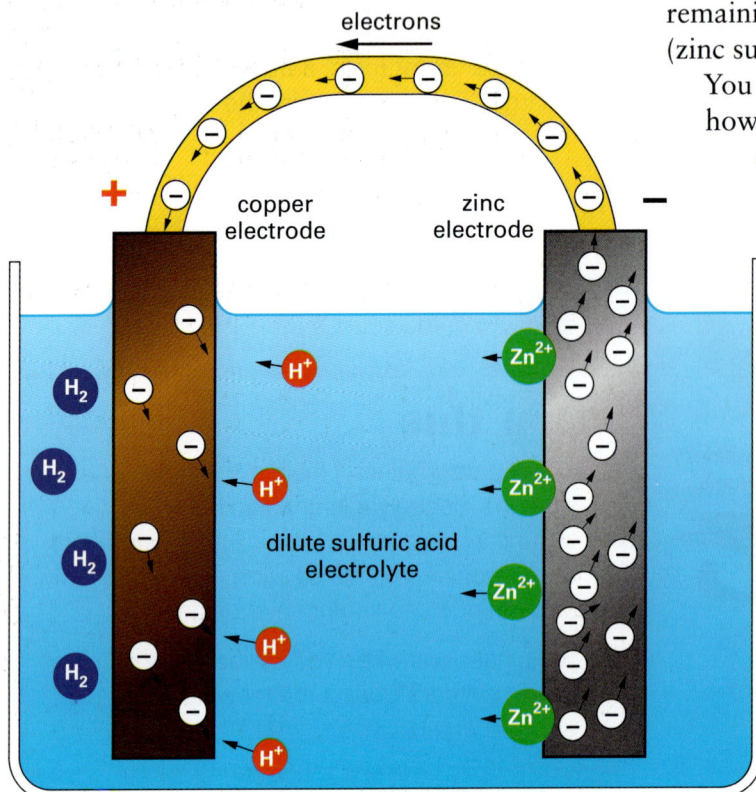

Fig 5 How a simple electric cell works

Dry cells

The cells used in torches and portable radios are called **dry cells**. This is because the liquid electrolyte has been replaced by a moist electrolyte paste in a sealed container.

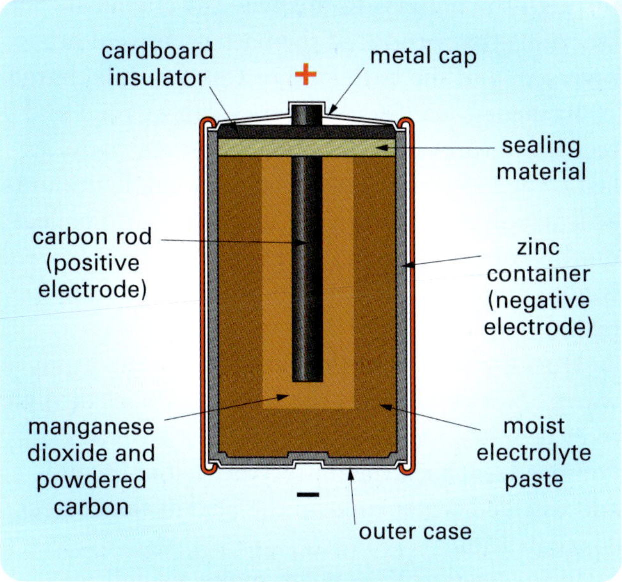
cardboard insulator
+
metal cap
sealing material
carbon rod (positive electrode)
zinc container (negative electrode)
manganese dioxide and powdered carbon
moist electrolyte paste
−
outer case

The outside case is made of zinc. This is the negative electrode, and it loses electrons (oxidation) to form zinc ions.

$$Zn \rightarrow Zn^{2+} + 2e^-$$

The positive electrode is a carbon rod surrounded by manganese(IV) oxide. (Carbon is a good conductor of electricity.) The reduction reaction at this electrode is complicated, but it can be simplified as:

$$Mn^{4+} + e^- \rightarrow Mn^{3+}$$

The manganese dioxide also removes any hydrogen formed at the positive electrode by reacting with it. The electrolyte paste conducts the electricity.

A carbon–zinc dry cell produces 1.5 volts. Batteries are made by connecting several cells together. For example, a 9 V battery consists of six 1.5 V cells connected together as shown in Fig 7 (6 × 1.5 volts = 9 volts). In everyday language the word battery is also used for a single cell.

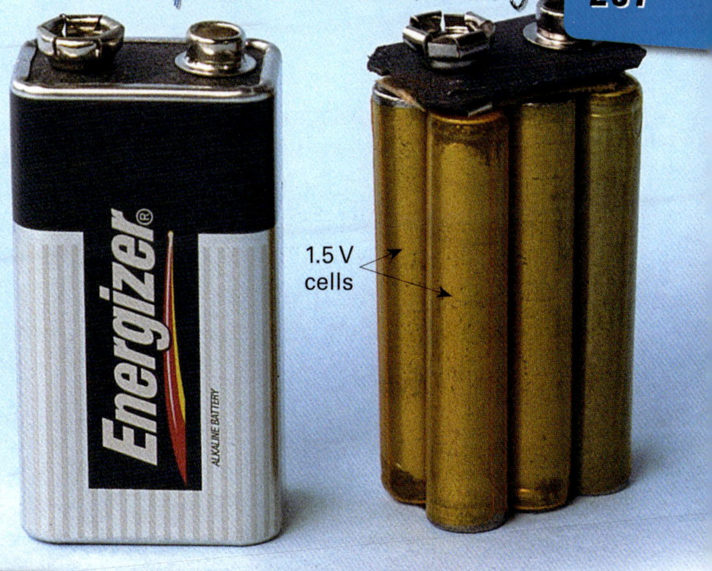
Energizer
ALKALINE BATTERY
1.5 V cells

Fig 7 A 9 V battery cut open showing the six individual 1.5 V cells

Suppose you have a CD player that needs six 1.5 V dry cells. The cells have to be connected in series so that the top positive terminal of one touches the bottom negative terminal of the next. In the appliance illustrated below there are two rows of 3 cells, one row on top of the other. The total voltage is 1.5 V × 6 = 9 V.

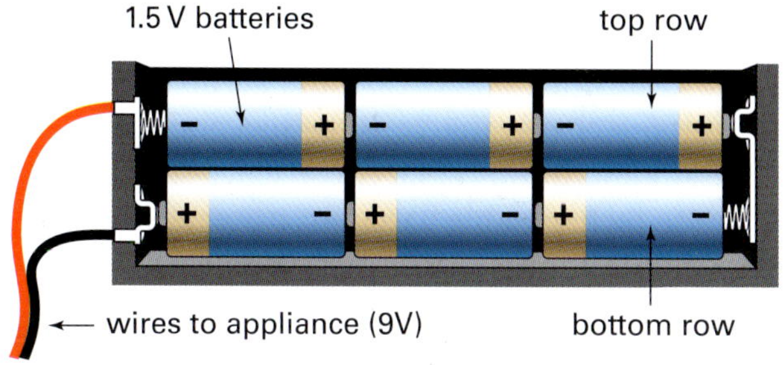
1.5 V batteries
top row
wires to appliance (9V)
bottom row

Fig 9 When putting batteries into an appliance you must be careful to put them in the right way round.

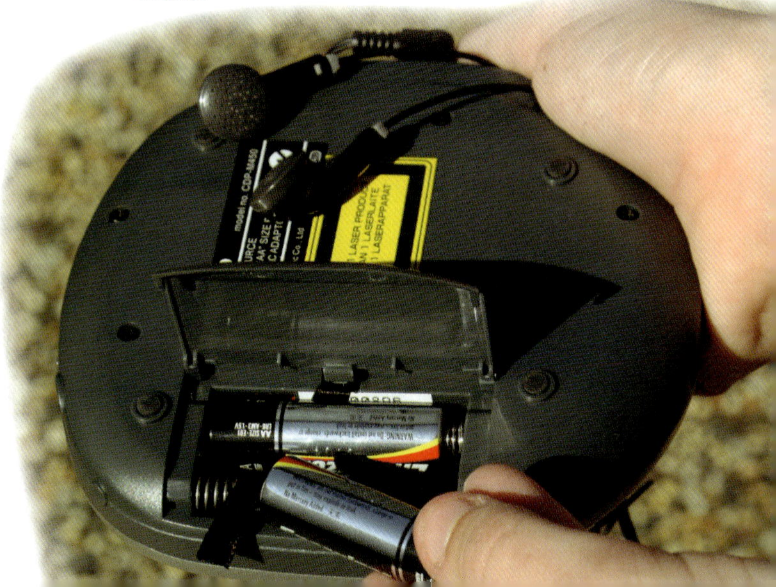

Small button cells are used in watches, calculators, cameras, hearing aids and hand-held electronic games. One type consists of an outer container of nickel or steel, with zinc powder and silver oxide separated by an electrolyte. The zinc is oxidised and the silver ions in the silver oxide are reduced to silver atoms.

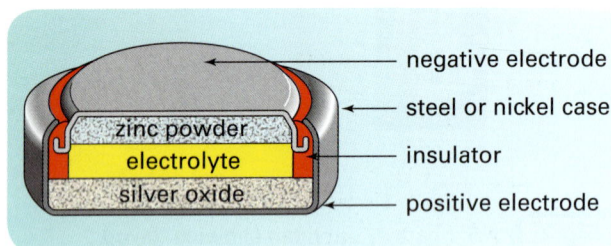

negative electrode
steel or nickel case
zinc powder
electrolyte
silver oxide
insulator
positive electrode

Rechargeable batteries

The cells discussed so far have a major disadvantage. Once the chemicals in them have reacted the cells go 'flat' and have to be thrown away. However, with some cells it is possible to reverse these reactions by passing electricity through them in the opposite direction. Rechargeable cells are widely used in mobile phones, laptop computers, cordless drills and radio-controlled model cars and aeroplanes. Two common rechargeable cells are nickel-cadmium (NiCad) and lithium ion. Most space satellites also use rechargeable batteries, using electricity produced by solar cells to recharge them.

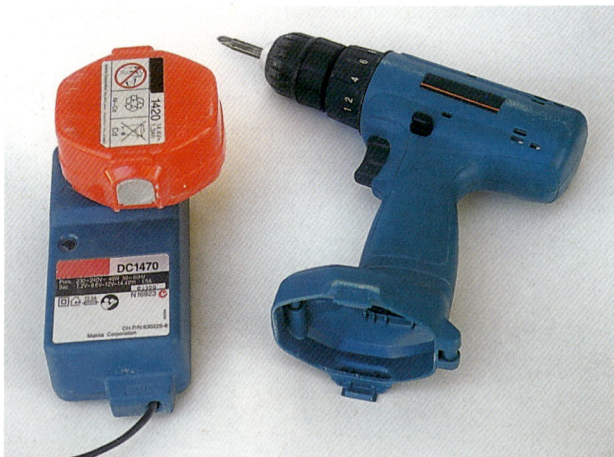

Fig 11 When this red nickel-cadmium battery is recharged, the chemical reactions that produced electricity in the electric drill are reversed.

The most common rechargeable battery is the car battery. It has electrodes of lead and lead oxide (PbO_2) in a sulfuric acid electrolyte. The battery produces an electric current to start the engine, but once the engine is running, an alternator (generator) is used to pass current back through the battery. In this way the chemical reactions that produced the battery current are reversed, and the battery is restored to full charge.

In theory, lead–acid batteries can be used and recharged forever. In practice, however, batteries last only 2–5 years. This is because small amounts of lead sulfate fall from the electrodes and collect on the bottom of the cells. Eventually there is not enough lead sulfate to produce lead on recharging.

During recharging the battery becomes quite warm, causing some of the water in the electrolyte to evaporate. This is why with most batteries you need to check the battery occasionally and add distilled water to keep the acid at the correct concentration.

In Investigate 27 you can make a small lead–acid battery and charge and discharge it.

Fig 12 Topping up a car battery with distilled water

⭐ extra *for* experts

A car battery consists of six cells connected together, as shown on the right. Each cell produces about 2 volts and contains two electrodes. The negative electrodes are lead and the positive electrodes are lead(IV) oxide PbO_2. These electrodes are immersed in fairly concentrated sulfuric acid, containing H^+ ions and SO_4^{2-} ions.

At the negative electrodes the lead atoms lose electrons (oxidation) to form lead ions.

$$Pb \rightarrow Pb^{2+} + 2e^-$$

At the positive electrodes Pb^{4+} ions gain electrons (reduction) to form Pb^{2+} ions.

$$Pb^{4+} + 2e^- \rightarrow Pb^{2+} + 2H_2O$$

During discharge the Pb^{2+} ions react with the sulfuric acid to form lead sulfate (an insoluble white solid) which builds up on the electrodes. The reverse reaction occurs when the battery is recharged (whenever the engine of the car is running).

When you recharge a battery or jump start a car, the water in the battery is electrolysed to hydrogen and oxygen gases. For this reason it is important to leave the caps off and keep away from any sources of ignition such as a burning cigarette.

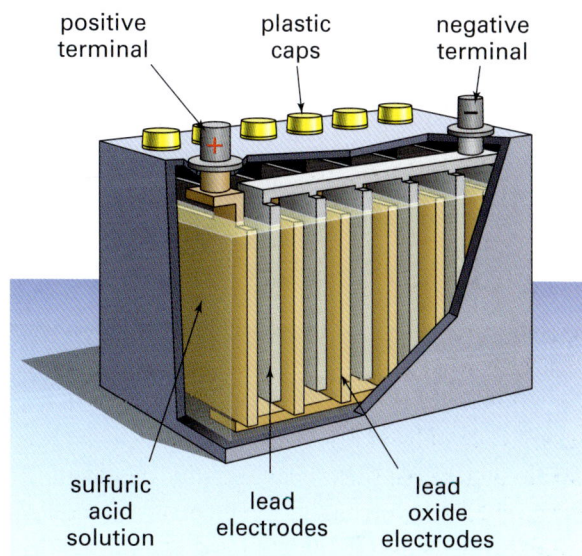

positive terminal   plastic caps   negative terminal

sulfuric acid solution   lead electrodes   lead oxide electrodes

🌡️ Science in action

Batteries for hybrid cars

With the cost of petrol increasing and carbon dioxide from car exhausts contributing to global warming, more people are buying hybrid cars. These cars have an electric motor as well as a normal petrol engine. They also have a battery pack which fits under the floor in the back. When you accelerate, the battery powers the electric motor. When you reach cruising speed the petrol engine starts up as well. Then, when you slow down, the electric motor acts in reverse. It acts as a generator and recharges the battery. This way you use much less petrol and produce less exhaust gas. Hybrid cars at present use nickel-metal hydride battery packs. For example, the Toyota Prius has a sealed 168-cell nickel-metal hydride battery which produces 201.6 volts. Scientists and technologists are constantly experimenting with new types of batteries.

Fig 14 The dashboard display in a Toyota Prius hybrid car

Investigate
27 A MODEL CAR BATTERY

Aim

To make a model lead–acid car battery and investigate how it works.

Materials

- 2 clean **lead** strips, **Toxic** eg 5 cm × 1 cm
- 100 mL beaker
- power pack
- 5 connecting wires
- 1.5 volt torch bulb in holder
- voltmeter or multimeter
- switch
- 1M **sulfuric acid** **Corrosive**

lead strips

6 V DC

sulfuric acid

switch

Wear safety glasses.

light bulb or voltmeter

Planning and Safety Check

- 1M sulfuric acid is very corrosive. If any is spilt, what should you do?
- Why should you wash your hands well after handling the lead strips?
- Why is it important to make sure that the lead strips do not touch during charging or discharging?

Method

1 Connect up the electric circuit as shown, and have your teacher check it. The lead electrode connected to the positive terminal of the power pack is the positive electrode.

2 Set the power pack to 6 V DC and turn it on to charge your 'battery'.

3 After 5 minutes, turn off the power pack and turn on the switch to connect the battery to the light bulb. The battery is now discharging.

How long does the bulb glow?

4 Recharge the battery by turning off the light bulb switch and turning the power pack on again for 5 minutes.

5 Remove the torch bulb and replace it with a voltmeter. Make sure the positive terminal of the voltmeter is connected to the positive electrode of the battery.

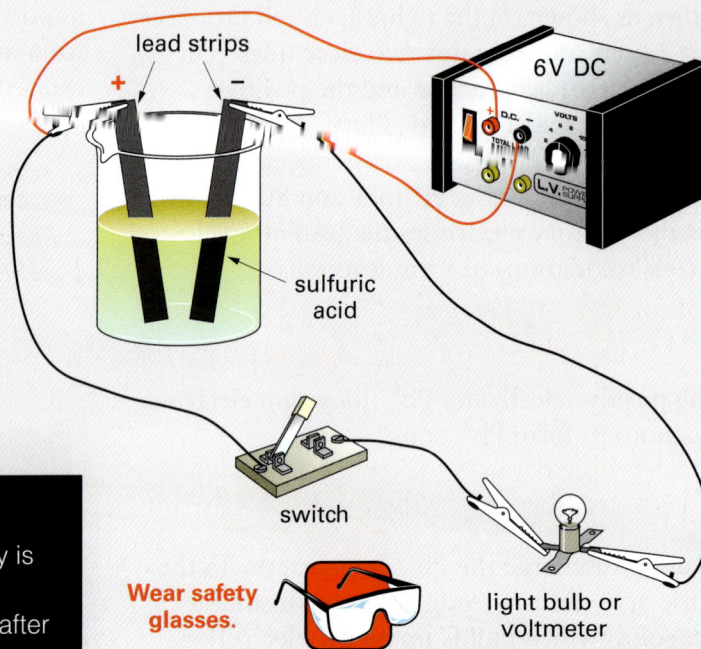

6 Switch on the voltmeter circuit.

Record the voltage of the battery.

What happens to the voltage as the battery continues to discharge?

Discussion

1 What evidence of chemical reactions did you observe during charging and discharging?

2 Explain in your own words the difference between charging and discharging.

3 Would you get as much energy out of the battery as you put into it? Explain your answer.

try this

Use your battery to investigate the effect of one or more of these variables on its performance:

- the charging time and voltage used
- the distance between the lead strips
- the size of the strips.

Fuel cells

Fuel cells are electrochemical cells that produce electricity continuously and do not need to be recharged.

Hydrogen–oxygen fuel cells were used on the *Apollo* missions which put people on the Moon, and they are currently used in the Space Shuttle. Each cell consists of two electrodes separated by an electrolyte (see Fig 16). Hydrogen (the fuel) is fed into one electrode and oxygen (air) into the other.

At the negative electrode the hydrogen gives up electrons (is oxidised):

$$2H_2 \rightarrow 4H^+ + 4e^-$$

At the positive electrode the oxygen accepts electrons (is reduced):

$$O_2 + 4H^+ + 4e^- \rightarrow 2H_2O$$

Adding these two equations together, the overall reaction is:

$$2H_2 + O_2 \rightarrow 2H_2O$$

A big advantage of this fuel cell is that the only waste product is water. In fact, the fuel cells on the Space Shuttle are used to produce drinking water as well as electricity. At present fuel cells are too expensive for general use, but they are being trialled in buses in Perth. It may not be long before they are widely used, eg in hydrogen cars and mobile phones.

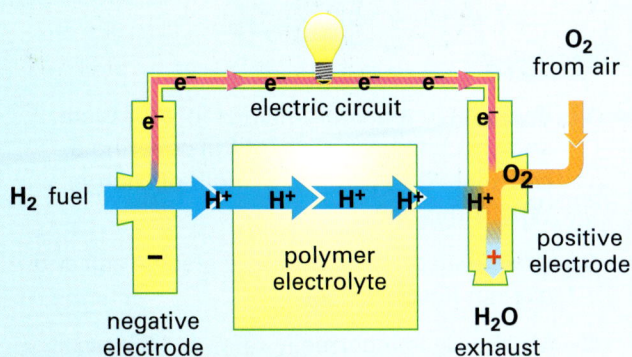

Fig 16 This type of fuel cell generates 0.7 volts. The electrodes contain a platinum catalyst and the electrolyte is made of a conducting plastic similar to Teflon. Many of these cells stacked together can be used to power a hydrogen car (below).

WEBwatch

Use the internet to research fuel cells and write a report which includes:

• types of fuel cells
• their advantages and disadvantages
• where they are used.

Go to www.scienceworld.net.au and follow the links to these useful websites:

Fuelling the 21st century

Fuel cell technology

How fuel cells work

Fig 17 How a hydrogen car works

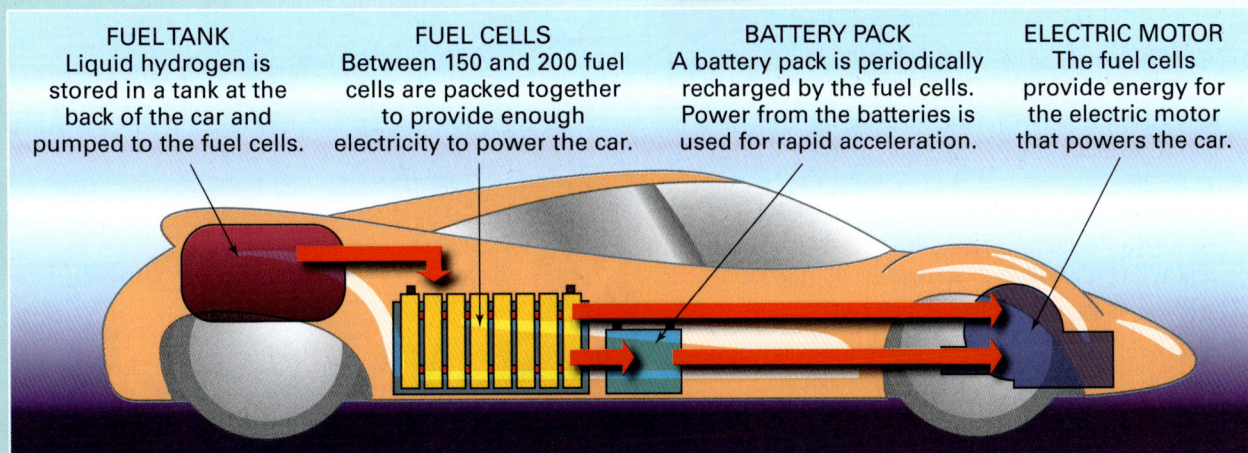

FUEL TANK
Liquid hydrogen is stored in a tank at the back of the car and pumped to the fuel cells.

FUEL CELLS
Between 150 and 200 fuel cells are packed together to provide enough electricity to power the car.

BATTERY PACK
A battery pack is periodically recharged by the fuel cells. Power from the batteries is used for rapid acceleration.

ELECTRIC MOTOR
The fuel cells provide energy for the electric motor that powers the car.

Check!

1   If you have amalgam fillings in your teeth and you bite on a piece of foil covering a chocolate bar, you feel a tingle of charge. Why is this so?

2   Draw a diagram of a simple electric cell and explain how it works.

3   Most people incorrectly refer to 1.5 V dry cells as batteries. Why is this incorrect?

4   How could you make a 4.5 V battery from 1.5 V dry cells?

5   What are the two electrodes in a dry cell made of?

6   What is the electrolyte in a car battery?

7   Why are lead–acid batteries often referred to as storage batteries?

8   What has happened when a battery is flat?

9   Explain how the flow of electric current in an electrolyte differs from that in the wire connecting the electrodes.

challenge

1   I-Chung put a zinc strip and a copper strip in a test tube and added water. When he connected a voltmeter the reading was zero. How can you explain I-Chung's result?

2   Tanya decides to make a simple cell spillproof by sealing it with a rubber stopper. However, the rubber stopper keeps popping out. Suggest why this happens.

3   A copper–zinc cell gives a voltage of about one volt while a copper–lead cell gives a voltage of less than 0.5 V. Write an inference to explain these observations.

4   Alistair wants to recharge his car battery using a battery charger.

   a   To which battery terminals should the positive and negative terminals of the battery charger be connected?

   b   What would be the effect on the battery if the charger was connected incorrectly?

   c   Why is it important to remove the plastic caps on each cell of the battery during recharging?

   d   Explain why smoking during this procedure is hazardous.

5   In Getting Started you made an electric cell by putting a copper wire and a magnesium strip in a lemon (containing citric acid). Use what you have learnt in this section to answer these questions.

   a   What is the electrolyte in this cell?

   b   What reaction occurs at the magnesium electrode? Is this electrode positive or negative?

   c   What reaction occurs at the copper electrode? Is this electrode positive or negative?

6   A torch bulb is connected to a copper–zinc cell. At first the bulb glows brightly, but it gradually becomes dimmer. Explain why this happens.

7   In 1780 Luigi Galvani investigated animal electricity. He connected different metals such as copper and iron to the hind legs of dead frogs, as shown in Fig 18. He found that the legs twitched.

   a   Use what you have learnt in this chapter to explain Galvani's observation.

   b   Look at Fig 9 in the illustration below. It shows an iron bracelet (A) connected to a copper bracelet (C) by a curved wire. Redraw this, labelling the two electrodes and the direction of the current flow.

Fig 18   Galvani's experiments on animal electricity

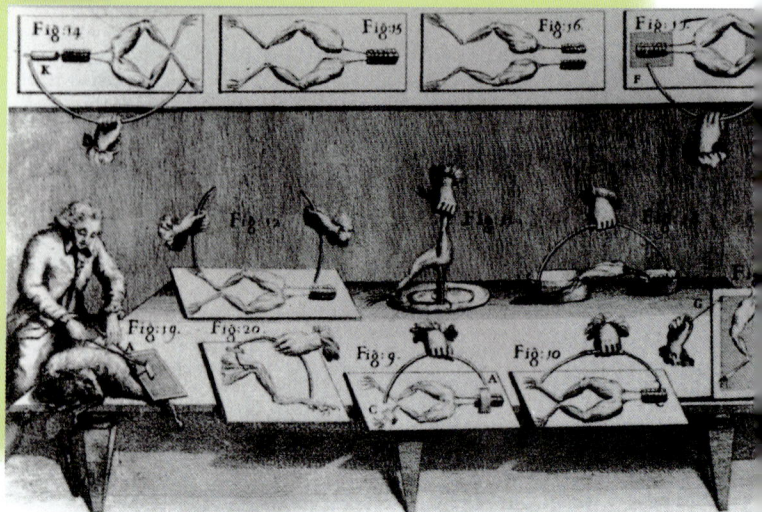

12.2 Electrolysis

Electroplating

If you browse through a jeweller's shop you will find many shiny 'silver' articles such as bracelets, necklaces, cutlery, trays and jugs. The silver on these objects is usually only a thin coating about 0.01–0.05 mm thick on top of an inexpensive metal such as copper, zinc or nickel. The coating has been put on by electrolysis, a process in which electricity is used to cause chemical reactions. It is the reverse of what happens in electric cells.

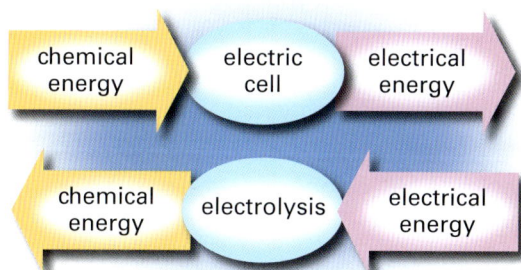

chemical energy → electric cell → electrical energy

chemical energy ← electrolysis ← electrical energy

Putting a layer of metal on the surface of another metal is called **electroplating**. To put a coating of silver on a teapot you would use the apparatus in Fig 21. The teapot is connected to the negative terminal of a power supply and immersed in an electrolyte such as silver nitrate, which contains ions of the metal that is to form the coating. The positive electrode is a rod of silver. When the power is turned on, the positive silver ions in the electrolyte are attracted to the negative electrode (the teapot), where they accept electrons and are reduced to silver atoms.

$$Ag^+ + e^- \rightarrow Ag$$

At the positive silver electrode the silver atoms release electrons and are oxidised to silver ions.

$$Ag \rightarrow Ag^+ + e^-$$

The negative nitrate ions move towards the positive electrode but do not take part in any reaction. The overall result is that the silver rod slowly dissolves, and the teapot is coated with silver.

Fig 20 This motorcycle fuel tank has been electroplated with a thin layer of chromium (chrome) by placing it in a vat containing chrome solution and passing an electric current through it.

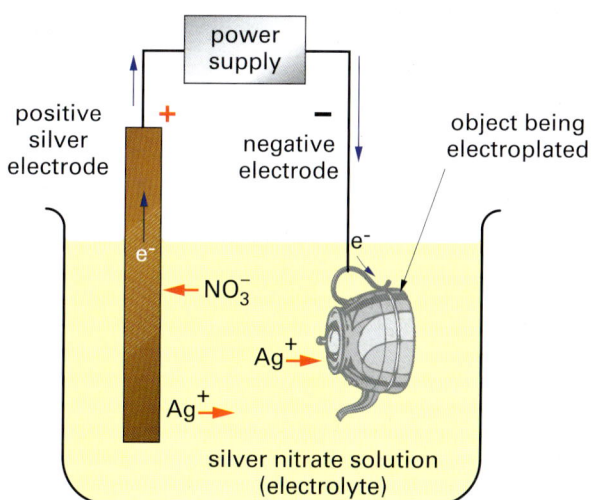

Fig 21 This teapot is being electroplated with a layer of silver.

Investigate
28 COPPER PLATING

Aim

To investigate the electrolysis of copper sulfate solution.

Materials

- **acidified copper sulfate solution** (1M)
- 250 mL beaker
- carbon rod
- copper strip
- power pack
- 2 connecting wires

Toxic

Planning and Safety Check

- Read the investigation carefully and design a suitable data table to record your results.
- What safety precautions will be necessary?
- Discuss with your teacher how you will dispose of the copper sulfate solution.

Method

1 Set up the equipment as shown, with the carbon electrode connected to the negative terminal of the power supply.

2 Set the power supply to 2 V DC and turn it on for 3 to 4 minutes. *Don't let the electrodes touch.*
   📋 Observe the electrodes while the current is turned on.

3 Remove the electrodes, wash and inspect them.
   📋 What do you think the coating on the negative electrode is?

4 Reverse the connections to the electrodes so that the carbon electrode is connected to the positive terminal.

5 Allow the current to flow for 3 or 4 minutes.
   📋 Describe what happens this time.

Discussion

1 What ions are present in the copper sulfate solution?

2 Which electrode is negative in Step 2? Write an equation for the reaction that occurred there.

3 The copper sulfate tends to lose its blue colour after a while. Write an inference to explain this.

4 Did you observe bubbles of gas at the positive electrode? Infer what this gas is and where it came from.

5 How could you test your inference in Question 4?

6 Explain what happened in Step 5 when you reversed the connections.

7 The copper is always deposited at the same electrode. Which one is it—the positive or the negative?

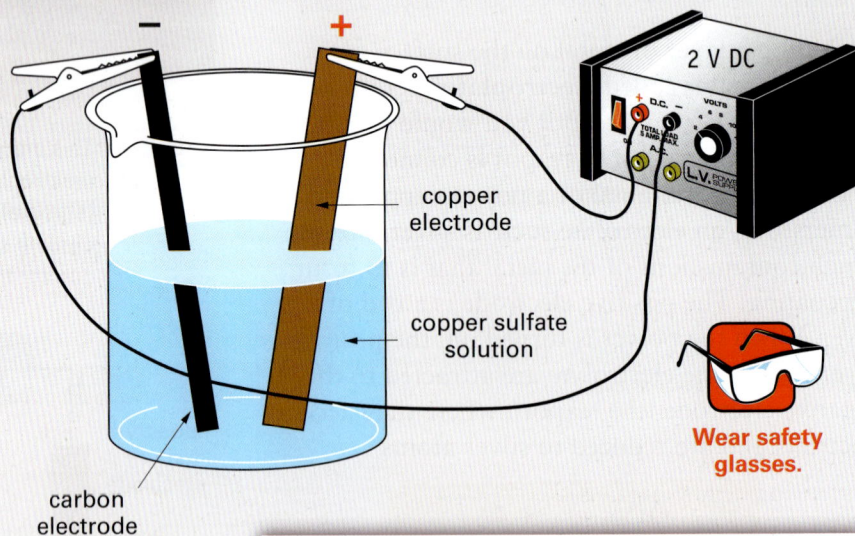

−   +

2 V DC

copper electrode

copper sulfate solution

Wear safety glasses.

carbon electrode

⊙ try this

Plan and carry out an experiment to electroplate various metal objects with copper. To get an even coating of copper, clean the metal to be plated with steel wool or dip it in nitric acid (caution) before you start. Use a low voltage (2 V DC) and leave for at least 20 minutes.

Electrolysis in industry

Electrolysis is widely used in industry to produce the materials we use in everyday life. For example, if you melt sodium chloride it conducts an electric current and can be electrolysed as shown on the right. The electrodes are made of an unreactive material such as carbon.

The positive ions move to the negative electrode where they accept electrons to form sodium metal.

$$2Na^+ + 2e^- \rightarrow 2Na$$

The molten sodium is less dense than the molten sodium chloride and floats to the top of the cell, where it can be collected.

The negative chloride ions move to the positive electrode, where they give up their electrons to form chloride atoms which immediately form molecules of chlorine gas.

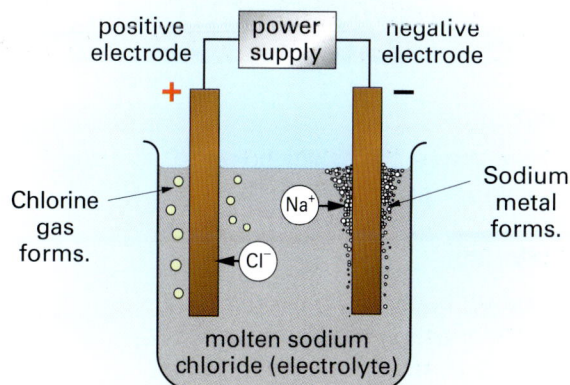

$$2Cl^- \rightarrow Cl_2 + 2e^-$$

Sodium is a very reactive metal. It is used in sodium vapour lamps. Chlorine is a toxic greenish-yellow gas used to sterilise drinking water and in the manufacture of polyvinyl chloride (PVC) and various pesticides.

science bits

Hair removal by electrolysis

Linda is always pulling hairs from her face, and has gone to the beauty salon to have the hairs removed permanently. The beautician uses a very fine gold needle which she connects to the negative terminal of a 9 V power supply. The positive electrode is a shiny metal cylinder which Linda holds in her hand. The beautician gently pushes the needle into the hair follicle and turns on the power for about 10 seconds. This is repeated 3 or 4 times. Finally, tweezers are used to remove the hair easily and painlessly. But how does the process work?

Your body tissues contain water, and dissolved in this water is sodium chloride,

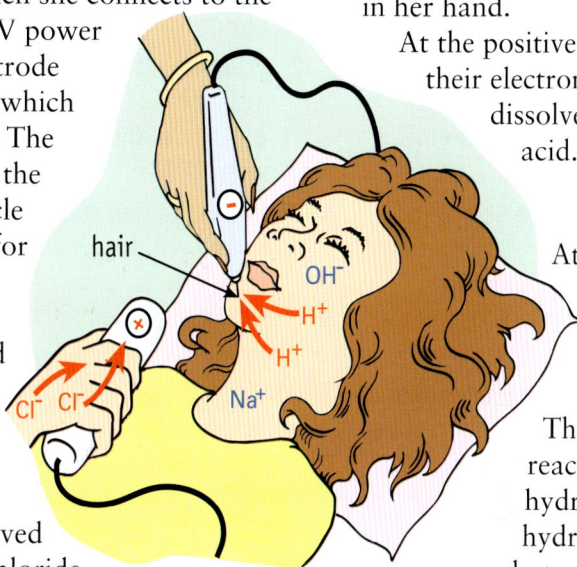

present as Na^+ ions and Cl^- ions. Some of the water molecules also break into H^+ ions and OH^- ions. So, when the electrolysis equipment is connected and turned on, Linda's body conducts an electric current. The positive ions move to the negative electrode in the hair follicle, and the negative ions move to the positive electrode held in her hand.

At the positive electrode the Cl^- ions give up their electrons to form chlorine gas, which dissolves in water to form hydrochloric acid.

$$2Cl^- \rightarrow Cl_2 + 2e^-$$

At the negative electrode the H^+ ions accept electrons to form hydrogen gas.

$$2H^+ + 2e^- \rightarrow H_2$$

The Na^+ and OH^- ions do not react, but together form sodium hydroxide (NaOH). This sodium hydroxide is alkaline and gradually destroys the root of the hair.

Investigate
29 DRAWING BY ELECTROLYSIS

Aim

To electrolyse potassium iodide solution and explain what happens.

Materials

- power pack
- 2 connecting wires
- large evaporating basin
- large filter paper
- white tile or similar
- large shiny nail
- aluminium foil
- **potassium iodide** solution (0.5M)
- sodium thiosulfate solution (0.5M)
- starch suspension (1% freshly prepared)
- phenolphthalein indicator
- disposable gloves

Toxic ☠

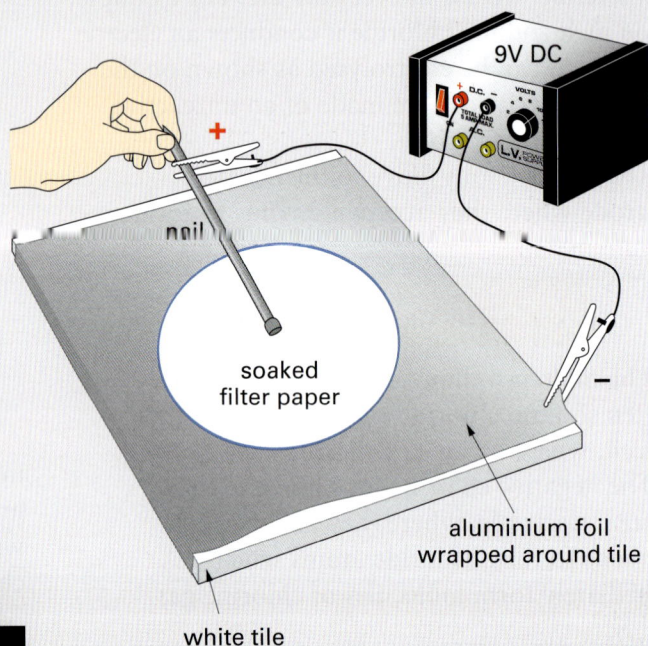

9V DC

soaked filter paper

aluminium foil wrapped around tile

white tile

Planning and Safety Check

Why is it important to wear disposable gloves for this experiment?

Method

1. Set up the equipment as shown.

2. Mix the following solutions in an evaporating basin:

   10 mL potassium iodide
   5 mL sodium thiosulfate
   5 drops starch
   5 drops phenolphthalein

3. Soak a large filter paper in the solution in the dish.

4. Wear gloves to remove the soaked filter paper from the dish, drain off any excess liquid, then place the filter paper on the aluminium foil wrapped around the tile. Press it down to make sure it has good contact with the foil.

5. Switch on the power pack and use the nail to draw a letter or shape on the damp filter paper. *Be careful not to tear it.*

6. Switch off, reverse the connections, and try again.

Discussion

To start with the filter paper contains equal numbers of K^+ and I^- ions from the potassium iodide. It also contains equal numbers of H^+ and OH^- ions from the water.

1. When the nail is positive it produces a blue-black colour where it touches the filter paper. What can you infer from this blue-black colour? (Hint: the solution on the filter paper contains starch.)

2. Write an equation for what happens when iodide ions I^- give up electrons at the positive electrode. (Hint: it is similar to what happens with Cl^- ions—see page 295.)

3. When the nail is negative it produces a pink colour. What can you infer from this pink colour? (Hint: the solution on the filter paper contains phenolphthalein, an acid–base indicator.)

4. Write the equation for the reaction when H^+ ions accept electrons at the negative electrode. (Hint: see page 286.)

5. If H^+ ions are removed at the negative electrode, why would the phenolphthalein indicator change colour from colourless to pink?

Check!

1. Explain the terms:
   a. electrolysis
   b. electrolyte

2. a. How is electrolysis different from what happens in an electric cell?
   b. Is electrolysis an exothermic or an endothermic reaction? Explain.

3. a. Which of the following materials could be used as an electrode for electrolysis: carbon, zinc, plastic, copper? Explain.
   b. Which of the following liquids could be used as an electrolyte in electrolysis: dilute sulfuric acid, distilled water, lead sulfate solution, methylated spirits, sugar solution.

4. Why is it that one Cu^{2+} ion combines with two electrons?

5. In the electrolysis of aluminium, aluminium ions Al^{3+} accept electrons to become aluminium atoms. Write an equation for this reaction.

6. How could you coat a spoon with copper?

7. a. Which ions exist in a copper sulfate solution?
   b. When electricity is passed through copper sulfate solution, what happens at the negative electrode? Write an equation.

challenge

1. A steel knife is to be electroplated with nickel using nickel sulfate solution.
   a. Draw a diagram showing how this would be done.
   b. What would the positive electrode be made of?
   c. Write equations for the reactions occurring at both electrodes. (Nickel ions are Ni^{2+}.)

2. Why is a direct current and not an alternating current used in electroplating metals?

3. Use the explanation of hair removal by electrolysis on page 295 to answer these questions.
   a. When the beautician is removing hairs from your face why do you need to hold the other electrode?
   b. Why is a shiny metal cylinder used as the positive electrode?
   c. Why does the area around the hair becomes quite warm during the treatment?
   d. What happens to the hydrogen gas produced at the negative electrode?
   e. Why is it that the root of the hair becomes alkaline during the treatment?
   f. The electrical connections are sometimes reversed briefly at the end of the treatment. Suggest a reason for this.

4. The gold pendant below was made from a leaf. Suggest how this would have been done.

5. In the electrolysis of molten sodium chloride (page 295), explain the following.
   a. Why is electricity conducted in the molten state but not in the solid state?
   b. Why are the products formed only around the electrodes and not throughout the liquid?
   c. What causes the electric current to flow in the liquid and in the connecting wires?
   d. What are the similarities and differences between the electrolysis of molten sodium chloride and hair removal by electrolysis?

6. Predict what would happen if you electrolysed molten lead(II) bromide $PbBr_2$. Write equations.

12.3 Corrosion of metals

Rusting

A big problem with metals is that they corrode; that is, they react chemically with moist air. Metallic corrosion and its prevention costs Australia hundreds of millions of dollars every year.

Corrosion is a reaction between a metal and moist air. For example, when iron rusts it reacts with oxygen to form iron oxide Fe_2O_3. This is the brown coating we call rust.

$$4Fe(s) + 3O_2(g) \rightarrow 2Fe_2O_3(s)$$

For rusting to occur both air and water are necessary. This is why objects made of iron and steel do not rust in the desert or in space.

The rusting of iron and steel is an electro-chemical process. Consider a drop of water on a piece of iron. The water, which contains dissolved carbon dioxide and other gases from the air, acts as the electrolyte. Near the centre of the drop the iron atoms lose electrons to form Fe^{2+} ions, which move into the water. The metal in the centre of the drop becomes negatively charged.

$$Fe \rightarrow Fe^{2+} + 2e^-$$

Electrons flow across the surface of the iron to the edges of the drop, which have a positive charge. Here there is a high concentration of dissolved oxygen, and the oxygen molecules gain electrons to form hydroxide ions.

Fig 27 When iron rusts it reacts slowly with air and water to form brown iron oxide. This ship was wrecked in 1893.

$$O_2 + 2H_2O + 4e^- \rightarrow 4OH^-$$

These OH^- ions then react with the Fe^{2+} ions to form iron hydroxide then iron oxide Fe_2O_3. Salt water accelerates the corrosion because it is a very good conductor of electricity.

The presence of carbon in steel tends to accelerate corrosion. Other metals can either accelerate or slow down the corrosion. If conditions favour the loss of electrons, the rate of corrosion is increased, but if iron can be prevented from losing its electrons, corrosion can be slowed down or prevented.

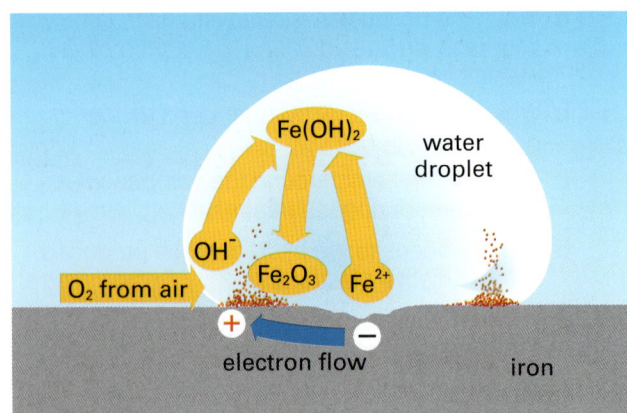

Fig 28 The corrosion of iron is similar to what happens in an electric cell.

298 Science World 3

Experiment
CORROSION OF IRON

Research questions

1 You suspect that iron rusts faster if you are near the coast where the air is salty. Is this true?

2 You have read that if iron is touching another metal it rusts faster or slower, depending on the metal. Is this true?

Design your experiment

1 Work in a small group to design an experiment to answer the two questions above. Use the diagram and the hints below as a guide.

2 Write out the method for your experiment. Make sure your tests are fair. Which variables will you control? Which variable will you change?

3 Make a list of the materials you will need.

4 Discuss how you are going to record your observations. You could use a digital camera to record the corrosion of the nails.

5 Do a risk assessment for your experiment.

Hints

1 Use steel wool to clean the nails, copper and magnesium thoroughly before you start.

2 The copper and magnesium need to be in tight contact with the nail.

3 It is best to continue the experiment for several days, up to a week. You will need to put your experiment somewhere it will not be disturbed.

Discussion

1 Use your results to answer research Question 1 —does iron rust more rapidly in salt water? Are your results reliable? Should you do more tests?

2 What effect did the copper have on the rusting of the nail? What effect did the magnesium have?

3 Write inferences to explain why copper and magnesium affect the rusting of iron.

4 Use your results to list the three metals (iron, copper and magnesium) from most reactive to least reactive.

5 If you did the experiment again, could you improve your method? Explain.

6 Can you suggest ways of extending your experiment? Suggest other questions you could investigate.

Write your report

Write a full report of your experiment, using the usual headings. In your conclusion, make sure you answer the two research questions.

Applying what you have learnt

1 Where would you expect iron to rust more rapidly—in a river or in the ocean? Explain.

2 Predict what would happen if you used copper screws in a steel boat in salt water. Explain your prediction.

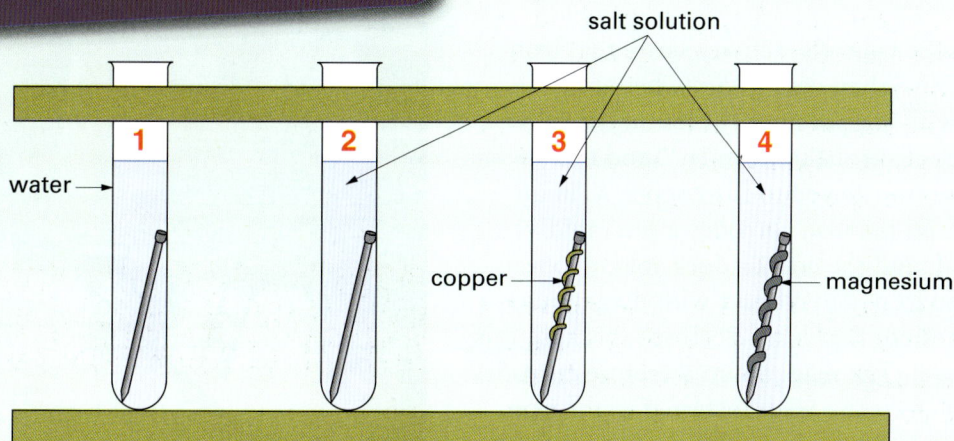

Preventing corrosion

The results of your experiment from the previous page can be explained in terms of how chemically reactive the metals are.

Sodium and gold are both metals. Yet sodium reacts so quickly with air that it has to be stored in kerosene. On the other hand, gold and silver coins can lie on the ocean floor for hundreds of years without corroding. The metals can be arranged in a list with the most reactive at the top and the least reactive at the bottom. This is the **activity series**. It can be used to predict reactions of metals, eg which will react most rapidly with an acid.

Activity series

most reactive
(lose electrons most readily)

potassium	$K \rightarrow K^+ + e^-$
calcium	$Ca \rightarrow Ca^{2+} + 2e^-$
sodium	$Na \rightarrow Na^+ + e^-$
magnesium	$Mg \rightarrow Mg^{2+} + 2e^-$
aluminium	$Al \rightarrow Al^{3+} + 3e^-$
zinc	$Zn \rightarrow Zn^{2+} + 2e^-$
iron	$Fe \rightarrow Fe^{3+} + 3e^-$
tin	$Sn \rightarrow Sn^{2+} + 2e^-$
lead	$Pb \rightarrow Pb^{2+} + 2e^-$
copper	$Cu \rightarrow Cu^{2+} + 2e^-$
silver	$Ag \rightarrow Ag^+ + e^-$

least reactive

You can see from the activity series that iron is more reactive than copper. So, when iron is in contact with copper in salt solution the iron rapidly loses electrons to form Fe^{3+} and the electrons are transferred to the copper, as in an electric cell. So the iron corrodes more rapidly than normal, and the copper does not corrode.

When the iron is in contact with magnesium, it is the magnesium that loses electrons (because it is more reactive). The magnesium therefore corrodes rapidly and electrons are transferred to the iron, stopping it from corroding. This process is called

sacrificial protection because the magnesium is sacrificed to protect the iron

Another metal that slows down the corrosion of iron is zinc. Iron used on roofs is coated with zinc or a zinc–aluminium alloy to prevent the iron corroding. This zinc-coated iron is called galvanised iron, and a coloured version is available as *Colorbond*. Because the zinc is more reactive than iron, it slowly corrodes in preference to the iron.

Lumps of zinc or magnesium are often attached to the steel hulls of ships to protect them from rusting. Because zinc is more reactive than the iron, it is corroded in preference to the iron. Once the zinc blocks have corroded they have to be replaced.

Tin cans are made of iron (steel) coated with a thin layer of tin. Tin is a very unreactive metal, so it corrodes very slowly. The inside of the can is often coated with a thin layer of plastic to give extra protection from corrosion. However, if the can is damaged the plastic and tin layers may be

Fig 31 The zinc blocks fitted to this ship corrode in preference to the steel in the hull.

broken, exposing the iron. Iron is higher on the activity series than tin, so it reacts rapidly with the contents of the can. Poisonous gases may be produced and these may get into the food. So beware of scratched and dented cans.

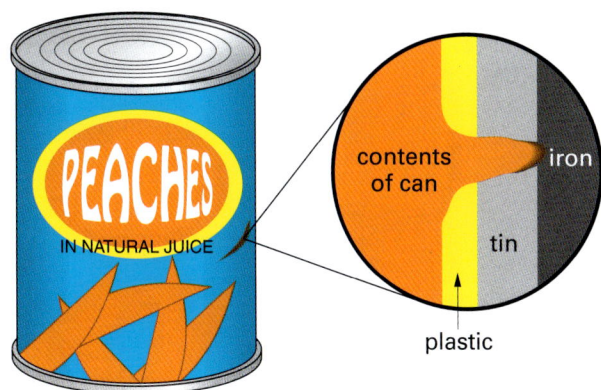

Fig 32 Magnified cross-section of the wall of a damaged tin can. When this happens the contents of the can may react with the iron.

Corrosion of aluminium

Aluminium is a very reactive metal yet it does not seem to need any special protection from corrosion. The secret is a very thin layer of aluminium oxide which forms on the surface of a freshly cut piece of aluminium when it is left in air. This layer of oxide sticks to the aluminium and prevents water and air attacking the uncorroded aluminium underneath. The aluminium has formed its own protective layer. See the diagram below.

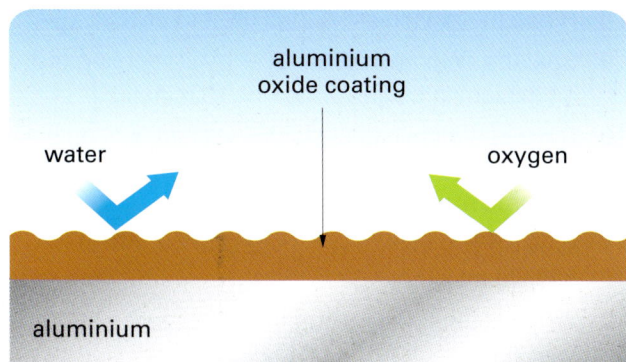

To protect the aluminium even more, the oxide layer can be made thicker. This is done by an electrolysis process called **anodising**. The aluminium article is thoroughly cleaned and dipped in a dilute sulfuric acid electrolyte. It is then made the positive electrode (anode) by connecting it to the positive side of a power supply. Hydroxide ions from the water are attracted to the positive electrode where they give up electrons and form oxygen atoms.

$$2OH^- \rightarrow O + H_2O + 2e^-$$

These oxygen atoms then react with the aluminium anode to form aluminium oxide. This oxide coating can be dyed, so aluminium articles can be anodised different colours.

Fig 34 Anodised cups

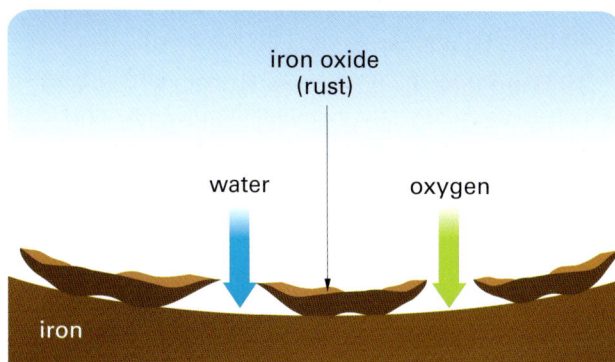

Fig 33 Aluminium oxide forms a protective coating on aluminium, but rust is flaky and does not keep the air and water from the iron underneath.

Aim

To anodise a piece of aluminium.

Materials

- piece of aluminium, eg 5 cm x 1 cm
- aluminium foil
- 2 beakers (100 mL)
- **2M sulfuric acid**   **Corrosive**
- metal tongs
- safety glasses and disposable gloves
- hotplate (or burner, tripod and gauze)
- power pack and connecting wires
- fabric or food dye solution
- stand and clamp
- detergent
- bench mat
- tissues

Wear safety glasses.

Wear a lab coat or apron.

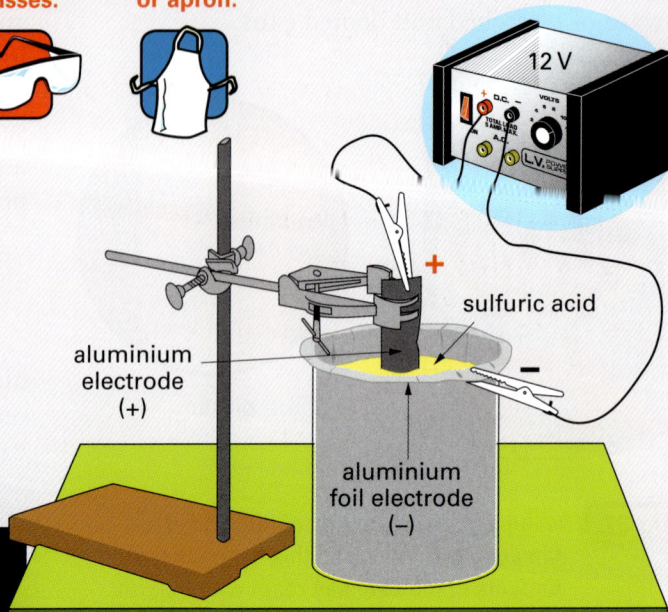

12 V

+

sulfuric acid

aluminium electrode (+)

−

aluminium foil electrode (−)

Planning and Safety Check

- Read the investigation carefully before you start. There are many steps and you will need to be very safety conscious and well organised. You may want to do the investigation as part of a science project on anodising.
- Ask your teacher what you should do with the leftover sulfuric acid.

Method

1 Line a beaker with aluminium foil, then carefully three-quarters fill it with 2M sulfuric acid.

2 Connect the aluminium foil to the negative terminal of the power supply (without allowing the alligator clip to dip into the acid).

3 Thoroughly clean the piece of aluminium to be anodised. Scrub it with warm water and detergent and dry with a tissue. Once cleaned, the aluminium must be handled only with clean metal tongs.

4 Use the stand and clamp to suspend the piece of aluminium in the centre of the beaker *so that it does not touch the aluminium foil*. Connect the piece of aluminium to the positive terminal of the power pack.

5 Turn on the power supply and increase the voltage slowly to 12 volts. Leave for about 15 minutes, then use the tongs to remove the piece of aluminium and wash it in water.

What did you observe during the electrolysis?

How has the aluminium changed?

6 In a second beaker heat a prepared dye solution until it is almost boiling.

7 Immerse the anodised aluminium in the dye solution and leave for 10 minutes, or until the aluminium has a permanent colour.

8 Rinse the aluminium and allow it to cool.

9 Seal the coloured oxide layer by immersing the aluminium in boiling water for 10 minutes.

10 Rinse the aluminium in water and dry it.

Discussion

1 Why do you think it was necessary to clean the aluminium in Step 3?

2 Why shouldn't you touch the aluminium with your fingers after Step 3?

3 Are you happy with your final product? Could you improve your method? How?

Check!

1 An iron bar might last 20 years, a bar of aluminium 100 years and a gold bar thousands of years. Why is this so?

2 Use the activity series to place these metals in order from most reactive to least reactive:

   copper gold magnesium sodium zinc

3 What is the chemical formula for rust?

4 a Which two substances are needed for rusting to occur?
  b List two things that speed up the rusting of iron.

5 How does painting iron and steel prevent it from rusting?

6 What is the process of galvanising? How does it prevent iron from rusting?

7 The Water Board wants to protect its steel pipes from rusting. To do this they want to attach blocks of another metal to the pipes. They are considering three different metals—lead, magnesium and zinc. Which would be the best metal to use? Why?

8 Why does metal guttering on houses near the coast rust more quickly than guttering on houses in inland areas?

9 Alfredo left some lead sinkers in the bottom of his aluminium dingy the last time he went fishing.
  a Write an inference to explain why his boat leaked the next time he used it.
  b Design an experiment to test your inference.

challenge

1 If you were going to put aluminium sheeting on a roof, would you use iron nails? Explain.

2 Why does iron rust more rapidly if the air is polluted?

3 Bethanie wonders why food cans are not covered with zinc, like galvanised iron roofs. Explain why zinc-coated cans wouldn't work.

4 Infer how rust bubbles form under paint.

5 Sue bought an expensive piece of art made from iron. To stop it rusting she attached a small block of zinc to it by wire.
  a How does this prevent the iron art from rusting?
  b Predict what would happen if she used a block of lead instead of zinc.
  c Suggest other ways Sue could stop the art from rusting.

6 When iron rusts what change takes place in the iron atoms? Write an equation.

7 Write a balanced equation for the corrosion of aluminium when it reacts with oxygen. (Hint: the valency of aluminium is 3+.)

8 Look at your results from Investigate 26 showing the voltages produced by different pairs of metals. How can you use the activity series to predict which pair of metals will produce the highest voltage?

9 Design a controlled experiment to compare the rate of corrosion of aluminium, copper and iron indoors and outdoors. If possible, carry out your experiment.

MAIN IDEAS

Copy and complete these statements to make a summary of this chapter. The missing words are on the right.

1 An electric _____ consists of two different conductors (electrodes) immersed in a conducting solution (_____).

2 Most dry cells cannot be _____, but the lead–acid batteries used in cars can be.

3 _____ is the process in which electricity is passed through an electrolyte to cause _____.

4 _____ is an electrolysis process in which a metal is coated with a thin layer of another metal.

5 In an electric cell and in electrolysis, _____ are lost at one electrode (oxidation) and _____ at the other electrode (reduction).

6 Iron and aluminium corrode by reacting with _____ in moist air to form _____.

7 To prevent iron rusting it is essential to stop oxygen and _____ from reaching the metal.

8 The _____ series lists the metals from the most reactive to the least reactive. When two different metals are in contact in moist air or in water, the more _____ metal corrodes.

activity
cell
chemical reactions
electrolysis
electrolyte
electrons
electroplating
gained
oxides
oxygen
reactive
recharged
water

Try doing the Chapter 12 crossword on the CD.

Working with technology

REVIEW

1 Predict which of the following metals will react most rapidly with dilute sulfuric acid.
   A aluminium
   B magnesium
   C lead
   D silver

2 To coat a piece of zinc with copper, which liquid would you use in the electroplating bath?
   A copper sulfate solution
   B zinc sulfate solution
   C hydrochloric acid
   D distilled water

3 Predict which set-up on the right will act as an electric cell. Explain why each of the other set-ups will *not* work.

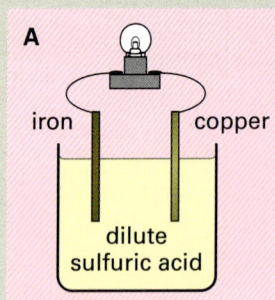

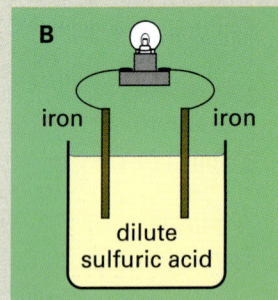

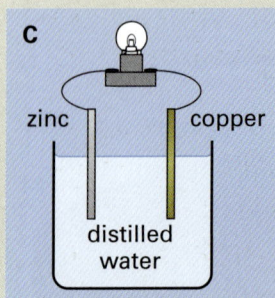

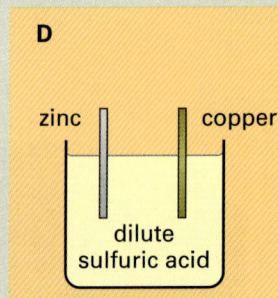

A
iron   copper
dilute sulfuric acid

B
iron   iron
dilute sulfuric acid

C
zinc   copper
distilled water

D
zinc   copper
dilute sulfuric acid

4 To investigate the corrosion of metals Allison set up four test tubes as shown below.

a Use the activity series on page 300 to work out which strip of tin would corrode the most.

b Which strip of tin would corrode the least? Why?

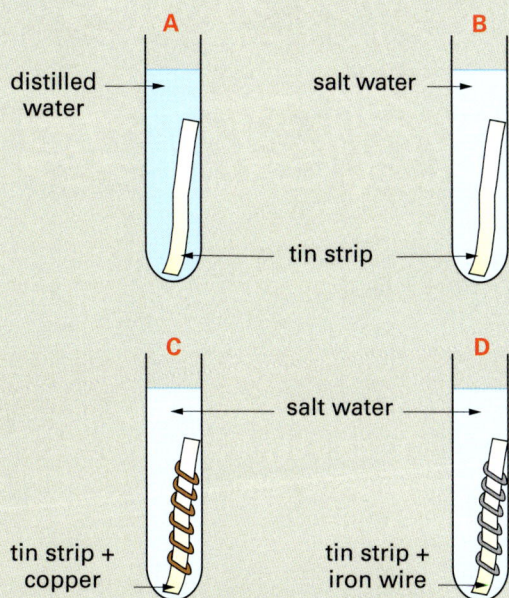

5 If an electric current is passed between two carbon electrodes placed in concentrated sodium chloride solution, chlorine gas is produced at the positive electrode. Which one of the following inferences best explains why this happens?

A Chlorine gas is dissolved in the solution, and when an electric current is passed through it, chlorine gas is forced out.

B Hydrogen ions from the water react with chloride ions to form hydrochloric acid, which in turn forms chlorine gas.

C When an electric current is passed through water, gases are given off and one of these is chlorine.

D Negative chloride ions from the solution move to the positive electrode and release electrons to form chlorine gas.

6 List at least three important differences between a car battery and a torch cell.

7 Consider this list of metals and alloys: aluminium, bronze (copper-tin), calcium, gold, iron, magnesium, steel, tin.

a Three of these are more resistant to corrosion than the others. Which are they?

b Suggest why each is resistant to corrosion.

c Which one of the other metals or alloys will corrode most quickly? Explain your answer.

8 Magnesium chloride is melted and electricity passed through the liquid.

a Which ions will be in the liquid?

b At which electrode will magnesium metal be formed? Explain your answer.

c Which element will be formed at the other electrode? Write an ionic equation for the reaction that occurs.

9 The photo below shows an iron pillar in Delhi in central India. It shows little sign of rust, even though it is about 1500 years old. Write at least one inference to explain the absence of rust.

Check your answers on page 339.

13 Space science

Getting Started

Form a group of three or four people and discuss the questions below.

1. You are standing in a lift on a set of scales. The scales read 50 kg. Suddenly the lift moves upwards. What happens to the reading on the scales? Why?

2. You tie an object to a piece of string and whirl it around your head. You then let the string go. In which direction will the object travel? Draw diagrams to help your explanation.

3. You drop two objects at the same time from a very high cliff. They are the same size but one is five times as heavy as the other. Which reaches the ground first?

4. You are on a space walk alongside the Shuttle's cargo bay 400 km above the Earth. You let go of the handrail. Will you fall back to Earth? Explain.

13.1 Getting into space

How high can you jump vertically when you stand on the ground with your feet together? Fifty centimetres? The reason why you cannot jump any higher is because the force of gravity attracts you to the Earth. To get into space you have to overcome this force. To do this, rocket engines have to supply a force greater than the downwards force of gravity. When the engines in a rocket ignite, the force generated by the engines accelerates the rocket upwards.

Science in action

The first rocketers

The Chinese are credited with the invention of rockets, which were used in warfare and in religious ceremonies. The rockets were made of bamboo tubes filled with gunpowder. In warfare they were attached to arrows, and in ceremonies they were attached to bamboo sticks to help them steer a straight course.

The legend of Wan-hu

Legend has it that Wan-hu, a lowly government official in the Ming Dynasty (early 16th century), was intrigued with rocketry, and he thought rockets could be used for transportation. Wan-hu was also a keen astronomer and dreamed that rockets could take him to the stars.

He built a special chair with 47 rockets and two kites attached to it. At the appointed time, Wan-hu sat in the chair and gave the order for his assistants to light the fuses. Moments later there was a massive explosion. When the smoke and dust cleared, Wan-hu and the rocket chair were gone. The world's first want-to-be astronaut was gone.

I'm gonna be as famous as Wan-hu.

....and just as dead!

Busting the myth of Wan-hu

The *Mythbusters* team decided to try to recreate the Wan-hu rocket chair using the same sort of materials available to Wan-hu. They used a crash test dummy instead of a human.

The chair exploded on the launch pad and the dummy suffered severe burns. The team then tried modern rockets, but the chair only rose a few metres before going out of control and crashing. The team concluded that rockets cannot supply enough force to lift a rocket chair very far away from the Earth's surface.

WEBwatch

Go to www.scienceworld.net.au and follow the links to the websites below.

Brief history of rockets

An interesting, easy-to-read account of the history of rocketry from early times to the present.

Chinese fire-arrows

The story of Wan-hu, and links to the history of rocketry and other sites.

The History of Rocket Science

Detailed information on the history of the science of rockets and rocket design.

Force, mass and acceleration

When the engines in a rocket ignite, the force generated by the engines accelerates the rocket upwards. How quickly a rocket lifts off depends on the mass of the rocket and the force generated by its engines.

In Chapter 5 you learnt that the acceleration of an object is directly proportional to the force acting on it and inversely proportional to its mass. That is:

$$\text{acceleration} = \frac{\text{force}}{\text{mass}}$$

$$a = \frac{F}{m}$$

$$\text{or} \quad F = ma$$

For example, the upwards force produced by a rocket of mass 10 000 kg being accelerated at 10 m/s^2 is:

$$
\begin{aligned}
F &= ma \\
&= 10\,000 \text{ kg} \times 10 \text{ m/s}^2 \\
&= 100\,000 \text{ N}
\end{aligned}
$$

Fig 4 The force generated by a rocket's engines accelerates the rocket upwards.

Weight is a force

If you hang an object on a spring balance the spring stretches. This shows that there is a downwards force. If a larger mass is hung on the balance the spring stretches further, showing that the force is greater. F = ma can be rewritten as:

$$W = mg$$

where **W** is the weight force and **g** is the acceleration due to gravity

Acceleration due to gravity

When you hang a 1 kg block on a Newton spring balance, the dial reads 9.8 N. This means the weight of the 1 kg block is 9.8 N. If the block is unhooked from the spring balance, it will fall to the ground. The acceleration of the block is:

$$
\begin{aligned}
g &= \frac{W}{m} \\
&= \frac{9.8 \text{ N}}{1 \text{ kg}} \\
&= 9.8 \text{ m/s}^2
\end{aligned}
$$

So the acceleration due to gravity at the Earth's surface is 9.8 m/s^2.

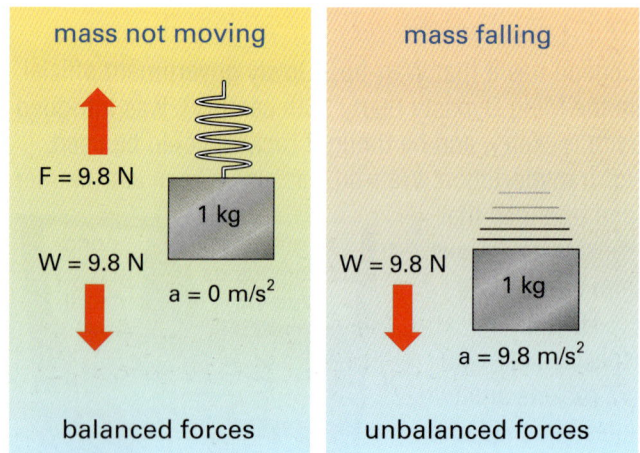

mass not moving — mass falling

F = 9.8 N
1 kg
W = 9.8 N
a = 0 m/s^2
balanced forces

W = 9.8 N
1 kg
a = 9.8 m/s^2
unbalanced forces

Fig 5 When the mass is hooked on the spring, the forces are balanced and there is no motion. When it is unhooked it falls with an acceleration of 9.8 m/s^2.

What happens if a 2 kg block falls to the ground? When the block is attached to the spring balance it reads 19.6 N. If the block is unhooked from the balance, the acceleration of the 2 kg block is:

$$g = \frac{16.9\ N}{2\ kg}$$
$$= 9.8\ m/s^2$$

The heavier block still falls with the same acceleration as the lighter one. In general, the acceleration due to gravity is the same for all objects on the Earth's surface. Why then does a tennis ball fall faster than a piece of paper? Falling objects are slowed down by friction due to the air around the Earth, and the amount an object is slowed down depends on its shape. So in real life, different objects do not all fall with the same acceleration.

The acceleration due to gravity is not the same everywhere. It decreases as you move away from the Earth. So when the force of gravity decreases, the acceleration also decreases. This means that if you travel away from the Earth your weight will decrease. The table below shows how gravity and weight decrease with increasing distance from Earth for a 50 kg person.

Location of 50 kg person	Acceleration (m/s²)	Weight (N)
On the Earth's surface	9.8	490
100 km above Earth	9.6	480
500 km above Earth	8.3	415
1000 km above Earth	6.8	340

The force of gravity also depends on the mass of the planet or moon. You can investigate the differences in the acceleration due to gravity on different planets in the activity below.

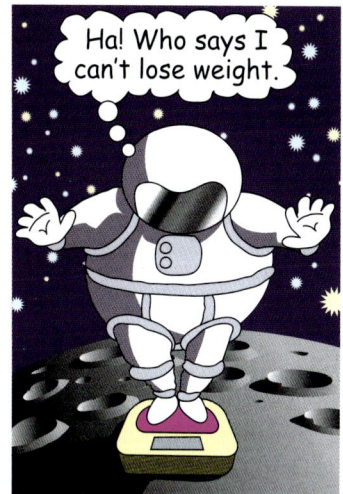

Activity

Suppose you are on the surface of Planet X and you are curious to find out how the weights of various masses on the surface of this planet are different from those on Earth.

The table below shows the results for Planet X.

Mass (kg)	Weight (N)
2	39.2
4	78.4
6	117.6
8	156.8

📋 Use the formula W = mg to find the acceleration due to gravity on Planet X.

📋 Suppose you took the four masses in the table back to Earth. Find the weights of the masses on the Earth's surface.

📋 The acceleration due to gravity on Jupiter is 25.5 m/s². Calculate the weights of the 2, 4, 6 and 8 kg masses in the table.

📋 Write a generalisation about the relationship between weight and gravity.

📋 If the force of gravity is directly proportional to the mass of the planet, work out which planet (X, Jupiter or Earth) has the smallest mass and which has the greatest.

📋 How much would you weigh on Planet X? How much would you weigh on Jupiter?

Rocket science

The cartoon below illustrates Newton's third law of motion.

When the man fires the gun, the bullets go in one direction and the gun moves in the opposite direction. Newton's third law of motion states:

> **For every force there is an equal and opposite force.**

The two forces in this law are often called the *action* force and the *reaction* force. You can investigate these forces in the activity below.

The action–reaction principle is used in rockets. Rockets shoot out hot exhaust gases from their engines. The force of the exhaust gases shooting out (the action) pushes the rocket forwards (the reaction). This is why rockets are sometimes called *reaction engines*. And the faster

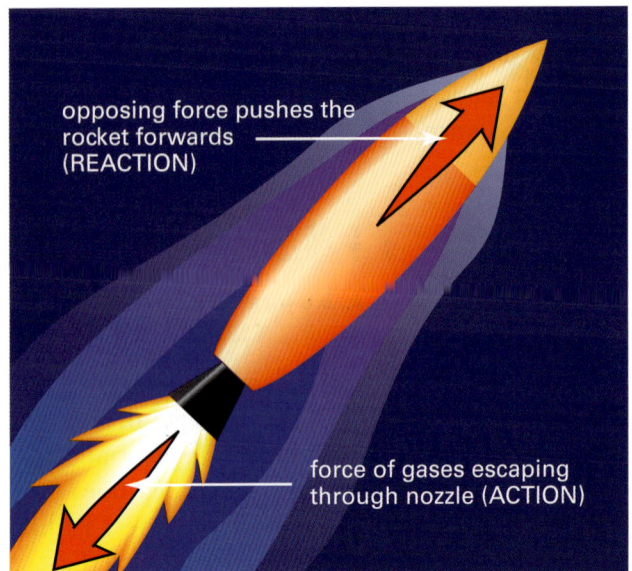

Fig 8 A rocket works on the principle of action and reaction.

the hot exhaust shoots out, the faster the rocket moves in the opposite direction.

All aircraft use the action–reaction principle. The blades on propeller-driven aircraft spin rapidly and push the air backwards (action), thus pushing the aircraft forwards (reaction). The engines on jet aircraft take in air at the front. This is mixed with jet fuel, ignited, and then the hot exhaust gases are forced out of the back of the engine. This pushes the aircraft forwards.

Activity

For this activity you need a heavy ball (medicine ball) and a skateboard or skates.
1 Stand on the skateboard facing the front and hold the medicine ball at chest level.
2 Throw the ball horizontally to another person without bending your legs or pushing the skateboard.
   📋 Describe what happens.
   📋 In what way is this similar to the gun cartoon above?
   📋 Which is the action force and which is the reaction force?

3 Find out what happens when you throw the ball harder.
   📋 Interpret your results.

Experiment
MODEL ROCKETS

Planning and Safety Check
- Carefully read through Part A and Part B. Work in a small group to design the tests for both types of rockets.
- Make a list of the equipment you will need for each part of the experiment.
- Design and draw up data tables for your results.
- Discuss the safety precautions necessary in this experiment. Draw up a risk assessment sheet listing all the safety hazards and the precautions you will need to take.

PART A
Balloon rockets

The task
Your task is to design an efficient balloon rocket which will be propelled along a length of nylon fishing line. The efficiency of the rocket will be tested in two ways:
- how far the rocket goes along the nylon fishing line
- how fast the rocket goes in the first 5 metres.
You are to use simple materials in your test—balloons, drinking straws, adhesive tape and nylon fishing line.

Discussion
1 Compile class results of the two tests.
2 Which design features are important in making a balloon rocket?
3 What caused the motion of the rocket?
4 How well would your rocket go in space? Explain.
5 How would you design your rocket to test whether altering the size of the jet (where the air comes out of the balloon) has an effect on the speed of the rocket? Try it!

PART B
Water rockets

In this part of the experiment, your task is to find out which variables affect the motion of a water rocket.

Use the diagram below to build a water rocket. Your teacher will help you fit a car valve extension tube through a rubber stopper. (You can also purchase commercial water rockets.)

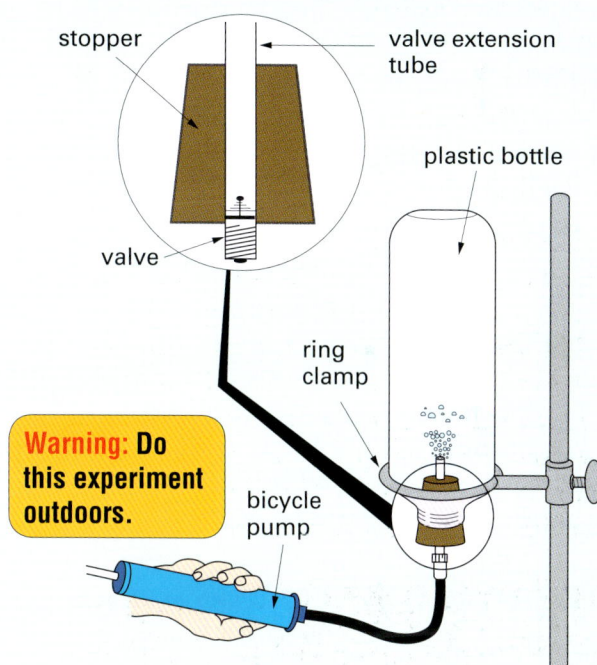

Warning: Do this experiment outdoors.

Experiment with the water rocket to find out how the following variables affect its motion.
- the amount of water in the bottle
- the size and shape of the container

Discussion
1 Write a report of your findings.
2 Explain in detail what caused the motion of the water rocket. In which ways is this similar to the motion of the balloon rocket? In which ways is it different?
3 Is water necessary for the operation of the water rocket? Test your prediction.

Rocket motion

In Part A of the experiment the balloon rocket moved forwards (the reaction force) because air was forced out of the balloon in the opposite direction (the action force). The water rocket in Part B shot upwards (the reaction force) because the compressed air in the bottle forced water out of the mouth in the other direction (the action force).

In a space rocket, the fuel burns in a combustion chamber. The burning fuel produces hot gases which are forced out of the nozzle at great speed. The force of the escaping gases produces an equal and opposite reaction which pushes the rocket upwards. This force is called the **thrust**. Applying Newton's second law of motion (F = ma), the thrust of a rocket is equal to the mass of the escaping gases multiplied by the acceleration of the gases.

The net force accelerating the rocket from its launch pad is the thrust minus the weight of the rocket.

net force = thrust of engines − weight

For example, a 2 000 000 kg rocket has engines that develop a thrust of 69 600 000 N. What is the acceleration of the rocket at lift-off?

Weight of rocket	=	2 000 000 kg × 9.8 m/s^2
	=	19 600 000 N
Thrust of engines	=	69 600 000 N
Net force	=	thrust − weight of rocket
	=	69 600 000 − 19 600 000 N
	=	50 000 000 N
acceleration	=	$\dfrac{\text{net force}}{\text{mass of rocket}}$
	=	$\dfrac{50\,000\,000 \text{ N}}{2\,000\,000 \text{ kg}}$
	=	25 m/s^2

Space engineers design engines that develop as much thrust as possible, while at the same time they try to reduce the weight of the rocket.

Rocket engines

All rocket engines work on the same principle: they burn fuel to produce fast-moving exhaust gases which push the rocket forwards.

As well as the fuel, space rockets have to carry a source of oxygen because there is no air in space in which to burn the fuel. There are two types of rocket engine—the *solid-fuel engine* and the *liquid-fuel engine*.

The solid-fuel engine uses a solid fuel mixed with an *oxidiser* much like a fireworks skyrocket. A spark ignites the mixture and the explosive reaction produces gases which are forced out of the engine's nozzle. The solid-fuel engine is very simple in construction and very powerful for its weight, and is used mainly in booster rockets to lift heavy payloads into space. However, like the skyrocket, it suffers one major disadvantage—once ignited it cannot be extinguished until the fuel has been used up.

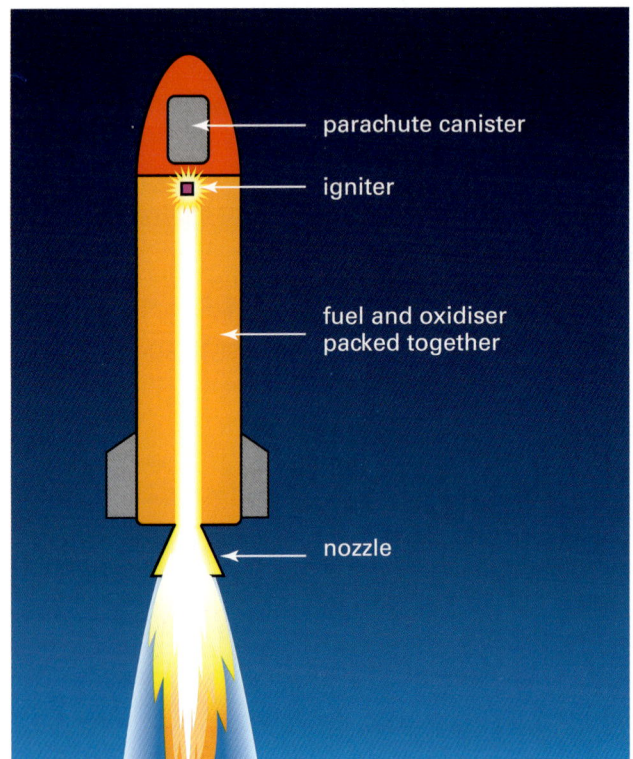

Fig 11 A solid-fuel rocket engine has solid fuel and oxidiser packed together. When ignited, the fuel burns, sending high speed gases out through the nozzle. The parachute enables the rocket to be recovered for reuse.

The liquid-fuel engine needs complicated pipework and pumps to force the liquid hydrogen fuel and the oxidiser (liquid oxygen) into the combustion chamber. Here they are ignited and burn explosively. The advantage of this type of engine is that it can be throttled back, or turned on and off, to control the rocket's speed.

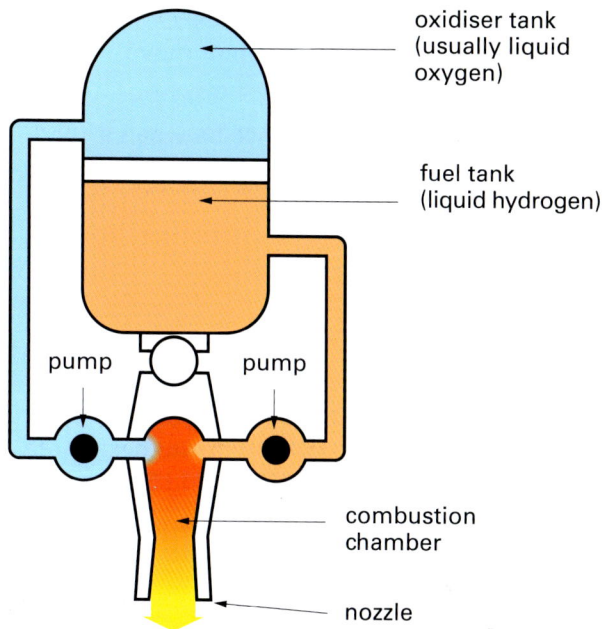

Fig 12 A liquid-fuel rocket engine. This engine is more complicated and expensive to build than the solid-fuel engine, but its thrust can be controlled.

Rocket designs

Since gravity is greatest at the Earth's surface, the most powerful engines in a rocket have to be used at lift-off. Space rockets usually use two to four solid-fuel booster engines alongside the main liquid-fuel engine. However, two minutes after lift-off the solid-fuel boosters have used up all their fuel. To reduce the mass of the rocket, engineers design parts of the rocket to fall away when they are no longer needed. Most rockets have this design and are called multistage rockets.

About 10 minutes after lift-off the main rocket engines also run out of fuel. This first stage, which is the largest part, then detaches and burns up in the atmosphere as it falls to Earth. Engines in the second stage then ignite and carry the rocket further into space.

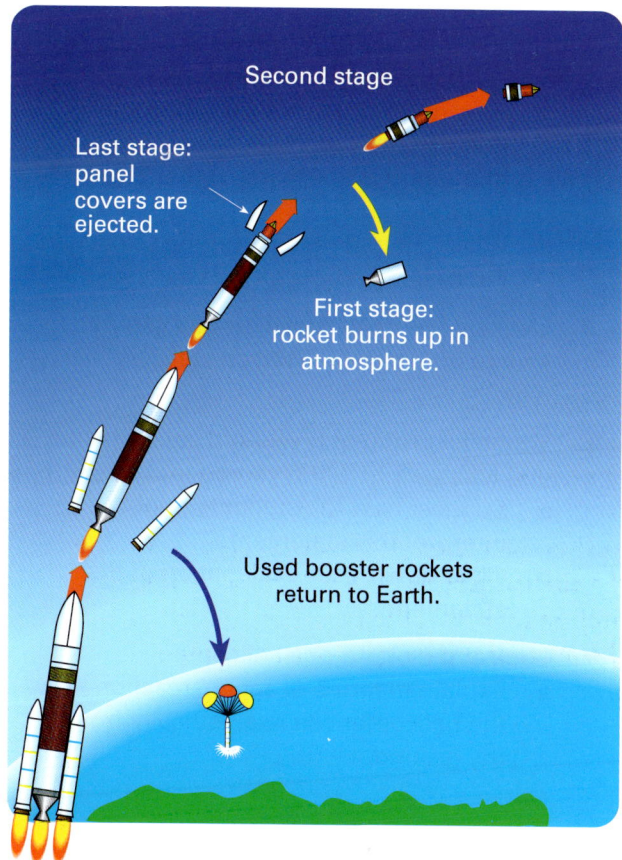

Fig 13 Sections of a multistage rocket detach and fall away after use. This helps to keep the mass of the rocket as small as possible while gaining maximum acceleration.

Check!

1 a You simultaneously drop a 2 kg rock and a 10 kg rock from a high cliff. Why should they hit the ground at the same time?
  b You then drop a piece of paper and a small pebble from the cliff at the same time. Will they hit the ground at the same time? Explain.

2 How does Newton's third law of motion explain how a rocket moves?

3 A bag of sand is attached to a spring balance. The dial reads 147 N. What is the mass of the bag of sand?

4 Look at question 1 in Getting Started.
  a What is the mass of the person?
  b How much does this person weigh?
  c Suggest why weighing scales are graduated in kilograms rather than newtons.
  d Why does the reading on the scales increase when the lift moves upwards?

5 Unlike jet aircraft, space rockets carry a source of oxygen as well as fuel. Explain why.

6 You tell a group of 8-year-old students that you lose weight when you go into space.
  a Suggest how the students might interpret this statement.
  b Write down your explanation of the statement.

7 Look at the photo of a helicopter.
  a Explain in terms of action–reaction how the helicopter can rise vertically from the ground.

  b How does the helicopter move forwards?

8 a Explain the difference between a solid-fuel rocket engine and a liquid-fuel engine.
  b The last stage of a multistage rocket contains a small liquid-fuel engine. Why is the engine small, and why does it use liquid fuel and not a solid fuel?

9 In this chapter and the last chapter you have learnt Newton's three laws of motion. In your own words write down these three laws. Check pages 117, 122 and 310.

challenge

1 A man has a mass of 85 kg. Use the table on page 309 to calculate:
  a his weight on Earth
  b his weight 1000 km above the Earth

2 The rockets that carried the Apollo missions into space had a thrust-to-weight ratio of 12:1.
  a What does this statement mean?
  b Suggest what would happen to the acceleration of the rocket if the thrust-to-weight ratio was larger.

3 A lunar lander of mass 3000 kg lands on the Moon's surface. When they are ready for lift-off, the astronauts fire the lander's rockets which develop a thrust of 15 300 N. If $g = 1.6$ m/s^2 on the Moon, calculate the acceleration with which the lander leaves the Moon's surface.

4 The Space Shuttle and the booster rockets pictured on page 307 have a combined mass of 2 200 000 kg. The acceleration on lift-off is maintained at 2.5 g for 50 seconds (g = acceleration due to gravity on Earth).
  a Calculate the net upwards force on the Shuttle at lift-off.

  b Find the thrust developed by the engines.

5 The graph below shows a plot of weight versus mass for a number of objects. Use the graph to work out whether the readings were taken on the Moon ($g = 1.6$ m/s^2), on Mercury ($g = 4.1$ m/s^2) or on Saturn ($g = 10.8$ m/s^2). Explain how you arrived at your answer.

6 Leon stands in a lift and hangs a 5 kg bag of potatoes on a spring balance. The dial reads 42.5 N. Describe the motion of the lift. As a challenge calculate the acceleration of the lift.

13.2 Orbiting the Earth

If you look at the Moon on successive nights, you will see that its position in the sky changes. This is because of the Earth's rotation, and also because the moon revolves around the Earth in its orbit. An **orbit** is a path taken by an object as it moves around another object.

Satellites

Objects that orbit planets are called **satellites**. The moon is Earth's natural satellite. The first artificial satellite to orbit the Earth, called *Sputnik 1*, was launched in October 1957 by the then Soviet Union. Since then more than 4000 artificial satellites have been launched into orbit. Hundreds of communications satellites relay radio and television information between the continents on Earth 24 hours a day.

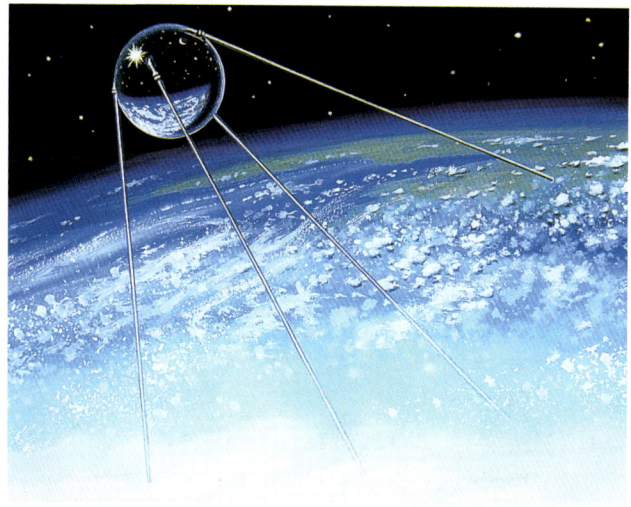

Fig 16 *Sputnik 1* was the Earth's first artificial satellite. It was relatively small with a mass of 84 kg and a diameter of 53 cm. Its four aerials beamed back information about the temperature and density of the upper atmosphere.

Investigate
31 ORBITS

Aim

To use a model to show the forces acting on a body in orbit.

Materials

- 1.5 m length of nylon fishing line
- plastic tubing (about 15 cm long),
- rubber stopper with a hole in it
- brass hanger and some brass masses

Planning and Safety Check

- Carefully read through the investigation. Then tell your partner what you have to do, what you have to record and what safety precautions you have to take.
- It is best to do this investigation outdoors.

Method

1 Tie the rubber stopper to the end of the fishing line. Thread the other end of the fishing line through the plastic tube.

2 Hold the end of the fishing line below the tube and whirl the stopper around in a circle as shown in the diagram below. Now let the fishing line go.

In which direction did the stopper travel? Draw a sketch to show this.

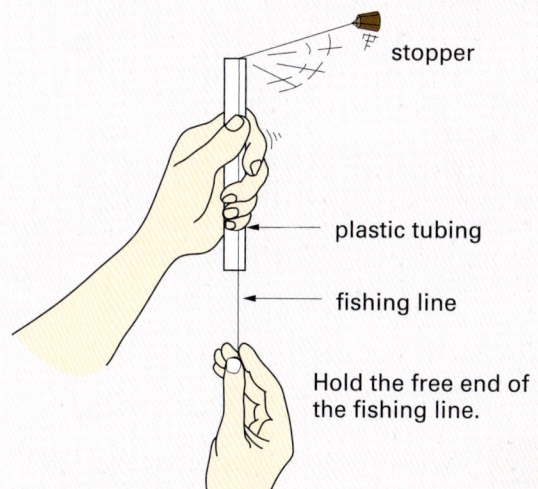

stopper

plastic tubing

fishing line

Hold the free end of the fishing line.

3 Thread the fishing line through the tubing again. Then tie the brass hanger to the free end.

4 Add some masses to the hanger and whirl the stopper so that it orbits at a constant distance and the masses do not move up or down. This may take a little practice.

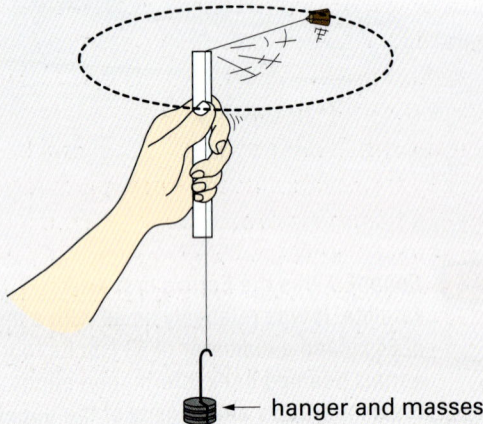

← hanger and masses

📋 Record the radius of the orbit.

5 Now speed up the orbiting stopper.
📋 Record what happens to the masses.

6 Add masses to the hanger so that the stopper orbits at the same radius orbit as in Step 4.

7 What will happen if you decrease the speed of the orbiting stopper? Test your prediction.

Discussion

1 Why did the stopper fly off when you let the string go in Step 2?

2 What happens to the rotating stopper when its speed increases? How could you keep it rotating at the same radius of orbit?

3 What keeps a spacecraft in a circular path when it is in orbit?

In the investigation you just did, you should have concluded that the revolving stopper is being pulled towards the centre of the circle by the force along the fishing line. This force keeps changing the *direction* of the stopper's motion. And if this force disappears the stopper flies off in a straight line. The stopper is not pulled in towards the tubing, because it has sufficient orbital speed (inertia) to keep it in 'orbit'.

In the same way, the gravitational force pulls an orbiting satellite towards the centre of the Earth. The satellite does not fall to Earth, because it has sufficient speed to stay in orbit.

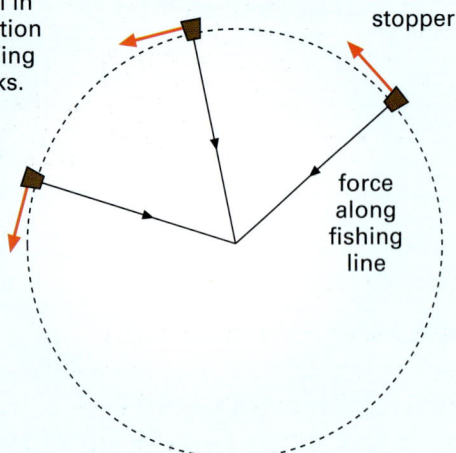

The stopper will travel in this direction if the fishing line breaks.

stopper

force along fishing line

Fig 19 The inwards pulling force along the fishing line constantly changes the direction of the stopper's motion.

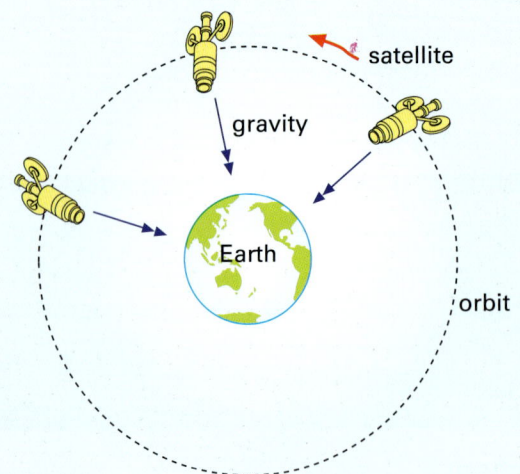

satellite

gravity

Earth

orbit

Fig 20 The satellite is being pulled towards Earth by the force of gravity, but its motion (inertia) keeps it in orbit.

Types of orbits

You found out earlier that the Earth's gravity is strongest at the surface and decreases with altitude. (In outer space gravity is zero.) This means that satellites in a low Earth orbit will experience a stronger gravitational pull than satellites in higher orbits. To overcome this problem, satellites in low Earth orbits have to have a greater orbital speed, otherwise they fall back to Earth. In general, the higher the altitude of the satellite the slower its orbital speed.

Low Earth Orbits

Low Earth Orbits (called LEOs) are usually at altitudes of about 400 km. At this height, 99.9% of the Earth's atmosphere is below you, so satellites avoid the problem of friction with the Earth's atmosphere. LEO satellites move at high speeds of about 8000 m/s, and include the Earth-monitoring and 'spy' satellites. Because of their low altitude, LEO satellites can take very clear pictures of objects as small as 3 m across on the Earth's surface. They usually have a much shorter life than other satellites because even the tiny amounts of gases in the upper atmosphere gradually slow them down. As the satellite's

Fig 21 During the Iraq war, low orbit US spy satellites were used to pinpoint military targets, in this case in Baghdad.

speed decreases it loses altitude and eventually falls to Earth where it burns up in the more dense atmosphere.

LEO satellites can be linked to form information networks in space. For example, twenty-four LEO satellites have been placed above the Earth to form the Global Positioning System (GPS). Sailors, airline pilots or even motorists driving along central Australian outback roads can find their position on the Earth's surface using a small portable receiver.

Even though LEO satellites have a much shorter life than high altitude ones, placing satellites in the lower orbit is much cheaper. This is because large, powerful and very expensive rockets are needed to launch the high altitude satellites. Sometimes the high altitude satellites are 'parked' in low orbit, before they are boosted into higher more useful altitudes.

Fig 22 This scientist in Antarctica is using a hand-held GPS receiver to accurately plot his position.

Polar orbiting satellites

Polar orbits are special low Earth orbits which carry satellites in a circle over the North Pole and South Pole. These high-speed satellites complete about 14 revolutions of the planet every 24 hours. As the satellite revolves from pole to pole, the Earth rotates beneath it. In this way, the satellite 'sees' every part of the Earth's surface at relatively close range.

Geostationary orbits

A satellite placed in orbit 36 000 km above the Earth's equator takes exactly one day to complete an orbit. During this time, the Earth also turns once on its axis. This means that the satellite remains over the same point on the Earth's surface. Orbits at this altitude are called **geostationary orbits** or sometimes, geosynchronous orbits. Satellites in this orbit travel at about 3200 m/s, less than half the speed of the LEO satellites.

Geostationary satellites are used to beam everything from commercial radio and television broadcasts to navigational and weather information. However, there are so many satellites in this orbit that its use is now governed by international regulations.

Aussat and Intelsat satellites relay TV channels to subscribers all over Australia. To receive these broadcasts, subscribers have a satellite dish pointing towards a geostationary satellite above the equator.

Fig 24 An image from the GMS Japan geostationary satellite positioned in orbit to the north of Australia

Fig 23 A satellite dish on this school is used to receive TV channels from geostationary satellites.

The weather information that is continuously beamed down to Australian weather forecasters comes from one of five geostationary satellites that form a network around the equator. The GMS Japan satellite is positioned over the equator to the north of Papua New Guinea. This satellite sends information and pictures to forecasters who then send them on to radio and TV stations as well as newspapers.

WEBwatch

1 Weather satellites

You might like to look at some images from weather satellites. Go to www.scienceworld.net.au and follow the links to the websites below.

JCU MetSat

The lastest GMS Japan satellite image of Australia can be found on this website.

Australian Region Satellite Images

This Bureau of Meteorology site provides satellite images and state-by-state weather forecasts in Australia.

2 Google Earth

Would you like to see a satellite's view of your neighbourhood, or even a close-up of your house? Go to www.scienceworld.net.au and follow the links to **Google Earth**.

You can use this link to download the Google Earth application onto your computer. Then you can scan almost everywhere in the world and zoom in to see details of cities, mountains, lakes and oceans.

The Space Shuttle

The Space Shuttle is a reusable rocket about the size of a small airliner. Its cargo bay is large enough to carry a school bus. The original purpose of the Space Shuttle was to carry large instruments into space at a far cheaper cost than by conventional rocket. For example, the Space Shuttle can carry thirteen times the payload of a conventional Delta multistage rocket at only one and a half times the cost.

The main role of a Shuttle mission is to place satellites into orbit, retrieve and repair damaged satellites, and transport crew and parts to and from the International Space Station (ISS). For example, in August 2006, *Atlantis* delivered a second set of solar panels that will double the power output on the ISS.

After the mission, which lasts for up to 10 days, the Shuttle is ready for re-entry. Some of its 44 small rockets fire to slow the orbiter down from an orbital speed of 28 000 km/h. At an altitude of 120 km friction begins to generate a large amount of heat. The temperature on some of the Shuttle's surfaces can reach close to 1500°C, as shown in the diagram below.

The lightweight aluminium shell of the Shuttle is covered with thousands of heat-insulating tiles. The orbiter enters the atmosphere belly first, with the nose, the front of the wings and tail and the underside exposed to most of the heating. The tiles are designed to perform 100 missions before they are replaced.

There are four main types of tiles, each of them being able to withstand different temperatures. For example, composite carbon tiles can withstand temperatures of 1650°C before breaking down. These tiles are thick and reasonably heavy, and are costly to make. The tiles are designed to re-radiate heat so quickly that a tile heated in a kiln and glowing white-hot at 1250°C can be held in your hand 10 seconds after being removed from the kiln.

Fig 25 During re-entry, the nose, the front of the wings and tail, and the underside of the Space Shuttle are exposed to most of the heating.

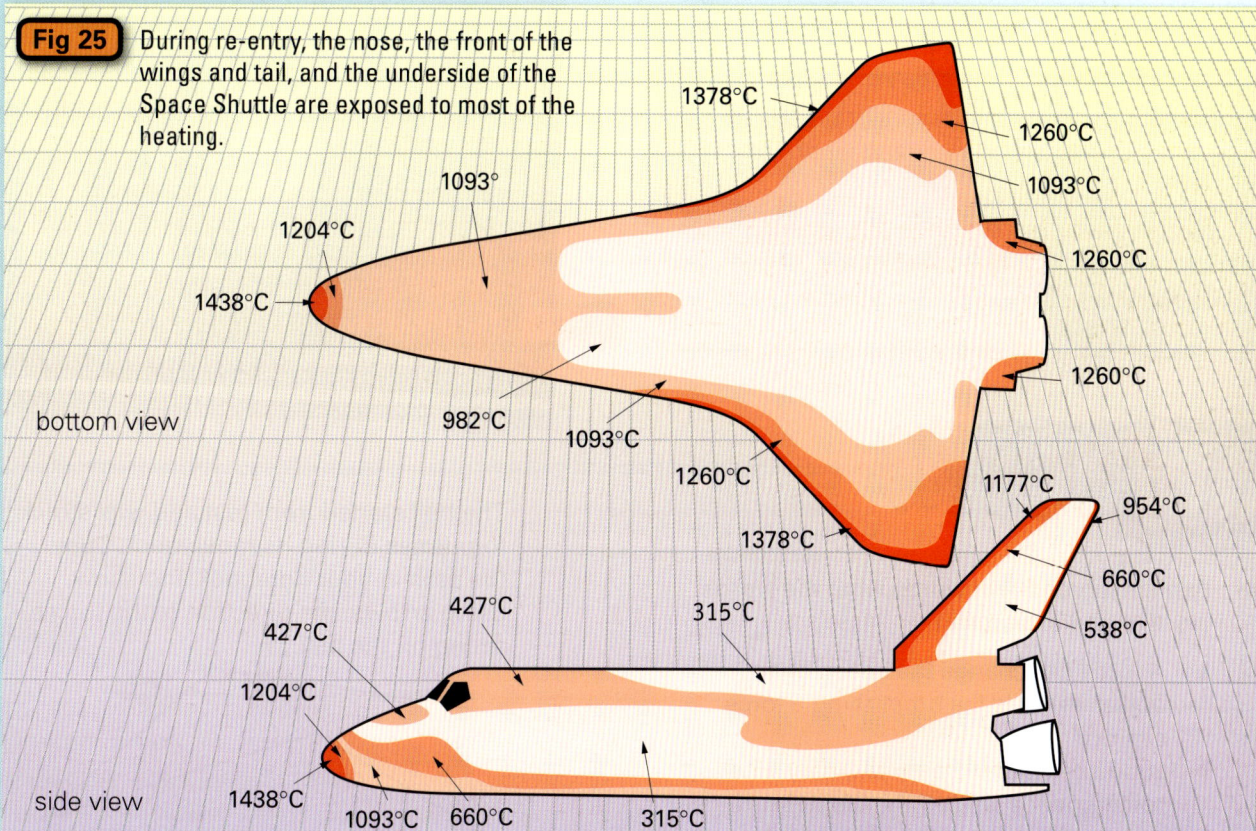

Activity

In this activity, you need to imagine you are a space engineer. Your task is to determine where each of the four types of heat-insulating tiles will have to be placed on the Space Shuttle.

1 Trace the bottom-view and side-view outlines of the Shuttle on the previous page.

2 Use the information in the data table and the heat contour diagrams to indicate the position of each type of tile on your orbiter outlines.

3 When determining the distribution of tiles, remember that the tiles with the best heat insulation properties also are the heaviest and are the most expensive.

Type of material used in tile	Breakdown temp (°C)
heat resistance felt	370
light-weight silica	650
heavy-weight silica	1350
composite carbon	1650

✍ Make a list of all the factors you have to take into account when deciding where to place the tiles.

✍ Suggest why a metal skin (for example titanium alloy which was used in the *Apollo* spacecraft) is not used on the Shuttle.

WEBwatch

Go to www.scienceworld.net.au and follow the links to the websites below.

Office of Space Operations

Gives comprehensive information on the Space Shuttle, International Space Station, Questions and Answers, meet the space crews of the Shuttle missions and details of space missions.

The future of flight?

Gives details of the Crew Exploration Vehicle design by Lockheed Martin which is to replace the Space Shuttle.

Crew Exploration Vehicle

Has information on the proposed Crew Exploration Vehicle, and has links to other sites.

How the Orion CEV will work

Has interesting information on the proposed Crew Exploration Vehicle and launch rockets.

Fig 26 The Orion Crew Exploration Vehicle

Check!

1 Explain in your own words what the words *revolve* and *orbit* mean.

2 a A force can change the speed of an object. What is the other thing a force can do?

b Leon sketched the path taken by a ball rolling over a smooth horizontal surface.

The ball started from rest and was struck four times during its movement. Copy the path in your notebook and show, using arrows, the direction of the forces acting on the ball.

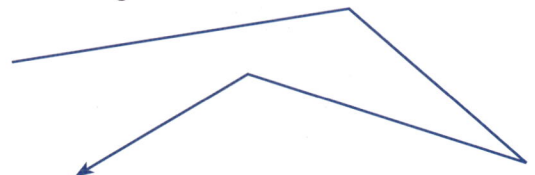

3 Mariela whirls a tennis ball attached to a string around her head in a horizontal circle.

   a Explain in terms of force why the tennis ball moves in a circle.

   b What would happen to the ball if the string broke?

4 What is a geostationary satellite? How is it different from other types of satellites?

5 **a** A low Earth orbit (LEO) is usually about 400 km above the Earth's surface but very rarely below this altitude. Why?

   b Why do satellites in LEOs have to have high orbital speeds?

   c What is the main advantage of placing a satellite in LEO?

6 How is a polar orbiting satellite different from a geostationary satellite? What are the advantages of placing satellites in polar orbits?

7 What was the purpose of building the Space Shuttle?

8 **a** What causes the temperature on the Shuttle's surface to rise on re-entry?

   b Which parts of the Space Shuttle are reusable, and which have to be replaced before the next launch?

challenge

1 The map shows the five overlapping areas serviced by the geostationary weather satellites.

   a Which satellite's data would be used to determine the weather patterns for each of the following—Sydney, Perth, New York, Singapore and Hawaii?

   b What is the advantage of a geostationary satellite?

   c Why are these satellites unsuitable for obtaining weather data about Norway or Alaska? Suggest a way of obtaining data about these regions.

   d Geostationary satellites send weather data to Earth 24 hours a day. Suggest how they obtain weather data at night.

2 The tennis ball that Mariela is whirling around her head in Check 3 above does 10 revolutions in 8 seconds.

   a If the string is 2 metres long, how fast is the ball travelling in its circular path?

   b Calculate how long the ball will take to do 10 revolutions if it travels at the same speed but the string is 3 metres long.

3 It is cheaper to launch a satellite-carrying rocket in an easterly direction than in the opposite direction. Suggest why.

4 A satellite is moving with an orbital speed of 8000 m/s in a low Earth orbit at an altitude of 450 km. Assuming the Earth is circular with a radius of 6380 km:

   a calculate the time it takes for the satellite to orbit the Earth

   b find out how many times the satellite orbits the Earth in 24 hours.

5 *Columbia* was the first in NASA's fleet of Space Shuttles. It was launched on 9 April 1981 and landed again two days later. However, on 1 February 2003, it disintegrated on re-entry and all seven astronauts perished. Use your internet browser to research this Space Shuttle, and write a short story about its achievements.

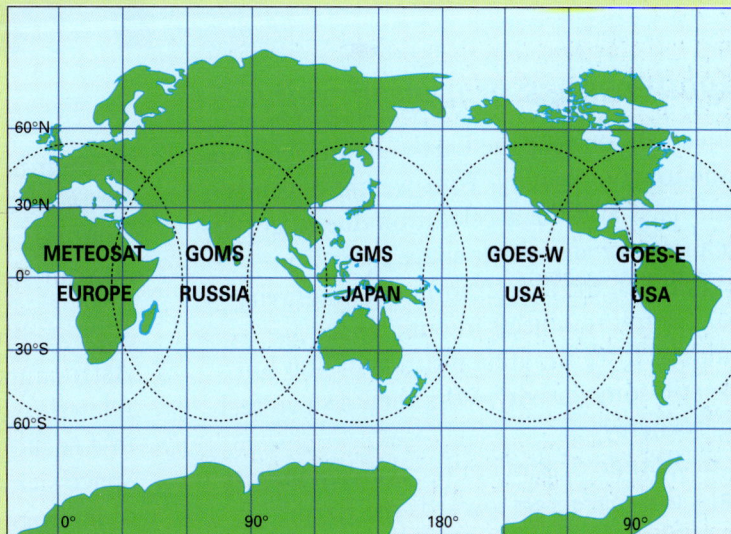

13.3 Living in space

As the giant rocket blasts off from the launch pad, the astronauts aboard the space module feel the effects of the tremendous force of the rocket engines. One hour later the space module is in orbit 400 km above the equator. At this altitude the astronauts feel 'weightless'. Outside the space module there is no air and no protection from the Sun's radiation. Let's look at some of the problems of living in space.

Fig 29 An astronaut catches a weightless sandwich during a snack on board the Space Shuttle *Atlantis*.

Weightlessness or microgravity

All objects on or near the Earth are attracted to it by the force of gravity. Your weight depends on your mass and the acceleration due to gravity. When an object is in outer space there is no gravity; that is, the acceleration due to gravity is zero. Therefore objects in outer space are weightless. However, at an altitude of 400 km there is still some gravity. Why then do you feel weightless here?

At an altitude of 400 km the reduced gravity still pulls the spacecraft towards the Earth. However, the spacecraft is moving fast enough to keep it moving in a circular orbit. So the spacecraft and everything inside it is effectively in free fall. This is why astronauts feel weightless when in orbit.

Weightlessness is not really the correct word for this effect. Objects in orbit still have some weight, although very small. **Microgravity** is a more precise word that describes the lack of weight.

Advantages of microgravity

You can move in any direction with just a little push in the opposite direction. You can work upside down without the feeling of blood rushing to your head. And you can sleep horizontally or vertically, although you have to be strapped into your bed to avoid floating away when you move in your sleep.

Disadvantages of microgravity

Astronauts often get space sickness. This is related to the motion sickness some people feel in a rocking boat or when travelling in a car. Space sickness may also be caused by the effects of microgravity on the balancing organs inside the ear.

Eating and going to the toilet also have their problems in space. You have to drink all liquids through a straw from a closed container. In an open cup the liquids form drops and float around the compartment. Food is packed in individual serving pouches on trays that have magnets on them to hold them firmly on a table or wall or wherever you wish to eat.

In the Shuttle toilet, air draws the faeces and urine into a bowl underneath the seat. Blades shred the solid wastes, which are then dried when exposed to the vacuum of space. Urine and other waste water is periodically dumped overboard where the material instantly vaporises in space.

Air and water

The air in the crew compartment of the spacecraft is similar to that on Earth. The air pressure is maintained at 1000 hectopascals (1000 hPa) —the same as at sea level.

The composition of the compartment's air is 79% nitrogen and 21% oxygen. Carbon dioxide, given off as a waste product of respiration, is monitored very closely. An excess of CO_2 in the air can make you drowsy and sleepy and this could be dangerous for the crew. Canisters filled with lithium hydroxide absorb the CO_2. The CO_2 reacts with the lithium hydroxide to form lithium carbonate and water vapour. Other canisters filled with activated charcoal absorb odours from the compartment.

Electrical power in the spacecraft is generated by fuel cells. In these devices, oxygen and hydrogen are chemically combined to produce electricity and about 3 litres of water per hour as a by-product. The water is stored and is used for drinking, for the toilet and for the air control system, which maintains the relative humidity at about 55%. Any excess water is dumped overboard where it vaporises and disperses into space.

Maintaining fitness

When you have been in space for a period of time, the microgravity affects your body in a number of ways.

1. One of the most noticeable effects is that the liquids in your body redistribute themselves. The liquids in the upper part of your body increase, causing your face to puff up and some stuffiness in your sinuses.
2. Your posture alters with the low gravity. When you relax, your arms float away from your body, your knees bend and your toes point, making walking difficult. To overcome this, you can wear suction cups on your shoes.
3. The microgravity affects your heart in a similar way to being bedridden for a long period of time. Your heart and pulse rates decrease, as does your blood pressure. To overcome this problem you have to exercise for at least 30 minutes each day on the treadmill or rowing machine.
4. The most serious problem for space travellers is the demineralisation of bones. Weightbearing bones lose calcium and phosphorus during long periods of microgravity, and this causes a weakening of the bones in the skeleton.
5. Long periods of microgravity also decrease muscle tissue. The Russian cosmonaut Yuri Romanenko lost 15% of the muscle tissue in his legs during an 11-month stay aboard the Mir space station.

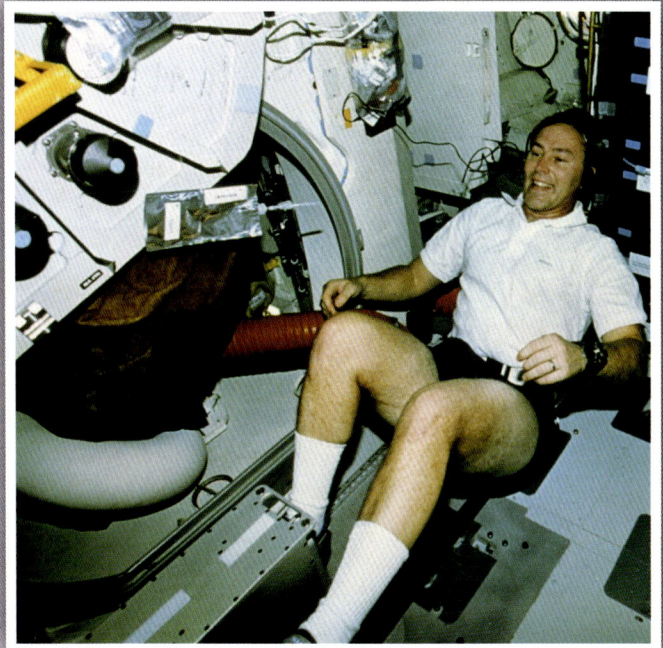

Fig 30 Astronaut Jerry Ross exercising on a bicycle ergonometer on the Space Shuttle *Atlantis*.

Heat and radiation

At an altitude of 400 km the temperature in space can be as high as 250°C in the sunlight and as low as −150°C in the shade. The crew compartment of the spacecraft is maintained at a constant temperature and pressure, but any space walks require special clothing. To overcome the extreme temperature changes in space, the undergarments of the spacesuits are equipped with water-cooling and ventilation.

On Earth, the atmosphere absorbs much of the harmful high-energy radiation from the Sun, but in space there is no such protection. This radiation can cause cancer and changes to the chromosomes in your sex cells. Spacesuits therefore have to be designed to reflect this dangerous radiation.

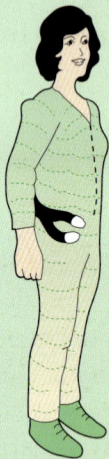

1 The spacesuit's under-garment is made from Spandex mesh with plastic tubing woven into it. The tubing circulates cool water from the life-support backpack.

2 The outer suit comes in two sections and can be put on in less than 5 minutes. The suit contains oxygen-filled pressure bladders that help to keep its shape.

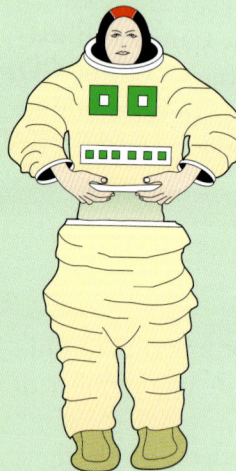

3 When the torso section is put on, the cooling tubes from the undergarment are connected to the tubes that flow to the life-support backpack. The trousers are then joined to the torso section by a rigid aluminium ring.

4 The life-support backpack contains oxygen, water, batteries, and communication equipment. The space-suit is designed to be re-used and should last 15 years.

Activity

Astronaut's diary

Use the information on pages 322–324 to write a 24-hour diary in the life of an astronaut orbiting the Earth in a space station. For this task, work in a group of three or four people. Use the following ideas in your diary.

- How many hours do you allocate for sleeping, exercising, working and relaxing?
- List the difficulties you face when doing everyday activities in microgravity. For example, washing, cleaning your teeth, eating and drinking, and using the toilet.
- What are the problems of working in a spacesuit and doing jobs in space?
- Describe the experiences at lift-off from Earth and in re-entry.

Space stations

In early 1971 the Russian spacecraft *Salyut 1* became the first space station to be put into Earth orbit. Since that time a number of improvements have been made to make them more liveable for the astronauts who spend an extended period of time in them.

The unmanned *Salyut 6* space station was sent into orbit in 1978. Two months later, two cosmonauts on board a Soyuz spacecraft docked with the Salyut space station and entered it via the docking bay. Three months later they were visited by two other cosmonauts in another Soyuz supply vehicle. This was the first time a space station had been supplied with fresh provisions, and unwanted materials removed.

In 1988 Musa Manarov and Vladimir Titov became the first people to spend more than a full year away from Earth on board the Mir space station. But after nearly 15 years in space Mir crashed back to Earth in March 2001.

The International Space Station (ISS)

In 1998 a new space station was born. On 20 November, space scientists from 16 countries throughout the world watched as the Russian Proton rocket carried the first section of the International Space Station (ISS) to an orbit 400 km above the Earth. The ISS is the largest international space project in history.

The ISS is in orbit at an altitude of 360 km, and orbits the Earth every 92 minutes. By June 2006 it had completed over 42 000 orbits since its launch.

In 2006, additional solar panels were installed to increase electrical power, and further modules will be added until it is complete some time in 2012.

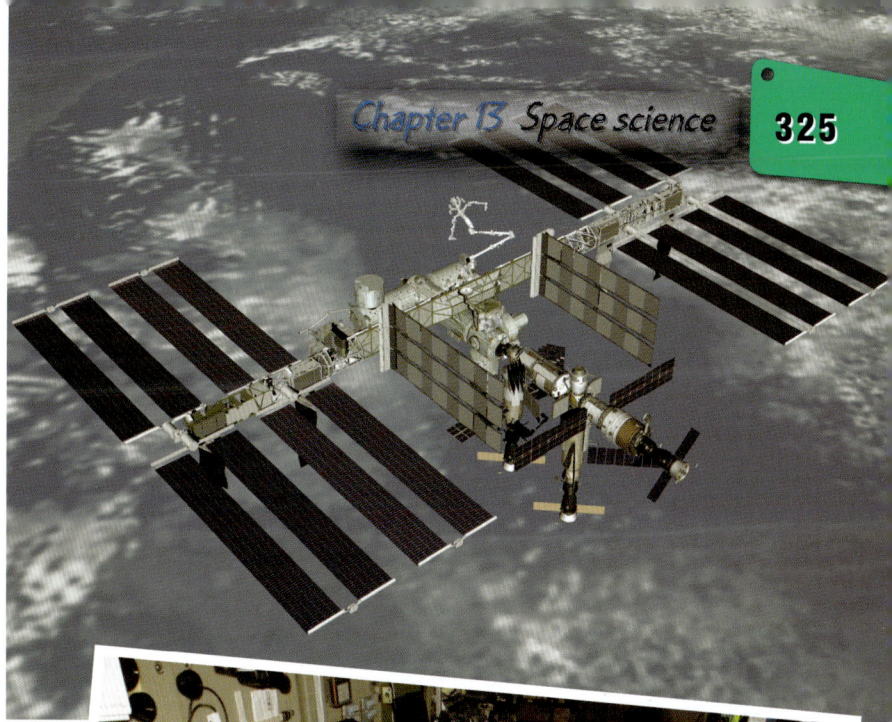

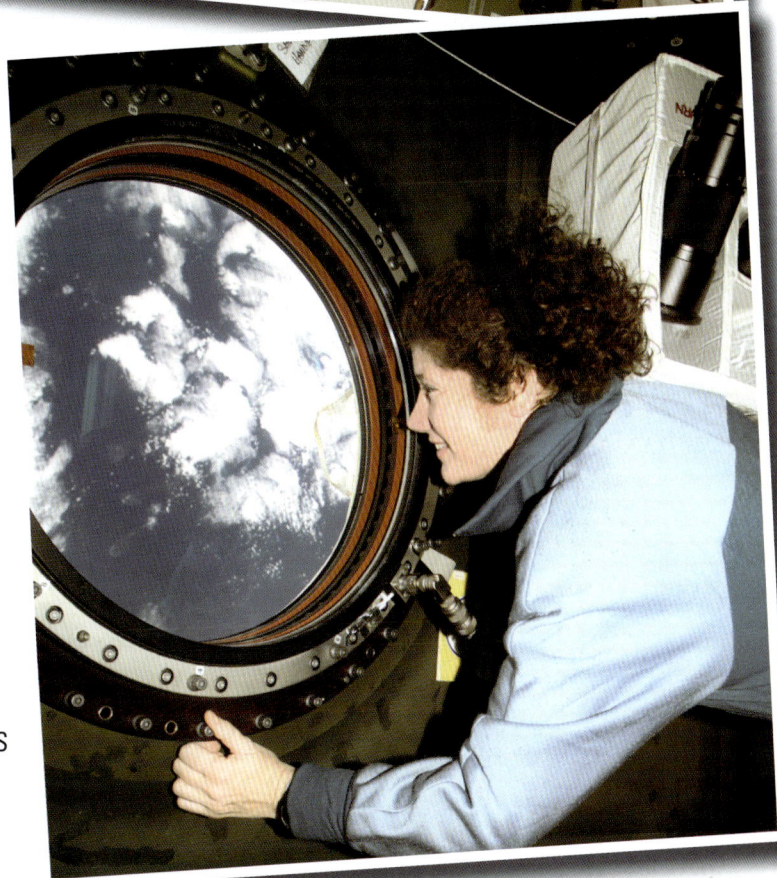

Fig 32 (*top*) The International Space Station in orbit 360 km above the Earth's surface
(*middle*) Russian ISS commander Pavel Vinogradov and other crew members in the Zvedna Service Module
(*bottom*) US astronaut flight engineer Susan Helms looking at Earth from a window in the ISS

Artificial gravity

The one factor that causes most problems for humans in space is the lack of gravity. Serious health problems such as the demineralisation of bones, weakening of the heart and loss of muscle tissue occur when people spend long periods of time in space. Many of the experiments on board the ISS are designed to look at these problems, but they may only be solved if artificial gravity can be created in space stations. How can space stations be designed to create artificial gravity? Try the activity below.

Fig 33 An artist's impression of a space station spinning around a central axis to create artificial gravity

Activity

Your task is to design a space station that will generate artificial gravity and will have facilities for an extended stay by the people on board. Use the internet, books and magazines to help you with this task.

Use the statements below as a guide in your design. As well as describing your design, write a report detailing the various features of the space station and how its inhabitants can survive in space.

- Describe the overall shape of the space station.
- Is it necessary to create artificial gravity in the space station? If not, how will the people on board overcome microgravity problems?
- How will light and electricity be provided for the occupants?
- How will the space station be built? Remember the present-day Shuttle can carry a maximum load of 20 tonnes.
- How will the space station be supplied with food, water, oxygen and fuel, and how will unwanted materials be removed?
- How will the space station be protected from radiation and from meteorites?

WEBwatch

Go to www.scienceworld.net.au and follow the links to the websites below.

Inside the space station
Has a description and tour through the different modules in the ISS.

International Space Station
Comprehensive information about the ISS.

Life on the Space Station
Interactive tour of the ISS, as well as an interview with an astronaut, and links to other sites.

Space Station
NASA's space station site.

Science in action

Andy Thomas: Australian astronaut

Andy Thomas is the only Australian to have orbited the Earth. He began his training with NASA in 1992 and flew his first flight into space on board the Space Shuttle *Endeavour* in May 1996.

In 1998 he spent 141 days and 2250 orbits of the Earth aboard the Mir space station and was the last US-trained astronaut to stay on Mir.

He blasted off into space again in 2001 on board the Space Shuttle *Discovery* along with three other crew, and headed towards the International Space Station. Three Space Station crew on board *Discovery* replaced three others who had been working on the ISS. Andy and

fellow astronaut Paul Richards had to walk in space to attach a platform and pump to the outside of one of the modules on the ISS. In 2005 Andy visited the ISS again on board *Discovery*.

For more information about Andy Thomas, go to www.scienceworld.net.au and follow the links to these websites:
Andrew S. W. Thomas
Mission Specialist Andy Thomas

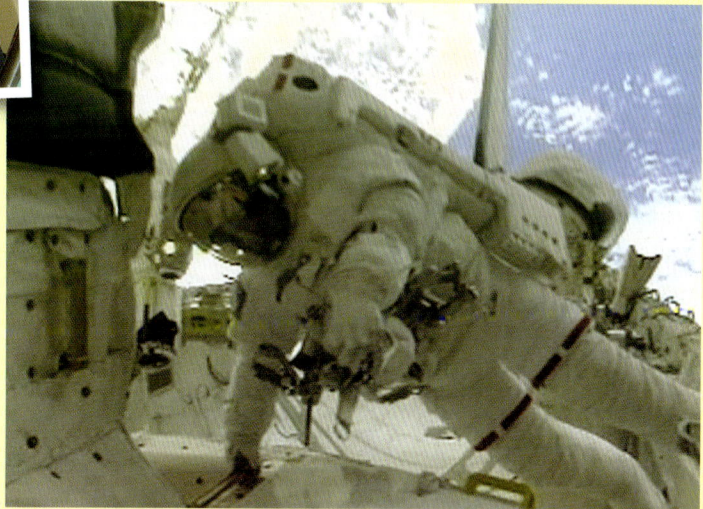

Fig 35 Andy Thomas gathers equipment in the cargo bay of Space Shuttle *Discovery* at the end of his space walk in March 2001.

Check!

1 What is meant by free fall? Where on the Earth's surface could you demonstrate free fall?

2 Explain the term *microgravity*. Are there any places in the solar system that would have zero gravity? Explain.

3 The photo on the right shows a handwashing station inside the Space Shuttle. Suggest reasons for the design of this piece of equipment.

4 In which ways is the air in a spacecraft's crew compartment similar to the air on Earth? In which ways is it different?

Fig 36 Washing your hands on the Space Shuttle

5 All items of equipment, including knives and forks, pens and scissors, that are used during a space mission have small Velcro pads on them. What is the purpose of these pads?

6 Why is the level of carbon dioxide in the air of the crew compartment monitored carefully?

7 The fuel cells in spacecraft produce electricity when hydrogen and oxygen combine. The two gases would take up a huge amount of space on the spacecraft. Suggest how space engineers have overcome this problem.

8 You have put on your spacesuit and are now ready to go outside into free space to begin repairs to a damaged satellite. Write a short story about how you would get out of the spacecraft, and what it might be like outside in space.

challenge

1 The manned manoeuvring unit or MMU allows an astronaut to move from a spacecraft to other places, say, another orbiting satellite. The propellant is simply nitrogen gas.

   a Suggest how this propellant might move you through space.

   b How do you think you would be able to control the speed of the MMU?

2 a How is carbon dioxide removed from the air in a spacecraft?

   b Write a word equation for the reaction that occurs when carbon dioxide is removed from the air in the spacecraft using lithium hydroxide.

3 Suggest why the outside temperature at an altitude of 400 km can be as high as 250°C in the sunlight and −150°C in the shade.

4 Electrical power for the Space Shuttle is produced in fuel cells. Each cell generates 1.2 volts DC and there are 24 cells in each battery. Each cell produces about 20 watts of electrical power.

   a What is the total voltage produced by each battery?

   b What power (in watts) can be produced by each of the Shuttle's batteries?

5 Suggest why water vaporises immediately it is released into space from a spacecraft.

6 The International Space Station will cost about $150 billion to build. The Human Genome Project cost $45 billion.

   a Compare and contrast the benefits of these two science projects to humankind.

   b What is your opinion about the statement that these projects are examples of 'scientists spending money on themselves and not on the people who really need it'?

7 Use the internet and other library resources to write a brief history of space stations. Find out how many space stations have been built and put into orbit, what functions they served, and what has happened to them.

8 Before humans went into space, small Rhesus monkeys were placed in orbit for various periods of time. Even recently monkeys have been used in a number of space experiments.

   Discuss with others the pros and cons of using animals in space experiments. You might like to organise a debate on this subject.

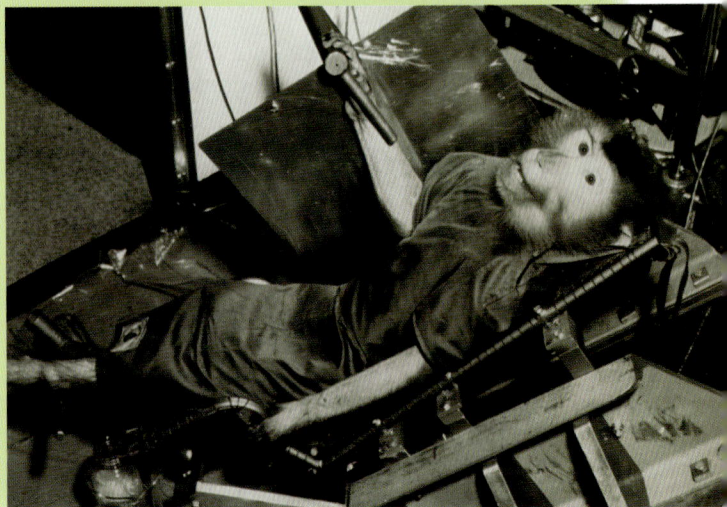

MAIN IDEAS

Copy and complete these statements to make a summary of this chapter. The missing words are on the right.

1. There are a number of problems to overcome when living in space: you need a supply of air and water, protection from _____ and extremes of temperature, and dealing with 'weightlessness' or _____.

2. The weight of an object is a _____ and it is found by multiplying its _____ by the acceleration due to gravity.

3. The acceleration due to _____ on the Earth's surface is 9.8 m/s², and it _____ as you move away from Earth.

4. The force or _____ developed by a rocket's engines is due to the exhaust gases moving backwards (the _____) and pushing the rocket forwards with an equal force (the _____).

5. The net force on a rocket at lift-off is equal to the thrust of the engines minus the _____ of the rocket.

6. Gravity pulls a satellite towards the Earth, but its _____ (motion) keeps it in orbit.

7. _____ in low Earth orbits, where the gravity is stronger, have much greater _____ than satellites in higher orbits.

action
decreases
force
gravity
inertia
mass
microgravity
orbital speeds
radiation
reaction
satellites
thrust
weight

Try doing the Chapter 13 crossword on the CD.

Working with technology

REVIEW

1. You are standing on some scales in a lift. The scales read 60 kg. The lift suddenly accelerates downwards. The reading on the scales will be:
   A 60 kg
   B less than 60 kg
   C more than 60 kg
   D 60 × 9.8 kg

2. In 1975 *Apollo 15* astronaut Scott Irwin dropped a hammer and a feather while standing on the Moon's surface.
   a Why did they both hit the ground at the same time on the Moon but not on the Earth's surface?
   b Would the hammer fall faster or slower on the Moon than on the Earth? Explain.

3. Jilly stands on ice wearing ice skates. She throws a heavy weight out in front of her.
   a In which direction does she move?
   b Explain what would have happened if Jilly had thrown the object with more force.

4. Which one of the statements is correct?
   A Liquid-fuel rockets are cheap to make and are very simple in construction.
   B Solid-fuel rockets have to carry a source of oxygen but liquid-fuel rockets do not.
   C Once ignited solid-fuel rockets cannot be extinguished.
   D Most liquid-fuel rockets burn hydrogen and nitrogen gas in the combustion chamber.

5 Two satellites are in orbit around the Earth. Satellite A is at an altitude of 400 km while satellite B is at an altitude of 900 km. Explain why satellite A has to have a greater orbital speed than B.

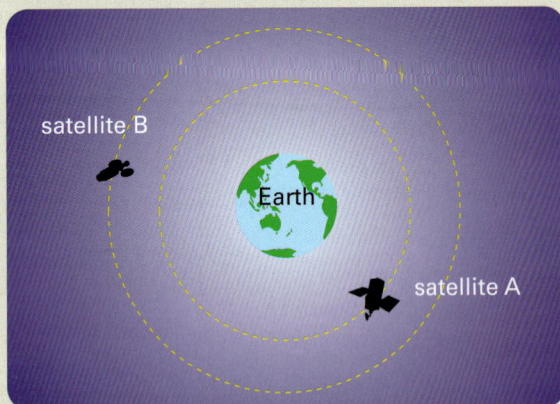

6 You are in the Shuttle ready for lift-off. The engines that fire for lift-off are solid-fuel engines. The last stage is powered by liquid-fuel engines.
  a Why do space rockets have to carry their own source of oxygen as well as the fuel?
  b What is the advantage of using solid-fuel engines for lift-off?
  c The engine in the Space Shuttle is a liquid-fuel type. Suggest why this type of engine is used.

7 Spending long periods of time in microgravity causes problems for the heart, weight-bearing bones and muscle tissues. Describe how microgravity affects these parts of the body.

8 Imagine you are a crew member of Shuttle mission STS-120 to the International Space Station. You make the following observations:
  a When the Shuttle reaches the ISS in orbit, you notice that your face and neck become 'puffy' and you feel a fullness in your head.
  b In the ISS crew compartment, you can drink liquids upside down as easily as right-side up.
  c Inside the orbiting ISS, you sneeze and you crash backwards into the compartment wall.
  d During re-entry you notice the tiles on the nose of the orbiter glow red hot.

Write an inference for each observation.

9 The table gives the acceleration due to gravity for a number of bodies in our solar system.

Planet or moon	Acceleration due to gravity (m/s^2)
Mars	4.1
Earth's moon	1.6
Saturn	10.8
Pluto	0.3
Ganymede (moon of Jupiter)	3.9
Uranus	8.9

  a On which planet would your weight be about half of what it is on Earth?
  b Astronaut Ziro's weight is 88 N on Earth's moon. What is his mass on Mars? What is his weight on Uranus?
  c A rocket of mass 75 000 kg blasts off from Ganymede with an acceleration of 5 m/s^2. Calculate the thrust developed by the rocket's engines.
  d Will the same rocket be able to lift off from the surface of Uranus? Explain.

10 An astronaut in a manned manoeuvring unit (MMU) or 'space scooter' has a total mass of 110 kg. Each of the twenty-four jet nozzles around the base of the MMU can produce a thrust of 9 newtons.
  a What would the astronaut's weight in newtons be on Earth?
  b The astronaut goes for a space walk and fires one jet nozzle. How fast would she accelerate?
  c If the astronaut stood on the Earth's surface and fired all the jet nozzles downwards, would the MMU develop enough thrust to lift her off the ground?
  d Would the astronaut lift off if she fired all the MMU's jets on the Moon?

Check your answers on pages 339–340.

Answers to Reviews

If your answer does not agree with the answer given here, go back to the chapter and read the relevant section again. Your answers may be slightly different from the answers given here. If in doubt, check with your teacher.

Chapter 1 Science is investigating

1 **B**

2 **C**

3 **C**—If the researchers know who gets the lotion containing Z and who doesn't, this may influence their observations of the effect of the lotions. To overcome this problem a procedure called a double-blind experiment is used (see page 7).

4 **A**

5 You catch, count and tag a sample of mullet (eg 20) in that section of the river. You then release the tagged mullet back into the river. After some time you catch a second sample (eg 10) and count how many are tagged (eg 2) and untagged (eg 8).

Proportion of tagged mullet in 2nd sample = proportion of tagged mullet in river

So $\dfrac{2}{10} = \dfrac{20}{\text{total}}$

Therefore   total $= \dfrac{20 \times 10}{2} = 100$

So you estimate there are 100 mullet in this section of the river.

6 **a** Total number of periwinkles = 120
   b Total area = 100 m^2
   Area of 1 quadrat = 1 m^2
   Area of 10 quadrats = 10 m^2
   population = no. of periwinkles in 10 quadrats
   $\times \dfrac{\text{total area}}{\text{area of 10 quadrats}}$
   $= 120 \times \dfrac{100}{10}$
   = 1200 periwinkles
   c The quadrat method was used because the periwinkles are not mobile—they are fixed in position on the rocky platform.

7 **a** The uncontrolled variables were the type of bicycle, the condition of its brakes, the mass of the rider, the speed of the bike and how hard the rider braked.
   b It would be best for the same person to test each bike, travelling at the same speed and braking the same way on both bikes. Ideally the bikes should be the same, with different-sized wheels, but this is not possible.

8 **a**

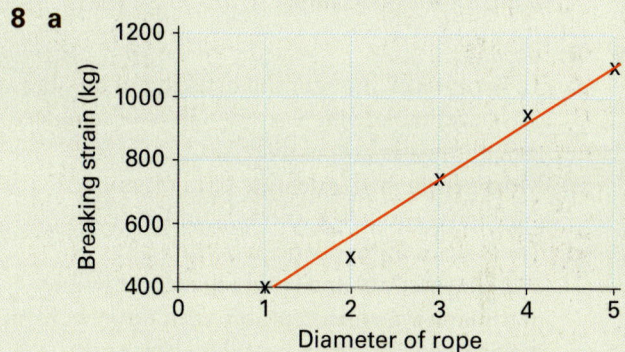

Note that the line does not go through all the points, but it goes close to them.
   b As the diameter of the rope increases, the breaking strain also increases. (If you wanted to be quantitative you could say that the breaking strain increases by about 175 kg when the rope diameter increases by 1 cm.)

Chapter 2 Consumer science

1 **a** objective   **e** subjective
   b objective   **f** subjective
   c subjective   **g** objective
   d objective

Whether the answer is objective or subjective depends on the details of the test. For example, it is possible to obtain objective results for question **c**.

2 **a** loss of mass = 1.676 g
   b Evaporation of some of the liquid ingredients in the lotion would explain the loss of mass.
   c The rate of moisture loss was decreasing. On the first day the loss was 0.444 g but on the last day the loss was only 0.257 g.
   d Unless the moisture loss for the lotion is compared with that for other lotions, the experiment does not prove that the lotion 'holds its moisture longer'.

3 a The reliability of the cars was measured by counting the number of cars which did not have breakdowns or days off the road, and converting this to a percentage of the total number of cars of that make.
b Mazda
c about 1.5 years old
d about 7 years
e After about 12 years the reliability is about the same for all three cars.

4 a 10%
b 32% of males thought the drinking of alcohol was acceptable, whereas only 20% of females thought it was acceptable.
c Most people had a definite opinion on marijuana (only 4% and 6% undecided).
d There were more people who thought drinking alcohol and smoking cigarettes and marijuana was unacceptable than there were who thought it was acceptable. Drinking alcohol was thought to be more acceptable than smoking cigarettes or marijuana. There were no large differences between males and females, although drinking alcohol was more acceptable to males than to females.

5 a deck, trucks, wheels, bearings and skidpads/noseguards
b The bearings are to help the wheels turn freely (by reducing friction).
c The best wheels have a 'high rebound factor'. You can test a wheel by dropping a marble onto it and measuring how high it bounces.
d The variables you need to control are the plastic tube, the marble and how you dropped the marble.
e The cheapest skateboard would be $160. The most expensive would be $365 (or more).

6 a The independent variable (the one you vary) is the brand of correcting fluid.
b The dependent variable is the drying time.
c You will need to control how you apply the correcting fluid to the paper, eg one small drop. All drops need to be tested on the same paper, under the same conditions (eg no blowing, same day).
d 1 Put a drop of correcting fluid on a piece of paper.
  2 Measure how long it takes to dry. (You need to decide how you will tell when it is dry.)

3 Test drops of other types of correcting fluid in exactly the same way.
4 Record all results and decide which type dries most quickly.

Chapter 3 Light and sound

1 B—Only for this ray (AX) is the angle of incidence equal to the angle of reflection.

2 D—See page 58.

3 A

4 D—The light rays are refracted through a rectangular glass block as shown in **A**, but the rays that come out the other side of the block are always parallel to the incoming rays.

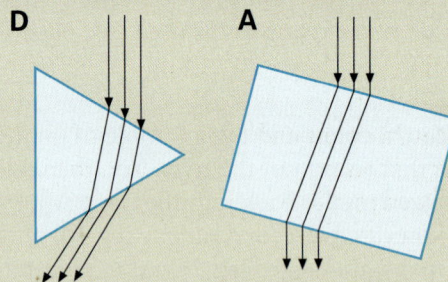

5 a 15 cm
b Lens B will be less curved and thinner.

6 a green light only
b red and violet light
c The filter is green because a green filter will transmit its own colour and absorb the others.

7 White light is shining in your eye because it contains green, blue and red light, affecting all three types of colour vision receptors.

8 When different coloured lights pass through a prism, red light is refracted least, and blue the most, with green in between. So if beam C is green, then B must be yellow (between red and green).

9 a The sound wave that returned in 0.10 seconds came from the shoal of fish.
b The sound wave took 0.05 seconds to travel to the fish. If sound travels 1450 m each second, then the fish are 1450 × 0.05 = 72.5 m below the ship.

c The table on page 66 shows that the speed of sound in water is less at lower temperatures. Therefore as the temperature decreases the speed of sound also decreases. The sound wave will take longer to return, and the fishermen may therefore think that the water is deeper than it is.

Chapter 4 Communications technology

1 C

2 **1** diode
2 LED
3 capacitor
4 transistor
5 resistance
6 current
7 LDR

3 **a** speaker
b phosphor
c brightness control
d electron gun
e deflecting coil
f antenna

4 **a** The light bulb will glow only in circuit B where the negative end of the diode (the straight line in the symbol) is connected to the negative side of the battery (short fat stroke).
b Circuit A has the largest current. This is because it has the largest voltage and the resistance in each circuit is about the same. To calculate the actual current in each circuit you can use Ohm's law.

5

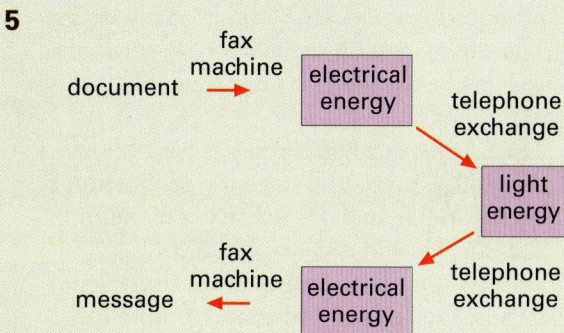

6 **a** D
b D
c B

7 **a** 1 Hz (1 wave per second)
b

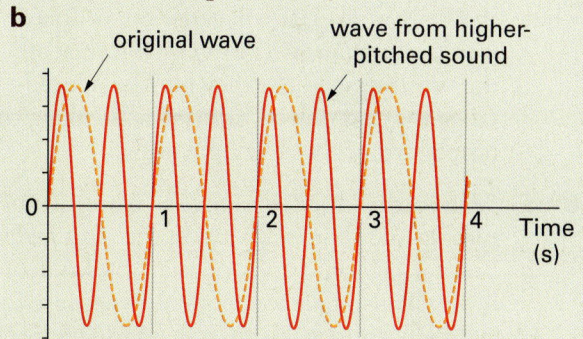

8 The sound waves cause the paper cone to vibrate. This causes the coil to move in and out of the magnet. This movement then creates an alternating current in the wires.

Chapter 5 Road science

1 D

2 $v_{av} = \dfrac{d}{t}$ so $t = \dfrac{d}{v_{av}}$
$= \dfrac{280 \text{ km}}{80 \text{ km/h}}$
$= 3.5 \text{ h}$

3 **a** C
b A or the first part of B
c D or the second part of B
d B

4 The furniture van would require more force to stop it because its mass is greater.

5 Before Scott braked, the golf clubs were moving with the car—at the same speed as it. When he braked, the seatbelt held him in his seat, but there was nothing to stop the clubs continuing to move forward, due to inertia.

6 Reaction distance depends on the driver and on the speed, so it would be the same for the motorbike, car and semitrailer. Braking distance, however, depends on the vehicle, especially its mass. So the braking distance would be shortest for the motorbike and longest for the semitrailer.

7 **a** When a stationary car is hit from behind by another car, the inertia of the people in the car causes them to move backwards into their seats. If they do not have head restraints they may suffer whiplash injury.

b The car that hit the stationary car will stop suddenly, so inertia will cause the people in it to continue moving forwards. If they are not wearing seatbelts they may be injured when they hit objects in front of them, eg the dashboard or the steering wheel.

8 a When a car's brakes 'lock', the wheels stop turning and slide (skid) across the road surface.
b The car may skid and you may lose control of it. It will also take longer to stop because the sliding friction is less than the static friction that exists when the wheels are rolling.
c Car designers have developed an antilock braking system (ABS) which senses when a wheel is about to lock up and pumps the brake off and on rapidly.

9 You need two different equations to solve this problem.

$$a_{av} = \frac{v - u}{t} = \frac{0 - 15 \text{ m/s}}{3 \text{ s}} = -5 \text{ m/s}^2$$

$$F = ma$$
$$= 80 \text{ kg} \times -5 \text{ m/s}^2$$
$$= -400 \text{ newtons}$$

(The force is negative because it is a braking force.)

10 a Initially the lift accelerates (upwards slope); it then continues to move at a constant speed (flat part of graph); finally the lift decelerates (downwards slope) and stops.
b To find the acceleration you calculate the slope of the graph.

$$a_{av} = \frac{10 - 0 \text{ m/s}}{1.7 \text{ s}}$$
$$= 5.9 \text{ m/s}^2$$

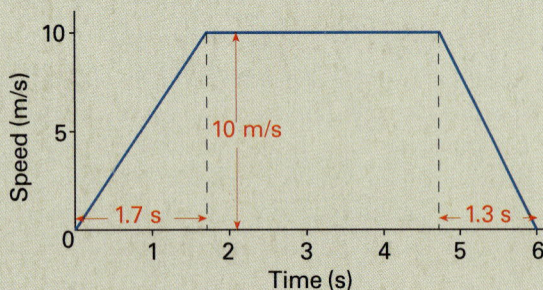

c Deceleration $= \dfrac{0 - 10 \text{ m/s}}{1.3 \text{ s}} = -7.7 \text{ m/s}^2$

Chapter 6 Our energy future

1 C

2 A

3 B

power of sunlight   = 500 watts/m²

power of cell (10% efficient) = 50 watts/m²

area of solar cells required $= \dfrac{1000 \text{ watts}}{50 \text{ watts/m}^2}$
$= 20 \text{ m}^2$

4 a solar cell—light energy
b coal-burning power station—chemical energy
c wind generator—kinetic energy
d hydro-electric power station—potential energy
e geothermal power station—heat energy

5 a about 8.6×10^9 tonnes oil equivalent per day
b 2003
c You would need to extrapolate the graph to the year 2015. This prediction would be unreliable, however, because you do not know how steeply the curve will rise. It could even fall.

6 The electricity we use at present comes from coal-burning power stations which release huge amounts of carbon dioxide into the atmosphere. The petrol we burn in our cars also produces carbon dioxide. So by cutting down our use of electricity and petrol we reduce our greenhouse gas emissions and consequently global warming.

7 a 'Energy demand' is how much energy is required. 'Energy supply' is the energy produced from local or imported resources.
b The energy gap on the left is only small and was probably filled by importing oil, coal or natural gas.
c The surplus is where supply is greater than demand. During this stage the production of energy in Bananaland reached a maximum.
d The surplus will end about 2009.
e about 150 million tonnes of oil equivalent
f Import fuel, decrease demand, find more fossil fuel reserves, use nuclear energy, use alternative fuels (eg ethanol), use alternative sources (eg solar, wind, tides).

8 There are a number of serious problems with the use of nuclear power, but it is a possible solution to our ever-decreasing reserves of fossil fuels and rising greenhouse gas emissions.

9 Wind, geothermal and tidal energy can be used only in certain areas—where there are strong winds, volcanic action or hot rocks, or large tides.

10 You could use a Remote Area Power Supply (RAPS) to generate electricity from solar cells and a wind generator (see page 149), if there was enough sunshine and wind. You could use a solar hot water system, and heating costs could be reduced by the house design described on page 147.

Chapter 7 Responding

1 C

2 B

3 **a** Involuntary actions include heartbeat, breathing, digestion and balance (see page 157).
   b The cerebellum and the brain stem coordinate involuntary actions.

4 **A** flash of light   **E** motor neuron
   B receptors in eye   **F** pupil
   C sensory neuron   **G** pupil decreases
   D spinal cord

5 Hormones can act on the whole body, on body systems or on individual organs. On the other hand, nerves act only on muscles and glands.

6 **a** Animals A, B and C are mammals or birds because they have a constant body temperature.
   b 40°C
   c Animal B is probably a human because the set-point temperature is about 37°C.
   d The body temperature of animal D increases during the morning as the outside temperature increases. Its body temperature decreases when the outside temperature decreases in the afternoon.

7 **a** Experiment 1: The cells that produced the growth hormone were removed, so the growth of the shoot stopped.

   Experiment 2: The growth hormone in the extract acted on the cells below the cut and growth continued.

Experiment 3: The aluminium cap stopped the light getting to the cells in the tip, which in turn stopped the production of growth hormone, and growth stopped.

   b There are several possible designs. Here is one way:
- Cut the tip off one plant, crush it and place the extract on the cut shoot (as in Experiment 2).
- Cut the tip off a second plant and crush it. Then cut off another piece of the shoot to expose the cells further down. Place the extract on this shoot.
- The first plant should grow while the second one will not.

8 **a** Hormone X stimulates the kidney to reduce the amount of sodium being filtered out of the blood and therefore increases the amount of sodium in the blood.
   b the receptors in the brain
   c

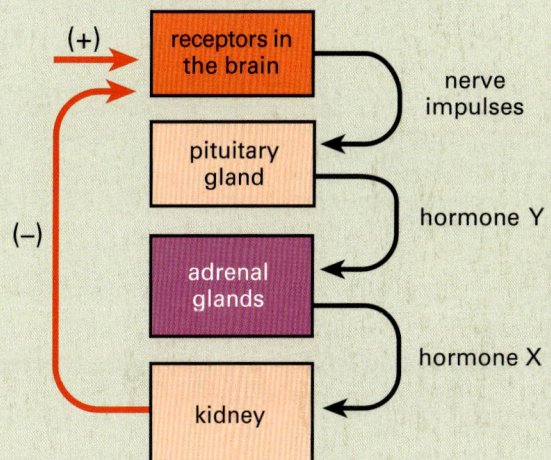

Chapter 8 Inheritance

1 B

2 C

3 C

4 **a** 32 pairs
   b 32 single chromosomes
   c An X chromosome and 31 others, or a Y chromosome and 31 others.

5 **a** TTCAG

b The two strands of DNA are held together by weak bonds between the base pairs on each strand.

6 a 7 amino acids
 b asparagine-serine-glutamic acid-phenylalanine-proline-arginine-serine
 c The mutation will change the phenylalanine in the sequence to leucine.
 d The change in the amino acid sequence might stop the action of the gene and hence your blood would not clot when your skin was cut or damaged.

7 a The gene for blood type O is recessive, therefore Mrs Sloan with blood type O is definitely homozygous.
 b The daughter's genotype is oo. One of these genes came from her father. Therefore, Mr Sloan's genotype must be Ao.
 c Baby Sloan has a 50:50 chance of having A type blood (as shown below).

father

	A	o
o	Ao	oo
o	Ao	oo

mother

8 a SS
 b The plant would have smooth seeds because the gene S is dominant.
 c ss
 d The gene for wrinkled seeds (s) is recessive. Therefore for a plant to have wrinkled seeds its cells would have to contain two genes for wrinkled seeds (ss).

9 a The genotypes of the parent plants are TT and Tt. They are both tall.

	T	T
t	Tt	Tt
T	TT	TT

 b All the plants are tall.

10 Suppose the gene for tongue-rolling is T and the gene for non-tongue-rolling is t. Then the phenotype for the daughter and son who cannot roll their tongues is tt. The father and mother must have genotypes Tt because they can both roll their tongues and have children who cannot.

The purple circles and squares indicate those who can roll their tongues.

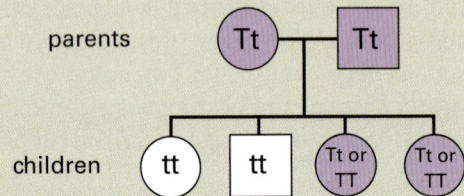

parents Tt — Tt

children tt | tt | Tt or TT | Tt or TT

11 Suppose a woman with a gene for colour deficiency on one X chromosome (XX^c) has children with a man with normal colour vision (XY). The Punnett square below shows (in theory) that the female children will have normal vision but half of them will carry the colour-deficiency gene. In the male children, 50% of them will be colour deficient.

female with normal vision — male with normal vision

	X	Y
X	XX	XY
X^c	XX^c	X^cY

carrier female with normal vision — colour-deficient male

12 The characteristic is definitely recessive. If you represent the alleles as A and a, then the people with aa genes have the characteristic. You can see from the pedigree that this characteristic has 'skipped' a generation. The child in the bottom row has it, while her parents in the line above do not.

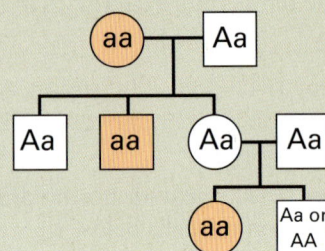

aa — Aa
Aa | aa | Aa — Aa
aa | Aa or AA

Chapter 9 Species survival

1 B—see page 219

2 A

3 C

4 The ancestors of the domestic dog were selectively bred (artificially selected) by humans to produce breeds with the required characteristics. For example, the greyhound was bred for speed while the golden retriever was bred for hunting.

5 Two plants from the same stock have the same genotypes. However, if they are planted in different areas where the climate is different, then the environmental conditions will produce different characteristics (phenotypes).

6 Fruit flies born with curly wings cannot fly. Hence, they would die of starvation or would be easy prey for predators.

7 C—The other alternatives could change the gene pools and hence the characteristics of the organisms. For example in A most insects would die, but the naturally resistant ones would survive and hence the gene pool might change.

8 If the mainland finch was the ancestor of the Galapagos finches, then the DNA of each finch would be very similar. The higher the percentage similarity, the more Darwin's inference is supported.

9 See the diagram in Exercise 6 on page 232. Instead of the foreign DNA you would use the gene for human growth hormone.

10 Here is one suggestion for an experiment, although you may have a different design. If so, ask your teacher to check it.

In a very large cage (aviary), place a number of model tree trunks—all made from dark-coloured material (dark bark). Release 50 dark-coloured moths and 50 light-coloured ones. Also release a small number of birds. After a number of hours, remove the birds and record the number and colour of the wings of moths that have been eaten.

Repeat the experiment this time using light-coloured model tree trunks, the same number of moths and the same number of birds.

By tabulating the number and colour of the moths' wings in each case, you should be able to see whether birds act as selection agents by eating light-coloured moths on the dark bark, or the dark-coloured moths on the light bark.

11 **a** The selection agents are temperature and availability of water.

b Over a long period of time, the trees have spread over both sides of the mountain, but only those trees best suited to the conditions in each of the locations have survived and reproduced.

c The trees at X are separated from the trees at Z by the cold conditions on the high parts of the mountain, and it is unlikely that trees at X and Z would interbreed. Therefore, if the gene pools of each group are isolated from each other for a long period of time, trees at X and Z could form two different species. On the other hand, trees at Y are not totally isolated from the trees at Z and might still interbreed.

Chapter 10 Explaining reactions

1 **a** When an atom loses one electron its charge is 1+.

b When an atom gains two electrons its charge is 2−.

2 **a** C, D and E—since they contain only one type of atom

b A and B

c D and F

d A, B and E

3 B

$$2+ \qquad 1-$$
$$Mg_{\,1} \underset{\times}{\overset{\times}{\longleftarrow}} (OH)_2$$
$$Mg\,(OH)_2$$

4 **a** Three—Cu, S and O

b Cu^{2+} and SO_4^{2-} ions (see page 244)

c Ionic

5 **a** Ionic compounds are held together by the attraction between oppositely charged ions (see page 237).

b Covalent compounds are held together by the sharing of electrons (see page 240).

6 **a** $C + 2Br_2 \rightarrow CBr_4$
    b $Fe_2O_3 + 3C \rightarrow 2Fe + 3CO$
    c $P_4 + 6H_2 \rightarrow 4PH_3$
    d $C_4H_8 + 6O_2 \rightarrow 4CO_2 + 4H_2O$
    e $Al_2(SO_4)_3 + 3Pb(NO_3)_2 \rightarrow$
                           $3PbSO_4 + 2Al(NO_3)_3$

7 **a** $MgSO_4 \rightarrow Mg^{++} + SO_4^{--}$
       $KOH \rightarrow K^+ + OH^-$
       (See the table on page 172.)
    b

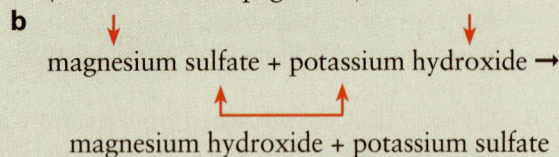

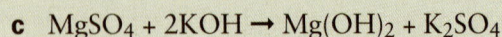

    magnesium sulfate + potassium hydroxide $\rightarrow$

       magnesium hydroxide + potassium sulfate

    c $MgSO_4 + 2KOH \rightarrow Mg(OH)_2 + K_2SO_4$

8 When copper sulfate dissolves in water, Cu^{2+} and SO_4^{2-} ions are formed. These ions are free to move and conduct an electric current.
    Distilled water contains uncharged H_2O molecules which do not conduct an electric current.

9 X has a valency of 1–. (You can tell this from the formula HX, since H has a valency of 1+.)

    Y has a valency of 2+ (because of YX_2)

    Z has a valency of 2– (because of YZ)

10 **a** The nitric acid reacts with the copper to form copper ions which make the solution blue.
     b Nitrogen dioxide (formula NO_2) contains nitrogen and oxygen atoms. These atoms must have come from the nitric acid (HNO_3).

11 **a** The blue colour is due to copper ions in solution. Since copper was produced in the reaction, you can infer that the copper ions changed to copper atoms. This is why the solution lost some of its blue colour.
     b If copper is formed then you are left with iron sulfate.

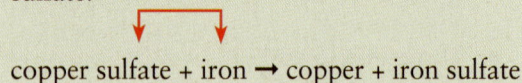

    copper sulfate + iron $\rightarrow$ copper + iron sulfate

       $CuSO_4 + Fe \rightarrow Cu + FeSO_4$
    (assuming a valency of 2+ for iron)
    or $3CuSO_4 + 2Fe \rightarrow 3Cu + Fe_2(SO_4)_3$
    (assuming a valency of 3+ for iron)

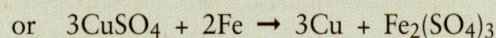

Chapter 11 Metals and non-metals

1 D

2 A

3 B—see pages 274 and 275

4 B—would seem to be the best alternative
    A—could have serious effects on the economy
    C—expensive and only shifts the problem elsewhere
    D—only decreases the size of the problem
    E—not a long-term solution and the SO_2 is still being released into the atmosphere
    (Different people may have different opinions.)

5 **a** The copper goes into solution as copper ions Cu^{2+} which move to the negative terminal, where they accept electrons to form copper metal. (See Fig 33 on page 276.)
    b The silver is very unreactive and simply falls to the bottom of the container.

6 **a** B and F
    b A, B and C; or D and E
    c B and C
    d A, D, F and H are all metals
    e F and H are transition metals
    f C
    g A
    h G
    i The reactive metals on the left of the periodic table (A and D) are likely to react with the non-metals on the right (B, E and G).

7 **a** zinc (most reactive), then copper, and then platinum (least reactive)
    b Platinum would make the best mirror because it does not corrode and hence its surface stays shiny.

8 If you go to the last element (111) in the periodic table and start numbering to the right, element 117 fits into group VII. You would therefore expect it to be very reactive, like the other halogens in Group VII. Element 118 fits into Group VIII so you would expect it to be unreactive, like the other noble gases in Group VIII.

9 Using the flow chart on page 280 as a guide:

copper ore (chalcopyrite) → *smelting* (SO₂) → impure copper → *electrolysis* → pure copper; impurities

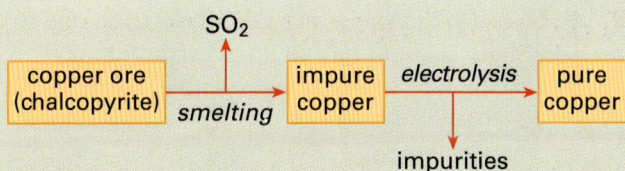

10 In copper the electrons are not firmly bound to the atomic nuclei and can move freely in the spaces between the atoms (see page 266). Hence copper is a good conductor of electricity. In diamond all four of carbon's valence electrons are involved in strong covalent bonds with other carbon atoms (see page 271). Hence diamond does not conduct electricity.

11 a

Element	Symbol	Atomic number	1st shell	2nd shell	3rd shell
hydrogen	H	1	1		
carbon	C	6	2	4	
neon	Ne	10	2	8	
sodium	Na	11	2	8	1
chlorine	Cl	17	2	8	7

(No. of electrons spans 1st, 2nd, 3rd shell columns)

b carbon
c neon
d 1
e hydrogen, sodium and chlorine

Chapter 12 Electrochemistry

1 B—using the activity series on page 300

2 A—The electroplating solution must contain copper ions.

3 A—will work
B—will not work because the metal strips are the same
C—will not work because distilled water is a poor conductor of electricity
D—will not work because the metal strips are not connected.

4 a C—The tin and copper in contact in salt water act like an electrochemical cell. Because the tin is more reactive than copper it corrodes rapidly.

b D—Because the iron is more reactive than tin, it corrodes in preference to the tin. Hence the tin corrodes only slowly.

5 D

6

Car battery	Torch cell
number of connected cells	single cell
usually 12 volts	usually 1.5 volts
can be recharged	cannot be recharged
contains acid	dry cell (no liquid)
bulky and heavy	compact

7 a aluminium, bronze and gold
b Aluminium forms a protective layer of aluminium oxide (see page 301). Bronze is an alloy of copper and tin. Gold is a very unreactive metal.
c Calcium is very reactive and will therefore corrode quickly.

8 The electrolysis of molten magnesium chloride is similar to the electrolysis of molten sodium chloride (see page 295).
a Magnesium ions Mg^{2+} and chloride ions Cl^-.
b Magnesium metal will be formed at the negative electrode since the Mg^{2+} ions are attracted to it.
c The Cl^- ions will be attracted to the positive electrode where they give up electrons to form chlorine gas: $2Cl^- \rightarrow Cl_2 + 2e^-$

9 Some possible inferences are:
• It is very dry in central India (very little water in the air to cause rusting).
• The iron is very pure (contains no carbon).
• The iron has a coating of oil from people's hands which acts as a protective coating.

Chapter 13 Space science

1 B

2 a On Earth falling objects are slowed down by the friction due to the air. Because the feather has a large surface area, there is more air resistance and the feather falls more slowly than the hammer. On the Moon, where there is no air, the hammer and the feather fall together.

b The hammer (and the feather) would fall more slowly on the Moon because the acceleration due to gravity is less.

3 a Jilly moves backwards if she throws the heavy weight forwards. This is due to action and reaction. (See page 310.)

b If the action force increases, the reaction force also increases. Therefore, Jilly would have moved backwards much more quickly.

4 C

5 Satellite A is closer to the Earth and will experience a greater gravitational pull than satellite B. Therefore, to stay in orbit satellite A will have to have a greater orbital speed than satellite B.

6 a There is no oxygen in space in which to burn the fuel. Therefore oxygen has to be carried.

b The solid-fuel rocket engine is more powerful than a liquid-fuel engine of equivalent weight.

c The Shuttle uses a liquid-fuel engine because it can be adjusted or turned off and on to control the Shuttle's speed.

7 Microgravity causes the heart and pulse rates to decrease as well as blood pressure to decrease.

The bones tend to lose calcium and phosphorus during long periods in space. This causes a weakening of the bones.

Because of the lack of exercise of the weight-bearing bones, the body's muscle tissue tends to decrease. This is a similar effect to being bedridden for a long period of time.

8 a In microgravity, the blood and other liquids in your body flow to places like the neck and the head, causing puffiness and fullness in these parts.

b In the Shuttle there is no 'down' because the spacecraft is in 'freefall'. Therefore drinks will not flow 'downwards' and can be drunk in any position.

c When you sneeze in microgravity, the action of the air being forced out of your mouth in one direction pushes your body in the opposite direction.

d As the Shuttle enters the Earth's atmosphere, the friction of the air created by the speed of the Shuttle causes the tiles on exposed surfaces such as the nose to glow red hot.

9 a Mars (4.1 m/s^2)—since the acceleration due to gravity is about half that on Earth (9.8 m/s^2)

b Use the formula W = mg to find Ziro's mass.

$$W = mg, \quad so \quad m = \frac{W}{g}$$
$$= \frac{88 \text{ N}}{1.6 \text{ m/s}^2}$$
$$= 55 \text{ kg}$$

His mass is 55 kg on Mars (or anywhere else). On Uranus his weight is:

$$W = mg$$
$$= 55 \text{ kg} \times 8.9 \text{ m/s}^2$$
$$= 489.5 \text{ N}$$

c Weight of rocket on Ganymede:

$$W = 75\,000 \text{ kg} \times 3.9 \text{ m/s}^2$$
$$= 292\,500 \text{ N}$$

Net force accelerating rocket—

$$F = 75\,000 \text{ kg} \times 5 \text{ m/s}^2$$
$$= 375\,000 \text{ N}$$

Net force = thrust − weight
so, thrust = net force + weight
$$= 375\,000 \text{ N} + 292\,500 \text{ N}$$
$$= 667\,500 \text{ N}$$

d On Uranus the rocket's weight is—

$$W = 75\,000 \text{ N} \times 8.9 \text{ m/s}^2$$
$$= 667\,500 \text{ N}$$

The weight of the rocket is equal to the thrust, so there is zero net force and the rocket will not be able to leave the surface of Uranus.

10 a On Earth the weight of the astronaut is 110 kg × 9.8 m/s^2 = 1078 N

b $a = \frac{F}{m} = \frac{9 \text{ N}}{110 \text{ kg}}$
$$= 0.08 \text{ m/s}^2$$

c The total thrust developed by the 24 rockets is 24 × 9 = 216 N. This is much less than the astronaut's weight (1078 N), so the rockets would not lift her off the ground.

d On the Moon the astronaut's weight is 110 × 1.6 = 176 N. This is less than the total thrust developed by the rockets, so she would lift off from the Moon's surface.

Glossary

The words in this list occur in **dark type** throughout the book. The number after each entry gives the page where you will find more information. For some words the pronunciation is given. The syllable in capitals should be stressed; for example, evaporation (e-VAP-or-AY-shun).

acceleration: the rate at which an object speeds up or slows down; average acceleration (in m/s^2) is calculated by dividing the change in speed by the time. 104

activity series: a list of the metals arranged from the most reactive to the least reactive. 300

addition: making colour by adding different coloured lights together. 61

alkali metals: very reactive elements in Group I of the periodic table, eg sodium and potassium. 268

alkaline earth metals: reactive metals in Group II of the periodic table, eg magnesium and calcium. 268

alleles (a-LEELs): different forms of the same gene; each allele produces variations in inherited characteristics, eg eye colour. 195

allotropes: different forms of the same element; for example, diamond, graphite and buckyballs are allotropes of carbon. 271

AM (amplitude modulated): radio stations that broadcast using a type of wave whose frequency is constant but whose amplitude varies. 94

amplitude: the size of a signal or the loudness of a sound, measured by the height of the wave above or below the zero point. 75

analog (AN-a-log) signal: a wave signal used in communication devices, that varies in value at different points in time. 76

anodising: an electrolytic process which thickens the protective film of oxide on the surface of aluminium. 301

artificial selection: the selection and breeding of particular organisms to produce offspring with desired characteristics. 225

atomic number: the number of protons in the nucleus of an atom; equal to the number of electrons. 262

auxins (ORK-sins): a group of hormones responsible for the growth of cells in the stems and roots of plants. 168

biomass: plant and animal material used as a source of renewable energy. 140

bit: a binary digit, with the value 1 (on) or 0 (off). 76

blind experiment: a controlled experiment involving people, where the subjects do not know who is in the control group and who is in the test group. 7

brain: the main organ of the nervous system, which controls all the systems in the body. 156

brain stem: the base of the brain which controls involuntary actions such as breathing and heartbeat. 157

byte: a unit of information, usually eight bits, used in communications technology. 76

capacitors: electronic components that store charge in a circuit. 83

cathode ray tube: a glass tube in which an electron beam is produced and controlled to form a pattern of light on a fluorescent screen. 90

cerebellum (ser-a-BELL-um): a small, crinkly part at the lower back of the brain which controls involuntary actions such as balance and coordination. 157

cerebrum (ser-EE-brum): the largest part of the brain; it controls memory, speech and voluntary actions, and receives information from sense receptors. 157

chemical bonds: attractive forces between atoms holding them together. 236

chromosomes: objects found in the nucleus of a cell that carry the genetic information. 180

clones: organisms that have identical genes to their parents. 230

co-dominance: where the genes for a particular characteristic combine to give features of both the individual genes. 200

communication: the sending of a message, verbally or non-verbally, to another person who understands the message. 74

correlation: how closely two variables depend on each other. 14

corrosion: the process in which water and air react with metals; rusting is the corrosion of iron. 298

covalent bond: a chemical bond formed by the sharing of electrons between two or more atoms. 240

digital signal: a wave signal used in communication devices; it has one of two values—zero or one. 76

diode: an electronic component that allows current to flow in one direction only. 82

dispersion: the splitting up of white light into the colours of the spectrum. 58

DNA (deoxyribonucleic acid): the complex chemical

compound found in chromosomes that contains the genetic code. 186

dominant gene: a gene for a particular characteristic that completely hides or masks the alternative (recessive) gene. 195

double-blind experiment: an experiment in which neither the subjects nor the experimenters know who is in the control group and who is in the test group. /

dry cells: electric cells that contain a moist paste rather than a liquid electrolyte. 287

electric cell: an electrochemical cell that converts chemical energy into electrical energy using chemical reactions. 284

electrodes: conductors that allow electric current to flow into or out of an electrolyte. 284

electrolysis (ee-lek-TROL-e-sis): the process of passing an electric current through an electrolyte to produce chemical reactions at the electrodes. 276

electrolyte (ee-LEK-tro-lite): a substance in solution or molten that conducts an electric current and is decomposed in the process. 284

electromagnetic spectrum: the full range of electromagnetic radiation, such as heat, light, ultraviolet and X-rays. 67

electroplating: depositing a thin layer of metal on another using electrolysis. 293

emulsifiers (ee-MULL-si-fiers): substances which can turn mixtures into emulsions (colloids with tiny droplets of one liquid, eg oil, spread through a second liquid, eg water). 43

endocrine glands: glands found in various places in the body, which produce hormones and release them directly into the blood. 162

endocrine system: system consisting of a number of endocrine glands throughout the body. 156

evolution: a process in which species change over time and develop into new species. 219

extrapolating (ex-STRAP-oh-late-ing): using a graph to predict a value beyond the range of a set of measurements. 13

FM (frequency modulated): radio stations that broadcast using a type of wave whose amplitude is constant but whose frequency varies. 95

focus: the point at which rays of light meet after reflection from a curved mirror, or refraction by a lens. 49

frequency: the number of waves that pass a certain point in one second; it is measured in hertz (Hz). 94

friction: a force that opposes motion of one surface across another; before sliding occurs you have **static**

friction, and once sliding occurs you have **sliding friction**. 113

fuel cell: an electric cell in which the reactants are supplied continuously; in a common fuel cell, hydrogen and oxygen react to produce water. 150

gene pool: the sum of all the genes in a population of a particular organism. 219

genes: segments of DNA that carry genetic information from one generation to the next. 186

genetic engineering: the common term for a technique in biotechnology of inserting desired genes from one species into the chromosomes of another species. 226

genome: the total genetic material in an organism. 191

genotype (JEE-no-type): the type of genes in an organism. 197

geostationary orbits: orbits at a particular altitude such that a satellite remains over the same point on the Earth's surface. 318

geothermal power stations: power stations which use hot water or steam from deep within the Earth to generate electricity. 141

half-life: the time it takes a radioactive substance to lose half of its radioactivity. 130

halogens: very reactive non-metals in Group VII of the periodic table, eg chlorine and iodine. 270

heterozygous (HET-er-o-ZYE-gus): where the genes for a particular characteristic are different; a hybrid. 197

homozygous (HO-mo-ZYE-gus): where the genes for a particular characteristic are the same; a pure breeder. 197

hormones: chemical messages that control important processes of an organism, such as growth. 156

incomplete dominance: where the genes for a particular characteristic are neither dominant nor recessive but combine to give a mixture or blend of characteristics. 200

inertia (in-ER-sha): the tendency of a body to stay at rest or continue its motion, unless acted on by a force; this is called Newton's first law of motion. 117

interpolating (in-TERP-oh-late-ing): using a graph to predict a value between two or more measurements. 13

ions (EYE-ons): atoms or groups of atoms that have a positive or negative charge, caused by the loss or gain of electrons. 236

ionic bond: a chemical bond resulting from the attraction between oppositely charged ions. 237

law of reflection: the angle of incidence of a light ray is equal to the angle of reflection. 49

line of best fit: a line which is closest to most of the plotted points on a graph; it shows the relationship between two variables. 11

liquid crystal displays (LCDs): displays which use liquid crystals sealed between two glass plates; used in digital watches, calculators and flat screen TVs. 93

meiosis (my-OH-sis): the process of cell division that produces sex cells with half the number of chromosomes that body cells have. 182

microgravity: a term that describes the apparent weightlessness of an object that is in orbit. 322

minerals: metal compounds found in the Earth. 273

momentum: the mass of a moving body multiplied by its speed. 117

mutations: permanent changes in genes; they may be caused by exposure to radiation or chemicals. 188

natural selection: the process in which the best adapted individuals survive in a particular habitat (often called survival of the fittest). 213

negative feedback system: a system of control in the body in which the response acts as a stimulus to oppose the change caused by the original stimulus. 171

nervous system: system consisting of the brain, spinal cord and nerves that run to all parts of the body. 156

neuron (NEW-ron): the basic unit of the nervous system; a nerve cell. 158

noble gases (or inert gases): unreactive gases in Group VIII of the periodic table, eg helium and neon. 270

non-renewable energy: energy resources that are not replaced as they are used; for example, coal and oil. 130

nuclear fission: the splitting of the nucleus of a large atom such as uranium into smaller atoms, with the release of a large amount of energy. 130

nuclear fusion: the combining of nuclei of small atoms, such as hydrogen, into larger nuclei, with the release of large amounts of energy; the process occurs in stars. 132

objective tests: tests where the results are based on measurements rather than people's opinions. 28

optical fibres: cables made of thin pure glass fibres which allow the transmission of digital light pulses over long distances. 77

orbit: the path followed by an object in space as it moves around another object. 315

ores: mineral-containing rocks that are suitable for mining and mineral extraction. 273

pedigree: a family tree, showing the inheritance of particular characteristics from one generation to later generations. 198

periodic table: a listing of the elements in order of their atomic numbers; elements are grouped according to their chemical properties. 262

phenotype (FEE-no-type): the physical appearance or characteristics of an organism. 197

phosphors (FOS-fours): substances, coated on the inside of a cathode ray tube or plasma screen, that glow when struck by electrons. 91

pituitary (pit-YOU-it-tree) gland: an endocrine gland, located on the underside of the brain, that controls other endocrine glands. 163

placebos (pla-SEE-bows): substances that have no chemical effect on the body; given to a subject in a blind or double-blind experiment. 7

quadrat: a small measuring area which can be used to sample the organisms in a particular area. 17

reaction time: the time it takes you to respond to a stimulus; for example, the time between seeing a red light and applying the brakes. 111

recessive gene: a gene for a particular characteristic that is completely hidden or masked by the alternative (dominant) gene. 195

recombination: the process by which offspring have a combination of genes from each parent. 210

reflex action: an automatic response to a stimulus without involving the brain. 160

refraction: the bending of light which occurs when light passes from one transparent substance to another. 51

renewable energy: energy resources that can be replaced as they arc uscd; for example, wood and solar energy. 130

replication: the process by which DNA makes identical copies of itself. 187

resistors: poor conductors used to reduce the amount of current flowing in an electric circuit. 82

sample: a small part of anything, intended as representative of the whole, eg a sample of city voters. 29

satellite: a natural or artificial object that orbits a planet. 315

scatter graph: a graph where you plot many points to see if there is any correlation between two variables. 14

scattering (of light): the bouncing of light from particles such as dust or smoke. 63

semiconductors: substances, for example silicon and germanium, that have properties between conductors and insulators and that are used to make diodes and transistors. 87

smelting: the process of extracting metals from their ores through melting. 274

solar cell (or photovoltaic cell): a device containing a semiconductor which absorbs solar energy and converts it directly to electrical energy. 135

species: a population of organisms that have similar features and can interbreed. 210

spectrum: the rainbow colours produced when white light is split up after passing through a prism or raindrops. 58

speed (average): the total distance travelled, divided by the time it takes to go that distance; usually measured in m/s or km/h. 102

subjective tests: tests where the results are based on people's opinions rather than on measurements. 28

subtraction (of colour): making colours by mixing different paints or pigments together. 61

survey: a method of obtaining information which involves looking at a sample of a larger group. 28

thrust: the force developed by a rocket's engines to move it forward. 312

total internal reflection: occurs when light hits a boundary between two transparent substances at a large angle of incidence and is reflected, with none transmitted. 54

transistor: an electronic component that acts as a switch or an amplifier in a circuit. 83

transition metals: the elements found in the middle of the periodic table; they include common metals such as iron and copper. 269

valency: the number of electrons an atom gains, shares or loses when combining with other atoms. 243

valence electrons: the electrons in the outer shell of an atom; these electrons participate in chemical reactions. 264

viscosity: a measure of how easily a liquid flows. 35

X-linked: genes that are found on the X chromosome but have no equivalent on the Y chromosome. 202

Index